BLUE GUIDE

LONDON

EMILY BARBER, JUDY TITHER, ANNABEL BARBER

with photographs by
The Athenaeum Photographic Group

SOMERSET • LONDON

Nineteenth edition

Published by Blue Guides Limited, a Somerset Books Company
Unit 2, Old Brewery Road, Wivesliscombe, Somerset TA4 2PW
blueguides.com
'Blue Guide' is a registered trademark.

ISBN 978–1–916568–01–3

A CIP catalogue record of this book is available from the British Library.

Distributed in the United States of America by
W.W. Norton & Company, Inc.
500 Fifth Avenue, New York, NY 10110.

The authors and the publishers have made reasonable efforts to ensure the accuracy of all the information in *Blue Guide London*; however, they can accept no responsibility for any loss, injury or inconvenience sustained by any traveller as a result of information or advice contained in the guide.

Blue Guides, their authors and editors, are prohibited from accepting any payment from any restaurant, hotel, gallery or other establishment for its inclusion in this guide, or for a more favourable mention than would otherwise have been made.

Every effort has been made to contact the copyright owners of material reproduced in this guide. We would be pleased to hear from any copyright owners we have been unable to reach.

Maps by Dimap Bt.
Architectural line drawings: Michael Mansell RIBA & Gabriella Juhász © Blue Guides.
Floor plans and watercolours: Imre Bába © Blue Guides.
All material prepared for press by Anikó Kuzmich.

Printed in Hungary by Dürer Nyomda Kft., Gyula.

Your views on this book would be much appreciated. We welcome not only specific comments, suggestions or corrections, but any more general views you may have: how this book enhanced your visit, how it could have been more helpful. Blue Guides authors and editorial and production team work hard to bring you what we hope are the best-researched and best-presented cultural guide books in the English language. Please write to us by email (editorial@blueguides.com), via the comments page on our website (blueguides.com) or at the address given above. We will be happy to acknowledge useful contributions in the next edition, and to offer a free copy of one of our titles.

Emily Barber studied History of Art at UCL, is an independent valuer for the Treasure Valuation Committee of Great Britain and a Freeman of the Goldsmiths' Company, City of London. She has worked in the international jewellery industry at auction for 25 years and has been involved with the research and sale of many valuable and historic jewellery collections. She has taught and lectured on the history of jewellery and her opinion is regularly sought by museums and institutions. **Judy Tither** is an editor with more than 30 years' experience and was Assistant Editor on Blue Guides for 15 years. She is now freelance and works on academic titles and play-scripts. **Annabel Barber** is Editorial Director of the Blue Guides, author of *Blue Guide Budapest* and co-author of *Blue Guide Rome* and *Blue Guide Lombardy*. She is a member of the British Guild of Travel Writers.

Special thanks are due to **Charles Freeman**, freelance academic historian and historical consultant to the Blue Guides. His *Egypt, Greece and Rome, Civilizations of the Ancient Mediterranean* (Oxford University Press, 3rd ed. 2014) is widely used as an introductory textbook to the ancient world and is supported by his *Sites of Antiquity: 50 Sites that Explain the Classical World* (published by Blue Guides). He is a Fellow of the Royal Society of Arts.

Grateful thanks also go to the following for contributions, comments and corrections: Philip Antscherl, Andrew Bano, Tabitha Barber, Alan Crockard, Timothy Duke, Sarah Harrison, James Howells, Simon Ingram-Hill, David Natali, Anthony Pacitto, Michael Partington, Ann Rossiter, Carol Wright.

4

CONTENTS

MAPS AND PLANS

INTRODUCTION

L ondon's history spans two millennia. Ever since the Romans set up camp on the banks of the Thames in AD 43 this great city has sprawled along the river in both directions, up and down residual Roman roads and over the intervening fields and countryside, swallowing up disparate villages whole. This is London's essence: its complex, complicated, convoluted spread.

London is the seat of the British government as well as the British monarchy and as a consequence is rich in tradition, pomp and ceremony. By 1800 London was the largest and most important city in the world; throughout the 19th century the Victorians built on these advantages and London became the nucleus of the vast British Empire.

London is a global financial centre as well as a cultural capital. In London you will find four World Heritage sites, internationally famous attractions and some of the best art, theatre, music, entertainment and shopping in the world. London has hosted the Olympic Games three times in its history, most recently in 2012, the success of which gave the city a boost. London is also a food-lovers paradise and has over 70 Michelin-starred restaurants. It has numerous parks and green spaces and its river and waterways are open for boating, walking and cycling. It has one of the most extensive public transport systems of any modern metropolis as well as Europe's busiest international airport. Here too you will find the finest taxi drivers, who have passed the rigorous and celebrated 'Knowledge' exam, which demands an intimate acquaintance with London's complicated street layout. London cabbies pride themselves on being able to pick you up and take you anywhere you want via the best route—without the aid of GPS.

London has formulated and distilled many great inventions: penicillin, fire insurance, the daily newspaper, canned food, traffic lights, the electrical generator, the first television, the Internet—the list is impressive. London is so proud of its luminaries that buildings are riddled with plaques proclaiming the great and the good, the venal and the virtuous, who have once lived in them.

Today, London is truly a stimulating, cosmopolitan and thoroughly modern metropolis. When the last edition of this book went to press, over eight million people lived here. Today that figure stands at almost ten million. Thousands of daily commuters work in London. Foreign visitors arrive here in large numbers as tourists, expatriates and students. Many people from around the globe have chosen to make this city their home. London is always busy, always crowded, always buzzing. Londoners seldom conform to stereotype: they rarely form an orderly queue for the bus, never wear bowler hats and generally prefer coffee to tea; but what they excel at is adapting to change. As the modern city strives to accommodate its burgeoning population and update its infrastructure, London is constantly evolving and transforming itself. Geographically, London may not be in the centre of Europe, but in terms of diversity and innovation, it is at the centre of the world.

LONDON CHRONOLOGY

55–54 BC Julius Caesar's invasions of Britain

AD 43 The Romans invade Britain again. They find the Thames to be fordable, near the present site of London Bridge.

AD c. 50 The Romans found Londinium, on the site of the City of London

AD 61 Roman London is burnt by Boudica

410 Rome is sacked by the Goths. The Romans begin their withdrawal from Britain, leaving the people to organise their own defence. Decline of Londinium begins

597 St Augustine lands in Kent on a mission to convert the people to Christianity

604 Augustine appoints Mellitus Bishop of London

619 Mellitus becomes Archbishop of Canterbury. As soon as he leaves London, the people resume their pagan ways

731 Bede describes Lundenwic, on the site of today's Covent Garden, as 'a trading centre for many nations'

872 The Danes occupy London

886 Alfred the Great takes London and recognises Danish control of eastern England. Watling Street is the frontier

c. 960 Founding of the Benedictine Abbey of Westminster

1014 Battle of London Bridge. King Olaf II of Norway joins forces with the Saxon Ethelred against the Danes

1066 Death of Edward the Confessor. Harold fails to retain the crown, and William the Conqueror is crowned in Westminster Abbey

1106 Building of Southwark Cathedral begins

1123 Foundation of St Bartholomew's Hospital and priory

1161 Henry II orders the building of a new shrine to Edward the Confessor

1176 Old London Bridge is begun, on the site of an ancient crossing

c. 1078 William begins the White Tower

1215 King John signs *Magna Carta*

1225 Franciscans arrive in London, establishing themselves at Greyfriars

1269 Consecration of Henry III's splendid new Westminster Abbey

1274 Edward I makes a grant of land to the Dominicans, who build a friary in the area now known as Blackfriars

1290 Edward I begins his attempts to conquer Scotland. He turns to Italian money-lenders for funding and expels the Jews from London

1296 Edward I removes the Stone of Destiny from Scone and brings it to London

1305 William Wallace is executed at Smithfield. The following year Robert the Bruce becomes King of Scotland and open revolt begins against King Edward I

1348 The first outbreak of plague, known as the Black Death

1362 English replaces French as the official language of Parliament

1381 The Peasants' Revolt enters London, demanding an end to serfdom. Richard II negotiates with them and their leader, Wat Tyler, is killed

1397 Richard Whittington becomes

Mayor of London for the first time

1411 Building of the London Guildhall begins

1414 Lollards seize London and attempt to capture Henry V

1440 Foundation of Eton College

1450 Jack Cade's rebellion against Henry VI. Fierce fighting in London

1460 The Duke of York arrives in London announcing a claim to the throne. Beginning of the Wars of the Roses

1471 Lancastrian defeat at the Battle of Barnet secures the throne for York's son, Edward IV

1476 William Caxton sets up his printing press at Westminster

1483 Mysterious death of the Princes in the Tower

1496 Henry VII empowers John Cabot to set up trading links with those countries he discovers on his voyages of exploration

1500 Wynkyn de Worde sets up a printing press in Fleet Street

1509 Henry VII's death at Richmond is met with public rejoicing. The canny king, who had done so much to set England on her mercantile career, is succeeded by Henry VIII. Little do the people know what is in store

1510 Founding of St Paul's School

1512 After a fire at Westminster, Henry VIII moves his court to Whitehall

1513 Henry VIII establishes the Royal Naval Docks at Deptford

1521 Lutheran books are burned in London and Henry VIII receives the title 'Defender of the Faith' from Pope Leo X

1527 Copies of Tyndale's Bible are burned in St Paul's

1529 Wolsey fails to obtain a divorce for Henry VIII. Thomas More becomes Chancellor

1534 Act of Supremacy: Henry VIII is supreme head of the Church of England

1536 The Dissolution of the Monasteries begins, with the crown seizing Church land and property. Many areas of London that are public parks today are appropriated by Henry VIII as hunting grounds

1547 The House of Commons makes the Palace of Westminster its meeting place instead of the Chapter House of Westminster Abbey

1552 Edward VI founds St Thomas's Hospital

1553 Mary I becomes Queen and sets about restoring the old religion

1558 Elizabeth I succeeds to the throne and re-suppresses the religious houses re-opened by Mary

1565 Thomas Gresham founds the Royal Exchange

1576 The Theatre playhouse opens in Shoreditch

1577 An institute for the teaching of science is established by the will of Sir Thomas Gresham

1581 Francis Drake is knighted at Deptford. He returned from his circumnavigation the previous year

1582 The first houses in London to receive pumped water

1585 Shakespeare arrives in London

1587 Mary, Queen of Scots is executed, having been implicated in a plot to kill Elizabeth I, the culmination of many decades of intriguing, with alliances signed and broken, between England, Scotland and France

1588 Defeat of the Spanish Armada. English dominance of the seas is assured

1595 Hungry Londoners riot

1598 John Stow publishes his *Survey of London*

1599 The Globe Theatre opens in Southwark

1600 Founding of the East India Company on Leadenhall Street

1603 James VI of Scotland becomes James I of England, thus uniting the two kingdoms; Sir Walter Raleigh founds the Mermaid Tavern club

1604 The Treaty of London brings peace with Spain and a trade agreement with France

1605 The Gunpowder Plot, a Catholic conspiracy to blow up Parliament

1608 Foundation of the Royal Blackheath Golf Club

1613 The New River is constructed, to bring drinking water from Stoke Newington

1615 Tobacco vending machines are introduced in taverns; James I issues a proclamation to the effect that London is to be transformed into a 'truly magnificent city comparable to the Rome of the Emperor Augustus'

1617 The first attempt is made to create one-way streets in London

1619 Inigo Jones begins the Banqueting House

1620 The *Mayflower* sets sail for Plymouth from Rotherhithe

1621 John Donne is appointed Dean of St Paul's

1632 Van Dyck becomes court painter to Charles I

1633 Bananas are first displayed in a London shop window by the herbalist Thomas Johnson

1634 Opening of Covent Garden Market

1642 Parliament takes control of the army; Charles I leaves London; beginning of the Civil War

1645 The group of scientists who are later to become the Royal Society begin to meet informally in London and Oxford

1649 Charles I is beheaded at Whitehall. The loyal Scots promptly declare Charles II king

1654 Treaty of Westminster ends the first Anglo-Dutch war over trade routes

1657 Velho Sephardic cemetery opened on Mile End Road

1658 Oliver Cromwell dies at Whitehall. He is buried in Westminster Abbey. The effigy in his funeral procession is dressed in full royal regalia. He is succeeded by his son

1660 Pepys writes the first entries in his diary; Charles II enters London and the monarchy is restored

1661 The first postmarks in the world are struck in London

1662 Queen Catherine of Braganza introduces tea-drinking to the London court

1665 The Great Plague

1666 The Great Fire

1676 The 'Little Fire of London' devastates Southwark

1671 Captain Blood attempts to steal the Crown Jewels from the Tower

1673 The Test Act: Catholics and nonconformists may not hold public office

1674 The Treaty of Westminster brings peace with the Dutch. New Amsterdam becomes New York

1675 The Royal Observatory is founded at Greenwich

1677 The Monument, the tallest free-standing column in the world, is inaugurated as a memorial to the Great Fire

1680 Henry Purcell becomes organist at Westminster Abbey

1681 Charles II offers sanctuary to the

Huguenots, French Protestants facing persecution at home

1682 Spitalfields Market is established

1685 The Duke of Monmouth's rebellion against James II is crushed. Judge Jeffreys presides over the Bloody Assizes, condemning his supporters to death. Monmouth himself is beheaded

1688 James II attempts to force Church leaders to support his Liberty of Conscience declaration; William of Orange is invited to take over the throne; James leaves for the Continent: the 'Glorious Revolution' is over

1693 William III borrows £1 million, with interest, to fund the war with France: this signals the beginning of the National Debt, which Disraeli in his novels will excoriate as the 'Dutch system'

1694 The Bank of England is founded, to obtain interest on government money

1696 Great Howland Dock is built, the largest commercial dock in the world

1698 Opening of White's, London's oldest gentlemen's club

1699 Free fish market established at Billingsgate

1702 Britain's first daily newspaper, the *Daily Courant*, is founded in Fleet Street

1704 Britain is victorious over France at Blenheim

1706 Thomas Twining starts his tea importing business

1707 Union of the English and Scottish parliaments

1711 The new St Paul's Cathedral is formally declared complete; the New Churches Act is passed, more churches are to be built to serve the rapidly growing city: they become known as 'Queen Anne churches'

1720 The South Sea Bubble hoax ruins many London investors

1721 Robert Walpole becomes the first British Prime Minister

1723 Handel is appointed composer to the Chapel Royal

1731 Downing Street becomes the official residence of the Prime Minister

1734 A group of Grand Tourists found the Dilettanti Society, aimed at promoting a taste for Classical antiquities

1739 Establishment of the Foundling Hospital, the first secular institution of its kind

1750 The first umbrella is sported in London by Jonas Hanway. He is roundly ridiculed

1751 Robert Clive establishes control of southern India

1753 Founding of the British Museum

1754 Outbreak of the Seven Years' War, a tussle between the Great Powers over colonisation and the division of territory

1755 Samuel Johnson publishes his Dictionary

1761 Ashkenazi burial ground opens on Brady Street

1764 London introduces a system of house numbering

1768 Founding of the Royal Academy

1770 Construction of London's first canal, the Limehouse Cut; Captain Cook lands at Botany Bay and claims it for Britain

1776 American Declaration of Independence

1780 Outbreak of anti-Catholic protests, known as the Gordon Riots

1783 The last execution at Tyburn

1787 Founding of the Association for the Abolition of the Slave Trade

1788 The first shipment of convicts from Millbank arrives in Australia

1799 Death of Tipu Sultan; the British consolidate their position in south India

1801 Birth of the United Kingdom with the union of Britain and Ireland; Pitt wants to make provisions for Catholics but George III refuses

1802 Madame Tussaud arrives in London; West India Dock is built: it will quickly be followed by a succession of others; following the Treaty of Alexandria signed with France the previous year, treasures including the Rosetta Stone arrive at the British Museum

1805 Battle of Trafalgar: victory over Napoleon; Nelson is killed

1807 Pall Mall is the first London street to be lit by gas

1813 Bryan Donkin sets up the fist meat cannery in Bermondsey; Spencer Perceval, the only British Prime Minister to be assassinated, is shot

1815 Battle of Waterloo ends the Napoleonic Wars

1816 The British Museum purchases the Parthenon Marbles from Lord Elgin; economic depression following the Napoleonic Wars leads to poverty and rioting, which is met by increasingly repressive government measures

1817 Dulwich Picture Gallery opens, the first public art gallery in Britain

1820 The Cato Street conspiracy, a plot to assassinate the entire Cabinet, is foiled; the cause of reform is retarded by fears of public radicalism

1824 Founding of the National Gallery

1829 Catholic Emancipation Act: the first Catholic MP takes his seat in Parliament; London begins its first scheduled omnibus services

1832 The Reform Bill is passed, greatly augmenting the electorate

1833 Abolition of the Slave Trade

1836 The first London railway is built between Deptford and Bermondsey (London Bridge)

1837 Queen Victoria makes Buckingham Palace her London residence

1840 The last ever Bartholomew Fair is held at Smithfield

1841 Fenchurch Street Station is the first to be built in the City

1843 Opening of the Thames Tunnel between Rotherhithe and Wapping

1846 Famine strikes Ireland; the first operation under ether to be performed in Europe is carried out at University College Hospital

1847 The British Museum opens

1848 Founding of the Pre-Raphaelite Brotherhood; Chartist meeting on Kennington Common, a prelude to delivering to Parliament a petition demanding better rights and enfranchisement for the working man

1849 Charles Henry Harrod sets up his famous store in Knightsbridge

1851 The Great Exhibition is held in Hyde Park

1853 Beginning of the Crimean War

1857 The Indian Mutiny (Uprising)

1858 Queen Victoria is proclaimed sovereign of India; the *Great Eastern* is launched

1860 Henry Poole invents the dinner jacket (renamed the 'tuxedo' in New York) in Savile Row

1861 Lagos in Nigeria is proclaimed a crown colony

1863 The churchyard of St Botolph-without-Bishopsgate is the first to open as a public garden; the first Tube line, the Metropolitan, runs from Paddington to Farringdon

1864 The first Christmas Day swim in the Serpentine takes place

1865 The Salvation Army is founded in Whitechapel

1868 Britain's last public execution takes place outside Newgate; its first traffic roundabout comes into operation at Parliament Square

1875 London's first commemorative plaque is set up (in Leicester Square, to Sir Joshua Reynolds)

1876 Alexander Graham Bell makes the first UK demonstration of his telephone from Brown's Hotel

1877 Queen Victoria is declared Empress of India; Dr Barnardo opens his 'Ragged School' in the East End

1880 All clocks in the country are set to Greenwich Mean Time

1895 Oscar Wilde is sentenced to Pentonville Prison

1897 Queen Victoria celebrates her Diamond Jubilee

1901 Death of Queen Victoria

1904 'Entente Cordiale' between France and Britain, aimed at solving colonial disputes in Africa

1907 The 5th Russian Labour Party congress is held in Whitechapel

1909 Selfridges opens on Oxford Street

1912 Suffragettes invade the House of Commons

1913 A suffragette plot to bomb St Paul's is foiled

1914 A suffragette slashes the *Rokeby Venus* with a meat cleaver; Britain declares war on Germany following the German invasion of Belgium

1916 The Easter Rising in Ireland; Daylight Saving is introduced; Battle of the Somme; Mark Gertler paints his *Merry-go-Round*

1917 The Royal Family abandon their German title, becoming the House of Windsor; the Balfour Declaration supports the founding of a Jewish homeland in Palestine

1918 Women over 30 are enfranchised; the German army surrenders on 11th Nov: the date is still commemorated every year as Remembrance Day

1919 The Irish Republican Army (IRA) is founded and begins a campaign of political murders and aggression against British targets; the Cenotaph is unveiled on Whitehall; Nancy Astor becomes the first female MP

1920 The Unknown Soldier is buried in Westminster Abbey

1921 The province of Northern Ireland is formed; Gandhi stages a mass repudiation of the Prince of Wales in Calcutta

1922 Founding of the BBC and of the Irish Free State

1924 Britain elects its first ever Labour government: one of its first acts is to recognise Bolshevik Russia, which Lloyd George had previously refused to do

1925 British Summer Time is instituted on a permanent basis; J.L. Baird gives the first public demonstration of his new television, at Selfridges

1926 The British Commonwealth recognises a number of dominions as being exempt from British legislative control

1928 The Thames floods, drowning four people in London. Many artworks are damaged at Tate Britain

1929 The Dorothy Warren Gallery in Mayfair is raided by police: it is exhibiting erotic art by D.H. Lawrence which is deemed obscene

1932 Oswald Mosley founds the British Union of Fascists; Sir Thomas Beecham founds the London Philharmonic Orchestra

1934 The Bauhaus architect Walter

Gropius comes to London, fleeing Nazi persecution. He stays in the capital for three years

1936 The first high-definition TV broadcasts are made from Alexandra Palace; Battle of Cable Street in the East End between police and opponents of the Fascists; Edward VIII abdicates

1938 Sigmund Freud comes to London, fleeing persecution in his native Vienna

1939 IRA bombs are detonated at Tottenham Court Road and Leicester Square Underground stations; Britain declares war on Germany following the latter's invasion of Poland

1940–1 London is badly damaged in the Blitz

1943 The *Scharnhorst* is sunk by British ships, among them HMS *Belfast*

1945 The end of the Second World War

1946 The new Labour government begins a programme of nationalisation

1947 George VI renounces the title Emperor of India; India gains independence

1948 The *Empire Windrush* brings 500 Jamaican immigrants to London; London hosts the Olympic Games; end of the British mandate in Palestine: the state of Israel is declared; the National Health Service is set up

1949 Strike by London dockworkers

1950 Britain sends troops to Korea; Scottish nationalists steal the Stone of Destiny from Westminster Abbey (it is recovered soon after)

1951 The Festival of Britain opens

1952 Accession of Queen Elizabeth II; Agatha Christie's *The Mousetrap* begins its theatre run

1954 Roman temple of Mithras discovered in the City

1956 The Clean Air Act is passed in an attempt to deal with London's

notorious 'pea-souper' smogs; the Suez Crisis results in the Prime Minister's resignation

1957 Ghana and Malaya achieve independence

1958 Race riots in Notting Hill

1961 Closure of the Victualling Yard at Deptford

1962 Planning laws capping the height of buildings at 80ft are lifted, paving the way for the towering constructions of the future

1963 Kenya achieves independence

1964 Martin Luther King preaches at St Paul's Cathedral

1965 Winston Churchill is accorded a state funeral

1967 London Bridge is sold to an oil magnate in Arizona

1968 Closure of St Katharine Docks

1969 The Aviva Tower becomes the first building to be taller than St Paul's; abolition of the death penalty for murder

1971 Decimal currency is introduced in Britain and Ireland

1972 Ugandan Asians arrive in Britain, expelled from their country by President Amin

1973 Britain joins the EEC, the forerunner of the EU; IRA bombs are discovered at Baker Street and Sloane Square Tube; the government promises to tax the rich 'until the pips squeak'; the three-day week comes into force

1974 Covent Garden Market moves to Nine Elms, Battersea

1976 More IRA bomb attacks on the London Tube; the Brick Lane synagogue becomes a mosque; the National Theatre is opened

1977 The Queen celebrates her Silver Jubilee

1978 'Winter of Discontent': freezing

temperatures and repeated strikes and Trades Union disputes

1979 Margaret Thatcher becomes Britain's first female Prime Minister

1981 A development corporation is set up to repurpose the London docks; Tower 42 becomes the tallest office block in Europe; race riots in Brixton

1982 Billingsgate fish market moves to West India Dock; opening of the Barbican Centre; beginning of the Falklands War; opening of the Thames Barrier; an intruder is found in the Queen's bedroom in Buckingham Palace

1983 IRA bombs explode on Oxford Street and outside Harrods

1985 The East London Mosque opens on Whitechapel Road; further riots in Brixton

1986 The 'Big Bang' deregulation of the London Stock Market: the resulting boom leads to many companies moving from the cramped City to former dockyard premises; Richard Rogers's Lloyd's Building is opened; the first newspaper companies move from Fleet Street to Wapping

1987 Smoking is banned on the Underground following a fire at King's Cross

1989 The Truman Brewery on Brick Lane ceases production

1990 Crowds take to the streets to demonstrate against the government's Community Charge or 'poll tax'

1991 More IRA bomb attacks on the London Tube; One Canada Square becomes the tallest building in Europe; beginning of the Gulf War

1992–3 Irish terrorist bombs explode in the City causing fatalities and damage to historic buildings; fruit and vegetables cease to be traded at Spitalfields Market; fire at Windsor Castle; Buckingham Palace is opened to visitors

1996 The Stone of Destiny is officially moved from London to Edinburgh

1997 The Prime Minster, Tony Blair, throws a 'Cool Britannia' party in Downing Street, to which rock stars, fashion designers and left-leaning literary luminaries are invited; Diana, Princess of Wales dies in a car crash in Paris

2000 London celebrates the Millennium

2003 Britain supports the US invasion of Iraq

2004 Norman Foster's 'Gherkin' opens

2005 Islamic terrorists detonate bombs on the London Underground: over 50 people are killed and many more injured; Reuters moves out of Fleet Street, the last remaining newspaper business to do so

2011 Heron Tower becomes the tallest building in the City

2012 Renzo Piano's Shard is the tallest building in the European Union; London hosts the Olympic Games

2013 The London Mithraeum is discovered under Walbrook Square; former Prime Minister Margaret Thatcher is granted a ceremonial funeral

2020 The 2016 Brexit vote comes into force in January and London becomes the capital of a UK outside the EU

2022 Queen Elizabeth II celebrates her Platinum Jubilee; she dies in September

2023 Coronation of King Charles III; 22 Bishopsgate, the City's tallest building, rises over 900ft into the sky. Eleven new towers, some even taller, are projected by 2030.

THE CITY OF LONDON

The City is London's most ancient quarter and a global financial centre: for over two millennia it has been closely connected with international trade and commerce. The tightly built 'Square Mile' of small streets, crooked alleys, squares, courts, churches, civic buildings and offices stretches from the Royal Courts of Justice in the Strand (Temple Bar) to Aldgate in the east and from the Thames in the south to City Road in the north. It is a

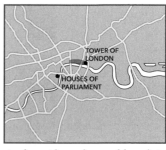

concentrated area in constant flux, where ancient jostles with modern—although in recent years, the modern has begun elbowing the ancient out of the way, as giant, mixed-use towers soar ever higher above the narrow alleys, claiming a place on the skyline from the spires, steeples and rooflines of older structures.

Some highlights of the area

✦ **St Paul's Cathedral**, the masterpiece of Sir Christopher Wren and one of the great works of English Baroque architecture;

✦ The myriad smaller **City churches**, numinous and atmospheric;

✦ The **Guildhall Art Gallery**, with a fine collection of paintings and sculpture and remains of the amphitheatre of Roman Londinium.

The City of London Corporation is keen to attract visitors and much investment has gone into hotels and shopping complexes. Though the City's demographic is changing, its worker : resident ratio is still weighted towards the former and it is much busier on weekdays, when the streets and alleyways hum with business while tucked away in the oases of quiet, leafy courtyards, office and construction workers take coffee breaks and eat their lunchtime sandwiches. Although weekends offer relatively quieter streets, be aware that many bars and restaurants may be closed, and though most tourist attractions are open, the City's beautiful and historic churches are very often not. Weekdays are the best time to visit these, from around 10am to early afternoon.

CITY INFORMATION CENTRE

St Paul's Churchyard. Map p. 638, C3. You can book City walks and buy travel cards and tickets. cityoflondon.gov.uk.

The Walkie-Talkie looms over the Thames, with the Scalpel puncturing the sky beside it. On the waterfront are the blue glass Northern & Shell building and Old Billingsgate, with its fish weather vane and dolphin finials. Between them is the graceful lead spire of St Margaret Pattens.

HISTORY OF THE CITY OF LONDON

London first became a port of wealth and prominence under Roman occupation (AD 43–410). In the 2nd century, the Romans built a towering defence wall around the City, 20ft high and 8ft wide, as impressive as Hadrian's Wall in the North. It formed the foundations for the medieval city wall that was restored by King Alfred in the 9th century and remained standing until the 18th and 19th centuries. The legacy of this defensive circuit loosely defines the perimeters of the City to this day and significant remains may still be seen at Tower Hill, the Barbican and on the modern road called London Wall.

After the Norman Conquest of 1066, William the Conqueror built three mighty fortresses in the City to subdue its citizens (the Tower, officially outside the City's limits, is the only one that remains). However, William also recognised the City's value to the wealth of the country and approved a London charter which upheld previous Saxon rights and privileges. In the 12th century, the City was granted the autonomy of self government, a privilege that continues today. Many of the City's grand livery companies (*see below*) were founded in the 12th–13th centuries. By the 15th century the City was home to flourishing trading firms and in 1600 the great East India Company was established. In 1565, Sir Thomas Gresham founded the Royal Exchange, opened by Elizabeth I. The Plague of 1665 reduced the population by one fifth and then in 1666 the Great Fire reduced five-sixths of the medieval city to ashes, destroying 86 out of 107 parish churches and the halls of 44 livery companies. Although the chief architect, Christopher Wren, wished to restructure along more planned, Enlightenment lines, the urgent need to rebuild meant that the City was re-erected over its medieval footprint, within the outline of the old Roman walls.

After the Fire many wealthy inhabitants moved west, but the City remained a great commercial centre. The Bank of England was founded in 1694 and this and other major civic buildings such as the Mansion House, the official residence of the Lord Mayor, were constructed. By the 19th century, the Port of London was the largest in the world and the fulcrum of the British Empire. The expansion of the Victorian era saw the demolition of residential areas, including many historic buildings, to make way for commercial premises and the railway. Fenchurch Street, Cannon Street, Blackfriars and Liverpool Street stations were constructed and with them came new, wider thoroughfares such as Queen Victoria Street, lined with banks and warehouses.

In the Second World War, the City was subjected to terrific assault during the Blitz. German aircraft used the Thames to navigate their way to London and whole areas were laid waste by incendiary bombs. After the War, the City was painstakingly rebuilt and since the 1980s, high-rise buildings began to arrive. The soaring towers of the 21st century have changed the landscape once more.

Today the City is one of the most important financial centres in the world. Statistics from the City of London website at the time of writing recorded over

500,000 workers making the weekday commute from outside its boundaries and ten million annual visitors to its tourist attractions. In comparison, realtively few people actually live here; the City only has about 9,000 residents.

THE CITY OF LONDON CORPORATION AND LORD MAYOR

In the 12th century, in recognition of its importance as a trading centre, the City of London was granted the right to run its own affairs by the Crown. Today it is still a city in its own right and a ceremonial county, with its own local government and police force. The City's boundaries are delineated by plaques bearing its coat of arms: the shield of St George borne by dragons. The City motto, *Domine dirige nos* (Lord, direct us), is to be seen inscribed upon many buildings and monuments. The City is divided into 25 districts, known as Wards, each of which is represented by elected councillors and an Alderman.

The City of London Corporation is headed by the Lord Mayor (a role distinct from the Mayor of London), who is elected annually and whose role is unsalaried and non-party political. Only the Sovereign takes precedence over the Lord Mayor in the City. The Lord Mayor's role is essentially that of an ambassador, promoting the City's interests both abroad and at home, and he (or she) presides over of the Court of Aldermen and the Court of Common Council (the Ward representatives), who meet in the Guildhall. The City Corporation is proud to be the oldest continuously elected governing body in the world.

The Lord Mayor's Show, held annually in November since 1215, is the official procession from the City to the Royal Courts of Justice in Westminster, where the Lord Mayor takes the oath of office and swears allegiance to the Crown. The procession is over three miles long and the Lord Mayor rides in a historic gilded state coach, accompanied by sheriffs, aldermen, the Sword Bearer and the Common Cryer. The City's livery companies and regiments also participate. On the way, the procession stops at St Paul's Cathedral, where the Lord Mayor is blessed by the Dean.

The livery companies

The City has over 100 livery companies, all of which are linked to its medieval trading past when guilds were set up as fraternities for its tradesmen. The guilds maintained professional standards, regulated crafts and provided support, education and places of worship for their members. They were also fiercely protectionist, limiting all activity in each sphere to guild members. In the 21st century they no longer hold a monopoly over trade but are committed to upholding excellence and funding educational and charitable projects. The Worshipful Company of Goldsmiths is still responsible for regulating the gold standard and its Hall is home to the London Assay Office. Some livery companies, such as Maltmen, Bonnet Makers, Pinmakers, Soapmakers, Hatband Makers and Galochemakers, have ceased to exist.

The order of precedence, originally based on financial and political influence, is now based on the antiquity of the company. The Great Twelve are as follows:

1. **Mercers**. Hall on Ironmonger Lane (*map p. 639, D3*)
2. **Grocers**. Hall on Princes Street (*map p. 639, D3*)
3. **Drapers**. Hall on Throgmorton Avenue (*map p. 639, E2*)
4. **Fishmongers**. Hall at London Bridge (*map p. 639, D4–E4*)
5. **Goldsmiths**. Hall on Foster Lane (*map p. 638, C2*)
6. **Skinners**. Hall on Dowgate Hill (*map p. 639, D3*)
7. **Merchant Taylors**. Hall on Threadneedle Street (*map p. 639, E3*)
8. **Haberdashers**. Hall on West Smithfield (*map p. 638, B2*)
9. **Salters**. Hall on Fore Street (*map p. 639, D2*)
10. **Ironmongers**. Hall in Shaftesbury Place (*map p. 638, C2*)
11. **Vintners**. Hall on Upper Thames Street (*map p. 639, D3*)
12. **Clothworkers**. Hall in Dunster Court (*map p. 639, E3*).

Freedom of the City gave a member of a guild or livery company the right to carry out their trade within the Square Mile, the right to vote, immunity from conscription into the armed forces and the right to marry in St Paul's Cathedral. Freedom is still granted and ancient surviving privileges still permit a freeman (or woman) of the City to herd a flock of sheep over London Bridge and a flock of geese down Cheapside. Entry to the livery companies' premises is not open to the public; to visit their halls one must apply in person directly. See the website for further details (*cityoflondon.gov.uk*) or ask at the City Information Centre (*p. 16*).

AROUND FLEET STREET & LUDGATE HILL

Map p. 638, A3–B3. Underground: Temple, Blackfriars.

Fleet Street, which runs from Temple Bar to Ludgate Circus, is the ancient road that linked Westminster with the City of London. It derives its name from the River Fleet or Holbourne, an underground river (parts of which are now a sewer) which rises at Hampstead and Highgate Ponds, flows down the Holborn Valley and joins the Thames near Blackfriars Bridge.

Fleet Street has long been associated with both the legal profession and the printing trade, hence its names the 'Street of Shame' and the 'Street of Ink'. Legal London continues to survive, thrive and expand here and until the late 1980s, Fleet Street was the centre of Britain's newspaper industry (the first newspaper, *The Daily Courant*, was set up in 1702). At one time nearly all national newspapers and international journals were printed in the area. In its 20th-century editorial heyday, when hard-bitten, hard-drinking journalists delivered copy either longhand or banged it out on old-fashioned typewriters, the line between workplace and watering hole was remarkably blurred. Each newspaper had a pub regarded by its staff as its own and many had a nickname. For example, the *Mirror*'s hacks could be found in the 'Stab in the Back' (the White Hart, off Fetter Lane; now demolished). The neighbourhood was especially frenzied late at night, when the dailies went to press with their first editions and the great presses rumbled in the basements. Today, all newspapers have moved their printing plants and editorial offices elsewhere. Reuters, the last to remain, left in 2005. Fleet Street is now an ordinary Monday-to-Friday working area of London with some interesting sights and a few historic pubs on the way to St Paul's Cathedral.

FROM TEMPLE BAR TO YE OLD CHESHIRE CHEESE

At no. 1–2 Fleet St, at the junction with the Strand, is the former **Child's Bank**, in a building of 1878–80. Child & Co. was founded in the 17th century, some decades before the Bank of England (it was in fact the third oldest bank in the world; the Child family home at Osterley, with interiors by Adam, can be visited; *see p. 528*). Latterly part of the NatWest banking group, it closed its doors forever in the summer of 2022. The square blue plaque low down on the wall confirms that this was also once the site of the Devil Tavern, demolished in 1787, a literary haunt where Ben Jonson reigned supreme in the 'Apollo Club'. A mock ode under a bust of the god apostrophised wine as 'the true Phoebeian liquor: cheers the brains, makes wit the quicker.' Luminaries of the succeeding generation who drank here included John Aubrey and John Evelyn.

The half-timbered house at **no. 17 Fleet St**, with a projecting upper storey and pairs of oriel windows, dates from 1610 and is one of the few buildings to have escaped the Great Fire. Its lower floor, built of stone, is the entrance to the Inner Temple and Temple Church (*see p. 215*). Built as the Prince Henry pub (presumably named after the elder son of James I), the first floor, known as Prince Henry's Room, has a Jacobean plaster ceiling with the Prince of Wales's feathers and the initials PH. In the 17th century the pub was known as the Fountain Inn and in 1661 was visited by Samuel Pepys, who 'stayed till 12 at night drinking and singing'. The building is now Catalonia House.

Ye Olde Cock Tavern, a short way on at no. 22, preserves some 17th-century interior fittings from the original inn that stood on the other side of the road. In the 1880s it was rebuilt on the current site. Also on the south side is **Hoare's Bank** (no. 37), founded in 1672 by Richard Hoare, a goldsmith and dealer in precious gems, who moved to Fleet Street in 1690. Still run by the Hoare family, it is the only remaining private bank in the UK. The Neoclassical building of Bath stone was designed by Charles Parker in 1829–30 to incorporate an office, strongroom and living space. Famous customers have included Catherine of Braganza, Sir Godfrey Kneller, Samuel Pepys, Lord Byron and Jane Austen. The marvellously old-fashioned banking hall exudes an air of quiet gentility and old-world Englishness.

Opposite Hoare's Bank is the neo-Gothic church of **St Dunstan-in-the-West** (*stdunstaninthewest.org*), which has a fine openwork lantern tower and centralised octagonal interior lit by windows high up in the walls. The medieval church, founded c. 1170, was rebuilt by John Shaw in 1830–3 and completed by his son. John Donne was vicar here in 1624–31. The tower was restored in 1950 after bomb damage during

World War Two. The famous clock to the right of the tower is by Thomas Harris. Dating from 1671, it was the first clock in London to have a minute hand. It is also the oldest performing clock in London: the hours and quarters are struck by two club-wielding giants (thought to represent Gog and Magog). The church is also famed for its exterior statue of Elizabeth I (1586), the only one known to have been carved during her reign and which previously stood on top of the Ludgate (an entrance to the City demolished in 1760). In the octagonal interior, the carved wooden high altar and reredos date from the 17th century and many of the monuments are from the original church. On the left side in an amusing monument to Hobson Judkin, 'the honest solicitor', and on the right the bust of Edward James Auriol, the 17-year-old only child of a rector of St Dunstan's, who drowned in the Rhône in Geneva in 1847. St Dunstan's is home to the Romanian Orthodox Church in London and the limewood painted iconostasis (c. 1860) was brought from Antim Monastery near Bucharest in 1966.

CITY CHURCHES

In 1665, at the time of the outbreak of the Great Fire, there were 107 churches in the City of London. 86 were destroyed and only 51 rebuilt, many of them by Sir Christopher Wren, his pupil Nicholas Hawksmoor, and his assistant, the exceptionally gifted Robert Hooke. Of the resultant new total of 72 churches, 25 were demolished during the rapid development and of London in the later 19th century, reducing the number of churches to 47. Luftwaffe bombs wreaked havoc during WWII. Eighteen churches were utterly destroyed, and of those, eight were never rebuilt: at certain points in the City, isolated towers still stand, forlorn reminders of a former church. Today there are 39 churches in the City. The most complete surviving examples by Wren are St Martin-within-Ludgate and St Margaret Lothbury. St Mary Woolnoth is the only City church entirely by Hawksmoor (though altered) and the only one to have escaped the Blitz unscathed. Generally the City churches are open on weekdays (there is typically a half-hour Communion service at lunchtime). Not all are used for regular Anglican worship: some have become study centres or spiritual retreats; others offer a home to other congregations. For information, see *london-city-churches.org.uk*.

Sweeney Todd, the Demon Barber of Fleet Street, is reputed to have had his shop near St Dunstan's, where he murdered his clients and made them into pies. Further along on the opposite side, **El Vino's wine bar**, founded in 1879 and a Fleet Street institution, served generations of newspapermen, who thronged the bar each evening, mingling with barristers and lawyers, picking up useful gossip. Until 1982, women were not allowed to stand and drink with male colleagues and would only be served at tables in the back room. El Vino's still has an extensive wine list (*davy.co.uk*). Behind it, Old Mitre Court is the **site of Serjeants' Inn**, seat of the former Serjeants-at Law, senior barristers who were gradually superseded by QCs and KCs. The Inn closed in 1871.

Stay on the north side of the road as you round the gentle curve of Fleet Street, to appreciate the celebrated view of St Paul's Cathedral rising over the Fleet valley, loomed over now by the behemoth of 22 Bishopsgate. The small alleys opening off Fleet Street—Johnson's Court, St Dunstan's Court, Bolt Court, Hind Court, Wine Office Court—are part of London's pre-Great Fire street pattern and probably originated as gardens. **Ye Olde Cheshire Cheese** (*145 Fleet St; ye-olde-cheshire-cheese.co.uk*) is an atmospheric 17th-century pub (rebuilt in the year after the Great Fire) with 18th-century additions. It is possible that one of its past patrons was Samuel Johnson, who lived in Gough Square just beyond it (*see below*). Other luminaries who certainly drank here include Dickens, Tennyson, Thackeray, Mark Twain, Conan Doyle and W.B. Yeats. Inside, the fittings are mainly 19th-century and the myriad small rooms are hung with mementoes. The parrot, Polly (d. 1926, now stuffed), was notoriously foul-mouthed and enjoyed imitating customers. On Armistice Night, 1918, she apparently mimicked the sound of popping champagne corks as bottles were opened to celebrate the end of the WWI. The Cheshire Cheese today aims to continue the venerable London tradition of the chop house, serving simple, meaty English food.

Statue of Queen Elizabeth I on the exterior of St Dunstan-in-the-West. Known to have been carved during the monarch's lifetime (1586), it once stood on Ludgate, an ancient entrance to the City.

DR JOHNSON'S HOUSE
Tucked away behind Fleet Street in Gough Square is the handsome red-brick house of c. 1700 where the great lexicographer Dr Samuel Johnson lived from 1748–59 (*map p. 638, A2–A3; drjohnsonshouse.org*).

Originally from Lichfield in Staffordshire, Johnson moved to London with his friend, the actor David Garrick. A struggling journalist when he first occupied the house, he produced *The Rambler* here and wrote *The Vanity of Human Wishes*. It was also while living here that he was commissioned to compile the celebrated Dictionary. Published in two volumes in 1755, it went through four editions in Johnson's lifetime and instantly became the standard authority. A congenial man with a wide circle of friends, Johnson nevertheless did not enjoy great wealth. He lived simply at Gough Square with his wife, Elizabeth Porter, 20 years his senior, until her death in 1752, and later his Jamaican servant, Francis Barber, joined him.

The house is unostentatious and pleasing. On the ground floor is the **Parlour**, with a portrait of Francis Barber. The stairs lead to a landing with hinged partitions, allowing the staircase to be blocked off and one large room created from the **Withdrawing**

Room and **Miss Williams's Room**. The authoress Anna Williams was a friend of Mrs Johnson and companion to Dr Johnson after his wife's death. The portrait of her was painted by Sir Joshua Reynolds' sister Frances. By all accounts Miss Williams became foul tempered in later life, perhaps owing to a failed cataract operation which left her blind. Francis Barber fled the household twice because of her; but the breach was healed and 'Frank' was the main beneficiary of Johnson's will.

At the top of the house is the **Garret**, where the Dictionary was written and where, at long tables, six clerks took down Johnson's succinct and often witty definitions. Throughout the rooms are period furnishings and objects, several of them personal to Johnson or to his close friends. Johnson's own walking stick is on show, as is his piece of 'healing gold', a medal he received when as a young child he was touched for the King's Evil by Queen Anne.

Facing the house, at the east end of Gough Square, is a modern **sculpture of Dr Johnson's cat**, Hodge, sitting with oyster shells by his side. Johnson regularly bought oysters for him; in those days they were cheap, not the luxury they have become.

SOME SPLENDID FORMER PRESS PALACES

Peterborough Court, the huge **former Daily Telegraph building** (135–141 Fleet St), with lateral doorways marked 'In' and 'Out', was completed in 1928–31 by Elcock & Sutcliffe with Thomas Tait. It is an Art Deco fusion of monumental classical motifs (twin Mercurys scurrying East and West, with a map of Britain and Ireland behind them) and giant Egyptian-style columns in the central section. The huge clock is by the Birmingham Guild of Handicraft. The building is now owned by the Qatari royal family.

Further down, at 120–129 across Shoe Lane, are the **former offices of *The Daily Express***, a sleek and sensational Art Deco building with bands of clear glass and black Vitrolite (opaque tinted glass made by Pilkington) set in chromium strips. Designed by Sir Owen Williams in 1930–3, it is London's earliest curtain-walled building and has a sumptuous Art Deco entrance hall by Robert Atkinson. It was built when the *Daily Express*, owned by the press baron Lord Beaverbrook, was Britain's most popular paper. Evelyn Waugh briefly worked here in 1938 and went on to lampoon the experience in his novel *Scoop*. At the time of writing, the building was undergoing redevelopment.

Directly opposite the *Daily Express* building, the huge stone edifice with an oculus above the doorway occupied by a bugle-blowing herald angel is the **ex-headquarters of Reuters**, designed by Sir Edwin Lutyens in 1935. Reuters left in 2005.

ST BRIDE'S

Directly behind the Reuters building is Wren's church of St Bride (*map p. 638, B3; stbrides.com*), the 'spiritual home of the media' since Wynkyn de Worde, the first printer to set up in Fleet Street in 1500, was buried in the churchyard. Samuel Pepys was baptised here. The church was rebuilt after the Great Fire, in 1671–8, and the soaring, telescopic steeple was added in 1701–3. It is the tallest of all Wren's spires (226ft) and has launched a thousand similes, the most famous of which likens it to a tiered wedding cake. The church was gutted by bombs in 1940 but the steeple remained standing

Mercury figures hasten from the British Isles to spread news around the globe. Detail of the façade of the former *Daily Telegraph* building (1931).

despite a raging fire which caused its bells to melt and fall. The church was rebuilt from 1954 by Godfrey Allen, an authority on Wren. The *trompe l'oeil* behind the altar, giving the impression of an apse, is by Glyn Jones. To the left of the high altar is the **Journalists' Altar**, commemorating those in the news industry who have died, been kidnapped or are missing in the field. Prior to reconstruction, the site was excavated by F.W. Grimes and Roman remains were discovered, along with the foundations of six previous churches on the site as well as thousands of human skeletons, many believed to belong to victims of the Great Plague. An exhibition in the **crypt** displays selected finds (including an iron coffin with a lock, designed to deter graverobbers). Among the old memorials is one to the composer Thomas Weelkes, who was buried here in 1623. Four hundred years later, a motet by him was sung at the coronation of King Charles III.

Behind the church, St Bride's Passage leads to Bride Lane, with the red-brick and stone **St Bride Foundation**, founded in 1891 as a social, cultural and recreational centre for locals and for those in the printing trade. On the upper level is the St Bride Library, with important collections relating to printing, publishing, typography and the graphic arts.

LUDGATE HILL
Ludgate Circus is the busy traffic junction of Farringdon Street, Ludgate Hill and Fleet Street. Its name commemorates the ancient Lud Gate, popularly believed to be named after King Lud, mythical founder of London, but more likely to derive from the Old English *hlid*, a gap or opening, or *hlið*, a slope or hillside, since the gate stood at the site of an ascent to the City's highest point. It was the first curfew gate in London to be closed at night. Statues from it, notably that of Elizabeth I, may be seen at St Dunstan-in-the-West on Fleet Street (*see p. 23*). Fleet Place off Limeburner Lane is named to commemorate the **site of the Fleet Prison**, which stood on the east side of the Fleet

river and was used for those committed by the Star Chamber and for debtors. The prison was twice rebuilt, after destruction in the Great Fire (1666) and again in the Gordon Riots (1780); it was finally pulled down in 1844–6.

Ludgate Hill rises towards St Paul's Cathedral. Some way up on the left, next to Ye Olde London pub, a slender lead spire marks the church of **St Martin-within-Ludgate** (*open weekdays 11–3*), so named because it stood just within the Roman wall, close to Lud Gate. The church was rebuilt after the Great Fire by Wren, probably with Robert Hooke, in 1677–86 and has an original font, reredos and pulpit of 1680. Other fine woodwork includes a doorcase (right of the entrance) with the peapod emblem of Grinling Gibbons, though the carving is attributed to William Emmett, Gibbons's predecessor as Master Carver in Wood to the Crown. The 17th-century breadshelves against the left-hand wall are originally from St Mary Magdalen, Fish Street. Wealthy parishioners would leave food for poorer members of the parish on these shelves. Captain (later Admiral) William Penn, father of the founder of Pennsylvania, was married in the former church in 1643. Although the roof was damaged during the Blitz, the church was the least damaged of Wren's City's churches during World War Two. A Chinese Christian congregation gathers here every Sunday.

Further up again, in Ave Maria Lane, is **Stationers' Hall**, the guildhall of the Stationers' Company. The fine Neoclassical stone-faced east front, facing the outer courtyard, is by Robert Mylne (1800). The Stationers' Company, founded c. 1402, was incorporated by royal charter in 1557 and for a time it preserved the sole right of printing in England (apart from the presses at Oxford and Cambridge), retaining a monopoly on the publishing of almanacs until 1771. Until the passing of the Copyright Act of 1911, every work published in Great Britain had to be registered for copyright at Stationers' Hall. In 1933 the company was amalgamated with that of the Newspaper Makers. A plane tree in the court behind the Hall marks the spot where seditious books used to be burnt.

Behind Stationers' Hall is **Amen Court**, a quiet little nook that escaped WWII bombing. Nos 1–3 were built in 1671–3 as dwellings for the Canons Residentiary of St Paul's. The Black Dog of Newgate, a fearsome ghostly hound, is reputed to haunt the high wall that backs onto the site of Newgate Prison.

The names of the streets here—Paternoster Lane, Amen Court, Amen Corner, Ave Maria Lane—come from the prayers that the canons would chant as they processed to St Paul's Cathedral, which stands at the top of Ludgate Hill.

ST PAUL'S CATHEDRAL

Map p. 638, C3. Underground: St Paul's. Services only (no sightseeing) on Sun. This is a very popular destination; it is worth booking online to avoid the queue: stpauls.co.uk. Ticket prices are hefty. Leave plenty of time for your visit: visitors are ejected promptly at closing time and even before that, vergers begin roping off sections of the building. Guided tours of the cathedral and crypt can be taken for no extra charge (ask at the guiding desk; no advance bookings). The Triforium Tour (fee) includes the Trophy Room with Wren's Great Model (to book, see website).

ST PAUL'S CATHEDRAL: WEST FAÇADE

St Paul's Cathedral stands on the top of Ludgate Hill, which at 58ft above sea level shares with the summit of Cornhill the accolade of being the highest point in the City. St Paul's is the largest and most famous of all the City's many churches, the cathedral of the Bishop of London and the English Baroque masterpiece of Sir Christopher Wren, built between 1675 and 1711. Wren deliberately designed it to dominate the City landscape and until the construction of the Aviva Tower (1 Undershaft) in 1969, it was the tallest building in the City, complemented by the myriad spires of surrounding churches, designed by Wren and others. Today, despite the St Paul's Cathedral Preservation Act of 1935, its impact is drastically lessened by recent high-rise eruptions and at the time of writing, the Aviva Tower itself was due to be demolished and replaced by an even taller successor. Nevertheless, St Paul's is a true icon of London and fulfils Wren's belief that architecture, especially public architecture, has the power not only to establish a nation but also to induce its people to love their country. The surrounding area was devastated during the Blitz but St Paul's survived thanks to the St Paul's Watch, a group of volunteers who defended it during incendiary bombing raids. The cathedral is built of gleaming

Portland stone adorned with fine 17th-century carving. It is worth spending several hours in this magnificent place—but be prepared for large crowds at all times of year and queues to climb the dome.

HISTORY OF ST PAUL'S

There is no evidence to support the theory that a Roman temple stood on the commanding site now occupied by St Paul's, although Roman artefacts have been found in the area and Londinium's western hilltop would have been a logical site for a capitolium. What is certain is that a Christian church was founded here in AD 604 by Mellitus, a missionary companion of St Augustine who later became Archbishop of Canterbury. The earliest buildings were frequently destroyed by fire and Viking attacks. In 1087 Bishop Maurice, chaplain to William the Conqueror, founded the church which went on to become, after much rebuilding, the splendid medieval cathedral of Old St Paul's. It was the longest cathedral in England (600ft) and the central tower was surmounted by a steeple which at the lowest estimate was 460ft high—but destroyed by lightning in 1561 and never re-erected. Today St Paul's is one of the great churches of the Protestant world, but it is worth remembering that until the reign of Henry VIII it was a Catholic cathedral where Mass was celebrated and where saints were venerated. In Old St Paul's John Wycliffe was tried for heresy in 1377 and Tyndale's New Testament was publicly burned here in 1527. By the 17th century it had become sadly neglected and restorations were begun under Charles I. Inigo Jones added a classical portico to the west front, one of his objects being to banish from the church the 'secular rabble' that for over a century had used the nave (Paul's Walk) as a place of business (and frequently intrigue). Jones's restorations were halted by the outbreak of Civil War in 1642. Parliamentarians seized control of the cathedral and it was used as a barracks for 800 horses. After the Restoration in 1660, plans to restore and repair the cathedral were once again considered until the cathedral practically burned down in the Great Fire of 1666. Wren conceived several designs for a new building, including the so-called Great Model (housed in the Trophy Room), which, like Michelangelo's design for St Peter's, was in the form of a Greek Cross. As had happened with St Peter's likewise, the design was modified to a Latin Cross and finally, nine years after the Fire, work commenced on Sir Christopher Wren's new St Paul's; the first cathedral to be built in England since the Reformation. Building costs were largely met by a tax on sea-borne coal entering London. The cathedral was declared complete in 1711.

Exterior of St Paul's

The exterior of St Paul's consists throughout of two orders, the lower Corinthian, the upper Composite. On the north and south sides the upper order is merely a curtain wall, not corresponding with the height of the aisles and concealing the flying buttresses that support the clerestory of the nave. The balustrade along the top was added against the wishes of Wren, who cynically remarked that 'ladies think nothing well without an edging'. The west front, approached by a broad flight of steps and flanked by two towers, has a lower colonnade of twelve columns and an upper one of eight. In the pediment, sculpture by Francis Bird (1706) depicts the *Conversion of St Paul*. Above the pediment stands the figure of St Paul, flanked by other apostles and the four Evangelists, also by Bird. Bird also carved the statue of Queen Anne that stood by the west front (the current statue is a copy). Anne was the reigning monarch at the time of the cathedral's completion. In the northeast tower is a peal of bells and in the southwest tower are Great Paul (a bell weighing nearly 17 tons, the largest bell in the UK) and Great Tom, a bell tolled on the death of senior members of the Royal Family, the Archbishop of Canterbury, the Bishop of London, the Dean of St Paul's or the Lord Mayor of London.

The famous **dome**, built to rival that of St Peter's in Rome and one of the largest cathedral domes in the world, lifts its cross 365ft above the City. The outer dome is of wood covered with lead. Between it and the painted inner dome is a cone of brick which rises between them and bears the weight of the elegant lantern on the top.

Interior of St Paul's

The interior, though 'classical' in detail, still retains the general ground plan of a Gothic church—nave and aisles with triforium and clerestory, transepts and a deep choir— with, however, the great dome-space at the crossing. Against the massive piers rise Corinthian pilasters and stone enrichments relieve the wall-spaces. The monuments in the cathedral are eloquent of the nation's history, commemorating men of art and invention as well as victors in war.

On entering St Paul's, the visitor should first walk up the centre of the nave to the great space beneath the dome, where the huge proportions of the church are especially impressive.

The dome (A): The inner cupola of the dome soars 218ft above you, resting upon massive supports, of which the four chief ones, at the angles, afford room in their interiors for the vestries and the library staircase. Nineteenth-century mosaics executed by Salviati of Venice fill the spandrels, traditionally seen as linking spaces between the heavenly realm above and the earthly realm below and thus decorated with images of those who transmitted God's message to mankind: here on the west we see Old Testament prophets (from south to north, Isaiah, Jeremiah, Ezekiel and Daniel, designed by Alfred Stevens and partly executed by W.E.F.

Britten). The other spandrels show the Evangelists: SS Matthew and John (by G.F. Watts) and SS Mark and Luke (by Britten). In the quarter-domes, at a lower level, are more recent mosaics by Sir W.B. Richmond (d. 1921).

Above the arches is the Whispering Gallery (*see p. 34*), above which again are recesses with 19th-century marble statues of the Fathers of the Church. The cupola, above, was decorated by Sir James Thornhill with eight scenes in monochrome from the life of St Paul. Monochrome was used deliberately in a carefully planned scheme for the decoration of the new church, which was to be Anglican in spirit: dignified, dedicated to the glory of God, neither Roman Catholic (too gaudy) nor Puritan (too plain). Later decorations have eclipsed the original intent to a great degree. The spandrel mosaics are a marked example.

Quire (B): Although a Luftwaffe bomb struck the east end of the quire, bringing down tons of masonry onto the sanctuary, the priceless carvings escaped almost undamaged. Above the high altar is a carved and gilded baldachin of marble and oak, by Godfrey Allen and S.E. Dykes Bower, replacing the reredos damaged in 1941 and serving as a memorial to Commonwealth citizens of all creeds and races who lost their lives in the two World Wars. The tall bronze candlesticks in front are copied from four now in St-Bavon in Ghent, which were made by Benedetto da Rovezzano for the tomb of Henry VIII at Windsor but were sold under the Commonwealth.

The beautiful carved **choir stalls and organ case** are by Grinling Gibbons. The organ was originally built in 1695 by Father Smith (*see p. 218*) to John Blow's direction, and was played by Jeremiah Clarke at its inauguration.

The mosaics which decorate the vaulting of the quire were designed by Sir W.B. Richmond and were executed in 1891–1912. The central panel of the great apse shows *Christ in Majesty*, seated upon the rainbow: 'Behold, a throne was set in heaven, and one sat on the throne. And he that sat was to look upon like a jasper and a sardine stone: and there was a rainbow round about the throne, in sight like unto an emerald.' (*Revelation 4:2–3.*) In the shallow cupolas above the choir proper are (from west to east) the

Creation of the Beasts, *Creation of the Birds* and *Creation of the Fishes*.

North aisle: The **Chapel of All Souls (C)** was dedicated in 1925 to the memory of Field Marshal Earl Kitchener of Khartoum (d. 1916), with a recumbent figure by Reid Dick and a roll of honour of the Royal Engineers.

The **Chapel of St Dunstan (D)** has a memorial (under the first window) to Lord Leighton (d. 1896), painter and sculptor.

The **Monument to the Duke of Wellington (E)** is by Alfred Stevens. Above the pediments at either end are allegorical groups: *Truth Plucking out the Tongue of Falsehood* and *Valour Thrusting down Cowardice*. The equestrian statue on the top was executed by Tweed in 1912 from a sketch-model by Stevens.

Opposite it is the **Monument to General Gordon (F)** and further down on the left is the **Memorial to Lord Melbourne** (d. 1848) **(G)**, with *Two Angels at the Gate of Death* by Marochetti.

North transept (H): This part of the church was severely damaged by a bomb in April 1941, when the transept dome and the whole of the north porch, with the famous inscription from Wren's tomb: '*Si monumentum requiris, circumspice*' ('If you would see his monument, look around you'), fell into the crypt below. Here is William Holman Hunt's third version of his painting ***The Light of the World*** (1900). Commemorated here are the composer Sir Arthur Sullivan (of the Gilbert and Sullivan light operas); Sir Joshua Reynolds, with a monument by Flaxman; and Turner.

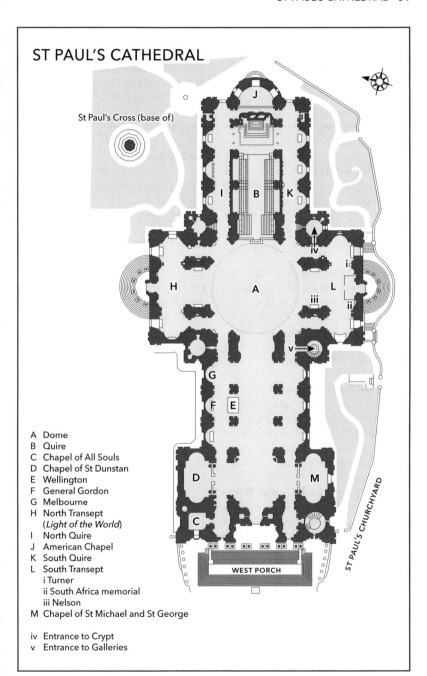

ST PAUL'S CATHEDRAL

St Paul's Cross (base of)

J

I B K

H A L

iv

i

iii

ii

v

G

F E

A Dome
B Quire
C Chapel of All Souls
D Chapel of St Dunstan
E Wellington
F General Gordon
G Melbourne
H North Transept
    (*Light of the World*)
I North Quire
J American Chapel
K South Quire
L South Transept
    i Turner
    ii South Africa memorial
    iii Nelson
M Chapel of St Michael and St George

iv Entrance to Crypt
v Entrance to Galleries

D M

C

ST PAUL'S CHURCHYARD

WEST PORCH

North quire (I): At the entrance to the north quire aisle are gates by Jean Tijou (c. 1712) and a statue of Samuel Johnson in a Roman toga, by Bacon. The choir screen, formed of the original altar rails, is also by Tijou. The Chapel of the Modern Martyrs commemorates Anglican martyrs since 1850.

American Chapel (J): The chapel which occupies the cathedral apse is the memorial to America's fallen in the Second World War, with a roll of honour containing 28,000 names of those who fell in operations based on Britain.

South quire (K): In the aisle is the figure (clad in a shroud) of John Donne (1573–1631), poet and Dean of St Paul's, the only comparatively uninjured monument (by Nicholas Stone) to have survived the destruction of Old St Paul's. It still shows traces of fire.

South transept (L): Here is the entrance to the crypt (*see below*), beyond which, at the angle of the dome-space, is a statue of the prison reformer John Howard (1726–90), the first monument admitted into the new St Paul's.

On the south wall of the transept is a memorial to **J.M.W. Turner (i)**. On the other side of the door is a bronze **memorial (ii) by Princess Louise**, the sculptor daughter of Queen Victoria, to the Colonial Troops who fell in the second South African War. On the west wall of the transept is a **monument to Lord Nelson (iii)**, shown leaning on an anchor, by John Flaxman; the reliefs on the pedestal represent the Arctic Ocean, the North Sea, the Nile and the Mediterranean.

Chapel of St Michael and St George (M): This chapel has since 1906 been occupied by the Most Distinguished Order of St Michael and St George, with the banners of the Knights Grand Cross (GCMG). The order (instituted in 1818) is conferred for distinguished services in colonial or foreign affairs. The prelate's throne is a memorial to Lord Forrest (d. 1918) of Bunbury, Western Australia, the first Australian peer. On the left is the door to the Geometrical Staircase—a spiral of 92 stone steps and an iron balustrade by Tijou (*accessible only on a guided tour*).

St Paul's Crypt and Trophy Room

The crypt (*entrance in the south transept*) corresponds in size with the upper church. Here are the graves of many of those whose monuments are above, as well as many additional monuments and graves to those who made outstanding contributions to the nation. Below the south choir aisle, at the foot of the staircase, is a bust of Sir John Macdonald (1815–91), first Prime Minister of Canada. In the second bay are monuments to the painter Sir Edwin Landseer and the hymn-writer and Bishop of Calcutta Reginald Heber (d. 1826), by Chantrey. In the pavement is the tomb of Sir Lawrence Alma-Tadema. In the next bay is the **tombstone of Sir Christopher Wren**, above which is the original tablet with its famous epitaph (*see North Transept, above*).

This bay and the one to the north are known as '**Painters' Corner**', for here rest Lord Leighton, Benjamin West, Sir Thomas Lawrence, Landseer, Millais, Turner, Reynolds and Holman Hunt. On the walls are memorials to William Blake, Van Dyck, Constable

Detail of the dome of St Paul's with Sir James Thornhill's monochrome scenes of the life of St Paul: *Conversion on the Road to Damascus* (right); *Shipwrecked on Malta* (centre) and *Attempting to convert Agrippa* (left).

and Lutyens. John Singer Sargent is commemorated by a relief group of the *Redemption*, which he designed.

The chapel at the east end of the crypt, formerly called St Faith's, was dedicated in 1960 as the Chapel of the Order of the British Empire. Further west a wall tablet marks the grave of Sir Alexander Fleming (d. 1955), discoverer of penicillin.

In the west portion of the crypt is the colossal porphyry **sarcophagus of Wellington** and further on a memorial to Florence Nightingale (1820–1910). Below the centre of the dome, **Lord Nelson** rests in a coffin made from the mainmast of the French ship *L'Orient*, enclosed in a sarcophagus of black and white marble originally designed for Cardinal Wolsey (*see p. 560*). In recesses to the south and north are other military heroes and a bust of Lawrence of Arabia (d. 1935).

A plaque commemorates 5,746 men of the garrison of Kut (Iraq) who died in 1916. In the adjoining recess is a memorial to the Labour politician Sir Stafford Cripps (d. 1952), with a fine bust by Epstein. Opposite is a bust of George Washington near a tablet to William Fiske, Olympic bobsleigh medallist and the first US citizen to join the RAF. He lost his life in the Battle of Britain, 'an American citizen who died that England might live'. The memorial to the poet and critic W.E. Henley (d. 1903) has a bust by Rodin.

In the **Trophy Room** is Wren's Great Model, the vast maquette of the projected cathedral, that was produced for King Charles II in 1673.

The galleries

The upper parts of the cathedral are reached by a staircase from the south aisle (*marked on the plan on p. 31*). Be warned: once committed to the ascent, it is not possible to turn back. First (easy to climb to) is the **Whispering Gallery**, 112ft in diameter, which runs within the lower dome. It takes its name from the fact that words whispered near the wall on one side can be distinctly heard at the other side: but the pressure of crowds often makes it difficult to test this. However, this is the best point from which to admire Thornhill's monochrome paintings in the dome.

Further up is the **Stone Gallery**, the exterior gallery around the base of the dome, which commands a fine view of London. Finally, up 528 steps from ground level (not recommended to anyone who suffers from claustrophobia or vertigo), is the **Golden Gallery**, a narrow ledge running around the base of the lantern. From here one is rewarded by panoramic views.

PATERNOSTER SQUARE & ST PAUL'S CHURCHYARD

North of St Paul's Cathedral is **Paternoster Square** (*map p. 638, C3*), where printing and publishing warehouses were based until their annihilation during the Blitz. Post-war rebuilding was contentious and generally disliked, until redevelopment by Sir William Whitfield in 2000 finally created a worthy setting for Wren's great masterpiece. The tripartite stone gateway at the south edge of the square is **Old Temple Bar**, originally erected in Fleet Street after the Great Fire (*see p. 219*). In the pedestrian-only piazza, modern buildings fan out from a central column topped by a flaming gilded urn. *Paternoster*, the bronze sculpture of Christ and his sheep, is by Elisabeth Frink (1975).

Worn 17th-century relief of a boy on a basket in Panyer Alley.

The London Stock Exchange relocated to Paternoster Square in 2004. Paternoster Row leads out of the square into **Panyer Alley** where, embedded in the wall, is a damaged 17th-century relief of a boy sitting on a woven basket (pannier). Some scholars have taken this to refer to a nearby former bread market. The inscription underneath the basket reads: 'When ye have sought the Citty round, yet still this is the highest ground. August the 27 1688'.

In the northeast part of St Paul's Churchyard stood **St Paul's Cross** (a column topped by a gilded statue of St Paul). In the 16th century it functioned as an open-air rallying point where members of the public could come to hear the Word. East of the cathedral is **St Paul's Cathedral School** (founded 1123; current buildings 1960s, incorporating the surviving tower of St Augustine, Watling Street). Across the street to the south, the distinctive angular tent-like structure is the **City of London Information Centre**, with useful visitor information on all things City-related. Standing with your back to the south porch and looking straight ahead along the stepped St Peter's Hill (at the top of which is a monument to City firefighters of WWII), you can see down to the Millennium Bridge (*described on p. 446*), built to connect St Paul's with Tate Modern and the South Bank. There is usually a steady stream of foot traffic using this thoroughfare. From here, it is an easy stroll to see the old Choir School in Carter Lane and the Old Deanery in Dean's Court (*described on p. 37*).

WHITEFRIARS & BLACKFRIARS

Map p. 638, B3. Underground: Blackfriars.

WHITEFRIARS

The plot between Bouverie Street and Whitefriars Street, south of Fleet Street, is the **site of the medieval monastery of Whitefriars**, so-called because the Carmelite monks wore white. Scant remains of the crypt may be seen behind a glass wall in a sunken courtyard off Magpie Alley (from Bouverie St) or Ashentree Court (from Whitefriars St). The chamfer-fronted Art Deco building on the corner of Tudor St and Whitefriars St is **Northcliffe House**, former headquarters of the *Daily Mail*, built in the 1920s.

Carmelite Street leads south towards the Embankment, past surviving Victorian buildings in red brick and pale stone. At the end of the street on the left is the neo-Gothic **Sion College** (Sir Arthur Blomfield, 1887), founded c. 1630 for the benefit of the Anglican clergy. Its chief glory was its library of 300,000 volumes, which possessed many rarities but suffered considerable war damage. The building was sold in 1996 and the books and manuscripts were split between Lambeth Palace and King's College Library. The view of the Thames is now overwhelmed by glassy towers. Where John Carpenter Street meets the Embankment you will see Seward Johnson Jr's amusing statue of a city worker attempting to hail a cab. *Taxi!* (1983) formerly stood in New York City and was originally painted all over in realistic colours. Now everything except the moustachioed executive's shirtfront has gone back to bronze. It belongs to the art collection of JP Morgan Chase and was brought to London in 2014.

Next door is the neo-Renaissance former City of London School for Boys (Davis & Emmanuel, 1882). On the curve of the street stands **Unilever House** (1932), with its long Ionic loggia, commissioned by the Lancashire soap manufacturers Lever Brothers after their merger with the Dutch margarine company Margarine Unie. More than one commentator has pointed out the irony of Seward Johnson's *Taxi!* being sited so close to this, since Seward Johnson was heir to the rival pharmaceutical company Johnson & Johnson.

New Bridge Street leads north from the Thames, on a line with Blackfriars Bridge. The buildings embraced by **Bridewell Place** mark the site of Bridewell Palace, possibly founded in Norman times but renovated by Henry VIII for official use during the early years of his reign. Holbein's *The Ambassadors*, which hangs in the National Gallery, was painted in Bridewell Palace. Edward VI granted the palace to the City of London and it became a house of correction for wayward women and afterwards the notorious Bridewell Prison. It was pulled down in the 19th century.

BLACKFRIARS

Blackfriars, to the east of New Bridge Street around Blackfriars Station, takes its name from the Dominicans, who wore black habits and who established extensive monastic buildings between the Thames and Ludgate Hill. Edward I granted them the land in 1274 and allowed them to rebuild the City Wall around this area. It was customary in medieval cities for the two mendicant orders to set up houses close to the city walls. Thus the Dominicans were at Blackfriars, near Ludgate and the mouth of the Fleet river, while the Franciscans (Greyfriars) occupied the areas around Newgate and Aldgate. The Carmelites (Whitefriars) had their monastery just to the west (*see above*). The Blackfriars buildings were used for state occasions and meetings of the Privy Council. A synod here in 1382 condemned Wycliffe's teaching as heretical. It was also here that a decree of divorce was heard between Henry VIII and Queen Katherine of Aragon. The friary was closed in 1538, during the Dissolution of the Monasteries.

Blackfriars Station is today a major terminus with entrances on both the north and sound sides of Blackfriars Bridge. Blackfriars Pier is a stop for river bus services.

BLACK FRIARS LANE

When the wide thoroughfare of Queen Victoria Street was created in 1867–71, it sliced through many ancient streets and alleys and as a result created wedge-shaped sites on which triangular buildings were built. One of the last remaining is the **Black Friar pub**, opposite the station on the corner of New Bridge Street. The sculpture over the main door is of a rotund, black-robed friar smiling beatifically down on passing traffic. Built in the 1870s, the pub has a unique Arts and Crafts interior dating from 1905 (restored 1983) of polychrome marble slabs and beaten bronze bas-reliefs of jolly friars at work. In the restaurant, there are red marble columns, an arched mosaic ceiling and further decorative figures.

From the pub, cross under the railway bridge and immediately on the left is Black Friars Lane, leading into **Playhouse Yard** (*map p. 638, B3*), where Richard Burbage's theatre once stood. Further up Black Friars Lane on the right is the **Apothecaries' Hall**, dating partly from the 1660s, partly from the 1780s. It is built on the site of the friary guest house.

CARTER LANE

Carter Lane, leading right out of Black Friars Lane, is an atmospheric street of mainly pre-20th-century buildings with narrow alleys leading off it. It has managed to survive destruction and escape development, and is favoured by TV crews when a location redolent of yesteryear is required. The **former St Paul's Choir School** (F.C. Penrose, 1874–5), at the end of the street on the left (corner of Dean's Court), has been a youth hostel since 1975. The neo-Renaissance building is reminiscent of an Italian *palazzo* and would not look out of place amongst the buildings commissioned by Prince Albert in South Kensington. The sgraffito Latin frieze running along the first storey is from St Paul's letter to the Galatians, 6:14: 'MIHI AUTEM ABSIT GLORIARI NISI IN CRUCE DOMINI NOSTRI JESU CHRISTI / PER QUEM MIHI MUNDUS CRUCIFIXUS EST ET EGO MUNDO' (But God forbid that I should glory, save in the cross of our Lord Jesus Christ, by whom the world is crucified unto me, and I unto the world).

In Dean's Court itself, behind a parapet wall with pineapple finials, is the **former St Paul's Deanery** (1672), designed by Wren. The two-tone red-brick façade, with sash and dormer windows, is a vision of restrained elegance. John Donne, when Dean, lived in the earlier house on the site. Since 1996, this has been the official residence of the Bishop of London.

ST ANDREW-BY-THE-WARDROBE

Retracing your footsteps down Carter Lane, go down Addle Hill and then into Wardrobe Terrace to reach the church of St Andrew-by-the-Wardrobe (*closed for refurbishment at the time of writing; standrewbythewardrobe.org*), perched above Queen Victoria Street. It was rebuilt by Wren in 1685–94 and is one of his plainer churches (restored in 1961 after war damage). It took its name from the proximity of the King's Great Wardrobe, the Crown's store of arms and clothing that used to be in the area until 1666, when it was destroyed by the Great Fire. The only part of the former Royal Household to remain in the City is the College of Arms (*see below*).

QUEEN VICTORIA STREET

The **College of Arms**, occupying a handsome building on Queen Victoria Street, is the official heraldic authority for the UK and much of the Commonwealth (*college-of-arms.gov.uk*). The College was first incorporated by Richard III in 1484 and its heralds received a new charter from Queen Mary I (and a building on the present site) in 1555. This was destroyed in the Great Fire and the present building (1671–88) was designed by Francis Sandford, Rouge Dragon Pursuivant, and Morris Emmett, the King's bricklayer. Splendid 19th-century wrought-iron gates, formerly at Goodrich Court, Herefordshire (demolished), were given to the College in 1956.

The Officers of Arms are appointed by the Crown on the advice of the Duke of Norfolk as hereditary Earl Marshal, whom they assist in planning and participating in ancient and splendid ceremonies including the State Opening of Parliament, state funerals and the monarch's coronation. They consist of three Kings of Arms (Garter, Clarenceux and Norroy & Ulster), six Heralds (Windsor, Somerset, Richmond, York, Chester and Lancaster) and four Pursuivants (Bluemantle, Portcullis, Rouge Croix and Rouge Dragon). Since the 15th century at least, the Kings of Arms have been responsible for granting coats of arms on behalf of the Crown to eminent persons and organisations. A right to arms by inheritance is established by proving and recording at the College a descent from someone already on record as being entitled to bear arms. Suitably qualified American citizens who can prove descent from someone once a subject of the Crown may be granted honorary arms. Visitors can see the Earl Marshal's Court with its throne (Court of Chivalry). The heraldic and genealogical records and collections compiled over the course of more than five centuries are unique (*no public access except for groups by arrangement*). The officers will make searches and undertake genealogical enquiries.

The church of **St Benet Paul's Wharf** stands marooned in traffic between Queen Victoria Street and Upper Thames Street, a roaring modern thoroughfare not particularly pleasant for the pedestrian. The original 12th-century church was destroyed in the Great Fire and its successor was built by Wren's associate Robert Hooke in 1678–84. It is now used by Welsh Anglicans and services are in Welsh. Inigo Jones (d. 1652) was buried in the earlier church (monument destroyed in the Fire). The 17th-century Restoration interior escaped both Victorian improvements and Luftwaffe bombing.

At no. 101 Queen Victoria Street (corner of Peter's Hill) is the **International Headquarters of the Salvation Army**, a quasi-military Christian movement founded in 1865 by the Methodists William and Catherine Booth to help those in need. The current building, the third on the site (Sheppard Robson, 2004), fulfils the brief 'modern in design, frugal in operation, evangelical in purpose'. Each year millions pass by the fritted glass premises with Gospel texts on its windows, since Paul's Hill leads directly to the Millennium Bridge (*see p. 446*), meaning that footfall is substantial.

Beyond, on the other side of the road, is the church of **St Nicholas Cole Abbey** (*stnickschurch.org.uk*), an elegant balustraded box with elaborately pedimented arched windows, built by Wren in 1672–8 on the site of its pre-Fire predecessor. It is now a centre for spreading the message of Jesus and weekday lunchtime talks are held both here and at other locations. Note the richly-coloured glass of the east windows, by Keith New (1962), who also contributed to the post-War Coventry Cathedral. There is some fine surviving wood carving in the church. The floor of the WCs is a *terrazzo* assortment of tombstone fragments.

South down the curving Lambeth Hill is the tower of **St Mary Somerset**, in a small patch of green above Upper Thames Street. The rest of the church, built by Wren in 1695, was taken down c. 1870. The Baroque urns and crocketed obelisks are noteworthy.

ON & AROUND CANNON STREET

Map p. 639, D3. Underground: Cannon Street, Mansion House.

Cannon Street is a corruption of Candlewick Street, after the wax chandlers who worked here. At the St Paul's end, at 10 Cannon St (between Distaff Lane and Friday St), is the former *Financial Times* building, **Bracken House** (Sir Albert Richardson, 1955–9, redeveloped by Hopkins & Partners, 1988–91), a striking construction in dark pinkish stone and sandstone with an interesting astrological clock by Philip Bentham: at its centre, in a sunburst motif, is the face of Winston Churchill (a friend of Brendan Bracken, Chairman of the *FT*). It is said that pink sandstone was chosen for the building because of the famous salmon pink colour of the *Financial Times* newsprint.

Mascaron of Winston Churchill as the sun within an astrological clock, on the pink sandstone Bracken House.

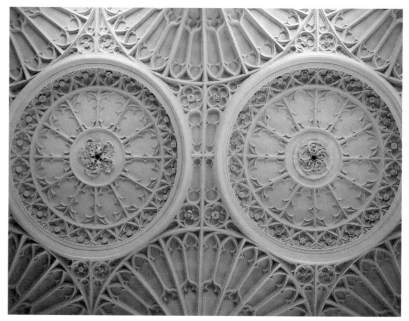

Detail of the fan-vaulted ceiling of St Mary Aldermary.

At 30 Cannon Street, the **former Crédit Lyonnais building**, built in the 1970s by Whinney, Son & Austen Hall, fills the triangular space. Each floor has a wide projecting cornice and is clad in cast sections of glass-fibre-reinforced concrete, giving the impression of a tiered confection dripping in icing. Viewed from certain angles, it looks like a hybrid of a cruise liner and the Leaning Tower of Pisa (though by today's London standards, it can hardly be classed as a tower). In the round-arched building facing it in the opposite intersection triangle is **Sweeting's fish restaurant**, which began life as an oyster bar in 1839 and is still going strong serving lobster bisque (*39 Queen Victoria St, sweetingsrestaurant.co.uk*). Opposite, in Queen Victoria Street, is the church of **St Mary Aldermary** (so called, according to the antiquary John Stow, because it is 'elder than any church of St Marie in the City'). It was rebuilt by Wren's office after 1679 (tower 1704) and is an important surviving example of 17th-century neo-Gothic architecture. Inside, the elaborate white plaster fan-vaulted ceiling is especially noteworthy. Milton married his third wife here in 1663. The church is involved in active outreach programmes and is home to the Host café, which serves 'divine' coffee and cakes and which charmingly allows people to sit and congregate in the pews with their teacups.

ST JAMES GARLICKHYTHE AND VINTNERS' HALL

In Garlick Hill is the church of **St James Garlickhythe** (*map p. 639, D3*), so called because this was once an important Roman or Saxon harbour (hithe) where garlic was traded. Wren rebuilt the church after the Fire in 1672–82 and the complex steeple (1713–17) is thought to be after a design by Hawksmoor. The use of clear glass clerestory windows and high ceilings gave the church its nickname, 'Wren's Lantern'. It is a traditional Anglican church, noted for its music. The interior has fine 17th-century wood-carving and ironwork. The organ, of 1718–19, is probably by Knopple but has previously been attributed to Father Smith (*see p. 218*).

The church looks down over the relentless traffic of Upper Thames Street, and opposite, to the Neoclassical façade of **Vintners' Hall**. This is one of the larger livery halls and has occupied this site since 1446. It was rebuilt in the 1670s, after the Great Fire, and escaped World War Two bombing with superficial damage. Its collections include fine tapestries and paintings. The company, one of the original Great Twelve (*see p. 20*), is still linked to the UK wine trade. Together with the Crown and the Worshipful Company of Dyers, the Vintners share ancient custody of Britain's Mute swan population and take part in the annual Swan Upping ceremony, which is a census of the swan population on the Thames (*see p. 562*). The custom dates from the 12th century, when swans were considered a tasty and exclusive delicacy and the Crown claimed possession of them to ensure that the royal banquet table was duly provisioned.

THE THAMES RIVER WALK AROUND CANNON STREET

The river walk stretching east and west is highly recommended. Wharves and warehouses may have gone, but narrow lanes bearing historic names run down to the Thames. Cross Upper Thames Street on the pedestrian bridge, which takes you into narrow **Queenhithe**, a landing place dating from the re-colonisation of the Roman City by Alfred the Great in AD 886. It later became an important medieval dock and was named after Queen Matilda, wife of Henry I. Henry III decreed that all grain ships should discharge here. As you walk down to the water you pass a **mosaic timeline of London** from the Roman conquest to Queen Elizabeth II's Diamond Jubilee of 2012. Head left (east) and the walk takes you all the way to the Tower of London, with interesting detours back into the City along the way. **Southwark Bridge**, with its green and yellow colour scheme, was originally the work of John Rennie, designer of Waterloo Bridge (1813–19), but was entirely rebuilt in 1912–21 by Sir Ernest George. Excavations in the vicinity unearthed evidence of the Roman quay and remains of three Saxon ships and other Roman and Saxon finds. Beneath the bridge on the north side is **Fruiterers Passage**, its name commemorating the Fruiterers' Company whose guildhall used to stand nearby. The passage today is lined with images of the bridge and local vicinity in cream, sepia and black tile. In **Walbrook Wharf**, with the Banker Pub on the river, is the entrance to **Steelyard Passage**, a shadowy route beneath the Victorian turrets of Cannon Street Station, with glowing circular floor lights and echoing with the clanging and clinking sound effects of metal being forged. The Hanseatic League's trading colony had their base here from the 13th century.

Angels adoring the Name of God (1708), in the painted dome of St Mary Abchurch.

UPPER THAMES STREET AND DOWGATE HILL

On Upper Thames Street (*map p. 639, D3*) is **Whittington Garden**, a patch of green commemorating Sir Richard Whittington (1354–1423), merchant, politician, philanthropist, four times Mayor of London and the inspiration for the folk tale of 'Dick Whittington and his Cat'. The church of **St Michael Paternoster Royal**, rebuilt by Whittington in 1409, is also his burial place. The name derives from the rosary (paternoster) sellers who used to live in the area. Destroyed in the Fire, it was rebuilt by Wren in 1685–94, one of the last of the City churches to be rebuilt. The fine steeple (1713–17) is possibly by Hawksmoor. It was also one of the last churches to be restored after the Blitz and in 1968 was re-dedicated as the chapel and headquarters of the Mission to Seafarers, an Anglican charity serving merchant sailors around the world. Inside are vivid stained-glass windows by John Hayward, including one of Dick Whittington and his cat. In College Hill a blue plaque records the site of Whittington's house in 1423.

Three more livery halls are in Dowgate Hill just before Cannon Street: note the decorative entrances to the halls of the **Tallow Chandlers** (no. 4), the **Skinners** (no. 8) and the **Dyers** (nos 11–13). Excavations in this area in 1965 revealed traces of a Roman governor's palace of AD 80–100, overlooking the Thames beside the mouth of the Walbrook stream, which entered the Thames at Dowgate. At a lower level, timber foundations suggested that this was the earlier site of a Roman fort. Further excavations in 1988–9 revealed a late Roman building.

THE LONDON STONE AND A GROPIUS SHOPFRONT

Opening off Cannon Street, the narrow Salters' Hall Court leads to **St Swithin's Church Garden**, nestled in the lee of the bulbous backside of Walbrook House. St Swithin's Church, which once stood here, was rebuilt by Wren after the Fire but so badly damaged during the Blitz that it was demolished in 1962. Facing Cannon Street on the building between Salters' Hill Court and St Swithin's Lane is the **London Stone**, an unremarkable-looking lump of blackened limestone immured in the wall at ground level behind glass. The stone is of ancient yet contradictory provenance. Some believe it to have been the *miliarium* of Roman London, from which all distances on the Roman high roads were measured. Others claim it as the stone from which King Arthur drew *Excalibur*. In 1450, rebel leader Jack Cade, who marched 5,000 men to London in revolt against King Henry VI, struck the stone with his staff, exclaiming 'Now is Mortimer Lord of this City'.

On the further corner of St Swithin's Lane is a building dated 1870 and with painted wrought-iron rams' heads at pavement level. Next door at no. **115 Cannon St**, the Art Deco shopfront in black Vitrolite (1936) is by the great 20th-century modern architect and founder of the Bauhaus School, Walter Gropius. German-born Gropius sought refuge from the Nazis in London in 1934–7, where he worked with Maxwell Fry before emigrating to America.

ST MARY ABCHURCH

St Mary Abchurch on Abchurch Lane (*map p. 639, D3*) was rebuilt by Wren in 1681–6 and restored by Godfrey Allen (1945–57). In the interior, the **dome**, with its four oval windows is an architectural *tour de force*. The painted decoration that adorns it is by William Snow (1708): it shows angels adoring the Name of God, which appears in Hebrew in a burst of golden sunlight. The splendid **limewood reredos**, with a gilded pelican in her piety (1686), is a superb work by Grinling Gibbons. The City churches are rich in fittings either traditionally or hopefully attributed to the great wood carver, but not many are actually confirmed as being by his hand. Gibbons was greatly admired for his exquisite and realistic limewood carvings, often of fruit and flowers: he was the unsurpassed master of this medium. Other examples of his work may be seen in St Paul's Cathedral, Hampton Court Palace and St James's Piccadilly. The V&A has several pieces, including a wooden 'filigree' cravat resembling Venetian lace, which was one of Horace Walpole's prize possessions (he would wear it on occasion at his home, Strawberry Hill).

WALBROOK & MANSION HOUSE

Map p. 639, D3. Underground: Bank.

Walbrook, which leads north from Cannon Street, takes its name from the Walbrook stream, one of London's numerous hidden rivers, whose waters now flow underground from Finsbury to the Thames, emerging at Walbrook Wharf (*see p. 41*).

THE LONDON MITHRAEUM

The triangle between Queen Victoria Street, Cannon Street and Walbrook is occupied by the Bloomberg London events space. Here, at 12 Walbrook, is the entrance to the London Mithraeum (*londonmithraeum.com*). This is an area rich in Roman remains.

In 1889 three sculptures, including the relief of *Mithras Slaying the Bull* (now in the Museum of London), were unearthed, leading to speculation that there must have been a Temple of Mithras on this site, dedicated to the ancient mystery cult. During post-war reconstruction work in 1954, the remains, dating from AD 240 and consisting of a rectangular hall with two longitudinal rows of columns and an apsidal end, were duly discovered. Initially re-erected on a different site close by, they have now been returned to their original location and are open to the public.

In 2013, contractors digging foundations for the Bloomberg building stumbled upon remains of timber structures that once stood on the banks of the Walbrook stream, as well as over 10,000 objects, both decorative and everyday, in metal, glass, ceramic, wood and leather. These included writing tablets, earrings, remains of sandals and a gladiator's amber amulet, beautifully preserved in layers of Walbrook mud. Items from this important discovery, dubbed the 'Pompeii of the North', are on show in a glass cabinet on the ground floor.

The Mithraeum remains are two floors down. Visitors to the 'Temple Experience' are conducted into a darkened chamber, where the temple foundations can be seen, to hear a recorded recreation of what a Mithraic feast may have involved, with a priest making a solemn roll-call of attendees from all seven grades of initiation (*see box opposite*).

ST STEPHEN WALBROOK

The church of St Stephen Walbrook was rebuilt by Wren in 1672–80 but is now ignominiously dwarfed by the monstrous, bulgy Walbrook House office block next door. The noble interior, with its circular dome supported on eight arches, is one of the architect's masterpieces, his dress rehearsal for St Paul's Cathedral. It was carefully restored after its partial destruction in 1941. The church's later restoration in 1978–87 was led by the property developer and arts patron Peter Palumbo (later Baron Palumbo of Walbrook), a churchwarden, who also commissioned the **central altar, by Henry Moore** (1972–83). Made of travertine, it is the only piece of church furniture Moore designed and its installation caused controversy because it contradicted Wren's Restoration vision, whereby the altar was placed at the east end and not in the centre of the church. After a hearing at the Court of Ecclesiastical Causes Reserved, Moore's altar was finally allowed to remain, though it is still not universally liked and has been compared to a ripe camembert cheese.

The 17th-century stone font is by Thomas Strong, with a fine wood cover by William Newman, and the wooden reredos and pulpit (also 17th-century) are by Thomas Creecher, William Newman and Thomas Maine. A memorial on the south wall, decorated with angel musicians in glass mosaic, commemorates the composer John Dunstable (d. 1453), 'the father of English harmony'. Sir John Vanbrugh (d. 1726), playwright and architect of Blenheim Palace, is interred here without a monument.

THE CULT OF MITHRAS

The cult of Mithras was one of the most popular foreign cults to spread in the Roman Empire in the 2nd and 3rd centuries AD. Its origins were in Persia, where worship of the god is said to have been founded by the sage Zoroaster. Mithras was associated with the sun and with cattle-herding or stealing, and the most common representation of him, found in reliefs or statues in all Mithraic temples, shows him astride a large bull which he is stabbing in the neck.

There is much debate over how and why Mithraism spread from Persia, and the extent to which the Romans developed the cult for their own ends. In the Western Empire, Mithraism was especially popular among soldiers, slaves and ex-slaves. Women seem to have been excluded. Members met in small groups of up to 35, in sanctuaries which were designed to resemble caves, the traditional haunt of the god. At the eastern end there would be a relief or statue of Mithras, surrounded by symbols of constellations and two deities carrying torches. This was the 'light' end of the sanctuary, which contrasted with the 'dark' western end and made the point that this was a saviour god who brought the initiate from darkness into light. During ceremonies the initiates would recline on platforms along the side walls of the sanctuary and enjoy a ritual meal. Some 400 Mithraic sanctuaries are known, a high proportion of them in Rome, but they are also found in army camps along the northern border of the Empire from Britain to the Danube.

The most important feature of Roman Mithraism was its series of graded initiations, each associated with a planet. The highest grade was the 'Father'. Inscriptions show that there might be one or two 'Fathers' in each group and its status was such that it could be recorded on an initiate's tombstone. It has been suggested that the disciplined ascent through the grades appealed to soldiers because it mirrored their ascent through the ranks to officer; and to slaves hoping to make a similar transition into freedom.

MANSION HOUSE

Mansion House (*map p. 639, D3*) is the official residence of the Lord Mayor (*guided tours can be arranged for groups; cityoflondon.gov.uk*). A Palladian edifice, with an imposing Corinthian portico, it was erected by George Dance the Elder in 1739–52, with alterations by Dance the Younger from 1795. The pediment, depicting the *City of London Receiving Gifts of Plenty*, was sculpted by Sir Robert Taylor. The splendid Egyptian Hall on the first floor is the scene of banquets, balls and other functions. Dance modelled it after the so-called 'Egyptian Hall' as described by Vitruvius, taken to mean a large central space surrounded by colonnaded walkways. It contains some 19th-century sculptures. Also included in the tour are the Long Parlour, with a remarkable coffered ceiling; the Saloon, adorned with plasterwork, tapestry and sculpture; and the State Drawing Room.

Facing Mansion House, on the corner plot with Princes Street, is Sir Edwin Cooper's **National Westminster Bank** (1929–32). On this site the world's first postmarks were struck in 1661 (plaque on the Princes Street side of building).

POULTRY, OLD JEWRY & GUILDHALL

Map p. 639, D3–D2. Underground: Mansion House, Bank.

POULTRY

The short street leading almost directly westwards from Mansion House is known as Poultry, from its early occupation by the shops of poulterers, who drove their flocks from Essex with special cloth coverings over their webbed feet. The pink and cream striped corner building in the angle between Poultry and Queen Victoria Street is **No. 1 Poultry**, a Post-modern office block by James Stirling (1998), which King Charles once deprecated as looking like a radio. The Coq d'Argent French restaurant is at the top, with a roof terrace and garden (*coqdargent.co.uk*). Opposite it, at 27–35 Poultry, is the **former Midland Bank headquarters** by Lutyens (1924–37). It is now a hotel, The Ned, with its own private members' club. Elizabeth Fry, the women's prison reformer, lived on this site in 1800–9; the poet Thomas Hood was born here in 1799. He is probably best known for his 'Song of the Shirt', in which he imagines a poor seamstress toiling for a pittance from dawn to dusk:

> With fingers weary and worn,
> With eyelids heavy and red,
> A woman sat in unwomanly rags,
> Plying her needle and thread—
> Stitch! stitch! stitch!
> In poverty, hunger and dirt,
> And still with a voice of dolorous pitch,—
> Would that its tone could reach the Rich!—
> She sang this 'Song of the Shirt!'

The church of St Mildred, Poultry was also here (it was pulled down in 1872). Grocer's Hall Court, off Poultry, leads to the **hall of the Worshipful Company of Grocers**, second in order of precedence and one of the original twelve (*see p. 20*). Its main entrance is on Princes Street.

OLD JEWRY

Old Jewry was the area set aside for Jews since William the Conqueror encouraged them to settle in England soon after 1066. In 1290, after two centuries of intermittent support punctuated by outbreaks of persecution, they were expelled by King Edward I, an edict that remained in place until Oliver Cromwell formally invited Jews back to

England from 1655, in the hope that they would reinvigorate the country's finances. In **Frederick's Place**, a small Georgian cul-de-sac, Disraeli worked at no. 6 from 1821–4. The building is now the **Mercers' Hall**, belonging to one of the richest of the City livery companies, the first in order of civic precedence, still committed to education and charitable works. A mercer was a dealer in fine fabrics.

A blue plaque on the wall opposite the entrance to **St Olave's Court** commemorates the site of the Great Synagogue that stood here until 1272. St Olave's Court leads past what remains of **St Olave Old Jewry**, its tower a relic of the Wren church demolished in 1887. Memorials and furnishings from it can now be seen in St Margaret Lothbury (*p. 58*). A Roman pavement and vessels were discovered beneath it. In **Ironmonger Lane** are more buildings belonging to the Mercers, with their emblem of the 'Mercers' Maiden', the badge of the Mercers' company. A plaque on the corner of Ironmonger Lane and Cheapside, together with a relief plaque of a mitred head, commemorates St Thomas à Becket, who was born in a house near this spot.

GUILDHALL

Guildhall (*map p. 639, D2*) is the ceremonial and administrative centre of the City of London Corporation. It is built over the largest Roman amphitheatre discovered in the UK, part of which is on view beneath the Guildhall Art Gallery (*see overleaf*). The complex has many entrances but is best approached from Gresham Street through to Guildhall Yard. Stand with the church of St Lawrence Jewry behind you and the entrance to the Guildhall Art Gallery on your right, to admire the façade of the Great Hall, which dates from 1411 with a 'Hindoo Gothic' porch added in 1788 by George Dance the Younger. Surmounting the porch is the City coat of arms, with the motto *Domine dirige nos*: Lord, direct us. Much damage was sustained in the Great Fire in 1666 and again during WWII. In the 1860s Sir Horace Jones restored its Gothic splendour and restoration in the 1950s was undertaken by Sir Giles Gilbert Scott and later by his son Richard. This is the only secular pre-Fire stone building remaining in the City.

Great Hall and Crypt
Entry by guided tour. These are held once a month and fill up quickly. See cityoflondon.gov.uk
The **Great Hall** is approached down a glass and concrete ambulatory—a 1970s' interpretation of a medieval cloister by Richard Gilbert Scott. The Great Hall (151.5ft long, 48ft wide and 89ft high) was built in 1411–29 by John Croxton as the third guildhall on this site, and the largest. The huge tracery windows are in essence 15th-century but much restored. The 19th-century hammerbeam roof was destroyed in 1940 and has been replaced by stone arches with a panelled ceiling (1954). The hall is used for Court of Common Council meetings, for City ceremonies such as the election of the Lord Mayor and sheriffs, and state banquets hosted by the Corporation. The most important of these is the banquet given in November, by the new Lord Mayor and sheriffs, for the members of the Cabinet, when the Prime Minister makes an important speech. At an earlier period the hall was used also for major trials (recorded on a panel), including that of Lady Jane Grey, the 'Nine Days' Queen' in 1553.

Against the walls are a statue of Winston Churchill sprawled in an armchair (by Oscar Nemon) and monuments to Nelson (inscription by Sheridan), Wellington, Chatham (inscription by Burke), William Pitt (inscription by Canning) and Lord Mayor Beckford; the famous giants Gog and Magog, by David Evans (above the entrance at the west end), replace those burned in 1940. Gog and Magog have been regarded as guardians of the City since the reign of Henry V and played a traditional role in welcoming kings and queens to London. Two wicker effigies of them feature in the Lord Mayor's Show (*see p. 586*). Neil Simmons' larger-than-life-size Carrara marble statue of Margaret Thatcher, famously decapitated in 2002 and since repaired, was put back on display in the Guildhall Art Gallery in a strong Perspex box before being taken in 2015 to an out-of-the-way location where it could only be viewed on request. At the time of writing it was reported to have been spotted in the Guildhall itself.

In the basement, the **Crypt** is an important survival of the buildings of 1411 and is the largest medieval crypt in London. The East Crypt is borne by clustered columns of Purbeck marble (restored in 1961). The West Crypt (restored 1973) has octagonal stone columns supporting a plain vault.

Guildhall Art Gallery

Housed in a building designed by Richard Gilbert Scott (with D.Y. Associates), with rather clownish statues of London notables, including Dick Whittington and his cat, under the porch, the **Guildhall Art Gallery** (*free except for temporary exhibitions; cityoflondon.gov.uk*) displays around 250 pictures at any one time from the Corporation of London's collection of over 4,000 works. During construction work in 1987, the astonishing discovery was made of London's Roman amphitheatre. The remains have been preserved and can be visited.

The gallery has display spaces on three floors: small rooms on the ground floor and basement, and a gallery with a raised balcony on the floor above. The interesting and varied collection includes works commissioned and collected by the Corporation since the 16th century and others presented or bequeathed to it. Works are displayed on a rotating basis and it is not possible to know what will be on show at any one time. Among the portraits are eminent City officeholders, such as John Michael Wright's full-length portraits of two of the Fire Judges appointed to assess property claims following the Great Fire of 1666. Topographical views of London include Jan Griffier the Younger's *The Thames during the Great Frost* and John Atkinson Grimshaw's *The Thames by Moonlight with Southwark Bridge*, as well as other views of the City both historic and contemporary. Works celebrating national victories and events include John Singleton Copley's enormous *Defeat of the Batteries at Gibraltar*, commissioned by the Corporation in 1783 and completed in 1791. It is one of the largest pictures in the country and a particular requirement of this building was that it should have a wall large enough to accommodate it.

Other works include Constable's full-size sketch for *Salisbury Cathedral from the Meadows* and many fine Victorian pictures, in which the collection is particularly rich. Among them is Hugh Goldwin Rivière's charming *The Garden of Eden*, showing a young couple with eyes only for each other amid grey London gloom, and Frederic Leighton's

Virtual pugilists in the Roman amphitheatre underneath the Guildhall.

The Music Lesson, with the actress and Gaiety Girl Connie Gilchrist modelling as the young pupil. Well known Pre-Raphaelite works include Millais' *My First Sermon* (a little girl sitting alert) and *My Second Sermon* (the same girl fast asleep); Holman Hunt's *The Eve of St Agnes*; and Rossetti's *La Ghirlandata*. Other notable works are Tissot's popular *Too Early* (1873), showing a lady in pink looking awkwardly at the floor, having arrived at a dance in unfashionably good time. Marianne Stokes's *The Net Mender* shows a cottage interior in the Netherlands.

The Roman amphitheatre

The dark, spot-lit Amphitheatre Chamber is on the lower ground floor. Do not expect Capua or the Colosseum: the remains are extremely scanty, consisting of parts of the stone-built eastern entrance and some well-preserved sections of wooden sump drains and water conduits. The theatre was first constructed c. AD 70, with a timber superstructure, and was capable of seating some 6,000 spectators at a time when the population of Londinium would only have been around four times that number. Elliptical in shape, more than 100 yards long and 90 yards wide, it would have been used mainly for animal fights and public executions, rarely for expensive gladiatorial contests. In the 2nd century it was improved with stone, and abandoned at some time in the 4th century. Curious luminous green silhouettes of pugilists evoke the atmosphere of the ring in full cry.

ST LAWRENCE JEWRY AND ALDERMANBURY

On the corner of Aldermanbury and Gresham Street stands **St Lawrence Jewry** (*map p. 639, D2; stlawrencejewry.org.uk*), rebuilt by Wren in 1671–7 and well restored after war damage. A showcase at the west end has porcelain vitrified by fire during the Blitz and a vellum baptismal register which shrank instead of burning. This is the official church of the City Corporation and has a fine white and gold interior. The Trumpeter's Gallery is used on ceremonial occasions and the Lord Mayor's sword rest against the front right-hand pew is a copy of the original. Pepys records a visit to the church 'for curiosity' and his disappointment with the sermon. Sir Thomas More delivered a series of lectures here. The 'Spital' sermon is preached here in Feb or March, attended by the Lord Mayor, sheriffs and aldermen, who cross Guildhall Yard in a colourful procession. The service was originally preached to the governors of the Royal Hospitals, from an open-air pulpit at St Mary Spital (no longer extant). Note the weather vane in the shape of a gridiron, the attribute of St Lawrence, who was roasted alive on one in Rome in 258.

On the corner of Aldermanbury and Love Lane is a small garden on the **site of St Mary Aldermanbury**. Destroyed in the Great Fire, rebuilt by Wren and destroyed again in the Blitz, its remains were shipped in the 1960s to the campus of Westminster College, Fulton, Missouri as a memorial to Winston Churchill (who made his famous Iron Curtain speech at the College). The memorial is to the actors John Heminge and Henry Condell, editors of Shakespeare's First Folio (of which the Guildhall Library has a copy). Judge Jeffreys (*p. 11*) was buried here, having died in the Tower in 1689. At no. 20 Aldermanbury is the **Insurance Hall**, former headquarters of the Chartered Insurance Institute, founded in 1873. Much of its business pertained to fire insurance (*see p. 391*)The Institute sold the building in 2018.

In Aldermanbury Square is the **Brewers' Hall**, built in the 1960s following the destruction of the livery company's earlier building. Behind it, facing the road named London Wall, is a small garden with a statue by Karin Jonzen (1972) entitled *The Gardener*. On the other side of London Wall are the scant **remains of Elsing Spital**, an Augustinian priory founded in 1329 'for the sustentation of a hundred blind men' and dissolved in 1536.

CHEAPSIDE & ALDERSGATE

Cheapside (*map p. 638, C3*) was a busy market from Saxon times (*chepe* in Old English means market) and a higgledy-piggledy medieval street of retailers that was laid waste by the Great Fire. The names of the cross-streets indicate the position of the different traders: bakers in Bread Street, ironmongers in Ironmonger Lane, fishmongers in Friday Street, dairymen in Milk Street, etc. Sir Thomas More was born in Milk Street in 1478. The 'prentices of Chepe,' Chaucer tells us, 'were long notorious for their turbulence'. Two of London's famous Elizabethan taverns, The Mitre and the Bull Head, were located here.

In Bread Street, to the south, stood a third, the Mermaid Tavern, famous for the club founded in 1603 by Sir Walter Raleigh, whose members included Ben Jonson, Donne and Shakespeare. 'Have ye tippled drink more fine than mine host's Canary wine?' mused Keats. 'Souls of Poets dead and gone, what Elysium have ye known, happy field or mossy cavern, choicer than the Mermaid Tavern?' All three watering holes, Mitre, Bull Head and Mermaid, were destroyed in the Great Fire. John Milton was born in Bread Street in 1608. Also in Bread Street stood Wren's St Mildred's church, where Shelley and Mary Godwin were married in 1816. It was destroyed in WWII.

Cheapside also runs through the heart of Roman London. A public bath of c. AD 100 was found nearby, and to the south the main Roman road through the City was discovered during excavations. Watling Street was a major thoroughfare, leading from Londinium to Dubris, the port of Dover. In 1912, a priceless cache of 16th- and 17th-century jewels and gems was discovered hidden in a Cheapside basement. The collection, known as the Cheapside Hoard, is part of the holdings of the Museum of London (*see p. 399*).

Chaucer's 'turbulent prentices' are alive and well today, since retailing has come home to Cheapside. **One New Change**, a mall complex by Jean Nouvel (2010) nicknamed the 'Stealth Bomber', has shops, restaurants, bars and offices. The glass panels are designed to reflect the sky and a cut in the building frames a view of St Paul's Cathedral (the roof gallery, open seven days a week, offers a fine prospect of St Paul's dome). Placed just inside the cut in the building, facing St Paul's across New Change, is Gavin Turk's **Nail** (2011), a sculpture of exactly that, a giant nail banged into the ground. The connotations of both artisanal workmanship with organic materials, as well as Christianity and the Cross, are impossible to ignore in this brash, glassy, materialist context.

On the **corner of Cheapside and Wood Street** are three small shops, all re-fronted, though what lies behind the frontages are rare 17th-century survivors of post-Fire re-building. Behind them, an immense plane tree grows on the **site of the church of St Peter Cheap**, destroyed in the Fire and not rebuilt. The tree is believed to have inspired Wordsworth's 'The Reverie of Poor Susan' (1797), a poem about a country girl working in London in whom visions of remembered bucolic sweetness are awakened by the dawn trilling of a thrush from a tree at the corner of Wood Street.

ST MARY-LE-BOW

According to tradition, 'Cockneys' are born within the sound of Bow Bells, the bells of St Mary-le-Bow (*map p. 639, D3; stmarylebow.org.uk*). At one time they could be heard in Hackney Marshes but today, surrounded as the church is by tall buildings, not many Londoners get an opportunity to be born real Cockneys. The famous bells also called back Dick Whittington to be four times Mayor of London. They were destroyed in the Great Fire and their successors suffered in the Blitz, but new ones have been recast from those salvaged. The Pearly Costermongers' Harvest Festival, held at the church on the last Sun in Sept, affords an opportunity to hear the bells ring out: and ring out they do, gloriously, for several hours. Pearly kings and queens (*see overleaf*) from various London boroughs, along with donkeys and dogs pulling carts of autumnal produce, gather at the Guildhall before processing with City dignitaries behind a marching band along Cheapside to the church.

The Virgin Mary cradles the church of St Mary-le-Bow in her arms. On either side of her, each steeple represents a City church bombed during WWII. Stained glass by John Hayward (1964).

PEARLY KINGS AND QUEENS

Pearly Kings and Pearly Queens have their origins in London's costermongers, the itinerant traders, barrow boys and vendors whose famous cries of 'Come and buy!', 'Cherry ripe!' once filled the City streets—and on market days in some areas, still do. In the 19th century the costermongers of each borough began to elect a 'king' to represent them to the authorities and to defend their patches against other traders. They began to distinguish their dress by stitching rows of mother-of-pearl buttons along the seams of their trousers. The full Pearly costumes that are seen today evolved after the 1880s, when a rat-catcher named Henry Croft covered an entire suit with pearl buttons arranged to form patterns and the slogan 'All For Charity'. Soon all the 'Pearlys' were at it, constructing ever more elaborate attire for themselves to be worn in their pageants and processions. Today there are several Pearly groups, all of which devote their efforts to raising money for the city.

St Mary-le-Bow was one of the first churches to be rebuilt after the Fire, by Wren, in 1670–80. It succeeds the older medieval church of Sancta Maria de Arcubus, 'of the arches'. The name derives from the Deanery of the Arches, a group of thirteen parish churches under the jurisdiction of the Archbishop of Canterbury, not the Bishop of London. Their council, the Court of Arches, traditionally met here.

The fine Neoclassical **steeple**, erected in 1678–80, is 224ft high, second in height of the London steeples after St Bride's. Inside the tower entrance, a haunting photograph taken after the Blitz shows the area's devastation. The church was gutted in 1941 and the interior restoration, completed in 1964 by Laurence King, is to Wren's design, though the furnishings are in a very different style. The decorative, brightly-coloured **east windows** are the work of John Hayward (1964). The window on the left represents the bombed City churches grouped around the Virgin, who holds the church of St Mary-le-Bow in her arms. Note the bosses on the keystones of the arches, carved with the portraits of past rectors. At the west end is the memorial bust of Admiral Arthur Phillip (1738–1814), founder and governor of the first colony of British settlers in Australia (1788), who was born in Bread Street. The bust was salvaged from St Mildred's church.

Below the church, the Norman **crypt** (c. 1077–87, incorporating Roman bricks) is one of the oldest and most important ecclesiastical structures in the City. The Chapel of the Holy Spirit occupies the part formerly used as a burying place and as the meeting place of the ecclesiastical Court of Arches (*see above*). In 1914 an ancient stone from this crypt was placed in Trinity Church, New York, in reference to the fact that William III granted to the vestry of that church the same privileges as those of St Mary-le-Bow.

John Milton is commemorated by a tablet on the church's exterior west wall. In the **churchyard** is a statue of Captain John Smith, founder of the Colony of Virginia, erected in 1960. It is a copy of the statue in Jamestown by William Couper. Smith is buried in St Sepulchre-without-Newgate (*see p. 231*).

ST VEDAST ALIAS FOSTER

In Foster Lane, which leads off Cheapside to the north opposite One New Change, stands the boxy church of St Vedast alias Foster (*map p. 638, C2; vedast.org.uk*), noted for its Baroque steeple with obelisk spire that has been attributed to Wren's pupil, Hawksmoor. The unusual dedication to a 6th-century Frankish bishop from Arras, northern Gaul, points to a post-Conquest founding. St Vedast was venerated in England from the 12th century where he was known as St Foster. The church was rebuilt after the Fire by Wren's office in 1695–1701 (steeple 1709–12) and it was restored after the Blitz in 1953–63 under the direction of its rector, Canon Mortlock, and the architect Stephen Dykes Bower. The pews face the nave, collegiate style. Cleaning in 1992–3 revealed the medieval fabric of the walls. On the list of vicars in the entrance, note Foulke Bellers (1643–61), presented as a 'Commonwealth Intruder'. The *Journal of the House of Commons* for August 1643 notes that, 'an Order for sequestring the Rectory of the Parish Church of St Vedast, alias Fosters, London, whereof James Batty is Rector, to the Use and Benefit of Foulke Bellers, Master of Arts, a godly and orthodox Divine; who is thereby authorized and required to officiate the said Cure, as Rector; and to preach diligently there; was this Day read; and, by Vote upon the Question, assented unto.' The ousted Batty had been a staunch Royalist.

The quiet courtyard, Fountain Court, with entrances from the church vestibule and the street, displays a section of Roman mosaic pavement, a profile in carved stone of Canon Mortlock by Jacob Epstein and an ancient Syrian brick presented to Canon Mortlock and found during Sir Max Mallowan's (Agatha Christie's husband's) dig at Nimrud in the 1950s/60s. The cuneiform inscription translates: 'Shalmaneser Mighty King, King of the World, King of Assyria, Son of Ashurnasirpal, Mighty King, King of the World, King of Assyria, son of Tukulti-Ninurta who was also King of the World, The facing of the Ziggurat of the City of Kalhu.'

GRESHAM STREET AND THE APPROACH TO LONDON WALL

Gresham Street (*map p. 638, C2*) takes its name from the old Gresham College (now based at Barnard's Inn; *see p. 229*). On the corner of Foster Lane stands the neo-Renaissance **Goldsmiths' Hall**, by Philip Hardwick (1835). The Worshipful Company of Goldsmiths was founded in 1327 and is one of the original twelve great livery companies (*see p. 20*). It is also one of the richest and its hall has a fitting gilded interior and an opulent collection of plate, which is brought up from the vaults for sumptuous livery dinners. The Goldsmiths' Company is responsible for maintaining standards in gold, silver, platinum and palladium and its headquarters are home to the London Assay Office. Although it is not open to the public, it holds bi-annual exhibitions and entry to these is usually free (*thegoldsmiths.co.uk*).

Next to Goldsmiths' Hall, on the other side of Gutter Lane, is the **Wax Chandlers' Hall**, built in 1958 though the company has had a hall on this site since 1501. Opposite is a small garden on the **site of St John Zachary**, a church destroyed by the Fire and not rebuilt. Left of the garden, on the corner of Gresham and Noble streets, is the small red-brick **church of St Anne and St Agnes**, designed on a Greek cross plan by Wren's office (1680) and restored in 1963–8. Noble Street itself boasts a large exposed section of the **old City wall** (*see p. 71*). Opposite it, Oat Lane takes you past the **Pewterers' Hall** (1961), next to which a small garden in the midst of a modern office block commemorates the **site of St Mary Staining**, a church destroyed in the Fire and not rebuilt. A passage (St Alban's Court) leads through the office block to Wood Street. Here, directly opposite, is the **tower of St Alban**, the only remaining part of Wren's neo-Gothic church rebuilt after the Fire in 1685. It is now a private house and notoriously difficult to let, marooned as it is on a traffic island. Almost all the buildings in this street, assemblages of concrete verticals with plate glass between them, were built in the last few years. At the end of Wood Street on the left, **no. 88 Wood Street** is an office block with glass walls extending floor-to-ceiling in a cascading design, by Richard Rogers, completed in 2001. The huge blue and red funnels at ground level that look like comedy periscopes are for ventilation.

Wood Street leads onto **London Wall** and the Barbican (*see p. 74*). Nearby, substantial sections of the **old City wall** may be seen.

ALDERSGATE AND POSTMAN'S PARK

Foster & Partners designed the billowing, glassy **One London Wall** (corner of Aldersgate Street; completed 2004), which incorporates **Plaisterers' Hall** (1972). Behind it, on Noble Street, are the remains of an ancient Roman fort.

St Botolph-without-Aldersgate escaped the Great Fire but was entirely rebuilt in 1788–91. It is noted for its 18th-century interior (*stbotolphsaldersgate.org.uk*). The Aldersgate of the name refers to the old north City gate (pulled down in 1761).

Postman's Park was laid out in the 1880s in the churchyard of St Botolph-without-Aldersgate and the former burial grounds of Christ Church Newgate Street and St Leonard Foster (a church not rebuilt after the Fire). It is higher than street level because, due to overcrowding, bodies were laid flat and covered with earth rather than buried. On the north side (right as you enter from Aldersgate Street) is the Watts Memorial, a lean-to with a wall covered in Arts and Crafts ceramic tiles made by Royal Doulton. Each tile commemorates 'those who have heroically lost their lives trying to save another'. Unveiled in 1900, the idea was suggested by the painter G.F. Watts, who believed 'everyday heroes provide models of exemplary behaviour and character'. The tributes are charming: we read, for example, of a 19-year-old railway clerk who drowned while 'trying to save a lad from a dangerous entanglement of weed'.

Exit Postman's Park onto King Edward Street and turn left for the former General Post Office building, the **King Edward Building** (1911), by Sir Henry Tanner. The foundation stone was laid by King Edward VII. The statue in front is of Sir Rowland Hill, whose postal reforms led to the introduction of the first postage stamp, the Penny Black. The building stands on the site of Christ's Hospital, the famous 'Blue Coat School', founded by Edward VI in 1552 to educate City orphans. The foundation included St Thomas's Hospital for the sick and Bridewell Hospital for idle vagabonds. The school moved to West Sussex in 1902. The bust of a famous former pupil, the essayist Charles Lamb, was moved to the Watch House, Giltspur Street, in 1962 (*see pp. 231–2*). Opposite is another former post office building, originally known as **GPO North** (Sir Henry Tanner, c. 1895), with a façade extending onto St Martin's le-Grand.

On the junction of Newgate and King Edward streets stands the shell of **Christ Church Newgate Street** (*map p. 638, C2*), on the site of Greyfriars church, a Franciscan foundation of 1225 and the largest church in London after St Paul's Cathedral until its destruction in the Fire. Wren and Hooke re-built it in 1667–87 on a reduced footprint over the old choir, and the tall trees in the churchyard to the west mark where the former 300ft medieval nave was. The church was badly bombed in World War Two, but the tower was restored in 1960 and is now a private house. The ruined nave is now Christchurch Greyfriars Garden and the pergolas with their tumbling wisteria and roses mark where the nave piers once stood. The remains of the east wall were lost during road-widening in the 1970s but a low wall, erected in 2001 by Merill Lynch, marks the line.

THE BANK OF ENGLAND, LOTHBURY, THROGMORTON STREET & OLD BROAD STREET

Map p. 639, D3–E2. Underground: Bank.

THE BANK OF ENGLAND

The Bank of England building covers a three-acre quadrilateral area between Lothbury, Bartholomew Lane, Threadneedle Street and Princes Street. It is the central bank of the United Kingdom, founded in 1694 by William Paterson, backed by powerful City men to regulate monetary policy. The bank became state-owned in 1946 and in 1997 gained operational independence. Its affairs are managed by a board consisting of a Governor, Deputy Governors and a Court of Directors appointed by the Crown. After the Gordon Riots (1780), the Bank was protected nightly until 1973 by a detachment of armed guards. The Bank is the banker to the Government and on its behalf manages the National Debt and the UK's gold reserves, sets interest rates and has the sole right to issue banknotes in England and Wales. Its first polymer banknotes were issued in 2016, and a new set of notes with the head of King Charles III in 2024 (though in London today, cash is increasingly rarely seen).

The building

The first building on this site was in Palladian style by George Sampson (1732–4 and 1745–51), with additions by Sir Robert Taylor from 1765. It was replaced by a curtain-walled Neoclassical building, with top-lit banking halls, by Sir John Soane (1788–1833). It was rebuilt by Sir Herbert Baker in 1925–39; only the sheer, unseeing outer wall remains from Soane's design, although this too did not escape Baker's modifications. The loss of Soane's masterpiece is now considered an architectural tragedy and drawings of his interiors are held at the Sir John Soane Museum in Lincoln's Inn Fields. The bank's façade is best viewed across Threadneedle Street, from the steps of the Royal Exchange. The wall, decorated with a Greek key motif, is punctuated

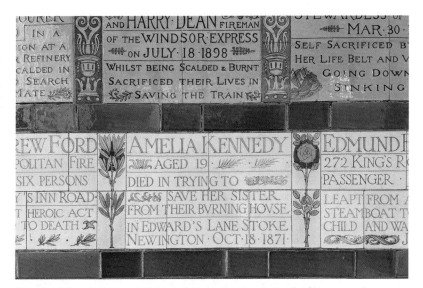

Ceramic tributes in Postman's Park, commemorating heroic deeds of bravery and self-sacrifice on the part of ordinary Londoners.

by Corinthian columns and forbidding bronze doors with caducei, the attribute of Hermes, the god of trade and protector of trade routes (his symbol also peppers the exterior of the Royal Exchange). From within, Baker's building rises seven storeys above ground and descends three levels below (the Bank secures the gold reserves of the UK and other countries in an immense vault which takes a 3ft long key to open; it is the outline of this vault which determines the curvature of Bank Underground station, necessitating the famous admonitions to 'Mind the Gap'). The six huge sculptures are by Sir Charles Wheeler (who executed all the external sculpture as well as the bronze doors) and in the pediment appears the 'Old Lady' of Threadneedle Street, as the bank is popularly termed. From Threadneedle Street, walk clockwise around the bank to admire **Tivoli Corner**, at the junction of Princes Street and Lothbury. This survivor from Soane's bank, modelled on the Temple of Vesta at Tivoli, near Rome, was retained and 'improved' by Baker. The gilded figure of Ariel that surmounts it is by Wheeler.

The Bank of England Museum

The Bank of England Museum (*entrance on Bartholomew Lane; bankofengland.co.uk/ museum*) illustrates the Bank's history and role. The collection includes prints, drawings and paintings illustrating the building and its history, as well as caricatures and cartoons of the 'Old Lady of Threadneedle Street'. This nickname of the Bank goes back to an 18th-century cartoon by Gillray showing the Prime Minister, William Pitt the Younger, attempting to ravish the Bank, who is depicted as an elderly lady desperate to hold on to her honour (and gold). Here too is an iron chest-safe dating from 1700, goldsmith's receipts (the earliest form of banknote) and the Royal Charter of 1694. Here you will find the world's finest collection of Bank of England notes, including counterfeits. A 13kg gold bar, which one may handle, is part of the eye-popping gold display. The bank has more than 400,000 gold bars in its care.

LOTHBURY

Rounding the Bank's 'Tivoli Corner' takes you into Lothbury (*map p. 639, D2*), a short street connecting Gresham and Throgmorton streets. In an alcove in the Bank's blank wall is a **statue of Sir John Soane**, enveloped in a voluminous cloak. The name Lothbury probably derives from 'Lattenbury', a place where copper- and tinsmiths worked, and the church of **St Margaret Lothbury** (*stml.org.uk*), re-built by Wren in 1683–92, displays the armorial bearings of the Worshipful Company of Plate Makers. Its medieval foundations demonstrate that it once stood on the banks of the Walbrook stream (*see p. 43*). The obelisk lead spire, attributed to Robert Hooke, was completed in 1698–1700. The church is notable for its fine 17th-century fittings, including an exquisite font carved with biblical scenes (previously attributed to Grinling Gibbons due to its similarity to the one at St James's Piccadilly) and a rare chancel screen of an eagle with outstretched wings, carved by Woodruffe and Thornton in 1683–4 (the only other surviving chancel screen in a Wren church is at St Peter-upon-Cornhill; *see p. 61*). Most of these furnishings are not original to the church but are re-housed refugees from All Hallows the Great and St Olave Jewry, Wren churches torn down by the Victorians.

Next to the church, at no. 7 Lothbury, is the tall, narrow Venetian Gothic **former Overseas Bankers' Club** (now flats), by George Somers Clarke Sr (1866), in Portland stone and pink sandstone. With its traceried windows and barley-twist columns, it appears transplanted from the canals of the *Serenissima*, or at the very least from the pages of Ruskin's *Stones of Venice*. Next door again, at 41 Lothbury, the former headquarters of NatWest Bank (Mewès & Davis, 1921–32), redeveloped as offices, curves gently into Throgmorton Street.

THROGMORTON STREET

Throgmorton Street (*map p. 639, D2–E2*) is named after Sir Nicholas Throckmorton, a courtier of Elizabeth I and her envoy to Mary Queen of Scots. By the time he died in 1571, he had lost Queen Elizabeth's favour. His tomb may be seen in the church of St Katherine Cree (*p. 69*). On your left, past Angel Court and Throgmorton Avenue, is **Drapers' Hall**, with two huge atlantes flanking the entrance. The hall, dating in part from 1667 though practically rebuilt in 1866–70 and restored in 1949, stands on the site of Thomas Cromwell's mansion and preserves his courtyard plan. After Cromwell's execution, Henry VIII sold it to the Drapers.

In Austin Friars, a snaking alleyway (*entrance on the corner of Throgmorton St and Old Broad St*), stands the **Dutch Church** (Arthur Bailey, 1950–4; *dutchchurch.org.uk*). This lofty church, with its graceful flèche, replaces the 13th-century building—originally the nave of a priory of Augustinian friars—that was assigned by Edward VI in 1550 to Protestant refugees and was ultimately left exclusively to the Dutch. The old church was completely destroyed in 1941 and the great west window, by Max Nauta, shows

Edward VI and Princess Irene of the Netherlands. The latter laid the foundation stone of the new church. Beneath the Communion table is the altar stone of the priory church of 1253.

NETHERLANDERS IN BRITAIN

A distinct feature of the artistic community in England in the 16th and 17th centuries was the presence of foreign artists and craftsmen, of which the majority were Netherlandish. England had enjoyed commercial and artistic links with Flanders since the Middle Ages and the city of Antwerp was a base for English bankers and merchants, particularly those in the cloth trade. Netherlandish artists and craftsmen, who provided a level of skill which to some extent native artists lacked, were encouraged to settle in England and to work for the court and for private patrons. Guillim Scrots, formerly court painter to the Habsburg court at Brussels, worked for Henry VIII and Edward VI, while Hans Eworth, from Antwerp, was painter to Mary I. Religious and political events in the Low Countries provided added reasons for Netherlanders to emigrate. Large numbers of Protestant refugees arrived from those parts of the Low Countries under Habsburg rule. The etcher and painter Marcus Gheeraerts the Elder fled to London from Bruges in 1568 and his son, Marcus Gheeraerts the Younger, was to become the leading artist under Elizabeth I. John de Critz, whose sister married Gheeraerts the Elder, arrived from Antwerp and headed an artistic dynasty active in England for several generations. Legislation designed to protect native workers restricted the activities of 'alien' artists and craftsmen, who could only set up workshops if they assumed English citizenship. Many therefore lived in parishes beyond the jurisdiction of the City guilds.

The focus of London's Netherlandish community was the Dutch Church, Austin Friars (*see opposite*). Not all Netherlandish artists and craftsmen were religious refugees, however. London offered career opportunities for artists such as Daniel Mytens and Van Dyck, as well as for specialists in genres other than portraiture. The renewed cultural programme of the court following the Restoration of Charles II in 1660 attracted skilled artists and craftsmen, and Dutch and Flemish artists were at the forefront of the development of British marine and landscape painting.

OLD BROAD STREET

The triangular space at the junction of Threadneedle Street and Old Broad Street (*map p. 639, E2*) is occupied by a dignified, stone-faced building of 1903. This is the face of a more down-to-earth era, before today's airy palaces of glass rose up to fill the sky. The **former Stock Exchange Tower** at no. 125 (the current Stock Exchange is at Paternoster Square outside St Paul's) was built in 1972 as a seven-sided concrete block. Damaged by an IRA bomb in 1990, it was completely remodelled in glass in

2004–8 for office and retail use. A sculpture of an angel's wing is outside. Further up Old Broad Street at no. 19 is the elegant, cream-coloured **City of London Club** (Philip Hardwick, 1833–4), which narrowly escaped demolition in the 1970s to make way for the building next door at no. 25. At 600ft, **Tower 42** (formerly the NatWest Tower; R.Seifert & Partners, 1970–81) was the tallest office block in Europe until One Canada Square in Docklands was completed in 1990—and it is now dwarfed entirely by the gigantic 22 Bishopsgate behind it (over 900ft high). The Tower, severely damaged by the Bishopsgate bomb in 1993 (*see p. 69*) and by then considered outdated in any case, was recommended for demolition. When this was deemed too expensive, it was refurbished instead.

THREADNEEDLE STREET, CORNHILL & THE ROYAL EXCHANGE

Map p. 639, D3–E3. Underground: Bank.

Threadneedle Street runs from the Bank of England and Royal Exchange all the way to Bishopsgate. At no. 30 is the **Merchant Taylors' Hall**, the largest of the livery company halls, on this site since 1347 (*for the livery companies, see p. 19*). It was damaged by the Great Fire, gutted in the Blitz and re-opened in 1959. The 14th-century crypt survives. The activity of the Merchant Taylors and the Needlemakers (whose hall was nearby) probably gave Threadneedle Street its name.

Diagonally opposite at no. 38, in rusticated Palladian style, is the **former British Linen Bank** (1902–3), by Macvicar Anderson, currently a restaurant. It is built on the site of South Sea House, the South Sea Company's headquarters, where the 'South Sea Bubble' speculation scandal burst in 1720. Note the stone relief of two sailors over the archway at the end, where it meets the splendid, single-storey **Gibson Hall** (John Gibson, 1864–5), built as the National Provincial Bank's headquarters and now a private events venue curving onto Bishopsgate. The exterior is rich in sculptural ornament. The reliefs by John Hancock represent Industry and the statues ranging on the top of the building, covered with netting to deter London's omnipresent pigeons, from left to right, represent Manchester, England, Wales, Birmingham, Newcastle and the potteries, Dover, the shipbuilding towns, the mining towns and London.

Opposite is the massive, glassy **22 Bishopsgate**. Its viewing platform on the 58th floor, Horizon 22, was, at the time of writing, the highest in the UK (*horizon22.co.uk*).

CORNHILL

The junction of Cornhill with Gracechurch Street (*map p. 639, E3*) is a good place to pause to get one's bearings. If you stand with Leadenhall Street ahead of you, you can see the Lloyd's building straight ahead (*see p. 66*), with the Scalpel behind it and the Cheesegrater and Gherkin lurking to the left. The skyscraper nicknamed the Walkie-Talkie, on Fenchurch Street (*see p. 66*), looms to your right. To your immediate left are 22

Bishopsgate (*see above*) and Tower 42. Cornhill, Lombard Street and King William Street fan downwards from Gracechurch Street in an area that for centuries has been one of the chief banking and financial centres of London. Between them, a meandering network of narrow passages and alleys evokes the old, densely-packed City where coffee houses, taverns and chop houses were located and where today one still chances upon hidden pubs and shops. They are particularly lively at lunchtime on weekdays, when crowds of City workers fill them, loudly chatting and laughing, clutching their prandial pints.

CITY ALLEYS

Change Alley (*entered from Cornhill and Lombard St*) saw scenes of wild speculation during the South Sea Bubble excitement in 1720. Jonathan's Coffee House, the principal meeting place of stockbrokers, was located here from 1680–1778. 'London's oldest chop house', founded in 1757, was Simpson's, off Cornhill (closed at the time of writing). In Castle Court is The George and Vulture pub, founded in 1600 and mentioned in Dickens's *Pickwick Papers*: 'Mr Pickwick and Sam took up their present abode in very good, old-fashioned, and comfortable quarters, to wit, the George and Vulture Tavern and Hotel, George Yard, Lombard Street'. A good view of the back of the building is from Bengal Court. A print shop in George Yard was the scene of the first meeting of the Society for Effecting the Abolition of the Slave Trade (*see p. 65*). Set in a wall in Corbet Court is a stone carving of the Mercers' Maiden, the earliest surviving property mark of the Mercers' Company dating from 1669 and installed here in 2004. In St Michael's Alley is St Michael's churchyard and the Jamaica Wine House (1885; *jamaicawinehouse.co.uk*), on the site of London's first coffee house, the Pasqua Rossee's Head, founded in 1652.

Cornhill, named after a long-extinct grain market, is a low eminence standing at 58ft above sea level: together with Ludgate Hill it is the highest point in the City. **St Peter-upon-Cornhill**, with large windows facing Gracechurch Street and its tower visible behind the 19th-century shopfronts of Cornhill, was rebuilt by Wren in 1677–84 and contains a carved wooden choir screen, one of only two such screens in Wren churches (the other being in St Margaret Lothbury; *see p. 58*). Wren is known to have been reluctant to divide the interior space in this way; this screen was installed at the insistence of rector William Beveridge, a fervent believer in the sanctity of Communion. The church is used by the benefice of St Helen's Bishopsgate as a Bible study centre and youth group meeting point, and there is a service for Mandarin-speaking Christians on Sun. Otherwise the interior must be viewed by appointment (*stpeteruponcornhill. org.uk*). The small garden behind, in St Peter's Alley, is the old burial ground, alleged to have been founded by the British early Christian ruler Lucius in AD 179 (the historical existence of Lucius is contested by scholars, though Bede mentions him).

Back on Cornhill, opposite St Peter's, stands the tall, slim, neo-Venetian Gothic **Shanghai Commercial Bank**, built by Edward I'Anson (1870). In an earlier building on

The Royal Exchange (1844), serene Classicism amid the ceaseless hubbub of London traffic and the skyward burgeoning of shimmering new towers. The tallest one shown here is 22 Bishopsgate, completed in 2020.

this site were the offices of Smith, Elder & Co., publishers of Thackeray and the Brontës.

St Michael's Church, with an unexpectedly tall tower (a survivor of the Great Fire), was rebuilt by Wren and Hawksmoor in 1670–1724 and restored by Sir George Gilbert Scott in Gothic style in 1857–60. It stands on one of the oldest Christian sites in Britain, dating back to the Roman occupation, and today offers a traditional Anglican service following the Book of Common Prayer. The sky-blue and gold interior houses a sculpture of a terrifying-looking pelican in her piety. The church is known for its weekly organ recitals (*st-michaels.org.uk*). Next door, the neo-Renaissance former Union Discount Company of London building (c. 1890), with granite columns the colour of liver sausage, occupies the site of the house (burned down in 1748) in which the poet Thomas Gray was born in 1716.

THE ROYAL EXCHANGE

Standing at the entrance to the Royal Exchange (*map p. 639, E3*), you are in the most ancient part of the City and at the centre of Roman London. The steps afford a fine view of the Mansion House (*see p. 45*), NatWest and the Bank of England (*see p. 56*), as well as straight ahead to No. 1 Poultry (*see p. 46*).

The **forecourt** features twelve Victorian-style lamps, donated by the twelve great livery companies (*see p. 20*), each with a brass plate and company motto and surmounted by a spiky dragon rampant. The **equestrian statue of Wellington** (Chantrey and Weekes, 1844) was cast from French cannon. The war memorial commemorates Londoners who fell in both World Wars.

The first Royal Exchange, inspired by the Bourse at Antwerp, was built in 1566 by Sir Thomas Gresham (1519–79), a rich merchant, member of the Mercers' Company and valued royal agent instrumental in reducing the royal debt. He acted as agent for King Henry VIII in the Low Countries (a fine portrait of him can be seen in the Rijksmuseum in Amsterdam). The Exchange acted as a commercial forum for merchants to meet and do business in convivial surroundings. It was destroyed in the Great Fire in 1666 and rebuilt in 1669. This second building burned down in 1838 but some of the sculptures survived. The current building, designed in classical style by Sir William Tite, was opened by Queen Victoria in 1844. The richly decorated exterior, essentially a Victorian classical pastiche with caducei (symbol of Hermes, patron of trade), is well worth inspecting. The impressive tympanum group above the Corinthian portico, by Sir Richard Westmacott (1844), represents *Commerce holding the Charter of the Exchange*, attended by the Lord Mayor, British merchants and natives of various foreign nations. The Wren-like campanile has a statue of Gresham on its east face and a large golden grasshopper vane (Gresham's badge), said to be from the post-Fire building.

The Royal Exchange ceased operating as a bourse in 1939. It was used by the London International Financial Futures until the late 1990s, its trading floor constructed as a separate shell within the existing building. In 2002, the Royal Exchange was remodelled as a luxury retail mall and shops, cafés and a Fortnum's bar and tearoom now occupy the central mosaic courtyard. Panels originally commissioned to line the walls of the courtyard are now in the first-floor gallery. They include one of Lord Leighton's few murals, *Phoenicians Bartering with Ancient Britons* (1894–5).

Around the Royal Exchange, the statue on the traffic island on Cornhill is of Sir Henry Greathead (1844–96), chief engineer of the City and South London Railway and inventor of the travelling shield that enabled the deep-level cutting of the Tube system. His plinth is positioned over a ventilation shaft for Bank Underground station.

On the wall of the Royal Exchange along Threadneedle Street are statues erected in 1844 to Sir Hugh Myddleton and Richard Whittington.

In the passage at the rear of the building is a granite column topped by a statue of Baron Paul Julius Reuter, who founded the Reuter's News Agency at the Royal Exchange in 1851 (Michael Black, 1976); a seated figure of George Peabody, founder of the charitable Peabody Trust (1869) and a fountain-group, *La Maternité*, by Dalou (1877–9).

LOMBARD STREET

Lombard Street, once a street of banks, derives its name from the 'Lombard' money-lenders from Genoa and Florence, who held financial sway here from the 13th–16th centuries. The first Lloyd's Coffee House (1691–1785) was founded on Lombard Street and during the 1930s the street was paved in rubber from British Malaya to muffle the sound of traffic so as not to disturb its moneymen. The phrase 'Lombard Street to a China orange' means heavily-weighted odds, with 'Lombard Street' being taken to signify value and the 'China orange', a trifle. **Number 1 Lombard St**, part of the curving building overlooking the Bank of England and Mansion House, stands on the site of the Smith, Payne & Smith bank, where the father of Charles Dickens's first love, Maria Beadnell, worked.

Since de-regularisation, the banks have deserted Lombard Street. However, a number of colourful hanging signs commemorate the historic institutions once based here: note the enormous **gilded grasshopper**, the badge of the great financier Sir Thomas Gresham, founder of the Royal Exchange, with the initials TG and the date 1563, hanging outside no. 68.

The church of **St Mary Woolnoth** (*map p. 639, D3; stml.org.uk*), which forms a monumental bastion between King William Street and Lombard Street, is a building of great originality. It is Nicholas Hawksmoor's only City church, erected in 1716–27 and restored and altered in 1875–6 by William Butterfield. It was the only City church to remain intact throughout the air raids of 1940–5. The porch new serves as a takeaway café. The interior contains an elaborate reredos and ornamental woodwork. On the south wall is a memorial to Edward Lloyd, founder of the first Lloyd's coffee house (*see Lloyd's of London, overleaf*). From the pulpit John Newton helped to set William Wilberforce and Hannah More on their abolitionist and philanthropical paths.

The church of **St Edmund the King**, rebuilt by Wren (and possibly Hooke) during the 1670s, is now home to the London Spirituality Centre. The spacious interior houses excellent carved woodwork, including a font cover topped with gilded apostles, and has a fine display of Church silver.

At the end of the street, **no. 54 Lombard St**, on the corner of Gracechurch Street, with Post-modern curved glass rooftops (GMW Partnership 1986–94), is the former headquarters of Barclays Bank. The Walkie-Talkie is prominent from here.

LOMBARD STREET, ST MARY WOOLNOTH AND THE SLAVE TRADE

St Mary Woolnoth, which styles itself the 'Embassy of Amazing Grace', is strongly bound up with the abolitionist cause. In 1780 a new rector came here, John Newton, a man who had had an extraordinary career and had recently been curate in the parish of Olney, Buckinghamshire, where he had befriended the poet William Cowper. Newton was born in Wapping, in London's Docklands, in 1725. Naturally enough, he turned seawards for a career, becoming both the captain of a slave ship and ending up himself enslaved, to a West African princess. In 1748, during a mighty storm in the Bay of Donegal, he had a spiritual experience that led to his conversion. On returning to dry land, he embarked on a course of theological study. Newton was never to be a conventional clergyman, however. His temper was ardent and sudden and he was drawn to the Evangelical movement. With Cowper he wrote the 'Olney Hymns', the most famous of which is *Amazing Grace*. As a preacher, he was charismatic. William Wilberforce, the great abolitionist, himself a clergyman, sought advice from Newton when he felt that his faith was wavering. The inaugural meeting of the Society for Effecting the Abolition of the Slave Trade was held in a printer's shop off Lombard Street, in George Yard, in 1787. The movement gained much impetus the following year when Thomas Clarkson, also a Church of England vicar, used the same printer's shop to issue thousands of copies of a line drawing of the slave ship *Brooke*, which he had obtained from Olaudah Equiano, former slave, freedman and eloquent abolitionist. It shows hundreds of human beings crammed into the hold with scarcely any space to move. All at once it became impossible for people to turn a blind eye to what was happening or to pretend that they did not know. Newton was vocal in his descriptions of conditions on board the slave ships, which he had witnessed first hand. His testimony helped to turn parliamentary opinion. The Abolition of the Slave Trade Act was finally passed in 1807. Newton died in the same year and is buried in St Mary Woolnoth and is commemorated by a tablet on the north wall. The epitaph was written by himself.

LEADENHALL STREET & BISHOPSGATE

Map p. 639, E3. Underground: Bank, Monument.

LEADENHALL MARKET, THE WALKIE-TALKIE AND LLOYD'S

Leadenhall Market, with its elaborate arcaded buildings of glass and painted steel, is the work of Sir Horace Jones (1880–1), architect of Smithfield and Billingsgate markets. A meat and game market existed on the site from medieval times and in 1663 Pepys bought 'a leg of beef, a good one, for sixpence' here. Jones retained the medieval street plan when his new market was erected. It was built over part of a Roman basilica of AD 150, one of the largest buildings of its kind in the Roman Empire, which closed one side of the forum. Substructures were unearthed during modern excavations and reputedly survive in the basements of no. 90 Gracechurch St and 21 Lime St, both sites now smothered in new building. Today the market, open 24hrs a day as a thoroughfare, houses shops, bars and restaurants (*leadenhallmarket.co.uk*) and nearby office workers are its clientèle.

The East India Company was founded on Leadenhall Street in 1600. The essayist Charles Lamb and economists James Mill and his son John Stuart Mill once worked as clerks in East India House (demolished 1862), which stood on part of the site where the Lloyd's Building is now (*see below*).

Walk straight through the market to come out onto Lime Street. Here, a right turn takes you down to 20 Fenchurch Street, one of London's most controversial skyscrapers: the 37-storey **Walkie-Talkie** (Rafael Viñoly; *map p. 639, E3*). This enormous building, with its unique shape, bulging in different directions depending on your angle of view, rears above the City skyline like a leviathan. In the summer of 2013, while it was still unfinished, sunlight reflected down from its curved glass surface caused the panels of a car parked in Eastcheap to melt. Its shape has attracted cynical comments: flaring upwards to allow larger surface areas on the upper levels, where higher rents can be charged for the premium of a splendid view. The Sky Garden on the top floor can be visited free of charge but you do have to book a slot (*skygarden.london*).

On Lime Street in the other direction (at no. 1) is the main entrance to the stainless steel, glass and concrete tubular edifice of **Lloyd's of London**, designed by Richard Rogers and opened by in 1986. A building of 1928, designed by Sir Edwin Cooper and which Lloyd's had long outgrown, was demolished to make way for the new tower in 1979. Lloyd's, the great international association of underwriters and insurance brokers, transacting most kinds of insurance, began in 1688 as a gathering of merchants in Edward Lloyd's coffee house in Tower Street (later in Lombard Street and in the Royal Exchange); its original business was marine insurance. Rogers's building was designed with a dealing room that could expand or contract according to market conditions by means of a series of galleries around a central space. The Lloyd's Building is considered one of the greatest buildings of the 1980s and has achieved listed status. It is a leading exponent of what is sometimes termed 'Bowellism', architecture that places functional elements such as elevators and air-conditioning pipes on the exterior so as to maximise space inside. Rogers was memorably parodied by the television show *Spitting Image* as a puppet with his internal organs on the outside, an apostle of form reflecting function.

1 UNDERSHAFT, THE CHEESEGRATER AND THE SCALPEL

Standing across Leadenhall Street from the Lloyd's Building is another skyscraper designed by Richard Rogers, the Leadenhall Building, familiarly known as **The 'Cheesegrater'** due to its wedge shape. The nickname was coined after the City of London's chief planner saw a model and commented that it was the sort of thing one might use to grate parmesan. Standing tall at 48 storeys, it is—unusually—designed not to rely on concrete foundations. Instead the glass and steel megaframe, by Arup, provides stability. Behind it, at the time of writing, stood the 28-storey Aviva or St Helen's Tower (**1 Undershaft**; *map p. 639, E3*), set back from the road in an open piazza. Clad in tinted brown glass, influenced by similar office blocks in mid-town Manhattan, it was built in the 1960s as the Commercial Union Insurance building. In its time it was a landmark structure, the first of a succession of skyscrapers that rose into the sky after regulations capping the height of construction at 80ft, to protect the historic skyline, were scrapped. At the time of going to press, a new building over 1000ft high was projected for the Undershaft site—and its nickname had already been chosen: The Trellis.

Facing the piazza, on the other side of Lime Street from Lloyd's, is **The Scalpel** (*52 Lime St*; Kohn Pedersen Fox, 2018), another multi-storey tower, deliberately designed to lean out of the frame for anyone approaching St Paul's up Fleet Street. Next to it, the skyscraper with the concave frontage and triple-tiered roofline with deep setbacks is the **Willis Building** (*51 Lime St*; Norman Foster, 2008). Between the two stands a

St Andrew Undershaft, its ancient name descriptive once again, as it cowers beneath the 'Gherkin'.

stainless steel sculpture entitled *Roundhouse* (2018), by the New York-based metalsmith Joel Perlman. It embodies everything that The Scalpel and Willis Building are not.

ST ANDREW UNDERSHAFT AND THE GHERKIN

At the corner of Leadenhall Street and St Mary Axe stands the church of **St Andrew Undershaft** (*map p. 639, E3*), now dwarfed by the Gherkin, which rises directly behind it. It was built in Perpendicular style in 1520–32, though a church has stood on this site since the 12th century. The name is derived from the ancient practice (discontinued in 1517) of erecting a 'shaft' or maypole, taller than the tower, in front of the south door. The last maypole survived, slung under the eaves of a neighbouring cottage, until 1549, when a zealous cleric declared it to be idolatrous and it was taken down and burned. The church falls under the jurisdiction of St Helen's Bishopsgate: to visit the interior you must make an appointment (*st-helens.org.uk*). It survived both the Fire and the Blitz but was grievously damaged in the Baltic Exchange bombing (*see below*) and its rare surviving 17th-century stained-glass window of portraits of monarchs was blown out. The organ was installed by Renatus Harris (*see p. 218*) in 1696. The alabaster monument to the historian and antiquary John Stow, author of the *Survey of London* of 1598, holds a quill pen which is ceremonially renewed every three years in an event organised in part by the Merchant Taylors' company. Stow was born in Cornhill and died in Lime Street.

Further up St Mary Axe, on the site of the former Baltic Exchange building of 1903, stands one of London's architectural icons, 30 St Mary Axe, fondly known as **The Gherkin** (*map p. 639, E2–F2*). It was built in 2004 to the designs of Foster & Partners. This distinctive structure, covered in diamond-shaped panes of glass, lends itself to an environmentally-friendly spiralling ventilation system. During construction, the grave of an unknown Roman girl was discovered on the site and this is commemorated on the low wall surrounding the piazza (plaque in the pavement opposite Holland House). The Baltic Exchange Building, headquarters of a body of merchants and brokers dealing in air and sea cargoes which was severely damaged in an IRA bomb attack of 1992, was demolished and not rebuilt. Surviving stained glass panels are kept in the National Maritime Museum (*p. 493*).

Holland House, on Bury Street, with its western façade facing the Gherkin, was built in 1914–16 by pre-eminent Dutch architect Hendrik Petrus Berlage. A Modernist symphony in black granite and green Delft ceramic tiling, it is the architect's only London building and very unusual. Commissioned by the Muller shipping company, it features a large ship's prow in granite on the southeast side. Peer through the entrance on the west (Gherkin) side to see the mosaic De Stijl interior.

BEVIS MARKS SYNAGOGUE

In Duke's Place just north of Aldgate (which takes its name from the 'old gate' which guarded the road out of London to the east) stood the Great Synagogue of London, established in 1690 and destroyed during the Blitz. What survives, in a little gated courtyard facing Heneage Lane, is the Spanish and Portuguese Synagogue or Bevis Marks Synagogue (*map p. 639, F2; sephardi.org.uk/bevis-marks*), a handsome building in red brick looking rather like a Wren church or Nonconformist chapel but also bearing resemblance to the Spanish and Portuguese Great Synagogue of 1675 in Amsterdam. Built in 1699–1701, it is probably by Joseph Avis, a carpenter who worked for Wren. The interior is very fine, with seven brass chandeliers representing the seven days of the week, 18th-century wooden seating and an elaborate oak Torah Ark (Ehal) at the east end. The twelve columns that support the women's gallery symbolise the Twelve Tribes of Israel and are painted to resemble marble. This is the oldest synagogue in Great Britain and was founded by Sephardic Jews who had fled Spain and Portugal to escape the Inquisition. It was the synagogue of Isaac d'Israeli, a talented poet and essayist of Italian Jewish ancestry, who quarrelled with the synagogue in 1817 and baptised his sons as Christians. The eldest of those sons was Benjamin, who later rose to become Prime Minister and Earl of Beaconsfield. The building was damaged by IRA bombing in the early 1990s but has been faithfully restored.

ST KATHARINE CREE

On the corner of Creechurch Lane and Leadenhall Street is the church of St Katharine Cree (*map p. 639, F3; stkatharinecree.org*). The name is a corruption of Christchurch, a priory of the Holy Trinity, founded by Matilda, consort of Henry I, in 1108. The church was rebuilt in 1628–30, retaining the medieval tower of 1504. It is the only surviving Jacobean church in London. William Laud, bishop of London, consecrated the church in 1631 and the form of service he used was later judged heretical and popish by the Puritans at his trial in 1644. A chapel commemorates both Laud and his patron, Charles I. The church is now a guild church (*see Glossary*).

The stained-glass rose window at the east end incorporates glass from the 1630s and is said to have been modelled on the one in Old St Paul's Cathedral (destroyed in the Fire). The font dates from c. 1631 and the restored organ has 17th-century pipes by Father Smith (*see p. 218*). Both Handel and Purcell played on the original instrument. An unverified tradition has it that Hans Holbein the Younger (d. 1543) was buried in the earlier church. The chest tomb with recumbent effigy of Sir Nicholas Throckmorton (d. 1570), the Elizabethan statesman after whom Throgmorton Street is named, survives.

The 'Lion Sermon', held annually around 16th Oct, commemorates the escape from a Syrian desert lion of fishmonger Sir John Gayer, Lord Mayor of London and founder of the Levant Company, who held office in Charles I's time. The church also holds an annual memorial service, in June, for the 9,000 people who lost their lives in the wreck of the *Lancastria*, a British troopship destroyed by German bombs off the coast of Brittany in 1940. A window of 1963, showing Christ walking on the water in front of a stricken ship, commemorates the tragedy.

BISHOPSGATE

Bishopsgate (*map p. 639, E2*) is the main commercial artery on the eastern side of the City, running north over the old Roman road that led from London to York, later known as the Old North Road or Ermine Street, now, more prosaically, the A10. Busy with vehicular traffic today, it was once threaded by a network of small alleys and courts with coaching inns and merchants' houses. Only the fabric of the medieval churches and a few small streets survive from its historic past, although one merchant's house, Crosby Hall, is now in Chelsea (*see p. 356*).

In April 1993, an IRA bomb exploded in Bishopsgate. One person was killed and 44 were injured and the blast and shockwaves caused £350 million worth of damage, especially to historic buildings and churches. The attack followed an earlier bombing the previous year in St Mary Axe, which had not only undermined the structure of the old Baltic Exchange but had caused £800 million worth of damage and cost three lives. The plethora of new building and the clusters of high-rises in this area, most notably at the southern end of Bishopsgate (*described above*), is in part due to the fabric of many buildings having been damaged by these terrorist attacks.

On the corner of Leadenhall Street is the 50-storey **8 Bishopsgate** office building (WilkinsonEyre architects), designed to make maximum use of natural light. At the top is The Lookout viewing gallery, which you can book to visit (*8bishopsgate.com/lookout*).

ST HELEN'S BISHOPSGATE

Beside the enormous 22 Bishopsgate (*see p. 60*), the alley known as Great St Helen's passes under the skyscraper's colour-spattered glass canopies to the church of St Helen's Bishopsgate (*st-helens.org.uk*), for which the Gherkin forms a backdrop. The small square in front of the church, with a tomb chest in the centre, is sheltered by plane trees. The church is a relic of a Benedictine nunnery founded c. 1210. The nunnery and its church were built alongside an existing parish church, hence the peculiar arrangement of the present structure, which has two parallel naves (one the former nuns' choir). The south transept and two chapels were added in the 14th century. The church was remodelled in the 15th and 17th centuries and restored by Pearson in 1891–3, in the Gothic style. Badly damaged by both the 1992 and 1993 bombs, the interior was restored and re-arranged again by the architect Quinlan Terry to accommodate a larger, evangelical congregation, work whic included controversially levelling the floors.

Nonetheless, the medieval interior houses an important number of surviving pre-Fire monuments, including the altar-tomb of Sir Thomas Gresham (d. 1579). In the north wall is the nuns' night staircase, an Easter Sepulchre and a 'squint' (peephole). In the chancel are some fine 15th-century stalls brought from the nuns' choir and a rare wooden sword rest (1665). Beyond the tomb chest of Sir John Crosby and his wife (d. 1475; of Crosby Hall; *see p. 356*), the Chapel of the Holy Ghost contains fragments of 15th–17th-century glass. The fine brasses (15th–16th centuries) include a lady in a heraldic mantle (c. 1535). Beside the south entrance is the fine restored monument of Sir John Spencer (d. 1609). The Jacobean font, pulpit, poor box and doorcases (west end) are noteworthy.

LEATHERSELLERS' HALL, ST ETHELBURGA AND HERON TOWER

Back on Bishopsgate, in the middle of the curving Palladian façade of nos 52–68 (Mewès & Davis, 1926–8), is the iron-gated entrance to St Helen's Place and the **hall of the Leathersellers' Company**, incorporated in 1444.

Facing Bishopsgate is the small ragstone façade of **St Ethelburga**, a brave little survival amid the towers of glass and steel. This 15th-century church escaped the Great Fire but was almost completely destroyed by the 1993 bomb. The exterior has been faithfully restructured and the church is now a centre for peace and reconciliation.

The old Bishop's Gate (pulled down in 1761) stood at the junction of Camomile Street and Wormwood Street, on the line of the old London wall. Both streets are named after popular medicinal herbs. Wormwood, in this case probably *Artemisia vulgaris* or mugwort, was used in beer-making before the advent of hops. The site of the old city gate is commemorated with a bishop's mitre fixed on the wall of a building on the Wormwood Street side. A short way down Wormwood Street, after it turns into London Wall, is the Neoclassical church of **All Hallows-on-the-Wall** (1765–7; *map p. 639, E2*) by George Dance the Younger. Completed when the architect was in his mid-20s, it was admired by his pupil, John Soane. The church, still consecrated, is now the offices of the Urban Youth Charity XLP and viewing of the unusual interior is by appointment only (*xlp.org.uk*). Part of the medieval City Wall may be seen in the churchyard.

Back on Bishopsgate is **Heron Tower** (Kohn Pedersen Fox, 2011), 46 storeys high, incorporating offices and a restaurant and sky bar. At ground level, Heron Piazza forms a new network of public squares and gardens on Houndsditch.

THE OLD CITY WALL

London was first encircled by walls by the Romans c. AD 200. These defences, pierced by numerous gates and posterns, were maintained throughout the Middle Ages. Only in the 18th century did they begin to be dismantled, as the capital expanded and its walls and gates became obstacles to traffic as well as to urban expansion. Sizeable sections of wall can still be seen and the London Wall Walk follows the line of the wall from the Tower of London westwards for about two miles, with a series of panels pointing out sites of interest along the way. The main gates were as follows (clockwise from the west): Newgate, Aldersgate, Cripplegate, Bishopsgate, Aldgate and Ludgate. Moorgate was added in medieval times. There were also water-gates on the Thames, such as Billingsgate, Queenhithe, Dowgate and Bridegate.

ST BOTOLPH-WITHOUT-BISHOPSGATE

Facing Heron Tower is the church of **St Botolph-without-Bishopsgate** (*map p. 639, E2; botolph.org.uk*). First mentioned in 1213, it was rebuilt in 1725–8 by James Gould and a team of masons, including his son-in-law George Dance the Elder, and then restored by the Roman Catholic architect J.F. Bentley in 1890–4. It was much damaged by both Bishopsgate bombs. Keats was baptised here in 1795 in the present font.

The churchyard has been a public garden since 1863 and was the first churchyard to be so transformed. It backs onto the line of the old City wall. The **church hall**, formerly a primary school, is of c. 1861 and the two Coade Stone (*see p. 466*) statues of charity children on either side of the entrance date from 1821.

Continue down the churchyard until you come to the **Victorian Bath House** (1895), nestled in front of glass office blocks. Owned by Henry and James Forder Nevill, who owned other Turkish baths in London, and designed by Harold Elphick, the Moorish kiosk is really the tip of the Turkish iceberg, as the rooms extend below ground. It is in part modelled on the shrine at the Church of the Holy Sepulchre, Jerusalem, and is richly decorated with terracotta, faïence, mosaic and stained glass. The onion dome, with star and crescent finial, housed the water tanks. Until relatively recently, the baths housed a Turkish restaurant and underground belly-dancing venue.

Off Bishopsgate, opposite Liverpool Street, is Devonshire Row, leading to **Devonshire Square** (*map p. 639, F2*), with shade trees and two fine 18th-century houses: Osborne House at no. 12 and **Coopers' Hall** at no. 13. Further down, an office, residential and retail development occupies former warehouses of the East India Company and Port of London Authority.

LIVERPOOL STREET STATION AND BROADGATE

Liverpool Street Station (*map p. 639, E2*) stands on the site of the first hospital of St Mary Bethlehem (1247–1676). A *tour de force* of Victorian Gothic cast iron and brick by Edward Wilson (1875), it was modernised and expanded in 1985–91 and then again in the 21st century to accommodate the Elizabeth Line. During successive phases of the construction work, remains of a large common burial ground were unearthed. Today Liverpool Street is the busiest transport hub in the City, gateway to Essex. The adjoining hotel, formerly the Great Eastern (Charles Barry, 1884), is now the Andaz, part of the Hyatt chain, re-opened in 2000 after a £70-million refurbishment. Inside, the opulent interior retains many original features, including a Masonic temple of 1912 on the first floor. Just outside the main station entrance (on the Liverpool St and Sun Street Passage corner) is an open space dubbed Hope Square. In it you will see the **Kindertransport Memorial**, a statue of children and their luggage who have just arrived in London, fleeing persecution in Nazi Germany. The statue is the work of Frank Meisler, who himself arrived at Liverpool Street on a *Kindertransport* train in 1939. His parents perished in Auschwitz.

The massive 30-acre **Broadgate development** surrounding Liverpool Street was initially conceived to provide modern office space for financial companies following the deregulation of the stock markets known as the 'Big Bang', which took place during Margaret Thatcher's government in 1986. In a major property deal, Broadgate was built over the former Broad Street Station (demolished 1985), which had opened in the mid-19th century to transport goods from the East End Docks to the Midlands. Built in phases, it is now a vast pedestrianised mixed-use area, an office city with plenty of shops and public spaces, overhung with greenery, where one can eat and drink (*broadgate.co.uk*). It is built in a mixture of architectural styles and is the work of several architects including Arup Associates and latterly Skidmore, Owings and Merrill. Much has been invested in public art: among the works are *Rush Hour*, influenced by T.S. Eliot's *The Waste Land* (George Segal, 1987); *Fulcrum*, colossal sheets of rusting steel (Richard Serra, 1987); the *Broadgate Venus* (Fernando Botero, 1989); *Bellerophon Taming Pegasus* (Jacques Lipchitz, 1966); *East End Venus* (Jim Dine, 1989).

THE NORTHERN REACHES OF BISHOPSGATE

At no. 202 Bishopsgate (corner of Middlesex St; *map p. 639, F2*) is **Dirty Dick's** pub of c. 1870. The pub is named after 18th-century City merchant Nathaniel Bentley, who on the death of his fiancée became a recluse with questionable personal hygiene. It is said that Bentley inspired Dickens's character of Miss Havisham in *Great Expectations*. Further up at no. 230 Bishopsgate (near the corner of Brushfield St) is the **Bishopsgate Institute**, opened in 1895 to bring educational and cultural opportunities to the people of this once-deprived area. The driving force was the Rev. William Rogers, the rector of St Botolph for 30 years. Charles Harrison Townsend designed the building in Art Nouveau style with a terracotta exterior of meandering trees and foliage, topped by twin turrets. It has notable similarities with his slightly later Whitechapel Art Gallery (*see p. 104*). The library (*free admission; bishopsgate.org.uk*) has important collections

'Hope Square' outside Liverpool Street Station, with Frank Meisler's *Kindertransport* Memorial (*The Arrival*), commemorating Jewish children who arrived here by train in the years immediately preceding the Second World War, escaping Nazi persecution.

relating to the history of London and lectures, concerts and events are usually held in the Great Hall. The vista down Brushfield Street is closed by the silhouette of Hawksmoor's magnificent Christ Church Spitalfields (*see p. 108*).

The City now merges imperceptibly with the area traditionally known as the East End of London. However, the local authority boundary is quite clearly marked with dragons, emblems of the City of London, and roughly coincides with a line linking Liverpool Street Station, Aldgate, Fenchurch Street Station and Tower Hill. There is one such dragon, proudly striding with bright red extended tongue, at the corner of Bishopsgate and Worship Street (*map p. 639, F2*).

THE BARBICAN, MOORGATE & THE NORTHERN CITY LIMITS

Map p. 639, D1–D2. Underground: Moorgate, Barbican.

John Betjeman has a famous mock-heroic image of a commuter slogging out his days in the City and dreaming of his cosy suburban home: 'And all that day in murky London Wall, the thought of Ruislip kept him warm inside...' London Wall, the street that loosely follows the boundary of the Roman city, is somewhat murky, though redevelopment has brightened it considerably. The Barbican, on its north side, is a multi-arts and conference venue (*main entrance to the events spaces is on Silk Street. barbican.org.uk*), with theatres, a concert hall, cinemas, exhibition halls, bars and restaurants. It is home to the London Symphony Orchestra and the Guildhall School of Music and Drama as well as to over 4,000 residents, who live in the three towers and 21 residential blocks. The Conservatory (*for opening times see Barbican website*) houses 2,000 species of tropical plant along with finches, quail and fish. The L-shaped artificial lake at the centre of the complex, with fountains and lakeside seating, alleviates the concrete harshness.

HISTORY AND DEVELOPMENT OF THE BARBICAN CENTRE
Prominent remains of a Roman/medieval bastion (the 'barbican' of the name) lie at the south edge of the site and can be seen from the Bastion Highwalk. The Roman city ended here. Subsequent development and habitation in what became the parish of Cripplegate was destroyed by Luftwaffe bombs in 1940 and only the church of St Giles-without-Cripplegate was left standing. During the 1950s, designs were proposed to redevelop the 60-acre site as a centre for the arts and entertainment and also as living and recreation space. London Wall, the road running between Aldersgate, Moorgate and Bishopsgate, was realigned in 1957–76. Building of the controversial complex behind it, in concrete Brutalist style, by Chamberlin, Powell and Bon, went ahead in 1971–81. The complicated structure on eight levels, three of which are underground, was opened by the late Queen Elizabeth II in 1982: she dubbed it 'one of the modern wonders of the world'. An integrated series of identical high-rise blocks lined the road; parking was underground and pedestrian access was at first-floor level via staircases, walkways and bridges. The plan, inspired by the ideas of Le Corbusier, had been to segregate pedestrians and traffic but the result was to allow traffic free rein along London Wall, turning it into a pounding, dual-carriage highway while the raised 'pedways', with decks for shops, gave the historic buildings and gardens at ground level an abandoned, sunken appearance. By the later 1980s, the taste for Modernism had soured and many walkways were abandoned. Today new raised pedestrian bridges of pre-rusted steel have been created, rebranded the Barbican 'Highwalk'. From them, you get a good view of the site.

LIVERY HALLS AND THE ALDERSGATE FLAME

The ruins of the **church of St Alphage**, with a collapsing 14th-century tower, stand in a little area of garden where you will find Michael Ayrton's bronze sculpture *Minotaur*. From the Highwalk here there is a good view of **Salters' Hall** (1976; based on designs by Sir Basil Spence) with its coat of arms and motto *Sal sapit omnia*, 'salt gives flavour to everything'. Beyond the ruins of the curved bastion (*see History, above*) are the former premises of the Museum of London, a building which in its day was a vision incarnate of Modernism (Powell & Moya 1968–76), white-tiled above and of black bricks below. Directly outside it stands the **Aldersgate Flame**, a bronze sculpture erected in 1981 on the approximate site of the house where Wesley felt himself converted to faith in Christ on 24th May 1730. In Wesley's own words: 'In the evening I went very unwillingly to a Society in Aldersgate Street, where one was reading Luther's Preface to the Epistle to the Romans. About a quarter before nine, while he was describing the Change which God works in the heart thro' Faith in Christ, I felt my heart strangely warm'd. I felt I *did* trust in Christ, Christ alone for Salvation: and an Assurance was given me, that He had taken away my sins, even mine, and saved me from the Law of Sin and Death.'

Other livery halls in the Barbican are the **Barber-Surgeons' Hall**, on Monkwell Square off Wood Street, rebuilt after War damage and opened in 1969; and the **Ironmongers' Hall**, a neo-Tudor edifice of 1925 in Shaftesbury Place.

ST GILES TERRACE

Lying at the heart of the Barbican complex, on the south side of the lake terrace, this paved piazza is the site of the restored church of **St Giles-without-Cripplegate** (*map p. 639, D2; stgilesnewsite.co.uk*), the Barbican's parish church and one of the few remaining medieval churches in the City. When built, it originally stood outside the City's walls, near the Cripplegate (the name probably deriving from the Old English *crepel*, a burrow or low opening). The piazza has been formed from its churchyard and weathered tombstones have been set into raised rectangular sections. The Great Plague was at its worst in the parish of St Giles, and plague burials fill nearly a folio volume of the parish register for 1665. The documents are now in the Guildhall Library.

The stone tower and the nave belong to the church of 1390 (the brick top storey of the tower was added in 1682–4 by John Bridges). After a fire in 1545 and alterations in the 17th–18th centuries, the church was badly damaged by bombs in 1940 but amazingly remained standing when everything else within a half-mile radius was destroyed. In the 1960s it was restored; the east and west windows were renewed and the organ (incorporating an 18th-century case) was installed.

Few monuments survive and most are in fragment form. A plaque beside the north (entrance) door recalls 'Men of Mark' connected with the parish, who include Sir Martin Frobisher, seaman and explorer (d. 1594); John Foxe, martyrologist (d. 1587); John Bunyan (d. 1688) and Daniel Defoe (d. 1731; the parish register records his burial in Bunhill Fields). Shakespeare attended the baptism of his nephew in this church in 1604, while lodging in Silver Street (now subsumed by the Barbican) with Christopher Montjoy, a Huguenot and 'tire maker' whom he had known 'for the space of tenne yeres or thereaboutes'. Oliver Cromwell was married here in 1620. Busts of Defoe, Bunyan,

Milton and Cromwell, presented to the Cripplegate Free Library by the philanthropist John Passmore Edwards, stand at the west end. Contemporary sensitivities at the time of writing had seen the bust of Cromwell, a representative of 'violence, anti-Irish prejudice and cruelty', endowed with a trigger warning. A plaque in the south aisle records the burial of Milton, whose *Paradise Lost* was printed by an Aldersgate printer. He died in Bunhill Row in 1674 but lived in several houses in the area and was buried in the same grave as his father. One night in 1790, a group of scamps, growing warm with beer at the home of the church overseer in nearby Beech Street, hatched a plot to disinter the poet's remains. According to Philip Neve in his *A Narrative of the Disinterment of Milton's Coffin*, the unearthed sarcophagus was concealed under a pew and Mrs Grant the gravedigger charged visitors tuppence to view the body. The bust of Milton that now surmounts the plaque was made by John Bacon, three years after this ignominious event. A window on the opposite side commemorates Edward Alleyn (*see p. 501*), a parishioner and benefactor.

MOORGATE AND THE NORTHERN CITY LIMITS

Map p. 639, D2–D1. Underground: Moorgate.

Moorgate is mainly a street of offices, leading north towards Islington and Hackney. Some of the buildings date from the late 19th century, some from the early 20th century and many from the 1980s. In Great Swan Alley, on the east side, is the **Institute of Chartered Accountants** (main façade on Moorgate Place), a Renaissance-style building by John Belcher (1890–3; extended 1930 by J.J. Joass), in part inspired by Genoese *palazzi*. The carving is by Harry Bates and the sculpted frieze, deliberately placed above the first-floor windows so as to be comprehensible from the ground, is by Hamo Thornycroft. The 1970s' extension is by William Whitfield. Moorgate Place leads out onto Moorgate, where at no. 36 is the **former Ocean Accident building** (1928) by Aston Webb & Son (currently Habib Bank). Note the capitals designed as ships' prows and the sculpture of a lighthouse in an alcove on the corner of Moorgate Place.

The Moor Gate itself, from which the street takes its name, was a 15th-century postern in the City Wall. It was pulled down in 1762. At 118 London Wall, next to the Globe pub on the corner, is the **former Fox umbrella shop** (1934) in black Vitrolite with two stainless steel foxes cavorting either side of the pink neon sign. The shop closed in 2011 and is now a wine bar, but Fox Umbrellas still exists: their workshop is near Croydon (*foxumbrellas.com*).

Across Moorgate is **Electra House**, a seeming monolith of a building surmounted by a bronze dome, completed in 1903 by Belcher and Joass for the Eastern Telegraph and Allied Companies. Occupied until 2019 by the London Metropolitan University, it was undergoing refurbishment for mixed use at the time of writing. Next door is **Britannic House**, built by Lutyens in 1924 for the Anglo-Persian Oil Company (later BP). With its Corinthian order and sculpture (including Britannia with her trident by Derwent Wood, on the corner of Finsbury Circus), it was the first of his grand City buildings.

Finsbury Circus was laid out in 1815–17. None of the original gentlemen's houses remains but the fine gardens in the centre are still preserved.

MOORFIELDS AND FINSBURY SQUARE

Moorfields (*map p. 639, D2*) is today commemorated in the name of a small street behind Moorgate Underground station, running parallel with Moorgate and leading into Ropemaker Street, where Daniel Defoe died in 1731. This was once marshy open land, the resort of beggars, highwaymen and prostitutes. In Thackeray's *Vanity Fair*, Becky Sharpe is recommended to read *The Blind Washerwoman of Moorfields*. Here the Royal London Ophthalmic Hospital was established in buildings by Robert Smirke in 1821. In 1899, Moorfields, as the hospital came to be known, outgrew its premises and moved to its current headquarters on City Road. The poet John Keats, the son of an ostler, was born in 1795 in a house in this area and was baptised at St Botolph (*see p. 71*).

Until the Catholic Relief Act of 1791, public Catholic worship was illegal. **St Mary Moorfields**, at 4–5 Eldon St, is the only Roman Catholic church in the City (and is only just within its limits: on Moorgate, just before the junction with South Place, stands a **City of London Dragon**, marking the municipal boundary). Completed in 1903 by George Sherrin, the architect of the dome of the London Oratory, St Mary Moorfields is easily missed but the sculpture of the *Virgin and Child* above the entrance points the way to a flight of steps leading down to the candlelit sanctuary.

Finsbury Pavement leads north to **Finsbury Square** (*map p. 639, E1*), where City Road leads into old London from the north. The square was laid out by George Dance the Younger in 1777, in an area until then notorious as a cruising ground (the road along the south side of the square replaces a pathway which in the early 18th century acquired the name of 'Sodomites' Walk'). No original buildings survive from Dance's design. One was Lackington's bookshop, the 'Temple of Muses', established in 1778 and known as a sight of London. Its memory survives in the name of nearby Lackington Street to the south. On the north side of the square, at nos 22–25, is **Royal London House** (Belcher/Joass, 1928), with a skyrocketing tower.

ARMOURY HOUSE AND THE HAC

City Road continues northwards, away from the official boundaries of the City, past the entrance to the drill-ground and headquarters (**Armoury House**; Thomas Stibbs, 1735; *map p. 639, D1*) of the Honourable Artillery Company of the City of London (HAC), the oldest military body in the country and the second oldest in the world. A private museum tells the history of the HAC and can be viewed by appointment with the archivist (*hac.org.uk*). The HAC is now a registered charity dedicated to 'military exercise and training and better defence of the realm'.

HAC was incorporated by Henry VIII in 1537 under the title of the Guild or Fraternity of St George. It has been established at its present home since 1642, and since 1660 the captain-general has usually been the Sovereign or the Prince of Wales. Officers for the Trained Bands of London were supplied by this company, in whose ranks Milton, Wren and Pepys served. The HAC has the rare privilege of marching through the City of London with fixed bayonets. On 15th September 1784, Vincent Lunardi made a balloon ascent from the HAC ground and travelled 24 miles, becoming the first aerial traveller in the English atmosphere and spawning a fad for ballooning. With him in the basket were a cat, a dog and a pigeon in a cage. The cat apparently became airsick and needed to be set down.

BUNHILL FIELDS AND WESLEY'S CHAPEL

Immediately to the north, between City Road and Bunhill Row (formerly Artillery Walk), lies **Bunhill Fields** (*map p. 639, D1*), the famous cemetery of the Nonconformists. Until its closure in 1854, approximately 123,000 people were buried here, among them Daniel Defoe (d. 1731; obelisk), John Bunyan (d. 1688; worn recumbent effigy), Susannah Wesley (mother of the Methodists John and Charles) and William Blake (exact location unknown but a gravestone beside the Defoe obelisk commemorates him). Two tombs commemorate descendants of Oliver Cromwell. There has probably been a burial ground here since Saxon times and the name probably derives from 'Bone-Hill' Fields. Today the quiet graveyard is a sanctuary from the surrounding inner-city sprawl and the mature trees of plane, oak, lime and ash provide shelter and a haven for birds, bats and ground fauna. Fenced plots surround grids of 18th- and 19th-century gravestones and underground vaults in varying stages of deterioration.

Milton wrote *Paradise Regained* and died in 1674 at a house in Bunhill Row (no. 125; demolished). In the **Quaker Gardens**, across Bunhill Row, laid out as a garden in 1952 and surrounded by flats, is the grave of George Fox (1624–91), founder of the Society of Friends (Quakers).

On the opposite side of City Road, at no. 49, stands **Wesley's Chapel**, built in 1778 by George Dance the Younger. A statue of John Wesley (1703–91), the founder of Methodism, is at the front and his grave is at the rear. Wesley's House adjoins the chapel and includes the Museum of Methodism, with a collection of Wesleyana and Methodist art. Wesley moved here in 1779 and it is furnished with many of his belongings. His small prayer room is on view (*wesleyschapel.org.uk*).

EASTCHEAP, THE MONUMENT, LONDON BRIDGE & LOWER THAMES STREET

Map p. 639, E3–E4. Underground: Monument.

The exits from Monument Tube station emerge above ground at a busy crossroads. On Clement's Lane, which opens off King William Street (and which offers a good view of the spire of St Edmund the King) is **St Clement Eastcheap**, rebuilt after the Fire by Wren and later Victorianised. It contains handsome 17th-century wood furnishings, including a carved and gilded font cover depicting a dove with an olive branch (not always on display), and a fine organ case of c. 1695. Samuel Pepys and John Evelyn worshipped here. The church claims to be the St Clement's in the nursery rhyme 'Oranges and Lemons'—but so does the church of St Clement Danes (*see p. 204*). The parish was merged with that of St Martin Orgar (possibly the church whose bells claimed the debt of five farthings in the same nursery rhyme), badly damaged in the Fire and eventually demolished, apart from the **bell-tower**, which was used to ring St Clement's bells. Rebuilt in an Italianate style in the 1850s, it still stands on Martin Lane, south of Cannon Street. Next to it, the empty plot with a central crooked tree marks the site of St Martin's churchyard.

ON AND AROUND EASTCHEAP

It is thought that somewhere near the point where Cannon Street, King William Street, Gracechurch Street and Eastcheap meet, stood the Boar's Head Tavern, where Falstaff and Prince Hal carouse in Shakespeare's *Henry IV Part I*. 'Come sing me a bawdy song,' cries Falstaff in Act III Scene 3, 'make me merry.' The building at **nos 33–35 Eastcheap**, an extravagant display of Victorian Gothic architecture at its most eccentric (R.L. Roumieu, 1868), was the London base for Hill & Evans, makers of vinegar. In its exterior decoration it makes reference to the legacy of the Boar's Head with a roundel of the said boar's face above the middle pair of windows in the centre. Another piece of Victoriana celebrating an animal tale can be seen at **23 Eastcheap** (built in 1862 for Hunt & Crombie, spice merchants), on the corner of Philpot Lane. Look up at the Philpot Lane elevation. Just above the right-hand scallop shell (marked with the name of the architects, Young & Son) you will see two tiny sculptures of brown mice fighting over a piece of yellow cheese. The story goes that two workmen on the building came to blows over a missing sandwich, only to discover that the culprits were a pair of mice.

ST MARGARET PATTENS
In a charming cluster of low-rise buildings at the corner of Rood Lane, where Eastcheap becomes Great Tower Street, is the church of St Margaret Pattens (*map p. 639, E3; stmargaretpattens.org*). Destroyed in the Fire, rebuilt by Wren in 1684–7, the soaring lead-covered spire (1698–1702) is the third highest in the City after St Bride's and St Mary-le-Bow. The church escaped the Blitz and has been a guild church since 1954. Its name is thought to derive from the pattens (undershoes raised on iron struts attached to the soles to protect the wearer from muddy roads) once made and sold in the lane. A sign asking women to remove their pattens used to hang on the church door. Today it maintains close links with the Worshipful Company of Pattenmakers and the Worshipful Company of Basketmakers (there is a small display dedicated to both guilds in the vestibule).

The two 17th-century churchwardens' canopied pews on either side of the entrance to the nave are unique survivals in London. The carved wooden reredos is a fine work; the small, square altarpiece of the *Agony in the Garden* is attributed to Carlo Maratta, a classically-inspired artist of the Roman school. Left of the altar is the original enclosed Beadle's pew. The church owns a rare silver gilt Communion cup of 1545, reputed to be the oldest in the City. A copy of the cup is used at a special service held on 30th Jan each year (or nearest Thur) in memory of King Charles I, the Martyr.

PUDDING LANE

In the Middle Ages, Eastcheap was the City's chief meat market. Animal entrails (puddings) were carried down **Pudding Lane**, on the right, to be disposed of in the river. It was in this lane that one of the worst disasters ever to befall London is said to have begun: the Great Fire, which started on 2nd September 1666, in the bakery of one Thomas Farriner. Pudding Lane today is architecturally extremely undistinguished: not surprisingly, not a stick or stone of its pre-Fire buildings survives.

Samuel Pepys on the Great Fire

Sunday 2nd September, 1666 (Lord's day). Some of our maids sitting up late last night to get things ready against our feast today, Jane called us up about three in the morning, to tell us of a great fire they saw in the City. So I rose and slipped on my nightgown, and went to her window, and thought it to be on the backside of Mark Lane [*map p. 639, F3*] at the farthest; but, being unused to such fires as followed, I thought it far enough off; and so went to bed again and to sleep. About seven rose again to dress myself, and there looked out at the window, and saw the fire not so much as it was and further off. So to my closet to set things to rights after yesterday's cleaning. By and by Jane comes and tells me that she hears that above 300 houses have been burned down tonight by the fire we saw, and that it is now burning down all Fish Street, by London Bridge. So I made myself ready presently, and walked to the Tower, and there got up upon one of the high places, Sir J. Robinson's little son going up with me; and there I did see the houses at that end of the bridge all on fire, and an infinite great fire on this and the other side the end of the bridge; which, among other people, did trouble me for poor little Michell and our Sarah on the bridge. So down, with my heart full of trouble, to the Lieutenant of the Tower, who tells me that it begun this morning in the King's baker's house in Pudding Lane, and that it hath burned St Magnus's Church and most part of Fish Street already. So I down to the water-side, and there got a boat and through bridge, and there saw a lamentable fire. Poor Michell's house, as far as the Old Swan, already burned that way, and the fire running further, that in a very little time it got as far as the steelyard, while I was there. Everybody endeavouring to remove their goods, and flinging into the river or bringing them into lighters that lay off; poor people staying in their houses as long as till the very fire touched them, and then running into boats, or clambering from one pair of stairs by the water-side to another. And among other things, the poor pigeons, I perceive, were loth to leave their houses, but hovered about the windows and balconies till they were, some of them burned, their wings, and fell down.

THE MONUMENT

At the junction of Monument Street and Fish Street Hill, immediately opposite the site where the Great Fire of London is said to have started, stands the Monument (*map p. 639, E3*), a colossal Doric column, 202ft high, erected from the designs of Wren and

King Charles II, in Roman guise, directs the resuscitation of London, while Fire, an aged hag, breathes brimstone from below. Relief by Caius Gabriel Cibber on the Monument.

Hooke in 1671–7 to commemorate the catastrophe. Largely concealed today by the surrounding high-rise blocks, it is only when you come upon it that you realise it is there—but still, a sense of how colossal it must originally have seemed still prevails. The Monument stands on the site of St Margaret's Church, New Fish Street, the first to perish in the Fire. The point where the Fire started, on 2nd September 1666 in Pudding Lane, was exactly 202ft from the Monument, hence the Monument's height.

In all, the Fire raged for three days and was reported to have covered 373 acres inside the City walls and 63 acres outside, destroying 13,200 houses, 44 livery halls and 86 churches. The number of human casualties was astonishingly small: only nine people died.

The Monument is built of Portland stone with a pedestal 21ft square and 40ft high and a fluted shaft 120ft high and 15ft in diameter. Latin inscriptions record the Fire. The bas-relief by Caius Gabriel Cibber (father of the later Poet Laureate Colley Cibber) represents the King consoling the City—the female figure in the ruins—while Fire, a ghastly crone, breathes smoke from below. The four dragons are by Edward Pierce. Inside the column (*for access, see themonument.info; no large bags*) a winding staircase of 311 steps leads to the caged gallery, though the views which it commands are less wide and striking than they once were. The gallery was first enclosed in 1842 to prevent suicides. The flaming gilt urn surmounting the Monument is 42ft high.

LONDON BRIDGE

London Bridge (*map p. 639, E4–D4*) divides the Thames into 'above' and 'below' bridge. Downstream is the Port of London. The reach immediately adjacent to the bridge is known as the Pool of London, while upstream is the King's Reach. The present bridge (Mott, Hay & Anderson with Lord Holford, 1967–72) is a box girder structure borne on three shallow arches of pre-stressed concrete faced with granite. It is 105ft wide. In the summer of 2017, Islamic extremists drove a van into pedestrians on the bridge, then drove to the south of the river, where they began a stabbing attack in Borough Market.

PREVIOUS LONDON BRIDGES

A wooden bridge across the Thames existed by the 1st century AD. This probably survived until 1176, having been repaired by the Saxons. The popular rhyme 'London Bridge is Falling Down' may date from this time, when it was resolved to 'build it up with stone so strong'. The new bridge, about 100ft west of the old, was begun in 1176 by Peter of Colechurch, at the instance of Henry II, but it was not completed until 1209 in the reign of King John. It stood close to the west end of the church of St Magnus. Rows of wooden houses sprang up on each side, and in the middle was a chapel dedicated to St Thomas à Becket. At each end stood a fortified gate, on the spikes of which the heads of traitors were exposed. The Thames under the bridge was notoriously difficult to navigate because of the narrow passage between the starlings and the force of the ebb tide. After a fire in 1758, the last houses were demolished and the bridge was partly reconstructed and opened in 1763. It was the only bridge over the Thames until the opening of Putney Bridge in 1729. Most Thames crossings were made in wherries rowed by watermen. The penultimate bridge on this site, 100ft upstream from Old London Bridge, was designed by John Rennie and completed by his son in 1832. It was sold in 1967 to an American oil tycoon for £1,025,000, dismantled into 10,000 granite slabs which were numbered and then shipped to Lake Havasu City, Arizona, where the bridge was re-erected over an artificial lake..

On the west side of London Bridge is **Fishmongers' Hall**, commonly known as Fish Hall, one of the grandest livery halls, with a fine Neoclassical façade on the river. It was built in 1831–5 by Henry Roberts and George Gilbert Scott and was badly damaged in 1940 (an earlier hall was also burnt down in the Great Fire). The Fishmongers' Company is one of the richest as well as one of the oldest of the twelve great livery companies (*see p. 20*). Its origin is lost in antiquity though it certainly predates the reign of Henry II. The fine interior has been restored in its former style. It contains Pietro Annigoni's 1955 portrait of Queen Elizabeth II, on which stamps and banknotes issued during her reign were modelled, and a fine portrait of Sir William Walworth, the Mayor who killed Wat Tyler in 1381 (as well as the dagger with which he is supposed to have done the deed).

ON AND AROUND LOWER THAMES STREET

From London Bridge, look down onto Lower Thames Street, once cobbled and now a roaring modern highway. Geoffrey Chaucer is said to have lived in this street from 1379–85, during part of which period he was Comptroller of the Petty Customs in the Port of London. Abutting the bridge is **Adelaide House**, by Burnet and Tait, a partnership known for their Modernist and Art Deco constructions. This was the first steel-framed block in London, the tallest in the city when it was completed in the mid-1920s. It takes its name from an earlier building named in honour of Adelaide of Saxe-Meiningen, queen of King William IV (Adelaide in Australia is also named after her).

Next to Adelaide House is the church of **St Magnus-the-Martyr** (*map p. 639, E4; stmagnusmartyr.org.uk*), on the site of the old approach to London Bridge: a hunk of blackened timber, part of the old Roman wharf, is placed under the bell-tower entrance porch and stone portions from earlier London bridges are in the churchyard. The church was destroyed in the Fire (Pepys mentions it by name in his Diary) and its rebuilding was completed by Wren in 1671–4; the later steeple (1703–6), 185ft high, is considered one of Wren's masterpieces. The church has been much altered over the centuries and today the pleasing, compact interior, with fine woodwork, continues an Anglo-Catholic tradition assumed between the two World Wars. Miles Coverdale (d. 1569), translator of the first complete English version of the Bible (1535), was rector of St Magnus in 1563–6 and is commemorated by a neo-Gothic tablet of 1837, right of the high altar. In the right-hand aisle is a painted wooden sculpture of the titular saint himself, Magnus Earl of Orkney (died c. 1117), depicted as a horned-helmeted Viking jarl. Also in the church is a wooden scale model (not entirely historically accurate) of Old London Bridge.

OLD BILLINGSGATE AND CUSTOM HOUSE

Next to the Northern & Shell Building, a product of the 1980s in blue reflective glass (and home to a publishing company once largely known for 'glamour' magazines), is the **former Billingsgate Fish Market** (*map p. 639, E4*), designed in 1874–8 by Sir Horace Jones. It took its name, according to Stow, from an old gate supposedly named after Belin, a legendary king of the Britons, first built here in 870. Billingsgate Wharf, said to be the oldest on the river, was used from very early times (perhaps indeed from the 9th century) as a landing-place for fishing boats and other small vessels. It now forms part of the Thames Path along the waterfront, accessed by Old Watermen's Walk or Old Billingsgate Walk. The free fish market was established here in 1699. Anyone could land their fish here and sell it in the market. Today, from the spacious waterfront terrace, you have a good view of the river façade, with fishy wrought ironwork and twin gilded fish weather vanes. In its heyday, Billingsgate claimed to be the only market in which every variety of fish was sold—'wet, dried, and shell'. The porters wore 'bobbing hats', round, hard-topped leather hats for carrying loads of fish. The market moved to the Isle of Dogs in 1982 and the old building is now an events venue.

Next to the old market, the large Neoclassical edifice behind blue railings, screened from the Thames behind an avenue of plane trees, is **Custom House**, by David Laing

(1812–17) and Sir Robert Smirke, who redesigned the central section after subsidence in 1825–8. The first custom house was established here in the 14th century to collect duty on trade on the river. Wren designed the replacement building after the Great Fire, but it burnt down in 1715.

ST MARY-AT-HILL

On the narrow, cobbled Lovat Lane, approached from opposite Old Billingsgate on Lower Thames Street, is the church of **St Mary-at-Hill** (*map p. 639, E3; stmaryathill. org*), rebuilt by Wren and Hooke in 1670–4 from the medieval church destroyed in the Great Fire. Later fires in 1848 and 1988 damaged the noteworthy woodwork, the box pews and other interior features, including the organ by William Hill (deemed one of the ten most important organs in the history of British organ building). The church has a distinguished musical tradition: Tallis and Mundy sang in the church choir in the 16th century. Today, the church is the venue for the annual Fish Harvest on the second Sunday in October, a celebration of the bounty of the sea.

In winter the church is entered via the small churchyard garden off the cobbled St Mary at Hill (note the 17th-century relief carving of the *Last Judgment* in the entrance/exit passage). Further down St Mary at Hill from the church is a doorway surmounted by a skull and crossbones, marking another way into the churchyard and charnel house. At the bottom of the street is the charming **Watermen's Hall**, built in 1780, the only Georgian hall in the City. Note the morose-looking carving of Old Father Thames above the entrance and the fish in the Ionic pilasters. The Company of Watermen and Lightermen of the River Thames, without livery for historic reasons, was founded in 1514 to regulate the trade of watermen and bargemen. Watermen (or wherrymen) were employed to carry people and their belongings on the Thames; lightermen carried goods from one ship to another or to shore (to 'lighten' meaning to unload). In 1598, London chronicler John Stow recorded there being 40,000 men earning their living on or along the river. A guild was formed in 1514, to regulate their operation on the Thames, and apprenticeships were introduced to teach the skills of the river. The Company still examines and approves all apprentices who wish to work on the river.

At the corner of St Mary at Hill and Lower Thames Street, a Roman bath house was discovered in 1969, part of a private residence of c. AD 200. Finds on the site showed the house to have been occupied until the second half of the 5th century.

ST DUNSTAN-IN-THE-EAST

A narrow alley, St Dunstan's Lane, leads from St Mary at Hill to Idol Lane and the ruined church of **St Dunstan-in-the-East**, on St Dunstan's Hill. The medieval church, damaged in the Fire, was restored and a fine tower added by Wren in 1695–1701. The body of the church was then rebuilt by Laing, architect of the Custom House, in 1817. The tower escaped the Blitz and now, as All Hallows House, houses the Wren Clinic, a centre for natural health and counselling, offering therapy for stressed-out City workers. The rest of the church was severely damaged in 1941 and has been turned into a wonderfully peaceful public garden with vines and creepers twining over the walls and windows; flowers and exotic plants and a pair of splendid oak trees adorn the ruined shell. Winter's bark (*Drimys winteri*), of which there is an example in the lower garden, was once eaten to prevent scurvy as its leaves are high in Vitamin C. Here also is a fig tree commemorating the coronation of George VI in 1937.

In Harp Lane, a little further east, is the **Bakers' Hall** (no. 9; 1963) with windows by John Piper commemorating the burning of the former hall.

ON AND AROUND FENCHURCH STREET

Until the Reformation, numerous religious orders were based in the area of London near **Mincing Lane** (*map p. 639, E3*), whose name comes from the Old English *mynecen*, a nun. It once led to the Benedictine priory of St Helen's Bishopsgate. Later it became the headquarters of the wholesale tea trade and was also a centre of the opium trade. Reginald Wilfer, in Dickens's *Our Mutual Friend*, was a clerk here, 'in the drug-house of Chicksey, Veneering, and Stobbles.' Today the giant marble and granite complex known as Minster Court, in surging Post-modern Gothic style (GMW Partnership, 1987–91), occupies much of the street.

The **Clothworkers' Hall** in Dunster Court was rebuilt in 1956 after its destruction in 1941. It is the sixth hall on this site since 1456. The archives and the plate, among which is a loving cup presented by Samuel Pepys, Master of the Company in 1677, were saved. Nearby in Mark Lane (where Pepys first thought he saw the Great Fire; *see p. 80*), is the surviving 14th-century **tower of All Hallows Staining**, which is maintained by the Clothworkers' Company.

Across Fenchurch Street is **Fen Court**, where a landscaped garden marks the churchyard of St Gabriel Fenchurch (destroyed 1666; not rebuilt). A sculpture here was unveiled by Archbishop Desmond Tutu in 2008 to celebrate the abolition of slavery. Entitled *Guilt of Cain*, by Michael Visocchi with text by Lemn Sissay, the sugar-cane-shaped uprights are a deliberate play on words.

At no. 71 Fenchurch St, on the corner with Lloyd's Avenue, is the **Lloyd's Register of Shipping building**, a society founded in 1760 (distinct from Lloyd's of London; *see p. 66*). The late Victorian building, its roof surmounted by an appropriate gilt weather vane, has been extended by Richard Rogers.

Fenchurch Street Station was the first station to be built in the City, in 1841. The current façade dates from the 1850s, with 20th-century modifications and extension.

HART STREET

St Olave Hart Street (*map p. 639, F3; saintolave.com*) dates from the 13th century and is a rare surviving medieval parish church in the City. Small and humble, it is immensely atmospheric. It is dedicated to King Olaf II of Norway, who fought with King Ethelred against the Danes at the Battle of London Bridge in 1014. In 1666 the Great Fire came within 100m of the church before the wind changed direction, thereby saving it from being engulfed in flames. The church was not so lucky during World War Two and sustained two direct hits during bombing raids. Although 90 percent of the façade was reduced to rubble, enough of the original masonry survived and it was rebuilt and the interior restored in the 1950s. King Haakon VII of Norway laid a stone from Trondheim

Above the gateway to St Olave's churchyard, skulls which in their time spooked both Samuel Pepys and Charles Dickens.

Cathedral in the sanctuary during its re-dedication. The original stained-glass windows were all destroyed except for the 19th-century window on the north side with coats of arms; it was away having another coat of arms added when the church was bombed. Samuel Pepys lived and worked in this area and worshipped in this church. Both he and his wife are buried here: high up on the north chancel wall, left of the altar, is a bust of Elizabeth Pepys (d. 1669); there is a tablet to Samuel Pepys in the south aisle. Other monuments include a wall tablet, right of the southeast window, commemorating (in lengthy Latin) William Turner (d. 1568), Dean of Wells, militant Protestant and father of English botany. Left of the southeast window is an early 17th-century painted alabaster portrait bust of Turner's son, Peter, 'Doctor in Physick', who attended Sir Walter Raleigh in the Tower. Peter Turner also wrote a treatise on plague cakes: little phials of arsenic to wear around the neck in order to combat infection. His effigy (c. 1614) disappeared from the church during the confusion of the Blitz and resurfaced in 2010 at public auction. In 2013 it was reinstalled after a 70-year absence, in a partial recreation of the original monument. The vestry, where Samuel Pepys paid his poll tax, has a 17th-century plaster ceiling depicting an angel. A memorial service dedicated to the great diarist is held here annually.

SEETHING LANE AND CRUTCHED FRIARS

The three 17th-century stone skulls in the pediment of the churchyard gate, overlooking **Seething Lane**, captured Pepys's imagination and later that of Charles Dickens. Pepys is purported to have safeguarded his parmesan cheese from the ravages of the Fire by burying it on or near Seething Lane gardens. The name Seething comes from an Old English word for chaff, a reference to the cornmarket in nearby Fenchurch Street.

When Pepys was Secretary of the Admiralty, the Navy Office stood in **Crutched Friars**, the prolongation of Hart Street to the east. It is named after an order of mendicants, the Friars of the Holy Cross or *Fratres Cruciferi* (of which 'Crutched' is a corruption). The continuation of Crutched Friars, Jewry Street, follows the line of the old City Wall.

THE TOWER OF LONDON, & ST KATHARINE DOCKS

The Tower of London, one of the metropolis's oldest and most famous landmarks, is built on the easternmost of the City's three hills. Spanning the Thames to the east of it is Tower Bridge, a magnificent feat of engineering and a tourist attraction in its own right. Just beyond the bridge are St Katharine Docks, former wharves and warehouses now filled with places to eat and drink.

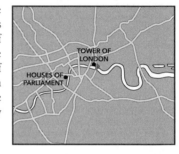

TOWER HILL

Historic Tower Hill (*map p. 639, F3; Underground Tower Hill, DLR Tower Gateway*), encompassing Trinity Square, was until 1747 a place of high-profile public execution. Among those put to death here were Sir Thomas More, George Boleyn (brother of the unfortunate Anne), Bishop John Fisher and Archbishop Laud.

Just outside Tower Hill Underground station is a large **sundial** (Edwin Russell, Mike Duffie & John Chitty, 1992) with engravings that give a chronological history of London. From here there is a good view of the Tower of London as well as an impressively large section of the **Roman and medieval wall**. It acts as a backdrop for a bronze statue of the emperor Trajan (d. AD 117; statue believed to be 18th century), shown in the act of addressing his troops. Another stretch of the wall, with windows and a sentry walk along the top, may be seen in a courtyard off Cooper's Row (the street leading north towards Aldgate). The remains of a medieval postern gate can be seen before the underpass from Tower Hill station to the Tower of London.

TRINITY SQUARE

Trinity Square Gardens (*map p. 639, F3*) are filled with memorials to mariners of the Merchant Navy who died with 'no grave but the sea'. Lutyens's **Mercantile Marine Memorial** (1928), designed as a Greek temple, honours those who perished during WWI. The peaceful sunken garden extension, which commemorates the merchant seamen lost in WWII, is by Sir Edward Maufe, with reliefs by Sir Charles Wheeler.

Behind, on Trinity Square itself, is the elegant **Trinity House** (Samuel Wyatt, 1793–5), with a rusticated ground floor and Ionic columns and pilasters above. It is the headquarters of the General Lighthouse Authority of England, Wales, the Channel Islands and Gibraltar, founded in 1514 when Henry VIII granted a Royal Charter to a fraternity of mariners called the Guild of the Holy Trinity, to 'regulate the pilotage of ships in the King's streams.' Pepys was Master as, later, was the Duke of Wellington.

Just beyond, the dominating Neoclassical edifice with a tower and sculpture and a giant order of Corinthian columns, stretching onto Muscovy Street, is **10 Trinity Square**, the former Port of London Authority building (Sir Edwin Cooper, 1922). It is now a luxury Four Seasons hotel and private members club. Inside, ancient artefacts discovered during the hotel's renovation are displayed. The ballroom, with walnut panelling and rich carving, that hosted the first reception for the United Nations in 1946, has been restored.

ALL HALLOWS BY THE TOWER
The church of All Hallows by the Tower (*map p. 639, F4; ahbtt.org.uk*) is the oldest surviving church in the City, founded in 675 for the tenants of the Saxon Barking Abbey. It survived the Great Fire when Admiral Sir William Penn and his sailors blew up houses around the church to create a firebreak, but it was largely destroyed in the Second World War (although the tower and the exterior walls survived). The brick tower is thus the same one from which Pepys watched the progress of the Great Fire: it is an important surviving example of Cromwellian church architecture in London. Pepys wrote, 'I up to the top of Barkeing steeple and there saw the saddest sight of desolation that I ever saw. Everywhere great fires, the fire being spread as far as I could see it.' Today's copper spire, in the manner of Wren, dates from post-war restoration work. Also during restoration, a large Saxon arch, with Roman masonry, was fully uncovered at the west end.

William Penn, son of the firefighting Admiral Penn, was born on Tower Hill in 1664 and was baptised in All Hallows. Here also John Quincy Adams, sixth president of the United States, was married to Louisa Johnson in 1797. All Hallows is the guild church of Toc H, a Christian organisation founded in 1922 by a former Army chaplain, the Rev. Philip ('Tubby') Clayton, whose effigy can be seen in the north aisle. In the south aisle, in the **Mariners' Chapel**, is a Crucifix whose Cross is made of wood from the *Cutty Sark*. The ivory Christ is said to be a devotional figure from the Spanish Armada's flagship. The font is of Gibraltar limestone and the fine **font-cover** of limewood is attributed to Grinling Gibbons. The tombs and brasses in the Sanctuary and Lady Chapel survived the bomb damage or were reconstructed. In the Sanctuary is the **Resurrection Brass** (c. 1500), showing Christ rising from the tomb; in the Lady Chapel the **Toc H Lamp of Maintenance** still burns. Here too is the **Tate Panel**, four wings from a dismembered triptych arranged in their current formation by Horace Walpole. They are thought to be the work of an early 16th-century Flemish master.

The Undercroft
The **Oratory of St Clare**, in a former burial vault, is dedicated to the Toc H Women's Association. The **St Francis Chapel** has a 13th-century barrel-vaulted roof. The **Undercroft Chapel** contains the ashes of members of Toc H. The plain crusading altar is from Richard I's castle at Athlit in Palestine. The remains of Archbishop Laud were

temporarily laid here after his beheading in 1645 (they were removed to St John's College, Oxford in 1663). In the **Crypt Museum** there is a tessellated Roman pavement—probably the floor of a Roman house—as well as many other Roman remains, including fragments of pottery and ashes from the city burned by Boudica in AD 61. The barrel is the crow's nest from the ship *Quest*, used by Sir Ernest Shackleton for his last Antarctic expedition in 1921–2.

THE TOWER OF LONDON

Map p. 639, F4. Underground: Tower Hill. DLR: Tower Gateway. hrp.org.uk.

His Majesty's Royal Palace and Fortress, the Tower of London, has been at the centre of English national consciousness for over 900 years, not only as a palace and stronghold but also as a prison, treasury, mint, records office, menagerie and wharf. Today it attracts over two million visitors a year: be prepared for crowds at all times but especially during high season and school holidays. It is one of London's four World Heritage Sites: the eruption of plate-glass and steel skyscrapers in the vicinity is perceived by some as careless city planning, having posed a threat to the Tower's World Heritage status.

HISTORY OF THE TOWER OF LONDON

The distinguishing 11th-century keep known as the White Tower rises at the centre of the 18-acre complex and is a superb—and complete—example of Norman castle-building. It is one of the most important and largest of William the Conqueror's castles and was purpose-built both to subjugate and to defend London following the Norman Conquest of 1066. The massive stone edifice would have towered over the city's low-rise timber buildings, visible for miles from land and water.

A programme of enlargement and reinforcement was initiated in the 12th century during the reign of the great warrior king Richard I (The Lionheart); by 1350 the Tower had become a mighty citadel. Framing the White Tower are the 13th-century concentric curtain walls built by Henry III and Edward I. The wall around the Inner Ward has 13 towers; the wall of the Outer Ward has six. From their names, one may deduce what some of them were used for. The rolling turf surrounding these fortifications was once a deep moat. This was not only the Tower's outermost defence system but also served as a fishpond, millpond and rubbish dump for those living within its precincts. It was drained in the 19th century and during World War Two was planted as an allotment.

Although never seriously assaulted, the Tower was besieged during the Peasants' Revolt of 1381. A detachment of rebels gained entry, abused the King's mother (Joan, the 'Fair Maid of Kent') and put to death the Archbishop of Canterbury.

Under the Tudors, when it was used as an armoury and munitions store and less as a royal residence, the Tower gained its reputation as a terrifying state prison and place of torture. Anne Boleyn was both crowned and executed here; her daughter, Princess Elizabeth, was held captive; and a later wife of Henry VIII,Catherine Howard, was also beheaded here.

Charles I lost control of the Tower at the beginning of the Civil War in 1642. In 1661 Charles II (the last monarch to sleep in the Tower) processed from here to Westminster Abbey to be crowned, a tradition that had obtained since the 14th century.

During the 19th century, after the relocation of many of the Tower's institutions (such as the Royal Mint), the Gothic Revival architects Anthony Salvin and John Taylor undertook a programme of re-medievalisation. Buildings were pulled down and rebuilt and the Tower was restored to its 'authentic' former glory. It was during the 19th century that the Tower became a thriving tourist attraction.

ENTRANCE AND OUTER WARD

The western entrance was built in the 13th century by Edward I. The barbican known as the **Lion Tower (1)**, where the Tower's beasts were kept (*see Royal Beasts Exhibition, p. 96*), no longer exists but its excavated remains can be seen on the left, with Kendra Haste's life-size wire sculptures of lions on top of them (more sculptures of former animal inmates, including a polar bear, are dotted around inside).

Pass through the **Middle Tower (2)** (1280, partially rebuilt 1717): on this causeway the Yeoman Warders' guided tours start. Moving on, **Byward Tower (3)** (1280) has one surviving portcullis. Inside are rare surviving fragments of a 14th-century wall painting of the *Crucifixion*, known as The Byward Angel (c.1393–4), and though it is not open to the public, it may be viewed online (*https://artsandculture.google.com*).

Once in the Outer Ward, **Water Lane** continues straight ahead, running parallel with the Thames. It is so called because Edward I successfully reclaimed it from the river. On the left is **Mint Street**, where the Yeoman Warders and their families live. The Mint was in operation here from 1279 to c.1810 and may be explored via interactive exhibition.

SOUTH WALL WALK

The 12th-century **Bell Tower (4)** is the second oldest building in the complex after the White Tower; it is here that the curfew bell is rung. Sir Thomas More and Bishop Fisher were confined here for refusing to recognise Henry VIII as head of the Church. As a princess, Elizabeth I was held captive in the Bell Tower by her half-sister Mary I.

St Thomas's, Wakefield and Lanthorn towers were once royal lodgings and together they form the Medieval Palace Exhibition. **St Thomas's Tower (5)** (1275–9) and the water entrance known as **Traitors' Gate (6)**, were built by Edward I. The name Traitors' Gate was coined because Tudor prisoners accused of treason arrived here by barge, having first passed under London Bridge, where the heads of recently executed

THE TOWER OF LONDON

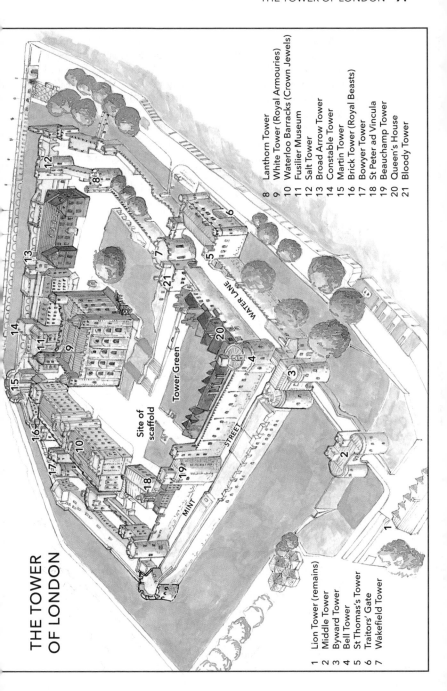

1 Lion Tower (remains)
2 Middle Tower
3 Byward Tower
4 Bell Tower
5 St Thomas's Tower
6 Traitors' Gate
7 Wakefield Tower

8 Lanthorn Tower
9 White Tower (Royal Armouries)
10 Waterloo Barracks (Crown Jewels)
11 Fusilier Museum
12 Salt Tower
13 Broad Arrow Tower
14 Constable Tower
15 Martin Tower
16 Brick Tower (Royal Beasts)
17 Bowyer Tower
18 St Peter ad Vincula
19 Beauchamp Tower
20 Queen's House
21 Bloody Tower

WATER LANE

Tower Green

Site of scaffold

MINT STREET

prisoners were displayed on pikes. Inside St Thomas's Tower, Edward I's bedchamber has been reconstructed, complete with royal bed and crackling faux fire. The peaceful oratory would have overlooked the Thames. A 19th-century covered bridge leads from St Thomas's Tower to **Wakefield Tower (7)**, one of the oldest parts of the medieval palace built in 1220 by the Warrior King, Henry III (Edward I's father), and which he could have entered via private stairs from his water-gate. Inside is a replica throne, a restored fireplace and a chapel. In 1471, at the end of the Wars of the Roses, Henry VI was murdered here whilst at prayer and a plaque on the chapel floor commemorates this. **Lanthorn Tower (8)** was built as lodgings for Henry III's queen and later housed a lantern by which boats could navigate the Thames by night. It was gutted by fire in the 18th century and the present building dates from the 19th century.

CUSTODIANS OF THE TOWER AND THE TOWER RAVENS

Today the Tower is cared for by Historic Royal Palaces but because it is home to the Crown Jewels, it is also a high-security garrison looked after by a unit of the Tower Guard. Once the tourists have departed, the night watch is reputed to be an eerie duty and numerous ghostly sightings have been reported by the Tower's small resident community. Distinct from the Tower Guard are the ceremonial custodians of the Tower, the Yeoman Warders, a body of about 40 men and women chosen from retired warrant and non-commissioned officers of the Army. They wear historic costume, said to date from the time of Henry VII or Edward VI, and are familiarly known as 'Beefeaters', probably derived from the rations once served to them. The Yeoman Warders provide free guided tours in English during the day and participate in the Ceremony of the Keys each evening, a ceremony dating from the 14th century that secures the Tower for the night.

Black ravens have always lived at the Tower and are attended by the Yeoman Warder Ravenmaster, who feeds them fresh meat and other treats. According to legend, the kingdom will fall should the ravens leave the Tower, so their flight wings are clipped. The longest-lived raven, Jim Crow, died aged 44 in 1924.

THE WHITE TOWER

The White Tower **(9)**, begun c. 1078, once dominated the London skyline. It is one of the most important surviving 11th-century buildings in Europe. Standing 90ft high, with walls 15ft thick in places, it was built using London labour to the Norman specifications of Gundulf, Bishop of Rochester. Caen limestone was imported from France and Kentish ragstone came up river by barge. Originally it incorporated parts of the Roman city wall in its defences (the ruined Wardrobe Tower outside the entrance was built on a Roman bastion). It received its name after Henry III limewashed the façade in 1240. The leaden onion tops to the turrets were added by Henry VIII in the 1530s. Of the four turrets, the round one was once an observatory. The windows were enlarged in the 17th–18th centuries.

The White Tower, a superb example of Norman architecture, with the water entrance known as Traitors' Gate below it.

The tower was a military storehouse from the 14th century and since the reign of Henry VIII a showcase for armour and weapons. Today it is home to important items from the collections of the **Royal Armouries**, the national museum of arms and armour. The roofs of the upper floors were created during the reign of Henry VII and are constructed from massive load-bearing beams—some of the largest single timbers ever used in wooden roof construction in England.

Entry is via a wooden staircase on the south façade (probably how the Tower was originally entered, the idea being that if under attack, the staircase could easily be destroyed and the stone keep secured).

Entrance floor: On show is Henry VIII's skirted field armour (including horse armour) in silvered steel (1515). The engraved Tudor rose and Spanish pomegranate motifs, with the initials H and K, celebrate his union with Katherine of Aragon, whom he married here at the Tower. Also here is the tournament armour that Henry wore as an older and bulkier king in 1540. Both suits were probably made at Henry's Greenwich workshop.

The exquisitely tooled and gilded armour of Charles I is probably of Netherlandish origin, made c. 1612 for his older brother Henry, Prince of Wales, the promising heir to the throne who died aged 18. The Japanese Samurai armour (1610) was a diplomatic gift to James I.

The 'Line of Kings' is an exhibition of life-size models of carved and painted horses together with surviving sculpted heads and hands of England's monarchs, some by Grinling Gibbons. The exhibition was conceived by Charles II at the Restoration and this is a partial re-creation of the original 17th-century display.

First floor: The **Norman chamber** has one of the earliest fireplaces in the country and early indoor lavatories built into the thickness of the walls. This room would originally have been open to the rafters but an additional floor was added in the 15th century.

St John's Chapel is one of the most beautiful and complete examples of Anglo-Norman church architecture in England. Henry VI lay in state here in 1471 as did Elizabeth of York, mother of Henry VIII, in 1503.

The **Great Hall** next door would

have been used for ceremonies and receptions. It exhibits further treasures from the Royal Armouries. Tiny armour, once believed to have been made for Queen Henrietta Maria's dwarf, stands next to a giant steel suit made for a man of 6'8", thought to be from Brunswick.

Second floor: The interactive exhibition 'Power House' tells the history of the White Tower's institutions, including the Ordnance Office, Ordnance Survey, the Royal Mint, Record Office, the Jewel House, Menagerie and Royal Observatory. Don't miss the executioner's block, complete with axe.

Basement: The spiral staircase in the round tower takes you down to the basement, where there is a collection of 17th–18th-century weaponry.

THE CROWN JEWELS

The Crown Jewels are housed in the **Waterloo Barracks (10)**, a building conceived by the Duke of Wellington around the time of the Chartist riots in 1848. There is nothing understated about this priceless collection of diamonds, historic gems and plate; the quantity and sheer size of the gemstones are astonishing. Unlike most other European crown jewels (notably the fabled French and Russian treasures, which were broken up and sold off following the revolutions of the 19th and 20th centuries), the British gems are still in use as important elements of an ancient Christian ceremony that can be traced back to the crowning of King Edgar at Bath in 973. The tradition of being crowned at Westminster Abbey was begun by William the Conqueror in 1066.

The exhibition, refreshed since the death of HM Queen Elizabeth II in 2022 and the coronation of King Charles III and Queen Camilla in 2023, is designed to evoke the pageantry of the Coronation procession and explain the uses of the regalia during the ceremony.

The royal regalia: Only four pieces of pre-Civil War regalia survive: the **three swords** (of Temporal Justice, Spiritual Justice and Mercy) made for Charles I's coronation in 1626 and the 12th-century silver gilt **Coronation Spoon**, used to

anoint the Sovereign with holy oil from the **Golden Ampulla**. Oliver Cromwell melted down and sold the rest during his calculated disposal of the late king's goods. The Coronation Spoon was bought in 1649 by a Royalist sympathiser and returned after the Restoration. The rest of the collection—the orb, sceptres, crown, spurs and armills—dates from the reign of Charles II and was later supplemented with the spoils of Empire.

The Crown Jewels: The jewels are viewed from slow-moving travelators which pass along the glass cases. It is worth taking several turns in order to absorb the magnificence.

The great diamond, Cullinan I, the First Star of Africa, was set in the **Sovereign's Sceptre with Cross** in 1911. At 530 carats, it is the largest top-quality white diamond in the world. It was one of several large diamonds cut by the Asscher Diamond Company from the Cullinan crystal, which weighed a colossal 3106 carats. Cullinan II (317.40 carats) is in the Imperial State Crown (*see below*).

Cullinans III and IV (weighing a total of 158 carats; inherited by Elizabeth II after the death of her grandmother Queen Mary and often worn as a brooch affectionately referred to as 'Granny's Chips') and Cullinan V (18.80 carats; also owned and worn by Elizabeth II) are now in the **Crown of Queen Mary** (the consort crown made in 1911; altered and worn by Queen Camilla in 2023).

The **Imperial State Crown of India**, made in 1911 for George V's coronation as Emperor of India, has over 6,000 gems and has only been worn once. The **Crown of Queen Elizabeth, the Queen Mother** is set with the luminous Koh-i-Noor ('Mountain of Light') diamond, a historic 15th-century Mughal gem said

to have been owned by Emperor Shah Jahan in the 17th century. The Mughals deliberately left the diamond in as natural a state as possible so as to retain its magical-religious properties. However, after it was presented to Queen Victoria, it was re-cut (in 1852) according to 19th-century European ideals and lost over 40 percent of its weight. A replica of how the diamond looked before re-cutting is set in an Indian armlet. In the same case is the miniature diamond crown that Queen Victoria wore as a grieving widow.

The **Imperial State Crown** stands alone at the end of the exhibition. Made for George VI's coronation in 1937, it incorporates gems of thrilling provenance: St Edward's Sapphire, in the centre of the Maltese Cross, was removed from a ring found in Edward the Confessor's tomb in Westminster Abbey; the large uncut spinel, known as the Black Prince's Ruby, was given to the Black Prince by Pedro the Cruel in 1367 and was worn by Henry V in his helmet at the Battle of Agincourt; some of the natural pearls are believed to have belonged to Mary, Queen of Scots, Catherine de Medici and Elizabeth I. The massive 317-carat Cullinan II or Second Star of Africa is at the front of the crown. The Stuart Sapphire is at the back.

Also on display is the gold Modernist **crown used for the investiture of the Prince of Wales** in 1969 (designed in 1914–16 by Louis Osman). The perfect orb is in fact a gold-plated ping pong ball engraved with the constellation of Scorpio (King Charles's star sign).

The **Fusilier Museum (11)**, in the headquarters of the Royal Regiment of Fusiliers, has uniforms, medals, equipment and relics relating to the history of the regiment from 1685 to the present.

EAST WALL WALK

Salt Tower (12) contains interesting prisoner graffiti, including Hew Draper's astrological sphere of 1561 (Draper had been imprisoned for sorcery). **Broad Arrow Tower (13)** is where Sir Everard Digby, one of the conspirators in the Gunpowder Plot, was held. **Constable Tower (14)**, rebuilt in the 19th century on the site of one of Henry III's mural towers, has a display relating to the Peasants' Revolt of 1381. **Martin Tower (15)** was the scene of Colonel Blood's bold and nearly successful attempt to carry off the State Crown in 1671. In the 19th century the Crown Jewels were displayed here in a cage and the public were allowed to reach through the grille to touch them. Security was heightened in 1815 after the arches of the State Crown were crushed by overzealous fondling.

ROYAL BEASTS EXHIBITION AND BOWYER TOWER

The Beasts Exhibition is housed in **Brick Tower (16)**. The Tower Menagerie originated during the reign of Henry III, when he received diplomatic gifts of exotic animals, including leopards, a lion, an elephant and, in 1252, a polar bear from Haakon IV of Norway. The bear was tethered to a long rope and allowed to swim and fish in the Thames. By the early 19th century, the menagerie of over 60 species had outgrown the Tower and in 1830 was given to the Zoological Society, who used it to form London Zoo.

Bowyer Tower (17), with a medieval vaulted ceiling, is where George, Duke of Clarence drowned in a butt of Malmsey wine in 1478. A plasma video screen fitted into the top of a large wooden keg ghoulishly reconstructs his misadventure.

TOWER GREEN, BEAUCHAMP TOWER AND THE QUEEN'S HOUSE

Seven executions took place on **Tower Green**: those of William Hastings, 1st Baron Hastings (1483); Queen Anne Boleyn (1536); Margaret Pole, Countess of Salisbury (1541); Queen Catherine Howard (1542); Jane Boleyn, Viscountess Rochford (1542); Lady Jane Grey (1554) and Robert Devereux, Earl of Essex (1601). A modern memorial marks the site of the scaffold. To the north is the Chapel Royal of **St Peter ad Vincula (18)**, rebuilt in 1307 and again by Henry VIII in 1520. Within are buried Anne Boleyn, Catherine Howard, Lady Jane Grey, Essex, Monmouth and other illustrious victims. The chapel holds services for the Tower's resident community and may be visited outside these times as part of a Yeoman Warder tour.

Across Tower Green is **Beauchamp Tower (19)**, notable for its 13th-century brick interior. The walls are covered with the inscriptions and carvings of former prisoners. Guildford Dudley, husband of Lady Jane Grey, was imprisoned here by Mary I and is believed to be the author of the engraving 'JANE'. Philip Howard, Earl of Arundel, was incarcerated here for ten years under Elizabeth I.

In the southwest corner of the Green is the **Queen's House (20)** (*no admission*), built in 1530 and one of the few houses to have survived the Fire of London. Reputed to be the most haunted of the Tower's buildings, it is the residence of the Resident Governor and incorporates the Bell Tower. The Tower's last state prisoner, Rudolf Hess, Deputy Führer, was held here in May 1941.

THE BLOODY TOWER

The Bloody Tower **(21)**, begun by Henry III as a water-gate and completed by Edward I, was the prison of Cranmer, Raleigh, Laud and Judge Jeffreys. Sir Walter Raleigh's room has been reconstructed. During his internment, he wrote his *History of the World* (Vol. I of the 1614 edition is on display). Up a short but steep spiral staircase, the 'Princes in the Tower' exhibition is designed as a medieval whodunnit.

TOWER BRIDGE

Map p. 639, F4. Underground: Tower Hill; DLR: Tower Gateway.

The area of the Thames known as the Upper Pool stretches from London Bridge to just below Tower Bridge on both sides of the bank. Once an area of working docks, there is now a riverside walk and new buildings rub shoulders with old warehouses and wharves now converted into living units, offices, shops and restaurants.

Tower Bridge is one of the most famous bridges in the world and an ingenious feat of late Victorian engineering. Completed in 1894, it fulfilled the urgent contemporary need for a Thames crossing east of London Bridge in order to counter heavy traffic and congestion. It was decided that its appearance should be in keeping with its neighbour, the Tower of London, and although not without its critics, this fanciful neo-Gothic

Tower Bridge, with a Thames Sailing Barge passing beneath it. The last such barge was commissioned in 1938 and 30 remain on the water today.

design (by architect Horace Jones and civil engineer John Wolfe Barry) was chosen. The resulting combined suspension and bascule bridge took eight years to build and its 11,000-ton steel core is clad in Cornish granite and Portland stone. The carriageway between the towers is composed of two bascules (or drawbridges), which are raised to allow tall ships to pass through. The original steam pumping engines used to provide hydraulic power to raise the bascules were replaced in 1976 by electric motors. The two high walkways between the towers were constructed to allow pedestrians to cross uninterrupted when the bascules were in operation. However, pedestrians preferred to cross at road level and the walkways became the haunt of unsavoury characters, leading to their closure in 1910. Although river traffic in this part of the Thames has diminished since its 19th-century heyday, the raising of the bascules is still an impressive sight (*a timetable of bridge lifts may be found on towerbridge.org.uk*).

VISITING TOWER BRIDGE

Entry to the Tower Bridge Exhibition is via the North Tower (*for times, and details of special tours, see towerbridge.org.uk*). The two walkways (now covered, and which also serve as exhibition space) afford impressive panoramic views of London; worth the entry fee alone. The glass floor has become famous. You descend to road level via the South Tower and then follow the blue line on the pavement to the final part of the tour, the Victorian Engine Rooms, which are situated on the south side of the river (Shad Thames). Here one can see the enormous pumping engines, accumulators and boilers that were originally used to raise the bascules. An interactive model of the bridge allows you to raise the bascules via both steam and modern hydraulic methods. Exit via the gift shop. You can either explore the south side of the river from here (*see p. 457*) or return across the bridge to St Katharine Docks.

ST KATHARINE DOCKS

Map p. 637, E3. Underground: Tower Hill; DLR: Tower Gateway.

St Katharine Docks were the first to be regenerated into commercial and leisure space after the demise of London's shipping industry. Today, instead of being filled with hubbub and hurly burly, the waterside expanse is leisurely and there is even an exclusive marina. This is a good place to come for a drink or a bite to eat after visiting the Tower. On the waterfront by the boat pier is a monumental sculpture, ***Girl with a Dolphin*** (David Wynne, 1973). The model for the girl was the tennis champion Virginia Wade, who went on to win the Wimbledon women's singles title in 1977. Another dolphin sculpture by Wynne can be seen in Chelsea (*p. 355*).

VISITING ST KATHARINE DOCKS

The only surviving original warehouse is **Ivory House**, occupying the centre of the docks, surmounted by a squat clock-tower. Built in 1852, it used to be the warehouse through which not only ivory but all manner of other luxury commodities passed. It has now been converted into apartments, boutiques and eateries. The Dockmaster's House by Philip Hardwick was demolished to make way for Devon House, an office building with views over the Thames. The **gates towards East Smithfield**, adorned with two elephants raising their trunks, remain, while Hardwick's other warehouses were destroyed during the War and subsequent redevelopment. The Dickens Inn, another former warehouse, was moved here from its original site further west.

The luxury Tower Hotel, on St Katharine's Way, was built during the first phase of the docks' restoration. This 1970s' concrete bastion, probably once considered a perfect foil for the Tower, has in its time been voted one of the ugliest buildings in Britain. However, the interior affords excellent river panoramas and the view of Tower Bridge when illuminated at night is especially good seen from the Xi Bar's picture windows.

HISTORY OF ST KATHARINE DOCKS

A dock has existed here since 1125. In 1147–8, a hospital and priory were founded on the land under the patronage of Queen Matilda, wife of King Stephen, who referred to it as 'my hospital by the Tower'. The priory escaped dissolution thanks to Katherine of Aragon, by then its patron. She remained in the role, even after her divorce from Henry VIII, until her death. By the end of the 18th century some 3,000 people lived and worked in the precincts of the ancient hospital and church and thousands more continued to settle here, turning the area into a densely-built slum. In 1825 the area was taken over for development as a dock and the inhabitants were unceremoniously evicted.

St Katharine Docks as they exist today opened in 1828. They were built by Telford as two connected basins accessed via a lock at the entrance to the Thames. A range of warehouses by Philip Hardwick lined the quays so goods could be unloaded straight into them; the docks specialised in wine, brandy, tea, rubber, marble, ivory, sugar and other valuable commodities. After fire damage in the Second World War, and also because modern steam and container ships were unable to enter the docks, they finally closed as a commercial enterprise in 1968. Their redevelopment has been cited as a model for urban regeneration.

On East Smithfield is the **Royal Pharmaceutical Society** (*entrance on John Fisher St.; map p. 637, E2*). It has a small museum on the history of British pharmacy (*rpharms.com/ about-us/museum*) which includes examples of 'Lambeth Delftware' apothecary jars. On Dock Street is the **former church of St Paul**, a 'church for seamen', built in an age when London's communities felt that they had too few churches rather than too many. The foundation stone was laid by Prince Albert in 1846. At the time of writing it was in use as a nursery school. Next door is the charming old Rectory, by the engineer William Cubitt.

THE EAST END & DOCKLANDS

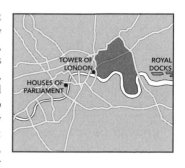

The City of London merges almost imperceptibly with the area traditionally known as the East End: Whitechapel, Spitalfields, Shoreditch and Bethnal Green. This is traditionally the heartland of London's Cockneys, born within earshot of Bow Bells, the 'great bell of Bow', which in the nursery rhyme can give no assurance that riches will ever materialise. Few Cockneys live in the East End today, however: most of the old families have moved further out, to Essex, and their place has been filled by newer arrivals. The East End has long played host to immigrant groups, bringing with them specific skills, and other Londoners now choose to live here over areas further west, where rents have climbed too high. Lining the waterfront are the famous Docklands, once receivers of tangible cargoes and now home to trading of a more electronic kind.

Some highlights of the area

✦ The atmospheric **Dennis Severs' House**, imaginative recreation of a Huguenot family's residence in historic **Spitalfields**, close to Hawksmoor's architecturally important **Christ Church**;

✦ **Brick Lane**, perhaps the best known street in the East End, a street which has inspired a novel and a monograph;

✦ Busy **Canary Wharf**, one of the first parts of the old docks to be redeveloped, home to the **Museum of London Docklands**.

EAST OF ALDGATE

Map p. 639, F3–F1. Underground: Aldgate.

'Always carry a firearm east of Aldgate, Watson.' Thus Sherlock Holmes admonishes his friend and partner in the 1991 television adaptation of the famous Conan Doyle stories. London's East End is a concept as much as a geographical location: the cliché view of it is as a place that is tough, poor, densely populated and vividly alive. This has certainly been true in the past. Spitalfields and Whitechapel were long centres of the rag trade. Huguenots came here in the 17th century, escaping persecution in France, and set up

Petticoat Lane Market (Wentworth Street), with a view of the 'Can of Ham' backed by 22 Bishopsgate and other City towers.

looms in their attics. Then came Jewish tailors (in 1897 the social researcher Charles Booth noted the presence of Welsh cowmen who supplied them with kosher milk). In the 19th century, thousands of Polish Jews fleeing Russian oppression settled here. Most of the descendants of those families have now dispersed to other parts of London and beyond and in the later 20th century the Jewish tailors' businesses were supplanted by Bangladeshi sweatshops: while at the end of the 19th century there were 80 synagogues here, now the East London Mosque lifts its minaret over Whitechapel Road.

Political refugees have found sanctuary in the East End too. Whitechapel prides itself on being the place where Lenin first met Trotsky. The 5th Congress of the Russian Social Democratic Labour Party was held here in 1907.

The East End is often regarded through rose-coloured glasses, as an example of triumphant multiculturalism. There are tensions, though. Somewhere in a refuse-blown street on the borderlands of Spitalfields, Shoreditch and Bethnal Green, a spraypaint sloganist has called for 'Death to hipsters!' Jack the Ripper may no longer stalk the streets and the Kray Twins are no longer at large; but at times a kind of latent turbulence is still to be felt here.

AROUND ALDGATE SQUARE

Busy Houndsditch (*map p. 639, F2*), dominated by the catenary curve of the '**Can of Ham' Tower** (Foggo Associates, 2019), follows the course of the old moat outside London's city wall. At Houndsditch's southern end is the bright blue **St Botolph Building** (Grimshaw Architects, 2011), in whose glossy panels is reflected the now diminished-in-stature spire of the church of St Botolph-without-Aldgate, which stands on **Aldgate Square**. The square marks the site of the Aldgate, or 'old gate', which guarded the road out of London to the east. Geoffrey Chaucer leased the house above the Aldgate from the City of London in 1374. A 'draught on Aldgate Pump' (which still stands on a peninsula of pavement at the junction of Fenchurch St and Leadenhall St) was once a cant expression for a worthless bill. Overlooking Aldgate Square to the west is the **Aldgate School**, in a handsome building of 1908 by A.W. Cooksey. Formerly Sir John Cass's Foundation Primary School, it was established in 1710 by John Cass, alderman and sheriff (the two figures of a charity boy and girl (1710–11) are from the original building). Cass died in 1718 (memorial in St Botolph's church opposite). On the annual Founder's Day (20th Feb), children and guests would wear a red feather in honour of Cass, who suffered a fatal haemorrhage whilst writing the will by which he funded the school, staining his white goose quill red with blood. In 2020 the school dropped his name because of concerns over links with the slave trade.

At the main entrance to St Botolph's churchyard, built into the perimeter wall, is an old **Metropolitan Drinking Fountain** of 1906, still with its iron cup on a chain.

ST-BOTOLPH-WITHOUT-ALDGATE

The current building is by George Dance the Elder (1744) but a church was first built here over 1,000 years ago, outside the old City gate so that travellers could pray on arrival and departure. Botolph is the patron saint of wayfarers; relics of his were kept at churches dedicated to him at Aldersgate, Aldgate, Bishopsgate and Billingsgate (the last of those four churches is no longer extant, having perished in the Great Fire).

In the **octagonal vestibule** is a handsome font and cover. There are memorials to Robert Dow (d. 1612), a benefactor, with an anxious-looking portrait bust, his hands clamped upon a complacently grinning skull, as well as to Sir John Cass (d. 1718), the founder of the Aldgate School (*see above*), and to Thomas Darcy and Sir Nicholas Carew, both beheaded on Tower Hill in 1538. Carew was executed for alleged complicity in the Exeter plot to depose Henry VIII, while Darcy's sentence was for taking part in the Pilgrimage of Grace against the same king's dissolution of the monasteries. Both men are buried in the churchyard.

The church interior is by J.F. Bentley (1888–95), with a broad upper gallery and a ceiling decorated with fine stucco angels. The **organ**, one of the oldest in the country, was a gift from Thomas Whiting in 1676 and is attributed to

Robert Dow, Merchant Taylor, apparently not sanguine about what the afterlife will bring. Memorial in St Botolph-without-Aldgate.

Renatus Harris (*see p. 218*). William Symington, pioneer of steam navigation who built the *Charlotte Dundas*, the world's first properly successful steamboat, died here 'in want' in 1831 and is buried in the church (tablet on the west wall). Thomas Bray, founder of the Christian publishers SPCK and SPG, was vicar here from 1708–22. There is a tablet to him in the glassed-in end of the left aisle, where a window commemorates Sir James Shaw, Lord Mayor in 1805–6, with his amusing motto, 'I mean well'. In the south aisle is a finely-carved panel of David playing the harp which, together with the lectern, dates from the early 18th century. Jeremy Bentham, the founder of Utilitarianism, was christened here in 1747 (*for the fate of his body after death, see p. 374*).

The fine peal of eight bells was cast in the 18th century at Whitechapel Bell Foundry (*see p. 115*). Daniel Defoe was married here in 1683: he mentions Aldagte and its church frequently in his *Journal of the Plague Year*, noting that a plague pit was dug in the churchyard. 'A terrible pit it was…The mark of it was many years to be seen in the churchyard on the surface, lying in length parallel with the passage which goes by the west wall of the churchyard out of Houndsditch, and turns east again into Whitechappel, coming out near the Three Nuns Inn.' The Three Nuns, at 10–12 Aldgate High Street, was demolished in the 1960s.

Daniel Defoe on asymptomatic transmission in St Botolph's

When people began to be convinced that the infection was received in this surprising manner from persons apparently well, they began to be exceeding shy and jealous of every one that came near them. Once, on a public day, whether a Sabbath-day or not I do not remember, in Aldgate Church, in a pew full of people, on a sudden one fancied she smelt an ill smell. Immediately she fancies the plague was in the pew, whispers her notion or suspicion to the next, then rises and goes out of the pew. It immediately took with the next, and so to them all; and every one of them, and of the two or three adjoining pews, got up and went out of the church, nobody knowing what it was offended them, or from whom...I observed that after people were possessed with the belief, or rather assurance, of the infection being thus carried on by persons apparently in health, the churches and meeting-houses were much thinner of people than at other times before that they used to be.

A Journal of the Plague Year, 1722

Beyond Aldgate Square, among massive new office blocks and thundering traffic, the street name **Minories** recalls a pre-Reformation London: it is named after the Minoresses, nuns of the Franciscan order of the Poor Clares. St Clare Street is another reminder of the sisters' presence here, until their nunnery was dissolved under Henry VIII. The coffin of Anne de Mowbray, which once lay in the church crypt, was found during construction work in the 1960s. Anne, who died at the age of eight, was the child bride of one of the Princes in the Tower. The **Hoop and Grapes pub** on the corner of Mansell Street is one tiny reminder of the former scale of the buildings that once stood here. The pub has foundations going back to the 13th century and the building itself is probably of the late 17th century.

WHITECHAPEL HIGH STREET

The jumble of signs and advertisements on **no. 88 Whitechapel High Street** contains a certain amount of history. Above the doorway, note the metal relief with the Star of David and twin Lions of Judah. In 1934–5 the *Jewish Daily Post* had its editorial offices here. Albert's menswear has been in operation since the early 1940s. This is also one of the *loci* of the Jack the Ripper tour, since the narrow **Gunthorpe Street**, between no. 88 and the White Hart pub, was the scene of one of his murders.

The **Whitechapel Art Gallery** (77–82 *Whitechapel High St; map p. 637, E2; whitechapelgallery.org*), founded in 1901, hosts exhibitions of work by both established and aspiring artists. It is proud of its pioneering spirit: Picasso's *Guernica* has travelled to the UK only once, in 1939, and was shown here. The striking main building, with its Arts and Crafts façade of falling golden foliage, is by Charles Harrison Townsend. The adjacent wing, with its decorative frieze of rams' heads and putti, is the former Whitechapel Library, founded by the philanthropist John Passmore Edwards. The

The former offices of the *Jewish Daily Post* on Whitechapel High Street.
The next-door alleyway was the scene of one of Jack the Ripper's murders in 1888.

library closed in 2005. A blue plaque commemorates the poet Isaac Rosenberg, who came to study at the library and wrote 'A Ballad of Whitechapel':

The traffic rolled,
A gliding chaos populous of din,
A steaming wail at doom the Lord had scrawled
For perilous loads of sin.

And my soul thought:
'What fearful land have my steps wandered to?
God's love is everywhere, but here is naught
Save love His anger slew.'

The weather vane (Rodney Graham, 2009) is a self-portrait of the artist as Erasmus, seated backwards on a horse reading Erasmus' encomium to Sir Thomas More, *In Praise of Folly.*

Diagonally opposite the gallery, on the corner of Whitechurch Lane, is the site of St Mary's church, the eponymous 'White Chapel', which was destroyed in the Blitz. The churchyard is now the **Altab Ali Park**, commemorating a young Bangladeshi textile worker who was fatally stabbed by three teenage boys in a racially-motivated assault in 1978.

Whitechapel High Street now becomes Whitechapel Road (*see p. 115*), leading east towards Stepney Green.

BRICK LANE

The area north of Whitechapel High Street used to be known as Banglatown in honour of its Bangladeshi community. Brick Lane (*map p. 637, E1*), the street whose name became the title of a famous novel by the Dhaka-born writer Monica Ali, is the main artery of that district. Street signs were proudly put up in English and Bengali and Brick Lane itself became famous for its curry restaurants. Today all that is changing. The Bengali presence is more muted than it was, and though the street signs are still there, some of them are badly rusted. Many of the restaurants are still in business but they cater to an increasingly passing trade. Brick Lane has long been a place of change. A vestige of Cockney times can be descried where Osborne Street ends and Brick Lane begins: Ye Frying Pan tavern thrusts its crumbling brick crest into the sky—but the premises today house the Shaad Grill. In the 19th century and for the first part of the 20th, the businesses here would largely have been Jewish: the name CH N. KATZ, in black paint over the door of a former twine merchant at no. 92, is a lone reminder. Yet the fame of Brick Lane has helped to safeguard its physical integrity: it resembles, more closely than most other London streets, a traditional old-fashioned high street, with small individual shopfronts. There are no chain stores.

At no. 59, on the corner of Fournier Street, is the London **Jamme Masjid**, the congregational mosque, with a tall, cylindrical steel minaret. The building dates from 1743, when it was built as a church by the Huguenots, who adorned it with its sundial reminding passers-by of mortality: '*Umbra sumus*; We are but a shadow'. Methodists took over the building in early 19th century; then, in 1898, it was converted for use as a synagogue. Since 1976 it has been a mosque.

19 Princelet Street, once a Huguenot house, later a synagogue, is now a charity and educational resource centre dealing with themes of minority culture and belonging. It boasts the first museum of immigration and diversity in Europe (*visits by appointment; 19princeletstreet.org.uk*).

The **Vintage Market** at no. 85 attracts many visitors from around the world. Straddling the road beyond Hanbury Street is the former **Truman Brewery**. Beneath Brick Lane is an artesian-fed well, a good source of water, and a brewery was established here in the 17th century. Beer was still brewed here up until 1989. The site has now been redeveloped as offices, workshops, cafés and nightclubs. Some occupy the plane-shaded courtyard on one side of the street.

On Sundays Brick Lane comes alive with its famous **street market**. It developed during the 18th century, with farmers selling livestock and produce outside the City boundary. However, the main impetus came from the Jewish population, who were permitted to trade on Sundays. Stalls offer a mix of fruit and vegetables, clothes, household goods, books, bric-à-brac and antiques (be aware: provenance uncertain). The **Backyard Market** for arts and crafts operates at weekends.

SPITALFIELDS

The name Spitalfields (*map p. 639, F1–F2*) comes from the priory of St Mary Spital, founded in 1197, and where the 'Spital Sermon' (now delivered at St Lawrence Jewry; *see p. 50*) was first preached. The area was once occupied by silk-weavers, largely descended from Huguenot (French Protestant) refugees who arrived after the Edict of Nantes, which had given them rights and protection, was revoked in 1685. Further north is Bethnal Green, once home to closely built streets of weavers' cottages, commemorated in the park now known as Weavers Fields.

PETTICOAT LANE

The association of the East End with cloth and clothing began in the 16th century, when traders moved here from London Bridge. A map of 1603 refers to 'Petticoat Lane', named thus because of its clothes stalls. The official name of the road is Middlesex Street (*map p. 639, F2*) and it is still lined with textile emporia. The surviving **Petticoat Lane Market** operates in the side streets to the east of it, notably in Bell Lane and Wentworth Street. Vans arrive in the morning to unload their merchandise: mainly clothing, but other items as well (*Sun 9–2; limited market Mon–Fri*). **Tenter Ground** (*map p. 639, F2*) takes its name from the frames on which weavers stretched their cloth (hence the phrase 'on tenterhooks'). The **Sandys Row Synagogue** (at no. 4a; *sandysrowsynagogue.org*), between the narrow, restaurant-filled Artillery Passage and Artillery Lane, was the first—and is now the last—fully-functioning Ashkenazi shul in London's East End.

Middlesex Street once offered lodging to the West African prince Ukawsaw Gronniosaw, who was captured and sold into slavery and afterwards made his way to Britain, where he married and struggled to make ends meet as a free citizen. Here he describes his arrival in London and his first meeting with his future bride:

Prince Ukawsaw Gronniosaw on Petticoat Lane

Mr Whitefield receiv'd me very friendly, was heartily glad to see me, and directed me to a proper place to board and lodge in Petticoat Lane, till he could think of some way to settle me in, and paid for my lodging, and all my expenses. The morning after I came to my new lodging, as I was at breakfast with the gentlewoman of the house, I heard the noise of some looms over our heads: I enquir'd what it was; she told me a person was weaving silk. I express'd a great desire to see it, and ask'd if I might. She told me she would go up with me; she was sure I should be very welcome. She was as good as her word, and as soon as we enter'd the room, the person that was weaving look'd about, and smiled upon us, and I loved her from that moment. She ask'd me many questions, and I in turn talk'd a great deal to her. I found she was a member of Mr Allen's Meeting, and I begun to entertain a good opinion of her, though I was almost afraid to indulge this inclination, lest she should prove like all the rest I had met with at Portsmouth etc. and which had almost given me a dislike to all white women. But after a short acquaintance I had the happiness to find she was very different, and quite sincere, and I was not without hope that she entertain'd some esteem for me...

Narrative, 1772

On Old Castle Street, **Calcutta House** is an old East India tea warehouse, now housing London Metropolitan University.

CHRIST CHURCH

When Christopher Wren surveyed Brick Lane in the 17th century, he found it 'unpassable for coach, adjoining to dirty lands of mean habitations, and far from any church.' That circumstance has now been altered: at the corner of Fournier and Commercial streets is Hawksmoor's masterpiece: Christ Church, Spitalfields (*map p. 639, F2; spitalfields.church*). It triumphantly and gloriously closes the vista down Brushfield Street, a truly spectacular sight, although the spiritual need that Christopher Wren perceived has waned and today it is more regularly used for events hire than for worship. The massive portico with its paired Tuscan columns takes the form of a vast Serlian window giving onto an eccentric, sandwich-board tower surmounted by

CHRIST CHURCH, SPITALFIELDS

a tapering spire. In the entrance vestibule are tablets commemorating ten evangelisers of the Jews, originally in the Episcopal Jews' Chapel in Bethnal Green but moved here in 1897. The 1720 interior features a flat coffered ceiling with stucco decoration, all painted bright white. The chancel screen is formed of four columns supporting an architrave surmounted by a Coade Stone Lion and Unicorn. On either side of the altar are funerary monuments by Thomas Dunn (right) and John Flaxman (left), both signed. The church is also home to a historic organ, made by Richard Bridge in 1735. It was restored in 2015 and frequent recitals are held.

On **Fournier Street** there are some fine surviving Georgian buildings, with tall windows and handsome doorways.

THE HUGUENOT CONTRIBUTION

Throughout the 16th and 17th centuries, large numbers of French Calvinist refugees found a safe haven in England. Many came to escape the French Wars of Religion and the 1572 Massacre of St Bartholomew, and numbers peaked sharply following the 1685 revocation of the Edict of Nantes, which removed Protestant freedom of worship. Huguenot communities were established in East Anglia, Kent and along the south coast, as well as in London. By 1700 Spitalfields, Leicester Fields and Soho had become distinct Huguenot areas. Spitalfields, being beyond the jurisdiction of the Weavers' Company in the City, became increasingly identified with the silk industry.

Many Huguenots were prosperous merchants who were able to escape with their goods intact. Their investments in London banking and insurance houses (several Huguenots were foundation subscribers to the Bank of England) contributed substantially to the capital's wealth, whilst marriage alliances created powerful trading and financial dynasties. A great many more Huguenots were skilled craftsmen, whose expertise and innovatory techniques had a profound impact on London's luxury trades. One such figure was Daniel Marot, a pupil of Louis XIV's *maître ornemaniste*, who worked at Hampton Court in the 1690s. Important carvers and gilders included the Pelletier family, who made furniture for Kensington Palace and Hampton Court, and a leading upholsterer was Francis Lapiere, based in Pall Mall. Many of London's finest 18th-century goldsmiths, such as Paul Crespin, Paul de Lamerie and the Rococo master Nicolas Sprimont, were second-generation Huguenots, while native masters such as George Wickes and Thomas Heming were Huguenot-trained. Today there is a registered charity, Huguenots of Spitalfields, which organises walking tours of the district and other events (*huguenotsofspitalfields.org*).

OLD SPITALFIELDS MARKET

A fruit and vegetable market on this site was first established under Charles II in 1682. The present covered market building (*map p. 639, F1*) dates from 1928. It closed as a wholesale market in 1992 and has found a new role as an arts, crafts, fashion and food market (*oldspitalfieldsmarket.com*).

DENNIS SEVERS' HOUSE

The extraordinary experience offered by this 1724 Georgian terrace house (*18 Folgate St; map p. 639, F1; booking essential, dennissevershouse.co.uk.*) is, in the words of its creator, Dennis Severs (d. 1999), 'a collection of atmospheres, moods that harbour the light and the spirit of various ages.' Unenamoured of the 20th-century world in

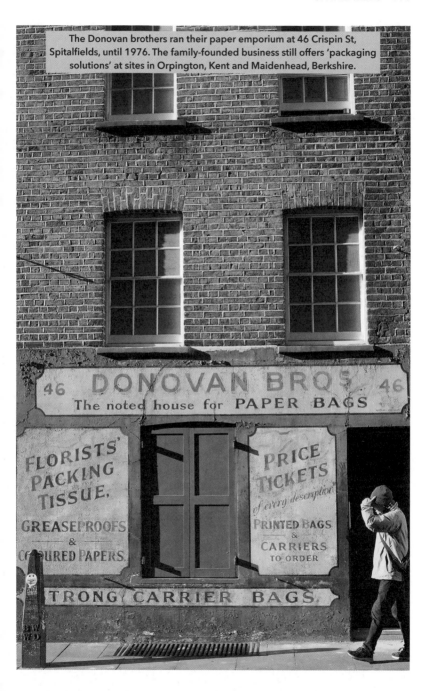

The Donovan brothers ran their paper emporium at 46 Crispin St, Spitalfields, until 1976. The family-founded business still offers 'packaging solutions' at sites in Orpington, Kent and Maidenhead, Berkshire.

which he lived, the US-born Severs sought to evoke the past through a collage of the senses and an assortment of locally-sourced objects (the emphasis is on atmosphere rather than precise historical accuracy). In 1979 he bought a dilapidated house on Folgate Street with a wonderful conceit in mind: to transform it into the living home of a fictional family of Huguenot silk weavers, the Jervises, spanning the years from 1724 to 1914. The tour includes ten rooms or 'spells', beginning with the Cellar and ending with the Back Parlour and following the history of Spitalfields from its origins to the Great War, taking in Hogarthian London along the way (The Smoking Room). The night-time candlelit itinerary is a sensory imaginarium, with open fires, chiming clocks, half-eaten plates of food and unfinished glasses of port, the smell of newly-peeled citrus fruit, rumpled and still-warm beds, and even a full chamber pot.

Elder Street (*map p. 639, F1*) leads out of Folgate Street. The house at no. 32 was once the home of the artist Mark Gertler, born in Spitalfields to Polish Jewish parents. He became the protégé of Lady Ottoline Morrell, who introduced him to members of the Bloomsbury group (Virginia Woolf found him a 'forcible young man' and egocentric). He committed suicide in 1939. The coal-hole cover outside the house is decorated with a detail from his famous anti-war painting *Merry-go-Round* (original in Tate Britain).

SHOREDITCH & HOXTON

Shoreditch is an area once famous for its cobblers and furniture makers, a place of wishful thinking, whose bells in the old nursery rhyme promise to pay 'when I grow rich'. Perhaps that is happening—at least if the cafés, galleries, artisans' boutiques and furniture stores on Redchurch Street and Calvert Avenue are anything to go by. **Redchurch Street** (*map p. 637, E1*), leading east from Shoreditch High Street, is a symbol of the accelerated gentrification of this area. It boasts a string of boutiques, including the storefront outlet of the tailor Timothy Everest, whose clients have included David Beckham, Mick Jagger and Tom Cruise. Everest first established his workshop in the historic textile district of Spitalfields.

North of Redchurch Street is the Boundary Estate, whose centrepiece, **Arnold Circus** (*map p. 637, E1*), is surrounded by red-brick mansion houses constructed from 1890 onwards on the site of the notorious Old Nichol slum. Rubble from the slum clearance was used to construct the high mound in the centre of the circus, which now supports a bandstand. Arthur Morrison, in his 1896 novel *A Child of the Jago*, calls the old slum 'the blackest pit in London'.

Opening off Shoreditch High Street in the other direction is **New Inn Yard** (*map p. 637, E1–D1*), which runs west to Curtain Road. This was once an insalubrious area bounded by a sewer and a horsepond, where James Burbage built his octagonal wooden Theatre in 1576. The site lay just outside the City, which had recently banned 'play-acting'. In 1597, after a dispute over the lease, the structure is said to have been pulled down overnight by Cuthbert Burbage, who used the salvaged planks to construct the

Globe Theatre in Southwark. Further south again was another wooden playhouse, the Curtain, also for a time managed by Burbage. In 2012 the foundations of the Curtain were discovered in Hewett Street, east off Curtain Road. It was found to have been a square structure, not circular as had previously been thought. Remains of ceramic money boxes were discovered in later excavations. These would have been used to collect ticket money, then taken to a central office, broken open and the money inside them collected together and counted. The term 'box office' derives from this custom. The multi-purpose high-rise property development named **The Stage** commemorates the old theatre. Excavated remains are preserved and at the time of writing there were plans to create a visitor centre.

One of the oldest monuments is **St Leonard's Church** (*map p. 629, D2; shoreditch. saint.church*) on Shoreditch High Street, which stands above the source of the Walbrook stream (*see p. 43*). The current building, with its plain Tuscan Doric porch, was built c. 1740 by George Dance the Younger. James Burbage and his sons Cuthbert and Richard (the friend of Shakespeare) are buried in the crypt, as is Gabriel Spencer, the actor whom Ben Jonson killed in a duel in Hoxton Fields in 1598.

The lively **Columbia Road Flower Market** (*Sun 8–3; map p. 629, D2; columbiaroad. info*) sells plants, bulbs, seeds, pots and garden tools and is worth a visit just for the atmosphere. There is more available here than horticulture; the street is lined with vintage stores, galleries, cafés and other boutiques. The phenomenon grew out of the huge Columbia Market that was built in 1869 by the philanthropist Baroness Burdett-Coutts to provide a place to buy cheap and nourishing food. It failed and the building was finally pulled down in 1960. As Charles Booth dryly noted, philanthropy and well-meaning alone are not enough: 'a market must grow by natural causes.'

MUSEUM OF THE HOME

Kingsland Road leads north from Shoreditch High Street to the iron railings, tall trees and low-lying buildings of the former Geffrye almshouses (c. 450 yds; no. 136), now housing the Museum of the Home (*map p. 629, D2; museumofthehome.org.uk*). The almshouses were the charitable foundation of Sir Robert Geffrye (1613–1704), a merchant with interests in India and the Far East, a Master of the Ironmongers' Company, a member of the Court of Aldermen, and Lord Mayor of London in 1685. In his will he left a sum of money for the establishment of almshouses. In 1712 a plot of land was purchased in what was then an area of market gardens and plant nurseries, and a simple but dignified building was constructed. Externally, the building is little altered. The statue of Sir Robert Geffrye in the niche above the central door caused controversy when the building reopened after refurbishment, as Geffrye's name has been linked to the slave trade. Calls were made for the statue to be removed. It is a copy after the 1723 original by John van Nost the Elder, which was moved in 1911 when the almshouses themselves moved to Mottingham, Kent, and in 1974 to Hook, Hampshire.

The almshouse pensioners, 43 of them when the building opened, received £6 each per year. Pensioners had one room each, where they would eat, sleep and live, with a fireplace and two windows overlooking the front gardens, with a small closet off it. The museum housed here today is devoted to the domestic space (both the house and the garden). Part of the displays consists of a succession of 'Rooms Through Time', from the 17th-century parlour, with its dark, heavy furniture and pewter plates, to the loft apartment of the late 20th century, with its atelier windows and open-plan design. The 'Gardens Through Time' series is along the same lines. In December the rooms are dressed for 'Winter Past', celebrating Christmas, wassailing, Hannukah, the Winter Solstice. The old Great Room, converted into a chapel in 1716, contains a fine marble monument to Geffrye and his wife, removed from Geffrye's local parish church of St Dionis Backchurch on its demolition in 1881. Geffrye's tomb is in the former Ironmongers' Graveyard in the museum grounds.

BETHNAL GREEN & WHITECHAPEL

Map p. 629, D2–E2 and p. 637. Underground: Bethnal Green, Whitechapel.

Bethnal Green was one of London's most crowded and poorest areas during the 19th century. On Charles Booth's famous Poverty Maps, it features large and black, denoting 'Lowest class: vicious, semi-criminal'. It was once an area of narrow streets of cramped weavers' cottages, each with wide upper-floor windows to let in the maximum amount of light. Its history is a story of the labouring poor, of Victorian social reformers, slum clearers and of optimistic post-war planners.

Very close to Bethnal Green Tube station, at the corner of Cambridge Heath Road and Roman Road, is the Anglo-Catholic **church of St John**, designed by Soane (1826–8), with an eccentric squat tower (*stjohnonbethnalgreen.org*). It contains a series of Stations of the Cross by contemporary artist Chris Gollon (2000). On the opposite side of the Green, a plaque on **no. 3 Paradise Row** commemorates Daniel Mendoza, English heavyweight boxing champion in the late 1790s, who lived here and wrote his *Art of Boxing*. Despite his many wins and his great fame, he died penniless in 1836.

YOUNG V&A

The Young V&A on Cambridge Heath Road, a branch of the V&A in Kensington (*map p. 629, E2; vam.ac.uk/young*), opened in 1872 as the Bethnal Green Museum, satisfying a desire first raised in 1851, in the wake of the Great Exhibition (*p. 329*), to establish a museum in the East End. The framework of the building is in fact a section of the Iron Building erected in 1857 as part of the South Kensington Museum, as the V&A was then known. In 1866 it was partially dismantled and re-erected here, with an outer façade of red brick designed by J.W. Wild. A series of mosaic panels decorates its two long sides, with scenes representing *Agriculture* on one side, and *Art* and *Science* on the other, all to the designs of Frank Moody. They were made by female students of the South Kensington Museum Mosaic Class under the supervision of Minton's. Inside, the museum reveals its delicate iron framework, its spacious central hall overlooked on either side by upper-level balconies. The monochrome mosaic floor was laid by female prisoners. The collection's focus on children dates from the 1920s and the museum now contains the national collection of childhood-related objects, dating from 1600 to the present. The museum is always filled with the sound of excited children's voices; but there is plenty of nostalgia value for adults, who will enjoy being brought face to face once more with the contents of long-forgotten toy chests.

WHITECHAPEL

Whitechapel is an area of narrow old streets intersected by wide arterial highways, shabby and ramshackle, its reputation partly clouded by the famous Jack the Ripper murders, the brutal serial killings of young women, mainly prostitutes, in 1888. The body of the first victim was found just behind Whitechapel Road in Durward Street. The perpetrator was never identified, although in 2023 researchers claimed to have found DNA evidence to link the deaths to a Jewish barber named Aaron Kosminski, who had come to London from Poland. Today there are companies offering Jack the Ripper tours, and at 12 Cable St, further south, you will find the **Jack the Ripper Museum** (*nearest station Shadwell, map p. 637, F2; jacktherippermuseum.com*). Also on Cable Street (*entrance on Graces Alley, off Ensign St*) is **Wilton's Music Hall**, dating from 1859. After it closed as a place of entertainment it became a Methodist meeting hall and then a warehouse. Today, after long years of dereliction, it is once again a theatre (*wiltons.org.uk*).

Another reminder of the area's lawless past is the attractive brick and stucco **Blind Beggar pub**, next to the entrance to the old Watney Mann Brewery (1902) near the corner of Cambridge Heath Road (*map p. 637, F1; 337 Whitechapel Rd; theblindbeggar. com*). The pub's name references the Blind Beggar of folk ballad, a knight blinded in battle in the 13th century and reduced to begging with his dog, at the same time trying to save his daughter from the clutches of unworthy suitors until such time as he providentially manages to find a large dowry for her. A statue of the beggar and his dog, by Dame Elisabeth Frink (1958), stands in the Cranbrook Estate (Skinner, Bailey and Lubetkin, 1964), north of Roman Road. The Blind Beggar pub has several claims to both fame and notoriety: William Booth, founder of the Salvation Army, preached his first sermon outside its doors; the Blind Beggar Gang was a posse of pickpockets who operated in the nearby streets at the turn of the 20th century; Ronnie Kray shot a man in the head with a Mauser here in 1966. Today the pub offers 'Gangster Tours'. The Kray twins and Aaron Kosminski are immortalised in wax at Madame Tussaud's (*p. 307*).

Whitechapel today has cast off its murky reputation and is a busy multicultural area with a large Muslim population. The large, yellow-brick **East London Mosque** (1985) with its slender minaret (*entrance to men's prayer hall from the main façade; women's prayer hall around the corner*) stands next to the London Muslim Centre at no. 46 Whitechapel Road. Close by at no. 34, on the corner of Fieldgate Street, is the site of the **Whitechapel Bell Foundry** (*map p. 637, F2*). Established in 1570, it moved here in 1738, into a former inn building of c. 1670. Bells of all sizes were made here, from tiny hand chimes to great clangers such as the Liberty Bell (1752) and Big Ben (1858). The foundry closed in 2017. At the time of writing, furious attempts were being made to preserve the site and the business and plans for a luxury boutique hotel had been rejected (*for details and updates, see thelondonbellfoundry.co.uk*).

Whitechapel Market occupies the northern side of the street between Vallance Road and Cambridge Heath Road. There are stalls of all kinds, selling dresses and scarves, pots and pans, fresh fish, fruit and vegetables and spices.

Opposite Whitechapel Tube station is the **Royal London Hospital**. When the original building was completed, in 1759, it was almost the only edifice on the street (then a highway along the course of the old Roman road). The case of Joseph Merrick (the Elephant Man) first came to the attention of a young surgeon at this hospital in 1884, when he saw the unfortunate Merrick exhibited at a freak show in a shop on Whitechapel Road (no. 259). Merrick died at the hospital in 1890, at the age of 27.

Off Brady Street is an **Ashkenazi burial ground**, one of two in this area. It is kept locked, though you can see the graves through the gate (*map p. 637, F1; entrance behind the new houses at nos 43–47; to visit, contact Bushey Burial Office, theus.org.uk*). It dates from 1761 and was closed to burials in 1858. Nathan Rothschild (d. 1836), founder of the family bank in London, is buried here.

MILE END & STEPNEY GREEN

Mile End Road (*map p. 629, E2*) is so named because it begins at the end of one mile from the old City Wall. It leads through the area known as Stepney to the south and Globe Town to the north. Just beyond the junction with Cambridge Heath Road, facing the traffic, is a bronze **bust of William Booth**, from whose open-air services in this neighbourhood in 1865 sprang the Salvation Army. A replica of the statue of him at Denmark Hill (*see p. 477*) was added in 1979, a little further along the road, to mark the 150th anniversary of his birth. Between the bust and the statue is the picturesque **Trinity Green**, whose almshouses were established in 1695 for '28 decay'd masters and commanders of ships or ye widows of such', a reminder that the docks are not far away. Look up to see the models of fully-rigged ships on either ends of the gables.

Further along at no. 81 is the **former Wickham's department store**, with its imposing Ionic columns. The department store came into being in 1927, when the Wickham family expanded their booming draper's business. Originally the store was designed to have a continuous street frontage, but plans were thwarted by the tenacity of a jeweller and watchmaker named Spiegelhalter, who had already moved once to make way for the Wickhams and refused to do so again. Undaunted, the department store—which, in its day, aimed to overtake Selfridge's in revenues and renown—built itself around the diminutive premises, shifting its planned central clock-tower a little to the left. Thanks to the success of local petitioning, the façade of the little **Spiegelhalter building** still stands today, comically and pluckily interrupting the storefront's grandiose colonnade.

STEPNEY GREEN

There are three Jewish cemeteries close to Stepney Green tube station. On Alderney Road is an **Ashkenazi burial ground** (*visits as for Brady St; see above*), its earliest gravestone dating from 1697. Prominent rabbis are buried here, including the first Chief Rabbi of England Aaron Hart (d. 1756). There are also two **Sephardic cemeteries** off Mile End Road. Behind Albert Stern House at no. 253 is the old cemetery, the Velho, founded in 1657. The much larger Nuevo Beth Chaim cemetery was established to the east in 1733. It is now within the grounds of Queen Mary, University of London. Some of the remains, including those of the boxer Daniel Mendoza (*see p. 114*), were moved to Brentwood. In both cemeteries the tombstones are laid flat, a symbol of the levelling power of death.

Tombstone in the Ashkenazi burial ground on Alderney Street.

Stepney Green itself, a wide street with some handsome 18th-century houses, leads past playing fields to the small **Stepney City Farm** on the corner of Stepney High Street. The farm, which boasts sheep, goats, rabbits and other animals, many of them rare breeds (for example the Buff Orpington ducks). The farm stands on the site of Worcester House, a moated manor built in 1597, as well as of a later building where the meeting was held which led to the Match Girls' Strike of 1888. A farmers' market is held on Saturdays and there is also a café (*stepneycityfarm.org*).

Opposite the farm is the ragstone and flint church of **St Dunstan and All Saints** (*stdunstanstepney.com*), mostly of the 15th century, though there has been a church on the site for much longer, since the late 10th century. Because of its great antiquity, St Dunstan's is proud to call itself the Mother Church of the East End and, because of its proximity to the London docks, the 'Church of the High Seas'. A sailors' memorial window, by Hugh Easton (1949), is in the north aisle. A Saxon relief of the *Crucifixion* (early 11th century) decorates the chancel. The bells in the tower, made in the nearby Whitechapel foundry (*see p. 115*), are those of the nursery rhyme 'Oranges and Lemons', anxiously wanting to know when the person addressed by the song will be rich enough to repay the five farthings. The doleful answer, 'I do not know', is given by the bell of St Mary-le-Bow in the City. Stepney church owes its large graveyard to extensions carried out at the time of the Great Plague of 1665. In fact, so great was the number of local deaths that it was feared that Stepney would no longer be able to furnish sufficient men for the English fleet. Today the churchyard has been mainly cleared of tombs but of the many laid to rest here were benefactors of Trinity Green almshouses (*see above*) and the 'wonder of the age' Roger Crabb, who had fought for Cromwell during the Civil War but then chose the life of a hermit, subsisting on a diet of 'mallows, docks and grass'. He died in 1680.

WAPPING, SHADWELL & LIMEHOUSE

Map p. 637, F3 and p. 625, A1. Overground: Wapping, Shadwell; DLR: Shadwell, Limehouse.

The London Docklands share geography as well as history with the East End. At one time, these docks were the largest and most impressive in the world, the nucleus of the British Empire, employing thousands in trade and the manufacturing industries.

HISTORY OF THE DOCKS

London's prosperity during the 16th and 17th centuries depended on its growing port, based on quays along the Thames such as Billingsgate and Queenhithe, and some deep-water moorings at the Tower, Wapping and Puddle Dock. Most moorings were in the Pool of London itself, the area of water east of London Bridge, with 'sufferance wharves' on both banks to take the overflow from the legal docks. The first commercial dock was the Great Howland (*see p. 481*). Enclosed docks began to be the norm in the 19th century, when trade—and pilfering—had increased and high-security berths and warehouses became a necessity to prevent ships lying idle in the Thames, waiting to unload and declare their cargoes. The City Corporation, which operated the Pool, resisted the building of docks which instead were developed piecemeal by private companies.

The first to be completed was West India Dock (1802). London Docks at Wapping followed in 1805, then the East India (1806), the Surrey Docks on the south bank (1807), St Katharine in 1828, Royal Victoria (1855), Millwall (1868), Royal Albert (1880) and King George V (1921). Each dock specialised in a particular type of trade and security was tight, with high walls, gates and even a drawbridge at West India Docks. The formation of the Port of London Authority in 1909 removed some of the destructive competition between each dock.

During WWII, Hitler attempted to disable Britain's economy by bombing the entire densely populated area: though rich in infrastructure, it was where the poorest communities in London lived and worked. For 57 consecutive nights incendiary bombs rained down. Post-war revival was stifled by new container shipping. By the 1960s trade had declined to such a low level that docks began to close. The increasingly titanic container vessels were better served at Tilbury and Felixstowe, which offered more up-to-date facilities and deep-water harbours. The decay was halted by the London Docklands Development Corporation (LDDC), which developed over 8.5 square miles of land and water-filled docks on both sides of the river, from Tower Bridge in the west to past the Thames Barrier at Woolwich in the east, to form an upmarket and desirable business and residential area. When the LDDC was set up in 1981 it was heralded as 'the most important inner-city development in Europe'. Parts of the docks have been filled in, but in the main, redevelopment has incorporated the large expanses of water.

View of Oliver's Wharf and one of the elegant Georgian houses of Pier Head. Between them is the narrow slit of Wapping Old Stairs, celebrated in legend and in folk song.

WAPPING

Wapping (*map p. 637, F3*) was once thronged with sailors, dockworkers and all manner of people connected with boats; former residents include Captain Cook and Vice Admiral William Bligh. London Docks opened here in 1805, covering 90 acres and specialising in wine, tobacco, rice and brandy; the bodies of water have been filled in except for Hermitage Basin near St Katharine Docks and Shadwell Basin. When in 1986 Rupert Murdoch moved his newspaper publishing company News International here from Fleet Street, the move was an important milestone in the history of industrial development and worker relations: computer technologies had made compositors and linotype machines redundant and many print workers lost their jobs. Today things have moved on once again and the 15-acre site, 'Fortress Wapping', was sold for residential and commercial redevelopment in 2012.

ALONG THE RIVER

Wapping's main attraction is probably the riverside stretch with its remaining historic pubs. It is possible to walk all the way from Wapping Lake to Canary Wharf, taking in Shadwell and Limehouse along the way.

In the Hermitage Riverside Memorial Garden, just south of Wapping Lake, stands the **Blitz Memorial** (Wendy Turner), the silhouette of a dove in flight cut out of a block of Portland stone. It commemorates those who died in the East End of London as a result of German bombing raids during WWII. From here you can walk along the Thames Path and Wapping High Street, past residential blocks to a charming enclave of yellow-brick buildings, the **Pier Head Conservation Area**. Georgian residences for senior dock officials, built in 1811–13, flank the dockside. The **Town of Ramsgate pub** (*62 Wapping High St, townoframsgate.pub*) lays claim to be the oldest pub on the Thames. Here in

1688, after the accession of William III, Judge Jeffreys, the loyal servant of James II who had presided over the Bloody Assizes, was arrested attempting to flee the country disguised as a sailor, and was brought to the Tower. Accessed via a small alley next to the pub, leading down to the river's edge beside the former Oliver's Wharf, are the **Wapping Old Stairs** of the eponymous ballad ('Your Molly has never been false, she declares, Since last time we parted at Wapping Old Stairs, When I swore that I still would continue the same, And gave you the 'bacco box, marked with your name...'). It is thought that the bottom of this slippery flight of steps may have been the site of the notorious **Execution Dock**, where Captain Kidd (executed 1701) and other notorious pirates were hanged and their bodies left until three tides had covered them. Slaves were also unloaded here.

In nearby Scandrett Street is the old **St John of Wapping School**. Founded in 1695 (though on a different site), it has twin entrances for boys and girls and statues of a 'bluecoat' charity girl and boy in niches above the doors. Just beyond it is the former St John's Church (now flats). The church was destroyed in WWII but its handsome clock-tower (1760) survives. On the corner of Green Bank is the charming **Turk's Head**, a former tavern where condemned pirates were served their last pot of ale before being hanged at Execution Dock. It is now an Anglo-French restaurant (*theturkshead.co.uk*). The park opposite used to be St John's churchyard and still preserves a few tombstones.

Further along Wapping High Street you pass the Waterside Gardens and Wapping New Stairs. Beside them are more old warehouses belonging to the **ex-Aberdeen, St John's and Phoenix wharves**. All are now converted into offices and flats. In the 19th century, this area was known as Sailor Town; a rough, frenetic neighbourhood of 36 taverns where sailors from all corners of the globe could quench their thirst and slake their ardour and where press gangs roamed. The **Captain Kidd pub**, a converted coffee warehouse, has good views from the riverside terrace and shares a claim with Wapping Old Stairs to be the site of Execution Dock (*see above*). The narrow King Henry's Stairs led down to the waterfront.

NORTH OF THE RIVERFRONT

Wapping Lane leads north past Watts Street, where the **Turner's Old Star pub** is reputed to have been owned by the painter J.M.W. Turner. Further north beyond Reardon Street, behind forbidding walls, is the expansive **Tobacco Dock** (D.A. Alexander, 1811–14; *map p. 637, F2–F3*), which linked Western Dock and Eastern Dock and was used to house tobacco, wool, wine and spirits. The buildings were redeveloped into a shopping and restaurant complex in the 1990s by Terry Farrell, utilising the original vaults, cast-iron columns and timber trusses. The development did not take off and the site is now an events venue. Two replica trading ships are moored here forlornly.

SHADWELL

The main thoroughfare of Shadwell is **The Highway** (*map p. 637, F2*), which runs eastwards from East Smithfield along the course of a Roman road. Excavations in the 1970s and again in 2002–3 uncovered Roman remains including a bath house, quarry, tower, drains, tanks, plots and a leather bikini. On the north side of The Highway is Hawksmoor's **St George-in-the-East**, with a massive 160ft tower and smaller 'pepperpot' turrets. Gutted in 1941, it has a modern interior but Hawksmoor's external shell, reminiscent of a Romanesque basilica, survives. It is one of the churches built after the New Churches Act of 1710–11, a scheme for 50 new churches to be built to spread the Word to new communities, often where immigrants were settling. When Charles Booth drew his portrait of East London in 1897, he noted that 'Each [district] has its charm except St George's, which has a squalor peculiar to itself.' The Church League for Women's Suffrage was founded here in 1909.

Shadwell, once a hamlet in its own right, became a seafaring community and then a slum and is now home to repurposed warehouses, glistening new office blocks, convenience stores, small shops and mosques (the area has a large Bangladeshi population). One of the famous businesses to operate on The Highway was Jamrach's Emporium, which traded in exotic animals and birds, many of them brought back by sailors from voyages around the world. A Bengal tiger once escaped from the shop and seized a young boy, carrying him off to Tobacco Dock (*see opposite*). The tiger was wrestled to the ground by Jamrach himself and the boy's life saved.

Charles Jamrach struggles with a tiger

One morning a van-load of wild beasts, which I had bought the previous day from a captain in the London Docks, who brought them from the East Indies, arrived at my repository in Betts Street, St George's-in-the-East. I myself superintended the unloading of the animals, and had given directions to my men to place a den containing a very ferocious full-grown Bengal tiger, with its iron-barred front close against the wall. They were proceeding to take down a den with leopards, when all of a sudden I heard a crash, and to my horror found the big tiger had pushed out the back part of his den with his hind-quarters, and was walking down the yard into the street, which was then full of people watching the arrival of this curious merchandise. As soon as he got into the street, a boy of about nine years of age put out his hand to stroke the beast's back, when the tiger seized him by the shoulder and run down the street with the lad hanging in his jaws. This was done in less time than it takes me to relate; but when I saw the boy being carried off in this manner, and witnessed the panic that had seized hold of the people, without further thought I dashed after the brute, and got hold of him by the loose skin of the back of his neck. I was then of a more vigorous frame than now, and had plenty of pluck and dash in me. I tried thus to stop his further progress, but he was too strong for me, and dragged me, too, along with him...

The Boy's Own Paper, 1879

Cable Street further north, running parallel with The Highway, is where the **Battle of Cable Street** took place (on Sunday 4th October 1936) between policemen and forces opposed to Oswald Mosley's fascist Blackshirts, who planned to stage a march through

Mural commemorating the Battle of Cable Street, when the East End was blocked to British Fascists in 1936.

the East End. A mural commemorating the event was painted in the 1980s on St George's Town Hall (*236 Cable St*), which faces St George's Gardens, the former churchyard.

AROUND SHADWELL BASIN

Shadwell Basin (*map p. 629, E2*) is a large expanse of water overlooked by **St Paul's church**, once known as the Church of the Sea Captains because over 70 were buried in the graveyard. Captain Cook and Thomas Jefferson's mother were both parishioners; John Wesley preached his last sermon here. The present 'Waterloo' church was built in 1820–1 to a design by John Walters. It is home to an Evangelical congregation. Shadwell Basin was formerly part of London Docks and is now a popular boating and water sports area with housing on three sides and, on the south side facing the street called Wapping Wall, near the Thames and the bright red ironwork bascule bridge, the **former Wapping Hydraulic Power Station**, dating from 1890. Formerly the provider of power for the docks' cranes, it was the last such power station still operating in the world before its closure in 1977. At the time of writing an extensive redevelopment project had been agreed for the building. Opposite, overlooking the river, is the ever-popular and picturesque **Prospect of Whitby pub** (*greeneking-pubs.co.uk*). Built in 1520, it was formerly called the Devil's Tavern because of the smugglers and thieves who drank here. The 'hanging' Judge Jeffreys was a customer, as were Samuel Pepys and later Dickens and Turner. Its current name was taken from a ship in 1777.

   King Edward Memorial Park, accessed across the red bascule bridge, marks the site of Shadwell fish market; it was landscaped in 1922 over slum dwellings. At its southern tip on the Thames Path is a circular red-brick rotunda, in fact a ventilation shaft for the Rotherhithe Tunnel. Against it is a little memorial to Willoughby, Frobisher and other 16th-century navigators who 'set sail from this reach of the River Thames near Ratcliff Cross to explore the northern seas'. Ratcliff was a former name for this area, derived from the red of the sandstone. The Thames Path leads east from here, past the massive 1980s red-brick kasbah known as **Free Trade Wharf** (a commercial/residential development that retains two original East India Company saltpetre warehouses), to '**Ratcliff Beach**', a section of pebbly waterfront that can be accessed down the appropriately named Narrow Street and which has excellent views of the Docklands skyscrapers.

North of Narrow Street, at 2 Butcher Row (*map p. 629, E2*), on the corner of St James Gardens, is one of England's oldest charities, the **Royal Foundation of St Katharine**. St Katharine's Royal Hospital was originally founded near the Tower in 1147 by Queen Matilda; in 1273 Queen Eleanor, wife of Henry III, took the wardenship and reserved the patronage for ever for the queens of England personally. However, after Queen Caroline's death in 1821, George IV took over and passed a controversial bill for destruction of the ancient precincts, in order for St Katharine Docks to be excavated in 1825. The Foundation removed to Regent's Park, only returning to the East End in 1950. The Warden's House occupies the former rectory of St James's church. The Foundation offers accommodation for those on retreat, on business or just on holiday.

LIMEHOUSE

Limehouse (*map p. 625, A1*), roughly the area between the Limehouse and Westferry DLR stations, takes its name from the lime kilns which manufactured quicklime for the building industry; from the 16th century it was one of London's main shipbuilding centres. Later the area became populous with labourers serving the West and East India Docks. A Chinese community established itself here in the 1890s, and the area gained a reputation for vice and opium dens which was enhanced and romanticised by writers including Oscar Wilde and Sir Arthur Conan Doyle, the books and films of Dr Fu-Manchu, and the press. The area was immortalised by Gertrude Lawrence in the popular song 'Limehouse Blues' (1922). London's Chinese community is now centred in Soho but there is still a small Chinese population in this area. Limehouse was also historically known for its lascars, sailors mainly from the Indian subcontinent who served on British ships and either failed to find a passage back or chose to stay and settle.

NEWELL STREET, LIMEHOUSE BASIN AND NARROW STREET

The church of **St Anne's Limehouse** (1730), reached from pretty, cobbled Newell Street, is considered one of Hawksmoor's masterpieces. It is another of the twelve churches built in this area as a result of the 1711 Act of Parliament. Badly damaged by fire in 1850, the church was restored by Philip Hardwick. Its clock is the highest church clock in London: designed as a special maritime clock, it used to chime every 15mins. The curious pyramid in the churchyard, contemporary with the church, is carved with 'The Wisdom of Solomon'. It is not known what the pyramid was for but some believe Hawksmoor intended it to be installed on top of the church.

On Newell Street, opposite the church, a path leads down to **Limehouse Cut** with its towpath, London's oldest canal, built in 1770. Bear left down the canal path to reach **Limehouse Basin**, formerly Regent's Canal Dock. Built in 1820, the dock was constructed to allow ships to unload cargoes onto barges for onward transport along the Regent's Canal. In this way, coal was supplied to the power plants along the canal and until the coming of the railway, the dock was the major entrance from the Thames to England's inland waterway network. The dock is also linked to the River Lee (or Lea) via the Limehouse Cut. Continuing left, the path skirts the Limehouse Basin marina and eventually comes out onto the **Thames Path**, where The Bread Street Kitchen (*junction of Narrow St and Horseferry Rd*) is in a former dockmaster's house. Follow the Thames Path east (left) along Narrow Street, with its fine 18th-century merchant's houses. The historic **Grapes pub** at no. 76 on the right was immortalised by Dickens as The Six Jolly Fellowship Porters in *Our Mutual Friend*. There is a good view up and down the river, including the glittering towers of Canary Wharf.

THE ISLE OF DOGS

Map p. 625, B2–B3. DLR: West India Quay, Canary Wharf; Underground: Canary Wharf.

The Isle of Dogs, once a boggy peninsula known as Stepney Marsh, remained relatively unpopulated until the docks were constructed here in the 19th century, bringing employment and industrialisation. Row upon row of Victorian terraces were built, at Poplar and the purpose-built estate called Cubitt Town, to shelter the humble dock- and ship-workers and their families. The name 'Isle of Dogs' may derive from the hunting hounds of Henry VIII, who came here for some sport from Placentia Palace across the river in Greenwich. However, this tongue of land was never really an island until the docks and canals were excavated. The West India Docks opened in 1802 as two rectangular basins, one for import and one for export. A shipping canal was cut across the peninsula in 1805 and was later incorporated as the South West India Dock. The huge L-shaped Millwall Dock, which now has a watersports and sailing centre, followed in 1868. All this caused the peninsula to become largely cut off from the rest of London. Only with the opening of the DLR and the Underground Jubilee Line extension in the late 20th century did getting here became relatively quick and easy. The Elizabeth Line has made things even quicker.

CANARY WHARF

The gleaming towers of Canary Wharf (*map p. 625, A1–B1*), not so long ago famed as London's Wall Street-on-Water, stand on the northern part of the Isle of Dogs, on a narrow piece of land between two of the West India Docks which once handled trade with the Canary Islands. After the last dock closed in 1980, the area became a wasteland. Today, the colossal development, with some of the earliest skyscrapers in the UK, comprises 14 million square feet of offices, flats, hotels, restaurants and shops.

The towers of Newfoundland Quay, including 'Newfoundland' itself, or the 'Diamond Tower', so named from its lozenge-patterned steel frame.

The expanses of water that formed the docks are now ornamental, the redundant cranes that used to hoist heavy cargoes frozen into pieces of public art. But it was not an easy transformation. After the 'Big Bang' deregulation of the City in 1986, Docklands was expected to become the stock-trading centre of London. Manhattan-style buildings soon began to fill the sky, but Paul Reichmann, the Canadian property tycoon who staked so much on the development, famously lost millions when the buildings failed to find tenants. Poor transport infrastructure was blamed (the Jubilee Line extension arrived too late and the Docklands Light Railway offered only a rickety, fairground ride). It was not until after 1999 that Canary Wharf began to take off.

All the major names in international finance are or have been represented at Canary Wharf and in its heyday over 60,000 employees made the Monday–Friday commute. Weekends, once quiet as office workers departed, are now busy since the arrival of well-appointed waterside apartment blocks. The view from Canary Wharf Pier takes in the skyscrapers of London's most famous financial hub: the City.

At the heart of Canary Wharf rises Cesar Pelli's 50-storey steel tower, known as 'Canary Wharf' but officially **One Canada Square**. Completed in 1991, it was then the tallest building in Europe and at 800ft high it is still prominent on the East London skyline, though no longer as dominant. The trellis-fronted **Newfoundland** (Horden Cherry Lee, 2020; *map p. 625, A2*), though not as tall, seems to stand out by virtue of it riverfront location. The winking lights at the apex of all the roofs are a warning to

Draped Seated Woman, familiarly known as *'Old Flo'*. Sculpture of 1957-8 by Henry Moore. Made for London's East End, she resided for some years in Yorkshire before being installed in Cabot Square, Docklands, in 2017.

aircraft passing by on their way to City Airport. Shops and cafés fill the arcades which lead from the DLR station, built into the base of the Tower, to **Cabot Square**. Here, as with the rest of Canary Wharf, a high standard of landscaping has been achieved with trees, sculpture and street furniture. One of the sculptures is Henry Moore's *Draped Seated Woman*, known familiarly as '*Old Flo*'. Created originally to adorn an East London housing estate, she languished unloved for some years until finally re-installed here.

The glass arc of **Canary Wharf Underground Station** (Jubilee Line) was designed by Sir Norman Foster. The vast interior, over 70ft below ground, features platforms that are as long as One Canada Square is high.

WEST INDIA QUAY
The broad West India Quay is north of Canary Wharf, linked to it by a footbridge. Overlooking the old import dock (North Dock), in a listed Georgian sugar warehouse, is the **Museum of London Docklands** (*map p. 625, A1; museumoflondon.org.uk/ docklands*), part of the wider Museum of London, which has both permanent and temporary exhibitions. The permanent galleries begin in the old No. 1 Warehouse and include themed displays exploring the relationship between London and its river, past life in the Docklands area, the history of trade—with all the good and ill that that entailed—which led to London becoming the 'warehouse of the world', and the story of the Docklands at war, including the destruction wreaked on 7th September 1940

by a Luftwaffe bombing raid. The final displays tell the story of the docks' rebuilding as a financial centre.

MILLWALL AND ISLAND GARDENS

Millwall is the area near the tip of the Isle of Dogs. The football club of that name was founded here in the late 19th century but last played in its home district in 1910. It is now based on the other side of the Thames. The 32-acre **Mudchute Park** (*map p. 625, B2–B3*) gets its name from the artificial landscape created by the silted mud dredged and dumped here from excavating Millwall Dock. It has been turned into a public open space and urban farm (*mudchute.org*).

Burrell's Wharf (*map p. 625, A3–B3*) on the waterfront is where the iron plates for the *Great Eastern*—the wonder and failure of her age—were manufactured. Isambard Kingdom Brunel and John Scott Russell designed the 629ft-long ironship, which was built between 1853 and 1858. It took three months to float her sideways into the Thames. As a cargo and passenger ship she proved of little use (too slow) and she was put to work laying Atlantic cables before being broken up in 1888. Some of the original buildings of the wharf survive (Plate House) and have been incorporated in the residential Burrell's Wharf complex. Further south, the **Great Eastern Launch Ramp**, which can be seen from the Thames Path, is the original timber slipway from which the *Great Eastern* was launched; Charles Dickens was among the crowd who came to enjoy the spectacle.

From **Island Gardens**, first laid out in 1895, there are good views of Greenwich and Deptford. The Greenwich Foot Tunnel under the river here opened in 1902 and replaced the ferry. The walk to Greenwich takes less than 10mins.

BLACKWALL AND THE ROYAL DOCKS

Blackwall is said to have taken its name from the colour of the river wall here in centuries past. It contains the tiny, narrow cobbled street named **Coldharbour** (*map p. 625, B2*), a rare survival amid the gleaming tower blocks. Further east on the Thames Path is the **Virginia Settlers Monument**, commemorating the 105 'adventurers' who set sail from a spot near here in December 1606 (over a decade before the *Mayflower*) and founded the settlement of Jamestown, Virginia. Captain John Smith was among them. Just beyond it is the sole surviving basin of **East India Dock** (*map p. 625, C1; DLR to East India*), now a wildlife sanctuary, home to newts and kingfishers, and just beyond that is Bow Creek, where the river Lea wriggles sinuously into the Thames.

Further east are the old **Royal Docks** (Royal Victoria, Royal Albert and George V docks; *map p. 629, F2*), the largest enclosed docks in the world with the largest man-made body of water. They are now a vast mixed-use facility with residential buildings, business parks, convention centres (the ExCeL), shopping malls, entertainment venues (the Brick Lane Music Hall), sports facilities (paddle- and wakeboarding) and London City Airport and its angular, glass-panelled City Hall. The **IFS Cloud Cable Car** service (*tfl.gov.uk*) operates between the Royal Docks (*Royal Victoria station on the DLR*) and Greenwich Peninsula (*North Greenwich on the Jubilee Line*). The experience is unique in London and there is a splendid prospect of the Thames Barrier (*see p. 500*).

Westminster Abbey quire.

WESTMINSTER & ROYAL LONDON

'Earth hath not anything to show more fair.' Thus wrote William Wordsworth in 1802, of the view from Westminster Bridge. Standing with the bridge behind you, Whitehall, with its government buildings, leads north, while sweeping away to your left is the magnificent 940ft façade of the Houses of Parliament. Head straight down Bridge Street to reach Parliament Square.

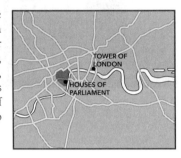

Some highlights of the area
✦ The **Houses of Parliament**, the seat of British government, a UNESCO World Heritage site covering eight acres, with 11 courtyards, 100 staircases, 1,100 apartments and two miles of passages;

✦ **Buckingham Palace**, the London residence of the British sovereign;

✦ The soaring Gothic **Westminster Abbey**, site of the coronation and burial of most kings and queens of England.

PARLIAMENT SQUARE

Map p. 635, F2. Underground: Westminster.

Parliament Square stands in an area that was once the desolate, marshy Thorney Island. Today it is overlooked by the austere bulk of HM Treasury as well as by the much more famous **Houses of Parliament (Palace of Westminster)**. The first Palace of Westminster (palace, monastery and church) was built here for Edward the Confessor (r. 1042–66) between the Thames and the Benedictine church of St Peter, founded AD 900, which later became Westminster Abbey. William the Conqueror made the palace his home and in 1097–9 his son, William Rufus (William II), added the magnificent Westminster Hall, one of the largest Norman halls in Europe. It remained the main residence of the kings of England until Henry VIII removed the court to Whitehall Palace after a fire in 1512. In 1547 the House of Commons transferred its meetings here from the Chapter House of Westminster Abbey. In 1834 the entire complex, by then a mix of Norman, medieval and later buildings, was burned down, with the exception

The river façade of the Palace of Westminster, a subtle mix of symmetry and asymmetry, begun c. 1840 by Charles Barry and Augustus Pugin.

of Westminster Hall, the crypt and part of the cloisters of St Stephen's Chapel, and the Jewel Tower across the road, which was a separate entity in any case. Reconstruction, in the prescribed neo-Gothic style, began c. 1840 and lasted about 30 years.

Parliament Square was laid out in 1868 as London's first traffic roundabout. It is always crowded with tourists and sometimes with demonstrations and protesters. In the central space are statues of eminent statesmen, including Winston Churchill (d. 1965) and Benjamin Disraeli (d. 1881), whose statue is decorated with primroses (his favourite flower) each year on 19th April, the anniversary of his death.

THE HOUSES OF PARLIAMENT (PALACE OF WESTMINSTER)
The building, which incorporates the ancient Westminster Hall and the crypt and cloisters of St Stephen's Chapel, was designed by Sir Charles Barry, at heart an Italian classicist, aided by Augustus Pugin, a zealous Gothicist. The result is a subtle and triumphant fusion of symmetry and asymmetry, rich in external decoration.

Besides the **House of Commons** in the north half (faithfully restored after complete destruction in WWII) and the **House of Lords** in the south half, the palace contains the homes of various parliamentary officials. Of the three towers, the huge, square **Victoria Tower** at the south end (right) is the highest; at its base is the Sovereign's Entrance to the House of Lords. The octagonal **Central Tower** rises above the Central Lobby and serves as a ventilation shaft. The other tower, the **Elizabeth Tower**, houses the Westminster Clock (still wound by hand), an authoritative time-keeper. It has four dials, each 23ft square; the Roman numerals are 2ft high and the minute-hands are 14ft long. **Big Ben**, the enormous 9ft bell which famously strikes the hour on an E note, was installed in 1858; it took 30 hours to winch it up the tower. Four years of restoration work began in August 2017, when the bells were silenced, but one clock face, its hands driven by a motor, was always visible and telling the correct time. The Ayrton Light above the belfry is lit when the House of Commons is sitting after dark.

THE WESTMINSTER SYSTEM

The Palace of Westminster gives its name to the 'Westminster system' of Parliamentary democracy, which exists in various forms in many countries of the world. In this system, the role of the head of state is largely symbolic and ceremonial, and actual government is carried out by ministers who are members of the country's legislature. In the United Kingdom (England, Scotland, Wales and Northern Ireland) the head of state is the hereditary monarch. Parliament consists of two chambers; the House of Lords consisting of hereditary peers, life peers and bishops of the Church of England, and the democratically elected House of Commons. The monarch appoints a prime minister, normally the leader of the largest political party in the House of Commons, who in turn appoints ministers. The most important ministers form a cabinet which, together with individual ministers, is collectively accountable to Parliament. The leader of the largest opposition party in the House of Commons, known as the 'Leader of the Opposition', appoints a 'shadow cabinet' and other shadow ministers to scrutinise the activities of each member of the cabinet and government department.

GUIDED TOURS OF THE HOUSES OF PARLIAMENT

Although security around the Palace of Westminster is tight and visible, there are guided tours on Saturdays throughout the year and on selected weekdays during parliamentary recesses. The tours are led by 'Blue Badge' guides and take approx. 75mins. For details, see parliament.uk/visiting. Buy/collect tickets at the kiosk adjacent to the Jewel Tower or from officials wearing jackets with the Houses of Parliament portcullis insignia. Only UK residents are admitted to the Elizabeth Tower and Big Ben; tickets may be requested through your local MP.

WESTMINSTER HALL

On Abingdon Street, once an ancient lane, the west façade of the Houses of Parliament (with Thornycroft's **statue of Oliver Cromwell** in front) is interrupted by the long line of **Westminster Hall**, a splendid and rare Norman survivor from the original Palace of Westminster. It is shown as part of the official guided tour (*see above*). The Hall is the oldest building on the Parliamentary estate and was witness to the trials of, among others, William Wallace in 1305, Thomas More in 1535 and King Charles I in 1649. It is here where foreign leaders address both houses of Parliament, and where monarchs have traditionally lain in state before their funerals.

A little further down, in Old Palace Yard, is an equestrian **statue of Richard the Lionheart**, holding his sword aloft, by Baron Carlo Marochetti (1856). It suffered during the Blitz when a bomb exploded nearby, apparently lifting it from the ground and bending the sword; traces of shrapnel are still visible on the plinth.

JEWEL TOWER

The small, ragstone **Jewel Tower** (*fee; english-heritage.org.uk*), opposite the House of Lords, is a rare survival of the medieval Palace of Westminster. It was built by the king's mason, Henry Yevele, for Edward III in 1356–66, as a royal treasure house, known as the King's Privy Wardrobe. After the devastating fire of 1512, when Henry's VIII's court moved from Westminster to Whitehall, the Tower was used to store a range of unwanted objects, including furniture, table- and bed linen, gaming tables and dolls used by his daughters, Mary and Elizabeth. From 1621 to 1864 it served as the Record Office of the Lords and thereafter (until 1938) as an assay office of weights and measures. Around the tower you can see the excavated remains of its moat and behind it part of the 10ft ragstone wall built in the 14th century to surround the precincts of Westminster Abbey.

Next to the Jewel Tower, in Abingdon Street Gardens, stands *Knife Edge*, a sculpture by Henry Moore (1967).

VICTORIA TOWER GARDENS

The entrance to Victoria Tower Gardens is next to the majestic Victoria Tower of the House of Lords. Just inside is a **statue of Emmeline Pankhurst** (1858–1928), the leader of the suffragettes, and a memorial to her daughter Christabel, by A.G. Walker (1930). Dominating the centre of the gardens is a **bronze cast of *The Burghers of Calais***, Auguste Rodin's famous group of 1889 depicting the six who surrendered themselves to Edward III in 1340 to save their city from destruction during the Hundred Years' War. This cast is dated 1908 and was installed in 1915; it is one of the official twelve casts the French Government allowed to be taken after Rodin's death. Continue through the gardens (there is a good view of the river and of Lambeth on the opposite bank) until you reach the jewel-like **Buxton Memorial Fountain**, by S.S. Teulon, which commemorates the abolition of slavery and the role of British parliamentarians in the ending of the slave trade. It has had a chequered life: the statues of British rulers were gradually stolen, even their later replacements were spirited away, and the drinking fountain ceased working. It was restored in March 2007 to mark the 200th anniversary of the Slave Trade Act.

WESTMINSTER ABBEY PRECINCTS

Map p. 635, F2–F3. Underground: Westminster, St James's Park.

At the end of Great College Street an archway (right) leads into Dean's Yard, once a portion of the Abbey Gardens. On the right are entrances to the cloisters and to **Westminster School**, one of the UK's great public (independent) schools, founded by Benedictine monks in 1179 and re-founded by Elizabeth I in 1560. The school is built around Little Dean's Yard on the site of the monks' quarters, relics of which remain. The College Hall, with a fine hammerbeam roof, dates from the time of Edward III and was formerly the abbey refectory. The main hall was the monks' dormitory. Ashburnham

House, the library, dates from 1400 but was rebuilt in 1660 as the home of the Earls of Ashburnham, probably to a design by John Webb, pupil of Inigo Jones. Westminster School now educates over 750 boys and girls. They enjoy certain privileges, such as shouting the 'Vivats' at coronations in the abbey, where they attend twice-weekly services. On Shrove Tuesday the 'Greaze' takes place in the main hall: a horsehair-reinforced pancake is tossed over a bar and the pupil securing the largest fragment is symbolically rewarded with a gold sovereign. On the long list of famous alumni are Ben Jonson, Dryden, Purcell, Wren, Judge Jeffreys, Charles Wesley, Gibbon, A.A. Milne, Sir John Gielgud, Kim Philby, Helena Bonham Carter, six prime ministers and two deputy prime ministers.

On the south side of Dean's Yard is **Church House** by Sir Herbert Baker (1937–40), the headquarters of the Archbishops' Council, the Church Commissioners and various other ecclesiastical boards. It is the meeting place, twice each year, of the General Synod of the Church of England. To the west is the **Abbey Choir School**, whose boys share the central green with Westminster School.

BROAD SANCTUARY

Broad Sanctuary, the name given to the road in front of Westminster Abbey, commemorates the tradition whereby fugitives from civil authority could claim sanctuary here, and protection by the Church (a privilege abolished by James I in 1624). The neo-Gothic red granite **Westminster Column**, opposite the west end of the Abbey, by Sir George Gilbert Scott (1861), was erected in memory of Westminster School alumni who fell in the Crimean War and the Indian Mutiny (the Uprising).

At the corner of Tothill Street and Storey's Gate rises the former Methodist **Central Hall**, with a huge lead dome, built in 1911 (Lanchester and Richards) as the headquarters of the Methodist Church and now also used for concerts, political rallies and public meetings. Speakers have included Mahatma Gandhi, Winnie Mandela and Mikhail Gorbachev. In January 1946 it became the first home of the General Assembly of the United Nations. Despite its neo-Renaissance appearance, it one of the earliest examples of steel-frame construction in London.

Next to it is the **Queen Elizabeth II Conference Centre** (Powell, Moya and Partners, 1986), an unobtrusive building on a potentially contentious site. It is the largest conference venue in Central London and is owned by the government. To its right are the Edwardian neo-Gothic buildings of the **UK Supreme Court**.

ST MARGARET'S CHURCH

In the shadow of the great Abbey stands the picturesque St Margaret's Church, dating from 1485–1523. It has been repeatedly altered and restored and the interior is adorned with Elizabethan and Jacobean wall monuments. It provides a welcome sanctuary from the throngs of people and vehicles outside.

St Margaret's was founded before 1189 as the parish church of Westminster, where local people would worship separately from the monks at the Abbey, and is also (since 1621) the 'national church for the House of Commons'. It has been described as being the last church in London to be decorated in the Catholic tradition, before the

Reformation. Samuel Pepys was married here in 1655; John Milton (for the second time) in 1656 and Winston Churchill in 1908. Sir Walter Raleigh, who was executed in 1618 in front of the Palace of Westminster, is buried in the chancel; and in the church or churchyard also rest William Caxton (1422–?91) and Wenceslaus Hollar, the Bohemian etcher who depicted London before the Great Fire.

At the east end of the south aisle is the notable chest tomb of Lady Dudley (d. 1600), and on the east wall, memorials to Caxton (whose first printing press was next to the Chapter House from 1476) and Raleigh, to whom the large west window is also dedicated. The window at the west end of the north aisle, with an inscription by Whittier, commemorates Milton. The richly-coloured east window, made in Holland before 1509, once believed to celebrate the betrothal of Katherine of Aragon to Prince Arthur, Henry VII's eldest son, in 1501, although after closer study, it was considered to represent Henry VIII. By the time the window was completed, however, Henry was already in pursuit of Anne Boleyn. Installed for a time in Waltham Abbey, it passed through various hands until it was bought for St Margaret's in 1758.

Outside, near the main west entrance to the church, a wall tablet commemorates 21 Parliamentarians who were originally buried in the abbey but who, on the Restoration of the Monarchy, were disinterred and reburied in an unmarked plot in the churchyard in 1661. On the external east wall is a lead bust of Charles I (c. 1800).

WESTMINSTER ABBEY

Map p. 635, F3. Underground: Westminster. Open to visitors Mon–Sat and for worship on Sun. The Abbey cloisters, Chapter House and museum all have different opening times, which are subject to frequent change. westminster-abbey.org. Hefty admission charge.

Westminster Abbey is officially the Collegiate Church of St Peter in Westminster, dedicated to the Apostle of the Gentiles (the other great Apostle, Paul, has his cathedral in the City). This great church holds a unique position in English history as the site of both the coronation and the burial of most English sovereigns. Though built at different periods, it is mainly (with the exception of Henry VII's magnificent Perpendicular chapel at the east end and the 18th-century west towers) in the Early English style, of which it constitutes one of the most impressive and best-preserved examples.

Special services are held in the Abbey throughout the year and include the opening of the Law Courts in October, when judges in their robes walk in procession from the House of Lords.

Interior of the Abbey

The abbey is 513ft long (including Henry VII's Lady Chapel), 200ft wide across the transepts and 75ft wide across the nave and aisles. The Chapel of Henry VII itself is 104½ft long and 70ft wide. As with all London's major historic attractions, the Abbey is crowded all the time (three million tourists pass through its precincts each year) and in order to deal with the numbers, each visit is designed to be simple and quick, to make sense of the daunting and important number of funerary and commemorative monuments by outlining only the essential. Visitors are encouraged to take a free audio guide or download the app to see the Abbey in a designated order. It is not easy to wander around at will; 'The Way' is clearly delineated and potential avenues for deviation are cordoned off. The description below therefore follows the trail of the audio tour and attempts to flesh out the information along the way. Remain patient: a visit to the Abbey is rewarding and should not be missed. If the audio guide appeals, the English-language version features the liquid diction of actor Jeremy Irons.

HISTORY OF WESTMINSTER ABBEY

According to tradition, a church on Thorney Island, or the Isle of Thorns, was built by the East Saxons and consecrated by Mellitus, first Bishop of London, in 616; but there is no authentic record of any earlier church than that of the Benedictine Abbey founded here in the 10th century and dedicated to St Peter. It received the name 'West Minster', or western monastery, probably from its position to the west of the City of London and its great cathedral of St Paul. King Edward the Confessor (d. 1066) rebuilt the Abbey on a larger scale, using money that he had originally set aside for a pilgrimage to Rome. His Romanesque church was consecrated in 1065, and when he died the following year, his body was laid to rest here while his throne was contested by both the Saxon Harold and the Norman William. At the famous Battle of Hastings, William defeated Harold, and the long years of Norman rule began. Edward was canonised in 1161, after cures began to be reported at his tomb. He received the epithet 'Confessor' (to denote a devout man who had not died a martyr's death), his body was placed in a new shrine, and the Abbey became a place of pilgrimage. Within this church, or its successor, every English sovereign since Harold (with the exceptions only of Edward V and Edward VIII) has been crowned. In 1220 the Lady Chapel was added at the east end, and in 1245 Henry III decided to honour Edward the Confessor by rebuilding the entire church in a more magnificent style, as it appears today. The architects were Henry de Reyns (1245–53), John of Gloucester (1253–60) and Robert of Beverley (1260–84). The influence of French cathedrals such as Rheims and Amiens and of the Sainte Chapelle in Paris can be seen in the height of the nave and the arrangement of the radial chapels at the east end.

In 1269 the new church was consecrated. From this time until the reign of George III the abbey became the royal burial church. In about 1388 Henry Yevele began to rebuild the nave for Archbishop Langham, and the work was continued after 1400 by William of Colchester; the design of Henry III's time was followed, with even the details little changed. The nave vault was completed by Abbot Islip in 1504–6. The new nave was hardly finished when the Lady Chapel was pulled down to make way for the magnificent Chapel of Henry VII (1503–19), attributed to Robert Vertue.

At the Dissolution (1536–41), the Abbey's community of Benedictine monks surrendered all their possessions, in perpetuity, to the king and his heirs. A new cathedral church was founded. Elizabeth I made the church a 'Royal peculiar' (directly responsible to the monarch) under an independent Dean and Chapter, whose successors administer it today. The extant monastic buildings date mainly from the 13th and 14th centuries, but there is Norman work in the Pyx Chamber and adjoining Undercroft.

Sir Christopher Wren was appointed Surveyor in 1698. Hawksmoor altered the west façade and added the towers (225ft high) in 1745. The Queen's Diamond Jubilee Galleries, the first significant addition for over two centuries, opened in 2018.

Central and North Nave: The nave appears to be homogeneously of the 13th century but is actually a mixture of dates: the east part is the earliest; the western section dates from the 14th–16th centuries. Its height is striking: separated from the aisles by a tall arcade supported on circular columns, around each of which are grouped eight slender shafts of grey Purbeck marble, it is the loftiest Gothic nave in England. Above the arches runs the double triforium with exquisite tracery and diaperwork and, still higher, the tall clerestory. Many monuments throughout the church commemorate people who are not buried in the abbey; burials in the nave took place only after the Reformation.

A few paces from the west door, in the centre of the nave, a slab of green marble is simply inscribed '**Remember Winston Churchill**' **(1)**. It was placed here 'in accordance with the wishes of the Queen and Parliament' on the 25th anniversary of the Battle of Britain. Churchill's body lies at Bladon, Oxfordshire.

Isolated by paper poppies in the centre of the floor is the **Tomb of the**

Unknown Warrior (2): the body of an unidentified soldier, chosen from four unknown combatants whose bodies had been exhumed from one of the main battlefields, the Somme, the Aisne, Arras and Ypres, was interred here on 11th November 1920 to represent all the nameless British dead in the First World War. 'They buried him among the kings because he had done good toward God and toward his House.' He rests in earth brought from the battlefields under a black marble slab from a quarry near Namur, Belgium. It has become a tradition for royal brides to send their wedding bouquets to be laid on the tomb, and Queen Camilla's coronation bouquet was laid here in 2023. In the centre of the nave, further east, is the **grave of David Livingstone (3)**, traveller and missionary in Africa (d. 1873).

The great benefactress Baroness Burdett-Coutts is commemorated near the west door. Across the front of the Belfry Tower is a bronze **effigy of Lord Salisbury (4)** (d. 1903). On the west wall is a bust of General Gordon (d. 1885), the defender of Khartoum, by Onslow Ford. Among the crowded monuments is one (east

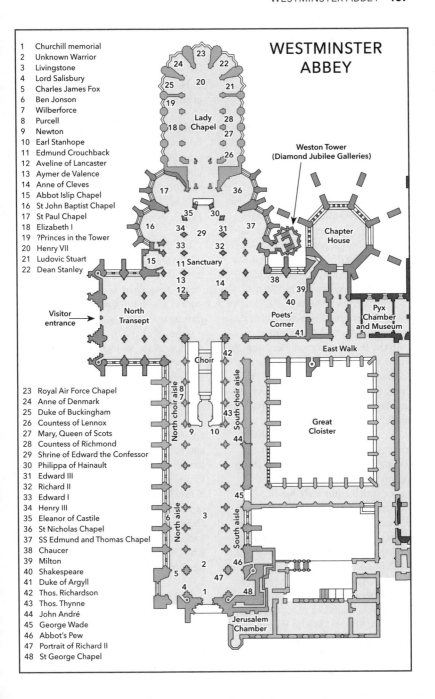

WESTMINSTER ABBEY

1 Churchill memorial
2 Unknown Warrior
3 Livingstone
4 Lord Salisbury
5 Charles James Fox
6 Ben Jonson
7 Wilberforce
8 Purcell
9 Newton
10 Earl Stanhope
11 Edmund Crouchback
12 Aveline of Lancaster
13 Aymer de Valence
14 Anne of Cleves
15 Abbot Islip Chapel
16 St John Baptist Chapel
17 St Paul Chapel
18 Elizabeth I
19 ?Princes in the Tower
20 Henry VII
21 Ludovic Stuart
22 Dean Stanley

23 Royal Air Force Chapel
24 Anne of Denmark
25 Duke of Buckingham
26 Countess of Lennox
27 Mary, Queen of Scots
28 Countess of Richmond
29 Shrine of Edward the Confessor
30 Philippa of Hainault
31 Edward III
32 Richard II
33 Edward I
34 Henry III
35 Eleanor of Castile
36 St Nicholas Chapel
37 SS Edmund and Thomas Chapel
38 Chaucer
39 Milton
40 Shakespeare
41 Duke of Argyll
42 Thos. Richardson
43 Thos. Thynne
44 John André
45 George Wade
46 Abbot's Pew
47 Portrait of Richard II
48 St George Chapel

Weston Tower
(Diamond Jubilee Galleries)

Lady Chapel

Chapter House

Sanctuary

North Transept

Visitor entrance

Poets' Corner

Pyx Chamber and Museum

East Walk

Choir

North choir aisle

South choir aisle

Great Cloister

North aisle

South aisle

Jerusalem Chamber

side) to Viscount Howe (d. 1758) by Scheemakers, erected by the Province of Massachusetts while it was a British colony.

North aisle: Across the head of the aisle is a large **monument to Charles James Fox (5)** (d. 1806). Floor slabs commemorate Ramsay MacDonald (d. 1937), Lloyd George (d. 1945), Ernest Bevin (d. 1951), Clement Attlee (d. 1967) and the noted Fabians Sidney and Beatrice Webb (d. 1947 and 1943), admirers of Soviet Russia who were buried here at the behest of George Bernard Shaw. On the wall is a monument to Campbell-Bannerman (d. 1908). Dean Stanley (Arthur Stanley, the liberal churchman who was Dean of Westminster from 1864–81) called this part of the abbey 'Whigs' Corner'.

In the third bay, a small stone upright in the wall at the bottom, inscribed 'O Rare Ben Johnson' [sic], marks the **grave of Ben Jonson (6)**, the poet and dramatist (d. 1637). The memorial was made, according to John Aubrey, 'at the charge of Jack Young (afterwards knighted) who, walking there when the grave was covering, gave the fellow eighteen pence to cut it.'

The **north choir aisle** has fine examples of early heraldry on the wall. A series of medallions under the organ (right) commemorate famous scientists, among them Charles Darwin (d. 1882; tomb in north nave aisle) and Lord Lister (d. 1912). Matching lozenges in the pavement honour men associated with music, including Elgar, Vaughan Williams, Britten, William Walton, Adrian Boult and C.V. Stanford. In the next bay **William Wilberforce (7)**, one of the chief opponents of the slave trade (d. 1833), and Sir Stamford Raffles (1759–1833), founder of Singapore, sit pensive in effigy above the tomb of **Henry Purcell (8)**, composer and organist at the Abbey (d. 1695).

Choir and sanctuary: The choir screen (1834, with medieval masonry) is by Edward Blore. Set into it are two impressive works by Rysbrack and Kent commemorating **Sir Isaac Newton (9)** (d. 1727) and **Earl Stanhope (10)** (d. 1721), faithful public servant of George I.

It is in the **sanctuary**, the raised space within the altar rails, that coronations take place. The **altar screen** is by Sir George Gilbert Scott (1867). In front is a beautiful **Cosmatesque pavement** of 1268, signed 'Odoricus'; it is thought to be by the hand of a member of the Roman Oderisi family. The original brass inlaid letters specified its intended cosmological significance: *Sphaericus archetypum globus hic monstrat macrocosmum* ('This round sphere represents a model of the Universe'): an appropriate place for the coronation and anointing of a temporal sovereign. On the left are three beautiful architectural tombs. Buried within them are **Edmund 'Crouchback' Plantagenet (11)**, Earl of Lancaster (d. 1296) , second son of Henry III and founder of the House of Lancaster; his first wife **Aveline (12)**, who died aged 15 in 1274; and **Aymer de Valence (13)**, Earl of Pembroke (d. 1324).

On the right side of the sanctuary are sedilia dating from the time of Edward I, with a 15th-century Florentine altarpiece of the *Madonna and Child* by Bicci di Lorenzo. Below is the tomb of **Anne of Cleves (14)**, fourth wife of

Henry VIII (d. 1557). The choir fittings were designed by Edward Blore in 1830.

North transept: The uniformity and proportions of the architecture in both transepts have been altered by the host of monuments and closures. Each transept is lit by a large **rose window**: the glass in the north transept is the oldest in the abbey, to a design of 1722 by Thornhill; below it on either side are exquisitely carved censing angels, sculpted by Master John of St Albans c. 1250.

Several eminent statesmen are commemorated here, including Richard Cobden, famous opponent of the Corn Laws (d. 1865; bust); Warren Hastings, Governor General of India (d. 1818); William Pitt, Earl of Chatham (d. 1778; huge monument); Lord Palmerston (d. 1865; statue) and Lord Castlereagh (d. 1821; statue). Towards the east wall are statues of George Canning (d. 1827) by Chantrey; Benjamin Disraeli (d. 1881) by Boehm; Gladstone (d. 1898) by Brock; and Sir Robert Peel (d. 1850) by Gibson.

The **Queen's Window**, unveiled in 2018, was designed by David Hockney to celebrate the reign of Queen Elizabeth II, the country's longest reigning monarch. It depicts Hockney's home county of Yorkshire, using his distinctively colourful palette, and reflects the late Queen's love of the countryside. It is the artist's first work in glass.

North ambulatory: The backs of the tombs of Aymer de Valence and Edmund Crouchback are well seen from here. Opposite the former, on the left-hand pier, is a plaque to Aymer's wife, Countess of Pembroke, who founded Pembroke College, Cambridge. Also on the left is an overwhelming monument to General Wolfe, in bas-relief by Joseph Wilton, commissioned by William Pitt to commemorate Wolfe's victory and death at Quebec in 1759. Behind are many monuments. To the left is a bust of Sir John Franklin, lost in the search for the Northwest Passage in 1847, with a noble verse by Tennyson: 'Not here: the white North has thy bones; and thou, heroic sailor-soul, art passing on thine happier voyage now toward no earthly pole...'. To the right lies Sir Francis Vere (d. 1609), a distinguished soldier of Queen Elizabeth I. His magnificent Renaissance tomb is modelled on that of Engelbert II of Nassau (d. 1504) at Breda, where kneeling knights also bear a canopy strewn with accoutrements. The tomb of Lady Elizabeth Nightingale (d. 1731), with a menacing figure of Death emerging from below to threaten the lady with a spear, is by Roubiliac, clearly inspired by Bernini's monument to Pope Alexander VII in St Peter's in Rome. Other memorials are to the actress Mrs Siddons (d. 1831), in her celebrated pose as the Tragic Muse (a bust by Chantrey after Reynolds); the actor John Kemble (d. 1823), designed by Flaxman; and the engineer and bridge-builder Thomas Telford (d. 1834).

The **Chapel of Abbot Islip (15)** is of two storeys: the lower chapel, seen through a screen, is where Islip is buried. Islip was one of the last abbots of Westminster before the Reformation (1500–32). The ceiling is decorated with his rebus of a boy falling from a tree and the motto 'I slip'. The upper chapel, re-dedicated to Florence Nightingale in 2010, the centenary of her death, is the **Nurses' Memorial Chapel**, commemorating members of the nursing profession who died in the Second World War. Next door, the **Chapel of St John the Baptist (16)** is entered through the tiny Chapel of Our Lady of the Pew. Above the entrance is a delicately carved alabaster niche from the demolished Chapel of St Erasmus (15th century); just inside is a modern alabaster carving of the Virgin. Traces of the painted vault remain from the late 14th century. The large monument to Thomas Cecil, Earl of Exeter (d. 1623), son of Lord Burghley, features his effigy and that of his first wife. His second wife refused to accept the less honourable position on his left hand and was buried in Winchester Cathedral.

Opposite outside is a staircase leading to the **Chapel of St Edward the Confessor (29)**, east of the high altar. Access is restricted but you can glimpse the Confessor's shrine at the centre and see the tombs surrounding it from the ambulatory (*a fuller description of the chapel is given on p. 142*); note the grate of Queen Eleanor's tomb, an admirable specimen of English wrought-iron work by Thomas of Leighton (1294). The back of Henry III's tomb is visible from the ambulatory.

The **Chapel of St Paul (17** has the restored, brightly-coloured tomb of Sir Lewis Robbesart, Lord Bourgchier (d. 1430), acting as a reminder that the medieval abbey would have been brightly painted. The chapel also contains a monument to Frances Sidney, Countess of Sussex (d. 1589), founder of Sidney Sussex College, Cambridge. The fine monument to Dudley Carleton (d. 1632) is by Nicholas Stone.

Henry VII's Lady Chapel: A flight of steps leads to the Lady Chapel or Chapel of Henry VII. Building began in 1503 but was not completed until 1516, six years after his death. It is the finest example in England of late Perpendicular or Tudor Gothic. Henry ordered it to be 'painted, garnished and adorned in as goodly and rich a manner as such work requireth and as to a king's work apperteyneth'. The culminating glory of its profuse decoration is the superb **fan vaulting**, hung with pendants in the nave, and stretched as a canopy to accommodate the bay windows in the aisles. The beautiful tall **windows**, curved in the aisles and angular in the apse, are particularly ingenious. The carving throughout is of the highest quality, and includes a series of 94 (originally 107) statues of saints popular at the time, with a frieze of angels and badges below.

The chapel was begun as a shrine for Henry VI, and carved stalls of the Knights of the Bath separate the nave from the aisles. In 1725, it became the chapel of the Order of the Bath (reconstituted by George I), with the Dean of Westminster its perpetual dean.

A doorway (left) leads to the north aisle, in the centre of which is the tall canopied **tomb of Elizabeth I** (d. 1603) **(18)**, erected by James I. Elizabeth rests here in the same grave as her half-sister Mary I (d. 1558); the Latin inscription translates: 'Partners in realm and tomb, here we sisters rest, Elizabeth and Mary, in hope of resurrection'. The marble figure is the work of Cornelius Cure (1605–7); Elizabeth's jewels are by the 20th-century British jeweller Sah Oved (1900–83). The east end of this aisle was called 'Innocents' Corner' by Dean Stanley, for here are commemorated two small daughters of James I (d.

1607), one represented in a cradle which is the actual tomb (the infant's effigy is seen in the mirror which has been placed opposite). In the marble urn between them, made to a design by Sir Christopher Wren, are some bones, claimed as those of the **Princes in the Tower (19)**, Edward V and his brother Richard, Duke of York, the young sons of Edward IV who disappeared from the Tower c. 1483. Edward V had been born in the Abbey sanctuary, where his mother had sought refuge from the Lancastrian faction. The Latin inscription on the urn expresses no doubt that the boys were suffocated in the Tower by order of their perfidious and usurping uncle Richard III. The jury is still out on this case.

Now proceed through oak and plated bronze doors to the **nave of the Lady Chapel**. The doors date from the 16th century and the heraldic devices that appear on them and recur elsewhere in the decoration of the chapel refer to Henry VII's ancestry and to his claims to the throne. The Welsh dragon indicates his Tudor father; the daisy (marguerite) and the portcullis refer to his Lancastrian mother, Margaret Beaufort; the falcon was the badge of Edward IV, father of Elizabeth of York, whom Henry married; the greyhound is that of the Nevilles, from whom she was descended. The crown on a bush recalls Henry's first coronation on Bosworth Field, when the defeated Richard's crown was plucked from a thorn tree; while the roses are those of Lancaster and York united by his marriage. Other emblems are the lions of England and the *fleur-de-lys* of France. On each side are the beautiful carved stalls of the Knights of the Bath, with the arms of its

successive holders emblazoned on small copper plates and the banner of the current holder suspended above. The lower seats are those of the esquires (no longer used as such) with their coats of arms. Beneath the seats are a number of carved misericords. A certain Thomas Rixon has carved his name on one of the seats on the south side.

The altar dates from 1935 but is a reconstruction of the original; the painting of the *Virgin and Child* is by the 15th-century Venetian artist Bartolomeo Vivarini. Beneath the pavement, lozenges with faded inscriptions mark the resting place of several Hanoverians, including **George II** (d. 1760; the last king buried in the abbey). Below the altar is the **grave of Edward VI** (d. 1553). Behind it, surrounded by a bronze screen, is the magnificent **tomb of Henry VII (20)** (d. 1509) and Elizabeth of York (d. 1503), an important work in marble and gilt-bronze by Pietro Torrigiano, completed c. 1518. The noble effigies of the king and queen lie on a black marble sarcophagus, with a carved frieze of white marble and adorned with gilt medallions of saints. They were the first monarchs in the abbey to be buried in a vault underground rather than above ground in a tomb chest. **James I** (d. 1625) is buried in the same vault as Henry VII and his queen. The first apse chapel on the south is filled by Le Sueur's gilt-canopied monument to **Ludovic Stuart (21)**, Duke of Lennox and Richmond (d. 1624), coloniser of Ulster and of Maine in the United States; in the next is buried **Dean Stanley (22)** (d. 1881), with a fine effigy by Boehm. Dean Stanley did much to rescue the abbey from neglect and disrepair.

The east chapel is the **Royal Air Force**

Chapel **(23)**. The window, by Hugh
Easton, commemorating the Battle of
Britain (July–Oct 1940), incorporates in
the design the badges of the 63 fighter
squadrons that took part. Flanking
the east window, two new windows
designed by Hughie O'Donoghue were
installed in 2013, to celebrate the 60th
anniversary of the coronation of Queen
Elizabeth II. Chiefly of rich blues, a
colour traditionally associated with
the Virgin Mary, the windows depict
emblems of the Virgin including stars
and lilies. The chapel keeps the Roll of
Honour (facsimile in adjoining chapel)
of the 1,497 airmen of Britain and her
allies who fell in the battle. Nearby is the
grave of Lord Dowding (d. 1970), who
commanded the air defence of Great
Britain, and on the south side is that of
Lord Trenchard (d. 1956), 'father' of the
RAF. In this chapel **Oliver Cromwell** (d.
1658) was buried (stone at entrance),
only to be exhumed after the Restoration
and symbolically hung at Tyburn. His
head was struck off and afterwards
exposed on Westminster Hall (*see also
Red Lion Square, p. 385*).

In the next chapel is a vault (usually
covered with an organ) with the graves
of **Anne of Denmark (24)** (d. 1619),
queen of James I, and Anne Mowbray,
the child wife of Richard, Duke of
York, the younger of the Princes in the
Tower. Anne died at the age of eight;
her remains were reburied here in 1965
(*see p. 104*). In the last chapel is the large
tomb by Le Sueur of **George, Duke of
Buckingham (25)**, the favourite of James
I and Charles I, assassinated in 1628,
with statues of his children by Nicholas
Stone.

In the south aisle is the tomb of
Margaret, Countess of Lennox (28)

(d. 1578). Her son, Henry Darnley, was
the second husband of Mary, Queen of
Scots and father of James I of England,
and his figure among the effigies of her
children on the sides of the tomb may be
identified by the (restored) crown over
his head (as Henry I of Scotland). Under
a tall canopy is the recumbent figure of
Mary, Queen of Scots (27) (1542–87),
whose remains were removed here from
Peterborough Cathedral in 1612 by
order of her son, James I. The work of
Cornelius and William Cure (1605–10),
this was the last royal tomb erected in
Westminster Abbey.

The tomb of **Margaret Beaufort,
Countess of Richmond (28)** (d. 1509),
mother of Henry VII, patron of Wynkyn
de Worde and founder of Christ's and
St John's colleges at Cambridge, has a
beautiful gilded effigy, a masterpiece by
Pietro Torrigiano of Florence, noted for
the delicate modelling of the deceased's
aging hands.

Chapel of Edward the Confessor: The
Chapel of St Edward the Confessor is
the most ancient, the most gorgeous
and the most sacred part of the church.
Visiting it is therefore restricted but
from the north and south ambulatories
one can peep in and recognise the
monuments. In the middle stands the
mutilated Cosmatesque **Shrine of St
Edward the Confessor (29)** (d. 1066),
erected in the late 13th century by 'Peter
of Rome', possibly the son of Odoricus,
who designed the floor of the sanctuary,
and showing traces of the original
mosaics. The upper part, now of wood
(1557), was originally a golden shrine
decorated with jewels and gold images
of saints, all of which disappeared at the
Dissolution. In the recesses of the base,

Tomb of Mary, Queen of Scots, in the Lady Chapel of Westminster Abbey.

sick people used to spend the night in hope of a cure.

On the south side of the shrine is the tomb of **Philippa of Hainault (30)** (d. 1369), wife of Edward III, with an alabaster effigy by Hennequin de Liège, a favourite sculptor of King Charles V of France. The elaborate **tomb of Edward III (31)** (d. 1377) has niches in which were statuettes of his 14 children, six of which remain (seen from south ambulatory). The last tomb on this side is that of **Richard II (34)** (d. 1400) and his first wife Anne of Bohemia (d. 1394), which is in the same style as that of Edward III. Their tomb was the first double royal tomb and they were originally depicted holding hands, at Richard's request, but their hands have long been broken. It is profusely decorated with delicately engraved patterns, among which may be distinguished the broom-pods of the Plantagenets, the white hart, the rising sun, etc. The beautiful paintings in the canopy represent the *Trinity*, the *Coronation of the Virgin*, and Anne of Bohemia's coat of arms.

At the west end is a beautiful **screen** (mid-15th century) with 14 scenes of the life of Edward the Confessor. In front are remains of the Cosmati pavement.

On the north side is the plain altar-tomb, without effigy, of **Edward I (33)** (d. 1307); in 1744 his body (6ft 2in long) was found to be in good preservation, dressed in royal robes with a gilt crown. Beyond are the Gothic tombs of **Henry III (34)** (d. 1272) and his daughter-in-law, **Eleanor of Castile (35)** (d. 1290), wife of Edward I. Both the bronze effigies, the earliest cast in England, are by William Torel, a London goldsmith.

South ambulatory: The **Chapel of St Nicholas (36)**, off the south ambulatory, is the vault of the Dukes of Northumberland, the only family with right of sepulture in the abbey.

The **Chapel of SS Edmund and Thomas the Martyr (37)** is separated from the ambulatory by an ancient oak screen and entered across a worn threshold. Inside to the right lies William de Valence, 1st Earl of Pembroke (d. 1296), half-brother of Henry III. This is the only example in England of champlevé Limoges enamel on a monument. The seated figure of Lady Elizabeth Russell (d. 1601), with her eyes closed and her foot upon a skull, is the earliest non-recumbent statue in the abbey. Beside the door is the tomb of John of Eltham (1316–37), second son of Edward II. This is the earliest alabaster effigy in the abbey and is interesting for the careful representation of the prince's armour. Opposite the entrance to this chapel is the outer side of Edward III's tomb, with finely worked little brass statuettes of his children, with enamelled coats of arms. The back of Richard II's tomb is also well seen.

South transept: The south transept is known as **Poets' Corner**, taking its name originally from the tombs of Chaucer and Spenser. Those commemorated here—now numbering over 100 writers and other creative artists—are chosen by the Deans of Westminster. Poets' Corner is officially full and the Abbey has further memorials in the two transept windows. The first to be unveiled (in 1996) commemorates the poet A.E. Housman (d. 1936). Memorials have also overflowed into the south end of the central aisle and John Betjeman

(d. 1984), former Poet Laureate, was squeezed in in 1996 with a small silver tablet on a pillar. On the end wall of the transept are two magnificent wall-paintings of *St Christopher* and *The Incredulity of St Thomas*, outstanding examples of the Westminster school of painting. Uncovered in 1936, they are ascribed to Walter of Durham (c. 1280).

There are too many memorials to enumerate. Those mentioned below are either actual burials or monuments of artistic importance: the bust of John Dryden (d. 1700; buried here) is by Scheemakers and that of William Blake (d. 1827) by Epstein. The Gothic **tomb of Geoffrey Chaucer (38)** (d. 1400), the poet of the *Canterbury Tales*, was erected 155 years after his death, though probably more because he was the Clerk to the King's Work and lived in the Abbey precincts than recognised as a poet. In front of Chaucer's tomb is the grave of Robert Browning (d. 1889) and a bust of Tennyson (d. 1892; also buried here).

Rysbrack's memorial to **John Milton (39)** (d. 1674) was only placed here in 1737, having been delayed by political feeling for over 60 years after the poet's death. Dr Samuel Johnson (d. 1784; buried here) is commemorated with a bust by Nollekens. The actors David Garrick and Henry Irving are also buried here, as are the ashes of Sir Laurence Olivier. Noël Coward, Dame Peggy Ashcroft and Sir John Gielgud, who was educated across the street at Westminster School, are also remembered here.

William Shakespeare (40) (d. 1616) is commemorated with a statue by Scheemakers, erected in 1740 with lines from *The Tempest*. At the corners of the pedestal are carved heads representing Elizabeth I, Henry V and Richard III. James Thomson (d. 1748), who wrote the words of 'Rule Britannia', is commemorated in a fine monument designed by Robert Adam. Above the door to the Chapel of St Faith is a portrait medallion by Nollekens of Oliver Goldsmith (1728–74; date of birth given wrongly in the epitaph), with an epitaph by Johnson.

The roster of famous names continues to the right of the chapel and includes John Ruskin (d. 1900), with a memorial roundel by Onslow Ford. Ruskin declined the offer of a Westminster Abbey funeral and was buried at his home at Coniston in the Lake District. The monument to **John Campbell, 2nd Duke of Argyll (41)** (d. 1743) is an exceptionally fine work by Roubiliac. Above on the west wall is Handel (d. 1759), also by Roubiliac, holding the script of *Messiah* (a slab in the floor marks his grave, and one beside it that of Charles Dickens). Also in the floor is a tablet commemorating Thomas Hardy (d. 1928), whose ashes are interred here, and the grave of Rudyard Kipling (d. 1936). Other memorials include Ted Hughes, Philip Larkin and C.S. Lewis.

South aisle: Opposite the east door into the cloisters is a good monument in black marble to **Sir Thomas Richardson (42)** (d. 1635), by Le Sueur. In his capacity as Chief Justice, Richardson refused to allow the assassin of the Duke of Buckingham (also buried here; no 25) to be tortured on the rack. Further on is a monument by Rysbrack to Sir Godfrey Kneller (d. 1723), the only painter commemorated in the Abbey. In the third bay is a tablet to William Tyndale (d. 1536), translator of the Bible. Under the organ loft is a monument to

Thomas Thynne **(43)** (d. 1682), with a bas-relief depicting his murder (he was shot in Haymarket in a love feud). Commemorated further on is **Major John André (44)** (d. 1780), hanged by Washington as a spy during the War of American Independence; the bas-relief shows Washington receiving André's vain petition for a soldier's death. Floor-slabs in front of the next bay mark the graves of Andrew Bonar Law (d. 1923) and Neville Chamberlain (d. 1944), prime ministers.

Above the West Cloister door is a dramatic monument by Roubiliac to **Field-Marshal George Wade (45)** (d. 1748), who provided the Scottish Highlands with roads and bridges in 1720–30. In the last bay is a small gallery of oak called the **Abbot's Pew** **(46)**, erected by Abbot Islip (16th century), and below, a memorial to the dramatist William Congreve (d. 1729).

On the first nave pier hangs a **portrait of Richard II (47)**, the oldest contemporary portrait of an English monarch. **St George's Chapel (48)** (*no entry*) is dedicated to all who gave their lives in the World Wars and contains a tablet to the million British dead. Here is the **Coronation Chair**, made in oak by Walter of Durham c. 1300–1. It has left the Abbey only three times: when Cromwell was installed as Lord Protector in Westminster Hall, and for safety during the two World Wars. It enclosed the famous Stone of Scone (*see below*), carried off from Scotland by Edward I in 1297 and used for all subsequent coronations of English monarchs.

THE STONE OF SCONE

This historic block of sandstone, on which all kings of Scotland were crowned from time immemorial down to John Balliol (1292), was traditionally identified with Jacob's pillow, upon which he rested his head when he had his famous dream, afterwards transported to Ireland, where it became the *Lia Fail* or 'Stone of Destiny' on the sacred hill of Tara. Historically it is recorded as being used for the enthronement of Macbeth's stepson at Scone in 1057, and was certainly in use there earlier. It was seized by Edward I, 'Hammer of the Scots', in 1297, and taken to London, where it was built into the Coronation Chair. Its sacred property as the *palladium*, or safeguard, of Scottish independence was supposed to have been vindicated when James VI of Scotland became James I of England in 1603. In 1996, the British Government ordered the stone's removal to Edinburgh Castle, with the provision that it should return to Westminster Abbey for future coronations. It was accordingly returned for the coronation of Charles III in 2023 and is now back in Edinburgh Castle.

CHAPTER HOUSE AND PYX CHAMBER

Entrance to the cloisters is by two doors from the south aisle. From them you have good views of the abbey's flying buttresses. The East Walk leads to the Chapter House, Pyx Chamber and Abbey Museum. The **Chapter House** is an impressive octagonal room,

56ft in diameter, built c. 1245–55 above the crypt of the Confessor's chapter house. The lofty roof is supported by a single central shaft, 35ft high, and it is lit by six huge windows. The tracery, like the roof, is modern, though copied from the blank window which escaped mutilation in the Reformation. The tiling at the centre is original. The arcading on the walls is adorned with medieval paintings (partly restored) of the life of St John and of the Apocalypse, with a frieze of animals below, presented by John of Northampton (1372–1404), a Westminster monk. The beautiful *Angel Gabriel* and *Virgin Annunciate* above the door date from 1250–3. The Chapter House is especially memorable as the 'cradle of representative and constitutional government throughout the world', for here the early House of Commons, separated from the House of Lords in the reign of Edward III, held its meetings until 1547, when it moved to St Stephen's Chapel at the Palace of Westminster. On your return to the cloister, note the wooden door on your left (c. 1050); the oldest door in London.

The **Pyx Chamber** is entered through a Norman archway and massive double door; each door has three locks. It was part of the 11th-century undercroft beneath the monks' dormitory and became the royal treasury in the 13th century. The altar is the oldest in the abbey. The word 'pyx' comes from the Greek word for box and refers to the wooden boxes in which silver and gold coins were kept before the 'Trial of the Pyx' when they were melted to test their purity.

THE QUEEN'S DIAMOND JUBILEE GALLERIES

The Abbey's greatest treasures are displayed in the 13th-century triforium, 52ft above the Abbey floor, once the Abbey's 'attic' where all manner of unwanted items were stored. Access is through the star-shaped **Weston Tower**, designed by Ptolemy Dean, Surveyor of the Fabric (*admission by timed ticket; stairs or lift*). Traditional and modern building materials have been sensitively used to blend in with the Abbey's Gothic architecture. The climb up the oak staircase is relieved by stunning views of the Palace of Westminster and the Chapter House through the hundreds of specially treated leaded-light windows; 12th-century fragments of glass found during excavation and conversion of the triforium have been incorporated in the windows between the Weston Tower lift and the galleries, merging old with new. The galleries were designed by MUMA (McInnes Usher McKnight Architects) and opened in June 2018. This is the first major addition to the Abbey for more than 250 years.

The galleries house some 300 objects covering 1,000 years of the Abbey's history and from them there are views down to the Great West Door and the Cosmati pavement. A **Roman sarcophagus** of c. AD 300–400, discovered in the Abbey's North Green, was probably from one of the city's Roman cemeteries and is one of only four inscribed coffins from that period found in the city. It was used for two burials: that of a wealthy Roman officer and later, in c. AD 900–1000, that of a Saxon monk or nobleman. A **scale model of the Abbey**, dating from 1714–16, shows it with a tower and spire at the crossing. It was commissioned by Sir Christopher Wren from the Abbey workshop and was an aid as he developed his plans. Had the tower been built, it would have measured 365ft, making it the tallest in London at that time. The **Westminster Retable**, richly painted and decorated, is the oldest altarpiece in England (c. 1270).

The surviving exquisite paintings depict St Peter, the Virgin, St John the Evangelist and some of the miracles of Christ. The **Litlyngton Missal** is a beautiful Latin manuscript, finely decorated using coloured inks and gold leaf. It was made between 1383 and 1384 and was the work of four craftsmen.

The Abbey's association with the monarchy is dramatically illustrated in the collection of **royal effigies**. These were wooden, and later wax, images of the monarch, used during the lying-in-state and laid on top of the coffin as it made its journey to the Abbey. Henry VII's bust, a painted gesso death mask applied over wood, is a powerfully realistic and skilled likeness (the death mask was the source for Pietro Torrigiano's celebrated terracotta sculpture of the King in the V&A; *see p. 339*). The **wax effigy of Nelson**, made while he was still alive rather than from a death mask, was modelled by Catherine Andras (1775–1860), a skilled and well-known worker in the medium, although the great admiral is shown blind in his left eye rather than his right. Emma Hamilton was satisfied with the likeness, however, once she had tweaked the hero's hair into the style he favoured. Nelson is dressed in some of his own clothes, including the shoe buckles he wore at the Battle of Trafalgar. Although he was buried in St Paul's, his effigy, like that of William Pitt, was made to attract visitors to the Abbey and to generate income.

VICTORIA EMBANKMENT

Map p. 635, F2. Underground: Westminster.

Victoria Embankment, which runs east from Westminster Bridge to Blackfriars Bridge, was completed in 1870 to a design by the civil engineer Sir Joseph Bazalgette. Bazalgette reclaimed 37½ acres of land to construct a road with a dual purpose: to relieve traffic congestion in the Strand and Fleet Street and to carry sewage beneath it. Previously all waste and effluent ran into the Thames and cholera was rife. Crisis was reached in 1858 when a scorching summer caused the unspeakable 'Great Stink', which was suffered acutely in Central London. The smell of the polluted Thames was so disgusting that MPs were driven from the House of Commons. From 1859 construction started and after completion around 1875, London's drinking water and riverscape were purified. Bazalgette's subterranean sewer network was a true wonder of the Victorian age and still serves London today, thanks to his deliberately extravagant pipe widths. As he rightly predicted, 'there's always the unseen'.

The section of Victoria Embankment described here is the stretch from Westminster Bridge to Charing Cross station. For Victoria Embankment Gardens, see p. 200.

Westminster Bridge was designed by Thomas Page in 1862. On the left-hand side of it is Thornycroft's **statue of Boudica** and her two daughters, driving her chariot (without reins) to victory against the Romans. Below is Westminster Pier, with boat services up and down river. Down by the water is the **Battle of Britain Monument**.

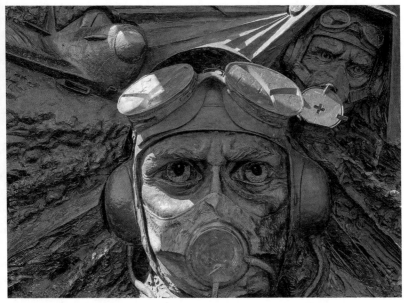

Detail of the Battle of Britain Monument (Paul Day, 2005), commemorating the aviators who fought the Luftwaffe in 1940.

Commemorating all those who took to the skies in defence of Britain from the Luftwaffe, it was unveiled in 2005 on the 65th anniversary of the battle. Overlooking the Thames at Whitehall Stairs is the **RAF Memorial**, a large gilded eagle on top of a Portland stone pylon, poised to fly ('I bare you on eagle's wings and brought you unto myself', *Exodus 19*), by William Reid Dick.

Lining the Embankment above the road are government office buildings. The corner site is occupied by **Portcullis House** (2001) on top of Westminster Underground station, its great bronze chimneys giving it the air of a neo-Tudor parliamentary factory. Next door, the pair of neo-Gothic buildings in red and white banded brick, the Norman Shaw Buildings (1887–1906), are named after the architect who built them. Curtiss Green Building is now the headquarters of the Metropolitan Police (the Met), with its iconic revolving sign.

Outside the Modernist Ministry of Defence building, in the somewhat clunkily-named 'Victoria Embankment Gardens, Whitehall Extension', the **Chindit Memorial** commemorates those who fought in North Burma during WWII. Surmounting the plinth is a mythical *chinthe*, the beast that guards Burmese temples and also features on the badge of the units. A blue plaque with the badge also carries the Chindit motto: 'The boldest measures are the safest'. Beyond the statue to Air Marshall Lord Hugh Trenchard (1873–1956), founder of the Royal Air Force, is the **Korean War Memorial**. The bronze statue of a British soldier, head bowed, stands in front of a Portland stone obelisk on a base of Welsh slate. It was the gift of the Government of South Korea and was unveiled in 2014. Nearby stands the hauntingly beautiful **Fleet Air Arm Memorial**, *Daedalus*, a slender stone column with a bronze statue of a naval airman, complete with helmet, flying suit and wings strapped to his arms, as though about to take flight. On the further corner are the fragmentary remains (reconstructed) of **Queen Mary's Steps**, part of a river terrace built for Mary II by Wren in 1691–3. In the 17th century, the steps would have provided direct access from the royal barge to Whitehall Palace.

The green stretch beyond Horse Guards Avenue is **Whitehall Gardens**, laid out in 1875 by Vulliamy. Overlooking the gardens is the elaborate, late 19th-century neo-Gothic façade of **Whitehall Court** (when viewed from the Blue Bridge in St James's Park it looks like every little girl's fantasy of a fairytale castle), with Alfred Waterhouse's **National Liberal Club** (1887) at one end. The major part, by Archer & Green (1892), was built as luxury flats and includes the five-star Horseguards Hotel. In front of Whitehall Gardens is a monument to Samuel Plimsoll (d. 1898), inventor of the Plimsoll Line, erected 'in grateful recognition of his services to the men of the sea of all nations'.

Over the road, in the river wall, is a **bust of Sir Joseph Bazalgette**, the Embankment engineer (George Simonds, 1899). Moored here are the *Tattersall Castle*, a Clyde paddle-steamer, now a pub, and the *Hispaniola*, a restaurant.

WHITEHALL

Map p. 635, F2. Underground: Westminster.

Whitehall, a name which has become the by-word for British governmental administration, is the wide boulevard that stretches for half a mile from Parliament Square to Charing Cross. It is lined on both sides by government offices and ministries. On this site, from the river to St James's Park, stretched Henry VIII's Palace of Whitehall, which burned down in 1698; today only archaeological fragments and Inigo Jones's Banqueting House remain from the great complex.

To explore Whitehall, start from Parliament Street—where tourists fall over themselves to photograph each other posing in old-fashioned red telephone boxes, historic London relics in their own right—and walk up towards Nelson's Column.

On your left are grandiose government complexes; the corner building overlooking Parliament Street and Parliament Square is the **Treasury** (Brydon, 1917), which connects via a bridge over King Charles Street to Sir George Gilbert Scott's **Foreign Office** of 1868. The building, in Inigo Jones style, covers 5½ acres. When the British Empire was at its height, it incorporated the Foreign Office, the India Office, the Colonial Office and the Home Office. During World War Two, a sprawling underground network of concrete-reinforced, bomb-proof rooms was built for Churchill's War Cabinet underneath the portion of these buildings that overlooks St James's Park. These now form an exhibition called the Churchill War Rooms (*see below*).

HISTORY OF OLD WHITEHALL PALACE

Whitehall Palace originated in a mansion purchased in 1240 by Walter de Grey, Archbishop of York, which became the London residence of his successors for nearly 300 years. When Cardinal Wolsey became archbishop, he embellished the palace (on the river side) with characteristic extravagance and Henry VIII seized the desirable property in 1529. He changed its name from York Place to Whitehall (a name then generally applied to any centre of festivities) and acquired more land towards St James's Park, on which he erected a tiltyard, cockpit and tennis courts. Whitehall became the chief residence of the court in London. Anne Boleyn was brought here on the day of her marriage to Henry in 1533 and in 1536 it was the scene of Henry's marriage to Jane Seymour. Henry died in the palace in 1547.

Masques by Ben Jonson, with sets by Inigo Jones and James Shirley, were frequently presented at the court in the time of James I and Charles I. Plans for a huge and sumptuous new palace for James I, drawn up by Inigo Jones and John Webb, were never carried out although the new Banqueting House (*described on p. 155*) was completed in 1622. Charles I was executed in front of it in 1649. Oliver Cromwell died in the palace in 1658. Under Charles II, Whitehall became the centre of revelry and intrigue described by Pepys, and James II fled into exile from here in 1688. The offering of the Crown to William and Mary provided the last great ceremonial function here in 1689. In 1698 the palace was accidentally burned to the ground and the royal residence was transferred to St James's Palace (*see p. 165*).

CHURCHILL WAR ROOMS

'This is the room from which I will direct the war,' announced Churchill on first visiting the Cabinet War Rooms, which are located 10ft underground, with reinforced concrete above—hence the nickname, 'The Slab' (*map p. 635, F2; admission charge; café; iwm. org.uk/visits/churchill-war-rooms*). Access is from Horse Guards Road by the Clive Steps, which has a statue of Clive of India and the Bali Memorial, commemorating those killed in the Bali bombings of October 2002.

Constructed between June 1938 and August 1939, and only completed a week before Britain's declaration of war, these rooms were the operations headquarters from which Britain's Second World War effort was directed during air raids. Much is still as it was during that time. The wall maps in the **Map Room**, for example, are punctured with pin marks representing the movements of the Allied convoys; and on a desk sit the variously coloured phones known as the 'beauty chorus', which connected the bunker to control rooms around the country. The **Transatlantic Telephone Room** was where Churchill spoke in private to President Roosevelt. The small permanent exhibition entitled 'Undercover: Life in Churchill's Bunker', tells of the day-to-day life of the people who often worked 16-hour shifts here, and includes **Churchill's office-cum-bedroom**, next to the Map Room, from which he made his four wartime broadcasts, though he seldom actually slept here. His wife Clementine's sitting-room is also preserved, with a comfy-looking chintz armchair, dressing table and washstand, and there is a rather spartan-looking **kitchen**, evidence of the domestic arrangements for everyone who worked here. Through oral histories and filmed interviews there are personal reminiscences, for example from Elizabeth Layton, one of Churchill's private secretaries and author of the memoir *Mr Churchill's Secretary* (1958). She recalls the wartime leader's towering greatness and character flaws in equal measure. The **Churchill Museum** documents Churchill's life, from young reporter, maverick politician, to wartime leader and latterly Cold War statesman.

DOWNING STREET
Tucked away behind wrought-iron gates (and a strong police presence), this narrow street (*map p. 635, F2*), built in the 1680s by Sir George Downing (a member of the first class to graduate from Harvard in 1642; later a profiteering soldier and diplomat who served both Cromwell and Charles II), is famous out of all proportion to its appearance as the residence of the British Prime Ministers since 1735. **No. 10 Downing St** became the property of the Crown in 1732 and George II offered it as a gift to Sir Robert Walpole, who accepted it for his office as First Lord of the Treasury. From that day it became the official residence of the Prime Minister, although many in the early years preferred to live in their own—often far grander—houses. William Kent redesigned the interior in 1732 and further alterations were made by Sir John Soane, who designed the impressive State Dining Room. The narrow front of the building belies its size; it is really two amalgamated houses containing 160 rooms and offices as well as the Prime Minister's private apartments. **No. 11 Downing St** became the residence of the Second Lord of the Treasury, the Chancellor of the Exchequer, in 1805.

Before Downing Street became the official residence of the Prime Minister, other well-known people lived in it, including James Boswell, who took lodgings here in 1762, and Tobias Smollett, who set up a doctor's practice here c. 1745–8.

WHITEHALL FROM THE CENOTAPH TO BANQUETING HOUSE
In the middle of Whitehall rises the **Cenotaph** (1920), Lutyens's monument to the Glorious Dead of the First World War. In its dignified simplicity it now commemorates the dead from all wars and is the UK's national war memorial. Every year the Remembrance Day ceremony takes place on the Sunday nearest to 11th November (Armistice Day). Members of the Royal Family, the Government and Opposition and other representatives lay poppy wreaths around the Cenotaph, and two minutes' silence are observed. Just beyond is the national monument to the Women of World War II, unveiled in 2005.

At no. 70 Whitehall, the 19th-century building with the Corinthian order and ornamental frieze is the **Cabinet Office** and former Treasury by Sir Charles Barry (1844–7), incorporating earlier parts by Sir John Soane and William Kent as well as excavated relics of Whitehall Palace, including Henry VIII's tennis courts. Next door, the Palladian **Dover House** is used by the Scotland Office. Designed in 1758 by James Paine for Sir Matthew Featherstonhaugh, it was remodelled by Henry Holland (portico

Horse Guards in the rain, with the mounted sentries of the Household Cavalry under the twin archways.

and dome) for Prince Frederick, Duke of York in 1792, then belonged to the Melbourne family until 1830. Opposite, in the middle of the road, is an equestrian statue of the First World War commander Earl Haig (d. 1928), erected in 1937.

The colossal **Ministry of Defence building**, headquarters of the British Armed Forces (E. Vincent Harris, 1939–59), dominates the east side of Whitehall as well as the river view. Inside are the remains of Cardinal Wolsey's wine cellar, later appropriated by Henry VIII. In front are statues of Field Marshals Montgomery (Oscar Nemon, 1980), Alanbrooke (Ivor Roberts-Jones, 1993) and Slim (with binoculars; Ivor Roberts-Jones, 1990). The main entrance is in Horse Guards Avenue (behind Banqueting House), flanked by colossal sculptures, *Earth* and *Water* (Sir Charles Wheeler, 1949–52).

Next door is the attractive **Gwydyr House** (1772), the Welsh Office; and then the only surviving part of Whitehall Palace: the Banqueting House (*described on p. 155*).

HORSE GUARDS PARADE

Opposite Banqueting House is **Horse Guards**, a white stone Palladian building with a central arch surmounted by a clock tower, built in the 1750s by William Robinson and John Vardy, influenced by the designs of William Kent. It is the official entrance from Whitehall to St James's Palace, via St James's Park, and the headquarters of the London District of the British Army and of the Household Cavalry. Two mounted troopers of the Life Guards or Royal Horse Guards (Blues and Royals) are posted here daily and there are two dismounted sentries within the archway. The former are relieved hourly, the latter every two hours (no doubt a welcome relief, as they are nearly always surrounded by tourists taking photos). During the Changing of the Guard, the guard on duty is relieved by a new guard of twelve men who troop in via the Mall.

The passage beneath the clock tower is the entrance to **Horse Guards Parade**, a wide parade ground on the fringes of St James's Park, formerly Henry VIII's tiltyard and the site of the celebrations held for Elizabeth I's birthday. In May and June the Parade Ground is used for the ceremonies of Beating the Retreat, when military music and parades are performed under floodlights in the early evening, and Trooping the Colour, the Sovereign's Official Birthday parade in June (*see p. 584*). The **Household Cavalry Museum** is also here (*householdcavalry.co.uk*), with displays on the history and day-to-day work of the King's mounted bodyguard, the focus of interest being on both the people and the horses.

Straight ahead is the **Guards' Monument** (1925–6). On the right-hand side, the vast neo-Wren wing in red brick and white stone with green copper domes is the **Admiralty extension** (1888–1905), connected to Admiralty Arch (*see p. 156*). On your left are the high-walled gardens of Downing Street and statues of Kitchener by John Tweed and Earl Mountbatten of Burma by Franta Belsky.

In front of the Horse Guards archway are two equestrian statues and the **Cadiz Memorial**, a huge mortar from Cadiz presented by the Spanish Government in 1814, mounted on the back of a winged dragon.

WHITEHALL FROM HORSE GUARDS TO CHARING CROSS

Beyond Horse Guards are more vast government complexes. The huge building with façades on Whitehall and Horse Guards Avenue is the **former War Office** (William Young, 1906). The building just before Great Scotland Yard is the **former Ministry of Agriculture and Fisheries** (John Murray, 1909).

Great Scotland Yard itself was the location of the headquarters of the Metropolitan Police until 1891. The street name originates from a mansion occupied before the 15th century by the kings of Scotland and their ambassadors when in London. Members of the retinue of James I are thought to have had their first kirk here. In popular parlance and crime fiction, Scotland Yard stands for anything connected with London policing and detective work.

Further up Whitehall, in the centre of the road, is a lifesize equestrian statue of George, Duke of Cambridge, a grandson of George III. It stands between the brown brick **former Paymaster General's Office** (John Lane, 1733) and the massive neo-Baroque **Old War Office**. Built in 1906 to designs by William Young, the latter building functioned as the War Office during both world wars and the Cold War: Asquith, Lloyd-George, Lawrence of Arabia and Winston Churchill all once worked here. It is now a Raffles hotel, the OWO (*theowo.london*).

On the left is the **Old Admiralty** or Ripley Building (Thomas Ripley, 1723–8), with a tall classical portico, its courtyard masked from the street by a Tuscan colonnaded screen with two seahorses (Robert Adam, 1760–1). This was the Admiralty of Nelson's time and it is here that his body lay in state in 1805.

BANQUETING HOUSE

The Banqueting House (*map p. 635, F2; hrp.org.uk*), on the corner of Whitehall and Horse Guards Avenue, is the most complete remnant of the old Whitehall Palace, the principal residence and seat of government of the Tudor and Stuart monarchy. The residential part was almost totally destroyed in a fire in 1698 but the Banqueting House was saved. In recent years, access to the public has been greatly curtailed (*see the website for open days*).

ARCHITECTURE AND HISTORY OF THE BANQUETING HOUSE

Erected in 1619–22, the building was conceived as a setting for formal spectacles and grand court ceremonies. The design was entrusted to the great architect Inigo Jones, whose approach to architecture, based on Classical Roman models, the mathematical principles of Vitruvius and the geometrically proportioned designs of Palladio, was revolutionary in Britain. Jones's strict use of the orders, Ionic below and Corinthian above, and of alternate triangular and segmental window pediments, produced a rational, measured and dignified building of tremendous impact. Externally the building has been altered: sash windows were installed in 1713 and in the 19th century it was given a Portland stone façade. Internally, however, it has been restored to how it would have appeared in early Stuart times, the double cube proportions of its main hall upstairs providing a fitting stage for state occasions. It was here that the sovereign touched for the King's Evil, an ancient ceremony performed for those with scrofula (last performed by Queen Anne; Samuel Johnson was a beneficiary); and it was also where the Maundy Thursday ritual of the washing of the feet of the poor and distribution of money was performed by the monarch. After the 1698 fire, William III had the building converted into the Chapel Royal, a function it retained until the 1890s. It is now used for formal royal and state occasions and banquets.

The main hall

The hall is approached by the main stairway, added in 1808–9 by James Wyatt to replace the original timber structure. Though the stairs are not the same as in Stuart days, the window aperture is the very one through which, on 30th January 1649, King Charles I was led out to the scaffold, built up against the exterior wall.

The king and court would enter the main hall at the north end, where the throne, under its symbolic canopy of state, was erected. The public was admitted from the south (still the case today). The glory of the hall is its magnificent painted ceiling.

Peter Paul Rubens, an artist already fêted by the courts of Europe and whom the Stuart monarchy was eager to engage, was commissioned in 1629–30. He presented to Charles I his great painting *Peace and War* (now in the National Gallery), was knighted, and then set to work on the nine Banqueting House canvases on his return to Antwerp. The completed works were installed by 1636 (Rubens was paid the princely sum of

£3,000 and never saw them *in situ*). Their theme was the glorification of the peaceful rule of James I: the canvases are filled with the kind of heavy allegory of wise and beneficent rule that was so popular at the courts of France, Italy and the Vatican but had yet to be seen in Britain. As you enter from the south, you are immediately struck by the central oval, the *Apotheosis of James I*, the king borne heavenwards by Religion and Justice, his temporal crown carried by putti while Minerva (Wisdom) holds out a wreath of laurel. Above the throne, visible the right way round to the visitor entering from the south, is the *Benefits of the Government of James I*. Peace and Plenty embrace, Minerva defends the throne against Mars (War). On either side are ovals with the *Triumph of Reason over Discord* and *Triumph of Abundance over Avarice*. At the north end, visible to the king seated on his throne, is the *Union of England and Scotland*, showing James I gesturing towards a child, the new-born fruit of the two countries' union, while Britannia holds the joined crowns above the monarch's head. To left and right are *Minerva driving Rebellion to Hell* and *Hercules beating down Envy*.

On the installation of the canvases, the Banqueting House ceased to stage court masques or theatrical spectacles which involved flaming or smoking torches.

THE MALL

Map p. 635, F2–E2. Underground: Embankment, Charing Cross.

The Mall is the spacious avenue lined with double rows of plane trees that skirts St James's Park on the north, exactly half a nautical mile from Admiralty Arch to the Victoria Monument in front of Buckingham Palace. It is London's only parade route, its pink tarmac a little like a red carpet (on official occasions barriers go up along the pavements), and it also provides an impressive finish for the London Marathon each spring. At the weekend this area is relatively quiet (*it is closed to traffic on Sun*), though full of visitors strolling in the park and along The Mall.

The sweeping curve of **Admiralty Arch** forms an impressive entrance to The Mall. This massive triumphal arch was designed by Sir Aston Webb as part of the national memorial to Queen Victoria, and was completed in 1912. It is on the processional route from Buckingham Palace to Whitehall and the City; the central archway is only used by royalty, while ordinary traffic passes through the two outer archways. From the arch there is a striking view down the 'triumphal avenue' to the Victoria Memorial and Buckingham Palace, which close the vista. This was once the official residence of the First Sea Lord, and it was used by the Admiralty for offices until 2011. The following year it was sold by the government and at the time of writing was being redeveloped as a luxury hotel.

The brown, bunker-like building on the left, covered in Virginia creeper, is the **'Citadel'**, a 'Cubist fortress' built in 1941–2 as an extension to the Admiralty to provide bomb-proof protection for the communications room. Across the footpath,

The Apotheosis of James I by Rubens, in the Banqueting House. The King looks distinctly wary as Justice manhandles him into position to receive the wreath of laurel borne by Minerva.

on the corner of the Mall and Horse Guards Road, is the **National Police Memorial**, commemorating more than 5,000 officers killed in the line of duty. Designed by Norman Foster and unveiled in 2005, it is incorporated into a ventilation shaft of the Bakerloo Line which cannot be removed. It consists of two elements: a large black rectangular block in which the roll of honour is displayed behind glass; and a tall glass stele, internally lit and standing in a reflecting pool. The bluish light it emits is said to be a reference to the blue lamp which traditionally hangs outside all police stations. This was the first memorial to be placed in St James's Park for 100 years.

On the other side of Horse Guards Road, elevated on a flight of steps, is the **South Africa Royal Artillery Memorial**, designed by W.R. Colton and commemorating the 1,083 soldiers of the Royal Artillery killed in the Second Boer War (1899–1902). A bronze horse, representing the spirit of War, is calmed and subdued by a winged figure of Peace.

Overlooking The Mall on the right is the honeysuckle-coloured stucco façade of Nash's Carlton House Terrace (*see p. 258*), once the smartest, most aristocratic address in London. Here is the entrance to the **Mall Galleries**, the exhibition space of the Federation of British Artists (*mallgalleries.org.uk*). Beyond, just before the Duke of York Steps, at Nash House (no. 12), is the **ICA** (Institute of Contemporary Arts). Founded in 1946, this organisation has a proud history of supporting living artists and launching their careers through its programme of exhibitions and films (*ica.org.uk*).

At the end of Carlton House Terrace, a double flight of steps (by De Soissons) leads to Carlton Gardens. At the top is a **statue of George VI** (W. McMillan, 1955) and below is a **statue of Queen Elizabeth, the Queen Mother** (Philip Jackson, 2009). Bronze friezes on either side of the steps (Paul Day, 2009) depict scenes from the life of the Queen Mother: on the left she and George VI are shown visiting the East End during the Blitz; on the right are vignettes of the Queen Mother as a widow, greeting members of the public, attending race meetings, and petting a beloved corgi.

MARLBOROUGH HOUSE

The Mall continues past the gardens of **Marlborough House** (*map p. 635, E2*). Built of Dutch red brick, it was designed by Christopher Wren in 1709–11 for Queen Anne's intimate friend and Mistress of the Robes, Sarah, Duchess of Marlborough, wife of the victor of Blenheim. Inside the house, on the staircase, are murals of the battles of Ramillies and Malplaquet, and in the Saloon, wall paintings of the Battle of Blenheim by Louis Laguerre. Also in the Saloon, about the cupola, is the ceiling painting *An Allegory of Peace and the Arts* (1635–8) by Orazio Gentileschi, removed from the Great Hall of the Queen's House at Greenwich. In the 19th century, Marlborough House was the home of dowager queens: Queen Adelaide (widow of William IV), Queen Alexandra (Edward VII) and Queen Mary (George V) all lived here. From 1965 it has been home to the Commonwealth Secretariat (*visits on weekdays only, secretariat. thecommonwealth.org*).

In Marlborough Road is the Symbolist **Queen Alexandra Memorial Fountain** (1932), in memory of the elegant, dignified and multiply-betrayed consort of Edward VII. It was completed by Sir Alfred Gilbert (who also made the famous '*Eros*' at

Piccadilly Circus) and was his last public work. The bronze sculpture portrays *Faith*, *Hope* and *Love* supporting an adolescent girl and leading her through the 'River of Life'; on the plinth one can read the words: 'Faith, Hope and Love: the Guiding Virtues of Queen Alexandra'.

CLARENCE HOUSE AND LANCASTER HOUSE

Back on The Mall are the entrances to two impressive mansions. **Clarence House**, in pale stucco, was built in 1825 by Nash for William IV when Duke of Clarence. It was formerly the residence of Queen Elizabeth, the Queen Mother and became the first primary London home of King Charles, while Buckingham Palace was under renovation. Next door, **Lancaster House**, dressed in Bath stone with a Corinthian portico, was built for the Duke of York by Benjamin Wyatt from 1825. After the Duke's death, it was completed in the 1830s for the Marquess of Stafford, later 1st Duke of Sutherland. Here the Sutherlands entertained lavishly until 1913 when it was bought for the nation by Lord Leverhulme. It is now an events venue managed by the Foreign and Commonwealth Office.

THE VICTORIA MEMORIAL AND CONSTITUTION HILL

The Mall's grand parade route culminates in a landscaped circus; at the centre is Aston Webb's **Victoria Memorial**. The backdrop is Buckingham Palace. The Memorial, executed by Sir Thomas Brock in 1911, shows Queen Victoria seated on the east side with groups representing *Truth*, *Motherhood* and *Justice* on the other sides, and is crowned by a gilt bronze figure of *Victory*. The tree-lined road on the right is **Constitution Hill**, said to be named after the 'constitutional' walks that Charles II used to take here in the company of his spaniels. It leads due west to Hyde Park Corner, with a sand-track for riders skirting Green Park. Here three attempts on the life of Queen Victoria were made (in 1840, 1842 and 1849), and here too, in 1850, Prime Minister Sir Robert Peel was fatally injured by a fall from his horse.

BUCKINGHAM PALACE,
THE ROYAL COLLECTION & ROYAL MEWS

Map p. 635, E2–E3. Underground: St James's Park, Victoria. Ticket office on Buckingham Palace Road. Tours from late July to end Sept each year, and sometimes in Dec and Jan—dates and details vary; rct.uk. Admission charge. Combined ticket with the Royal Collection art gallery and Royal Mews available. Garden café.

Buckingham Palace, impressively situated at the west end of the Mall, is the official residence of the British monarch (when the Sovereign is in residence, the Royal Standard flies from the roof). It is the Mall façade, from the balcony of which the monarch waves on great public occasions, that is best known to the world. A picturesque view of it, framed by trees, can be had from the bridge over the lake in nearby St James's Park. The façade dates from 1913 and was designed by Sir Aston Webb, who was also responsible for the spacious circus in front of the palace and the Victoria Memorial at its centre (*see above*). On the wide palace forecourt, behind the ornamental railings, the **Changing of the Guard** ceremony takes place (*11am, daily May–July, otherwise alternate days, weather permitting, see royal.uk or changing-guard.com*). The new guard, accompanied by a band with pipes and drums, marches from the nearby Wellington Barracks to relieve the old guard assembled on the forecourt. When the officers of the old and new guards advance and touch left hands, symbolising the handing over of the keys, the guard is 'changed'.

HISTORY AND ARCHITECTURE OF BUCKINGHAM PALACE

Buckingham Palace was originally Buckingham House, a private mansion built by John Sheffield, 1st Duke of Buckingham, in 1702–5. In 1762 it was purchased by George III and became the chief residence of Queen Charlotte, who had it enlarged and altered by Sir William Chambers. It was for George IV that the building was transformed into a palace; on his accession the new king signalled his intention to vacate his magnificent home, Carlton House, which overlooked the Mall (demolished 1826) and to rebuild Buckingham House on a grand and regal scale. Parliament voted £250,000 for the project, John Nash was the chosen architect and work began in 1825. On the king's death in 1830, with the palace still unfinished and costs having more than doubled, Nash was dismissed and Edward Blore, considered a safe pair of hands, was appointed in his place. Blore removed Nash's insubstantial and much criticised dome, added an attic storey, and in 1846–50 created the east wing across the forecourt, now hidden behind Webb's 1913 refacing. The new wing necessitated the removal of Nash's Marble Arch (*see p. 322*), designed as a ceremonial gateway to be topped by a statue of the monarch.

Tour of the palace

The tour (*approx. 1hr; visitors are free to tour the rooms at leisure, with an audio guide*) takes in the main State Rooms, the majority of them opulently conceived by Nash in the 1820s and completed by Blore. Nash's inventive interiors, with their gilded plaster ceilings, heavily decorated coves, wall hangings in richly-coloured silks and use of expensive materials (Carrara marble, gilt bronze), offered the unsurpassed grandeur sought by George IV. Many of the rooms were partially designed around the King's magnificent collection of pictures, furniture and porcelain from Carlton House, several items from which, together with other items from the Royal Collection, still furnish them.

Visitors enter the palace via the **Ambassador's Entrance** on Buckingham Gate, which leads to the courtyard behind the east wing. Here, Nash's building, in warm Bath stone, with Blore's alterations, is revealed. The sculptural theme is British sea power: in the pediment is *Britannia Acclaimed by Neptune*, designed by Flaxman, and inside Nash's two-storey columned portico is J.E. Carew's *The Progress of Navigation*. The friezes in the attic storey, *The Death of Nelson* and *The Meeting of Blücher and Wellington*, both by Westmacott, were added by Blore and were originally intended for the Marble Arch.

'They're changing guard at Buckingham Palace – Christopher Robin went down with Alice...'. Today great crowds assemble well before the ceremony is due to take place, jostling for a spot with good sightlines, smartphones at the ready.

The portico entrance leads into the **Grand Hall**, with mahogany furniture from Carlton House and Brighton Pavilion. From here, you approach the magnificent **Grand Staircase**, one straight flight leading to a landing and branching into two to the upper floor. The stairs are of Carrara marble, the intricate balustrade of gilt bronze, the work of Samuel Parker, who also made the gilt metal mounts for the mirror-plated doors which occur throughout the State Rooms.

The **Green Drawing Room**, with its deeply coved and bracketed ceiling, set off by silk hangings, is Nash's. It contains items from George IV's collection of Sèvres porcelain, the finest in the world, much of which was purchased from the French Royal Collection during the French Revolution. The **Throne Room** itself, with red silk wall hangings, was intended for investitures and ceremonial receptions. The throne (the chairs were made for Queen Elizabeth II's Coronation Ceremony of 1953) is divided from the rest of the room by a proscenium with two winged Victories holding garlands, modelled by Francis Bernasconi, the chief plasterer employed at the palace. The classical sculptural frieze, designed by Stothard, has a medieval theme: the Wars of the Roses. The **Picture Gallery**, 155ft long, is hung with works from the Royal Collection.

The **East Gallery** is the first of the rooms in the new block added by Queen Victoria in 1853–5 to designs by James Pennethorne. The interior decoration was overseen by the Prince Consort, although it is now much altered. Of the pictures usually on show, the most important is the familiar Franz Xaver Winterhalter's *Family of Queen*

Victoria (1846). The **Ballroom**, 123ft long, is where present-day investitures and other official receptions take place. The **State Dining Room** is hung with a series of full-length Hanoverian royal portraits. The room is used for official luncheons and dinners. Examples from George IV's magnificent silver-gilt service by Rundell, Bridge & Rundell are on show. The **Blue Drawing Room** is a magnificent, pure Nash interior, one of the finest in the Palace, with wide, flaring ceiling coves and coupled columns painted in imitation onyx. The delicate plasterwork reliefs show the apotheoses of Shakespeare, Spenser and Milton. The gilt sofas and armchairs are from Carlton House and the 'Table of the Grand Commanders', commissioned by Napoleon in 1806–12, with a top of hard-paste Sèvres porcelain with the head of Alexander the Great in the centre, was presented to George IV by Louis XVIII.

The **Music Room** is the most beautiful interior in the palace. Completed by Nash in 1831 and not much altered, it occupies the bow window, the central feature of Nash's west front, with views over the palace's private gardens. The large plate-glass windows were an innovation of the 1820s. The magnificent early 19th-century cut glass and gilt bronze chandeliers are from Carlton House.

The **Gardens** were landscaped by Nash and William Aiton of Kew Gardens, and include an ornamental lake, fed by the Serpentine. It is on these spacious lawns that the famous Royal Garden Parties take place. Nash's garden façade, a hidden and less familiar view of the palace, is worth a backward glance. Above the central bow is Westmacott's *Fame Displaying Britain's Triumphs*. The 'King Alfred' frieze, designed by Flaxman, is also by Westmacott.

JOHN NASH

'His style lacks grandeur, and great monotony is produced by his persistent use of stucco.' Thus the *Dictionary of National Biography* dismisses John Nash (1752–1835), the millwright's son who became one of the most distinctive of all British architects, whose grand, aspirational creations add character to much of London. There is more behind the portentous façades than meets the eye. Nash was a brilliant engineer and gifted town planner. He was chosen by the Prince Regent as architect of an ambitious project: developing a tract of former farmland into a graceful 'garden city', with a ceremonial avenue linking it with the prince's residence at Carlton House. Regent's Park, the layout of Trafalgar Square, and the graceful sweep of Regent Street (though altered since) are all legacies of this splendid scheme. When George became king, he retained Nash to transform Buckingham House into a palace of a splendour to rival Napoleon's Paris. Napoleon, by his own account, approved of what he saw, remarking that Nash had made London appear 'for the first time like a royal residence, no longer a sprawling city for shopkeepers'. Though Nash longed for a knighthood, he never received one. Wellington, the prime minister, refused to grant it so long as Buckingham Palace remained unfinished. And Nash never completed it.

THE ROYAL COLLECTION

Map p. 635, E2. Admission charge. Combined ticket with Buckingham Palace and Royal Mews available. Shop (free entry). rct.uk.

A gallery was first built here, on the site of the bomb-damaged private chapel once used by Queen Victoria, at the behest of Queen Elizabeth II and the Duke of Edinburgh. A subsequent redevelopment (John Simpson & Partners, 1998–2002), commissioned to mark Queen Elizabeth's Golden Jubilee, tripled the exhibition space. Winner of the Georgian Group Award for Best New Classical Building 2003 and described as 'high camp' by *The Guardian*, this grammatical Classical Revival gallery, partly inspired by the Greek temples at Paestum (the Doric portico and entrance hall) and the Temple of Isis in Pompeii (the garden pavilion elevation), as well as the work of Soane and Nash, is a permanent space for changing displays of objects taken from the outstanding and eclectic Royal Collection. Of particular note in the double-height entrance hall are the two winged genii bearing torches, which evidence the strong influence of Canova, and 70-ft long Homeric friezes which include allegorical representations of the Cold War (the *Iliad* panel) and the benevolent reign of Queen Elizabeth II (the *Odyssey* panel). They are all the work of Alexander Stoddart, who was Sculptor in Ordinary to The Queen in Scotland. The three main galleries are named after celebrated Neoclassical architects: Pennethorne, Nash and Chambers Gallery. Formerly known as the Queen's Gallery, the building was due at the time of writing to take the name The King's Gallery.

THE ROYAL COLLECTION

Formed through acquisitions and gifts, and held in trust for the nation by the British monarch, the Royal Collection is one of the most exquisite assemblages of fine and decorative arts in the world, and numbers over one million objects: paintings, sculpture, furniture, textiles, porcelain, clocks, miniatures, jewellery and Fabergé, books and manuscripts, maps and prints and arms and armour. Besides this gallery, where some 450 objects are on display at any one time, works from the Royal Collection are also displayed at other royal palaces and residences, national museums and galleries, on domestic touring exhibitions and on international loan exhibitions.

Though a few items date back to the reign of Henry VIII, the real origins of the collection began with Charles I, celebrated connoisseur and patron of art, who purchased part of the renowned Gonzaga collection of pictures and secured Anthony van Dyck as his court painter. Charles I's collection included works by Giulio Romano, Tintoretto, Titian, Raphael and Rubens, among many others. He acquired Raphael's important 'Acts of the Apostles' cartoons as well as Mantegna's *Triumphs of Caesar* (now at Hampton Court; *see p. 553*). Following his execution, King Charles's collection was dispersed by the Commonwealth government. However, many works were either bought back or returned to the restored Charles II by loyal supporters and constitute the core of the royal picture collection today.

The wider collection of objects is as diverse as it is large: Guido Mazzoni's *Henry VIII* (c. 1498), a terracotta bust of the boy-prince Henry; the armour of Henry VIII for the field and tilt (1539); Hans Holbein the Younger's chalk drawing of Sir Thomas More (c. 1526–7); Van Dyck's magnificent equestrian portrait of Charles I with M. de St-Antoine (1633); Vermeer's *A Lady at the Virginal with a Gentleman, 'The Music Lesson'* (c. 1662–5) and Queen Charlotte's tortoiseshell, gold and diamond notebook (c. 1765). The collection also contains gifts from Commonwealth countries, such as the Maori feather capes (*kahu kiwi*) and the 203-carat 'Andamooka' opal, presented to Queen Elizabeth II and the Duke of Edinburgh on the 1954 Royal Tour of New Zealand and Australia respectively.

THE ROYAL MEWS

Map p. 635, E3. Admission charge. Combined ticket with the Royal Collection gallery available. Shop (free entry). rct.uk.

The Royal Mews is a working department of the Royal Household, responsible for the maintenance of the Sovereign's horse-drawn carriages and other official conveyances, as well as livery, harnesses and other pieces of horse tack. Designed by Sir William Chambers in 1765–6, it was one of George III's early improvements to his new purchase, Buckingham House. The pediment was adorned in 1859 with a relief of *Hercules and the Thracian Horses*, the man-eating mares whom Hercules tamed by feeding them their master's flesh. Queen Victoria watched her nine children learn to ride here, and here royal horses are still trained to become accustomed to the sight and sounds of marching bands, crowds and flag-waving.

The **Irish State Coach** (1851) conveys the monarch to State Openings of Parliament. The **Glass State Coach** (1910) is used for royal weddings. The **Australian State Coach** (1988) is the most comfortable equipage, with electric windows, hydraulic suspension and heating. Also on display are some of the five royal **Rolls-Royce Phantoms IV to VI**. In place of the marque's 'Spirit of Ecstasy', a silver statuette designed by Edward Seago depicts St George and the Dragon.

The extraordinary **Gold State Coach** was built for George III in 1762 to a design approved by William Chambers. A fantastic showpiece designed to trumpet British sea power, the gilded body framework carved by Joseph Wilton comprises eight palm trees, each of the four corner trees rising from a lion's head and supporting trophies symbolising British victories against France in the Seven Years' War (1756–63). The body is slung on braces of morocco leather held by four gilded tritons, the front pair blowing conch shells, the winged pair behind holding trident fasces, symbols of maritime authority. Putti symbolising England, Scotland and Ireland stand at the centre of the roof, supporting the royal crown. The design of the wheels is based on those of an ancient triumphal chariot. It weighs almost four tons, requires eight horses to pull it, and has been used at every coronation since that of George IV in 1821. William IV likened the ride in it to 'a ship tossing in a rough sea'. After the death of Prince Albert, Queen Victoria refused to use it, complaining of the 'distressing oscillations'.

The **Diamond Jubilee State Coach** is the newest coach in the Mews, built to celebrate Queen Elizabeth II's Diamond Jubilee in 2012 and first used for the State

Opening of Parliament in 2014. It was made in Australia, combining traditional craftsmanship with modern technology. It has an aluminium body, balanced on six hydraulic stabilisers to prevent swaying. Panels inside were made from wood and other objects donated by 100 historic sites and organisations in the UK, including items from the royal palaces, 10 Downing Street and the Antarctic bases of Captain Scott and Sir Ernest Shackleton. The handrails are made of wood from the Royal Yacht *Britannia*, which was decommissioned in 1997. There is metal from a Spitfire, a Hawker Hurricane and a Lancaster, aircraft which played their part in the Battle of Britain, and a musket ball from the Battle of Waterloo. The friezes on the outside have representations of the emblems of the England, Wales and Scotland. On top, the gilt gold crown is of carved oak taken from HMS *Victory* with a camera hidden inside to record processions. It has only ever been used by the monarch and it was the coach which took King Charles and Queen Camilla from Buckingham Palace to Westminster Abbey for their coronation on 6th May 2023.

ST JAMES'S PALACE

Map p. 635, E2. Underground: Green Park. The public may attend services at the Chapel Royal and Queen's Chapel between Oct and Good Friday, 8.30am and 11.15am. The palace is not otherwise open to visitors. royal.uk.

The irregular brick building of St James's Palace was built by Henry VIII from 1531 on the site of a hospital for female lepers, St James-in-the-Field. The modest palace was perhaps never meant for the king himself, rather his illegitimate son Henry Fitzroy (d. 1536); however, it became the main London residence of the sovereign after Whitehall Palace burned down in 1698 and it was here that all official court functions were held. The current crenellated fabric is essentially 19th-century, but the distinctive Tudor Gatehouse overlooking St James's Street, with its polygonal towers, survives from Henry's reign, as does the Chapel Royal.

It is here that Queen Elizabeth I lodged during the crisis of the Spanish Armada and here that the marriages of George III to Charlotte of Mecklenburg-Strelitz and of Queen Victoria to Prince Albert took place. Queen Elizabeth II gave her first official speech here in 1952. Today it is the senior royal palace of the monarchy and although the sovereign has not lived here since Queen Victoria moved the royal family to Buckingham Palace, the British court is officially known as the Court of St James's; the title transfers to wherever the sovereign is located. All ambassadors and high commissioners to the UK are officially received at the Court and are grandly styled Ambassador to the Court of St James's. Members of the Royal Family and Royal Household live and have offices here.

THE CHAPEL ROYAL
The Chapel Royal has been greatly altered since it was built for Henry VIII. However, it preserves its fine painted timber ceiling (1540) by Hans Holbein the Younger, which

incorporates the mottoes and badges of Anne of Cleves, whose short-lived marriage to Henry VIII it honours. In 1836 the ciphers of William IV and his consort Queen Adelaide were added.

ORIGINS OF THE CHAPEL ROYAL
In origin the Chapel Royal was not, as it is now, a building, but a group of people, essentially the spiritual retinue of the monarch: a group of clergymen, lay clerks and choristers headed by a dean and sub-dean, who formed part of the Royal Household and travelled with the sovereign (in c. 1509, there were nine chaplains, 20 clerks and ten choristers; and in c. 1700 around ten men in orders and ten singers). The first explicit reference to this body of men as a 'portable chapel' came in a petition of 1295 from English prelates seeking to clarify who had jurisdiction of appointment to the Chapel.

The itinerant tradition continued right up to the Tudor period, with the monarch frequently on royal progresses during the winter months. It was only in the 17th century that the nature of the Chapel Royal changed, alternating between the palaces of Whitehall and St James's before finally coming to be based permanently at the latter in 1698.

At the core of the history of the Chapel is sacred music, which was at its zenith between the 16th and 18th centuries. Thomas Tallis (d. 1585), William Byrd (d. 1623), Orlando Gibbons (d. 1625) and Henry Purcell (d. 1695) all worked as organists here. Handel was appointed 'Composer of Musick of His Majesty's Chappel Royal' in 1723. In 1727 he composed his famous setting of 'Zadok the Priest' for the coronation of George II.

The Chapel Royal has witnessed many intimate spiritual struggles: it was here that Elizabeth I prayed on the eve of the Spanish Armada in 1588 and here that the martyr-king Charles I received his last Holy Communion on the morning of 30th January 1649, before his execution at Whitehall. In 1997, the coffin of Diana, Princess of Wales, lay for private respects to be paid by her family before her funeral at Westminster Abbey. The heart of Mary I, who died here, is buried under the choir stalls.

QUEEN'S CHAPEL
This second Chapel Royal, projected by Inigo Jones, was begun in 1623 for the Infanta of Spain, the intended wife of King Charles I, and was completed for Henrietta Maria of France, his eventual bride. Palladian in style, of yellow brick and edged with white quoins, it utilises a double-cube space like the Banqueting House at Whitehall. Its main architectural features are its barrel-vaulted ceiling and Venetian window. In 1642 it was used as a barracks by Cromwell's army. After the Restoration, it was refurbished by Wren for Catherine of Braganza, consort of Charles II.

To the west of St James's Palace is **Cleveland Row** (*map p. 635, E2*), where three mansions (now offices) overlook Green Park. The Reform Bill of 1832 was drafted in

St James's Palace, the senior palace of the British monarchy (though not used as a residence by the Sovereign). The complex is largely of the 19th century, with some Tudor survivals.

Stornoway House (Wyatt, 1794–6; rebuilt in 1959), which became the residence of Lord Beaverbrook in 1924 and housed his Ministry of Aircraft Production in 1940–1. Beyond the bow-fronted Selwyn House (1895) is Barry's huge and elaborate Italianate Bridgwater House (1849), built for the 1st Earl of Ellesmere on the site of a house presented by Charles II to his mistress Barbara Villiers, Duchess of Cleveland, who lived here in 1668–77.

ST JAMES'S PARK

Map p. 635, E2–F2. Underground: St James's Park.

St James's Park is the oldest of the royal parks. It extends over 57 acres from Horse Guards Parade on the east to Buckingham Palace on the west, and is bounded on the north by The Mall, on the south by Birdcage Walk. Laid out in English naturalistic style in a patrician environment of palaces and government offices, and commanding a famous view of Buckingham Palace, Horse Guards and Whitehall Court from the Blue Bridge, this park is one of the most picturesque in London, and in warm weather is a perfect spot to while away a few hours in a deckchair (*available for hire*).

Henry VIII laid out the watermeadows between his palaces at Whitehall and St James's in 1532 as a park in which to hunt deer. Under the early Stuarts it was the resort of the court and other privileged persons. One of these, during the Commonwealth, was the poet Milton, who lived in a house in Petty France overlooking the park from 1652 until the Reformation in 1660. In 1649, Charles I walked across the park from St James's Palace to Whitehall, on the morning of his execution, and here in 1660 Pepys had his first view of Charles II on his return to London: 'Found the King in the parke. There walked. Gallantry great'.

After the Restoration, the French landscaper André Mollet was employed to make 'great and very noble alteracions', and the scattered ponds were united to form a 'canal'. The park was then opened to the public; it remains the only large park in London which has not been enclosed by railings. It became a fashionable resort, where the King was frequently to be seen strolling unattended and feeding the waterfowl. The lake in the centre is still patronised by numerous water birds, for which Duck Island at the east end is reserved. Among the 'great variety of fowle' described by Pepys are the famous resident pelicans, descendants of those first presented by the Russian ambassador in the 17th century. For the Restoration poet Rochester, the park was little more than a profligate pimping ground, an 'all-sin-sheltering grove' where he looks on mortified as his beloved Corinna skips away into a hackney coach with three suitors: a 'Whitehall blade', a 'Gray's Inn wit' and a 'lady's eldest son' (the irony being that politicians (Whitehall) are not sharp; lawyers (Gray's Inn) are not clever or amusing; and the kind of eldest sons who frequent St James's Park are seldom yet of age). Until 1905, a dairy herd was grazed at St James's Park and milkmaids sold mugs of fresh milk, warm from the cow, to passers-by.

BIRDCAGE WALK AND THE GUARDS' MUSEUM

Birdcage Walk (*map p. 635, E2–F2*) skirts the south side of the park; its name recalls the royal aviary established here in the reign of James I. Overlooking it are the bow-fronted Georgian houses of Queen Anne's Gate (*see below*). Near the end of Birdcage Walk are the **Wellington Barracks**, the headquarters of the Household Regiments, spaciously laid out around a parade ground, dating from 1834. The **Guards' Chapel**, or Royal Military Chapel (*householddivision.org.uk*), is approached by a memorial cloister (1956) by H.S. Goodhart-Rendel, in honour of the Household Brigade in the Second World War. The chapel was wrecked by a flying bomb in 1944, during morning service, with the loss of 121 lives, including that of the chaplain. The altar candles remained burning, and the same candlesticks are used today. The present chapel, opened in 1963, is by George, Trew and Dunn; its austerity sets off the surviving ornate mosaic apse by G.E. Street. To the left of the chapel and in front of the cloister is the **Flanders Fields Memorial Garden**, designed by Belgian architect Piet Blanckaert, a gift of the people of Belgium, dedicated in 2014. The circular grass bed represents eternal life and contains soil from the 70 military cemeteries and battlefields in Flanders, collected by school children, and symbolises the return of the fallen. The words of the poem 'In Flanders Fields', by the Canadian doctor Lt. Col. John McCrea, are inscribed around the retaining wall and bronze regimental badges are set into the top. In front of the garden stands a statue to Field Marshal Harold Alexander, 1st Earl Alexander of Tunis, one of the great commanders of WWII, who fought in both wars.

Opposite is the **Guards' Museum** (*theguardsmuseum.com*), with artefacts pertaining to the five regiments of Foot Guards (Grenadier, Coldstream, Scots, Irish and Welsh), who furnish the troops that can usually be seen on parade, here and in front of Buckingham Palace, at the Changing of the Guard. Along with the cavalry regiments, the Blues and Royals and the Life Guards, they form the Household Division. Their duties are not merely ceremonial: all seven regiments of the Division are composed of fighting soldiers who have seen, or will at some time see, active service. The museum displays an annotated collection of uniforms, medals, silverware, weapons, colours, trophies and memorabilia. It also has a shop, the Toy Soldier Centre.

NEW SCOTLAND YARD, QUEEN ANNE'S GATE AND THE WESTMINSTER CHAPEL

The **former Blewcoat School** on Caxton Street (1709; *map p. 635, E3*) features a charming sculpture of a pupil in his uniform blue coat and yellow stockings.

At the north end of Broadway (no. 55), **St James's Park Underground station** occupies a massive and imposing building by Adam, Holden & Pearson with a lofty tower and relief sculptures by Jacob Epstein, Henry Moore and Eric Gill. At the corner of Petty France and Queen Anne's Gate is an ugly concrete turret by Sir Basil Spence (1976), housing the **Ministry of Justice**.

Queen Anne's Gate itself (*map p. 635, F2*) is a lovely enclave, its brown brick and stone-banded houses built in 1704 with the money of Charles Shales (who lived at no. 15) and probably also of William Paterson, 'founder' of the Bank of England (who lived at no. 19 in 1705–18). The houses have carved mascarons on the keystones and elaborate door cases with richly carved hoods, unique in London. There is an unfinished statue of Queen Anne at no. 13. The larger houses overlooking St James's Park are later, from about 1780. Lord Palmerston was born at no. 20 in 1784. No. 14, possibly designed by Adam, was home to the collector and early trustee of the British Museum Charles Townley; here he entertained friends, including the painters Reynolds and Zoffany, to excellent Sunday dinners.

A little further west, on Buckingham Gate (corner of Castle Lane) is the **Westminster Chapel** (*map p. 635, E3*), with a lofty interior and a horseshoe-shaped gallery. The building dates from 1865.

The Victoria Palace Theatre with its gilded statue of Anna Pavlova.

VICTORIA & PIMLICO

T he southern part of old Thorney Island, abutting the Thames, is now a dense urban network of busy roads with the frenetic hub of Victoria Station at the centre. There are some pockets of tranquillity: the streets, houses and gracious lifestyles of the residents of this part of London in the years immediately after WWI are evoked in Virginia Woolf's *Mrs Dalloway*. To the south is residential Pimlico, with attractive streets of terraced houses laid out in the early 19th century.

Some highlights of the area
✦ The beautiful, tenebrous, neo-Byzantine **Westminster Cathedral**, seat of the Roman Catholic Church in England;
✦ **Tate Britain**, home to the national collection of British art, with important works by Blake, Turner and the pre-Raphaelites.

VICTORIA

Map p. 635, E3–E4. Underground: Victoria.

The area around Victoria Station lacks charm, but it is difficult to avoid it: it is a bustling and important transport hub. This is one of London's busiest rail termini, serving Gatwick Airport, the south coast and the southeast suburbs. Victoria Coach Station on Buckingham Palace Road is the scene of incessant coming and going: the streets are choked with buses and coaches, thronged with people dragging wheelie luggage: there is an atmosphere of year-round transhumance.

North of Victoria Station, **Grosvenor Gardens** comprise two triangular patches of trees bisected by roaring roads. In the southern triangle stands Georges Malissard's equestrian statue of Marshal Foch, supreme commander of the Allied Forces in 1918. Shell-adorned *cottages ornés* stand on either side.

The northern triangle has a sculpture group of a lioness pursuing an antelope, by Jonathan Kenworthy (2000), commissioned by the Duke of Westminster.

On Victoria Street opposite the station is the **Victoria Palace Theatre**, which opened in 1911 on the site of an earlier music hall. It boasted a sliding roof which could be opened to allow cooling breezes to waft into the auditorium in hot weather. It is now known for its repertoire of musicals. The gilded ballerina on its summit, well seen against the blue glass of the office block next door, is a replica of the original 1911 statue of Anna Pavlova, which was removed for safekeeping during WWII and has mysteriously never been seen since.

WESTMINSTER CATHEDRAL

Map p. 635, E3. westminstercathedral.org.uk.

Facing a broad modern piazza off the south side of Victoria Street is Westminster Cathedral, dedicated to the Most Precious Blood of Our Lord Jesus Christ. It is the seat of the Cardinal Archbishop of Westminster and the most important Roman Catholic church in England. This extraordinary building—extraordinary, at least, in an English context—was completed in 1903 to designs by J.F. Bentley, who took his inspiration from early Christian basilicas, notably St Mark's in Venice and Haghia Sophia in Istanbul. The exterior of the church and its campanile are built in alternate courses of red brick and pale Portland stone. In the tympanum over the main entrance is a mosaic by Robert Anning Bell (1916) showing Christ flanked by the Virgin and St Joseph with St Peter and Edward the Confessor. The Latin inscription is from John: 'I am the door: by me if any man enter in, he shall be saved.'

Interior of Westminster Cathedral

The vast and numinous interior is beautifully proportioned, and all the more atmospheric for being incomplete: the domes were to have been clad in mosaic and—in theory at least—work is ongoing. New mosaics were produced by Boris Anrep and others have slowly been added since the 1980s. The walls and piers are revetted with coloured marbles, supplied from 24 countries and regions of the globe, including Greece, Italy and North Africa, by the Derbyshire-born marble merchant and stone carver William Brindley (who also worked on the Albert Memorial; *see p. 330*). Brindley personally travelled to Greece, Asia Minor and Egypt in search of the varieties of marble and other fine stone that had been popular in antiquity, among them porphyry, *cipollino* and *verde antico*. In total, over a hundred types of decorative stone were used. Bentley's plans for the decoration were detailed and specific: he wanted the lower parts to be clad in marble, while the decoration of the upper parts was to be of mosaic. Originally, the mosaic was created by hand with each individual piece being impressed directly into the plaster, giving the mosaic surface their distinctive shimmering appearance, best seen in the Lady Chapel and Holy Souls Chapel. Understandably this technique, the direct method, was both time-consuming and expensive, so in more recent times, to cut time and costs, the indirect method was used. Tesserae were placed face down, the image being built up in reverse on a temporary surface, such as paper, which was then transferred to the final location. The drawback is that the result on the surface is uniform and rather flat; something Bentley probably would not have approved of. One of the most recent mosaics, outside St Paul's chapel, is that representing St David,

Façade of the neo-Byzantine Westminster Cathedral (1903), its design inspired by Haghia Sophia in Constantinople and St Mark's in Venice.

depicted in glittering silver and gold. Designed by Ifor Davis, it was blessed by Pope Benedict XVI during his visit in 2010.

Nave: Two great **columns of red granite (1)**, emblematic of the Precious Blood of Jesus to which the cathedral is dedicated, stand at the head of the nave.

To the left is a bronze seated **statue of St Peter (2)**, modelled on that in St Peter's in Rome—and here, similarly, the faithful rub the saint's foot.

The **pulpit (3)** has fine Cosmati work. It is borne on twisted colonnettes reminiscent of those in the cloister of St John Lateran in Rome and is adorned with statues of the Evangelists. Against the pier beyond it is a much-venerated early 15th-century **Nottingham alabaster *Madonna and Child* (4)**.

WESTMINSTER CATHEDRAL

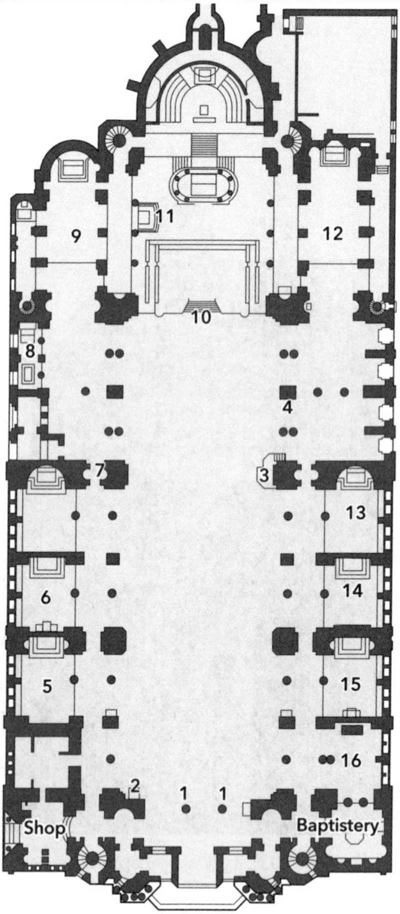

1 Red granite columns
2 Statue of St Peter
3 Pulpit
4 Alabaster *Madonna*
5 Holy Souls Chapel
6 Chapel of St George
7 *St Christopher* mosaic
8 Vaughan Chantry
9 Chapel of the Blessed Sacrament
10 Triumphal arch
11 Archbishop's throne
12 Lady Chapel
13 Chapel of St Paul
14 Chapel of St Andrew
15 Chapel of St Patrick
16 Chapel of SS Gregory and Augustine

The nave piers bear low reliefs by Eric Gill of the **Stations of the Cross** (1913–18), best seen early in the morning or late in the afternoon when the muted light beautifully emphasises them.

The intricate column capitals in the nave are of many types, all of them designed by Bentley based on the capitals in Haghia Sophia, with carved acanthus foliage deeply undercut so as to resemble lace.

North aisle: Though the architect Bentley died before the mosaic decoration could be carried out, he left instructions for it to be executed in a 'severe Greek style'. This is well seen in the **Holy Souls Chapel (5)**, where the scheme depicts the progress of the soul from the Fall (represented by Adam and the Tree) through the purifying fire of Purgatory (Shadrach, Meshach and Abednego in the Furnace) to the gift of eternal life (the Resurrected Christ). The Latin text, *Et sicut in Adam omnes moriuntur ita et in Cristo omnes vivificabuntur*, is from I Corinthians: 'For as in Adam all die, even so in Christ shall all be made alive.'

The next chapel, the **Chapel of St George (6)** has an altarpiece by Eric Gill showing *Christ Triumphant*, flanked by Thomas More and Bishop John Fisher. Here is displayed the body of John Southworth, a Catholic priest who was hung, drawn and quartered for his faith at Tyburn in 1654, during the Protectorate of Cromwell (*see p. 323*).

The **mosaic of *St Christopher* (7)**, in the narrow right-hand niche, is by Justin Vulliamy, assistant to Boris Anrep.

In the **Vaughan Chantry (8)** is the tomb of the founder of the Cathedral, Herbert Vaughan (d. 1903).

The **Chapel of the Blessed Sacrament** (**9**; reserved for prayer) is decorated with mosaics by Boris Anrep (1956–62): in the niches at either side of the entrance are a phoenix and a peacock, symbols of resurrection and eternal life.

East end: The great **rood** hanging from the triumphal arch **(10)** bears painted figures of Christ with the Evangelists in the terminals. The mosaic on the arch beyond shows Christ seated on the rainbow with the Twelve Apostles and the symbols of the Evangelists. The high altar is surmounted by a white marble baldachin supported on eight monolithic columns of yellow Verona marble on pedestals of *verde antico* marble. The **Archbishop's throne**, to the left **(11)**, is a smaller-scale copy of the papal chair in St John Lateran at Rome.

South aisle: The **Lady Chapel (12)** contains a mosaic of the *Madonna* by Anning Bell. Above, in the conch, is a mosaic of the *Tree of Life* inspired by early mosaics in Rome. The mosaics at the top of the walls show scenes from the life of the Virgin. The green and purple opus sectile floor is reminiscent of the pavements of Roman churches.

The **Chapel of St Paul (13)** has mosaics of the mid-1960s by Justin Vulliamy, to designs by Boris Anrep (who reportedly disliked them when installed). The **Chapel of St Andrew and the Saints of Scotland (14)** is decorated with beautiful, shimmering Byzantinesque mosaics by Robert Schultz Weir showing cities associated with the saint, including Patras, Constantinople and St Andrew's. In honour of the fisherman-saint, the floor is charmingly inlaid with motifs of fish and other sea creatures.

The **Chapel of St Patrick and the Saints of Ireland (15)** commemorates the Irishmen who fell in 1914–18. Each regiment has its own enamel plaque. The gilded bronze statue of the saint over the altar is by Arthur Pollen. The transenna that divides the chapel from the aisle features the shamrock of St Patrick and the oak leaves of St Bridget. Outside the chapel, between the aisle and the nave, is the tomb slab of Cormac Murphy O'Connor, the tenth Archbishop of Westminster (d. 2017).

The **Chapel of SS Gregory and Augustine (16)** contains the tomb-slab of Cardinal Hume (d. 1999), who served as both Archbishop of Westminster and Cardinal-Priest in Rome from 1976. When a year before he death he applied to Pope John Paul II for permission to retire, his request was refused.

ON AND AROUND HORSEFERRY ROAD

South of Victoria Street, the cobbled **Strutton Ground** (*map p. 635, F3*) hosts a street-market selling clothes, flowers and food (*weekdays until 3pm*). To the west in Greycoat Place is the **old Grey Coat Hospital**, founded in 1698 and still a school for girls. On the pedimented façade below the clock tower, in niches, are statues of a boy and a girl pupil.

Horseferry Road leads from Strutton Ground towards the river, passing the Channel 4 headquarters at no. 124 (Richard Rogers, 1994), with an exterior lift and high tension steel cables supporting the glass atrium. Opposite, at no. 95, in the Territorial Army Centre, is the small but comprehensive collection of the **Museum of the London Scottish Regiment** (*londonscottishregt.org*) in the drill hall of the regimental HQ.

Further south is **Vincent Square**, once a bear garden and now used as playing fields by Westminster School. On the north side, at no. 80, are the Royal Horticultural Society's Horticultural Halls (1904 and 1928), used as an events venue. On Recency Street (corner of Page St), the black-tiled Art Deco **Regency Café** is an old-fashioned 'greasy spoon', a traditional workers' café serving tea, black pudding and bubble and squeak.

At the end of Horseferry Road is **Lambeth Bridge** (Blomfield et al, 1932), replacing an earlier bridge of 1862 which in turn replaced an ancient horse ferry to Lambeth. For many centuries there has been a river crossing here, between the royal Palace of Westminster and the Archbishop of Canterbury's palace in Lambeth.

ST JOHN'S SMITH SQUARE

In the centre of Smith Square (*map p. 635, F3*) is the eccentric Baroque church of St John the Evangelist, known as St John's Smith Square (*sjss.org.uk*), with four massive towers topped by pineapples. The square was laid out by the Smith family, who owned the land, in 1726; the houses at nos 3–5 and 6–9 are original Georgian survivors. The church, now a noted Classical music and lecture venue, was completed in 1728 by Thomas Archer as one of the Commission for Building Fifty New Churches. Though it is one of the most elaborate, it has been much derided over the years: Dickens, in *Our Mutual Friend*, likened it (not particularly pithily) to 'a petrified monster on its back with its legs in the air'; some say the four angle towers were designed to ensure that the swampy foundations settled uniformly.

St John's has suffered over the centuries: a major fire in 1742 led to the extensive modification of Archer's original plan and in 1815 it was struck by lightning causing damage to the towers. In the early 20th century it was the target of a Suffragette bomb plot. Notwithstanding this, in 1928 Emmeline Pankhurst's funeral was held here (she is commemorated in Victoria Tower Gardens; *see p. 132*). The final blow was delivered on the last night of the Blitz, 10th May 1941, when the building took a direct hit from an incendiary bomb which completely gutted it. It lay empty until the threat of developing the site into a car park prompted locals to raise the funds for its restoration, which was completed in 1969. International stars have regularly performed here including Joan Sutherland, Pierre Boulez, Daniel Barenboim, Placido Domingo and Nigel Kennedy. There is a good café/restaurant in the crypt, which stays open until after the evening performance on concert days.

North of Smith Square is the pleasing **Lord North Street**, which dates from the 1720s (look out for the faded signs to WWII air raid shelters).

PIMLICO

Map p. 635, F4–E4. Underground: Pimlico.

The area hugged by the bend in the river between Lambeth Bridge and Chelsea Bridge is known as Pimlico, possibly named after a popular early 18th-century publican. Originally an area of marsh, it was developed from the mid-1820s for Richard Grosvenor by Thomas Cubitt, in a style less grand than that of Belgravia to the north, but perhaps less stand-offish and more pleasing. Many of Cubitt's porticoed and columned stucco houses and terraces have survived, and a **statue of Cubitt** himself (William Fawke, 1995) stands on the wedge-shaped corner where St George's Drive and Denbigh Street converge (*map p. 635, E4*). He is shown in the attitude of surveying, rod in hand.

Mozart composed his first symphonies at **no. 180 Ebury St** in 1764 at the age of eight and a sculpture of the boy prodigy (Philip Jackson, 1994) stands where Ebury Street meets Pimlico Road, at Orange Square (*map p. 635, D4*). Close by is the neo-Gothic church of **St Barnabas**, built in rusticated stone by Thomas Cundy in 1850 (spire rebuilt 2007). It was an early Anglo-Catholic foundation, which led to anxious mutterings about 'popery in Pimlico'. At a time when it was common practice for families or individuals to rent their pews, St Barnabas was the first church in London where pews were free.

St Saviour's Church in Lupus Street and **St Gabriel's** in Warwick Square are also by Cundy (*both map p. 635, E4*).

Fronting the river in Grosvenor Road is **Dolphin Square** (*map p. 635, E4*), an early condominium built in 1937, when it was the largest block of flats in Europe, with over a thousand apartments and its own swimming pool and restaurant. Because of its proximity to Westminster and to MI5, it was a popular London residence for politicians, civil servants, peers and intelligence officers. To the west sprawls the housing estate of **Churchill Gardens** (Powell & Moya, 1946–62). In its day it aspired to be Utopia made manifest and was heated, via its tall, cylindrical accumulator tower, by hot water from Battersea Power Station.

MILLBANK

Millbank (*map p. 635, F4–F3*), the busy highway that skirts the Thames, takes its name from a former mill belonging to the monks of Westminster. In Riverside Walk Gardens, a short way downstream (north) of Vauxhall Bridge, is Henry Moore's ***Locking Piece*** (1963–4). A flight of steps between two huge bollards once led to the water here. Convicts from Millbank prison (on the site of Tate Britain; *see below*) were led down the steps onto ships bound for Australia. A plaque fixed to the surviving bollard (beside the riverside parapet) commemorates this.

On the opposite side of the road, on the corner building of Atterbury Street, a sculpted bronze figure impetuously springs forth amid a seemingly artless twist of drapery (which actually pins him to his plinth). This is *Jeté*, by Enzo Plazzotta (1975), modelled on the great dancer David Wall, the youngest ever male lead in the Royal Ballet company (he was 21). Wall died in 2013.

TATE BRITAIN

Map p. 635, F3. Underground: Pimlico. Free (except for special exhibitions). tate.org.uk. Café. Tate Britain and Tate Modern are linked by the Tate riverboat service (every 40mins during gallery opening hours; tickets can be bought online). The exterior of the sleek catamaran (coloured spots) was designed by Damien Hirst.

Tate is in fact a family of galleries with a large collection displayed over four sites: Tate Britain and Tate Modern in London, as well as Tate Liverpool and Tate St Ives. Tate has two roles: it houses the national collection of British art, from 1500 to the present day, at Tate Britain; and the national collection of post-1900 international art at Tate Modern and outside London.

FOUNDATION, BUILDING AND GROWTH
Sir Henry Tate (1819–98), originally in the Liverpool grocery trade, began refining sugar in 1862 and was the pioneer producer, at his second refinery in London, of the new, patented commodity, cubed sugar. With the wealth this brought he began collecting modern British art and in 1889 he donated funds for the erection of a place to display it, as an annexe of the National Gallery. Work began in 1894 on the site of the old Millbank Penitentiary, formerly the largest prison in Europe, from where felons were dispatched to Australia. Sidney Smith's design, domed and temple-like, overlooks the river, its central portico surmounted by *Britannia*, flanked by the lion and the unicorn. This initial gallery has been added to many times to provide extra space for the expanding collection.

The gallery first opened in 1897 with displays of sentimental narrative pictures as well as Pre-Raphaelite works, including Millais' *Ophelia*. An increasing number of modern Continental works later came to be displayed here and in 1917 the Tate became the official home of modern foreign art as well as British. It was at the Tate that the great French Impressionist and Post-Impressionist pictures presented through the Hugh Lane Bequest and the Courtauld Fund were first shown. A conservative approach to modern art was, however, a defining feature of the Tate's early years. It was slow to acquire works by Cézanne; in the 1930s there was no German Expressionism and no Surrealism; and in the post-war years no Cubist works were purchased. This reluctance to engage with the avant garde hampered the formation of a modern art collection of weight and distinction.

Following the disastrous Thames flood of 1928, which engulfed the lower halls, damaged 18 works beyond repair and submerged J.M.W. Turner's portfolios and watercolours (which had to be spread out to dry on the upper floors), the art dealer Lord Duveen funded new exhibition rooms. Built in 1935–7 by the New York architect J. Russell Pope with Romaine-Walker and Jenkins, the imperious, monumental Duveens stretch like a great cathedral nave, vast and echoing, down the spine of the building.

Independence from the National Gallery came in 1955 and in the '60s and '70s the Tate became closely identified with contemporary art, staging live performance art and a succession of enthusiastically received exhibitions. Today Tate Britain is making up for past conservatism by becoming one of the state institutions most eager to decolonise and reinterpret its collection according to contemporary ideas of identity and victimhood.

The Turner Prize exhibition is held at Tate Britain every autumn, showing work by four shortlisted artists. The winner is usually announced in December.

The collection

The arrangement is chronological, devised as a 'Walk through British Art'. Each room has a different wall colour, title and theme, and the paintings are displayed in terms of their social context, showing how the artist responded to the economic, political, cultural and technological changes through which they lived and worked. Women artists have been brought to the fore with works by the country's first professional painters such as Joan Carlile (c. 1606–79) and Mary Beale (1633–99) through to modern and contemporary artists such as Gwen John (1876–19 39), Lubaina Himid (b. 1954), Rachel Whiteread (b. 1963) and Rachel Jones (b. 1991). The period rooms are interspersed with rooms devoted to single artists particularly associated with Tate.

Tudor and Stuart works

The earliest work in the collection is John Bettes' *A Man in a Black Cap* (1545), showing a plump man with an elaborately trimmed and parted beard. The fur around his neck is particularly well rendered. The wording running behind the sitter confirm the date he was painted and that he was 26 years old. The background colour was originally blue (a colour favoured by Hans Holbein the Younger, whose work may have influenced Bettes) but this has darkened to brown. *The Cholmondeley Ladies* is a regional portrait of two women born, married and brought to bed on the same day: they sit in bed, stiffly painted in large starched ruffs, holding their tightly swaddled babies. The full-length *James Hamilton, 1st Duke of Hamilton*, standing in a deeply shadowed interior in fine red stockings, was painted by **Daniel Mytens**, who brought to England a new realism. The *Portrait of a Young Girl* (c. 1681) is by **Mary Beale**, perhaps the most prolific female artist of this period. Her technique here was to paint swiftly in one session, rather than over several (more expensive) sittings. The sitter is unknown but may have been a family member or a studio assistant.

Anthony van Dyck, who became Chief Painter to Charles I, revolutionised portrait painting in Britain with his sophisticated handling of paint and the courtly swagger of his poses. The gallery also has a good collection of works by **Sir Peter Lely**, Chief Painter to Charles II; and an excellent collection of works by **Sir Godfrey Kneller**, the official painter of William and Mary, Anne and George I.

The second half of the 17th century witnessed a proliferation of new genres. *Monkeys and Dogs Playing* (1661) is by **Francis Barlow**, the first native-born landscape and animal artist; and there are still-life pieces by Edward Collier, collecting together objects symbolic of the transience of life.

The 18th century

One of the greatest painters of the Georgian age was **William Hogarth**, whose famous self-portrait, *The Painter and his Pug* (1745), has a palette in the foreground bearing the 'Line of Beauty', central to his ideas on harmony and beauty in art. Francis Hayman's portrait of the novelist Samuel Richardson, surrounded by his second wife and four daughters, is interesting for the clear influence it was to have on Gainsborough.

Grand Manner works from later in the century include portraits by **Sir Joshua Reynolds**, the Royal Academy's first President. Tate also has a large collection of works by **Thomas Gainsborough**, the other great portrait painter of the age (though his preferred inclination was landscape painting, of which the gallery has several important examples). Joseph Wright of Derby was another portraitist who turned his attention to other subjects, in his case the events and transformations of the Industrial Revolution and scientific invention. *An Iron Forge* (1772) is a superb example.

The lofty ideals of Neoclassical history painting are demonstrated in expansive images such as Benjamin West's *Pylades and Orestes brought as Victims before Iphigenia* (1766). In John Singleton Copley's large and famous *The Death of Major Peirson, 6 January 1781*, which commemorates the British defence of the island of Jersey against French invasion, the majesty of antiquity is applied to contemporary history.

There are also major works by the famous painter of horses, **George Stubbs**: *A Horse Frightened by a Lion* (1763) is among them, the horse's pose based on an antique sculpture. His *Haymakers* and its pendant *Reapers* show bucolic scenes in which the horse or horses are ancillary elements.

The Turner collection

Arguably the most famous of all British artists is J.M.W. Turner (1775–1851). His subjects were Classical mythology and history, contemporary events and natural disaster, painted with a concern for the changing atmospheric effects of light: golden sunsets, raging storms, tossing waves and enveloping mists. His early inspirations were Claude and Willem van de Velde the Younger: as his style developed, it became increasingly romantic and original, culminating in the great proto-Impressionist works for which he is so celebrated today. His brilliant image of the shadowy dome of the Salute looming out of the mist of the Venetian lagoon seems 'reminiscent' of

Monet, even though it pre-dates Monet by almost half a century. Some of his work, where concrete forms are dissolved and diffused by the effects of light and colour, are almost abstract in feel. The Tate's vast collection incorporates all periods and aspects of Turner's art, as well as personal items such as his paintboxes. Highlights include his self-portrait of c. 1799; *Snow Storm: Hannibal and his Army Crossing the Alps* and *Norham Castle, Sunrise*. There is also a wealth of watercolours and sketches demonstrating his evolution as an artist.

The Constable collection

John Constable (1776–1837) is one of Britain's most famous landscape artists. The collection ranges from early works painted in and around his native Suffolk to grander works, painted in London but based on previous sketches. Constable placed enormous emphasis on observation from nature, and on show are numerous rapidly executed and evocative sketches, either entire scenes or details such as scudding clouds. Highlights of the changing display include *Flatford Mill*; *Fen Lane, East Bergholt*; *Hampstead Heath with a Rainbow*; *Stoke-by-Nayland*; *The Valley Farm*; and the *Sketch for 'Hadleigh Castle'*, a full-size sketch for a work exhibited at the Royal Academy in 1829, a working method Constable used when creating his famous 'six-footers'.

The Blake collection

Works by the visionary genius, artist and poet William Blake (1757–1827) have been an important component of the collection from its earliest years. Included are Blake's illustrations to Dante's *Divine Comedy* and other works which demonstrate Blake's very personal philosophy and iconography. Highlights include the large, colour-print *Newton* and *Elohim Creating Adam* (1795).

The 19th century

Landscape painting includes monumental works such as James Ward's mighty *Gordale Scar*, of breathtaking proportions (sadly not on display at the time of writing). Not to be missed is Francis Danby's apocalyptic trio, *The Great Day of His Wrath*, *The Deluge* and *The Plains of Heaven* (1851–3). Richard Dadd's unfinished *The Fairy Feller's Master Stroke* was painted in Bethlem Hospital, where he was sent after murdering his father in 1843.

Tate's collection of **Pre-Raphaelite works** is outstanding. Among the many well-known major masterpieces are William Holman Hunt's *The Awakening Conscience* and Dante Gabriel Rossetti's *Ecce Ancilla Domini!*, *Beata Beatrix*, *Proserpine* and *Monna Vanna*. Sir John Everett Millais' *Ophelia* is one of the gallery's most popular pictures. Other familiar works are Henry Wallis's *Chatterton*, a romanticised view of the poet shortly after his suicide. Later works include Burne-Jones's extraordinary *Sisyphus* (c. 1870) and *The Golden Stairs* (1880), and Waterhouse's *Lady of Shalott* (1888).

The Tate's collection of **late Victorian works** includes paintings presented by G.F. Watts on the gallery's foundation and Frederic, Lord Leighton's heroic sculpture *An Athlete Wrestling with a Python*. William Powell Frith's *The Derby Day*, described by Ruskin as 'of the entirely popular manner of painting', created a sensation when exhibited at the Royal Academy in 1858 and was taken on a world tour.

James Abbott McNeill Whistler abandoned the Academy-led insistence on the importance of narrative and focused instead on the effects of light and atmosphere. His 'art for art's sake' aesthetic was fiercely attacked by Ruskin: *Nocturne in Blue and Gold: Old Battersea Bridge* (c. 1872–5) was painted as 'evidence' during the famous trial for libel after Ruskin had accused Whistler of throwing a pot of paint in the face of the public—a case which Whistler won, but received damages of just one farthing.

The Tate has an important collection of works by **John Singer Sargent**, including slick society portraits and the famous *Carnation, Lily, Lily, Rose* (1885–6), showing the pink glow of Chinese lanterns in the evening dusk.

Early 20th century

The response to Continental Post-Impressionism saw the emergence in England of a vigorous, innovative avant garde. The **Camden Town Group**, established in 1911 by Walter Sickert and others, produced sombre, realist, mainly urban scenes, including Sickert's own *Ennui* (1914). Everything in the painting—the subjects who face in opposite directions, the stuffed birds crammed under their glass dome and overall dun colour—suggests melancholy and boredom while in Harold Gilman's *Mrs Mounter at the Breakfast Table* (1916–17), the artist's landlady sits staring out over her very ordinary-looking tea pot, milk jug and cups with an almost blank expression, perhaps reflecting her mood.

Bloomsbury Group works, influenced by Cézanne and others, include paintings by Duncan Grant (*Bathing*, 1911) and Vanessa Bell (*Studland Beach*, c. 1912). Mark Gertler's highly original *Merry-go-Round* (1916) is a strident anti-war statement while Matthew Smith's *Nude, Fitzroy Street, No. 1* (1916), in its vivid use of colour, displays the influence of Matisse. Wyndham Lewis's *Workshop* (c. 1914–15), David Bomberg's *In the Hold*, and works by Christopher Nevinson and other **Vorticists**, with their diagonals, fragmented geometry and emphasis on urban industrialism, display the influence of Cubism and Futurism.

The years following the First World War saw a return to more traditional, figurative painting. The dominant figure was Stanley Spencer, whose greatest work, *The Resurrection, Cookham* (1924–7), is a personal, religious vision of modern life. Also in the collection are sleepy views of rural England by Paul Nash, including *Landscape at Iden*.

Mid-20th century

The great pioneers of **modern sculpture** in Britain were Jacob Epstein and Henri Gaudier-Brzeska. One of the most important and popular works is Epstein's massive *Jacob and the Angel* (1940–1), the angel's wings a great slab of alabaster.

Tate has an excellent collection of works by the outstanding figures of English abstraction, **Barbara Hepworth, Henry Moore, Ben Nicholson** and **Paul Nash**. Works include Nicholson's *1935 (white relief)*; Paul Nash's *Equivalents for the Megaliths* (1935); Edward Wadsworth's *Dux et Comes I* (1932), which is pure Surrealism; and Victor Pasmore's *Linear Motif in Black and White* (1960–1). Hepworth's *Three Forms* (1935), three white polished marble shapes of the utmost purity and simplicity, and

Pelagos (1946) reflect her preoccupation with form. Henry Moore was the foremost British sculptor of the mid-20th century and one of the leaders in the revival of direct carving. Tate has a large collection of important works, including *Recumbent Figure* (1938). By 1939 Nicholson and Hepworth had moved to Cornwall, near St Ives, where a younger generation of artists was attracted. The **St Ives School** included Patrick Heron (*Azalea Garden: May 1956*) and Roger Hilton, whose *Oi Yoi Yoi* (1963) shows his naked wife jumping with rage during an argument.

The large collection of works by one of the most important 20th-century British artists, **Francis Bacon**, includes *Three Studies for Figures at the Base of a Crucifixion* (c. 1944).

British **Pop artists** of the late 1950s and '60s include Peter Blake (*On the Balcony*, 1955–7) and Richard Smith (*Piano*, 1963). A second phase of Pop was taken up by a group of artists trained at the Royal College of Art, including **David Hockney** (his witty Californian work *A Bigger Splash*; 1967) and Patrick Caulfield (*Greece Expiring on the Ruins of Missolonghi* and *Ruins*, 1963 and 1964). The 'New Generation' of British sculptors, who moved from carved work to abstract constructions in industrial metals, brightly-painted steel, fibreglass and plastics, is represented by Sir Anthony Caro, Phillip King, Eduardo Paolozzi and William Turnbull.

Later 20th and 21st centuries

Works continuing the Realist or Figurative tradition include Graham Sutherland's landscapes and his portrait of Somerset Maugham; Lucian Freud's *Girl with a Kitten* (1947) and *Girl in a Striped Nightshirt* (1983–5); as well as works by Frank Auerbach, R.B. Kitaj and Leon Kossoff. The Tate has later important works by David Hockney, such as his enduringly popular *Mr and Mrs Clark and Percy* (showing the fashion designer Ossie Clark, a white cat on his lap, his toes buried in a hairy shagpile carpet, with his wife, the textile designer Celia Birtwell). Francis Bacon's *Triptych: August 1972* consists of three blurred and fused images of contemporary man based on the work of the pioneer stop-action photographer Eadweard Muybridge (*see p. 568*).

Since the 1970s, **conceptual art and installations** have been an important component of British modern art. Examples are Gilbert & George's 'sculpture on video tape' *In the Bush* (1972); Richard Long's sculptural interventions in the natural environment and indoor installations (*Turf Circle*, 1966); and Tony Cragg's *Stack* (1975). Sarah Lucas uses installation, sculpture and photography to explore self-perception and gender roles. In 2013 Tate stirred up controversy with its purchase of Martin Creed's *Work No. 227: The lights going on and off*, a Turner Prize-winner from 2001. It consists of an empty room where the lights flick on and off every few seconds. Other works acquired in the 21st century include Rachel Whiteread's *Untitled (Stairs)* (2001), a massive free-standing cast of a staircase, with three landings, which represents the comings and goings of daily life and Claudette Johnson MBE's *Figure in raw umber* (2018).

Putto with a wheatsheaf, on the Art Deco Adelphi building of 1938.

TRAFALGAR SQUARE & THE STRAND

This busy area of central London divides the Thames and its embankment from Covent Garden and London's West End theatreland. To the south lie the main office buildings of the United Kingdom's government. The wide street known as The Strand links Westminster with the City of London. At its west end is Trafalgar Square.

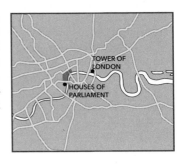

Some highlights of the area

✦ The perennially crowded **Trafalgar Square**, with Nelson's famous column and, filling its north side, the **National Gallery**, with its superb collection of Western European art;

✦ **Victoria Embankment Gardens**, a pool of quietude amid the hubbub, below the famous **Savoy Hotel**;

✦ The **Courtauld Gallery**, with some splendid works of the French Impressionist and Post-Impressionist schools in the architecturally important **Somerset House**.

TRAFALGAR SQUARE

Map p. 635, F2. Underground: Charing Cross.

Trafalgar Square is one of the focal points of London, always busy with traffic and filled with crowds who gather to watch the performance artists in the piazza in front of the National Gallery, and at other times of year for a great variety of events and festivals, including St Patrick's Day (17th March), the re-enactment of the Passion of Jesus (Easter); Diwali (Oct or Nov), Christmas carols beneath the tree (which is donated by the people of Norway in recognition of Britain's help during the Second World War) and New Year celebrations. Meanwhile, Nelson calmly surveys the scene from the top of his column. The square is named in honour of his naval victory over a combined French and Spanish fleet, fought on 21st October 1805 off Cape Trafalgar on the southern coast of Spain. While the victory ensured that Napoleon gave up all hope of invading England, it cost Admiral Nelson his life: he died on board his ship, the *Victory*, about three hours after receiving his fatal gunshot wound.

Trafalgar Square was described by Sir Robert Peel as 'the finest site in Europe'. The original layout, completed in 1844, is by Sir Charles Barry; redevelopment in 2003 removed much of the traffic chaos and turned it into a pedestrianised piazza—but this has brought chaos of a more human kind, with street performers and artists and crowds of tourists thronging the traffic-free space. The square was once well-known— even infamous—for the feral pigeons which flocked here in their hundreds but measures such as banning the sale of birdseed and the use of trained birds of prey have successfully reduced their numbers.

The two **fountains** in the square were designed by Lutyens in 1939. At the corners are **four tall plinths** topped by statues of two servants of the Empire, Sir Henry Havelock (by Behnes) and Sir Charles James Napier (by G.G. Adams); and by a monarch, George IV (by Chantrey; originally intended to surmount Marble Arch; *see p. 322*). An equestrian statue of William IV was intended for the fourth plinth but it was never installed due to insufficient funds. For 150 years the plinth stayed bare and now it is used for a changing series of contemporary sculptures and installations: the latest creation to adorn the 'fourth plinth' is now a subject of abiding interest. Against the north wall are bronze **busts of admirals**, pendants to the main Nelson monument in the centre.

NELSON'S COLUMN

The Nelson Monument, popularly known as Nelson's Column, commemorates the British naval hero of the Napoleonic Wars Admiral Lord Nelson (1758–1805). Standing 172ft high, it is by William Railton (1841) and carries a colossal 17ft statue of Nelson by E.H. Baily (1840–3). The statue shows him without his right arm, which he lost in a failed battle against Spain in 1797. The fluted granite column rises from a base guarded by four huge bronze lions couchant, popular with children (though the public is now strongly discouraged from climbing on them). These were modelled by Sir Edwin Landseer and cast by Marochetti in 1867. The four bronze reliefs are cast from French cannon captured at the naval battles they depict: Cape St Vincent, The Nile, Copenhagen, Trafalgar. The column has been scaled several times, by activists wishing to draw attention to causes ranging from Apartheid to air pollution. A petition to have the statue of Nelson removed, on the grounds that he was a racist and white supremacist, was rejected in 2020.

On the north side of Trafalgar Square is the National Gallery. As you face it, to the left (west), filling the block between Pall Mall and Cockspur Street, is the vast **Canada House** (Smirke, 1824–7; remodelled). Opposite its Cockspur Street flank, in the former headquarters of the Canadian National Railway Company, is **Hungary House**, a cultural centre for all things Magyar.

OLD CHARING CROSS

Charing Cross is officially not the open space in front of Charing Cross Station but the ancient road junction (now a circular traffic island) at the top of Whitehall, just south of Trafalgar Square. It was here, in 1291, that Edward I erected the last of the series of 13 crosses that marked the stages in the funeral procession of his greatly loved wife Eleanor of Castile from Lincolnshire to Westminster Abbey the previous year. The cross was destroyed in 1647 (a replica now stands in front of Charing Cross Station). Today, a plaque in the pavement marks the spot from which all distances to and from Central London are measured and here too stands a fine bronze **equestrian statue of Charles I** by Hubert Le Sueur (1633), which amazingly survived the Civil War. The pedestal is by Joshua Marshall, from a design by Wren. King Charles was known to have been a very small man and his monument today looks diminutive indeed amid the crowds and the endless double-decker buses, but he is not forgotten: a single rose is often to be seen attached to the side of the plinth and every year on the Sunday closest to 30th January, the anniversary of King Charles's execution in 1649, the English Civil War Society organises a march down The Mall in full period costume and the statue is adorned with wreaths. At the restoration of the monarchy in 1660, Charles II's triumphal procession was greeted here by 600 pikemen and later in the same year it was the scene of the execution of Thomas Harrison and seven other regicides, witnessed by Pepys, who wrote, 'I went out to Charing Cross, to see Major-general Harrison hanged, drawn, and quartered; which was done there, he looking as cheerful as any man could do in that condition. He was presently cut down, and his head and heart shown to the people, at which there was great shouts of joy...Thus it was my chance to see the King beheaded at White Hall, and to see the first blood shed in revenge for the blood of the King at Charing Cross.' (*Diary, 13th Oct 1660.*)

King Charles I's horse faces down Whitehall, a street whose name comes from the pale stone used to build Cardinal Wolsey's palace which once stood here. It is now associated with the offices and ministries of temporal government, although many of those have now moved away. At the top of the street, on the right-hand corner, is **Drummond's Bank**, founded as a private bank in 1717. Former account holders include George III, Alexander Pope, Robert Adam, Thomas Gainsborough and Beau Brummell. (*For other landmarks in Whitehall, see p. 150.*) Beyond the curved building on the opposite corner is **Northumberland Avenue**, a wide boulevard lined with imposing buildings over land anciently owned by the Dukes of Northumberland. It was created to connect the Trafalgar Square with the new Embankment.

ST MARTIN-IN-THE-FIELDS

The large church of St Martin-in-the-Fields (*map p. 635, F1; stmartin-in-the-fields.org*), at the northeast corner of Trafalgar Square, is known as the 'Church of the Ever Open Door', offering sanctuary to all and particularly known for its work with the homeless. The building is the work of James Gibbs (1722–6), modelled on a Classical temple with a hexastyle porch, behind which protrude the traditional tower and steeple. The church's design has been imitated across the USA and in India (St Andrew's Church, Edgmore, Chennai, built in 1821, is directly modelled on it). Inside, the ceiling is richly decorated by Artari and Bagutti. There is a tureen-shaped font (1689) from the previous church on this site, and a handsome 18th-century pulpit brought here after 1858. The pews have been retained, with 'closet' pews in the side aisles. The **east window**, by Iranian-born Shirazeh Houshiary (2008), has panes of clear glass divided by iron bars clustered and bending in the centre around a large hole, as if torn into the fabric of the regular grille. The original window was destroyed in WWII and the distortion of the new window evokes this, while at the same time the glazing bars are grouped to suggest the shape of a cross, a symbol of redemption.

In this church Charles II was christened and Nell Gwyn was buried. The burials of Roubiliac, Chippendale and John Hunter are also recorded. The first broadcast religious service took place here in 1924. The church is a regular venue for the memorial services of actors and politicians. It is also the parish church of the Royal Family and of no. 10 Downing Street.

St Martin divides his cloak, giving half to a beggar. Detail of the door of the church of St Martin-in-the-Fields.

The church provided the first home for the now world-famous Academy of St Martin-in-the-Fields orchestra. The musical tradition continues, with regular concerts. The brick-vaulted crypt is home to a popular café. Also in the basement are a bookshop, gift shop and brass-rubbing centre. Off the crypt is a gallery with early gravestones, an 18th-century whipping post and a statue of London's first Pearly King, Henry Croft (d. 1930; *see p. 53*), which was brought here in 2002 from St Pancras. The statue, commissioned in 1931 after Croft's death, shows him wearing the pearly costume which he donned in order to raise money for various hospitals and charities.

Further down (modern stairs beyond the brass-rubbing centre) is the Bishop Ho Ming Wah Chinese Community Centre, where people gather to do T'ai Chi; and the Dick Sheppard Chapel (1954), a memorial to the vicar who began the church's tradition of social service by giving refuge to soldiers on their way to fight in the trenches.

THE NATIONAL GALLERY

Map p. 635, F1–F2. Underground: Charing Cross, Leicester Square. Free. nationalgallery. org.uk.

The National Gallery's collection of Western European art, spanning the period c. 1250–1900, is one of the finest in the world. The Italian early and high Renaissance collection is particularly rich, with numerous works of international significance. There are also important early Netherlandish works; major holdings of 17th-century Dutch and Flemish masters, including Rembrandt, Rubens and Van Dyck; notable works by the French masters Claude and Poussin; as well as a significant collection of French Impressionist pictures. Although Tate Britain is the official home of British art, the National Gallery also has some seminal masterpieces of the British School.

Entrance to the National Gallery has always been free. Even during World War Two, when the collection was removed for safety to old mining caves in Wales, one masterpiece per month was shown at the gallery, at risk in the capital alongside Londoners. During its evacuation, much scholarly study of the collection was undertaken, resulting in published catalogues which set the international standard.

HISTORY OF THE GALLERY

Compared with other national galleries in Europe, this one was established relatively late. In 1824, the artist and collector Sir George Beaumont offered his collection to the nation with two provisos: that the government purchase the artworks of the wealthy banker John Julius Angerstein, one of the finest private collections in London, and that suitable accommodation be found for them. Angerstein's 38 Italian, Dutch, Flemish and British works form the core of the National Gallery's holding. Sebastiano del Piombo's magnificent *Raising of Lazarus* was officially the first work to enter the collection (it has the accession number NG1). In 1826 those first works were joined by Beaumont's own 16 pictures, which included several masterpieces: Canaletto's *The Stonemason's Yard*; Rubens' *View of Het Steen* (Beaumont considered Rubens 'the Shakespeare of painting'); and Beaumont's personal favourite, Claude's *Landscape with Hagar and the Angel*, which travelled with him whenever he left London for his country home.

In 1851 came J.M.W. Turner's overwhelming bequest of over 1,000 of his own watercolours, drawings and oils. In 1871 the collection of the late Prime Minister Sir Robert Peel came to the gallery, a distinguished assembly of mainly Dutch and Flemish pictures, including Hobbema's supreme *Avenue at Middelharnis* and Rubens' *Chapeau de Paille*. Since its foundation—and particularly from 1855, when Sir Charles Eastlake became Director—the gallery has also been making acquisitions of its own. Eastlake travelled throughout Italy purchasing important works, mainly early Italian 'Primitives'. Acquisitions continue—no longer solely of European art. In 2014 the first major American painting entered the collection: George Bellows' 1912 *Men of the Docks*, showing shipyard workers in Manhattan. The National Gallery celebrated its bicentenary in 2024.

The building: exterior

Built between 1833 and 1838 by William Wilkins, the building is dignified but somehow not imposing, its long façade punctuated with a central portico with Corinthian columns, and a dome and further porticoes to east and west, with column bases and capitals salvaged from the recently demolished Carlton House (*p. 160*).

A new east wing extension, designed by E.M. Barry, was completed in 1876. The building was further added to in 1907–11 with new galleries behind Wilkins' west wing. The Northern Extension was built in 1970–5. To the left of the main building, the Sainsbury Wing was completed in 1991 to designs by Venturi and Scott Brown, who won the commission after the original scheme, the winner of an architectural competition, was famously denounced by King Charles, when Prince of Wales, as a 'monstrous carbuncle on the face of a much-loved friend'. In a Postmodern classical style which acknowledges Wilkins' building, the new wing's main feature is a giant, broad and tall staircase which rises from the entrance foyer up to the main gallery level, with views over Trafalgar Square. Its Getty entrance and foyer (Dixon/Jones 2004) allows entry directly from Trafalgar Square, rather than up the main portico stairs.

The building: interior
Between 1885 and 1887 Sir John Taylor added the **Central Hall**, an architecturally important space with richly-coloured Venetian wall fabric, and the grand **Main Vestibule** (or Staircase Hall), whose pavement was later adorned by four **mosaic pavements by Boris Anrep**, commissioned in 1928–33. The foremost mosaicist working in Britain, Anrep's themes were *The Labours of Life* (west vestibule, 1928), *The Pleasures of Life* (east vestibule, 1929) and *The Awakening of the Muses* (portico entrance landing, 1933). *Modern Virtues* (north vestibule) followed later, in 1952. Anrep included many portraits of famous people (and also of his friends): Augustus John appears as Neptune; Margot Fonteyn (*Delectation*); Edith Sitwell (*Sixth Sense*); Bertrand Russell (*Lucidity*); Churchill (*Defiance*); Greta Garbo (*Tragic Muse*) and Virginia Woolf (*Muse of History*). The octagonal **Rotunda** at the centre of the 1870s' east extension to the main building has green Genoa marble columns, white and gilded plasterwork and a domed ceiling of etched glass panels.

The collection

Paintings are frequently moved, sent out on loan, or taken in for restoration, and extensive refurbishment was in progress at the time of writing, in connection with the gallery's bicentenary. To locate a particular work of art, ask at one of the information desks or download a floorplan from the website: nationalgallery.org.uk. The description below, ordered by date and school, covers the collection's highlights, many of which are long-established favourites.

Early Italy (13th–15th centuries)
The classic illustration of the **development of art in Italy** from the hieratic Middle Ages to the human focus of the Renaissance is furnished by Margarito of Arezzo's 1260s Byzantine icon-like *Virgin and Child*, the earliest Italian work in the collection; by Duccio's *Annunciation, Jesus Opens the Eyes of a Blind Man* and *Transfiguration*, predella panels from his masterwork, the *Maestà*, the high altarpiece of Siena Cathedral (1311); and lastly by Giotto's *Pentecost*. Leonardo da Vinci's large cartoon, *The Virgin and Child with St Anne and St John the Baptist* (c. 1499–1500), is a large-scale preparatory drawing for a painting commissioned by Louis XII of France.

Why bicker over white wine versus red when you can settle your differences and have both? Loretta Young as 'Compromise' in a mosaic by Boris Anrep in the pavement of the National Gallery Vestibule (1952).

Not Italian, but belonging to this period, is the outstanding **Wilton Diptych** (c. 1395), the highpoint of painting to survive from medieval England. Possibly of French authorship, it shows Richard II being presented to the Virgin and Child, accompanied by St John, St Edmund and St Edward the Confessor.

Early **Florentine works** include Lorenzo Monaco's brilliantly coloured *Coronation of the Virgin* (c. 1414); the only documented painting by Masaccio (a 1426 *Virgin and Child*, part of the altarpiece for the chapel of Santa Maria del Carmine, Pisa); and Fra' Angelico's *Christ Glorified in the Court of Heaven* (before 1435), with its ranks of angels.

Sienese art includes works by Sassetta, a leading artist of the early 15th century; and Giovanni di Paolo's *Scenes from the Life of St John the Baptist*, the desert realised as tall, craggy mountains. Uccello's *Battle of San Romano*, from Palazzo Medici, shows the mercenary general Niccolò da Tolentino in a magnificent head-dress on a rearing white charger (the other two parts of this painting are in the Uffizi and the Louvre).

Works by **Botticelli** include the *Mystic Nativity*, one of the gallery's best-known works, showing the Virgin kneeling in adoration, with a circle of dancing angels above the stable. Leonardo da Vinci's great *Virgin of the Rocks* (c. 1508), the central panel for the altarpiece of the oratory of the Milanese Confraternity of the Immaculate Conception, is one of the gallery's most renowned works.

From **Venice and the Veneto**, 1450–1500, are important works by Mantegna, including the *Agony in the Garden*, the slumbering Apostles in the foreground with rabbits hopping on the road along which Judas conducts the Roman soldiers; and works by the great Giovanni Bellini, Mantegna's brother-in-law, including the *Madonna of the Meadow* and his famous portrait of Doge Leonardo Loredan, in an expensive gold and silver damask robe, prominent against a blue background.

In a separate gallery are outstanding masterpieces by **Piero della Francesca**, who worked chiefly in his native Borgo Sansepolcro, Tuscany, and was recognised as a rare and extraordinary talent in the second half of the 20th century. The National Gallery has exceptional works by him, including the *Baptism of Christ*, a work of great delicacy, and *The Nativity*, an unfinished work allowing insight into his working methods.

Early Netherlands and Germany (13th–15th centuries)

Unlike early Italian works, which are painted in egg tempera, early Netherlandish and German works are in oil on panel. The technique, in fact, is thought to have been brought from the Netherlands to Italy by **Antonello da Messina**, who painted the famous *St Jerome in his Study*, with splendid architectural perspectives.

One of the greatest artists of his day was **Jan van Eyck**, who worked for Philip, Duke of Burgundy at Bruges. One of the most important of the National Gallery's pictures is his remarkable *Arnolfini Portrait*, probably a marriage portrait, the couple standing in a well-furnished room, their reflections seen in the round mirror in the background.

The outstanding Netherlandish painter of his time was **Rogier van der Weyden**, who worked in Brussels and probably for the Burgundian court. His beautiful *Magdalen Reading* (c. 1440–50) has been cut down from a once-large altarpiece. There are also works by Dieric Bouts, Memling and the leading Antwerp painter Quinten Massys.

Southern German painting includes *The Painter's Father* (1497), by **Albrecht Dürer**, one of the greatest European artists of his age.

Italian Renaissance works (16th century)

The National Gallery's Italian Renaissance collection is extensive and excellent. **Correggio**'s well known *School of Love* (c. 1525) was purchased in 1824. Major works by Florentine and Roman artists include **Michelangelo**'s unfinished *Entombment*; **Bronzino**'s outstanding *Allegory with Venus and Cupid*, the 'picture of singular beauty' mentioned by Vasari in 1568; **Raphael**'s large *Ansidei Madonna*; his beautiful *Mond Crucifixion* and *St Catherine of Alexandria*, shown twisted towards the sky in a position of holy rapture; his important and influential portrait of Pope Julius II; and the small and gentle *Madonna of the Pinks*, which caused controversy when it was acquired for £22m in 2004. Here also is **Sebastiano del Piombo**'s *Raising of Lazarus*, an 1824 Angerstein foundation work and officially the first to enter the Gallery.

The Gallery has some magnificent works by **Venetian artists**, including Veronese's enormous and impressive *Family of Darius before Alexander*; and *The Rape of Europa*, which came to the gallery in 1831 and was highly esteemed in the 18th and 19th centuries. Tintoretto, Jacopo Bassano, Palma Vecchio and Giorgione are also represented.

The Netherlands and Germany (16th century)

Among the fine collection of 16th-century Netherlandish pictures is **Jan Gossaert's** meticulous, tightly handled *Adoration of the Kings* (c. 1500–15), with angels hovering above the Virgin and Child, the kings bearing their costly gifts and dogs wandering across minutely observed cracked paving invaded by weeds. **Jan Brueghel the Elder's** later depiction of the same subject (1598) provides an interesting contrast. The collapsing stable roof, raised above the meagre hovel from which crowds bathed in holy light flock from all directions, is intensely memorable.

The collection of 16th-century painting from the Protestant states of what are now Germany and Switzerland is of particular note for its works by **Holbein**: *The Ambassadors* is one of the National Gallery's major masterpieces. Painted in 1533 for Jean de Dinteville, French Ambassador at the court of Henry VIII, it shows Dinteville standing with Georges de Selve surrounded by objects symbolic of Humanist learning. The perspective of the distorted skull, bottom centre, is corrected when viewed from the right. *Christina of Denmark* (1538), depicting a prospective bride of Henry VIII, is a rare, early example of full-length portraiture.

Dutch pictures (17th century)

Of the only 30 works known by **Vermeer**, the National Gallery has two: the outstanding *Young Woman Standing at a Virginal* (c. 1670) and *Young Woman Seated at a Virginal*. The two were perhaps intended as a pendant pair, personifying pure, monogamous love and coy licentiousness. **Pieter de Hooch's** *Courtyard of a House in Delft* (1659) seems to symbolise perfect motherhood and domestic order. Also on show is **Hoogstraten's** *Peepshow* (c. 1655–60), a painted box with two viewing holes through which the 3D illusion of a Dutch interior can be seen. From a black and white tiled floor a dog stares up at you, and through a doorway further rooms recede into the distance. On the other side a sleeping figure can be glimpsed in bed. Of such boxes to survive, this is the finest and most elaborate. Numerous works by **Gerrit Dou**, the principal artist of the Leiden *fijnschilders* ('fine painters'), are on show, including his *Poulterer's Shop* (c. 1670): game birds and a hanging hare are shown in a virtuoso performance of meticulous detail.

Works by **Cuyp** and the Dutch Italianate landscapists include Cuyp's brilliant *River Landscape with a Horseman and Peasants* (c. 1658–60), suffused with a beautiful golden light. It was bought by the Earl of Bute in the 1760s and is supposedly the picture that stimulated the admiration of Cuyp (and his landscapes populated by cows) among British collectors. **Hobbema's** *Avenue at Middelharnis* (1689), with its central avenues of trees receding into the distance, was formerly owned by Robert Peel and is one of the gallery's best-loved works. **Jacob van Ruisdael** was the most famous landscapist of his day and his *Landscape with a Ruined Castle and a Church* (c. 1665–70) is a famous work with light playing on the fields below scudding clouds.

The National Gallery has a large collection of **Rembrandt**'s works, both portraits and large-scale biblical pictures. The *Woman Taken in Adultery* (1644) was one of Angerstein's 1824 foundation works; the *Lamentation over the Dead Christ* was Beaumont's; and the famous *A Woman Bathing in a Stream* (1654), probably Hendrickje Stoffels, who lived in Rembrandt's household, came to the gallery in 1831. The important *Belshazzar's Feast* (c. 1635) is an early attempt by Rembrandt to establish himself as a large-scale history painter. He shows the moment when, having served wine in sacred vessels looted from the Temple in Jerusalem, Belshazzar observes the appearance of Hebrew writing on a wall predicting the fall of his kingdom.

Flemish pictures (17th century)

There is a large and impressive collection of works by the great Baroque artist **Rubens**. Many arrived at the gallery in the 19th century, including the *Rape of the Sabine Women* (1635–40), acquired in 1824; *A View of Het Steen in the Early Morning*, showing Rubens' country estate purchased in 1635 (part of the Beaumont bequest); and the important *Peace and War*, painted when Rubens was in England on a diplomatic mission to negotiate peace with Spain (presented by the Duke of Sutherland in 1828). Other works produced for English patrons include the portrait of the celebrated art connoisseur and collector Thomas Howard, Earl of Arundel. One of the most famous pictures in the National Gallery is *Le Chapeau de Paille*, part of the Peel collection purchased in 1871 (the name of the picture dates back to the 18th century). Other important works include *The Watering Place*, a landscape which inspired Constable's work of the same name.

Rubens' most famous pupil, **Van Dyck**, was also the most celebrated and influential artist working in Britain in the 17th century, official painter to the King, for whom he produced the enormous *Equestrian Portrait of Charles I* (c. 1637–8). He was knighted for his services.

Italian pictures (17th century)

By **Caravaggio** there is the early *Supper at Emmaus* (1601) as well as the late *Salome Receives the Head of St John the Baptist*, with theatrical, dramatic lighting and intense passion. Works by the **Bolognese school** (Annibale Carracci, Guido Reni and Guercino) are also on display. **Orazio Gentileschi**'s large and imposing *Finding of Moses* is an important work executed in England in the 1630s when the artist was in the service of Charles I and his queen, Henrietta Maria. His daughter and pupil **Artemisia Gentileschi**'s *Self-portrait as St Catherine of Alexandria* was acquired by the Gallery in 2017.

French pictures (17th century)

Rooms 19 and 20 are dedicated to the two great French landscape artists **Poussin** and **Claude**. Both the foundation Angerstein and Beaumont collections contained Claude, reflecting the high esteem in which British collectors held his work. *Landscape with Hagar and the Angel* was Beaumont's favourite picture. The gallery's collection of his hugely influential, poetic classical landscapes, peopled by figures from Classical mythology and the Bible, includes *The Enchanted Castle* (1664), which influenced Keats's 'Ode to a Nightingale'. When J.M.W. Turner bequeathed his pictures to the nation he stipulated that two of them, *Dido Building Carthage* and *Sun Rising through Vapour*, were to be shown alongside two of Angerstein's Claudes, *Seaport with the Embarkation of the Queen of Sheba* and *Landscape with the Marriage of Isaac and Rebekah*. They hang together, the modern genius alongside the influential predecessor.

Spanish pictures (17th century)
The highly individual style of **El Greco** is represented by *Christ Driving the Traders from the Temple* (c. 1600). Important works by **Velázquez**, expressing the dignity of the court of Philip IV, include the majestic 1630s full-length of the king, in a splendid costume with sparkling silver embroidery; and the exceptional *Toilet of Venus* ('*The Rokeby Venus*'; c. 1647–51), the only surviving female nude by the artist, famously slashed by a suffragette in 1914 and again attacked by eco-protesters in 2023. **Zurbarán**'s *St Francis in Meditation* shows the kneeling saint with uncompromising realism, in a stark interior, his face partially hidden by the dramatic shadow cast by his hood. **Murillo**'s more gentle works, with their soft style and colouring (known as *estilo vaporoso*), include his self-portrait, *Peasant Boy Leaning on a Sill* and the sweet and gentle *The Two Trinities* (1681–2).

Italy (18th–early 20th centuries)
Among many works by the Italian *vedutisti* are **Canaletto**'s excellent *Stonemason's Yard*, further Venetian views by Canaletto and **Guardi**, and two English works by Canaletto: *The Rotunda at Ranelagh* and *Eton College*. Canaletto owed his popularity in this country largely to the devoted patronage of Joseph Smith, Consul in Venice in the 1740s. **Tiepolo** is well represented with a good range of works, including the lovely and very characteristic *Allegory with Venus and Time*.

British School (18th–early 20th centuries)
Important full-length works include **Sir Thomas Lawrence**'s *Queen Charlotte* (1789–90), shown seated at Windsor Castle in expensive pearls, with a view of Eton College chapel through the window. **Hogarth's** *Marriage à la Mode* series, a moralising commentary on contemporary life, was part of Angerstein's collection.

   Gainsborough is represented by his early *Mr and Mrs Andrews*, showing a genteel couple outdoors in their park, and by his portrait of the actress Mrs Siddons, of whom he is said to have complained while painting it: 'Confound her nose, there's no end to it!' **Constable**'s well-known *Hay-Wain* and *The Cornfield* (1826) have done much to inform the quintessential idea of the English countryside. By Constable too is *The Cenotaph to Reynolds' Memory, Coleorton*. The monument had been erected in the grounds at Coleorton, Sir George Beaumont's country home, in 1812.

   Stubbs' monumental *Whistlejacket* shows a great rearing, riderless horse against a stark background. Other pictures include **Joseph Wright of Derby**'s famous *An Experiment on a Bird in the Air Pump* (1768) as well as **Turner**'s celebrated *The Fighting 'Temeraire', tugged to her Last Berth to be broken up* (1839) and his *Rain, Steam and*

Speed—The Great Western Railway (before 1844). Sargent's excellent *Lord Ribblesdale* (1902) is a likeness of a former trustee of the National Gallery.

France (18th–early 20th centuries)

French 19th-century Academy painting includes works by Géricault and **Delacroix**; and **Ingres**' *Mme Moitessier* (1844–56), the wife of a wealthy banker, shown seated in her finery. The picture, with its extraordinary porcelain finish, took Ingres twelve years to complete. **Rosa Bonheur**'s *The Horse Fair* (1853) was sensational in its day. To paint it, in the seething Boulevard de l'Hôpital in Paris, the artist had sought permission from the police to disguise herself as a man.

The gallery has an excellent Impressionist collection which includes several outstanding masterpieces: **Manet**'s *Music in the Tuileries Gardens* and his *Execution of Maximilian* (1867–68), the latter the second version he painted of the execution by firing squad of Archduke Maximilian, younger brother of the Emperor Franz Joseph of Austria, who had been installed as Emperor of Mexico by Napoleon III but was captured and executed by Mexican forces after the withdrawal of French troops. The mutilated fragments of the picture were rescued and pieced together by Degas.

Monet's work includes *Gare St-Lazare* (1877), *The Water-Lily Pond* (1879), *The Beach at Trouville* (1870) and *The Thames below Westminster* (1871). **Seurat**'s *Bathers at Asnières* is partly executed in his 'pointillism' technique. **Renoir**'s supreme *Les Parapluies* is also here.

The final decades of the 19th century are represented with works by **Cézanne**, including his well-known *Bathers*, '*Les Grandes Baigneuses*', one of three large works of the same theme. Of **Van Gogh**'s work, the gallery has one of the versions of his famous *Sunflowers* (1888), at which climate protesters hurled tomato soup in 2023, as well as *Van Gogh's Chair*, painted at Arles in November 1888 when he was working in the company of Gauguin. *A Wheatfield with Cypresses* was painted in September 1889 at the mental asylum at St-Rémy. **Henri Rousseau**'s *Tiger in a Tropical Storm* ('*Surprised!*') is the first of his over 20 jungle pictures (1891).

The Swiss painter **Ferdinand Hodler**'s *Kien Valley with the Blüemlisalp Massif* (1902) was acquired by the Gallery in 2022. Another recent acquisition is the *Portrait of Charlotte Cuhrt* (1910) by the German Expressionist painter **Max Pechstein**.

ON & AROUND THE STRAND

Map p. 636, A3–A2. Underground: Charing Cross.

The Strand is a major thoroughfare, curving east for nearly three quarters of a mile, between Trafalgar Square and Temple Bar, which marks the official boundary between Westminster and the City of London. This invisible line is marked by two boundary dragons, painted silver and red, who rear up proffering the City's coat of arms. The

Strand is the ancient link between the City and the Palace of Westminster and is still the official processional route between the two. Originally it ran along the banks of the Thames—hence its name—and from the 12th and 13th centuries bishops and royal courtiers built grand residences that led down to the water. These are now mainly referenced by street names and today, since the building of Victoria Embankment, the Strand is no longer on the river. When Charing Cross Station was first built, however, it provided a train-boat service to Europe; the popular turn-of-the-20th-century music hall song 'Let's All Go Down The Strand' tells of a group of tourists who planned to take it:

> One night a half a dozen tourists
> spent the night together in Trafalgar Square.
> A fortnight's tour on the Continent was planned
> and each had his portmanteau in his hand.
> Down the Rhine they meant to have a picnic
> 'til Jones said, 'I must decline.
> Boys you'll be advised by me
> to stay away from Germany,
> What's the good of going down the Rhine?
> Let's all go down the Strand (have a banana),
> let's all go down the Strand.
> I'll be the leader, you can march behind,
> come with me and see what we can find...'

ALONG THE STRAND TO THE NORTH

At the top of the Strand on the left facing Trafalgar Square is **South Africa House** (Sir Herbert Baker, 1933), decorated with elephant and antelope mascarons. From its balcony in August 1996, Nelson Mandela addressed a crowd of thousands. Beyond it, opposite Charing Cross Station, the cream stucco turreted façade with shops at ground level is Nash's **West Strand Improvements** of 1830–2. At the centre, behind a modern glass screen, is Coutts' Bank (established 1692), traditionally bankers to Britain's aristocracy although today, if you have at least £1 million in liquid funds, you might be considered as a client. The bank was at the centre of a furore in 2023 after it closed the account of prominent Brexit campaigner Nigel Farage.

Where the building ends, on Agar Street, is **Zimbabwe House**, designed by Charles Holden as the British Medical Association in 1907–8. Note the stained-glass Aesculapian snake above the doorway. The nude statues above the second-floor windows are by Jacob Epstein, apparently carved *in situ*. In 1937 their eroded parts were taken off, giving them their current maimed appearance. The building opposite it, with a little Doric porch, is the **former Charing Cross Hospital** (now a police station), its foundation stone laid in 1831.

In the block between Bedford and Southampton streets are two popular theatres: the Adelphi (1806; rebuilt twice) and the Vaudeville (1870): this was Victorian London's

Reminiscent of Michelangelo's half-finished *Slaves*: the mutilated nude figures by Jacob Epstein (1937) on the façade of Zimbabwe House.

theatre district, close to Covent Garden. In between, a narrow ceramic-tiled passage, Old Bull Yard, leads to the tiny Nell Gwynne pub. At no. 339 is Stanley Gibbons, 'the home of stamp collecting since 1856'.

ALONG THE STRAND TO THE SOUTH

CRAVEN STREET

Leading off the Strand towards the Thames is Craven Street, lined by simple terraced houses in dark brick. At no. 42 is the **British Optical Association Museum** (*open by appointment only; college-optometrists.org/the-british-optical-association-museum*), whose collection includes over 2,000 pairs of spectacles from the 17th century to the present as well as a portrait of Benjamin Franklin sporting a pair of *pince-nez*. Franklin is usually credited with the invention of bifocals.

It is appropriate that Franklin should be represented in the museum because at no. 36 is **Benjamin Franklin House** (*open for tours; benjaminfranklinhouse.org*), an elegant Georgian townhouse of 1730 and the only surviving London home of Benjamin Franklin, the great American statesman and scientist, who lived here from 1757–75. It was here that he sat at the windows 'air bathing', learnt to play the harp, guitar and violin, and conducted political negotiations with William Pitt the Elder on the eve of the American Revolution. While in London, Franklin forged friendships with many leading intellectuals and continued with his many writings and experiments, including the invention of the lightning conductor (it is also said that he performed alarming demonstrations of electricity at dinner parties). The staircase and much of the panelling is original. During restoration, a pit with human remains was discovered in the basement—probably connected to the anatomy school run by Franklin's friend William Hewson. Hewson is said to have died of blood poisoning after cutting himself during a dissection.

The German poet and essayist Heinrich Heine (d. 1856) lived at no. 32 Craven St and no. 25 was home to Herman Melville, author of *Moby Dick*.

CHARING CROSS STATION AND VILLIERS STREET

This busy commuter station (*map p. 636, A3*) brings passengers from southeast London and the south coast across the Thames via Hungerford Bridge. The **station** (John Hawkshaw, 1863–5) occupies the site of Hungerford Market (1682). The townhouse of Walter, 1st Baron Hungerford (d. 1449), a knight who fought at the Battle of Agincourt, stood here from 1425. The adjoining **former Charing Cross Hotel** (now the Clermont), with painted white, red and green decorative ironwork, was designed by E.M. Barry—it was one of the first buildings to be faced with artificial stone, in this case pale painted terracotta. In the paved forecourt, in front of the cab rank, stands an elaborate **neo-Gothic Cross** (E.M. Barry, 1865; restored) based on the original cross dedicated to Eleanor of Castile (wife of Edward I) which stood at the top of Whitehall to mark the last resting place of her bier on its journey from Lincolnshire to Westminster Abbey for burial in 1290 (*see p. 187*). Behind the station frontage, Terry Farrell's huge Post-modern office and shopping complex, **Embankment Place** (1986–91), stretches over the tracks and arches, down Villiers Street and all the way to Hungerford Bridge. The river façade, all curves and towers, is best observed from the Embankment (better still from the South Bank); it looks like a giant locomotive bursting out onto the Thames.

The part-pedestrianised **Villiers Street**, sloping down to the Thames, was once the site of York House, the residence of the Archbishop of York, owned from the 1620s by the royal favourite George Villiers, 1st Duke of Buckingham, and after the Civil War by his son, the 2nd Duke. At no. 47 in Kipling House (once the residence of the writer Rudyard Kipling) is **Gordon's**, London's oldest wine bar (est. 1890), a popular place for an after-work drink (its outdoor seating area overlooks Victoria Embankment Gardens).

VICTORIA EMBANKMENT AND GARDENS

The idea of creating an embankment along the Thames had been first suggested by Christopher Wren after the Great Fire but the ambitious piece of planning did not take shape until the mid-19th century, when it was carried out to a design by civil engineer Sir Joseph Bazalgette (*for the history, including the 'Great Stink', see p. 148*). The completed Embankment runs from Westminster Bridge to Blackfriars Bridge. The section that lies below the Strand begins at Charing Cross Tube station. Built into the river wall by **Hungerford Bridge** is a bronze portrait medallion of W.S. Gilbert (d. 1911), one half of the comedy-opera duo Gilbert and Sullivan, whose operettas were performed at the nearby Savoy Theatre. 'His foe was folly and his weapon wit'; the small sculptures represent *Tragedy* and *Comedy*.

Shell Mex House (1930s) and Cleopatra's Needle (1450 BC), on the Victoria Embankment.

Victoria Embankment Gardens are an elongated banana-shaped stretch of greenery planted with shrubs, trees, a small lily pond and flowerbeds, amongst which are several statues. Beautifully maintained, they are popular for sunbathing, picnicking, sitting and chatting or simply relaxing on one of the numerous benches. The gardens are overlooked by the façades of several of the Strand buildings, including the New Adelphi (*see below*), the Savoy Hotel (*see overleaf*) and the 1930s' **Shell Mex House**, with its distinctive, monumental façade and giant clock face.

Statues and monuments in the gardens include Robert Raikes, founder of Sunday Schools; a bronze fountain medallion of the blind campaigner for women's rights, Henry Fawcett (his blindness indicated by his closed eyes); and a bronze bust of Arthur Sullivan (the other half of Gilbert and Sullivan, d. 1900) by William Goscombe John (a topless maiden weeps against his plinth). In front of the Savoy is a small seating area and the D'Oyly Carte memorial.

On the river itself stands London's oldest monument: the so-called **Cleopatra's Needle**, an ancient Egyptian obelisk, erected in 1878 and now much weathered by acid rain and pollution. It is flanked by two large bronze sphinxes, c. 1882. The obelisk dates from 1450 BC and consists of a single piece of Aswan granite, quarried by Thutmose III. It was originally one of a pair at Heliopolis; the other now stands in New York's Central Park. The hieroglyphs were added by Ramesses II, 200 years later. Emperor Augustus had the obelisks moved to Alexandria, Cleopatra's city, in 12 BC. In 1819, Mohammed Ali, Viceroy of Egypt, presented the Needle to the British people in memory of Nelson and Abercromby and their successful Egyptian campaigns. However, it lay unclaimed in the desert until Prince Albert pressed for it to brought to London (Paris had been similarly presented with an obelisk and had already erected it). Eventually it cost £10,000 and six sailors' lives to tow the obelisk across the treacherous seas in a floating iron cylinder: at one point it was abandoned to the waves in the Bay of Biscay, but eventually recovered. It arrived in 1878 and after much disagreement, the site on the Embankment was chosen. The names of the sailors who died bringing the Needle to London are commemorated on a plaque at its base; beneath it is buried an 1878 time capsule, which includes photographs of beauties of the day.

The *pièce de résistance* of the gardens, however, the last relic of the Strand's historic past, when it was lined with courtly mansions, is the **water-gate of York House**. Built in 1626 by Nicholas Stone for George Villiers, 1st Duke of Buckingham, its rusticated Italianate façade, much eroded, is surmounted by two lions on either side of the Buckingham coat of arms. Before the Embankment was built, the Thames reached this point. Behind it is the narrow Watergate Walk (with the outdoor seating of Gordon's wine bar) and a flight of steps leading up to **Buckingham Street**, built on the site of York House. Here is an enclave of houses dating from the late 17th and early 18th centuries, many with fine doorcases. Samuel Pepys lived at no. 12 in 1679–88. Charles Dickens lived on the site of no. 15.

JOHN ADAM STREET AND THE ADELPHI

From the top of Buckingham Street, John Adam Street (*map p. 636, A3*) runs parallel with the Strand. On the site of no. 16 lived the caricaturist Thomas Rowlandson, who, along with Cruikshank and the bitingly satirical Gillray, lampooned English social and political life from the 1790s. Further on, the quadrangle made up of John Adam Street, Robert Street, Adelphi Terrace and Adam Street, is what remains of the **Adelphi**, an ambitious residential project built from 1768 by the four Adam brothers, John, Robert, James and William (Adelphi means 'brothers' in Greek). The development, on the site of Durham House, former residence of the Bishop of Durham, where Anne Boleyn had lived for a time, involved the building of high-quality residential streets, houses and terraces, all of uniform design, supported on an embankment of arches and subterranean vaults which were to be leased to river trade. Adelphi Terrace is the site of Royal Terrace, where 24 houses overlooked the river, their design inspired by the Palace of Diocletian at Split in Croatia. Directly behind and on either side were similar streets of quality housing. The project was a financial disaster, bringing near-bankruptcy on the brothers, and in 1774 a lottery was authorised by Parliament to rescue the enterprise. Among those who did come to live here, apart from the architects and builders themselves, were Sir Richard Arkwright, Charles Booth, Richard d'Oyly

Carte, David Garrick, Charles Dickens (the Adelphi features in *David Copperfield*), George Bernard Shaw, J.M. Barrie, H.G. Wells and John Galsworthy. In 1936–8 the entire central part was demolished and replaced by the **New Adelphi**, the current colossal Art Moderne office block, by Collcutt and Hamp, in brick, Portland stone and bronze, with much carved ornament (busy putti, signs of the Zodiac, etc.) and over the river terrace, huge sculptures representing *Dawn*, *Contemplation*, *Inspiration* and *Night*. Today, in the surrounding side streets, a few of the fine original houses survive; note those with stucco pilasters covered in Robert Adam's repeating anthemion motifs. At its base, between Savoy Place and York Buildings, is **Lower Robert Street**, one of the surviving vaults and now a narrow, winding cut-through and part of a London cab driver's 'Knowledge'. It is said to be haunted by a Victorian prostitute, 'Poor Jenny'. For security, the alley is closed at night.

The **Royal Society of Arts** (RSA) occupies a fine Adam building (no. 8 John Adam St) with an Ionic portico, Venetian window and statuary on the roof. The Society was established in 1754 to foster art, manufacture and trade. The equally fine interior may be visited by appointment or on designated open days (*thersa.org*). The Great Room features James Barry's painting cycle *The Progress of Human Knowledge*, hung below the cornice.

Adam Street leads back to the Strand. The enormous building with red granite columns at nos 77–86 is what remains of the **former Cecil Hotel**, the largest hotel in Europe when it opened in 1885, though eclipsed in grandeur just four years later by the Savoy (*see below*). A short way further up are the fine, decorated shopfronts of the Savoy Taylors Guild and the Coal Hole pub. In **Carting Lane**, a narrow side street leading down past the Coal Hole, a lone Victorian streetlamp survives from Bazalgette's time, ingeniously powered by methane gas rising from the sewers of the Savoy Hotel.

THE SAVOY HOTEL

The Savoy Hotel (*map p. 636, A2–A3*) opened in 1889. The block that faces the Thames is the original hotel; the block facing the Strand dates from 1904, though the entire building has been much altered from the original plans by Thomas Collcutt and the Arts and Crafts designer A.H. Mackmurdo. In a multi-million pound refurbishment in 2007–10, all the original contents were sold at auction and many of the interior spaces now aim to evoke the 'decadent' chic of the 1930s, though Collcutt's front hall, with its bas-reliefs of the Seasons, has been retained (and now has a painting of the Thames riverfront and York House with its water-gate; *see previous page*). Today the Savoy is still one of the most luxurious hotels in the world, managed by the Fairmont group. Afternoon tea at the Savoy, or drinks in its American Bar, or dinner at the Savoy Grill, remain near the top of many people's London 'to-do' list.

The hotel was conceived by the theatre impresario Richard d'Oyly Carte, renowned for his collaboration with the comic opera duo Gilbert and Sullivan (hence the monuments to all three in Victoria Embankment Gardens). Adjacent to the Savoy is D'Oyly Carte's earlier Savoy Theatre (1881; the first theatre to have electricity), built explicitly for the 'Savoy Operas' as they were then called (*The Mikado*, *The Pirates of Penzance*, *Iolanthe*, etc.). The Savoy was one of the first hotels to have private bathrooms with hot and cold running water, electric lifts and 24-hour room service. César Ritz was the first manager and Auguste Escoffier the first chef.

The hotel stands on the site of the Savoy Palace and on the left-hand side of the recessed entrance forecourt, above which are the famous green neon sign and a gilded statue of Count Peter of Savoy, are plaques noting important events in the palace's history. We learn that John of Gaunt, Duke of Lancaster and son of King Edward III, lived here in 'princely luxury' between 1362 and 1381, and that Geoffrey Chaucer often dined with him and wrote a number of his poems here.

Simpson's restaurant, to the left of the Savoy entrance, opened as a chess club in 1828 and became a bastion of English cuisine serving roast beef and Yorkshire pudding. It closed in 2020 and its famous trolleys and other furnishings began turning up for sale from antiques dealers. There are apparently plans to reopen in a new guise.

Gas lamp behind the Savoy Hotel powered by methane from the sewers beneath.

SAVOY PALACE AND CHAPEL

Savoy Palace, built in 1246, was given by Henry III to Peter II of Savoy, 1st Earl of Richmond (d. 1268) and uncle of Eleanor of Provence, Henry III's consort. The palace later passed into the possession of John of Gaunt, Duke of Lancaster, and was known for its magnificence until it burned down and was systematically destroyed during the Peasants' Revolt of 1381. John of Gaunt was the patron of Geoffrey Chaucer and part of *The Canterbury Tales* was written in the palace. John of Valois, King of France, taken prisoner at the Battle of Poitiers by the Black Prince, died here in 1364. On part of the site in 1640 was built Worcester House, home of Edward, 2nd Marquess of Worcester, where in 1660, James II (then Duke of York) married Anne Hyde. Their daughters Mary and Anne would later become Queens of England. In the house in 1658, Oliver Cromwell drew up the Confession of Faith; in 1661 Charles II ordered the Savoy Conference. The house and its grounds stretched all the way to the Thames waterfront and its garden was noted for a particularly luxuriant walnut tree which is said to have given rise to an altercation with the owners of the neighbouring property, whose view it obstructed and who wanted the tree to be cut down. The solution came with a fire in 1695, which carried away both tree and mansion.

Savoy Street leads south to the **King's Chapel of the Savoy**, entered from Savoy Hill (*map p. 636, A2; open Mon–Thur 9–4, Sun 9–1*). After Savoy Palace was destroyed in 1381, and following John of Gaunt's death in 1399, the manor was made over to the Crown. Henry VII built a hospital for the poor and homeless on the land in 1512. The chapel is all that remains of that hospital and was restored after a fire in the 19th century. It is the Chapel of the Royal Victorian Order and the stalls of the knights are marked by small copper plates emblazoned with the arms of the holder. A stained-glass window commemorates Richard d'Oyly Carte (1844–1901). The chapel is a royal peculiar, belonging to the King in his right as Duke of Lancaster.

ALDWYCH

The semicircular street looping south off the Strand, beyond the approach road to Waterloo Bridge, is **Aldwych** (*map p. 636, A2*), a piece of Edwardian town planning lined with grand, imperial buildings. It takes its name from an old colony (*ald wych*) of Danes who settled here before the Conquest. On the east corner, overlooking the church of St Clement Danes, is **Australia House**, built in 1911–18 as the office of the Commonwealth of Australia, utilising building materials especially imported from the Antipodes. High above, *Phoebus* drives the *Horses of the Sun*, who leap headlong out of the pediment. At the top of Aldwych, in the centre, is **Bush House**, designed as a trade centre by the American businessman Irving T. Bush. It was completed in 1935 to designs by Bush's fellow American, the architect Harvey Wiley Corbett. Once the headquarters of the BBC World Service, it is now part of King's College London. Two strategically draped male nudes on the façade lift a torch 'to the friendship of English speaking peoples'. The building faces Kingsway, a busy boulevard leading north to Holborn and Bloomsbury.

ST CLEMENT DANES

The church of St Clement Danes (*map p. 636, B2; sometimes closed for special events, stclementdanesraf.org*), a castaway on a traffic island, was designed by Wren and built in 1679–82 on the site of a much earlier building. It is traditionally believed to be the burial place of Harold Harefoot (King Harold I; d. 1040), son of Canute. The tower, added by James Gibbs in 1719–20, contains a famous peal of bells ('Oranges and lemons, say the bells of St Clement's'). In 1941, the church was gutted by fire and it has been restored as the church of the Royal Air Force. William Webb Ellis, the inventor of rugby football in 1823, was rector here (memorial tablet). Dr Johnson was a worshipper and is commemorated by a statue by Percy Fitzgerald (1910) outside the back (east end). His sculpted book was stolen by vandals and replaced in 1996 by the sculptor Faith Winter.

Before the entrance to the church are three sculptures. One is Hamo Thornycroft's 1905 memorial to William Gladstone, the liberal politician who was four times Prime Minister. His statue is surrounded by four groups of women and children representing *Education*, *Brotherhood*, *Aspiration* and *Courage*. The other two statues are by Faith Winter: Lord Dowding, commander of the RAF Fighter Command during the Battle of Britain, who was also a spiritualist, campaigner for the humane killing of animals and a believer in fairies and ghosts; and fighter pilot Sir Arthur 'Bomber' Harris, in charge

The church of St Clement Danes: interior view.

of Bomber Command during World War Two, who said of the Luftwaffe, 'they sowed the wind, now they are going to reap the whirlwind'.

ST MARY-LE-STRAND AND KING'S COLLEGE

In a pedestrianised enclave in the middle of the Strand stands the church of **St Mary-le-Strand** (*map p. 636, A2; open Tues–Thur 11–4, Sun 10–1; stmarylestrand.org*), with a classical portico and a steeple decorated with flaming urns. This was the first of the 'Queen Anne' churches erected under the 1711 New Churches Act, built by James Gibbs from 1714 and consecrated in 1723. The windows were designed deliberately high up so as to mitigate the noise of traffic. Its Italianate interior is derived from churches in Rome. It is now the church of the Women's Royal Naval Service.

The names of the side streets that lead south to the Embankment from this point, Arundel and Surrey, commemorate the sites of the townhouses of the Earls of Arundel. Adjoining Surrey Street is the Strand campus of **King's College London**, one of the incorporated colleges of the University of London, founded in 1829 by George IV and the Duke of Wellington in response to theological objections to the 'godless' London University (now UCL), founded in 1827. The 1971 façade conceals the interior buildings, built in the 1830s by Robert Smirke. Next door to King's College is Somerset House.

SOMERSET HOUSE & THE COURTAULD GALLERY

Map p. 636, A2. Underground: Temple.

Somerset House, built largely between 1776 and 1801, is the masterpiece of the architect Sir William Chambers, former architectural tutor to George III and from 1769 Comptroller of the King's Office of Works. The complex has two façades, one facing the river and the other facing the Strand. It was designed to house various government offices, in particular the Navy Office (which occupied the river block), as well as three learned societies under royal patronage: the Royal Society, the Society of Antiquaries and the Royal Academy of Arts (of which Chambers was a founder member). These societies moved out in the 19th century and the Courtauld Institute moved in in 1989–90. Their gallery has one of the finest collections in London.

The building

The current building stands on a site originally occupied by the townhouse of the Duke of Somerset (hence the name Somerset House), brother of Henry VIII's third wife, Jane Seymour. He became Lord Protector during the minority of his nephew Edward VI. His position was usurped by a rival and in 1552 he was executed on Tower Hill and his property was ceded to the Crown. In the 17th century Somerset House served as the official residence of successive Queen Consorts. Following the Restoration in 1660, the palace was refurbished for Henrietta Maria, the Queen Dowager, and included a

Cooling off in the Edmond Safra Fountain Court, Somerset House.

Catholic chapel. Samuel Pepys was a frequent visitor to Somerset House and found the new works 'mighty fine and costly'. Under Catherine of Braganza, the Portuguese consort of Charles II, Somerset House and its chapel remained a gravitational centre for Roman Catholics.

Chambers intended his new Somerset House to be a public showcase for English architectural and sculptural design. Its façades are enriched with the work of leading Royal Academician sculptors, exploring themes of maritime glory and royal patronage, symbolic of the building's function. Although probably by John Webb, Chambers believed the gallery, which along with the rest of the palace was demolished to make way for the new building, to have been the work of the revered Inigo Jones, and its pure Classicism inspired his **Strand façade**, which is surmounted by the arms of the British Empire, supported by *Fame* and the *Genius of Britain*, by John Bacon Sr (renewed in 1896). Below this stand *Prudence, Justice, Moderation* and *Valour* (by Agostino Carlini and Giuseppe Ceracchi), the qualities, according to a 1781 description, upon which dominion is built. The bearded heads on the keystones of the arcade, mainly by Joseph Wilton, represent Ocean and the great rivers of England.

Steep steps in front of the west wing lead down to a subterranean passage under the courtyard, the **Deadhouse**, where funerary tablets, the only remnants of the palace's religious past, can be seen (*guided tours only, on Thur and Sat; free; tickets from the Seamen's Hall*).

Between the Thames and Strand wings stretches a spacious central courtyard, the **Edmond Safra Fountain Court**. This is one of the most elegant public spaces in London, with café tables from which one can enjoy Chambers' dignified architecture as well as the rectangular 55-jet fountain (Dixon/Jones 1999–2000). Over Christmas and New Year the latter is covered with a temporary ice rink which, on a dusky winter afternoon with its lighted flambeaux, is extremely atmospheric in these Palladian surroundings.

THE COURTAULD GALLERY

Entrance from the Strand side of Somerset House. Admission charge; courtauld.ac.uk.

Part of the Courtauld Institute of Art, a leading college of art history and conservation, the Courtauld Gallery comprises a series of private collections, the foremost of which is the superlative Impressionist and Post-Impressionist collection of its founder, Samuel Courtauld. The gallery is highly enjoyable to visit. Some of the greatest masterpieces of French Impressionist and Post-Impressionist art are here installed in elegant 18th-century interiors, where they can be appreciated in an atmosphere of delightful calm.

HISTORY OF THE COLLECTIONS

Descended from a Huguenot family of silversmiths, silk weavers and textile manufacturers, Samuel Courtauld (1876–1947) was chairman of the multinational company which in the early 20th century had become a leading producer of the artificial textile rayon (the company still operates but the Courtauld name has been subsumed by mergers and acquisitions). As well as giving £50,000 to the nation for the purchase of works of art for the National Gallery and the Tate (among them Van Gogh's *Sunflowers* and Seurat's *Bathing Party*), Courtauld also built up a private collection, concentrating mainly on the 'modern' French school.

After the death of his wife in 1931, Courtauld gave over the majority of his collection (the rest was bequeathed on his death) to a new art history teaching school (there was no other in the country), which opened its doors as the Courtauld Institute of Art in 1932. Viscount Lee of Fareham was another of the founding fathers. As well as donating Chequers to the nation, for the use of Prime Ministers, he also gave his personal collection to the Courtauld. Wide-ranging, it included the richly carved and painted 1472 Morelli-Nerli *cassoni* (trousseau chests); masterpieces such as Rubens' sketch for *The Descent from the Cross*, the great altarpiece for Antwerp Cathedral; and Cranach's *Adam and Eve*. Most of the gallery's important British pictures also came through Lee.

The collections were further enhanced by the painter and art critic Roger Fry, who had advised Courtauld on his Impressionist purchases. As well as a number of his own works, he bequeathed Bloomsbury Group paintings and Omega Workshops ceramics, as well as works by other artists including Walter Sickert. Sir Robert Witt, the third player in the institute's foundation, gave over 4,000 Old Master drawings as well as his important photographic archive. Further gifts followed: the Mark Gambier-Parry bequest of 1966, consisting mainly of early Italian works; Dr Alistair Hunter's collection of British artists, including Ben

Theory of Painting by Sir Joshua Reynolds, first President of the Royal Academy, on the ceiling of a room in Somerset House once occupied by that learned society.

Nicholson's *Painting 1937*; and in the late 1970s came the major benefaction of the Anglo-Austrian connoisseur Count Antoine Seilern, known as the Prince's Gate Collection (from Seilern's London address). Astutely advised by curators, scholars and dealers, Seilern built up an exceptional collection of Old Master Dutch, Flemish and Italian paintings, extremely rich in works by Rubens and Tiepolo, but also including Oskar Kokoschka's 1950 *Prometheus* triptych, the artist's largest work, commissioned by Seilern for the ceiling of his Prince's Gate house.

Highlights of the collection

The collection is displayed in the **Fine Rooms**, designed by Chambers, with beautifully ornamented plasterwork ceilings. When the Royal Academy vacated the building, they took with them many of the works of art by Academicians, though Chambers' original colour scheme, with ceilings of pale green, pink and lilac, is preserved, and the rooms themselves, as well as the paintings displayed in them, are part of the exhibit.

The display is chronological and begins with **Medieval and Renaissance works**, many of them purchased in Italy in the 19th century. Particularly fine is the gold-ground triptych of the *Virgin and Child with Saints* by the Florentine painter Bernardo Daddi, a pupil of Giotto (1338), with scenes of the *Nativity* and *Passion* in the side leaves. There are also three predella panels by Fra' Angelico, also Florentine: a central *Pietà* with female saints on either side, including Margaret of Hungary in a Dominican habit.

There are more Florentine works (by Lorenzo Monaco) in the collection of **European Art from 1400–1800**. The *Entombment* by Lorenzo Lotto (1550–5) is a characteristically original work by this artist: men in turbans carry the dead body of Christ to the tomb, their way lit by children holding tapers while the Virgin swoons with grief in the background. Also here are a *Holy Trinity* by Botticelli (1490s), two works by Parmagianino and a good collection of Italian majolica.

Paintings of the **Northern Renaissance** include an exquisite *Virgin and Child with Angels* by Quinten Massys (1500–9); Hans Eworth's extraordinary allegorical portrait of Sir John Luttrell, rising half naked out of the sea with a shipwreck behind him (1550); and two very famous works: *Adam and Eve* by Lucas Cranach the Elder (1526) and *Landscape with the Flight into Egypt* by Pieter Brueghel the Elder (1563).

An entire room is devoted to **Rubens**, including an atmospheric *Conversion of St Paul* (1610–12), imagined as a night scene, along with its preparatory sketch.

From **18th-century Europe** come some fine portraits by Romney, Goya and Gainsborough (*Portrait of Mrs Gainsborough*, 1778–9), as well as Sir Joshua Reynolds's Cupid and Psyche (c. 1789), a study in chiaroscuro. In the centre of the ceiling of the first room, incidentally, is Reynolds's *Theory of Painting* (*illustrated on previous page*). Reynolds was the first President of the Royal Academy, who formerly occupied this building.

On the upper floor is the **Great Room**, where the Royal Academy Summer Exhibition took place from 1780–1836. The precipitous climb was wittily satirised by Thomas Rowlandson in his c. 1800 *The Exhibition Stare-case* (now hung outside the Great Room), showing eager exhibition visitors tumbling downstairs, with the billowing hindquarters of Albacini's completed *Venus Callipygos* in a niche, an amusing symbol of both exhibitionism and voyeurism. Above the door of the Great Room is the Greek inscription 'Let no one uninspired by the Muses enter here'. Inside are the great masterpieces of **Impressionism and the 20th century**. Manet's *A Bar at the Folies-Bergère* (1882), Monet's *Antibes* (1888), Renoir's *The Theatre Box* ('La Loge', 1874) and Cézanne's *The Montagne Sainte-Victoire* (c. 1887) are just a handful of the now internationally famous works from Courtauld's collection which can be admired here. Here too are paintings by Gauguin and Van Gogh (his *Self-Portrait with Bandaged Ear*, 1889), characteristic paintings and sculpture of ballet dancers by Degas, pointilliste works by Seurat, louche Parisian scenes by Toulouse-Lautrec and a Modigliani nude. Twentieth-century British artists represented here include Sickert, Frank Auerbach and Graham Sutherland.

The **Bloomsbury Room** recreates a simple living room in a bohemian townhouse of the kind that a member of the Bloomsbury Group might have inhabited, with paintings, textiles and ceramics, much of it by Roger Fry and the Omega Workshops. Fry's portrait of Nina Hamnett (1917) is here and alongside it hangs *A Conversation* by Vanessa Bell (1913–16).

LEGAL LONDON

Occupying land on the boundary between the City of London to the east and the City of Westminster to the west, the area around Chancery Lane, including Lincoln's Inn, Gray's Inn and the Inner and Middle Temples, can fairly be described as 'Legal London'. The Royal Courts of Justice are here as well as solicitors' offices and barristers' chambers. On weekdays the area is full of lawyers, hurrying to and from their chambers or

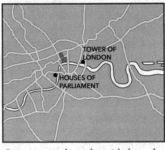

discoursing in small huddles. Life in the Inns of Court is conducted amid the calm of green and leafy quadrangles, with the lawyers' rooms opening off sequestered staircases, identical in design to the Oxford and Cambridge colleges from which many of the barristers graduated.

Some highlights of the area
+ The tranquil quadrangles of the **Inns of Court**;
+ The ancient and atmospheric **Temple Church**, with tombs of Crusader knights and warrior monks of the Knights Templar order;
+ The spacious **Lincoln's Inn Fields**, home to two excellent museums, the **Hunterian Museum** of the history of surgery and **Sir John Soane's Museum**, former home of one of England's most original architects, containing his eclectic and eccentric collection.

INNER & MIDDLE TEMPLE

Map p. 638, A3. Underground: Temple.

The Temple was originally the seat in England of the Knights Templar, the famous order of soldier-monks formed in 1118, originally to protect pilgrims to the Holy Land but who went on to amass impressive property holdings and to become the Christian world's first powerful bankers. On the dissolution of the Order from 1307, the Temple passed to the Crown and later into the possession of the Knights Hospitaller of the Order of St John, who continued at their priory in Clerkenwell (*see p. 402*) and leased the land to lawyers looking for premises near the courts of Westminster. In 1604,

Hare Court, Middle Temple, by night.

James I granted the land to the Inns of Inner and Middle Temple on the understanding that they provide accommodation and education for their members and share the maintenance of Temple Church.

Today this quiet enclave is shared by the Inns of Inner and Middle Temple, lying between the Thames Embankment and Fleet Street and the Strand. Here elegant chambers and courtyards, and the beautiful, historic Temple Church, lie within several acres of gardens. Widespread destruction in 1940–1 has been replaced with buildings in the traditional style by Sir Edward Maufe, Sir Hubert Worthington and T.W. Sutcliffe. Buildings belonging to the Inner Temple bear the device of the Winged Horse (Pegasus); those of the Middle Temple the Lamb and Flag.

TEMPLE PLACE AND MIDDLE TEMPLE

Essex Street is named after the townhouse of the Earls of Essex, which once stood here. On the corner of Milford Lane, at **2 Temple Place**, the richly ornamented neo-Elizabethan building is the former estate office of William Waldorf Astor, built in 1895 by Pearson. It is owned by the Bulldog Trust and viewing of the opulent interior is limited (*twotempleplace.org*). Exterior features include the bronze lamp posts, outside the main entrance, by W.S. Frith; one depicts a cherub on the telephone. The large gilded ship weather vane is of the *Santa Maria*, in which Columbus discovered America.

Moored on the river here is HQS *Wellington*, the last surviving wartime escort ship (she served in the Battle of the Atlantic and is now the headquarters of the Honourable Company of Master Mariners). The gate in the river wall, with a sombre *Old Father Thames*, commemorates the naming of this stretch of water as King's Reach, on the 25th anniversary of George V's accession.

Bounded by the Embankment and Middle Temple Lane are Middle Temple Gardens. **Middle Temple Hall**, a fine example of an Elizabethan chamber with double hammerbeam roof, was begun in 1562 under Edmund Plowden (commemorated in the Temple Church; *p. 216*). The interior, heavily damaged in 1941–4, has been rebuilt and restored. The High Table, at which benchers still dine, consists of three enormous planks cut from a single oak cut down in Windsor Forest and floated down the Thames, reputedly a gift from Elizabeth I. Sir Francis Drake was welcomed in this hall after returning from one of his expeditions; Shakespeare is said to have taken part in the première of *Twelfth Night* here in 1602 (*entry via pre-booked guided tour only, middletemple.org.uk/tours, events@middletemple.org.uk*).

INNER TEMPLE

Inner Temple Hall and Library, by Worthington (1952–6), replaces the 19th-century range destroyed in 1941. The refaced buttery at the west end and the crypt below it date from the 14th century (*not open to the public*). To the east is **King's Bench Walk**, with two houses ascribed to Wren (nos 4 and 5), popular locations for film companies. Towards the river lies the tranquil expanse of **Inner Temple Gardens** (*open weekdays 12.30–3, updates on Instagram @innertemplegarden*). Tudor Gate leads east onto Tudor Street towards Blackfriars; until the 18th century this was a lawless area known as 'Alsatia'.

Effigy of Gilbert Marshal, 4th Earl of Pembroke (d. 1241) in Temple Church. Knighted by King Henry III, against whom his family had previously rebelled, he died at a tournament in Hertfordshire as a result of a fall from his horse.

INNS OF COURT AND INNS OF CHANCERY

The four Inns of Court (Inner Temple, Middle Temple, Lincoln's Inn and Gray's Inn) are professional associations of barristers in England and Wales which have the exclusive right of calling persons to the Bar (originally the railing or 'bar' that separated the public and judicial areas of the courtroom), granting them the right to argue cases in court. The Inns originated in the 12th and 13th centuries, when lay people replaced clergy as lawyers in the secular courts. There are two ranks of barrister: 'juniors', who wear 'stuff' gowns, and King's Counsel (KC), who wear silk gowns and who are therefore often called 'silks'. The Inns' membership is made up of students, barristers and Masters of the Bench, or 'benchers', distinguished barristers or judges who form their Inn's governing body. Each Inn has a dining hall, library and chapel, surrounded by extensive gardens, and many barristers practise their profession from 'chambers' situated in one of the Inns of Court. The Inns' traditional role of training students has now been largely taken over by other bodies but students are still required to attend 'qualifying sessions' at their Inn, traditionally consisting of dinner at which talks are given on legal topics and students can take part in mock trials called 'moots'. (*Visitors are usually admitted to the quaint and quiet precincts of the Inns on Mon–Fri.*)

The nine Inns of Chancery originated as bodies which drew up documents connected with civil law. Later, they became associations and offices for solicitors but after the founding of the Law Society of England and Wales in 1825, they ceased to have any legal purpose. Clement's Inn, Thavie's Inn and Furnival's Inn now exist merely as names of modern buildings. Lyon's Inn, New Inn and Strand Inn have completely disappeared. The only surviving part of Clifford's Inn may be seen off Chancery Lane. The buildings of Staple Inn (c. 1585) survive on High Holborn (*see p. 228*). Barnard's Inn is now home to Gresham College (*see p. 229*).

TEMPLE CHURCH

Map p. 638, A3. Entrance via the south porch (fee). The church is noted for its music and holds services (most of them choral) according to the Book of Common Prayer. For details of concerts, and of opening times, see templechurch.com.

The Temple Church, or Church of St Mary the Virgin, belonging to the Middle and Inner Temples in common, is a 'peculiar', i.e. exempt from episcopal jurisdiction. The circular nave, known as the Round Church, is modelled on the Church of the Holy Sepulchre in Jerusalem, the holiest of sites where Jesus is believed to have been buried. It was consecrated in 1185 by Heraclius, Patriarch of Jerusalem, probably in the presence of King Henry II, and is in a transitional style between Norman and Gothic. The chancel was added in 1240. Henry III declared his intention to be buried here, although he was in fact buried in Westminster Abbey. The whole building was restored several times in the 19th century and then very seriously damaged in 1941, after which it was restored once again.

The Round Church

The arcading around the walls was replaced in the 19th century; the waggish carved heads, known as the **Grotseques (1)** (note the man having his ear chewed off by a creature) are copies of the originals. Arranged on the floor here are two groups of four 12th–13th-century recumbent marble effigies of knights in full armour, some with crossed legs, an attitude popularly—though probably erroneously—believed to signify that the deceased was a Crusader. The effigies were heavily restored, some reattributed, and rearranged in 1841 by Edward Richardson and casts of some of them were taken for display at the Great Exhibition of 1851. In 1941 an incendiary bomb caused the roof of the church to fall inwards and the effigies were caught up in the molten firestorm and badly damaged. They have since been restored and two of them lie next to their Victorian plaster casts (on long-term loan from the V&A), giving an idea of what they looked like prior to the war damage but after 19th-century restoration. The knights are all shown with open eyes and are all portrayed in the vigour of youth. The effigies, as the church itself once beautifully expressed it, 'are not memorials of what has long since been and gone; they speak of what is yet to come, of these once and future knights who are poised to hear Christ's summons and to spring again to war.' They include the following: **(2) effigy of William Marshal, 1st Earl of Pembroke** (d. 1219), soldier, statesman, expert jouster, negotiator of *Magna Carta* and Lord Protector of England during Henry III's minority. His feet rest on a lion; **(3) effigy of William Marshal, 2nd Earl of Pembroke** (d. 1231), eldest son of the 1st Earl; **(4) effigy Gilbert Marshal, 4th Earl of Pembroke** (d. 1241), third son of the 1st Earl and a less competent jouster than his father (he died after falling from his horse during a tournament); he is shown in the act of drawing his sword, his feet on a winged dragon; **(5) effigy of Geoffrey de Mandeville, 1st Earl of Essex** (d. 1144). He was one of the barons who spread anarchy throughout the land during the tussle for the throne between King Stephen and his rival Matilda and was killed while besieging a castle in Cambridgeshire.

Also on long loan from the V&A is the **cast of the tomb of King John (6)**, under whom *Magna Carta* was drawn up in 1215 (original tomb in Worcester Cathedral), and that of **King Henry III (7)**, who died in 1272 and had hoped to be buried in his church. He was eventually interred in Westminster Abbey.

The Chancel

Borne by clustered piers of Purbeck marble, from the same quarry as the originals, the wide chancel contains a number of monuments worthy of attention.

(8) Tomb of Edmund Plowden: This fine painted recumbent monument, with the hands, clasped in prayer, exquisitely rendered, commemorates the lawyer responsible for the beautiful Middle Temple Hall. Plowden (1518–85) was Treasurer of Middle Temple.

(9) Tomb of Richard Martin: A fine tomb chest and polychrome effigy.

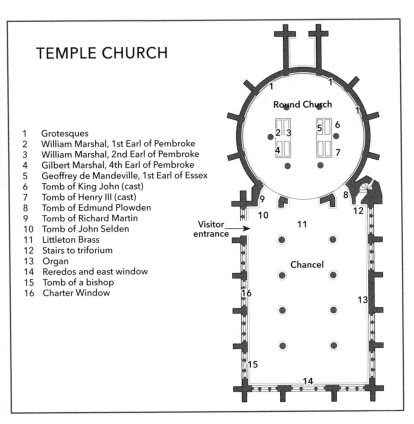

TEMPLE CHURCH

Round Church

1   Grotesques
2   William Marshal, 1st Earl of Pembroke
3   William Marshal, 2nd Earl of Pembroke
4   Gilbert Marshal, 4th Earl of Pembroke
5   Geoffrey de Mandeville, 1st Earl of Essex
6   Tomb of King John (cast)
7   Tomb of Henry III (cast)
8   Tomb of Edmund Plowden
9   Tomb of Richard Martin
10 Tomb of John Selden
11 Littleton Brass
12 Stairs to triforium
13 Organ
14 Reredos and east window
15 Tomb of a bishop
16 Charter Window

Visitor entrance

Chancel

Martin (1570–1618), shown kneeling at a desk, rose to be Recorder of London, in other words the senior judge of the criminal court.

(10) Tomb of John Selden: Set some way below the current floor level, beneath glass, is the black marble grave slab of the Middle Temple jurist John Selden (d. 1654), who dryly complained that 'Few men make themselves masters of the things they write or speak.' He was praised by Milton for his learning. Some of his books are now in the Bodleian Library in Oxford.

(11) The Littleton Brass: The monument takes the form of a stone slab with brass inlay. At the top is the coat of the arms of the Littletons, a prominent noble family whose members included a number of lawyers. Beneath the arms unfurls a long scroll, with individual shields on either side and a *memento mori* grinning skull at the bottom.

(12) Stairs to the Triforium: A narrow spiral stairway leads up to the triforium overlooking the nave. Halfway up, behind a narrow door, is a small space which has been identified as a **penitential cell** where Templar knights who had displeased the Master of the Order were confined as punishment. Walter le Bacheler is said to have been starved to death here in 1301. The Triforium floor is covered in 19th-century **Minton encaustic tiles**. They originally formed the paving of the church below; those that survived the Blitz were relaid here.

(13) **The Organ:** Originally made for Glen Tanar House in Scotland in 1926, the organ was installed here in 2012. It is the successor of the great Bernard Smith organ that was destroyed in WWII. Bernard ('Father') Smith and Renatus Harris, the two finest organ makers of their day, were each commissioned to make organs in 1683. The plan had been to erect them in the halls of the Inner and Middle Temples, where each was to be tested and a judgement formed as to which produced the finer sound. Both masters were irritated by the commission, each feeling that the contract should have been awarded to him alone, and each separately secured permission for his instrument to be set up in the Temple Church instead. Smith's was placed between the Round Church and chancel and Harris's at the opposite end. Such was the fury of the contest that acts of sabotage were even reported. The final verdict was passed in 1688, by Judge

Jeffreys (of Bloody Assizes fame, the trials of the rebels who attempted to overthrow James II in 1685). Smith's instrument was deemed the winner and Harris's was removed.

(14) **Reredos and East Window.** Designed under Wren's supervision in 1682, the reredos was removed during re-Gothicisation in 1840 and so escaped War damage. The 1950s' stained glass in the East Window is by Carl Edwards; Bradley notes that it is some of the best post-war glass in London.

(15) **Tomb of a Bishop:** The noble effigy depicts a 13th-century churchman, perhaps Sylvester de Everden, Bishop of Carlisle (d. 1254). When his coffin was opened in 1810, a child's skeleton was found at his feet; perhaps the remains of William Plantagenet, the fifth son of Henry III, who died in infancy. Next to the tomb is a Gothic piscina.

(16) **The Charter Window:** The stained glass, with the motto *Beati pacifici* (Blessed are the Peacemakers), is by Caroline Benyon (d. 2021), jeweller, silversmith and glass artist, daughter of Carl Edwards. Benyon trained with her father and worked with him on the west window of Liverpool Anglican Cathedral. This window dates from 2005.

The Churchyard

A **neo-Gothic column** topped by a horse and two knight-riders, emblem of the Templars, stands in the courtyard outside the church, at what was once the heart of the Templars' monastery. Sculpted by Nicola Hicks, it was erected in 2000 and also marks the point at which the Great Fire of 1666 finally ceased to spread. The **Master's House**, the home of the incumbent of the Temple Church, northeast of the church, was re-erected after the Great Fire and totally destroyed in 1941, but has been rebuilt in its 17th-century form.

AROUND TEMPLE BAR

The **Temple Bar Monument** (*map p. 638, A3*), a tall column in the middle of the road surmounted by a spiny dragon rampant, marks the boundary between the City of London and the City of Westminster. It was designed by Sir Horace Jones and erected in 1880. The statues of Queen Victoria and Edward VII (as Prince of Wales) are by Sir Joseph Boehm. The bronze dragon, proffering the arms of the City, is by Charles Birch. The two bronze reliefs depicting Queen Victoria visiting the City are by Charles H. Mabey and Charles Kelsey and refer to the ancient custom of the Lord Mayor granting the sovereign permission to visit the City and 'pass Temple Bar'. The custom is still observed on state occasions, when the Lord Mayor presents the sovereign with the Pearl Sword. The frontal relief, depicting Time and Fortune drawing a curtain over old Temple Bar, is also by Mabey. Old Temple Bar was a stone gateway erected on this site after the Great Fire and popularly believed to have been by Wren. By the 1870s it had become a traffic obstacle and was carefully taken down stone by stone. It was later re-erected at Theobalds Park in Hertfordshire, the country estate of Sir Henry Bruce Meux, where it mouldered for over a century. Since its rescue and restoration, it has been re-sited at the entrance to Paternoster Square, north of St Paul's Cathedral (*see p. 34*).

ROYAL COURTS OF JUSTICE AND CAREY STREET

The **Royal Courts of Justice**, or Law Courts, where the Strand meets Fleet Street, are home to the High Court, where civil cases are heard (criminal cases are heard at the Old Bailey; *see p. 232*), and the Court of Appeal, which has both civil and criminal divisions. The imposing Victorian-Gothic building, faced in Portland stone, was built in 1873–82 to the design of G.E. Street, who was responsible for both the exterior and the interior of the vast pile (so vast that a person was once found living in its basements—it has a thousand rooms and over three miles of corridors). The total cost for building was £1 million, excluding the £1,452,000 paid for the six-acre site and the demolition of 450 houses before work began. Street's untimely death, about a year before completion, was brought on by the strain of the monumental project and it was finished by his son, A.E. Street, and Sir Arthur Blomfield. Queen Victoria opened the building in December 1882. Members of the public are allowed free entry and may observe proceedings from the back of the court. Guided tours are also available (*see theroyalcourtsofjustice.com*). Once past the security system at the entrance, you are in the lofty Great Hall, which has a fine mosaic pavement. Official tours often include the opportunity of observing a High Court case from the public gallery.

Behind the Law Courts, north of the Strand, is **Carey Street**, its name synonymous with bankruptcy proceedings. The term 'in Queer Street', meaning in financial trouble, is thought to be a corruption of Carey. The small Seven Stars Pub (1602), one of the oldest in London, serves real ale and has an eccentric window display of dusty curios, including an animal skull sporting a barrister's horsehair wig and a lump of coprolite, a 'cretaceous turd from 146–66.4 million years ago'. Beyond the pub, on the corner of Serle Street, a niche above the door of a building belonging to Lincoln's Inn has a statue of Sir Thomas More (*see p. 357*), sculpted by George Sherrin. More was admitted to membership of Lincoln's Inn, where his father was a bencher (*see box on p. 215*) in 1496.

Beyond the 'Silver Mousetrap' (A. Woodhouse & Son, est. 1690), an attractive archway admits to the dignified 17th-century quadrangle of New Square, part of Lincoln's Inn (*see below*). A short way further up Carey Street is **Star Yard**, where you will find a rare surviving double-door Victorian urinal in green-painted cast iron.

LINCOLN'S INN FIELDS

Map p. 636, A2. Underground: Holborn, Chancery Lane.

This large, grassy expanse, just outside the City of London boundary, takes its name from Lincoln's Inn and was previously three fields called Cup, Purse and Fickett's, originally belonging to the Crown. In 1586 the Babington Plotters, who conspired against Elizabeth I in favour of Mary, Queen of Scots, were hung, drawn and quartered here. The site was laid out and developed in the 1630s by William Newton, with 32 houses surrounding a public open space, but the original plan is thought to have been by Inigo Jones. In 1666, the possessions of City inhabitants displaced by the Great Fire were secured at Lincoln's Inn Fields. In 1683 Lord William Russell was beheaded here for his part in the Rye House Plot, an attempt to assassinate Charles II. Charles' mistress Nell Gwyn lived here until 1687. By 1735, according to a government report, Lincoln's Inn Fields had become a favourite duelling-ground as well as a 'receptacle for rubbish, dirt and nastiness of all sorts' where vagabonds and beggars committed 'robberies, assaults, outrages and enormities'. The inhabitants had them enclosed and they remained under private stewardship until a campaign to restore public access was successful in 1894. Today it is the largest public square in central London, with paths in a cruciform layout, covering twelve acres with lawns and tennis courts. Once a fashionable place to live, the buildings surrounding it are now mainly offices and chambers, with solicitors taking advantage of the proximity to the Inns of Court. The LSE (London School of Economics) also occupies buildings here.

On the south side, the **Royal College of Surgeons** (nos 35–43) occupies a large building with an Ionic portico. The first building, erected in 1805–13, was by George Dance the Younger and Nathaniel Lewis. It was redesigned by Sir Charles Barry and rebuilt from 1834. The building was badly bombed during World War Two and only the library and portico survive. Within the college is the Hunterian Museum (*see below*).

The southwest corner of Lincoln's Inn Fields extends into Portsmouth Street where an old shop survives, a short way down on the left, claiming to be Dickens's **Old Curiosity Shop**, though it was named after the novel's publication. Nonetheless, this may well be the oldest shop in London, dating back to 1567. At the time of writing it sold handmade shoes.

On the west side of Lincoln's Inn Fields, **Lindsey House** (nos 59–60, c. 1640) is one of the few original buildings from the 17th century and was previously attributed to Inigo Jones. **Newcastle House** (no. 66 at the northwest corner) is a brick building with stone dressings of 1684–9 and was where the charter for the Bank of England was sealed. It was remodelled by Sir John Vanbrugh in the 18th century and again by Lutyens in 1930s. Since 1790 is has been the offices of Farrer & Co., solicitors, who numbered the late Queen Elizabeth II among their clients.

THE HUNTERIAN MUSEUM

This excellent museum of the history of surgery (*35–43 Lincoln's Inn Fields; hunterianmuseum.org*) is named after its founder, the celebrated surgeon John Hunter (1728–93), whose collection ran to over 70,000 specimens. The displays contain material on Hunter himself, as well as examples from his collection and exhibits on surgery through the ages.

The **Evelyn Tables**, mounted on the wall in the first room, are a set of four anatomical preparations on 6ft wooden boards on which dissected human nerves, arteries and veins are glued and varnished. Thought to be the oldest in Europe, they were acquired by the diarist John Evelyn in Padua in 1646 and subsequently used as teaching boards.

The Long Gallery displays thousands of Hunter's antique pickled specimens, both human and animal, ranged along the walls. All of them are fascinating, even though the blanched contents of the jars range from curious to freakish, showing examples of various pathologies from cancers to gall stones.

The historical displays include material on early pain relief, on cosmetic surgery (a skill which originated from work on rebuilding the faces of wounded soldiers from both world wars) and on modern transplants. Not only of consuming interest to the general visitor, the museum is also a valuable resource for medical students, as well as for artists who wish to settle knotty anatomical and biological questions.

The display of human remains is a sensitive issue today. The skeleton of Jonathan Wild, a receiver of stolen goods who was hanged at Tyburn in 1725, is on show. That of Charles Byrne is a different story. The wretched Byrne, a 7'7" Irish giant (d. 1783), made an unhappy living from his excessive height and drank himself to death at the age of just 22. He asked to be buried at sea so that his mortal remains could not be exploited. Against his wishes, surgeons vied for his body and 'surrounded his house just as harpooners would an enormous whale'. His remains are no longer on public display though they have been retained for research into acromelagy, the condition from which Byrne suffered, which causes the body to produce too much growth hormone.

SIR JOHN SOANE'S MUSEUM

Map p. 636, A2. 13 Lincoln's Inn Fields. Underground: Holborn. Free. There is limited capacity in the house and queues can form outside. You are asked to turn off your telephone and large bags are not permitted. A variety of tours, including candlelit tours and tours of the private apartments, are also offered. See website for details: soane.org.

This extraordinary house was the home of Sir John Soane (1753–1837), one of England's most important and original architects. The façade, of Portland stone and red brick, with its projecting loggia and incised lines representing pilasters, was daringly modern in its day—and considered a 'palpable eyesore' by many. The two large Coade Stone 'caryatids', based on those from the Erechtheion in Athens, give a foretaste of what can be expected within, in one of the most unusual interiors in London. The house was designed by Soane to house his ever-growing collection of antiquities and paintings, and the unusually-shaped rooms are crowded with works of art. Cunning use is made of surprise vistas and changes of level. Carefully positioned mirrors reflect both light and judiciously-placed possessions; ceilings are punched through to admit shafts of illumination at desired angles, dramatically falling on walls encrusted with sculpture and architectural fragments. Windows of rooms overlook courtyards packed with sculpture, and in the basement are solemn Gothic cloisters and cells, originally lit by light faintly penetrating through stained glass. The whole creates an overwhelming labyrinthine effect.

Soane's home is in fact spread over three houses, largely pulled to pieces and reconstructed to his own designs. He and his wife Eliza and their two sons lived in the house and Soane also had his architect's office here. Here he was able to continue and perfect architectural ideas he had used elsewhere: at the Bank of England (*p. 56*), his country villa at Ealing, Pitzhanger Manor (*p. 514*) and at Dulwich Picture Gallery (*p. 503*). Today the collection of Greek, Roman and Egyptian antiquities, casts, bronzes, gems and medals, ceramics, oil paintings and watercolours, 8,000 books, 30,000 architectural drawings (including many by Adam) and 150 architectural models, displayed in astonishing surroundings, is one of Soane's most extraordinary legacies. By the end of his life Soane was already referring to the ground floor of Lincoln's Inn Fields as 'the Museum'. He bequeathed it to the nation by Act of Parliament in 1833.

Tour of the house

To the right as you enter is the **Library and Dining Room**, conceived as one space with the Library at the front of the property and the Dining Room at the rear. Painted a rich, glossy Pompeian red, an arcaded division, suspended from the ceiling, articulates the two spaces, its two mirrored piers on either side of the room arranged with objects, including a model of the Soane tomb. Made in 1816 after the death of Soane's wife Eliza, the actual monument stands in the burial ground of St Pancras Old Church (*see p. 390*). Eliza Soane, Soane himself and their son John are buried there. Mirrors in the recesses above the bookcases, made for the room by John Robins, give an impression of a room beyond. The mythological ceiling paintings, with scenes from the story of Pandora, were commissioned from Henry Howard and positioned in 1834. Over the Dining Room chimneypiece is Sir Thomas Lawrence's portrait of Soane (1828–9), one of his last works, and below it a model of the Board of Trade offices which Soane designed at the entrance to Downing Street. Convex mirrors, canted forward, reflect the entrance from the Hall, and mirror-backed niches contain sculpture. It was in this room that Soane exhibited his large collection of antique vases, or 'Grecian urns', the most celebrated being the large 'Cawdor Vase', an Apulian volute krater of the late 4th century BC.

Approached from the Dining Room is Soane's **Study**, a tiny room also painted Pompeian red, crammed with marble fragments displayed on shelves and brackets of

Sir John Soane's Museum, characteristically Mannerist, with its caryatids bearing no loads and column capitals devoid of columns.

'bronzed' green. Above the door to the Dining Room is a large cast of the *Apotheosis of Homer*, taken from the marble relief purchased by the British Museum in 1819, originally in Palazzo Colonna, Rome. The oak-grained **Dressing Room**, with an elaborate ceiling in Soane's late manner, leads through into the **Corridor**, a forest of architectural plaster casts lit by a long skylight filled with tinted yellow glass, admitting a mellow light. The **Dome** continues the overwhelming assemblage of architecture and sculpture. Large and dominating is a cast of the *Apollo Belvedere* (formerly in the collection of Lord Burlington at Chiswick House), of which Soane was exceedingly proud, not least because of its provenance. Lined up on the balustrade, with a view down onto the Egyptian sarcophagus (*see below*), are antique vases and urns and Sir Francis Chantrey's bust of Soane. The **Ante-Room**, off the Corridor, contains a cast of the Michelangelo tondo now in the Royal Academy (*see p. 244*). The **Breakfast Parlour** remains almost unaltered from Soane's day. The ceiling is a beautiful flattened dome, almost floating in the air; to either side, openings rise to skylights with coloured glass. In the four corners of the ceiling are convex mirrors, and nearly 100 more punctuate the surfaces of the room, some merely small glittering orbs. On the north wall is a large watercolour of the Soane tomb, Flaxman's figure of *Victory* having been positioned in front of it by Soane just ten days before he died in 1837.

The **Picture Room**, its suspended ceiling a curious mix of Classical and Gothic forms, is where Soane displayed his best paintings, hung on an ingenious method of hinged panels which swing out, revealing different layers. Prized by Soane were his original ink-and-wash views of Paestum by Piranesi (1720–78) but the chief pictures are those by Hogarth: the celebrated eight-canvas *Rake's Progress* series (1732–3) and the magnificent four-canvas *Election* series (c. 1745). In addition Soane possessed watercolours by Turner; an oil sketch for Sir James Thornhill's Baroque ceiling for the Queen's State Bedchamber at Hampton Court; and a fragment of a tapestry cartoon, from the studio of Raphael, for the 'Life of Christ' tapestries for the Vatican. In the inner recess of the south wall is a plaster nymph by Sir Richard Westmacott, a friend of Soane's, who was invited to dinner to admire the placement of his sculpture.

In the basement is the **Monk's Parlour**, or the 'Parloir of Padre Giovanni' as Soane was amused to called it, the first of a series of theatrical spaces for his medieval and Gothic treasures, inspired by, and satirising, the taste for Gothick novels and medieval antiquarianism. It is an elaboration of the sombre, reclusive hermit theme begun at Pitzhanger (*p. 514*). Ancient stained glass and coloured glazing was set into windows and doors, rearranged in the 1890s for its greater protection, with yellow light filtering down from the Picture Room recess. The walls are covered with casts and genuine Gothic fragments, many from the old Palace of Westminster. In this odd, tenebrous environment, Soane would entertain close friends to tea.

The **Sepulchral Chamber**, where light floods down from the dome above, bouncing off the walls encrusted with marbles, sculpture and architectural fragments, is dominated by the colossal bulk of the alabaster **sarcophagus of Seti I** (d. 1279 BC; father of Ramesses the Great). This was Soane's most expensive and triumphant purchase, made in 1825. Huge and translucent, covered in hieroglyphs, it had been discovered by the Italian strongman and hydraulic engineer Giovanni Belzoni and offered to the British Museum by the British Consul-General in Egypt, Henry Salt, but was turned down on grounds of cost. In March 1825 Soane threw a three-day party to celebrate his purchase. Eight hundred and ninety guests, among them Turner, Coleridge and Sir Thomas Lawrence, viewed his home-cum-museum by lamp and candlelight, the flickering light shimmering in the mirrors and illuminating the spaces with dramatic chiaroscuro. The drama of the presentation was, of course, deliberate.

Returning to the inner hall, the stairs lead up to the Drawing Rooms, passing on the way the **Shakespeare Recess** and other niches with sculpture busts.

LINCOLN'S INN

Map p. 638, A2. Underground: Temple, Holborn, Chancery Lane. Precincts open Mon–Fri 7am–7pm. Buildings (except for the chapel, which is open Mon–Fri during working hours) are open for organised tours only. See lincolnsinn.org.uk.

Lincoln's Inn may derive its name from Henry de Lacy, Earl of Lincoln (1251–1311), adviser to Edward I in matters of law and a proponent of legal education; the Inn is near the site of his London mansion. It is more likely, though, that the name derives from Thomas de Lincoln, a serjeant at law during the 14th century. Formal records of the Inn date from 1422, although a body of lawyers is known to have practised here prior to this.

Between New Square and the Old Buildings to the east, is the **Old Hall** (c. 1489–90). It served as the Court of Chancery from 1733 to 1873 and is famously mentioned in the opening scene of Dickens's *Bleak House*.

The **Chapel** (1623) has been subsequently restored and enlarged. Its foundation stone was laid by Jonne Donne in 1620. The old tradition of ringing the chapel bell at midday to signify the death of a bencher of the Inn is thought to have inspired Donne's famous *Meditation XVII*:

No man is an island, entire of itself; every man is a piece of the continent, a part of the main. If a clod be washed away by the sea, Europe is the less, as well as if a promontory were, as well as a manor of thy friends or of thine own were. Any man's death diminishes me, because I am involved in mankind. And therefore never send to know for whom the bell tolls: it tolls for thee.

The chapel is built on a series of pillars and entry is via the double staircase. Thus the arcaded, open space below is in fact the crypt: inspection of the flagstones reveals them to be the weathered tombs of members of the Inn. In the 18th–19th centuries, unwanted babies were often left here and if adopted by the Inn were given the surname Lincoln.

The **Gate House**, which leads into Chancery Lane (*see below*), was commissioned in 1517–21 by Sir Thomas Lovell, Chancellor of the Exchequer to both Henry VII and Henry VIII. On the Chancery Lane side, it bears Lovell's arms as well as those of Henry VIII and Henry de Lacy. It was rebuilt in the 1960s but the oak doors are from the 16th century. To the west is the **Great Hall** (or New Hall), in red-brick Tudor style by Philip and P.C. Hardwick (1845). At the north end is the **Library**, extended in 1872 by Sir George Gilbert Scott. An archway with a second porter's lodge at the northwest corner of New Square leads into Lincoln's Inn Fields, with tall plane trees (*described below*).

CHANCERY LANE

Chancery Lane (*map p. 638, A2–A3*), which flanks Lincoln's Inn to the east, is named after the Court of Chancery, which dealt with disputes including land, property and trusts. The **Maughan Library** occupies the former Public Record Office, a fortress-like Gothic Revival building by Sir James Pennethorne and Sir John Taylor which stands on the east side of Chancery Lane, opposite the junction with Carey Street. Built in slow stages 1851–96, it was the first major neo-Gothic public building to be constructed after the Houses of Parliament and was conceived as 'the strongbox of the Empire' to secure the National Archives. It is built on the estate of the Master of the Rolls, including the Rolls Chapel, founded in 1253 by Henry III, originally as a *Domus Conversorum* (House of Converts) for Jews who had renounced their worldly goods in order to convert to Christianity. After the Archives' removal to Kew in 1997, the building was bought by King's College, London and reopened as a library after restoration. In the Western Room are remnants from the chapel; a 13th-century archway, three funerary monuments, stained glass and a mosaic floor. The monument to Dr John Yonge (d. 1516) is credited as the earliest Renaissance funerary monument in England and is attributed to Pietro Torrigiano, who was also responsible for Henry VII's tomb in Westminster Abbey. The 19th-century sculptures on the clock-tower are of four queens: Victoria, Elizabeth I, Anne and Maud (Matilda).

Opposite the Maughan Library is the **Law Society**, a Neoclassical building dating from 1832, which represents the interests of solicitors in England and Wales.

Chancery Lane houses a number of shops selling legal books and legal dress. Ede & Ravenscroft at no. 93–4 sells 'state, legal, municipal and academic' regalia, including horsehair wigs. At nos 53–64, further up on the opposite side beyond Cursitor Street (a 'cursitor' was a clerk in the Court of Chancery) are the **London Silver Vaults**, originally offering safe storage for household silver and now a shop with an Aladdin's Cave of antique and modern silver on sale in the basement (*silvervaultslondon.com*).

Ben Jonson in Chancery Lane

[Jonson's] mother, after his father's death, married a bricklayer; and 'tis generally said that he wrought sometime with his father-in-law (and particularly on the garden-wall of Lincoln's Inn next to Chancery Lane, and that a knight, a bencher, walking thro' and hearing him repeat some Greek verses out of Homer, discoursing with him, and finding him to have a wit extraordinary, gave him some exhibition to maintain him at Trinity College in Cambridge.

John Aubrey (1626–97), *Brief Lives*

Early 20th-century stained-glass window in Gray's Inn Chapel, showing the archway between South Square and Gray's Inn Square.

THE INNS OF HOLBORN & HOLBORN CIRCUS

Map p. 638, A1–A2. Underground: Chancery Lane.

GRAY'S INN
Known to have been occupied by lawyers by 1388, Gray's Inn (*entrance off High Holborn, beside the Cittie of York pub; Walks and Chapel open weekdays, graysinn.org.uk*) stands on or near the ancient manor of Purpoole or Portpool, owned by Sir Reginald de Grey, Chief Justice of Chester, Constable and Sheriff of Nottingham (d. 1308). The Inn was damaged by Luftwaffe bombing in 1941 and the Hall, Chapel and Library were burned out, along with 30,000 books. It was restored in a harmonious style in the 1950s.

The first quadrangle you come to, **South Square**, has a statue of Francis Bacon, one of the great names of Gray's Inn. Empiricist philosopher, statesman, lawyer and writer, he rose to become Treasurer of the Inn, retaining chambers here from 1577 until his death. In the Hall (1566, rebuilt 1951), Shakespeare staged the first performance of

The Comedy of Errors in 1594. John Bradshaw, who headed the court that tried King Charles I for treason, was called to the Bar at Gray's Inn. Luckily, during the Blitz, the stained glass had been taken to a place of safety, so much of it is original. Beyond South Square is **Gray's Inn square**, where the Chapel also preserves its early 20th-century glass.

The gardens, known as **Gray's Inn Walks**, or simply the Walks, entered along Field Court, were laid out by Francis Bacon in 1606 and altered in the 18th century. They consist of two sweeping parallel gravel drives bordered by plane trees, shrubs and sloping lawns. Many office workers choose to enjoy their lunch breaks here.

Francis Bacon on lawyers...

Notwithstanding, for the more public part of government, which is laws, I think good to note only one deficiency; which is, that all those which have written of laws have written either as philosophers or as lawyers, and none as statesmen. As for the philosophers, they make imaginary laws for imaginary commonwealths, and their discourses are as the stars, which give little light because they are so high. For the lawyers, they write according to the states where they live what is received law, and not what *ought to be* law; for the wisdom of a law-maker is one, and of a lawyer is another.

The Advancement of Learning, 1605

...and on gardens
God Almighty first planted a garden. And indeed it is the purest of human pleasures. It is the greatest refreshment to the spirits of man; without which, buildings and palaces are but gross handyworks.

Essay XLVI, 1625

STAPLE, FURNIVAL'S AND BARNARD'S INNS
The western limits of the City of London, known as **Holborn Bars**, are indicated by stone obelisks on the busy High Holborn, near Chancery Lane Underground station and opposite Staple Inn. In the roadway here stands the **War Memorial of the Royal Fusiliers** (City of London Regiment), by Albert Toft (1924).

On the south side of High Holborn is **Staple Inn**, the gabled and timbered façade of which, dating from 1586 (restored), is one of the oldest surviving buildings in London. The inn, which seems to have been a hostel of the wool staplers in the 14th century, was an Inn of Chancery (*see p. 215*) from the reign of Henry V until it was sold in 1884. It was severely damaged in 1944, when the fine 16th-century hall was demolished. This has now been rebuilt (with much of the old material) and is occupied by Staple Inn Chambers barristers, the Institute of Actuaries and other tenants. Dr Johnson lived here for a time in 1759–60 and here he is said to have written *Rasselas* in the evenings of a single week, to pay for his mother's funeral.

At **39 Brooke St**, leading off High Holborn opposite Staple Inn, the poet Thomas

Chatterton, the 'sleepless soul that perished in his pride' (Wordsworth's tribute), poisoned himself in 1770. He was 17.

Occupying the block between Brooke Street and Leather Lane is **138–142 Holborn**, a huge, neo-Gothic building in cinnamon-coloured brick, clad in terracotta by the same tiling firm that supplied the National History Museum. It was built as the headquarters of the Prudential Assurance Company (Alfred Waterhouse, 1879–1906; altered in the 1930s) and incorporated state-of-the-art Victorian gadgetry such as electric lighting and hot running water as well as a company chapel, restaurant, library and rooftop promenade for employees. It occupies the **site of Furnival's Inn**, in which Charles Dickens was lodging when he wrote the first part of *The Pickwick Papers* (memorial tablet and bust by Percy Fitzgerald, 1907, in the central courtyard). **Leather Lane Market** (*Mon–Fri 10–early afternoon*) has its stalls and cafés just beyond Waterhouse Square. A market has traded here for 400 years. The name has nothing to do with leather; it is probably a 14th-century derivative of the name of a local merchant. The market is known for its street food and on weekday lunchtimes streams of people can be seen coming away from the market with takeaway boxes.

On the opposite side of Holborn, at no. 23 near the corner of Fetter Lane, is the entrance to **Barnard's Inn**, with a device of the Mercers' Company ('Mercers' Maiden') in the pediment above the gateway. From 1894–1959 the defunct inn was occupied by the Mercers' School. The school was founded about 1450 and had Sir Thomas Gresham among its pupils. Since 1991, Barnard's Inn has been home to Gresham College, the institute of higher learning founded by Sir Thomas Gresham in 1579 for the delivery of lectures in Latin and English on 'divynitye, astronomy, musicke, geometry, law, physicke, and rhetoricke' by seven professors. The Chair of Commerce, funded by the Mercers' School Memorial Trust, has now been added to these seven ancient professorships. Gresham Professors and visiting guests still deliver free public lectures (*see gresham.ac.uk for upcoming events*), which are held in the Inn's old hall on a first come, first served basis. The restored hall dates from the late 14th century and has 16th-century linenfold panelling.

At no. 80 Fetter Lane is the Art Nouveau, neo-Perpendicular façade of the **former Buchanan's Distillery** by Henry J. Treadwell and Leonard Martin (1902). The name Fetter Lane derives either from the '*faitours*' (beggars) with which it used to swarm, or from a colony of '*feutriers*' (felt-makers).

HOLBORN CIRCUS AND ST ANDREW'S CHURCH

Beyond Barnard's Inn, Holborn ends at Holborn Circus, a busy road junction with an **equestrian statue of Prince Albert** (Charles Bacon, 1873) lifting his hat to the traffic that swirls around his horse's hooves. On the right is **Thavies Inn House**, which preserves the name of the now-defunct Inn of Chancery (*see p. 215*).

The **church of St Andrew** (*standrewholborn.org.uk*), rebuilt by Wren in 1684–7, is the largest of his City churches, with a lovely light interior. It was ruined in WWII and largely reconstructed, though the interior of the medieval tower, dating from 1446 and unaltered by Wren, survives. The 17th-century statues of a charity boy and girl on either side of the entrance door were brought here from a nearby charity school and

Day of Judgement relief above the north door of St Andrew's, Holborn (similar but not precisely identical to the one in St Mary-at-Hill in the City). It once marked the entrance to a burial ground, the last resting place of the poet Thomas Chatterton, to whom Keats dedicated his *Endymion*: 'A thing of beauty is a joy for ever: its loveliness increases; it will never pass into nothingness; but still will keep a bower quiet for us, and a sleep full of sweet dreams...'

chapel. Immediately inside to the left is the tomb of Captain Thomas Coram, erected when his remains were brought here from the Foundling Hospital (*see p. 382*). The church's other philanthropic link is with the surgeon William Marsden, who was so moved by the fate of a girl who died of exposure in the churchyard in 1827, with no hospital to take her in, that he founded the Royal Free Hospital the following year. In this church William Hazlitt was married in 1808 (Mary Lamb was bridesmaid and Charles Lamb the best man). In 1817 Benjamin Disraeli (at the age of twelve) was received into the Christian Church here. In the churchyard, above a doorway on the north side, note the splendid **stone relief of the *Day of Judgement***, with the Risen Christ flanked by angels sounding the last trumpets above a mass of coffins yielding up their dead. Thought to date from the 17th century, it once adorned the gateway of a burial ground attached to a workhouse in Shoe Lane, where Thomas Chatterton, the young poet who poisoned himself with arsenic, was buried in 1770. Henry Wallis's famous painting *The Death of Chatterton* can be seen at Tate Britain.

Behind St Andrew's is **Holborn Viaduct**, a road bridge 1400ft long and 80ft wide, constructed at the cost of over 4,000 dwellings and over £2 million in 1863–9. With its crimson and gold cast-iron railings, it was designed by the engineer William Haywood to carry the thoroughfare over the depression of the Holbourne stream, now smothered by Farringdon Street. The two bronze figures at each end are *Agriculture* and *Commerce* by H. Bursill and *Science* and *Fine Arts* by Farmer and Brindley (1868). The viaduct also crosses Shoe Lane, beyond which is the **City Temple** (Congregational), opened in

1874 under Dr Joseph Parker, for a congregation founded in 1640. Burnt out in 1941, it was rebuilt (apart from the façade) by Seely & Paget in 1956–8 and at the time of writing was being restored again.

NEWGATE & THE OLD BAILEY

Map p. 638, B2. Underground: Chancery Lane, St Paul's.

The Holborn Viaduct leads into Newgate Street. Here, at the junction with Old Bailey and Giltspur Street, is the church of St Sepulchre. On the corner, at 126 Newgate St, is the **Viaduct Tavern** (*viaducttavern.co.uk*), opened in 1869, the same year as the Holborn Viaduct, and well worth a pit stop. It occupies the site of the Giltspur Street Compter, a debtor's prison (there are still some cells in the basement), and was once a Victorian gin palace. Its ornate interior includes three gilded and painted panels of graceful, pre-Raphaelitesque maidens.

ST SEPULCHRE-WITHOUT-NEWGATE

St Sepulchre-without-Newgate (*generally closed Fri and Sat, see hsl.church/contact for updates*), the largest of the City's parish churches, was once closely associated with Newgate Prison. Until 1890 the bells of St Sepulchre (the 'Bells of Old Bailey' in the nursery rhyme 'Oranges and Lemons') were tolled when a prisoner was executed. Today it has happier connections and is the National Musicians' Church.

Dating back to the 12th century and named after the Holy Sepulchre in Jerusalem, the church was rebuilt in the 15th century and again after the Fire in neo-Gothic manner. In the **Musicians' Chapel** in the north aisle, a bust commemorates Sir Henry Wood (d. 1943), first conductor of the Proms (*see p. 585*), who at the age of twelve deputised for the organist. His ashes are buried here. A 1960s' stained-glass window commemorates the singer Dame Nellie Melba and the dessert named after her. In the same chapel, the remains of an **Easter sepulchre** are thought to mark the tomb of Roger Ascham (1515–68), tutor to Queen Elizabeth I. **Captain John Smith**, first governor of the state of Virginia, who sailed to America in 1607, is buried in the south aisle. A stained-glass window recalls how Princess Pocahontas freed him after his capture by Native Americans. Nearby, in a glass case, is displayed the **Execution Bell**. The bellman of St Sepulchre's would pass along an underground passage to Newgate Prison and ring it at midnight outside the condemned prisoner's cell, at the same time reciting a rhyme, the transcript of which is exhibited with it. The south aisle and chapel and the garden serve as a memorial to the Royal Fusiliers.

GILTSPUR STREET

King Richard II met the leaders of the Peasants' Revolt in Giltspur Street (*map p. 638, B2*) in 1381. A short way up the street, attached to the church of St Sepulchre, is the **Watch House** (1791, destroyed in the Blitz, rebuilt 1962), erected to deter the body

Sculpture by F.W. Pomeroy over the entrance to the Old Bailey, showing a sombrely hooded *Recording Angel* flanked by *Fortitude* and *Truth*. Fortitude clutches a sword; Truth gazes at her reflection in a looking glass.

snatchers who stole corpses from Newgate in order to sell them for dissection to St Bartholomew's Hospital opposite. The bust of English essayist Charles Lamb bears the inscription, 'Perhaps the most loved name in English literature who was a bluecoat boy here for 7 years. B·1775, D·1834.' It was moved here in 1962 from near the site of Christ's Hospital School (*see p. 55*), where Lamb was educated.

The junction of Giltspur Street with Cock Lane is known as **Pye Corner**. Mounted on the wall is a 17th-century gilded chubby cherub, known as the Golden Boy of Pye Corner, marking the spot where the Great Fire of 1666 supposedly stopped. The inscription beneath the monument reads, 'This Boy is in Memmory Put up for the late FIRE of LONDON Occasion'd by the Sin of Gluttony 1666' (a reference to the fire starting in Pudding Lane). In medieval times, prostitution was legal in Cock—Cokkes—Lane. John Bunyan, writer of *The Pilgrim's Progress*, died here in 1688.

THE OLD BAILEY

Map p. 638, B2. Generally open Mon–Fri 10–1 & 2–3.30 but check online. Closed Bank Holidays, reduced court sitting in Aug. Public galleries open for viewing of trials in session; no reserved seating. No children under 14, no electronic devices, bags, food or drink. No public access to the precincts of the Central Criminal Court. See cityoflondon.gov.uk for details or email ccc.enquiries@cityoflondon.gov.uk.

The neo-English Baroque Central Criminal Court, its façade inscribed with the motto 'Defend the Children of the Poor and Punish the Wrongdoer', is known as The Old Bailey. It is built on the site of the former Newgate Prison, which in turn stood on the site of New Gate, one of the gates in the Roman city wall. Newgate was an infamous and 'dreadful place of incarceration' from the 12th century until its closure in the early 20th century. The Museum of London (*see p. 399*) preserves a set of original iron doors from an old Newgate cell. Typhus, or 'gaol fever', was rife due to squalid conditions and overcrowding and in 1750 several judges, members of the jury and even the Lord Mayor died of it. Thereafter, strong-smelling herbs were spread around the court and judges carried posies. In 1768–75, new buildings by George Dance the Younger were erected in forbidding *Architecture terrible* style, designed to inspire awe in the convicted and deter would-be felons. Public executions, previously carried out at Tyburn (Marble Arch; *see pp. 322–3*), took place in front of Newgate from 1783–1868 and then within the prison until 1901. Elizabeth Fry, prison reformer, Quaker and helper of the homeless, helped found the Association for the Reformation of the Female Prisoners in Newgate in 1817.

Dance's buildings were demolished and replaced by the new Old Bailey (the current building) by Edward Mountford in 1900–7. A figure of *Justice* by F.W. Pomeroy (1907), cast in bronze and covered with gold leaf, stands on top of the dome. She wears a five-pointed star on her head and holds the Sword of Retribution in one hand and the Scales of Justice in the other. Pomeroy also sculpted the figures over the main entrance: *Fortitude* (left) and *Truth* (right) with the *Recording Angel* between them. The task of the Recording Angel, based on a text from the Old Testament book of Malachi, is to note down the deeds of men; such notes will form the basis for future reward or punishment. The main entrance is only used when the Lord Mayor visits in state as Chief Justice of the City. The Edwardian splendour of the Grand Hall is rarely open to the public. The extension on the south side of the Old Bailey, by McMorran and Whitby, was completed in 1972.

Britannia and her lion, protectively surveying Piccadilly Circus, viewed from Regent Street St James's.

PICCADILLY, ST JAMES'S & MAYFAIR

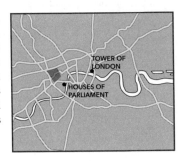

Piccadilly, a wide and busy thoroughfare, home to the Royal Academy and the Ritz, divides two of central London's most patrician districts, St James's and Mayfair. St James's is more old-fashioned and sedate, with its cluster of members-only clubs, its gentlemen's outfitters and its surviving long-established shops. Mayfair has luxury boutiques, famous hotels and fine dining.

Some highlights of the area
+ The old-fashioned shops of St James's, among them **Fortnum & Mason**, **Paxton & Whitfield** and **Berry Bros & Rudd**;
+ The **Royal Academy**, known for its excellent exhibitions of both old master and contemporary art and home too to a fine permanent collection;
+ **Green Park**, small and well kept, its greenery exceptionally welcome;
+ **Apsley House**, former home to the Duke of Wellington, victor of Waterloo, preserving his superb collection of paintings and other artefacts.

PICCADILLY CIRCUS

Map p. 635, E1. Underground: Piccadilly Circus.

Piccadilly Circus (*map p. 635, E1*), on which seven streets converge, is one of the most traffic-congested and animated intersections in London. Its most famous landmark is the **statue of 'Eros'**, which stands at the centre of the fountain. In reality, the precariously balanced archer, polythene-wrapped in winter to protect him from the cold, represents Anteros, the twin of Eros, who is 'love requited'. Made of aluminium (a novelty at the time, 1893), it was designed by Sir Alfred Gilbert to commemorate the philanthropic work of Anthony Ashley Cooper, 7th Earl of Shaftesbury, reformer of working conditions in factories, promoter of Ragged Schools (education for the children of the very poor) and campaigner for clean drinking water. Although condemned by contemporary critics, the statue has since been taken to the public's heart.

HISTORY OF PICCADILLY

The thoroughfare of Piccadilly, which leads southwest from the Circus to Hyde Park Corner, began life in 1612, when a certain Robert Baker bought a plot of land for £50 on the east side of the present-day Great Windmill Street. He built what was most likely a lodging-house, which became known locally as 'Pickadilly Hall', a nickname which may have originated as a joke, for Baker was by trade a tailor who made 'pickadils', scalloped frills at the armholes and necks of dresses, which were very fashionable at the time. The name caught on, and in 1627 for the first time, 'Pecadilly' was used to refer to the district to the north of Haymarket.

The nobility began to move to the area in increasing numbers, building mansions such as Burlington House (now the Royal Academy). But Piccadilly's real rise to importance began in the 19th century, with John Nash's 1811–13 Regent Street Plan, which aimed to create a *Via Triumphalis* by linking St James's Park and Carlton House (residence of the Prince Regent; since demolished) with Regent's Park. In the late 1870s and 1880s, Shaftesbury Avenue was created by cutting through Tichbourne Street into the Circus. The Circus quickly became a busy traffic nexus as well as a public space—somewhere to rest, drink (metal cups were provided, chained to the fountain), buy flowers, meet friends and lovers, pick up prostitutes (notably the 'Dilly Boys'; *see below*) or get a shoe-shine.

THE PICCADILLY LIGHTS

A central feature of Piccadilly is its world-famous Lights, the digital and LED video displays with the brand names of commercial products emblazoned on high for all to see. As far back as 1928, *The Times* referred to the then electric advertisements as a 'hideous eyesore which no civilised community ought to tolerate'. They are perfectly in keeping with the consumerist idiom of the place.

The first electric sign went up in 1890. In 1897 the New London Pavilion music hall (on the northeast corner, where the Trocadero amusement arcade is now) began advertising Spaten beer; and display space was being leased to anyone willing to pay for the privilege from around 1910 onwards. In 1922 illuminated signs went up advertising such household names as Bovril yeast extract, Schweppes drinks, Glaxo baby food and Pirelli tyres. Finally, in 1955, came the most famous advertising hoarding of all: the first Coca-Cola sign.

The advertising space has not only been used to sell products: the 1964 general election results were put up on the front of the **Criterion Theatre** building and, in 2002, the artist Yoko Ono paid £150,000 to erect a banner for three months with the words 'Imagine all the people living in peace' on it. The Criterion (on the south side of Piccadilly Circus) has a frontage designed by Thomas Verity in a French Renaissance style. It opened in 1873, to be followed a year later by the Criterion Long Bar (the restaurant has undergone several changes of ownership since then). During the Second World War the Criterion Theatre was used by the BBC to broadcast live light entertainment shows to keep up the morale of the nation. The core of the original premises, including the basement theatre and central staircase, has been beautifully restored (*criterion-theatre.co.uk*). Next to it, on the corner of Regent Street St James's, is the sporting department store **Lillywhites**, which opened in 1925.

THE DILLY BOYS AND 'PICCADILLY POLARI'

At the beginning of the 20th century, Piccadilly was the heartland of London's 'queer culture'. The most notorious denizens of the district were the so-called 'Dilly Boys', largely working-class teenage boys, often 'painted', who plied their trade up and down Piccadilly, in its shopping arcades and at the gates of the Royal Academy (the favoured spot of an infamous 'rouged rogue' named 'Gertie'). The distinguished homosexual Quentin Crisp (1908–99), author of *The Naked Civil Servant* (1968), was a Dilly Boy in the 1920s.

Dilly Boys had their own cant slang known as 'Piccadilly polari' (or 'parlare'), in which they communicated with their well-to-do customers. Part-Italian, part-Romany in origin, it was spoken in a sing-song manner as a 'vocal embodiment of their sexual character'. It also owed a lot to cockney slang, sailors' patois and the world of the theatre and the circus. While its heyday was in the 1920s, it underwent a public revival in the 1960s with the popular BBC radio comedy *Round the Horne*, in which two characters named Julian and Sandy spoke exclusively in this outrageous vernacular. Many words which were once the preserve of pre-Second World War underground gay culture are now common in everyday English: 'barney'=a fight, 'camp'=effeminate, 'clobber'=clothes, 'naff'=cheesily awful, 'rozzer'=policeman, 'scarper'=run, to name a few.

ALONG PICCADILLY TO THE ROYAL ACADEMY

Map p. 635, E1–E2. Underground: Piccadilly Circus, Green Park.

On the south side of Piccadilly (the left-hand side as you stand with your back to Piccadilly Circus) is the flagship branch of **Waterstones**, the largest bookshop in Europe. The building (Joseph Emberton, 1936) is a triumphant piece of Modernism, dynamically bringing together a Chicago steel frame, Art Deco and Bauhaus, faced in Portland stone. It has four floors plus a basement level of books and a café, bar and restaurant at the top, with views across the rooftops.

Just beyond Waterstones is the church of St James's Piccadilly (*described separately, below*), usually with a street market in its courtyard. Further up on the right, beyond Sackville Street, is Albany Close, with a handsome three-storey house, **Albany** (1771–4), in dark Flemish-bond brick with a Tuscan porch. Designed by Sir William Chambers as a town mansion for Peniston Lamb, 1st Viscount Melbourne (his son was the Whig prime minister, buried in St Paul's Cathedral, who gave his name to Melbourne in Australia), it served from 1792 as the residence of Frederick, Duke of York and Albany, second son of George III. In 1803 the Whig architect Henry Holland, who was also responsible for Brooks's club in St James's (*see p. 255*), converted the building into a series of bachelor pads—known as 'sets' and still in use today—by adding two apartment ranges to the sides of the main building. The covered walkway (where troughs of communal herbs are grown for residents and which you can glimpse through the open doorway) is known as the Ropewalk. Gladstone liked to stay here after a late-night House of Commons sitting. The poet Macaulay was another resident, as was the Conservative Prime Minister Sir Edward Heath. Byron, too, had a 'set' in Albany.

On the other side of the street is the **Princes Arcade**, containing 22 bow-fronted shops. Beyond it is **Hatchard's**, the oldest bookseller's in London (though no longer independent; it is owned by Waterstones). It is a five-storey building with a wooden shop front and four tall Corinthian columns uniting the central bays of the third and fourth floors. On 30th June 1797, John Hatchard wrote in his diary: 'This day, by the grace of God, the good will of my friends and £5 in my pocket, I have opened a bookshop in Picadilly [sic].' He need not have fretted. Hatchard's soon established itself as a supplier of books, pamphlets, magazines and newspapers to aristocrats and politicians of all persuasions; the Tory Robert Peel and the Liberal William Gladstone among them. It is certainly worth going in, if only to take a sweep up and down the central wooden staircase.

FORTNUM & MASON

Fortnum & Mason (*181 Piccadilly; fortnumandmason.com*) was founded c. 1707 by William Fortnum, footman to Queen Anne, and his landlord Hugh Mason, a shop-owner in St James's. By 1756, Charles Fortnum, also a royal footman, had premises in Piccadilly supplying foodstuffs to kings, queens and aristocrats (hence the royal coat of arms and Prince of Wales feathers on the façade). Every hour on the hour the clock (1964) reveals the figures of William Fortnum and Hugh Mason, who emerge to salute one another in fine gentlemanly fashion. Below them, perched on the canopy above the main door, is Lynn Chadwick's *Sitting Couple on a Bench*, nicknamed 'King and Queen', installed here in 2016. There is another variation on the theme at Canary Wharf.

The present exterior is mainly of the 1920s by the Scottish firm of architects Wimperis, Simpson & Guthrie. In 2007 it was refurbished by Jestico + Whiles and David Collins, among others, who added a four-storey atrium space, an elegant white volute staircase and a domed roof-light.

Throughout its history Fortnum & Mason has responded to customer needs and the demands of world crises: it trail-blazed the selling of teas and spices brought into the country through the East India Company in the mid-18th century; it innovated its own line of preserves for use by British soldiers during the Peninsular War (1808–14); a line in ready-to-eat dishes was developed for the Great Exhibition of 1851; and a huge quantity of concentrated beef tea for the troops was sent to Florence Nightingale in the Crimea. It is also Fortnum & Mason who historically supplied the gentlemen's clubs in

Pall Mall and St James's with their food parcels; they created 'concentrated luncheons' for shooting and fishing parties (the forebears of the modern-day hampers). In 1922 George Mallory took 60 tins of quail in foie gras and four cases of Montebello 1915 champagne from Fortnum's on his second (failed) attempt to scale Everest.

As a department store from the 1920s onwards, Fortnum's has also played an important role in encouraging the art of the window display. Its themed *montages* are famous. Today the store sells an array of goods from food, wines and spirits, tea and coffee, to household items and linens. There are also restaurants, a wine bar and tea salon.

ST JAMES'S PICCADILLY

The church of St James's (*map p. 635, E2; sjp.org.uk*) was one of approximately 50 churches projected from 1670 onwards by Wren's office as part of the scheme of rebuilding after the Great Fire of London: according to a paper written in relation to the scheme in 1711, Wren regarded it as the model church of its kind. Though devastated by bombing in 1940, it has been well restored.

A plain-looking building of brick with Portland stone quoins, St James's is based on a basilica plan. It is five bays wide, with a tunnel-vaulted nave but no chancel and no apse, with galleried aisles supported by Corinthian columns resting on square piers. The contrast between the simple exterior and rich interior is immensely rewarding. Central to the design was the aim of ensuring that the preacher and the celebrant be both audible and visible to the whole congregation, hence the spaciousness of the church, the large glass windows and the near absence of internal supports. Note the white marble **font** by Grinling Gibbons showing Adam and Eve standing by the Tree of Life, which is represented by the stem of the font itself, the snake curled lasciviously around it proffering an apple while the tree obligingly sprouts a branch to cover Adam's nakedness. The bas-reliefs on the bowl are, in an anti-clockwise direction, the *Baptism of Christ, Noah's Ark* and the *Baptism of the Treasurer of Queen Candace of the Ethiopians by St Philip*. Gibbons was also responsible for the organ case (made for the Catholic chapel of King James II at Whitehall in 1685; it was transferred here in 1691) and for the outstandingly beautiful **limewood reredos**, carved with flowers and fruit and acanthus whorls (the acanthus leaf is a symbol of rebirth and eternal life). John Evelyn was greatly taken with it (*see overleaf*).

As parish church of the Royal Academy, St James's has many artistic associations: William Blake was baptised in the font, and buried at the church are the caricaturist James Gillray (d. 1815) and the auctioneer James Christie (d. 1803), a close friend of Gainsborough (Christie's saleroom is still round the corner in King Street). At the end of the left-hand aisle is a plaque commemorating the painter Mary Beale (d. 1699), whose tomb here was destroyed in WWII. In the central entrance vestibule are memorials to the father-and-son painters of sea battles, the Elder and Younger Willem van de Velde, who both worked for Charles II and James II, and in the porch (Piccadilly side) the pavement slab of the artist Robert Anning Bell (d. 1933).

Today, St James's is much engaged with the local community, with outreach programmes providing help for the homeless (it is customary to find people sleeping in the pews). It is also home to the Blake Society (*blakesociety.org*).

John Evelyn on St James's Church

'I went to see the new church at St James', elegantly built, especially adorned was the altar, the white marble enclosure curiously and richly carved, the flowers and garlands about the walls by Mr Gibbons in wood, a Pelican with her young at her breast just over the altar in the carved compartments environing the purple velvet fringed with I.H.S richly embroidered. And most noble plate were given by Sir R. Geere to the value (as was said) of £200. Such an altar was nowhere in any church in England, nor have I seen any abroad more handsomely adorned.'

Diary, 7th December 1684

BURLINGTON ARCADE

The Piccadilly Arcade leads off the south side of Piccadilly. Opposite it, adjoining the Royal Academy in Burlington House (*described below*) is the more famous Burlington Arcade (*map p. 635, E2–E1*). Its Mannerist façade (c. 1930–1) by Arthur Beresford Pite is somewhat cumbersome but there is nothing heavy about the interior: a narrow passage under a glass roof, leading right through to Burlington Gardens and sheltering bow-fronted shops on both sides, most of them selling luxury goods. You can also get a shoe-shine here.

Built in 1819 by Samuel Ware under the patronage of Lord George Cavendish, son of William Cavendish, 4th Duke of Devonshire, Burlington Arcade was designed as a shopping centre, to provide a snug and bespoke experience. In 1925, the author of 'A Discourse on Shopping for the Elite' was moved to remark that: 'Whosoever finds in shopping a delight, whosoever is fastidious in his taste, whosoever values quality, distinction and style, will turn aside a moment from the roar of Piccadilly and saunter along the Burlington Arcade, for here is the shopping place of the true epicurean.'

From the first day until now, the arcade has been patrolled by its own police force, the Burlington Arcade Beadles, dressed in top hats and capes, who keep a watchful eye on the behaviour of shoppers. Originally the beadles were all members of the 10th Hussars (now The King's Royal Hussars), George Cavendish's own regiment, but are now ex-servicemen of all kinds.

THE ROYAL ACADEMY OF ARTS

Map p. 635, E1. Underground: Green Park, Piccadilly Circus. Restaurant and café. For opening times, exhibitions and guided tours, see royalacademy.org.uk.

The Royal Academy was founded in 1768 under the patronage of George III, in response to a petition signed by 36 artists desirous of 'establishing a society for promoting the Arts of Design'. Among these founder-members were Sir William Chambers, Thomas Gainsborough, Angelica Kauffman, Mary Moser, Sir Joshua Reynolds and Benjamin

West. Reynolds was its first President. The Royal Academy's aim was—and still is—the promotion of art and design through its teaching Schools, its Summer Exhibition of contemporary British work (an annual event since 1769) and via the staging of international loan exhibitions. It is for the last that the Royal Academy (RA) is perhaps best known today, being one of the principal venues in London for major national and international shows. The RA's first headquarters were in Somerset House (*see p. 206*), designed by Chambers. It moved to its present site in 1867 and now occupies two fine buildings, Burlington House facing Piccadilly, and Burlington Gardens immediately behind it.

The RA has always been a self-governing institution, its President elected from its body of Academicians (RAs) composed, since the 18th century, of leading painters, sculptors and architects and, from the 19th century, engravers. As well as Reynolds, past Presidents include Sir Thomas Lawrence, Lord Leighton, Sir Edwin Lutyens and Sir Hugh Casson.

SIR JOSHUA REYNOLDS

Joshua Reynolds (1723–92), the son of a Devon schoolmaster, was one of the pre-eminent society portraitists of his generation, first President of the Royal Academy of Arts and 'founder of the British School of Painting'. While on a tour of Italy as a young man, he had beheld with awe the works of Michelangelo, Raphael and Titian and returned home with the aim of raising the status of the artist in Britain.

Intellectually minded and sociable, Reynolds had a competitive relationship with other painters and was more at home with men from outside his field, the actor David Garrick and lexicographer Samuel Johnson among them. Indeed, he belonged, along with Johnson, to The Club, a group of a dozen or so men who met for supper and conversation at the Turk's Head Tavern in Gerrard Street, Soho.

Apart from his prolific output of pictures, Reynolds has left us his *Discourses on Art* (15 in total), mostly given by him at the annual prize-giving ceremony at the RA and touching on subjects ranging from colouring and the life model to art education and the work of Gainsborough. Not a good speaker, he was inaudible to many who attended his lectures, and those who could understand him did not always like what they heard—or read: William Blake notoriously wrote on his copy of the *Discourses*, 'This Man was Hired to Depress Art'.

Reynolds's chief inspiration never deviated from the Old Masters of Italy. His final remark to the RA was: 'And I should desire that the last words which I should pronounce to this Academy, and from this place, might be the name—Michael Angelo.' From an early age he had suffered from deafness (a silver ear-trumpet was never far from his side). This was compounded in later life by partial blindness. He died at the age of 69 and is buried in St Paul's Cathedral.

The Graces Unveiling Nature by the studio of Benajmin West (c. 1779), removed from the old Royal Academy in Somerset House and now in the ceiling of the Burlington House entrance hall.

BURLINGTON HOUSE

The present Burlington House, largely the work of Sydney Smirke (1866–76), encases a much older one, begun c. 1664 by Sir John Denham, then bought and completed in 1668 by the 1st Earl of Burlington. It was one of London's foremost private mansions. In the early 18th century it underwent radical alterations: first by James Gibbs for Juliana, Duchess of Burlington; and in 1717–20 by Colen Campbell for the Duchess' son, the famous promoter of Palladianism, the 3rd Earl of Burlington (*see Chiswick House, p. 511*). The current façade, which faces you as you pass through the central archway, has Campbell's Palladian ground and first storeys and Smirke's third storey, a heavy addition with niches containing statues of British and Italian Renaissance painters and sculptors. The wings creating the courtyard, by Banks and Barry in Italian

Renaissance style (1868–73), house learned societies: to the left, the Linnaean Society, Royal Astronomical Society and Society of Antiquaries; to the right, the Royal Society of Chemistry and the Geological Society. The fountain jets in the centre of the courtyard are placed, apparently, according to Reynolds's horoscope.

Entrance hall: The low-ceilinged entrance hall, remodelled in 1899, contains **ceiling paintings** by Benjamin West's studio (the central *Graces Unveiling Nature*, with the *Four Elements*) and roundels by Angelica Kauffman (*Composition*, *Design*, *Painting* and *Invention*), all removed from the RA's old meeting room in Somerset House on the Strand. A door at the right-hand end of the entrance hall leads into the **Keeper's House**, with cafés, bars and restaurants.

Main stairway: The central grand staircase by Samuel Ware (1815–18) leads up past bronze statues of Gainsborough and Turner. Here too are Sebastiano Ricci's grand Baroque paintings (***The Triumph of Galatea*** and ***Diana and her Nymphs***; 1713–15) and Kent's ceiling roundel of ***The Glorification of Inigo Jones*** (c. 1720).

The John Madejski Fine Rooms: The principal apartments of old Burlington House (*sometimes shown on guided tour*), were originally decorated—and perhaps designed—by William Kent for the 3rd Earl of Burlington. Some were altered by John Carr for the 3rd Duke of Portland in 1771–5 and then remodelled again by Samuel Ware in 1815–18 for Lord George Cavendish. The **Saloon**, with its pedimented doorcases, rich gilding and a ceiling by Kent (*The Marriage Feast of Cupid and Psyche*), is the most intact. The **Secretary's Room** has another Kent ceiling but others are by Ricci, taken, like the Riccis on the

current central stairway, from Gibbs's old staircase decorated for Juliana, Duchess of Burlington. The **Council Room** has Ricci's old staircase ceiling while the **General Assembly Room** has his *Triumph of Bacchus*, originally on the staircase wall.

Main Galleries: By Smirke, these consist of a central octagonal hall giving onto a succession of large, grand spaces. These galleries have witnessed spectacular crowds, especially in the 1880s and '90s during Leighton's successful presidency, when 350–400,000 visitors flocked

The Glorification of Inigo Jones by William Kent (c. 1720), ceiling roundel on the main stairway of Burlington House.

to see popular masterpieces such as Sargent's *Carnation, Lily, Lily, Rose* and Anna Lea Merritt's *Love Locked Out* (both now owned by the Tate). In was also here, in the octagonal hall in 1896, that Leighton's body lay in state. The Summer Exhibition still takes place here, as do the RA's excellent major loan exhibitions.

Sackler galleries: These third-floor galleries, by Norman Foster (1985–91)

have created additional exhibition space, dramatically approached via a glass capsule lift (or glass open-tread staircase) slotted into the narrow space between the back of Burlington House and Smirke's Main Galleries, affording an extraordinary close-up view of the architecture. Displayed in the shelf-like corridor outside the galleries is a collection of sculptural works of various periods.

BURLINGTON GARDENS

Burlington House is linked by an interior corridor to Burlington Gardens, a neo-Renaissance building whose exterior is adorned with statues of scientists and philosophers. It was built in 1866–70 by Pennethorne as the seat of London University and now belongs to the RA. Renovation was completed in 2018, the Royal Academy's 250th anniversary year.

The permanent collection

The RA's permanent collection includes diploma works presented by RAs on their election as members (a requirement since 1768). There are paintings, sculptures and works on paper, including portraits of RAs and other pieces either collected or bequeathed. Selected works from the collections are displayed in various parts of the building and can be viewed free of charge. These include casts of lapidary details of well-known Classical buildings (the Arch of Titus in the Roman Forum, the Temple of Vesta at Tivoli), many of them from the collection of Sir Thomas Lawrence; plaster casts after the antique (*Venus de Milo*, *Laocoön*, *Farnese Hercules*) and anatomical models (used for teaching in the RA Schools); works of original sculpture including plaster models by Flaxman for his frieze on the Covent Garden Theatre (surviving panels now decorate the Royal Opera House) and a model for the *Eros* statue in Piccadilly (the model had to pose for up to an hour with his leg in a sling).

Major highlights of the collection are exhibited in the **Collection Gallery** in Burlington Gardens. The display is arranged on a rotating basis and is beautifully lit and excellently captioned. Among the best known of the works is Reynolds' *Self-portrait with a bust of Michelangelo*; Sir Thomas Lawrence's extraordinary *Satan Calling his Legions* (1796–7), inspired by Milton's *Paradise Lost* and showing the outcast angel poised for battle, his face a travesty of a Classical Mars, standing nude and full-frontal with his sword and buckler somehow attached by a ribbon over his genitalia. Lawrence was very proud of it. The Royal Academy also has a collection of charming small paintings by Constable, including some fine cloud studies. Its only antique sculpture is a headless female figure of the 4th century BC. Its greatest treasure is **Michelangelo's 'Taddei Tondo'**, an unfinished marble *Madonna and Child with the Infant St John* (1504–5), a work of great beauty and spirituality, bequeathed to the RA in 1830.

PICCADILLY FROM THE RITZ TO HYDE PARK CORNER

THE RITZ

The most famous hotel in London, the Ritz (*150 Piccadilly; theritzlondon.com*) opened its doors on 25th May 1906 and immediately established itself as the best of the best. It was founded by the Swiss-born César Ritz, who worked himself up from (unsuccessful) wine waiter through manager of the Savoy in London to international hotelier with a chain of luxury establishments in Paris, London, New York and Budapest. He was dubbed, by no less a figure than King Edward VII, 'hotelier to kings and king of hoteliers'.

The hotel itself was designed by the Parisian architect Charles Mewès and his London-born pupil Arthur Joseph Davis. Ther pair had already worked together on the Paris Ritz and would later plan the Royal Automobile Club in Pall Mall. The Ritz is both modern and classical: it is actually constructed on a steel frame from Chicago, and while Portland stone was used on much of the façade, as was the fashion at the time, the ground-floor level is, more unusually, faced with Norwegian granite. The style of the interior is decidedly French, with its framed vista, grand enfilade and tribune and a grand staircase which sweeps down majestically into the vestibule.

The interior decoration can be appreciated in the **Palm Court** (*no sports clothing; men must wear a jacket and tie*), where afternoon tea is served. Inspired by an 18th-century French garden, it has a glass roof in a wrought-iron framework, hanging wrought-iron lamps, trellis-work painted in gold and exquisite French Neoclassical oval-backed armchairs, all separated from the vaulted corridor by a screen and two Ionic columns. In a central niche stands the gilded lead sculpture *La Source*, above which tritons blow caressingly into conch shells. In *A Dance to the Music of Time*, Anthony Powell describes the female figure thus: 'Although stark naked, the nymph looked immensely respectable; less provocative, indeed, than some of the fully-dressed young women seated below her.' The Art Deco-inspired **Rivoli Bar**, with glass panels, soft underlighting and scalloped ceiling domes, is recommended for a cocktail.

Hotel guests have included King Edward VII and his mistress Mrs Keppel, the Aga Khan (always dined at Table 1), Charlie Chaplin, Winston Churchill, Noël Coward, King Zog of Albania (and his eight bodyguards), Mahatma Gandhi, Nancy Mitford, Evelyn Waugh, Graham Greene, Tallulah Bankhead (who was famously photographed drinking champagne from a slipper at a reception party in 1951), Jackie Onassis (Table 9 by the window) and Bill Clinton. King Charles and Queen Camilla, when Prince of Wales and Duchess of Cornwall, made their first public outing together to the Ritz.

PICCADILLY MANSIONS

Piccadilly continues to Hyde Park Corner, with stately townhouses (now mainly offices and hotels) facing Green Park. The enormous **Devonshire House**, near Green Park Tube station, built in the 1920s with New York-inspired architectural touches, replaced the original Devonshire House, built by William Kent for William Cavendish, 3rd

Lazing in the deckchairs of Green Park.

Duke of Devonshire. When the 9th Duke found himself dogged by death duties, the house was abandoned and finally demolished in 1924. The **Devonshire Gates**, the magnificent former entrance gates to the mansion, which hang between sphinx-topped pillars, are now preserved across the road as an entrance to Green Park. They bear the motto of the Cavendish family (the Dukes of Devonshire), *Cavendo tutus*: Safety through circumspection. Opposite them, the Neoclassical **Cambridge House** (1758) at no. 94 was built for the Earl of Egremont. Formerly home to the Naval and Military Club (now in St James's Square), the instructions on the gateposts IN and OUT gave the club its nickname, 'The In and Out'. At the time of writing it was undergoing radical redevelopment as a private mansion.

Further along at **no. 106** (corner of Brick St) is the former town house of Lord Coventry, afterwards the St James's Club (which in 1978 merged with Brooks's; *see p. 255*), then a language school and now a secondary school. Its fine interior decorations, some by Robert Adam, survive. Beyond the **Park Lane Hotel** (or Sheraton Grand, 1927), on the corner of Old Park Lane, is the original **Hard Rock Café**, in a former car showroom of 1905.

GREEN PARK

Green Park (*map p. 635, E2*), properly The Green Park, is a triangular, 40-acre oasis of grassland and trees, without formal flowerbeds, extending from Piccadilly towards Buckingham Palace, from whose gardens it is separated by Constitution Hill. It is said that Thomas Wyatt's 1544 rebellion against Mary I's marriage to Philip II of Spain crossed this land. Charles II enclosed the park in 1668, constructing ice houses from which chilled drinks were served at royal picnics. By the 18th century Green Park was a fashionable pleasure garden: high society promenaded along **Queen's Walk** (named after Queen Caroline, wife of George II), which skirts the mansions of St James's on the eastern side. In the 1820s Nash landscaped the park and in 1826 it was opened to the public. In early spring, it is carpeted with daffodils. Under the wide pathway known as the **Broadwalk**, which bisects the park, flows the ancient Tyburn river. At the Buckingham Palace end of the Broadwalk is Canada Gate with, just inside it, the **Canada Memorial** (1994), a slanting sculpture with water gently lapping over bronze maple leaves and a central walkway, commemorating those in the Canadian forces who lost their lives during both World Wars. At the top of Constitution Hill are the **Debt of Honour Memorial Gates** (2002) commemorating all those from India, Pakistan, Bangladesh, Sri Lanka, Nepal, the Caribbean and former British colonies in Africa who fought with the British in both world wars.

HYDE PARK CORNER

Map p. 635, D2; Underground: Hyde Park Corner.

Hyde Park Corner is a busy road junction at the point where Piccadilly meets Park Lane. Right at its centre is the triumphal **Wellington Arch**. Formerly erected opposite the main entrance to Hyde Park, it was repositioned in 1883 to align with Constitution Hill and now forms part of a processional route from Buckingham Palace to Kensington Palace. It was designed by Decimus Burton in 1828 and is today open as a museum run by English Heritage (*joint ticket with Apsley House; see below*). The displays are arranged on three floors and cover the history of the Arch itself, as well as that of Marble Arch (*see p. 322*); the First World War; Napoleon and the Battle of Waterloo. A table-screen with audio commentary re-creates the battle. Original artefacts on display include the French-made sword carried by Wellington at Waterloo. From the exterior terraces there are good views towards Buckingham Palace on one side and of Apsley House (Wellington's former London home) and the **Lanesborough Hotel** on the other. The Lanesborough (William Wilkins, 1827, with later extensions) was formerly the St George's Hospital.

The Arch is surmounted by Adrian Jones' magnificently animated *Peace Descending on the Quadriga of War* (1912). This replaces M. Cotes Wyatt's much derided over-sized equestrian statue of Wellington (1838), described as 'a gigantic triumph of bad taste' (*Punch*) and 'a perfect disgrace' (Queen Victoria). Wellington himself was pleased with it and was upset at plans to remove it. It was taken down in 1883.

The **equestrian statue of Wellington** that faces Apsley House is by Boehm (1888). To the left of Apsley House is the tripartite **Hyde Park Corner Screen**, another work by Decimus Burton. Just inside it on the left is the pleasant Lodge Café.

APSLEY HOUSE

Map p. 635, D2. Admission charge. Joint ticket with Wellington Arch; english-heritage.org.uk.

Apsley House, once known as 'No. 1 London' since it was the first house after the turnpike from Kensington and Knightsbridge, was the town residence of Arthur Wellesley, 1st Duke of Wellington, the famous 'Iron Duke', victor of Waterloo and Prime Minister from 1828–30. It was built by Robert Adam in 1771–8 for Lord Apsley, later 2nd Earl Bathurst. In 1807 it was leased by the 1st Marquess Wellesley, Wellington's elder brother. Wellington himself bought it in 1817 and two years later commissioned Benjamin D. Wyatt to remodel some of the interiors. Further improvements were carried out in 1826–30 by Wyatt and his brother Philip. It was during this phase that the 90ft Waterloo Gallery was constructed, where, from 1830, the magnificent annual Waterloo Banquets took place to mark the anniversary of the great victory. By 1831 the Duke had apparently spent £64,000 on improvements and Wyatt's bill was three times over the original estimate, for which he was 'abused furiously'. Apsley House is the only historic London mansion to retain the majority of its contents, a circumstance which creates a unique opportunity: much trouble has been taken to restore the interiors to the aspect they would have worn in Wellington's day.

Ground floor

A large part of Wellington's magnificent collection of silver and porcelain is displayed in the **Museum Room**. Elaborate dinner services decorated with depictions of the Duke's exploits were presented to him by grateful crowned heads, including Franz I of Austria, Frederick Augustus of Saxony and Frederick William III of Prussia. Also here is the famous **Sèvres 'Egyptian Service'** (1809–12), its astonishing centrepiece based on the Temples of Karnak, Dendera and Philae, commissioned by Napoleon as a divorce present for the Empress Josephine, rejected, and presented to Wellington by Louis XVIII in 1818. Here too are the 'Wellington Shield' (c. 1822), designed by Thomas Stothard and made by Benjamin Smith; and gold and silver swords and daggers, including the sabre that Wellington carried at Waterloo.

Beyond the Inner Hall (the old entrance hall of the original Adam house) is the **Staircase**, remodelled by Wyatt after 1826. Its cast-iron stair-rail curves round the celebrated larger-than-lifesize **sculpture of Napoleon by Canova**, naked except for a figleaf and a draped cloak, and holding a small winged *Victory* in his right hand. Carved in 1802–6 from a single block of Carrara marble, it was disliked by Napoleon (allegedly because the *Victory* appeared to be flying away) and remained in storage in the Louvre until 1816, when it was purchased by the British Government and presented to Wellington by the Prince Regent.

Upper floor

The main showpiece apartments are here, some of which retain Adam features such as stucco grotesques (though these were all gilded by Wyatt when he remodelled the apartments in 18th-century French taste). The carpeting is a modern reweaving based on a fragment of the original discovered in the attics of the Duke's country house, Stratfield Saye, and some of the wall hangings reproduce the original fabrics. The paintings are very numerous. Many were purchased by the Duke himself, though some of the finest are from the Spanish royal collection, including works by Correggio, Murillo, Rubens and Velázquez. They were discovered rolled up in Joseph Bonaparte's captured baggage train following the French defeat at the Battle of Vitoria in 1808 and presented to the Duke in 1816 by Ferdinand VII of Spain. Lawrence's full-length **portrait of Wellington**, standing alone against a sombre sky, is one of the finest works of art in the house. Also here is Lawrence's famous half-length portrait of the Duke

(1815), arms folded, his right hand in a curiously truncated fist (shadows of fabric folds on the red coat sleeve look almost as if they might be fingers painted out).

The **Piccadilly Drawing Room** contains some of the finest pictures, including David Wilkie's *Chelsea Pensioners reading the Waterloo Despatch*, commissioned by Wellington in 1816 and completed in 1822. The scene is set in the King's Road, Chelsea, with the Royal Hospital to the left. When exhibited at the Royal Academy it created a massive stir and a protective barrier had to be erected. The **Portico Drawing Room** has a collection of personal items, including the Duke's false teeth and walking-stick-cum-hearing-trumpet, and an ink well made from the hoof of his beloved horse Copenhagen. Also here is his magnificent collection of 47 orders, decorations and medals.

The grand **Waterloo Gallery**, in Louis XVIII style with heavy gilding, was designed by Wyatt. It was here, from 1830–52, that the magnificent Waterloo Banquets took place. The east windows have mirrored shutters which, when drawn, transform the room into a supposed *Galerie des Glaces*: with the lighted candles and richly-adorned table, it must have been a sumptuous spectacle. Today slightly over half the paintings remain of the 130 that hung here in Wellington's day. According to the artist William Frith, it was the Duke's 'small weakness' when he had guests to identify the pictures in turn without consulting the catalogue. His favourite was the small *Agony in the Garden* by Correggio, showing Christ consoled by an angel while the disciples lie slumped asleep behind him. Goya's large equestrian portrait of Wellington is a rather hasty work painted in 1812, the likeness based on a chalk sketch Goya made of the Duke soon after the British army entered Madrid after the Battle of Salamanca. X-rays show that the head is painted over that of another sitter.

Wyatt's **Red Striped Drawing Room** contains Sir William Allan's *Battle of Waterloo* (1815), seen from the French side, as it stood at 7.30pm on 18th June 1815, when Napoleon, on the right, was making his last desperate efforts to turn the allied armies. Wellington found it 'Good—very good; not too much smoke'. The **Dining Room** was where the Waterloo Banquets were held before 1830. On the table is the 26ft silver parcel gilt centrepiece of the 'Portuguese Service', presented to Wellington by the Portuguese Council of Regency in 1816. On the walls are full-length portraits of European monarchs (many of them the same ones who donated all the dinner services downstairs), including Wilkie's kilt-clad *George IV*.

MONUMENTS NEAR APSLEY HOUSE

Behind Apsley House in Hyde Park (just inside Queen Elizabeth Gate to the right) is Westmacott's 18ft bronze *Achilles*, cast from cannon captured at the battles of Salamanca, Vitoria, Toulouse and Waterloo. It cost £10,000 and was paid for by 'the women of England'.

Close by, on a traffic island dubbed Achilles Way, formed by a loop in Park Lane, is Nic Fiddian-Green's colossal sculpture *Still Water* (2011), a bodiless horse-head, nose down as if in the act of drinking. At 33ft, it is London's tallest free-standing bronze and has led to a variety of spin-offs, including small crystal versions of it designed by the sculptor in tandem with Lalique.

Jermyn Street, home of men's quality tailoring (as well as the Redemption Roasters beside the church of St James's Piccadilly).

ST JAMES'S

Map p. 635, E2. Underground: Green Park, Piccadilly Circus.

The street layout of St James's has remained virtually as it was planned in the 1670s by Henry Jermyn, 1st Earl of St Albans, favourite of Queen Henrietta Maria, consort of Charles I (it was Jermyn who broke the news to her of the King's execution, one hopes tactfully and gently; he was described by Pepys as 'a fine civil gentleman'). Established as a residential district near the court of St James's (*see p. 165*), the area became famous in the late 18th century for its bachelor lodgings. From the reign of William III, the coffee and chocolate houses (the forerunners of today's clubs) were the rendezvous of aristocratic and learned London society, and specialist shops sprang up to serve both club members and courtiers. A number of such shops still survive: the area is well-stocked with purveyors of tobacco, shirts, hand-made shoes, perfumes and fine foods, as well as shooting and fishing accessories.

ON AND AROUND ST JAMES'S STREET

Berry Bros & Rudd, wine merchants, have traded at no. 3 St James's St since 1699; the shopfront retains its late 18th-century design. Today they run excellent wine courses (*bbr.com*). **Lock & Co. Ltd.**, hatters, were established at no. 6 in 1676. Nelson's hat (on his wax effigy in Westminster Abbey Museum) was made here. Further along, Byron House occupies the site where in 1812, after the publication of the third Canto of *Childe Harold*, Lord Byron 'awoke one morning to find himself famous'.

On the opposite side of the road, at no. 74, is the former Conservative Club in Palladian style (Basevi and Smirke, 1845). At nos 69–70 is the Carlton Club (*for this and the other gentlemen's clubs on St James's Street, see p. 254*).

King Street is pre-eminent among the art dealers and galleries in the area, with **Christie's** at no. 8, fine art auctioneers since 1766 (and in King Street since 1823). At no. 28 the modern Almack House stands on the site of the now defunct **Almack's** (1765–1871), the first club to admit both men and women. It was famous in Regency London for its aristocratic assemblies. Entry was by exclusive voucher and to qualify one was selected by the Club's formidable patronesses, who included Princess Esterházy, Sally Villiers, Lady Jersey and Emily Lamb, Lady Cowper. To be barred from attending Almack's was the ultimate social disgrace. The small 17th-century **Crown Passage**, with cafés, sandwich bars and a pub, links King Street with Pall Mall.

Back on St James's, on the west side is St James's Place, where two luxury hotels are discreetly located. **Dukes Hotel** is renowned for its Martinis; the **American Bar at the Stafford** has been serving cocktails since the 1930s (bar entrance at the back, in the tiny cobbled Blue Bell Yard, which has remains of 18th-century stables).

At the end of St James's Place, at no. 27, is **Spencer House**, a fine Palladian mansion built in 1756–7 by John Vardy, a pupil of William Kent, for John, 1st Earl Spencer. The interiors were completed by James 'Athenian' Stuart in 1766. It was considered one of the finest houses in 18th-century London and is the only 18th-century private mansion to survive intact. Today it operates mainly as a hospitality venue and the interior, notable for Stuart's Greek detailing, is open to the public on Sun by guided tour (*spencerhouse.co.uk*). The narrow passage past no. 23 leads to Green Park and a good view of the fine Neoclassical façade, with a palm-wreathed oculus and statuary over the pediment.

JERMYN STREET

Jermyn Street (*map p. 635, E2*) was one of the first streets to be laid out according to Henry Jermyn's plan. Historically it was a street of shirt-makers, hat-makers and boot-makers to the courtiers of the Restoration period. On the corner with St James's Street is Beretta, gunmakers since 1526 and also selling sporting accessories. The rest of the street is still filled with **gentlemen's outfitters**: old-fashioned shops here stock the kind of clothing that has apparelled the English gentleman for generations: Hilditch & Key (founded 1899), Charles Tyrwhitt, Thomas Pink, Hawes & Curtis (famous for introducing to the world the Duke of Windsor spread-collar) and Harvie & Hudson. New & Lingwood Ltd at no. 53 began life in 1865, serving scholars at Eton College. Diagonally opposite at no. 67 is Tricker's shoe shop, where you can still get a pair of bench-made brogues made to measure. The company was founded by a master shoemaker in 1829 and still operates its manufactory in Northampton, the traditional heartland of the English leatherworking industry.

Next to New & Lingwood is the entrance to the neo-Georgian **Piccadilly Arcade** (G. Thrale Jell, 1909). There are 16 shops in total, selling shirts, waistcoats, art books, watches, china and glassware. The Armoury of St James's at no. 17 has specialised for 30 years in regimental brooches. On the Jermyn Street side of the arcade there is a bronze statue (2002) of Beau Brummell, arbiter of St James's fashion.

BEAU BRUMMELL

The sculpture of George Bryan 'Beau' Brummell (1778–1840), based on a caricature of 1805 by Richard Dighton, shows the great dandy with artfully windswept hair, wearing fitted coat and trousers, top boots and an elaborate cravat. Brummell advocated simple but perfectly tailored clothing; it allegedly took him five hours each day to achieve sartorial perfection and his boots were polished with champagne. According to the *New Oxford Dictionary of National Biography*, 'His principal achievement while at Oxford was to perfect the "cut", the English art of ignoring people though conscious of their presence.' No one was his social inferior, not even a member of royalty. Promenading in St James's one day, he came across his one-time friend the—by then corpulent—Prince Regent, accompanied by Lord Monie. Ignoring the former, while acknowledging the latter, Brummell wondered aloud, 'Pray, who is your fat friend?' Alas, White's (*see overleaf*) proved his downfall: after losing £10,000 in a card game he was ruined financially and had to flee to France, where he remained for the rest of his life.

Other shops of note in Jermyn Street include **Paxton & Whitfield** (no. 93), 200-year old cheesemongers; **Floris** (no. 89), which has been selling fragrances, combs and shaving accessories on this site since 1730; **Geo. F. Trumper** (no. 20; corner of Duke of York St), traditional gentleman's barber and perfumer, selling all kinds of grooming products (the main shop is on Curzon Street; *map p. 635, D2*).

THE WHITE CUBE

Opening off Duke Street St James's is Mason's Yard (*map p. 635, E2*), named after Hugh Mason of Fortnum's (*see p. 238*), who ran a stabling and ostling business here. Today it is home to the White Cube gallery (*whitecube.com*). Founded in 1993 and run by the artworld impresario Jay Jopling, the White Cube has played an important role in exhibiting and publicising the work of a generation of British artists, most notably the 'YBAs' (Young British Artists), among them Tracey Emin and Damien Hirst. The original site of the White Cube was on Duke Street, a simple room within a room, hence the name. It moved here in 2006, to a purpose-built building on the site of an electricity substation (MRJ Rundell & Associates). The gallery has another exhibition space in Bermondsey (*see p. 460*) and another in Hong Kong.

ST JAMES'S SQUARE

This pleasant open space (*map p. 635, E2*), London's first West End square, was laid out in the 1670s as part of Henry Jermyn's development of the area. The original plan was to make it a piazza in the Italian and French style: symmetrical, 60ft wide, with four wide streets converging on the centre. In practice, three of the streets (Charles II Street, King Street and Duke of York Street) were shortened and one was eliminated completely and replaced by two smaller entrances which connect to Pall Mall, thus giving the square its slightly irregular shape and feeling of seclusion.

For the first 150 years of its life, the square—once known as the Place Royal—was a fashionable residential enclave. Today, none of the houses from the 17th century survives. From the mid-19th century, many private residences were taken over by businesses and institutions and in the 1930s new office blocks completely replaced some of the houses. Nonetheless, architecturally speaking, those that remain form an important group.

Shrouded by trees and bushes, in the garden at the centre of the square, is an equestrian **statue of William III** (John and Thomas Bacon, 1809). The king's death was precipitated after a fall from his horse, when the horse tripped over a molehill—'the little gentleman in black velvet', as the Jacobites toasted the innocuous culprit thereafter. In fact, on falling, King William only broke a collarbone; he died a few weeks later of pulmonary fever. The garden is open to all by day during the week and is a pleasant place to sit.

On the west side of the square, on the corner of Pall Mall, is the **Army & Navy Club**, (*men and women members*), familiarly known as The Rag, in a modern building of 1963. Next to it, at **no. 21**, the 1930s' building by Mewès & Davis (architects of the Ritz) stands on the site of old Winchester House, home to the War Office in the late 19th and early 20th centuries. It stood over a noxious cesspool and employees of the directorate regularly went down with 'Winchester House sore throat'. Across King Street at no. 16 is the **East India Club** (*male members only, women as guests*), in a handsome building of 1865. The club was formed by members of the East India Company in 1849. Over the years the club has incorporated a number of other smaller clubs, including the Sports Club, the Public Schools Club, the Devonshire Club and the Eccentric Club—once the favoured home-from-home of music hall stars. Next door is the **London Library** (*members only; londonlibrary.co.uk*), founded in 1841 by Thomas Carlyle (*see p. 355*) and based here since 1845. The house was remodelled as a steel-framed building in 1896–8. Deceptively small from the outside, it is a labyrinth within, with a unique and charmingly simple cataloguing system. It houses over a million books and has over 8,000 members, many of whom are writers. Past members include George Eliot, Charles Dickens, Sir Arthur Conan Doyle, George Bernard Shaw, Henry James, T.S. Eliot, Virginia Woolf and Agatha Christie.

At no. 12 is a blue plaque to Ada Byron (Lovelace), the mathematician who devised one of the earliest computer programs. Across Duke of York Street at no. 4, on the front of the **Naval & Military Club** building (familiarly known as the 'In and Out' after a building it formerly occupied on Piccadilly, with the entrance and exit gates thus boldly marked), is a plaque to the Virginia-born Nancy Astor, who in 1919 became the first woman to be elected a member of parliament in the UK. This is the Lady Astor who, so the story goes, once said to Winston Churchill: 'Winston, if I were married to you, I'd put poison in your coffee'; Churchill replied: 'Nancy, if I were married to you, I'd drink it.'

THE CLUBS OF ST JAMES'S

St James's is home to that peculiarly British institution: the gentleman's club. These elite bodies (literally so: you have to be elected to join) are discreet in the extreme—there are no name plates on the front doors and the very traditional ones have no website—and have a venerable history.

Inspired by Athenian symposia, the first recognisable 'club' in the metropolis was established at the Mermaid Tavern in Bread Street (*see p. 51*). Gentlemen's clubs in the 18th century evolved out of those taverns, supper houses and coffee houses, developing into the exclusive, polished and shuttered institutions of the 19th century and today. In spite of their misogynistic reputations, many clubs now admit women. The first to do so (after Almack's; *see p. 251*) was the aptly-named Reform Club in the 1980s. Today the clubs are valued for providing their members with affordable accommodation and dining in central London, and with comfortable public rooms in which to meet, relax and entertain.

White's: White's is the oldest surviving London club. Jonathan Swift called it 'the common rendezvous of infamous sharpers and noble cullies.' Indeed, it has been the area's chief gambling den (and a bolt-hole for prime ministers) for centuries. Politically, it has always been Conservative. The club rules date from 1736, the earliest extant of their kind.

White's began life in 1698 as a chocolate-house owned by Francis White (d. 1711), his name probably anglicised from Francesco Bianco or Bianchi (he is buried in St James's, Piccadilly). The original building burnt down in 1733 and in 1755 it moved to its present site in St James's. James Wyatt may have been the original architect; the bow window dates from c. 1811 and the façade is a mid-Victorian alteration.

Here George Harley Drummond of Drummond's Bank lost £20,000 to the professional dandy Beau Brummell. A later game proved Brummell's own ruin (*see p. 252*). *37–38 St James's St. Map p. 635, E2. Male members only.*

Boodle's: Established in 1762 in Pall Mall, this club, named after its former head waiter, Edward Boodle, is London's second oldest. It moved here in 1782. The building is of yellow brick, designed by John Crunden in the style of Robert Adam. Notice the beautiful fan-surrounded Venetian window.

This was the club of choice of Ian Fleming, author of the James Bond novels. Although it began life as a political club—an early member was the economist Adam Smith—its character soon became shaped by the comfortable country gentlemen who formed the bulk of its membership. *28 St James's St. Map p. 635, E2. Male members only.*

Brooks's: Founded in 1764, Brooks's moved to Henry Holland's purpose-built Palladian building in 1778. The club was a hotbed of Whig intrigue. Its founding members were all young Regency dandies who had been on the Grand Tour. It became a second home to Charles James Fox, who taught lessons in governance to the Prince Regent, the future King George IV, much to the chagrin of his father, George III. The

tutorials were given, so it is recorded, with Fox dishevelled, in his night-gown and open-breasted, still recovering from a heavy night of whist and piquet. A number of prime ministers have been members of Brooks's, as well as Gibbon, Macaulay, Reynolds, Garrick and Sheridan. It was bombed in 1974 by the Provisional IRA: Edward Heath, who was Prime Minister at the time, was dining nearby at Pratt's. *60 St James's St. Map p. 635, E2. Male members only.*

Pratt's: Tiny dining club founded in 1857 and named after William Pratt, who was attached to the household of the Duke of Beaufort. *14 Park Place. Map p. 635, E2. Men and women members.*

The Carlton Club: Formed in 1832 in direct opposition to the Reform Bill, the Carlton Club remains to this day the club home of the Conservative Party. It moved to its present location, a five-bay neo-Palladian building (1826) with a rusticated ground floor and first floor decorated with Corinthian columns, when its first building was destroyed in WWII. It was designed by Thomas Hopper (who would be defeated by Sir Charles Barry in the competition for the design of the Houses of Parliament). Despite being a bastion of conservatism, the Carlton Club could hardly have refused membership to Margaret Thatcher on her election as Conservative party leader in 1975; thus she 'joined the lads' as the BBC put it and became the first honorary woman member, the only woman afforded such a privilege until 2008, when women were permitted to become full members. *69 St James's St. Map p. 635, E2. Men and women members.*

PALL MALL & WATERLOO PLACE

Pall Mall (*map p. 635, E2–F2*) is named after a croquet-style game called *palla a maglio* ('ball to mallet') which was popular in the area during the 17th century (The Mall, leading up to Buckingham Palace, has the same derivation). Pall Mall is famous, like St James's, for its gentlemen's clubs, as well as for being the street in London where gas lighting was first demonstrated, by Frederick Winsor in 1807. The elaborate flambeaux which survive outside some of the buildings are still lit by gas on special occasions and for film shoots. By 1820 the whole of St James's was lit by gas; the area retains some of the oldest and most closely-spaced lamp posts in the city.

From 1774 until his death in 1788, Gainsborough lived in the west wing (no. 80) of **Schomberg House**, a 17th-century building of red brick with stone dressings (restored in 1956, when the rest of the house was rebuilt). The house at no. 79 (rebuilt) was given to Nell Gwyn by Charles II, with whom, according to Evelyn, she used to talk over the garden wall.

THOMAS GAINSBOROUGH

Born in Sudbury, Suffolk, the son of a cloth merchant, Gainsborough (1727–88) painted landscapes, portraits and genre scenes. Predominantly self-taught, he may have been apprenticed to a silversmith in London. His influences were less the Old Masters of Italy (as Reynolds's had been) and more 17th-century Northern European painters such as Rubens and Van Dyck. He frequently used models to draw from: coal for rocks and broccoli for trees were especial favourites. He did not enjoy being, as he put it, a 'phizmonger' (portrait-painter). Perhaps as a reaction to this, out of his landscapes he developed his so-called 'fancy pictures' (a term first applied to them by Reynolds), rustic genre paintings of peasant children and the deserving poor, which sought to evoke emotion and sympathy in the viewer. In this he was much influenced by Murillo. Tate Britain and Kenwood house have representative works. Shortly before his death he was visited by his rival Reynolds, to whom his last words are reputed to have been: 'We are all going to Heaven–and Van Dyck is of the company.' (*For Reynolds's own last words to the Royal Academy, see p. 241.*)

THE CLUBS OF PALL MALL

Royal Automobile Club: Founded in 1897, the RAC moved to this sumptuous French Renaissance-style building in 1911. It was built by Charles Mewès and Arthur Joseph Davis (who also collaborated on the Ritz), based, probably, on Ange-Jacques Gabriel's twin palaces of 1748 in the Place de la Concorde, Paris. There is a splendid two-storey domed, oval entrance hall in

Louis XVI style (which can just about be spied through the main door) and in indoor swimming pool with neo-Egyptian columns. General Charles de Gaulle used the club regularly during WWII. *89 Pall Mall. Map p. 635, E2. Men and women members.*

Reform Club: It was at this club that Jules Verne had Phileas Fogg accept the wager to attempt to travel around the world in 80 days. Built in 1841 by Sir Charles Barry, the Reform Club, like the Travellers Club next door, takes its inspiration from Italian *palazzi* and is perhaps Barry's masterpiece. As an institution, its origins lie in the Reform Bill of 1830–2. The Liberal prime ministers Palmerston and Gladstone were members, as was Isambard Kingdom Brunel. It was the first club to provide its members with bedrooms. *104–105 Pall Mall. Map p. 635, F2. Men and women members.*

Travellers Club: The club was established in 1814 by Robert Stewart, Lord Castlereagh, Marquess of Londonderry, the British Foreign Secretary who helped forge the European alliance against Napoleon. In the beginning membership was open to all men but those who 'shall not have travelled out of the British Islands to a distance of at least 500 miles from London in a direct line'. For most of its history it has been home to diplomats and explorers.

The premises were built in 1829 by Sir Charles Barry in the style of a Florentine palace. *106 Pall Mall. Map p. 635, F2. Male members only; women, no matter how well travelled, may only come as a member's guest.*

The Athenaeum: The Greek Revival exterior (1827–30) was conceived by Decimus Burton, who had worked with Nash on Regent's Park and Regent Street. The processional frieze (sculpted by John Henning) is copied from the Parthenon Marbles and the presiding figure of Pallas Athene (by E.H. Baily), goddess and patroness of learning, makes clear the club's intellectual bent. The Athenaeum was founded in 1824 as a club for artists, scientists and writers. Three of its founder members were Sir Thomas Lawrence RA, Sir Humphry Davy (the wheelchair in which he died is still kept in the club) and Sir Walter Scott. The president of the RA has always been an *ex-officio* member, and the club has had many other RA members in its long history, including J.M.W. Turner and Decimus Burton himself, as well as writers such as Dickens, Trollope and Macaulay. It has the best library of any club in London: Thackeray wrote some of his books here. *107 Pall Mall (facing Waterloo Place). Map p. 635, F2. Men and women members.*

WATERLOO PLACE AND CARLTON HOUSE TERRACE

On the corner of Pall Mall and Waterloo Place is the former United Service and Royal Aero Club, once the favourite haunt of the Duke of Wellington. It is now the headquarters of the **Institute of Directors**. The building, by Nash (1828), incorporates the main staircase from the demolished Carlton House. It was remodelled by Decimus Burton to match the Athenaeum opposite.

On Waterloo Place itself there are two **mounting blocks** formed of low, superimposed slabs. One is on the pavement outside the Institute of Directors and the other is opposite, outside the Athenaeum Club. They were installed here in 1830 by the Duke of Wellington, a founder-member of the Athenaeum, who was 61 at the time and not as spry as in the days of his youth.

In the middle of Waterloo Place is an equestrian statue of Edward VII. Further north, beyond Pall Mall, is the **Crimean War Memorial**, at the centre of which stands a female personification of *Victory*. The memorial, by John Bell, was first unveiled in 1861 to commemorate the Crimean War of 1853–6 and consisted of the central figure—then known as *Honour*—and the three guardsmen cast from three Russian cannons used during the Siege of Sebastopol. The statues standing to either side in front are later additions: Lord Sidney Herbert of Lea, Secretary at War (1867) by John Henry Foley (who also fashioned the sculptural group *Asia* and the figure of Prince Albert for the Albert Memorial; *see p. 330*) and Florence Nightingale (1915) by Arthur George Walker. The gas lamp with gilded finial dates from 1830. On the statue's right, at no. 16, is the **Iconic Images Gallery**, devoted to international photography (*iconicimagesgallery.com*).

At the bottom (south end) of Waterloo Place, at either side, are some fine bronze statues of soldiers and explorers, including Matthew Noble's sculpture of Sir John Franklin (d. 1847), the Arctic explorer who discovered the Northwest Passage. Just beyond are the Duke of York Steps, which lead down to the Mall and St James's Park (*see p. 167*). At the top of the steps stands the Tuscan granite **Duke of York Column** (1831–4), which commemorates Frederick, Duke of York and Albany, the 'grand old Duke of York', second and favourite son of George III. The column is by Benjamin Wyatt and the bronze statue by Sir Richard Westmacott. The Duke was Commander-in-Chief of the British Army until his death in 1827. Every officer and soldier in the Army forfeited a day's pay to provide funds for the monument to 'the soldier's friend'.

CARLTON HOUSE TERRACE

On either side of the Duke of York Steps stretches Carlton House Terrace (*map p. 635, F2*), once one of the most aristocratic places of residence in London, overlooking the Mall. Carlton House, which stood on this site, was a mansion built in 1709. It was the town residence of the Prince Regent, later George IV, from 1783. The Prince engaged Henry Holland to remodel the house in sufficiently opulent manner and it was here that he celebrated the news of his accession. Nash laid out Regent Street as a processional route to link the house with Regent's Park to the north, but the plan was never realised. Carlton House was demolished in 1827 and Nash's Carlton House Terrace (1827–33), with the Duke of York's column between, was built in its stead.

Under a tree on the right (west side) of the Duke of York Column is a small tombstone (behind glass) marking the grave of the German ambassador's terrier, Giro (d. 1934). The Prussian and later German Embassy was at nos 7–9 from 1849 until 1939.

The **Royal Society**, one of the most famous scientific bodies in the world, has occupied nos 6–9 (entrance at no. 6) since 1967. It originated from a group of eminent scholars who began to meet informally in London and Oxford in 1645. No. 5 was

View over Waterloo Place from the balcony of the Athenaeum. To the right—'a kind of vertical Athenaeum' (Ian Nairn)—rises the mid-20th-century bulk of New Zealand House.

formerly the residence of Lady Cunard and no. 2 was the home (in 1906–25) of eminent statesman and Viceroy of India, Lord Curzon, a statue of whom stands opposite.

Further west in **Carlton Gardens**, Lord Palmerston and Lord Balfour lived at no. 4 (rebuilt in 1933 by Sir Reginald Blomfield), where a tablet marks this as General de Gaulle's Free French headquarters from 18th June 1940. A statue of De Gaulle has been erected opposite (Angela Conner, 1993). A small square opens behind a statue of George VI, and stairs descend to The Mall. Lord Kitchener lived at no. 2 in 1914–15. No. 1 was occupied by Napoleon III in 1840–1; it is now the official residence of the Foreign Secretary.

MAYFAIR

Map p. 635, D2–D1. Underground: Hyde Park Corner, Green Park, Marble Arch, Bond Street.

Exclusive Mayfair, bounded by Oxford Street, Regent Street, Piccadilly and Park Lane, vies with Belgravia as the most prestigious address in London. The area offers a profusion of luxury boutiques, high-end jewellers, antique shops, art galleries and picture dealers. And after an extravagant retail spree, one can indulge in stylish drinking and fine dining in the area's smart hotels, bars, restaurants (several with Michelin stars) and clubs. Much interesting architecture survives, including original mews. Behind a discreetly elegant Georgian façade, you might catch a glimpse of an opulent private interior and in the narrower streets, large pockets of less grand houses, often in interesting, individual architectural styles, are to be found.

HISTORY OF MAYFAIR

Mayfair takes its name from the annual May Fair which was held around present-day Curzon Street and Shepherd Market from the late 17th century until 1764, when the area's well-to-do residents finally suppressed what was in reality fifteen days of rowdy and debauched revelry. The transformation into an elegant residential enclave then began. By the end of the 18th century this was largely complete. The streets and squares were laid out by wealthy landowners, among them Sir Richard Grosvenor (Grosvenor Square), the Lords Berkeley of Stratton (Berkeley Square) and the Earl of Scarborough (Hanover Square). The present Duke of Westminster, one of Britain's richest land and property owners, still owns large tracts of Mayfair.

Right up until the late 1930s, it was customary for members of the nobility and landed gentry to keep townhouses in Mayfair for use during the London Season. The 'season' was the annual period of several months (roughly January–June) in which the 'Ton', the fashionable *beau monde*, converged in 'Town' for an unremitting round of socialising and lavish entertainments. Daughters of marriageable age were presented at Court, thereby launching them into Society and into the paths of suitable husbands. Two world wars and subsequent shifts in society sounded the Season's death knell. The heads of the noble houses could no longer keep up their grand lifestyle and their magnificent town residences have now mostly been demolished. Many other former private houses have been converted into embassies, clubs or the offices of estate agents and financial or other institutions. The area commands some of the highest rents in London and ultra-rich foreign residents and 'new money' now tend to make up the population.

STREETS AND SQUARES OF WEST MAYFAIR

There is no 'right way' to visit this part of Mayfair, nor a correct order in which to approach what it has to offer. Below is a selection of its streets and squares, with their landmarks, described in alphabetical order by street name.

ALBEMARLE STREET

At the north end of the street (*map p. 635, E1*), behind an impressive rank of Corinthian columns modelled on the Temple of Antoninus and Faustina in the Roman Forum, is the **Royal Institution of Great Britain**, founded in 1799 to promote 'the application of Science to the common purposes of life'. A fascinating themed museum on three

Post-War vision of rectilinear symmetry: Ernő Goldfinger's 45–46 Albemarle St.

floors is devoted to the scientific discoveries of Michael Faraday (1791–1867), whose laboratory occupied the basement here (*21 Albemarle St; rigb.org*). Born the son of a blacksmith and initially apprenticed as a bookbinder, Faraday discovered electromagnetic rotation (the principle behind the electric motor) and—even more importantly for 19th-century industry—electromagnetic induction (the principle behind transformers and generators), as well as benzene, the magneto-optical effect, diamagnetism and field theory. The museum includes his restored laboratory as well as displays on Humphry Davy, whose assistant Faraday became, and Ada Lovelace, the mathematician and computer pioneer (and daughter of Lord Byron).

Brown's Hotel, at 33 Albemarle St, with a continuous first-floor balcony, was founded by James Brown, former valet to Lord Byron, in 1837; it is famous for its afternoon tea (*brownshotel.com*) and for the fact that Alexander Graham Bell made the first UK demonstration of his new invention, the telephone, from the lobby in 1876. Opposite is the entrance to the Royal Arcade, a glass-roofed parade of exclusive shops which opened in 1880.

The late 1950s building at nos. 45–46 is notable for being by Ernő Goldfinger, architect of Trellick Tower (*see p. 319*) as well as of his own home in Willow Road, Hampstead (*see p. 430*). Also on Albemarle Street, at no. 50, is the early 18th-century building that used to be the premises of John Murray, publishers of Byron, Jane Austen,

Darwin and Sir Arthur Conan Doyle. It was in this building that Byron's memoirs were burned after his death because they were thought too salacious.

BERKELEY SQUARE

Berkeley Square (*map p. 635, D1–E1*) was once one of the most elegant of London squares, laid out by William Kent c. 1739 on part of the gardens of Berkeley House. In the famous war song, Vera Lynn was 'perfectly willing to swear' that a nightingale sang here. It might have had its nest in one of the beautiful plane trees in the open garden in the centre (planted 1789).

On the west side of Berkeley Square, between Charles Street and Hill Street, the row of **fine Georgian buildings** dates from the 1740s. No. 44 (now the **Clermont Club**) is a survivor of Kent's original square, built in 1742–5 for Lady Isabella Finch; this 'finest terrace house in London' (Pevsner) possesses a beautiful interior with a Baroque-style

Original candle snuffer on the 'haunted house' on Berkeley Square.

staircase leading to a graceful drawing room. No. 45 was redecorated by Chambers for Clive of India in 1763 and was also the scene of Clive's suicide in 1774; in the 19th century Lady Dorothy Nevill received Gladstone and Disraeli and other celebrities of the day here. In the basement of no. 46 is the famous members-only nightclub **Annabel's**, the haunt of the 1960s' jet-set. Winston Churchill lived as a child at no. 48, and at no. 47 (now the exclusive J. Safra Sarasin Bank) William Pitt resided for a time with his brother, the 2nd Earl of Chatham. No. 50, previously the home of George Canning (plaque), is the so-called 'haunted house', which remained empty for long periods in the 19th century following numerous different sightings. Of particular note outside these buildings are the wrought-iron lamp holders, many of them complete with **original candle snuffers**; further examples may be seen in other streets in Mayfair.

In the far southwest corner, in Fitzmaurice Place, is the **Lansdowne Club**, begun in 1762 by Robert Adam for the Earl of Bute and sold in 1765 to the Earl of Shelburne, later 1st Marquess of Lansdowne. It became a club in the '30s; the façade is by Charles W. Fox. Blue plaques on either side of the entrance commemorate that the Marquess of Lansdowne lived here as well as Harry Gordon Selfridge, founder of the eponymous department store on Oxford Street.

BROOK STREET

Claridge's, in red brick on the corner of Davies Street (*map p. 635, D1*), is one of London's most exclusive hotels (built 1898, enlarged 1931) and frequently the choice of visiting heads of state and royalty. No. 41 is a 1720s' building Italianised by Barry. Jimi Hendrix lived at no. 23 for about 18 months in 1968–9. At no. 25 (plaque) Handel lived from 1725 until his death in 1759. It is now the **Handel House Museum** (*admission charge; handelhouse.org*). Handel ran his opera company from here, giving the first rehearsal of *Alcina* in 1735. His dining habits in these rooms are the subject of the following anecdote, reported by Charles Burney in 1785: 'During the repast, Handel cried out "Oh—I have de taught"...the company begged he would retire and write it down, with which request he so frequently complied that, at last, one of the most suspicious had the ill-bred curiosity to peep through the key-hole into the adjoining room, where he perceived that "dese taughts" were only bestowed on a fresh hamper of Burgundy.'

HANDEL ON BROOK STREET

From 1723, when he was appointed Composer to the Chapel Royal, until his death in 1759, Handel lived and worked in this Mayfair townhouse. Born in Saxony, Handel came to London in 1710, having been Kapellmeister to the Elector of Hanover, later King George I. What attracted him was the opportunity to stage Italian operas. In the next year his *Rinaldo*, at the Haymarket, proved a huge success. Naturalised a British citizen by Act of Parliament in 1727, he composed *Zadok the Priest* for the coronation of George II later in the same year. The words had been used at every coronation since that of King Edgar in 973; Handel's musical setting of them has been used at every coronation since that of George II. Concentrating increasingly on the composition of oratorios, Handel's work often drew parallels between British history and the Old Testament: they were patriotic pieces extolling by association the glories of the new Hanoverian dynasty. The most popular remains the *Messiah* (1741), of which regular Christmas charity performances in aid of the Foundling Hospital (*see p. 382*) were given after 1750. After 1751, unsuccessful operations on his cataracts left Handel completely blind. Until that time, he was exceptionally prolific, composing some 50 operas and over 20 oratorios, as well as cantatas, concerti and instrumental pieces—the majority of them while he was living in the rooms that can be seen here.

CARLOS PLACE

The **Connaught Hotel** (*map p. 635, D1*) dates to 1896, when it was known as the Coburg. It was the headquarters of General de Gaulle in the Second World War. It has a fine bar and an acclaimed restaurant. At no. 13 Carlos Place, **Hamiltons Gallery** occupies an unusual brick building with an open attic sporting lion's head roof blocks. This was Major Stephen Courtauld's racquets court (E. Vincent Harris, 1924). Originally the Carlos Place façade was without door or windows because the building extended back and adjoined Courtauld's residence at 47 Grosvenor Square. The large central niche, which has been extended into a door, formerly housed a bronze figure of St George, known to residents as 'Old George'.

CHARLES STREET

Charles Street (*map p. 635, D2*) preserves some original wrought-iron lamp holders and snuffers (e.g. at no. 40). Dartmouth House (no. 37) is home to the **English Speaking Union**, itself in the former home of Lord Revelstoke, of the Baring banking family and great-great-grandfather of the late Diana, Princess of Wales. From 1885, Revelstoke joined two 18th-century houses behind the present unified Anglo-French façade. The fine interiors were designed to show Revelstoke's art and furniture collection to advantage. Next door is the traditional **Chesterfield Hotel**, on the site of a house once occupied by the noted Regency dandy Lord Petersham, who owned a vast collection of snuff boxes and used a different one on every day of the year.

CURZON STREET AND SHEPHERD MARKET

Curzon Street (*map p. 635, D2*) has fine older houses on the south side. Disraeli died at no. 19 in 1881. No. 30, an Adam house (c. 1771), is home to the exclusive Crockford's private gambling club. The Curzon Cinema (1933, rebuilt in 1963) is almost opposite Crewe House (now the Saudi Embassy), a preserved stucco mansion set back from the road in its own grounds, designed c. 1740s, altered in 1810s by Edward Shepherd (*see below*) and occupied by the Marquess of Crewe from 1899. Opposite Half Moon Street is the large portico of the extraordinary **Third Church of Christ Scientist** (1910–12, tower c. 1932), its recessed entranceway emblazoned with the message 'Cleanse the leper, heal the sick, raise the dead'. Next door is **Geo F. Trumper**, barbers since 1875, still selling 'unique preparations for the hair and scalp, shaving creams and soaps of the purest qualities and all manner of toilet requisites'. Opposite at no. 46 is **Maggs Bros**, a long-established antiquarian bookseller, beside one of two archways leading into **Shepherd Market**, established by Edward Shepherd, builder and entrepreneur, and still retaining its 'village' atmosphere and 18th-century layout. It is filled with restaurants, pubs and a few small shops.

DUKE STREET

Brown Hart Gardens, on Duke Street (*map p. 635, D1*), is a public square laid out on the roof of an eccentric-looking neo-Baroque electricity substation in Portland stone (C. Stanley Peach, c. 1905). The gardens offer a café, spacious wooden seats, tubs of ornamental plants (including cabbages) and a good view of the Ukrainian church (*see below*). The substation replaced existing gardens at street level and after its completion, the Duke of Westminster ordered the creation of a public square to recompense the local, mainly working-class, residents who had lost their green space. Opposite the gardens is the red-brick **Cathedral of the Holy Family in Exile**, the mother church of the Ukrainian Greek Catholic Apostolic Exarchate of Great Britain, in a building of c. 1890 by Alfred Waterhouse.

FARM STREET

The main entrance to the Jesuit **Church of the Immaculate Conception** (J.J. Scoles, 1849) is here (*map p. 635, D1*), hence its familiar name of Farm Street Church. Evelyn Waugh mentions it in *Brideshead Revisited*. The entrance is flanked by statues of St

Interior of the Farm Street church, with its high altar by Pugin.

Anthony of Padua and St John of Nepomuk, finger to his lips. Catholic tradition sees John of Nepomuk as a martyr to the Seal of Confession, the bond by a which a priest may not divulge any secrets imparted to him in the confessional. In the chapel at the end of the north aisle is one of Timothy Schmalz's *Homeless Jesus* sculptures. The high altar is by A.W.N. Pugin, who designed the interiors of the Houses of Parliament. It is possible to walk through the church and out into Mount Street Gardens, which lead left onto South Audley Street.

GROSVENOR SQUARE

Upper Brook Street leads to Grosvenor Square (*map p. 635, D1*), laid out, with adjoining streets, in 1725–31 by Sir Richard Grosvenor. It covers six acres and is one of the largest of London's squares. The surrounding monumental terraces are mostly neo-Georgian blocks of apartments, offices and hotels built between the 1920s and 1960s; however no. 9 in the northeast corner survives from c. 1725.

On the west side is the **former American Embassy** (Eero Saarinen, 1958–61), a building lauded by many, though it was described by the architecture writer Ian Nairn as 'pompous and tragic...one of the biggest disappointments in London'. The square's garden was re-planned in the 1940s as a memorial to Franklin D. Roosevelt, President of the United States in 1932–44, and includes his statue by Reid Dick (1948). Facing it is a memorial to the Royal Air Force American Eagle Squadron: a Portland stone pillar crowned by a bronze American bald eagle by Elisabeth Frink, unveiled in 1986. There is also a memorial garden commemorating those who lost their lives in the terrorist attacks on the USA on 11th September 2001. It was partly the threat of terrorist attack that prompted the Embassy to leave Grosvenor Square for a purpose-designed moated building in Nine Elms (*see p. 469*). At the time of writing the Grosvenor Square property was being developed with Qatari money as The Chancery hotel.

HAMILTON PLACE

At no. 5 Hamilton Place (*map p. 635, D2*), the 19th-century building in French classical style is **Les Ambassadeurs Club**, a private-members' casino which featured in The Beatles' film *A Hard Day's Night* and in the James Bond film *Dr No*. The COMO Metropolitan Hotel, formerly the Londonderry, on the corner of Hertford Street, opened in 1967 on the site of Londonderry House, designed in the 1760s by James Stuart and reconstructed by Wyatt in the 1820s for the Marquess of Londonderry. Its grand staircase, magnificent ballroom and fine collection of statues all succumbed to the wrecking ball in 1962. Hamilton Place and Old Park Lane converge at the 30-storey **London Hilton** (1961–3), Mayfair's tallest point, where the rooftop bar and restaurant have good views.

MOUNT STREET

Mount Street (*map p. 635, D2–D1*) takes its name from 'Oliver's Mount', the defensive earthwork that was hastily thrown up in 1643 during the English Civil War when news spread that Charles I was approaching London after the Battle of Edgehill. Today it is fronted mainly by late 19th-century pink terracotta buildings housing shops and restaurants. Its famous butcher's shop selling Cairngorm-reared beef closed in 2015 and now the offering is mainly boutiques and dainty cafés, as well as Scott's, Mayfair's well-known fish restaurant. In Mount Street Gardens, a pleasant oasis, is the back of the neo-Gothic Farm Street Church (*see above*). At the end, on the corner of South Audley Street, is a good Victorian pub, The Audley. Diagonally opposite is Purdey's, founded as a showroom by the gunsmith James Purdey in 1880 and still going strong.

THE LONDON SQUARE

By the middle of the 19th century, London had upwards of a hundred squares. Some were fashionable, some were not, but all had a sward of green in the centre and were planted with trees and flowers, even adorned with statuary. The London square, claimed the writer, reformer and social researcher Henry Mayhew, was 'utterly unlike your foreign "*platz*", that bare paved or gravelled space with nothing but a fountain, a statue or a column in the centre of it.'

According to Todd Longstaffe-Gowan in *The London Square* (Yale, 2012), two main factors contributed to the development of the London square: the aim to enclose and safeguard common ground which people were in the habit of using for pasture and recreation; and the desire to create unified architectural ensembles to enhance the appearance of the city. Early prints show squares laid out with buildings of harmonious similitude surrounding a central area bounded by post-and-rail palisades. The apparent exclusivity of the square, however, was soon to be seen as a problem. Commentators complained that the common man was kept at bay while squares became the preserve of genteel children and their nurserymaids. Yet when private landlords were not in charge, the spaces often degenerated into squalor. Leicester Square was a famous example: it rapidly became a 'depository of refuse'.

Trafalgar Square remained an exception. No garden was ever planted there and old prints show it with not a shrub in sight yet plentifully supplied with pavement, fountains, statues and of course its column—decidedly 'foreign' and '*platz*'-like, Mayhew might have said. It quickly became—and still remains—a place of public congregation, often for leisure but also for political protest.

Today London's squares are sometimes private (Cadogan Square), sometimes public (Lincoln's Inn Fields) and sometimes a mixture of the two (St James's Square, open to all by day but locked at night, with the key held only by residents).

During the Second World War, many of the squares were dug up and planted with vegetables to feed the civilian population.

NORTH AUDLEY STREET

Leading out of the northwest corner of Grosvenor Square towards Oxford Street, North Audley Street (*map p. 635, D1*) boasts a fine set of manhole covers commissioned by the Grosvenor estate. Their motifs celebrate the trades and businesses that once flourished here. On the right as you head toward Oxford Street is the imposing neo-Grecian porch of the **ex-church of St Mark** (J.P. Gandy Deering, 1824–8), with a pierced stone tower rising above it. The church lay redundant for many years and is now filled with food and drinks stalls of Mercato Mayfair. None of the fixtures and fittings have been removed: with a wine bar in the Lady Chapel, a stand selling gin cocktails behind the pulpit and another selling craft beets in the chancel, it is a place to come to watch Mammon triumph amid the woodwork, mosaics, memorial tablets and fine stone inlay.

QUEEN STREET

The Regency courtesan Harriette Wilson lived in Queen Street (*map p. 635, D2*). She was born in Mayfair in 1786, the daughter of a Swiss clockmaker. Her announcement in 1825 that she planned to write her memoirs prompted a former client, the Duke of Wellington's famous reaction 'publish and be damned'. Harriette's response was that 'old frights like himself, who cannot be contented with amiable wives, but must run about to old procuresses, bribing them to decoy young girls, ought to pay us for the sacrifice they tempt us to make, as well as for our secrecy.' The memoirs are still in print. Wellington, we learn, was a dull companion, with whom conversation was 'very uphill work'. Queen Street today is home to two Michelin-starred restaurants, Tamarind (Indian) and Murano (modern Italian).

SOUTH AUDLEY STREET

The **Grosvenor Chapel** (*map p. 635, D1–D2*) is of plain brick with a quoin-edged tower (1730–1). Its foundation stone was laid by the landowner Sir Richard Grosvenor; it was used by US armed forces during the Second World War. Next to it at no. 19 South Audley St is Thomas Goode, china and glass specialists, occupying an elaborate building by Ernest George dated 1876 on the façade, which also sports three giant chinoiserie vases. At the time of writing, the company was under relatively new ownership and the building was due to be given an expensive makeover. At no. 72, beyond South Street, lived Charles X, last King of the Bourbons (r. 1824–30).

SOUTH MOLTON STREET

South Molton Street (*map p. 635, D1*) is a pedestrianised parade of shops. In the triangular site behind Bond Street Underground, on Davies Street and South Molton Lane, is **Grays Antique Centre**, a late 19th-century terracotta building, previously the headquarters of water closet manufacturers John Bolding & Son, and now a warren of 200 antique dealers. It is built over a tributary of the River Tyburn and in the basement a raised canal full of goldfish is fed with running water from the now underground source.

BOND STREET AND EAST MAYFAIR

Bond Street (*map p. 635, D1–E2*), divided into New Bond Street to the north and Old Bond Street to the south, was laid out by Sir Thomas Bond in 1686. Its name has been synonymous with fashion and shopping since the 18th century. Here was the place for dandies—known as 'Bond Street Loungers'—and it is here that they ogled promenading ladies through their quizzing glasses. Weston, famously the tailor to the leader of fashion himself, Beau Brummell (*see p.* 252), was located in Old Bond Street. Former residents include Jonathan Swift, James Boswell and Admiral Lord Nelson. Thereafter it became known as the centre of the London fine art world: long-established auctioneers **Sotheby's** and **Bonhams** both still have their flagship salerooms here. Today, this street of mainly 19th- and 20th-century façades is home to major international luxury brands. Gucci, Prada, Chanel, Versace and Louis Vuitton rub shoulders with traditional British brands such as upmarket stationer **Smythson** (no. 40). This is also the **jewellers'** street, where the most famous names in fine jewellery—Tiffany, Boucheron, Boodles, Cartier, Van Cleef & Arpels, Graff, De Beers—are represented one after the other and along the side streets. This is the only place in the world where dealers in the largest and rarest diamonds congregate in high concentration, giving the false impression that these extraordinary multi-million-pound gems exist in abundance.

Allies, at the junction of Old and New Bond Street, is a popular sculpture of Roosevelt and Churchill sitting casually on a bench (Lawrence Holofcener, 1995). It was unveiled to mark the 50th anniversary of the end of the Second World War.

CLIFFORD STREET AND CORK STREET
On **Clifford Street** (*map p.* 635, *E1*), which opens into Savile Row (*see below*), at no. 18, is **Buck's**, the gentleman's club on which P.G. Wodehouse modelled Bertie Wooster's rowdy club The Drones. It is famous for the Buck's Fizz cocktail, invented by its bartender in 1921. Also known as a mimosa, it is made of champagne and orange juice. Nearby **Cork Street** is a centre for the contemporary arts world, with many commercial galleries.

HANOVER SQUARE
Hanover Square (*map p.* 635, *E1*) is adorned with a bronze statue of William Pitt the Younger (Chantrey, 1831). The house at no. 21 was occupied by Talleyrand in 1835 (plaque). The church of **St George's, Hanover Square**, with a Corinthian portico, was built in 1724 to designs by John James, as part of the New Churches Act of 1711. Concerts are held regularly and a Handel Festival takes place each year (Handel worshipped here, being a neighbourhood resident; *see p.* 263). The register contains entries of the marriages of Sir William Hamilton and Emma Lyon or Hart (1791), Benjamin Disraeli and Mrs Wyndham Lewis (1839), 'George Eliot' and Mr J.W. Cross (1880), Theodore Roosevelt and Edith Carrow (1886) and H.H. Asquith and Margaret Tennant (1894); also of the remarriage of Shelley and Harriet Westbrook in 1814, legalising their Scottish elopement of 1811.

SAVILE ROW
Savile Row (*map p.* 635, *E1*) has been the home of British bespoke tailoring since the 1850s and it is here that the term 'bespoke' (used to signify when a particular cloth was already spoken for by a customer) was coined. Napoleon III and Winston Churchill (to name but two) were outfitted in Savile Row; the tuxedo was invented here in the 1860s. Sheridan lived at no. 14 (tablet) and died in 1816 in the front bedroom of no. 17.

Interior of the graceful Paul Hamlyn Hall, a former flower market of 1860, now part of the Royal Opera House.

THE WEST END, COVENT GARDEN & SOHO

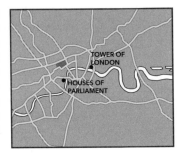

L ondon's 'West End', centred on Leicester Square, Soho and Covent Garden, is the city's entertainment heartland, home to theatres, clubs, restaurants and nightspots. Its streets, some of them narrow and cobbled, merit an unhurried wander: this is an area of historic and modern phenomena vying for attention by sight, sound and even smell. A good place to begin exploring these districts is the broad and busy Haymarket.

Some highlights of the area
✦ The **National Portrait Gallery**, a stone's throw from the entertainment hub of Leicester Square, where you come face to face with paintings, sculptures and photographs of some of the most influential men and women in British history;

✦ **Covent Garden**, once known for its produce and flower markets, now a centre for retail but still home to the **Royal Opera House** and site of the **Transport Museum** and the **'Actors' Church'**, with its memorials to stars of the stage and screen;

✦ This is an area of streets and squares with names hallowed by reputation: **Carnaby Street**, **Drury Lane**, with **Soho** itself as its throbbing heart, full of places to eat, drink and be merry.

HAYMARKET

Map p. 635, F1–F2. Underground: Piccadilly Circus.

Historically, Haymarket had an unsavoury reputation. In *Piccadilly in Three Centuries* (1920), Arthur Irwin Dasent remarked that 'Other and less innocent wares than hay were openly bought and sold in it until it became, in process of time, a recognised mart for human frailty.' Haymarket today is one of the main streets of London's West End theatre district.

At its northern end, where it meets Piccadilly and Coventry Street, are two works of sculpture positioned on a chamfered corner above and below a tall cylindrical window. On the roofline, poised as though diving down into the multitudes below, are the slender aluminium and gold-leaf figures of the **Daughters of Helios** (or '*Three Graces*'), by Rudy Weller (1992). Below, at street level, is the **Horses of Helios fountain**, also by Weller. The horses plunge through the water under a canopy.

Beyond the Art Deco **Haymarket House** (corner of Shaver's Pl.), Panton Street leads off to the left. Here you will find the **Harold Pinter Theatre** (Thomas Verity, 1881; *haroldpintertheatre.co.uk*), formerly the Comedy Theatre where the Watergate Club was established in 1956, allowing controversial plays to be performed to a 'club' audience as a way of circumventing censorship regulations.

Towards the lower end of Haymarket, on the corner of Charles II Street, is **His Majesty's Theatre** (*lwtheatres.co.uk*), conceived by Charles J. Phipps in French Renaissance style (1897), with four Corinthian columns enclosing an upper-floor loggia. George Bernard Shaw's *Pygmalion* premièred here in 1914. Today the musical is the staple fare: Andrew Lloyd Webber's *The Phantom of the Opera* has been running since 1987. Next to the theatre and looming above it is the glass and reinforced concrete bulk of **New Zealand House** (RMJM, 1963), home to the New Zealand High Commission. Standing 18 storeys high, not tall by modern standards (though conspicuously so for this part of London). It is a building with many detractors but just as many admirers, of whom the critic Ian Nairn was one: he found it 'thoughtful' rather than disruptive. Behind it, leading from Charles II Street through to Pall Mall, is the **Royal Opera Arcade**, the earliest covered shopping arcade of its kind in London (1816–18). Originally part of the Royal Opera House, it was designed by Nash in collaboration with his pupil George Stanley Repton. Commercial lets here come and go. At the time of writing, the Crown Estate and New Zealand government were working together to renovate both properties.

SUFFOLK PLACE AND SUFFOLK STREET

Diagonally opposite His Majesty's Theatre stands the **Theatre Royal Haymarket** (*trh. co.uk*), built in 1821 by John Nash as part of his ambitious development to link Carlton House with the new Regent's Park (*see p. 162*). Its Neoclassical façade is classic Nash, in clotted-cream-coloured stucco, with a portico borne by six Corinthian columns. The great actor-manager Sir Herbert Beerbohm Tree, founder (in 1904) of the Royal Academy of Dramatic Art (RADA), leased the theatre and managed it from 1887–97, establishing it as a centre for Shakespearian drama. In its distinguished history it has staged some important productions: in 1893, the premières of Oscar Wilde's *A Woman of No Importance* and *An Ideal Husband* were held here; in 1914, Ibsen's *Ghosts* was seen on the English stage for the first time.

Suffolk Place leads east from Haymarket to **Suffolk Street** (*map p. 635, F1–F2*), which remains (largely) unadulterated Nash, a sumptuous high-cholesterol stucco enclave of Classicism. The block on the west side, on the north corner of Suffolk Place, remains completely intact. The lower part of its façade is fronted by Doric columns topped by abaci (both witty conceits, as neither have true load-bearing functions) and

Clotted-cream-coloured stucco, the trademark of John Nash, on the corner of Suffolk Street and Suffolk Place.

a graceful wrought-iron balcony rail runs along the top. A plaque commemorates the radical free-trader Richard Cobden, who died here in 1865.

The blue plaque at no. 14 commemorates Richard Dadd (1817–86), the famous 'fairy painter' whose febrile imagination eventually broke down into schizophrenia, leading him to obey his 'voices' and stab his father to death in 1843, spending the rest of his days in the mental institutions of Bethlem and Broadmoor.

LEICESTER SQUARE

Map p. 635, F1. Underground: Leicester Square.

Leicester Square, at the heart of the West End, was laid out in the 1670s and named after Leicester House, built for Robert Sidney, 2nd Earl of Leicester, in 1635. It occupied the north side until its demolition in the late 18th century, after which fashion and respectability fled the area and it became popular with artists and entertainers. It was then that Leicester Square began to take on its present raucous flavour. Victorian music halls came and went, replaced by vast picture palaces. On Leicester Square itself, on the site of Leicester House, the first theatre to be repurposed was the **Empire**, which was rebuilt as a cinema in 1927. The building now also houses a casino, open round the clock. On the east side, the **Odeon Luxe** occupies the site of the Alhambra, which had hosted a distinguished Diaghilev season in 1921. Daly's Theatre, just off Leicester Square on Cranbourn Street, was completely rebuilt by its new owners, Warner Brothers, in 1937. It is now the **Vue West End** cinema and the façade retains sculptures of *Spirit of Sight* and *Spirit of Sound* (Edward Bainbridge Copnall, 1938).

The centre of the square is filled by a **garden**, where London plane trees are joined by palms. At the centre is a statue of Shakespeare (a 19th-century copy of the monument by Scheemakers in Westminster Abbey) and dotted around are bronze figures tracing a century of performing arts, unveiled in 2020. Among them are Bugs Bunny, Mary Poppins, Mr Bean, Paddington Bear—and Batman, who looks down from the Odeon cinema roof. TKTS operates the Half Price and Discount Theatre Ticket Booth in The Lodge, a pavilion on the south side of the garden (*tkts.co.uk*).

Sir Joshua Reynolds lived at no. 47 from 1760 until his death in 1792; this was the first house to acquire an official commemorative plaque (1875). At the time of writing it was occupied by a McDonald's. On St Martin's Street the **Westminster Reference Library** stands on the site of a house occupied by Sir Isaac Newton (1710–27) and Charles Burney (1774–94). Here Fanny Burney wrote *Evelina*.

From 1753 until his death in 1764, the artist William Hogarth had his townhouse on the opposite side from Reynolds, at the southeast corner (no. 30). Just beyond where it would have stood, **Irving Street** leads out of the square, its brick-and-stucco buildings filled with cafés and restaurants. At the far end, outside the entrance to the National Portrait Gallery, is a statue of the great actor Henry Irving (1838–1905, the first actor ever to receive a knighthood).

NATIONAL PORTRAIT GALLERY

Map p. 635, F1. Free. npg.org.uk.

The National Portrait Gallery was founded in 1856, the first establishment of its type in the world. The three men responsible for its foundation, the 5th Earl Stanhope, Thomas Macaulay and Thomas Carlyle, were all historians and biographers keenly interested in Britain's past and all three agreed that a National Portrait Gallery should not only illustrate British history but should celebrate the individuals who had contributed to Britain's pre-eminence, a view reflective of mid-19th-century British self-confidence. Carlyle, in his famous *On Heroes* (1841), had argued that 'the history of the world is but the biography of great men'. The new gallery was therefore to be a historical resource where images of the great and good could be venerated and could inspire emulation. The quest for role models is still perceptible today but contemporary attitudes to history are different and the perspectives of a post-Imperial audience are not shaped by Victorian certainty or self-belief.

The building

The building (1890–5) was designed by Ewan Christian and re-opened after important restoration in 2023. The entrance block, facing Charing Cross Road, is in Florentine Renaissance *palazzo* style while the side wing, facing St Martin's Place, is inspired by the delicate terracotta façade of Santo Spirito, Bologna. The façade is adorned with (named) portrait busts of significant figures in the museum's history (Stanhope, Macaulay and Carlyle) as well as noted artists, sculptors and historians. The main entrance doors, which resemble the bronze portals of a Roman basilica, contain panels of sketchy female portrait heads (all but one of them nameless) by Tracey Emin.

The most recent alteration and restructuring (Jamie Fobert Architects and Purcell) has been much praised for opening up the building to the light and restoring a sense of its former grandeur. The Portrait Restaurant on the fourth floor offers a famous bird's-eye panorama of Nelson on his column, with the Palace of Westminster and Big Ben beyond.

The collection

The foundations of the collection were laid by the etcher and illustrator George Scharf. The first acquisition was the 'Chandos' portrait of Shakespeare, after which the collection steadily grew from an original 57 pictures to over 1,000. Scharf's profound study of portraiture enabled him to authenticate as genuine or dismiss images, and his meticulous manuscript notebooks of portraits in private collections, with lively sketches and annotations, remain a valuable resource. Today the National Portrait Gallery holds over 200,000 images of famous figures from British history, many of them iconic. Visitors will inevitably have their own interests and specialisms. Nevertheless, an attempt to outline some of the highlights may be helpful. The collection is broadly chronological, within themes, beginning with the earliest works on the top floor and working downwards.

NB: Not all the collection can be shown at once. To minimise their exposure to light, miniatures, works on paper and photographs are shown in selected rotations.

Tudor and Stuart portraits

The collection of 16th- and 17th-century British pictures is one of the best in the world. The earliest portrait in the collection is the finely painted *Henry VII* (1505), his hand resting on a stone ledge, a composition taken from early Flemish portraiture. Another early work—probably, in fact, the most important work in the gallery—is Holbein's famous 'cartoon' for a mural in Whitehall Palace (since destroyed), celebrating the Tudor dynasty. King Henry VIII's commanding full-length pose served as the prototype for other images of him: a nearby portrait of Edward VI shows him imitating his father's swagger but it is a curiously anamorphic likeness, a distorted image which comes into line at one visual point. Other Tudor figures include King Henry VIII's wives; Thomas More (shown surrounded by his family in a copy after Holbein's lost portrait); Thomas Cranmer; and the full-length 'Ditchley Portrait' of Elizabeth I, by Marcus Gheeraerts the Younger, an exceptionally fine image of the deliberately ageless queen (c. 1592). It was painted to commemorate her stay at Ditchley, in Oxfordshire, as the guest of Sir Henry Lee. She stands on a globe, her feet on Oxfordshire, with lightning flashes behind her (banished by her radiance) and sunshine before, all typical of the symbolic portraiture so loved by the Elizabethans.

By James I's reign, canvas had become the most common support for painting, allowing for larger pictures. As well as James himself, by Daniel Mytens, are beautiful full-lengths by Robert Peake of Frederick, Prince of Wales and his sister Princess Elizabeth, in an intricately embroidered gown. From Charles I's reign are images of Charles himself (also by Mytens), Queen Henrietta Maria and Lord George Stuart, Seigneur d'Aubigny (c. 1638), a young royalist killed at the battle of Edgehill, an excellent late work by Van Dyck, who was Charles I's official painter. Sir Peter Lely, official painter to Charles II, is also represented. There are portraits of court wits such as the Earl of Rochester and of Samuel Pepys (the portrait by John Hayls that he mentions in his Diary) as well as of the king's mistresses. Nell Gwyn is shown with her chest bare and Barbara Villiers clasps her illegitimate son in imitation of an image of the Madonna and Child. Louise de Kéroualle poses with her arm around a black page girl who is holding a nacreous shell full of pearls (symbols of wealth) and a stick of coral (a symbol of diplomacy; the French court hoped that as the king's mistress, Louise could serve France's interests).

The later Stuart collection includes the ruthless Judge Jeffreys by John Michael Wright; a particularly beautiful Lely of Mary II, as Princess of Orange; and a very fine full-length of Queen Anne by Michael Dahl. Next to her is Anne's close friend, and later enemy, the powerful Duchess of Marlborough, shown with her gold key of office around her waist. Sir Godfrey Kneller's small allegorical oil sketch of the Duke of Marlborough shows the famous victor of Blenheim on a rearing horse.

18th- and early 19th-century portraits

There are portraits of George III and Queen Charlotte by Allan Ramsay and Sir Thomas Lawrence's autocratic profile oil sketch of George, the Prince Regent, with his hair brushed forward, Roman style, as well as his portrait of George's blowsy, unloved wife Caroline of Brunswick, but on the whole royalty cease to be the main subjects after Stuart times, as politicians come to the fore. Hung together are Kneller's important Kit-cat portraits, with their uniform frames, showing the politically Whig-minded members of the convivial drinking and dining club. The 18th-century collection includes portraits of scientists, artists and men and women of letters: Sir Christopher Wren; Hogarth (a terracotta bust by Roubiliac); the satirist and author of *Gulliver's Travels*, Jonathan Swift; the well-known, delicate sketch of Jane Austen by her sister Cassandra (an unsuccessful likeness, according to the family). Here too are Blake, Shelley, Byron (in 'magnifique' Albanian costume), Coleridge and Keats, and Benjamin Robert Haydon's portrait of the 72-year-old Wordsworth.

Naturally enough, from this period of British history, colonisation and conquest are much depicted. Also by Haydon are two memorable images of conquerors: Napoleon in exile and the Duke of Wellington surveying the field of Waterloo. Standing with their backs to us, both the victor and the vanquished look as lonely as each other. The expanding East India Company is the subject of Francis Hayman's important *Robert Clive Receiving the Homage of Mir Jaffir after the Battle of Plassey*. Works that reveal Britain's expanding global presence are numerous. Sir Joshua Reynolds's splendid *Portrait of Mai* (Omai) was jointly acquired by the NPG and the Getty in 2023. It is to be displayed on a rotating basis in the two galleries. Here too are likenesses of the great military and naval heroes of the day, the Duke of Wellington and Lord Nelson. Sir George Hayter's enormous *The Reformed House of Commons* (1833) was painted to commemorate the passing of the 1832 Great Reform Act, which widened the country's electorate. Portraits of campaigners for rights and justice include Mary Wollstonecraft (by John Opie), William Wilberforce (by Lawrence) and William Cobbett (possibly by George Cooke).

Victorian collection

The Victorian displays widen the genre from painting and sculpture to include photography. Staring out at us are the confident faces of Victorian statesmen, writers, artists, travellers, inventors and politicians. The British Empire's evangelising spirit is summed up well in Sir George Strong Nares' *The Secret of England's Greatness*, showing Queen Victoria presenting a Bible to a kneeling African convert.

Famous portraits include Branwell Brontë's painting of his sisters, Charlotte, Emily and Anne, a naïve work discovered folded up on top of a cupboard by the second wife of Charlotte Brontë's widower. There are fragile daguerreotypes of the British 'inventor of photography', Henry Fox-Talbot, from the 1840s. Also among the photographs is Robert Howlett's well-known 1858 image of Isambard Kingdom Brunel, standing before the massive anchor chains of his steamship *Leviathan* (later the *Great Eastern*). Works by Julia Margaret Cameron include her equally famous Herschel. Shown together are G.F. Watts' 'Hall of Fame' portraits of the great men of his day, which Watts bequeathed to the gallery. His belief in the importance to history of men of intellectual power and vision, close to Carlyle's theory of the Hero, chimed well with the founding mission of the gallery. Carlyle, of course, is included (he hated his portrait). The gallery

Crucifixion by Jean Cocteau (1960; detail), in Notre-Dame de France.

also owns Watts' famous image of his wife for one year, the actress Ellen Terry, shown at the age of 17 'choosing' (the title of the work) between the worldly camellia and the innocence of violets. Terry—who was 30 years younger than Watts—left her husband and returned to the stage.

John Singer Sargent's powerful and brilliant 1908 portrait of the Earl of Balfour, a pivotal figure in British politics from the 1880s, was thought by G.K. Chesterton to sum up not only the man but also the vague pessimism of the age. The gallery's other late Victorian and turn-of-the-century images include the Italian Boldini's dashing *Lady Colin Campbell*, socialite and journalist, shown in black chiffon with an impossible wasp waist; Napoleon Savory's photograph of his 'picturesque subject', Oscar Wilde, taken in New York in 1882; Virginia Woolf by her sister Vanessa Bell; Dame Laura Knight's famous portrait of herself in profile, in her studio painting a nude female model seen from behind; and Sargent's half-length portrait of Henry James, repaired after the suffragette Mary Wood attacked it (apparently at random) with a meat cleaver in 1914.

Modern and contemporary collection

Figures from the period of the First World War include the suffragette Emmeline Pankhurst and Sherril Schell's well-known photograph of Rupert Brooke. There are a great many portraits of politicians. Graham Sutherland's oil sketch of Sir Winston Churchill is a reminder of the original, disliked by Churchill and destroyed by his wife. Of the royal portraits, a standout is Pietro Annigoni's not-quite-full-length portrait of Queen Elizabeth II, upright and regal against an austere blank background. There are examples of works in many media: David Hockney's acrylic of Sir David Webster; Feliks Topolski's watercolour and gouache of Pandit Ram Gopal; Paula Rego's pastel of Germaine Greer; Gilbert and George's gelatin silver print self-portraits.

The final room contains a memorable display of **death masks**, including one of Keats and another of Wordsworth, by Benjamin Robert Haydon. It is interesting to compare them with the portraits, taken from life, upstairs.

ON AND AROUND CHARING CROSS ROAD

Map p. 635, F1. Underground: Leicester Square.

Charing Cross Road, which runs from Oxford Street in the north to Trafalgar Square in the south, is a major artery of London's West End. It dates in its present guise from the late 1870s, when buildings were demolished to allow the new road to materialise, in an effort to relieve traffic congestion. Today it fights its way north from Trafalgar Square past several landmarks or districts of interest. It is bisected in the centre by Shaftesbury Avenue, where more theatres cluster. Parallel to it at its southern end is another street of playhouses, St Martin's Lane.

NOTRE-DAME DE FRANCE

In Leicester Place, off the northeast corner of Leicester Square, is the lovely, peaceful French church of Notre-Dame de France (*map p. 635, F1; ndfchurch.org*), burned in 1940 and completely rebuilt in 1955. Above the stylised Serlian entrance door is a relief of the *Madonna of Mercy* (*Notre Dame de la Miséricorde*; Georges Saupique, 1953), holding open the folds of her mantle to offer welcome and sanctuary. Inside, over the high altar, is an Aubusson tapestry of the *Bride of Christ*, shown in a Paradise garden with a very fluffy, pompom-headed Lamb. In the chapel on the left side, the altar is decorated with a **mosaic of the Nativity** by Boris Anrep and the walls with **frescoes by Jean Cocteau** (1960). On the left is the *Annunciation*; on the right the *Ascension*; and in the centre a very original *Crucifixion*, showing only the lower register of the scene, with just the bleeding feet of Christ and the bottom of the Cross, the focus of attention being on the faces of the mourners and the gesticulating of the Roman centurions.

CHINATOWN

West of Charing Cross Road, below Shaftesbury Avenue, is London's Chinatown (*map p. 635, F1*), where many settlers from Hong Kong set up businesses after WWII. A large community displaced from Limehouse (*see p. 123*) also settled here. The district is more of a showpiece today but there are still restaurants, bakeries and supermarkets and places offering massage, acupuncture and Chinese medicine, and you will see delivery vans unloading sacks of jasmine rice and crates of pak choy. At Chinese New

Year (Jan/Feb) there are lion and dragon dances and entertainment. **Gerrard Street** is a pedestrianised Chinese avenue with large entrance gates, lion sculptures, paper lanterns and signs in Chinese. Here, inconspicuous on the façade of no. 43 (at the time of writing the Loon Fung Supermarket) is a plaque commemorating John Dryden, Poet Laureate under Charles II, who lived here. Lanterns and entrance gates are also a feature of **Lisle Street** and **Wardour Street**. The Cantonese restaurant Wong Kei on Wardour Street was once famed for having the rudest waitstaff in London. This is no longer the case, but the menu has not altered.

AROUND CAMBRIDGE CIRCUS

The busy Cambridge Circus (*map p. 635, F1*), with the Cambridge pub on one corner, is named after the 2nd Duke of Cambridge, who made the land over for development in 1887. The circus is dominated by the ruddy terracotta façade of the **Palace Theatre** (T.E. Collcutt, 1888; *palacetheatrelondon.org*). Built for Richard d'Oyly Carte (who was born in nearby Greek Street), it opened as the English Opera House in 1891 with Sir Arthur Sullivan's *Ivanhoe*. The great Russian ballerina Anna Pavlova made her first London appearance here. Today it is the home of the musical.

Opposite the Cambridge pub is the **site of Marks second-hand bookshop**, made famous by Helene Hanff in *84 Charing Cross Road* (plaque). Charing Cross Road was known in the past for its bookshops. Though Mark's closed in 1970 (and the building was, at the time of writing, occupied by a McDonalds), a small handful still survive,

Parasols in Chinatown.

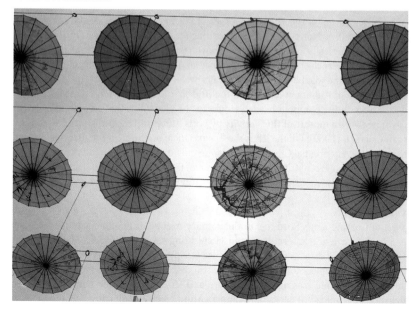

Detail of the frieze on the former Saville Theatre, showing drama through the ages. A character playing Shakespeare's Bottom is on the extreme left, and a flapper of the 1920s brings up the rear.

though sadly not the second-hand stalls where Giuseppe Tomasi di Lampedusa, author of *The Leopard*, apparently loved to browse.

Just north of Cambridge Circus, on Charing Cross Road on the left, is **Foyles** (*foyles.co.uk*), once known as 'the world's largest bookshop'. It was founded in 1906 by two brothers who sold off their textbooks after failing their civil service exams and then realised they had the start of a good business. The brand name Foyles remains, although the shop was acquired by Waterstones in 2018. It occupies a building that once housed two institutions, the **College of Distributive Trades** (left) and St Martin's School of Art (right). The doorway of the former is decorated with charming reliefs by Adolfine Mary Ryland showing a seamstress, a window dresser, grocer's assistant, draper and other occupations connected with retail.

The elegant **Phoenix Theatre** opposite (main entrance on Phoenix St) opened in 1930 with Coward's *Private Lives*. Beyond it, on the corner of Stacey St and New Compton St (entrance on St Giles Pl.) is the **Phoenix Garden**, a tiny jungle-like haven of birdsong with seats and benches scattered amid lush vegetation. It is overlooked by the back of the **Odeon Cinema** on Shaftesbury Avenue. Formerly the Saville Theatre, it has a long frieze on its main façade, by the sculptor Gilbert Bayes (1931), tracing the history of drama through the ages, from the Greek Chorus through Punch and Judy to

20th-century flappers. Brian Epstein, manager of the Beatles, leased the theatre in 1965 and introduced Sunday concerts. Procul Harum, Pink Floyd, the Rolling Stones and many others have played here. Plans to convert the building into a hotel were rejected in 2019. It has been a cinema since 1970 and at the time of writing was still operating as such. Opposite it is the red-brick **Chinese Church in London**'s outreach centre, formerly the Soho Baptist Chapel.

ST MARTIN'S LANE

West Street (*map p. 635, F1*), leading southeast out of Cambridge Circus, is home to a yellow-brick chapel with high arched windows, where Wesley preached. Its pulpit is now in St Giles-in-the-Fields (*see p. 367*). Here too are Ivy Restaurant (*the-ivy.co.uk*), popular with theatre-goers, and the Ambassadors and St Martin's theatres. The latter has been staging Agatha Christie's *The Mousetrap* for over 70 years: it is the world's longest-running play. West Street leads into **St Martin's Lane**. Its lower section, beyond Great Newport and Garrick streets, is still lined with attractive buildings, including more theatres: the Noel Coward and, at the bottom, the Coliseum, whose prominent globe-topped tower makes it a landmark from some distance. It was built in 1904 as a music hall and Ellen Terry, Lillie Langtry and Sarah Bernhardt all appeared on its elaborate stage. The English National Opera (*eno.org*) is now based here. The Duke of York's Theatre (1892) saw the first performance of Barrie's *Peter Pan*; diagonally opposite it is the St Martin's Lane Hotel, an Ian Schrager/Philippe Starck 'urban resort'.

In 1764 Mozart lodged in **Cecil Court**, now lined with print and second-hand book shops. The street was known as 'Flicker Alley' during the early 20th century, when the pioneers of newsreel film-making set up offices here. In St Martin's Court is Sheekey's fish restaurant and oyster bar, dating from 1896. A plaque on no. 60 St Martin's Lane (opposite the Noel Coward Theatre) marks the **site of Chippendale's workshop** from 1753, near the corner of New Row, which, together with the narrow **Goodwin's Court** (*a little further down, entrance well hidden up two steps*), leads through to Covent Garden. Goodwin's Court preserves some charming early Georgian bow-windowed shop-fronts.

COVENT GARDEN

Map pp. 635, F1–636, A2. Underground: Leicester Square, Covent Garden. NB: There are no escalators at Covent Garden station, only lifts. At busy times of year it is quicker to walk from Leicester Square.

Covent Garden, once a thriving fruit and vegetable market, is now an outlet shopping venue and crowds are drawn here at most times of the year, both to the old covered market hall itself and to the streets that surround it, which are filled with shops, theatres and restaurants, and lined by human statues, performers, hawkers and touts of all kinds. Much of the retail space in the old market hall is now occupied by global brands, but there is a handful of surviving individual stores (*coventgarden.london*).

HISTORY OF COVENT GARDEN

The name 'Covent Garden' comes from the area's origin as the kitchen garden of the 'convent' of Westminster Abbey. After the Dissolution of the Monasteries, in 1540, the 1st Earl of Bedford, John Russell, received the land from Henry VIII and constructed his Bedford House, whose garden continued to produce fruit and vegetables. In the 17th century the 4th Earl decided to take advantage of the growing demand for property and appointed Inigo Jones as architect to plan a new square. The resulting Piazza became one of the first and finest of its kind in London, focused on the portico of St Paul's Church on the west side. The north and east sides comprised porticoed houses with an arcaded walk underneath; the present buildings are a modern imitation. Behind them were service streets and stables. According to Todd Longstaffe-Gowan in *The London Square*, this was the earliest example of mews accommodation in the metropolis. The south side of the piazza was bounded by Bedford House gardens. Traders set up fruit and vegetable stalls against its perimeter wall and later, when Bedford House was demolished, market stalls began to appear in the centre of the Piazza.

During the 18th and 19th centuries, Covent Garden became known for its coffee houses, attracting the writers and artists of the day. One well-known establishment was Bedford's in the northeast corner of the Piazza and others were Will's, Button's and Tom's. Tom's quickly gained a reputation for being little more than a brothel, and as the area began to be a place of scandal and ill repute, so fashionable residents began to trickle away.

The 6th Duke of Bedford decided that the market needed a permanent hall and commissioned Charles Fowler to design the Central Market Building. This Neoclassical structure, supported on Doric columns, transformed the open square when it was completed in 1830. The iron and glass roofs were added by Cubitt between 1875 and 1889. By the middle of the 20th century the market activities had grown to such proportions that they were causing appalling congestion. In 1974, the market moved to a new site at Nine Elms, where it remains (*see p. 469*). Covent Garden, however, now a prime tourist attraction, remains as congested as ever.

THE PIAZZA AND 'ACTORS' CHURCH'

The **Piazza**—the area between the portico of St Paul's Church and the Central Market— is the setting for street entertainment continuing a long tradition, recorded by Samuel Pepys who watched a Punch and Judy performance here in 1662, the first recorded instance of such a show. Performances are generally of a high quality; an excellent view is afforded by the Balcony Bar of the Punch and Judy pub. The annual May Fayre still hosts traditional (and alternative) Punch and Judy shows.

The wide Tuscan portico of St Paul's Church, commonly known as the **'Actors' Church'** (*actorschurch.org*), is just a false front: the entrance is from the other side. You can walk through the churchyard, which has a sculpture of *The Conversion of*

St Paul by Bruce Denny. It was unveiled by Dame Judi Dench in 2015. Inigo Jones was given a very small budget for this church. When asked to keep costs down, he promised, undaunted, to build 'the handsomest barn in England'. It is not an unfitting description. And although most of the building was destroyed by fire in 1795, it was reconstructed by Thomas Hardwick to the original design.

The walls inside the church are covered with memorials: Vivien Leigh, Boris Karloff, Terence Rattigan, Charlie Chaplin and Noël Coward are all commemorated here, to name but a few. On the north wall is a plaque to Thomas Arne, composer of 'Rule Britannia', who was baptised and buried here. A silver casket mounted on the south wall of the chancel holds the ashes of Dame Ellen Terry (d. 1928). In the entrance vestibule is a carved limewood wreath from St Paul's Cathedral by Grinling Gibbons. It was placed here as a memorial in 1965 (Gibbons is buried here).

Covent Garden's acting tradition continues in **Garrick Street**, where the Garrick Club (the sombre building opposite the Floral Street corner) has attracted actors and writers since 1831.

The narrow Rose Street leads to the **Lamb and Flag pub**, which dates back to 1638, although the present building is 18th-century. The poet John Dryden was nearly assassinated here by thugs thought to have been hired by the Earl of Rochester, whom Dryden had mocked in his *Essay upon Satire* in 1679. The offending lines began 'Rochester I despise for want of wit.'

THE MARKET AND TRANSPORT MUSEUM

Shops and stalls are open daily. There are large map boards on site and an information office. For details and updates, see coventgarden.london.

The Central Market Hall is divided into three parts: a main central building and two lateral halls. The stalls in the **Apple Market** on the west side of the central building originate from the old Flower Market. They are fixed but the traders change, bringing a range of original British crafts and jewellery design.

The **Jubilee Hall** at the southwest corner of the Piazza was built in 1908 to house the imported fruit market. It has now been redeveloped behind its original façade, offering a general market, antiques and art and crafts on different days.

The **Flower Market** building in the southeast corner of the Piazza dates from 1872. It now houses the **London Transport Museum** (*map p. 636, A2; ltmuseum.co.uk*). The collection began to be formed in the 1920s by the London General Omnibus Company and constitutes a unique record of public transport from c. 1830 to the present day. Exhibits include splendid old buses, omnibuses, taxis and trains; a display on art and design, including the history of the London Transport 'roundel' (its logo) from its inception in 1908 to the present; Harry Beck's famous map of the London Underground; the Johnston typeface (*p. 509*); and some superb London Transport posters, which incorporate the work of leading British graphic artists of the 20th century. There is also a display on how the Underground was dug, with rotary excavators and tunnelling shields.

ROYAL OPERA HOUSE

Map p. 636, A2. Public areas open daily. For tours, see roh.org.uk. Restaurant and café.

Bow Street, which takes its name from its shape of a bent bow, is fronted by the impressive portico of the Royal Opera House, home of the Royal Ballet and Opera companies.

HISTORY OF THE ROYAL OPERA HOUSE
The first Royal Opera House was designed by Edward Shepherd (of Shepherd Market fame; *p. 264*) and opened in 1732. The actor and manager John Rich had a triumphant opening with a revival of Congreve's *The Way of the World*. There was lively rivalry with the Theatre Royal, Drury Lane (*see below*) over the next 150 years until the Opera House became the place for Italian opera. In the 18th century a disastrous fire destroyed the theatre and Handel's organ. The second theatre on the same site, by Robert Smirke, was modelled on the Parthenon and boasted a Classical frieze by John Flaxman and statues by Flaxman and Rossi. The *Annual Register* for 1809 describes the opening: 'The New Theatre opened on Monday night, with the Tragedy of *Macbeth*...It was crowded the instant the doors were open, and though on the steps of the portico the mob were exclaiming against the advance of prices, yet when they got into the theatre, they were silenced by the beauty of the spectacle they beheld.' The silence did not last—and the price riots continued for two months, until prices were reduced. Another disastrous fire followed in 1856 and the entire building was consumed. The present theatre, the third on the site, was designed by E.M. Barry and completed in 1860.

Behind the Corinthian-style portico are parts of Flaxman's frieze (*see box above*) and, in niches, Coade Stone (*p. 466*) statues of two Muses by John Rossi. These were the only elements salvaged from the predecessor of this building after the 1856 fire. The main entrance is to the left of the old portico, through the **Paul Hamlyn Hall**, built in 1860 as a market hall for exotic flowers. Pause to look up above the modern street front to see its graceful cream ironwork.

As well as the frieze and statues mentioned above, another element to survive the 1856 blaze was the foundation stone of the second theatre, laid by the Prince of Wales (the future George IV). It is now on display in the foyer vestibule (*ask a guard to let you in if locked*) and reads: 'LONG LIVE GEORGE PRINCE OF WALES'.

To the left of the Royal Opera House is the Linbury Studio Theatre. Archaeological excavations here in 1996 revealed parts of **Saxon Lundenwic**, the settlement which covered much of Westminster from the mid-7th century.

The Royal Opera House is linked to the Royal Ballet School by the accordion-like **Bridge of Aspiration** (WilkinsonEyre, 2003), which stretches across Floral Street.

Opposite the Royal Opera House is the **former Bow Street Magistrates Court**, completed in 1880 but representing a link with law and order that dated back to the first courthouse on the site in 1740. Here in 1749 the Fielding brothers (Henry and John) established the Bow Street Runners to catch thieves and villains; forerunners of the Metropolitan Police which followed less than 100 years later. The Magistrates Court, at which Emmeline Pankhurst, Oscar Wilde, Casanova and the Kray twins were all at one time defendants, closed in 2006. It is now one of the NoMad portfolio of luxury hotels, joining those in New York and Las Vegas.

DRURY LANE AND LONG ACRE

In Catherine Street (*map p. 636, A2*) is the entrance to the large **Theatre Royal, Drury Lane** (*lwtheatres.co.uk*), recently reopened after restoration. On the wall near the entrance is a bronze bust and stone plaque commemorating Sir Augustus Harris, owner-manager from 1879–97, set in an elaborate fountain by Thomas Brock. The present theatre was designed by Benjamin Wyatt in 1811–12; the portico was added ten years later and the colonnade in 1830. The pillars came from Nash's Quadrant in Regent Street. A ghost is said to haunt the Upper Circle. The theatre has an illustrious 300-year history; the first playhouse on the site was opened in 1663 for Thomas Killigrew's 'King's Company', under the first royal patent to be granted after the Restoration. Charles II was frequently in the audience and here he met and became enamoured of the actress Nell Gwyn, who had lodgings in Drury Lane (she is commemorated by the pub opposite: Nell of Old Drury). The theatre burnt down in 1671 and was rebuilt in 1674 to a design by Wren. The theatre's stormy history includes riots and attempted assassinations, including those of the future George II in 1716 and of George III in 1800 (after his assailant had been removed, the King calmly gave orders for the play to continue). From 1747 the great actor-manager David Garrick revived the works of Shakespeare here—though when Sheridan took over in 1776, it became a theatre of comedy, including his own *School for Scandal*. In 1809, despite its possession of the world's first ever safety curtain, the theatre burned to the ground. Sheridan watched the flames while sipping a glass of port in a coffee house across the road and said, 'Surely a man may take a glass of wine by his own fireside'. Brave words: he was ruined by the fire and died in want. In the Victorian era the theatre was known for its melodrama. Today it is famous for musicals.

Catherine Street is filled with places to eat and drink. On **Russell Street**, opposite the lateral flank of the Theatre Royal, is the Art Deco **Fortune Theatre** (1924). Beside it, in Crown Court, is the **Scottish Presbyterian kirk** (*crowncourtchurch.org.uk*), on this site since 1718. Scottish Presbyterians have had a place of worship in London since the early 17th century, when courtiers of James I established themselves in Scotland Yard (*see p. 154*).

Drury Lane itself is named after the Drury family, who were courtiers to the Tudor monarchs. In the 18th century the area was known for its gin shops and by the end of the 19th century it was one of the worst slums in London. The Peabody Estate on the east side was one of the many developments built for the poor during the 1860s and '70s by the American-born philanthropist George Peabody.

Coved ceiling of the Grand Temple in Freemasons' Hall, filled with esoteric symbols.

LONG ACRE

Drury Lane leads north to Long Acre. Look up Great Queen Street to the right and you will see the huge **Freemasons' Hall** (*map p. 636, A2*), the second on the site (H.V. Ashley and F. Winton Smith, 1933). It is the headquarters of the United Grand Lodge of England, established in 1768, and houses an exhibition of the history of English Freemasonry (*ugle.org.uk*). Adjoining it in Great Queen Street are the **Grand Connaught Rooms**, which incorporate some parts of the original Freemasons' Hall, including the fine banqueting hall designed by F. Cockerell. The rooms are named after the Duke of Connaught, who both laid the foundation stone of the new Hall and ceremonially opened it. He succeeded his brother Edward VII as Grand Master of the Lodge.

Historically **Long Acre** was known for the coach- and cabinet makers—including Chippendale—who settled here. At roof level at no. 31 you will see a surviving inscription: 'Carriage Manufactory'. Further down on the same side, the building at nos 12–14 housed **Stanfords**, the long-established and excellent travel bookshop (*stanfords. co.uk*), from 1852 until 2018, when it moved across the road to Mercer Walk (through Slingsby Place, diagonally opposite). On the corner building, a plaque commemorates the world's first TV broadcast, made from here by John Logie Baird in 1929.

NEAL STREET AND SEVEN DIALS

Neal Street (*map p. 635, F1*) is a long shopping street filled with shops in attractive former warehouses. The buildings of the picturesque enclave **Neal's Yard**, off Short's

Gardens, are painted in bright colours, as if in wishful imitation of La Boca, Buenos Aires. The yard has given its name to a commercial brand of herbal remedies and beauty products; their original shop is here.

Opposite the turning into Neal's Yard is the Seven Dials Market, in another large warehouse between here and Earlham Street. It is home to food stalls and eateries including the 'world's first cheese conveyor belt' at Pick and Cheese.

Both Short's Gardens and Earlham Street lead to the road junction known as **Seven Dials** (*map p. 635, F1*). A Doric pillar topped by six sundials was erected here in 1694. It was taken down in 1773, allegedly because of a rumour that treasure was buried beneath it, although it is more likely that its removal was an attempt to give undesirable loiterers nothing to loiter around: as Dickens noted in *Sketches by Boz*: 'It is odd enough that one class of men in London appear to have no enjoyment beyond leaning against posts.' The original pillar now stands on the green in Weybridge, Surrey. Its removal made no difference: 'Lounging at every corner, as if they came there to take a few gasps of such fresh air as has found its way so far, but is too much exhausted already, to be enabled to force itself into the narrow alleys around, are groups of people, whose appearance and dwellings would fill any mind but a regular Londoner's with astonishment.' Such was Seven Dials in the late 1830s. The area had the reputation of being a notorious thieves' quarter. A new **Sundial Pillar**, made by trainee masons, was unveiled by Queen Beatrix of the Netherlands in 1989, when she was in London to celebrate the tercentenary of the accession of William of Orange. The seven wedge-shaped house frontages that face the pillar are all different and all interesting. One of them is the Cambridge Theatre (1930); another the Mercer Street Hotel (the land here once belonged to the Mercers' Company); and low down on another, on the corner of Short's Gardens, is a plaque with complicated instructions for converting the solar readings on the dials to Greenwich Mean Time.

SOHO

Map p. 635, E1–F1. Underground: Leicester Square, Tottenham Court Road, Oxford Circus.

Soho, once the true epicentre of London's nightlife, is a cramped, lively district, bounded by Regent Street, Oxford Street, Charing Cross Road and Shaftesbury Avenue. The grids of small streets—some scruffy, some seedy, all of them crowded—are lined with bars, pubs, restaurants, cafés, delicatessens, clubs and other venues. Soho caters for everyone: rich or poor, gay or straight, local or tourist; and nearly every nationality is represented here. If you are looking for cheap eats, international cuisine or serious gastronomy, cocktails, pints of beer, comedy, jazz, theatre or dancing, to purchase vintage vinyl or to indulge in proclivities best not described, Soho can help. It also has a few stylish hotels and private members' clubs, and the district has a rich history. Plans to pedestrianise parts of Soho are cyclically shelved and the narrow roads simmer with traffic and garishly decorated, noisy cycle rickshaws.

HISTORY OF SOHO
Originally hunting grounds belonging to Henry VIII, the name is said to derive from an old hare-coursing cry of 'So-ho!' From the 1670s the land, along with the rest of the West End, began to be built up by wealthy landowners, who laid out streets and squares. Soho was mostly conceived by the bricklayer Richard Frith (a street is named after him) but unlike in neighbouring Mayfair and Bloomsbury, the rich and aristocratic did not linger long. Artists and writers settled here from the 18th century; an outbreak of cholera in the mid-19th century finally drove the better-off residents away. Soho is well-known for its immigrant communities, who have given the area its distinctive feel. Huguenots escaping persecution after the revocation of the Edict of Nantes at the end of the 17th century were the first to arrive, founding the French church in Soho Square. Then came Greeks, escaping the Turks (Greek Street commemorates them); and Italians, Hungarians and Jews all came here after being exiled by revolution and to escape persecution.

By the mid-20th century, Soho stood for all things bohemian, alternative and edgy. It was a place frequented by intellectuals, artists, writers, actors and musicians, who congregated here in search of inspiration—and while waiting for it to descend, consumed copious quantities of liquor. Dean Street's recently defunct Colony Rooms was Soho's famous and eccentric drinking den. It was founded in 1948 by Muriel Belcher, described by *bon viveur* jazz musician George Melly as 'a benevolent witch, who managed to draw in all London's talent up those filthy stairs'; she 'adopted' the artist Francis Bacon to tout for punters in exchange for free drinks. The exhaustive list of famous members and regulars, who crowded into the ghastly-coloured green bar (perfumed by alcohol with undertones of drains and vomit), included E.M. Forster, Lucian Freud, Peter O'Toole, Dylan Thomas, Tracey Emin and Damien Hirst. Princess Margaret, London's original It girl, once went for a pink gin.

Soho was also London's red light district and centre of the sex trade, acquiring a sleazy and sordid reputation that still lingers. Today, though, the area has been cleaned up considerably. Some strip clubs and clip joints still survive and the gay sex shop Prowler is still going strong on Brewer Street, but most of what Soho offers today is good eating. Those who truly walk on the wild side have moved further east. People working in the media, film, fashion and the arts tend to congregate and socialise in Soho. For the most part, it is a place to eat, drink and have a good time.

STREETS AND SQUARES OF WEST SOHO

Golden Square (*map p. 635, E1*), one of Soho's two squares, is home to a number of film, TV and radio companies. The artist Angelica Kauffman lived at no. 1. The statue of George II in Roman costume in the centre is by John Nost (1753). In Warwick Street, a peaceful Roman Catholic chapel, **Our Lady of the Assumption and St Gregory**, survives from 1790. Formerly the chapel of the Portuguese Embassy and then the Bavarian, its sanctuary and apse were built in the late 19th century. Echoing the style of early Christian Roman basilicas, it is clad with strips of pale grey marble and features a mosaic of the *Coronation of the Virgin*.

Carnaby Street (*map p. 635, E1*) runs behind Liberty's department store (*p. 296*) and, with the parallel Kingly Street, is the main shopping street of Soho, although independent boutiques are dotted around elsewhere. Carnaby Street was famous for its cutting-edge fashions in the Swinging Sixties and British designers such as Mary Quant set themselves up here. Today it a pale shadow of its former self, with generic brand outlets and a branch of the sandwich franchise Prêt-à-Manger.

In **Marshall Street** is a public leisure centre with a restored 1930s' swimming pool. It was also in this street that the poet and visionary artist William Blake was born in 1757: a concrete tower now stands on the site, on the corner of Broadwick Street. Blake later lived in **Poland Street**, where at no. 15 the poet Shelley took lodgings in 1811, after his expulsion from Oxford; one night he was found to have sleep-walked from Poland Street all the way to Leicester Square.

Off Great Marlborough Street, leading towards Oxford Street, is **Ramillies Street**, with the **Photographers' Gallery** (*16–18 Ramillies St; thephotographersgallery.org.uk*), the first exhibition space in the UK devoted entirely to photography and still the largest public gallery of its kind in the country.

STREETS AND SQUARES OF EAST SOHO

Old Compton Street is the centre of gay Soho. A plaque at no. 59, near the Wardour Street end, commemorates the 2i's ('two eyes') coffee shop, hailed as the birthplace of British rock 'n' roll, where many stars once performed.

Wardour Street (*map p. 635, E1*) was once the home of furniture makers, including Thomas Sheraton in 1793–5. The Marquee Club was based here in the 1960s, encouraging many new bands (The Who, The Rolling Stones) who have since become household names. In St Anne's Court, between Wardour St and Dean St, a plaque commemorates David Bowie, who recorded here. The **church of St Anne**, with a garden laid out around it, has a tower of 1685, partly by Wren; the rest was destroyed in 1940. The heavy steeple (1801–3) is by S.P. Cockerell and below is a monument to William Hazlitt (d. 1830). Dorothy L. Sayers, mystery writer and translator of Dante's *Inferno*, was a churchwarden here (*entrance to the church interior at 55 Dean St*).

Karl Marx lived in **Dean Street** c. 1850 (at no. 28, above the restaurant Quo Vadis), in two cramped rooms with his wife, a growing family and their housekeeper Helene Demuth. He walked daily to the British Museum Reading Room to write. The **French House** at no. 49 is a Soho institution. The pub began serving emigré French in 1914 and was the meeting place for the Free French during World War Two. Photographs of previous patrons—artists, writers, poets and journalists—line the walls. Beer is served by the half pint; mobile phones are banned. Die-hard regulars and professional soaks might still frequent the bar, but mainly today it attracts tourists, who are happy to queue up to get in.

'Look up! look up!
O citizen of London,
enlarge thy countenance.'

William Blake House on
Marshall Street, a housing
block of the 1960s on the
site of the house where
the great visionary poet
was born.

SOHO SQUARE

Soho Square (*map p. 635, F1*) was laid out from 1677. In 1764 Mozart (then lodging at no. 20 Frith St) taught music in the house (no. 22) of Lord Mayor William Beckford, brother of Richard (*see below*). The statue in the garden of Charles II is by Cibber (c. 1681). On the east side of the square, the Italianate **St Patrick's Church** (RC) opened in 1793 (rebuilt 1891–3). It is England's oldest place of worship dedicated to the great apostle of the Irish. The dark red-brick **French Protestant Church**, a reminder of Soho's Huguenot past, dates from 1893 and is by Sir Aston Webb. Services are conducted in French. The square was first surrounded by large mansions,

M. Georges Gaudin, riding in triumph on a gilded snailshell.

including one belonging to the Duke of Monmouth, who chose 'Soho' as his password at the Battle of Sedgemoor (1685). It soon became a fashionable area (the fictional Sir Roger de Coverley, invented by Josph Addison, had his town quarters here). In the 18th century it was a favourite residence of ambassadors. In 1777 Sir Joseph Banks came to live at no. 32 (rebuilt), which became the centre in London for the scientists of the time: the inaugural meeting of the Royal Institution was held here. In the southeast corner of the square, on the corner with Greek Street, is the **House of St Barnabas**, a Grade I listed Georgian mansion built in the late 1740s. Richard Beckford, wealthy Member of Parliament, lived here during the 1750s and was probably responsible for the fine Rococo plasterwork, wood carving and ironwork interior, one of the finest in London. The cantilevered staircase is particularly noteworthy. The Council Room on the first floor features an outstanding ceiling and a copy of the original fireplace. The Chapel dates from 1862. Since 1862, it has been occupied by a charity for the destitute and homeless. The building now operates as a private members' club with donations and subscription fees going towards the charity's outreach programmes.

GREEK STREET AND FRITH STREET

Greek Street (*map p. 635, F1*) is named after a colony of Greeks from the island of Milos whose church, founded c. 1680, was in the nearby Charing Cross Road. The fine restaurant **L'Escargot** was established in 1927 by Georges Gaudin, who had been serving French food to Londoners since 1896. Here he came up with the idea of farming his own colony of snails below stairs, thereby becoming the only English restaurant serving fresh snails. A plaster portrait of him riding a snail is above the main entrance—'slow and sure' was his motto. In 1754 the relentless Latin lover Giacomo Casanova lived in Greek Street; Thomas de Quincey lived here too for a time, in great poverty. It was in Soho that he befriended Ann, an ill and lonely sixteen-year-old prostitue, who later disappears without trace (*see below*). At no. 28 is Maison Bertaux, founded in 1871 and still serving mouth-watering French *patisserie*.

In **Frith Street**—which has many buildings dating from the late 17th and early 18th centuries—is the famous jazz club **Ronnie Scott's**, founded by the eponymous tenor saxophonist in 1959. At no. 6 (1718; partly rebuilt) Hazlitt died in 1830 (it is now a comfortable hotel of the same name). On the site of no. 20, Mozart stayed in the 1760s. Bar Italia, another Soho classic, founded by Italian emigrés in 1949, is still going strong serving good coffee, but is now very touristy. John Logie Baird demonstrated his television here in 1926.

Thomas de Quincey in Soho Square

One night, when we were pacing slowly along Oxford Street, and after a day when I had felt more than usually ill and faint, I requested [Ann] to turn off with me into Soho Square. Thither we went, and we sat down on the steps of a house, which to this hour I never pass without a pang of grief and an inner act of homage to the spirit of that unhappy girl...Suddenly, as we sate, I grew much worse...and all at once I sank from her arms and fell backwards on the steps...I felt an inner conviction of the liveliest kind, that without some powerful and reviving stimulus I should either have died on the spot, or should at least have sunk to a point of exhaustion from which all re-ascent under my friendless circumstances would soon have become hopeless. Then it was, at this crisis of my fate, that my poor orphan companion, who had herself met with little but injuries in this world, stretched out a saving hand to me. Uttering a cry of terror, but without a moment's delay, she ran off into Oxford Street, and in less time than could be imagined returned to me with a glass of port wine and spices; and for this glass the generous girl without a murmur paid out of her humble purse at a time—be it remembered!—when she had scarcely wherewithal to purchase the bare necessaries of life...I sought her daily [after this], and waited for her every night, so long as I stayed in London...So it was for years; but now I should fear to see her; and her cough, which grieved me when I parted with her, is now my consolation. I now...think of her...as one long since laid in the grave...taken away, before injuries and cruelty had blotted out and transfigured her ingenuous nature, or the brutalities of ruffians had completed the ruin they had begun.

Confessions of an English Opium Eater, 1821

Shaftesbury Avenue (*map p. 635, E1–F1*) forms the eastern border of Soho. It was laid out in 1886 and quickly superseded the Strand as London's theatre district. Today it is still home to a number of theatres. At the western end are four in quick succession: the Lyric (C.J. Phipps, 1889; refurbished in the 1930s); the Apollo (1901, in ornate French Renaissance style); the Gielgud (W.G.R. Sprague, 1906) and the Sondheim (1907), also by Sprague but given a new exterior by Sir Hugh Casson following bomb damage.

OXFORD STREET, MARYLEBONE, BAYSWATER & NOTTING HILL

Oxford Street and Regent Street make up London's busiest shopping district, frenetic at times: some boast that it offers the most intensive retail to be had in Europe. Just north of Oxford Street are regular, dignified streets and squares laid out in the late 18th and 19th centuries, expanding to engulf once-rural Marylebone and reaching west to Notting Hill. Further north are the canals of Paddington and Little Venice.

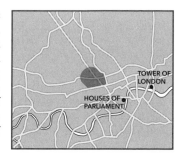

Some highlights of the area

✦ The curving sweep of **Regent Street**, an important piece of 19th- and early 20th-century town planning. Look up above the shopfronts to admire the eclectic architecture. **Liberty**, the old-established store famed for its 'Liberty print' fabrics, is just behind it;

✦ The **Wallace Collection**, in Manchester Square, with exceptional works of 18th-century fine and applied art and other important masterpieces;

✦ **Madame Tussauds**, the perennially popular waxworks museum.

REGENT STREET

Map p. 635, E1. Underground: Piccadilly Circus, Oxford Circus.

Regent Street, which ascends in a stately sweep northwards from Piccadilly Circus to Oxford Street, is named after the Prince Regent (later George IV) and was conceived from 1811–14 by the architect John Nash (*see p. 162*) as a ceremonial route linking the Prince's residence, Carlton House (since demolished), with Regent's Park. It was completed in 1825 and soon attracted wealthy traders and shopkeepers. By the late 19th century, however, Nash's buildings had deteriorated and the arches and colonnades were the haunt of streetwalkers and undesirables. A plan was made to

Prospero and Ariel by Eric Gill (1933) on the front of BBC Broadcasting House.

improve and modernise the vista, and from 1898 until about 1930, Nash's buildings were successively demolished and replaced by the current arc of grandiose edifices in British Imperial style. Sir Reginald Blomfield is recognised as the principal architect but Arthur Joseph Davis, Sir John James Burnet, Henry Tanner, John Murray and Ernest Newton all had a hand. The apparent homogeneity of Regent Street's Portland stone emporia is belied upon close inspection: despite being on the same large scale, the buildings are not identical and there is a diffuse range of ornament here, from Classicist to French to neo-Egyptian, the columns, balustrades and Dutch gables enhanced by Greek key patterns, palm leaves, swags, garlands and volutes. Regent Street remains a significant and historic example of town planning and the buildings along it have achieved listed status.

REGENT STREET FROM CAFÉ ROYAL TO LIBERTY

This first, curved section of Regent Street originally had colonnades protecting shoppers and, above, balconies fronting lodging houses. The new façades omitted the colonnades. At no. 68 is the **Café Royal**, established in 1865 and now a luxury hotel (David Chipperfield Architects; *hotelcaferoyal.com*). It was formerly a meeting place for artists and writers including Beardsley, Oscar Wilde, Whistler, Max Beerbohm, Sickert, T.S. Eliot, J.B. Priestley and Compton Mackenzie. **Veeraswamy**, at nos 99–101, is London's oldest Indian restaurant, founded in 1926 to serve Anglo-Indian cuisine (*entrance on Swallow St; veeraswamy.com*). Heddon Street leads to a quieter backwater of restaurants now known as Regent Street's 'food quarter'.

Hamley's (*hamleys.com*) is London's largest and most famous toy store and, as the descendant of a small shop founded by William Hamley in Holborn in 1760, the oldest toyshop in the world. At no. 218 on the same side, The Edwardian stone building with a concave, pillared frontage, is the original home of **Liberty** (*liberty.co.uk*), founded in 1875 by the draper Arthur Lazenby Liberty to sell his imported silks, fabrics and furnishings, capitalising on the contemporary taste for all things oriental. The vast sculptural group above the engaged Ionic colonnade depicts *Britannia with the Wealth of East and West*, a reference to the founding concept of the store as a bazaar for Eastern merchandise. The building is now occupied by other retailers. Behind it on Great Marlborough Street is the distinctive half-timbered mock Tudor extension of 1924 (Edwin Hall Sr and Jr), Liberty's current premises. The wooden beams are from the hulls of two 19th-century Royal Navy ships: HMS *Impregnable* and HMS *Hindustan*. Ruskin and members of the Pre-Raphaelites all flocked to Liberty's, which then went on to develop its well-known 'Liberty Style', via collaboration with the best Art Nouveau and Arts and Crafts artists and designers of the day. Its mass-produced enamelled jewels and silverware were marketed under the inclusive banner 'Cymric'. The **Liberty Clock** (1925, Edwin Hall Sr and Jr), on the archway into Kingly Street, is flanked by a sculpted rooster (daybreak) and owl (night) with, beneath them, a ribbon bearing the admonition 'No minute gone comes ever back again; Take heed and see ye nothing do in vain.' Above, a mechanical figure of St George rides forth every hour to slay a mechanical dragon. The interior of the shop is richly decorated with carved woodwork and boasts what has been claimed as the longest chandelier in Europe

Behind Regent Street, in the pedestrianised Argyll Street, is the **London Palladium**, founded in 1910, a large-capacity theatre with a 19th-century Neoclassical facade.

OXFORD CIRCUS AND LANGHAM PLACE

Facing Oxford Circus, solid and sedate, are four identical buildings making up the quadrant. North over the crossing, at 309 Regent St, the **University of Westminster**, formerly a polytechnic, was conceived in 1838 by British aeronautical engineer Sir George Cayley, to make scientific learning accessible. In 1882, the philanthropist Quintin Hogg continued its work providing 'mental, moral and physical development' for disadvantaged boys and young men. A statue of Hogg stands further on, in Great Portland Street.

At Langham Place (*map p. 632, C4*) is the only surviving Nash building from his *Via Triumphalis*, and also the only surviving Nash church: **All Souls** (1823; restored after World War Two; *allsouls.org*). It is built in Bath stone and, with its circular Ionic porch resembles an Italian *tempietto*, though it is crowned by a soaring steeple instead of a dome. The design and placement is deliberate: Nash intended it to be a landmark uniting Regent Street with what is now Great Portland Street, the last run-up to the green expanse of Regent's Park. Today it has an active evangelical congregation. In the porch is a bust of Nash by Behnes (1831).

Looming behind All Souls, the steel-framed Art Deco building faced in Portland stone, with a copy of a short-wave radio antenna on the roof, is **BBC Broadcasting House**, the headquarters of the BBC from where news, radio, television and online services are produced and digitally broadcast. It was designed and purpose-built by Colonel Val Myer and opened in 1932. The main exterior sculpture of *Prospero and Ariel* (the spirit Ariel was chosen to personify broadcasting on radio waves) is by Eric Gill (1933), with a further three friezes of Ariel, also by Gill. The modern, curving glass extension and piazza, known as the Peel Wing, was completed in 2010. On the roof, the ten-metre glass and steel sculpture entitled *Breathing* is by the Catalan artist Jaume Plensa. It is designed as a large listening glass, inscribed with the following poem: 'Life turns and turns on the crystal glass; breathing in our body; silence is a voice, our voice; silence is a body, our body', as a tribute to all journalists and technicians who have died carrying out their work. Each evening the glass is illuminated by a beam of light that travels through its centre, to coincide with the BBC's ten o'clock News broadcast. The interior of the building may be seen as part of a guided tour (*online pre-booking essential; bbc.co.uk/showsandtours*).

Diagonally opposite is the five-star **Langham Hotel**, by John James and Giles Murray, which opened in 1865 as the first purpose-built 'Grand Hotel' in London. The opulent interiors were decorated in marble with yards of silk, Persian tapestries and hand-printed wallpaper; it had the first hydraulic lifts in the world (known as 'rising rooms'), hot and cold running water, an early form of air conditioning and WCs in every bedroom. It had its own post office and travel agent (Thomas Cook & Son) and the corridors were wide enough for two women, when fashionably attired in the bouffant crinolines of the day, to pass each other with ease. Later in the 19th century the hotel kept abreast of modern developments by installing electric light and the telephone, and it proudly combined what it considered to be the best of English, French and American style, taste and service. Exiled emperors Napoleon III and Haile Selassie stayed here, as did poets and writers including Oscar Wilde, Mark Twain, Somerset Maugham, Sir Arthur Conan Doyle, Robert Browning and George Orwell. Wallis Simpson often stayed at the Langham while being courted by the Prince of Wales.

OXFORD STREET

Map p. 635, D1–E1. Underground: Marble Arch, Bond Street, Oxford Circus, Tottenham Court Road.

Oxford Street, London's most famous shopping street, stretches for about 1¼ miles between Marble Arch in the west and Tottenham Court Road to the east. It is interrupted by **Oxford Circus**, the junction with Regent Street and part of Nash's grand and uncompleted scheme for linking Regent's Park with Carlton House (*see p. 162*). The crossing is of the type known as a 'pedestrian scramble' or 'X-crossing'. It stops traffic completely and allows pedestrians to cross diagonally as well as laterally, in order to relieve congestion.

Around 300 shops line Oxford Street, among them major high-street names in fashion, some with more than one branch. The shopping here may not be as glamorous or exclusive as that in Mayfair and Knightsbridge, but the shops are open late, seven days a week. They seem to attract a perpetual swarm of shoppers and tourists, becoming exceptionally crowded during holiday seasons. If it is the mix of architectural styles you have come to see, these are not the streets for ambling: enjoy the buildings from the top of a double-decker bus. As traffic often slows to a crawl, you will have ample time to look around you.

HISTORY OF OXFORD STREET
Lying on the line of a Roman road and formerly known interchangeably as 'the road to Oxford', 'Tyburn Way' and 'Uxbridge and Worcester Road', Oxford Street, which is built over the River Tyburn, was properly established in the 18th century. It takes its name from the Earl of Oxford, Edward Harley, who married Lady Henrietta Cavendish Holles; their daughter married the Duke of Portland and the three families' names have lent themselves to streets throughout the area. Horse-buses arrived in 1833 and the Central Line in 1900, bringing carriage-loads of new customers to the shops. Every year in mid-November, the famous Christmas lights are switched on by a 'celebrity'.

OXFORD STREET SHOPS AND LANDMARKS
What once set Oxford Street apart were its giant flagship department stores, great emporia arrayed one after the other along the north side of the street, vying for

public notice and continually refurbished and upgraded to keep up with the thirst for disposable luxury and high-end brands. The Covid pandemic and its aftermath were not kind to high-street retail: of the five great department stores that Oxford Street once boasted (Dickins & Jones at Oxford Circus; and then John Lewis, House of Fraser, Debenhams and Selfridges in close succession on Oxford Street), only two remain. **John Lewis** (established 1864; *johnlewis.com; map p. 635, E1*), along with Peter Jones in Sloane Square, make up the John Lewis Partnership where the staff are partners in the business as well as employees. This quintessentially British emporium is the place to go when needing to choose fabric for new curtains, to chat to someone about the pitfalls of buying a new TV, to have an underwear fitting or to browse the latest fashions and skincare products. The current building dates from 1960; Barbara Hepworth's aluminium **Winged Figure** (1963) graces the façade overlooking Holles Street. At no. 16 Holles St (the site now engulfed by John Lewis), Lord Byron was born in 1788.

House of Fraser, a privately-owned chain of department stores first established in Glasgow in 1849, had its flagship store in an Art Deco building (1937) at no. 318 (corner of Cavendish St). It was the first in Britain to introduce the novelty of escalators (rather than elevators) to every floor. In 2021 plans were approved for redevelopment of the building and House of Fraser was given notice to vacate the site. The store closed in January 2022. Debenhams, which used to occupy the building at no. 334 (between Vere St and Marylebone Lane), was founded as a draper's shop on Wigmore Street by one William Clark in 1778. On receipt of financial support from William Debenham, the store changed its name to Clark and Debenham and as Debenhams continued trading until the financial difficulties of long lockdowns forced the closure of large numbers of stores in 2021.

Opposite Bond Street Underground, set back from the street, is **Stratford Place**, all that remains of Oxford Street's 18th-century past. It was built in the 1770s by Richard Edwin for the Hon. Edward Stratford, who went on to become the 2nd Earl of Aldborough. His Neoclassical mansion, Stratford House, is now home to the Oriental Club, founded in 1824 for 'noblemen and gentlemen associated with the administration of our Eastern empire, or who have travelled or resided in Asia, at St Helena, in Egypt, at the Cape of Good Hope, the Mauritius, or at Constantinople.'

St Christopher's Place (*map p. 635, D1*) connects Oxford Street with Wigmore Street. Here are narrow Victorian passages and courts with shops, boutiques, cafés and restaurants, some with outside dining.

Selfridges (*map p. 635, D1; selfridges.com*), the second largest department store in the UK after Harrods, was founded in 1909 by the innovative American businessman Harry Gordon Selfridge, who is credited with putting the 'fun' into shopping and who believed 'the customer is always right'. Setting up in London some 30 years after the first great department stores of Manhattan, Selfridge pulled in the crowds with the aid of several stunts, one of which was to exhibit Blériot's monoplane after his successful crossing of the English Channel in 1909. By the 1920s and '30s, the store was the last word in ultra-modern, Art Deco luxury: one of the original French lacquer lift panels of 1928 is in the V&A. The grand Ionic façade that shadows Oxford Street was designed by another American, Daniel Burnham, in 1928. It features a giant Art

Deco clock, 'Queen of Time', by Gilbert Bayes. The rooftop garden hosted fashion shows and was a popular place to relax, while the large windows at street level were—and still are—renowned for their innovative displays, especially at Christmas. Today, Selfridges continues to embrace the concept of luxury (in 2013 it became the first department store to instal a champagne-vending machine).

Across Orchard Street from Selfridges is (or was, at the time of writing) **Marks & Spencer** (*marksandspencer.com*). Known as 'M&S', 'Marks and Sparks' or simply 'Marks', the shop began life in Leeds in 1884 when Michael Marks set up his famous bazaar with the slogan 'Don't ask the price, it's a penny.' Ten years later he went into partnership with Tom Spencer. The result is a British retailing phenomenon, selling everything from evening gowns to ready meals, with stores now occupying high streets, airports and railway concourses up and down the land (not to mention their strong online presence). In 2023 M&S were refused permission to demolish the existing Art Deco building and redevelop the site. The campaign to save the building was won on eco grounds (demolition and reconstruction would release too much CO_2) rather than because of any aesthetic considerations. The current building, **Orchard House** (Trehearne and Norman 1929–30), is almost a stripped-down version of Selfridges next door. It has a narrow corner chamfer and elegant matching wings articulated by a giant order of Ionic pilasters. (M&S have another branch on Oxford Street, occupying a black granite building of 1937–8 called The Pantheon, because it is built on the site of James Wyatt's 'Pantheon' assembly room of 1772, 'the wonder of the 18th century'.)

Science, by Sir William Reid Dick (1937), bronze sculpture in the entranceway of Selfridges.

MARYLEBONE

Map p. 635, D1–E1 and p. 632, B4–C4. Underground: Bond Street, Oxford Circus, Baker Street, Marylebone.

The name Marylebone is a derivation of 'St Mary by the Bourne', a reference to the parish church which lay next to the Tybourne—or Tyburn—river. Variously pronounced ('Marry-le-bn'; 'Marly-bone'), Marylebone today is a well-to-do area bounded by Oxford Street to the south, Edgware Road (west), Marylebone Road (north) and Great Portland Street (east). In contrast to jostling Oxford Street, Marylebone has the feel of a genteel town, thanks to the orderly Georgian plan of its streets and squares, which retain remnants of elegant 18th-century terraces along with dignified late Victorian and Edwardian houses. The feeling is enhanced by the range of independent shops and boutiques, cafés and restaurants. The area is managed by its two principal landowners: the Howard de Waldens and the Portmans.

THE HOWARD DE WALDEN ESTATE

The area known as the Manor of Tyburn was recorded in the Domesday Book in 1086. By 1538, Henry VIII had created a royal hunting ground (now Regent's Park). After a succession of tenants, John Holles, Duke of Newcastle, acquired some of the land in the early 18th century. It then passed to his daughter, Lady Henrietta Cavendish Holles, whose husband, Edward Harley, 2nd Earl of Oxford, and the architect John Prince projected Cavendish Square and its surrounding grid of fashionable streets. After the 2nd Earl's death, the estate passed to his daughter, Margaret Cavendish Harley, who married the Duke of Portland. Building continued with Harley Street, Portland Place and Wimpole Street. In 1879, the 5th Duke of Portland died without issue and the estate passed to his sister, Lucy Joan Bentinck, widow of the 6th Baron Howard de Walden. Today the 90-acre estate is still managed and maintained by the De Walden family and is known as the Howard de Walden Estate. The streets, including Oxford Street, take their names from members of these families, their titles and possessions.

CAVENDISH SQUARE AND QUEEN ANNE STREET

Cavendish Square (*map p. 635, D1–E1*), behind the John Lewis department store on Oxford Street, was the first of John Prince's developments for the 2nd Earl of Oxford, begun in 1717. In the central garden is a bronze statue by Thomas Campbell (1851) of Lord George Bentinck, Conservative MP and horse-racing enthusiast. The pedimented façades of two of the houses on the north side, with engaged Corinthian columns, are relics of a noble mansion begun in the 1720s for James Brydges, 1st Duke of Chandos, politician and patron of the arts. It was never completed, though it has been suggested that the 'princely' Duke had plans to connect the proposed town mansion via a private road with Cannons, his grandiose Middlesex stately home (*see p. 564*) which Pope was accused of satirising as 'Timon's Villa' ('At Timon's Villa let us pass a day, Where all cry out, "What sums are thrown away!" So proud, so grand, of that stupendous air, Soft and Agreeable come never there.'). The archway connecting the two wings is adorned with a lead *Madonna and Child* by Jacob Epstein (1953). No. 20 on the west side, the Royal College of Nursing since 1926, is the former home of Liberal Prime Minister H.H. Asquith. Previous tenants at no. 5 opposite include the traveller and writer Lady Mary Wortley Montagu and Lord Nelson.

At the northeast corner of the square, Chandos Street leads to **Queen Anne Street** (*map p. 632, C4*). On the corner, at no. 2 Queen Anne St, is Chandos House, built speculatively by Robert Adam in 1769–71 in a fine, grey stone (Craigleith, from a quarry near Edinburgh that the Adam brothers had interests in). It was leased by the 3rd Duke of Chandos in 1774 and from 1814–43 was the home of the Austrian Embassy. Ambassador Prince Paul III Anton Esterházy entertained here in lavish style. The Howard de Walden Estate purchased the lease in 2002. Now beautifully restored, with many original Adam interior features, it is owned by the Royal Society of Medicine and serves as a meeting and events venue. **Mansfield Street**, leading north, has fine remaining Adam houses.

PORTLAND PLACE

The grand avenue known as Portland Place (*map p. 632, C4*), speculatively laid out in 1778 by Robert and James Adam for the Duke of Portland, stretches all the way to Regent's Park. It is very broad for a central London street because at the time of building, the southern end was taken up by Foley House, a large mansion within its own grounds, whose occupant, Lord Foley, insisted on retaining his uninterrupted view north. The completed street, over 100ft wide and lined on either side with elegant Adam houses, was splendid in proportion and scale, so splendid in fact that Nash would perceive it as the grand final section of his processional route from Regent's Street to the Park and he deliberately placed his church of All Souls at the bend with Langham Place to unite the vista. Today, the Adam terraces exist in fragment form and are interrupted by more modern buildings. No. 55 was presumably erected to fill a World War Two bombsite; note how the corner of the Adam pediment of the house next door, no. 61, looks as if it has been casually snipped off to accommodate it. At no. 63 lived the author Frances Hodgson Burnett, whose lesser-known adult novel *The Making of a Marchioness* (1901) was a great favourite of Nancy Mitford's.

The Art Deco building in Portland stone at no. 66 is the **headquarters of RIBA** (the Royal Institute of British Architects). It was a competition-winning design by C. Grey Wornum and opened in 1934. The exterior sculpture and reliefs are by Edward Bainbridge Copnall and James Woodford; the bronze doors depicting the River Thames and famous London buildings in relief are also by Woodford. The interior, open to all, houses a café/bar, restaurant, bookshop and library. Guided tours of the building are available (*see architecture.com*).

In the middle of the boulevard are several monuments: Quintin Hogg, founder of Westminster Polytechnic (George Frampton, 1906), who lived in nearby Cavendish Square, sits reading to two boys; an equestrian statue of the Army officer Sir George White (John Tweed, 1922); General Wladyslaw Sikorski, Prime Minister of the Polish

Government and Commander-in-Chief of the Polish Armed Forces, 1939–43 (erected 2000); and a bronze bust of Lord Lister, surgeon and founder of antiseptic medicine (by Thomas Brock).

Portland Place emerges into **Park Crescent**, where Nash's semicircular stucco composition of terraced houses (1812–22) is a fine prelude to Regent's Park itself. From the private garden, a statue of Prince Edward, Duke of Kent, 4th son of George III and father of Queen Victoria, surveys Portland Place.

HARLEY STREET AND WIMPOLE STREET

Harley Street (*map p. 632, C4*), running parallel with Portland Place to the west, has been synonymous with private healthcare since the 19th century. Here and in neighbouring Wimpole Street, doctors, surgeons and dentists have their practices. At nos 43–49 Harley St is Queen's College, an independent girls' school founded in 1848 by Frederick Denison Maurice, professor of English Literature and History at King's College London, to provide girls and young women with a serious education; it was the first institution in Great Britain where women could gain academic qualifications.

At the bottom of Wimpole Street the **chapel of St Peter** (facing Vere Street; *map p. 635, D1*), of brick with stone quoins and with a Doric porch, is by James Gibbs (1721). Now deconsecrated, and carpeted wall-to-wall in blue, it houses the Institute of Contemporary Christianity. No. 1 Wimpole St is the **Royal Society of Medicine**, in an Edwardian Baroque building (John Belcher, 1912), the entrance flanked by Rods of Asclepius in verdigris copper. At 64 Wimpole St is the **British Dental Association**, which has a small museum dedicated to the history of British dentistry. The museum was founded in 1919 by Lilian Lindsay, the first woman to qualify as a dentist, and entry is free (*bda.org/museum*). Opposite, at **no. 94**, what remains of the former Abbatt Toyshop frontage is Ernő Goldfinger's earliest work in London (1936). Further north, to the left off Wimpole Street at **no. 47 Queen Anne Street**, is the house where J.M.W. Turner lived and which he maintained as his gallery space until his death in 1851. The property, famously squalid and known as 'Turner's Den', was purportedly infested with Manx cats, and umbrellas were required indoors during wet weather.

No. **50 Wimpole St** is the address from which the poet Elizabeth Barrett eloped in order to marry Robert Browning in 1846; the couple then left for Italy and lived in Florence until Elizabeth Barrett Browning's death in 1861. Note the many mews in this area, narrow streets parallel with the main thoroughfares, once providing stables for horses and coaches, then garages for cars, and now sought after as homes and offices. At no. 17 **Wimpole Mews** lived the fashionable osteopath Dr Stephen Ward (d. 1963), with whom the showgirl and model Christine Keeler lived for a time. Ward became famous for his part in the Profumo Affair: he introduced MP and Secretary of State for War John Profumo to Keeler and the ensuing scandal of their brief liaison brought down the Conservative government.

WIGMORE STREET

Wigmore Street (*map p. 635, D1*) runs parallel with Oxford Street. The terracotta building at no. 36 is the **Wigmore Hall**, a recital venue for Classical soloists and chamber musicians, hosting over 400 concerts a year. It was built as Bechstein Hall by the eponymous German piano-makers (who had showrooms next door) in 1901. The interior, celebrated for its intimacy coupled with near-perfect acoustics, was designed by Thomas Collcutt, who had previously collaborated with Richard d'Oyly Carte on various theatre projects as well as the Savoy Hotel and the public rooms of many P&O liners. It is richly decorated in mahogany, alabaster and marble. The Arts and Crafts mural in the cupola above the stage depicts the 'Soul of Music'. It is the work of Gerald Moira, whose other public commissions included artworks for Lloyd's Register of Shipping and the Central Criminal Court. During the First World War, anti-German feeling in England led to the affairs of many German firms being wound up by the Board of Trade (Dame Nellie Melba was vilified for singing 'Land of Hope of Glory' to the accompaniment of a Bechstein piano) and the hall was sold at auction to Debenhams the department store, who at the time occupied no. 33 opposite (the huge Edwardian Baroque building clad in white Doulton tiles). In 1917 it re-opened under a new name: Wigmore Hall.

Marylebone Lane winds picturesquely north from Wigmore Street to join **Marylebone High Street** (*map p. 632, C4*), the heart of old 'St Mary by the Bourne', where the Tyburn flowed (*see p. 301*). Today it is marketed as 'Marylebone Village', a chic enclave with good shops, nice places to eat and desirable apartments to live in. Here, at no. 83–84, you will find **Daunt Books**, in a beautiful pre-WWI shop with balustered galleries. Originally specialising in travel, it now stocks a range of fiction and non-fiction and is usually deservedly thronged (*dauntbooks.co.uk*).

THE PORTMAN ESTATE

The western side of Marylebone extends for 110 acres from Marylebone High Street (*map p. 632, C4*) to Edgware Road (*map p. 632, A4*), incorporating Manchester, Portman, Montagu and Bryanston squares. The land has been owned by the aristocratic Portman family since the 16th century and was built up from the 17th century. Today, the estate is run by Christopher Portman, 10th Viscount Portman.

AROUND BRYANSTON AND MONTAGU SQUARES

Montagu and Bryanston squares were built by David Porter, c. 1810–15; the architect was Joseph Parkinson. **Bryanston Square** (*map p. 632, B4*) is named after the Portland family estate in Dorset while **Montagu Square** to its east takes its name from Elizabeth Montagu (*see Portman Square, below*), Porter's benefactor who helped him, a former chimney sweep, become a builder. Anthony Trollope lived at no. 39. After the death of William Pitt the Younger, whose social hostess she had been, Lady Hester Stanhope also lived in Montagu Square, before abandoning England for the Levant. The Neoclassical church of St Mary's (*entrance on Wyndham Place*), with its Ionic stone portico and tower, is by Robert Smirke (1824) and was built to seal the view from Bryanston Square. Along with All Souls, Regent Street, it is one of the Commissioners' or 'Waterloo' churches. At no. 1 Dorset Street lived the computer pioneer Charles Babbage (1791–1871).

On **George Street**, the Irish poet Thomas Moore had his first lodgings in London (site of no. 85). **Bryanston Court**, on the corner with George Street and Seymour

Detail of the back of the Raoul Wallenberg monument in Cumberland Place. Faithfully represented is a *Schutzpass*, the type of document issued by Wallenberg to Jews in Budapest in 1944, conferring Swedish diplomatic immunity on them to protect them from deportation to labour or concentration camps or from confinement in the ghetto.

Place, was home to Mrs Wallis Simpson in 1933–6; she entertained the Prince of Wales here before moving to Cumberland Terrace, Regent's Park.

At 33 Seymour Place is the **West London Synagogue** (1872; main entrance at 34 Upper Berkeley St), with a Byzantine/Romanesque interior. The **Western Marble Arch Synagogue** stands on the Cumberland Place hemicycle (*both synagogues map p. 634, C1*), with a monument to Raoul Wallenberg outside it (Philip Jackson, 1997). Wallenberg, a Swede who was in Budapest during WWII, heroically rescued many Jews from deportation and the death camps by issuing Swedish protective passes. Last seen alive in early 1945, he is presumed to have died a prisoner in the Soviet Union.

The **Edward Lear Hotel** at no. 28–30 Seymour St is the former home of writer and artist Edward Lear. The area around New Quebec Street and Seymour Place has been revitalised as a small shopping district with select shops, boutique hotels, pubs and restaurants and is now promoted as 'Portman Village'.

PORTMAN SQUARE

Portman Square (*map p. 635, D1*) was built from 1764. On the site of the Radisson SAS Portman Hotel stood a fine townhouse of 1781, by James 'Athenian' Stuart. The house, destroyed during a WWII bombing raid, was built for Mrs Elizabeth Montagu, wealthy widow, society hostess, bluestocking and close friend of Lady Margaret Harley, daughter of the 2nd Earl of Oxford and wife of 2nd Duke of Portland. She was careful never to invite 'idiots' to her literary soirées: guests included Joshua Reynolds, David Garrick, Samuel Johnson, Edmund Burke, George Lyttleton, Horace Walpole and William Wilberforce. Before her husband's death and prior to taking up residence in Portman Square, her salons were held at her home in Hill Street, Mayfair.

Home House (no. 20; 1773–7) is a fine surviving example of Robert Adam's work. It was commissioned by another wealthy widow, Elizabeth, Countess of Home. From 1789–94 it served as the French Embassy and from 1932–90 it was home to the Courtauld Institute of Art (the art historian and Soviet spy Anthony Blunt lived in a flat here during his tenure as Director). The splendid interior includes a flying staircase with glass dome, ceilings by James Wyatt (the architect originally commissioned) and walls decorated by Antonio Zucchi. It is now a private members' club, incorporating the Georgian townhouses on either side (nos 19 and 21).

BAKER STREET AND MARYLEBONE ROAD

Baker Street (*map p. 632, B4*), linking Oxford Street with Marylebone Road, is universally associated with Sir Arthur Conan Doyle's detective Sherlock Holmes and his assistant Dr Watson. The small **Sherlock Holmes Museum** (*admission charge; sherlock-holmes.co.uk*) in a Victorian house at no. 239 (north of Marylebone Road, near Regent's Park) tries hard to evoke the atmosphere of the novels by recreating the fictional detective's home based on descriptions in Conan Doyle's stories. Renumbered 221b (Sherlock Holmes's fictitious address), the detective's study and bedroom have been created and furnished with period memorabilia. The surreal experience is further enhanced on the upper floors, where die-hard fans takes smartphone videos of groups of waxworks.

Chiltern Street was, at the time of writing, being transformed into a street of independent shops, with a hotel in the old fire station. **Paddington Street Gardens**, which in the 18th century was a burial ground for Old Marylebone Parish Church, were converted into formal gardens in the 1880s. The remaining Neoclassical Fitzpatrick Mausoleum, in Portland Stone, dates from 1759.

On the south side of Marylebone Road (a roaring six-lane highway), at the junction with Gloucester Place, is Sir Edwin Cooper's **Old Marylebone Town Hall**, former headquarters of Westminster County Council (opened 1920), with a 1938 library extension next door. The huge building, with its giant Corinthian order, tower and pair of lion sculptures flanking the entrance steps, is now part of the London Business School.

West (left) along Marylebone Road is the terracotta-clad **Landmark Hotel**, built by Robert Edis in 1899. Inside is an impressive palm atrium where one can take afternoon tea (*landmarklondon.co.uk*). Behind the hotel is **Marylebone Station**, of the same date. **Dorset Square**, originally part of the Portman Estate, was the site of Thomas Lord's first cricket ground in 1787–1811. The Georgian terraced houses were built after Lord moved the eponymous ground to St John's Wood (*see p. 416*). The square is named after the Duke of Dorset, an early cricketing enthusiast. George Grossmith, actor in several of Gilbert and Sullivan's operettas and co-author of *The Diary of a Nobody*, lived at no. 28; Dodie Smith lived at no. 18.

MADAME TUSSAUDS AND THE ROYAL ACADEMY OF MUSIC

The corner building on Marylebone Road with a huge, distinctive green copper dome, formerly the London Planetarium, is now part of the eternally-mobbed tourist attraction known as **Madame Tussauds**, a waxworks museum (*map p. 632, B4; madametussauds. com*). It was founded in 1835 by Marie Tussaud, who had been taught the art of wax-modelling by Dr Philippe Curtius, a physician and her mother's employer, who left her his collection of models after his death. At the court of Louis XVI she had sculpted various famous personalities, including Voltaire, and during the French Revolution, though initially condemned to death, she was famously employed to take the death masks of guillotine victims. After fleeing France, she toured Europe with her collection of waxworks, before coming to settle in England in 1802. Few waxworks from Tussaud's lifetime remain; a fire in 1925 and bombing during WWII caused significant damage, although some of the casts still exist. The exhibition, now an international franchise and continually updated, focuses on waxworks of modern personalities: stars of film, stage, sport and music as well as royalty, politicians and comic-book superheroes.

Further along, on the corner with the York Gate entrance to Regent's Park, is the Royal Academy of Music, founded in 1822. The main building, in neo-Hampton Court style, is by Sir Ernest George (1912). The **Royal Academy of Music Museum** (*map p. 632, C4; free; ram.ac.uk/museum*) is in a part of York Gate designed by Nash. The museum collections include scores, manuscripts, letters, art, photography, memorabilia, and three floors of musical instruments. Highlights include Sir Henry Wood's conducting batons (made of poplar wood, painted white) and a violin of 1709 by Stradivari, which was once owned by Giovanni Battista Viotti, violinist to Marie-Antoinette.

ST MARYLEBONE PARISH CHURCH

Opposite the Royal Academy of Music is Thomas Hardwick's **St Marylebone parish church** (1817; *map p. 632, C4*), with an impressive Corinthian portico and cylindrical tower; the domed bell chamber is supported by gilded angel caryatids. This is Marylebone's fourth parish church; the first was built near Oxford Street (probably near the Marylebone Lane corner) c. 1200. This church, built on New Road (now Marylebone Road), faced towards open fields and was thought to be splendid enough for Nash to open up a view of it when he created York Gate opposite. Elizabeth Barrett and Robert Browning were married here in 1846. Next to the church a small public garden serves as a cut-through to Marylebone High Street where, hard right, is the **Memorial Garden of Rest**, the site of the previous parish church where Byron was christened and where Nelson worshipped and had his daughter Horatia baptised in 1803. The small garden, planted with shrubs and trees, is lined with weathered, lichen-covered tombstones. Beside the boundary with Marylebone High Street is the obelisk monument to Charles Wesley (d. 1788), parishioner, hymn writer, brother of John Wesley, and father of Samuel Wesley the organist and composer. Also buried here were James Gibbs, Allan Ramsay and George Stubbs.

SPANISH PLACE

Spanish Place is so named because after the Restoration, the Spanish Embassy used to stand nearby, on Manchester Square. In the late 18th century, when restrictions on Catholic worship were eased, a chapel was built here. Its successor, the large Roman Catholic **church of St James's Spanish Place** (*entrance at 22 George St; map p. 632, C4*) is a pure example of Gothic Revivalism (1890). The architect, Edward Goldie, borrowed details from 13th-century English Gothic cathedrals at Lichfield and Salisbury, as well as from Westminster Abbey. Inside, the reredos in the Lady Chapel is by J.F. Bentley (architect of Westminster Cathedral).

At no. 3 **Spanish Place** lived Captain Frederick Marryat, Royal Navy officer and novelist. His works include *Mr Midshipman Easy* and *The Children of the New Forest*.

THE WALLACE COLLECTION

Map p. 635, D1. Free entry to the permanent collection. Restaurant. wallacecollection.org.

The handsome Manchester Square, originally laid out in the 1770s, is famed chiefly for its mansion, **Hertford House**, built for the Duke of Manchester and now home to the Wallace Collection.

Built in 1776 for the 4th Duke of Manchester, Hertford House lies on the north side of the handsome Manchester Square. The collection that it contains was formed by successive members of the Seymour-Conway family, Marquesses of Hertford, and by Sir Richard Wallace, natural son of the 4th Marquess. Sir Richard Wallace's widow bequeathed the collection to the nation in 1897, on condition that nothing was added or removed from it. This stipulation was respected until 2019, when the Wallace Collection made its first ever loan, of Titian's *Perseus and Andromeda*, to the National Gallery, where it formed part of an exhibition reuniting a series of works based on stories from Ovid that Titian had produced in the 1550s for Philip II of Spain. Though temporary loans may now become more frequent (the *Laughing Cavalier* went out in 2023, again to the National Gallery), the Wallace Collection remains a splendid survival and its paintings, furniture and *objets d'art* are displayed in a manner fully evocative of the atmosphere of an aristocratic town mansion, as Hertford House was in its heyday.

The Marquesses and their collection

The Wallace Collection, like the Frick in New York or the Musée Nissim de Camondo in Paris, is a supreme example of a private art collection displayed in the home of its collectors. The museum is seldom crowded and a visit here is one of the great joys of London. The collection comprises important 18th- and 19th-century British portraits, mainly collected by the 1st and 2nd Marquesses, and a large collection of 17th-century Dutch and Flemish pictures, collected by the 3rd Marquess. Its chief importance and glory, however, is the exceptional collection of 18th-century French painting, sculpture, furniture, porcelain and *objets d'art*, amassed by the 4th Marquess and unparalleled in this country (in this area the Wallace Collection outdoes both the National Gallery and the V&A).

Richard Seymour-Conway, 4th Marquess of Hertford (1800–70), spent much of his life in France, in Paris in an apartment on Rue Laffitte, and at the Château de Bagatelle in the Bois de Boulogne. Collecting was an obsession, made possible through the extraordinary works of art on the market following the French Revolution. He purchased works by the leading 18th-century painters Boucher, Watteau, Fragonard, Lancret and Greuze, as well as items by the finest French cabinet makers such as Boulle and Riesener. On his death in 1870, Hertford House was bought by his illegitimate son, Sir Richard Wallace, from his cousin, the 5th Marquess. Wallace added an extensive collection of medieval and Renaissance works as well as the important collection of arms and armour, which is second only to that of the Royal Armouries.

WALLACE FOUNTAINS

Outside Hertford House stands a bright green Wallace Fountain, one of the type donated by Sir Richard Wallace in 1872 to the city of Paris, where they have become known simply as 'wallaces'. Designed by Charles-Auguste Lebourg, the fountains provided a free supply of clean water, and were enthusiastically received by Parisians. The fountain's ornamental dome is supported by four caryatids representing the gowned goddesses of Simplicity, Sobriety, Charity and Bounty, distinguishable by their knees, whether left or right, covered or bare. Eighty-two Wallace Fountains can be found in different parts of Paris, with at least six in other French cities and towns, and others in over 20 cities worldwide.

Detail of the Wallace Fountain outside Hertford House.

Richard Wallace inherited the estate of his father the 4th Marquess in 1870, and found himself caught up in the Siege of Paris and the painful birth of the Second Republic. Staying on in the city, he paid for an ambulance and a hospital bearing the Hertford name. Beleaguered by the Prussians and forced to accept a humiliating peace, the city's violent suppression of the Paris Commune in the following year persuaded Wallace to remove his art collection to London for safe-keeping, offering the fountains as a farewell gift.

Hertford House

Some of the rooms in the house contain surviving parts of the original decoration. Others have been decorated in a way that recreates their former appearance. On the ground floor, for example, Wallace decorated his **Smoking Room** with Turkish-design Minton tiles and a mosaic floor. A niched recess at one end contains pieces of the original wall revetment. The white marble **main staircase**, rising grandly to the first floor, has a magnificent balustrade (1719–20) of cast and wrought iron and gilt brass, originally from the stairs leading to Louis XV's Cabinet de Médailles in the Palais Mazarin, Paris. One of the finest examples of French metalwork of the period, it was sold as scrap in the mid-19th century, bought by the 4th Marquess and, in 1847, altered to fit Hertford House and installed by Sir Richard Wallace.

Upstairs, the **Large and Oval Drawing Rooms** were, at the time of the 2nd Marquess, magnificent ballrooms where, in 1814, a grand ball was held to celebrate the defeat of Napoleon. The **West Room**, Lady Wallace's bedroom, is decorated with curtains and wallpaper in the original blue colour scheme. In the **East Drawing Room** Isabella, wife of the 3rd Marquess, would entertain the Prince Regent on his daily visits between 1807 and 1820.

To contain the growing collection, Sir Richard and his French wife altered and extended the house, most importantly adding the **Great Gallery**, designed by Thomas Ambler. It extends the full length of the back of the house and was purpose-built, with top-lighting, for the display of pictures as well as for glamorous entertaining. A water-powered lift provided additional access.

More recent redevelopment (Rick Mather) has involved glazing the **central courtyard**, which is now home to the restaurant.

Highlights of the collection

The collection is so rich that only an attempt can be made to canvas its highlights. The Wallace Collection maintains an excellent website with a search function showing the location of each exhibited piece.

Sculpture, furniture and *objets d'art:* Sculptural highlights include **marble busts by Houdon** of Madame Victoire, one of Louis XV's daughters, and Madame de Sérilly, maid of honour to Marie-Antoinette. There is also a **bronze bust of Louis XIV** (c. 1699), of magnificent hauteur, by Antoine Coyzevox, the king's sculptor, and a marble version of the same likeness.

Among the medieval and Renaissance treasures collected by Sir Richard Wallace is a marble bust of Christ (c. 1515) by Pietro Torrigiano, from Westminster Abbey, as well as exquisite medieval ivories, enamels and miniatures.

The collection of **furniture** includes exceptional examples of the work of the cabinet maker André-Charles Boulle, veneered with *contre-partie* marquetry (sheets of turtleshell and brass glued together and a design cut out). There are also pieces once owned by Marie-Antoinette, including a small desk by Jean-Henri Riesener, the leading cabinet maker under Louis XVI, with marquetry water lilies and an elaborate perfume burner (1774–5) by Pierre Gouthière. An original poster of August 1793, advertising a sale of furniture and effects from the Petit Trianon, once belonging to the Queen, is also part of the collection. The delicate worktable

(1786–90) by Adam Weisweiler belonged to the Empress Josephine.

As might be expected, there are some splendid pieces of **porcelain**, including a Sèvres ice-cream cooler, part of a service made for Catherine the Great of Russia. There is also a large wine cooler (1574) from the collection of Cosimo de' Medici.

The astonishing collection of **arms and armour** was built up by Sir Richard Wallace. There is an exceptionally fine 17th-century Indian dagger, made for either Jehangir or Shah Jahan, with a solid gold hilt set with diamonds and a floral design of rubies, with leaves of emeralds; Tipu Sultan's *tulwar*, a type of scimitar; and the gold and ivory sword of Ranjit Singh. Memorable in the European Armoury collection is the equestrian armour for horse and rider, the horse's browplate equipped with a great ramming prong.

Paintings: Early works include Italian paintings of the Lombard, Venetian, Florentine and Sienese schools. There are fine views of Venice by Canaletto and Guardi. Among a number of works by Watteau is his well-known *Music Party* (c. 1718), with music-making on a palatial terrace. 'Fancy' pictures by Greuze include *The Broken Mirror* (1763), *Innocence* (a young girl holding a lamb) and *Fidelity* (a young girl holding a dog). Boucher's portrait of Madame de Pompadour shows her in her garden at Bellevue (the statuary group in the background, *Friendship Consoling Love*, is a reflection of her now-platonic relationship with the king). One of the Wallace's most famous paintings is Fragonard's *The Swing* (1767), purchased by the 4th Marquess. It is a picture full of artful abandon, flirtation and innuendo, the graceful, provocative girl poised in the air, the action of the swing tossing her delicate slipper in the direction of her lover and allowing him a tantalising view up her frothing skirts.

English paintings include *The Strawberry Girl* by Reynolds as well as his *Nelly O'Brien*, which shows the well-known beauty and courtesan seated with a pet dog in her lap, her face shaded by the brim of her hat. Gainsborough's *Mrs Robinson as Perdita* (1781) was commissioned by the Prince of Wales after he had seen the actress perform the role from Shakespeare's *The Winter's Tale* at Drury Lane; she holds the miniature of him he sent to her. Lawrence's slick portrait of George IV (1822) was thought by the artist to be his best likeness of the king, and is mentioned in Thackeray's *Vanity Fair*.

The collection of 17th-century Dutch and Flemish pictures includes two masterpieces by Pieter de Hooch: *A Boy Bringing Bread* and *A Woman Peeling Apples*, as well as typical genre scenes by Jan Steen. A particularly famous work is Rubens' *The Rainbow Landscape* (c. 1636), a late summer afternoon scene on the artist's country estate (it is the pendant to *Het Steen* in the National Gallery, which the Gallery had wanted to acquire but was outbid by the 4th Marquess). There is a self-portrait by Rembrandt as well as a portrait of his teenage son Titus. Probably the best-known item in the Wallace Collection is Frans Hals's *Laughing Cavalier*. Whichever angle you look at him from, his teasing eyes follow you. The 4th Marquess outbid Baron de Rothschild for the picture, paying six times its auction estimate, which of course added to the picture's celebrity. Painted in 1624, the identity of the man, neither a cavalier nor laughing, is unknown, although in 2012 the Dutch art historian Pieter Biesboer suggested that it might be the same sitter as the wealthy cloth merchant depicted by Frans Hals ten years later, in a portrait now in Cleveland, Ohio. The man in question is Tieleman Roosterman, who died in 1673.

Titian's *Perseus and Andromeda*, painted originally for Philip II of Spain and once owned by Van Dyck, was purchased by the 3rd Marquess in 1815. Poussin's exceptional *Dance to the Music of Time* is another well-known painting.

BAYSWATER, PADDINGTON & LITTLE VENICE

Map p. 634, A1–B1. Underground: Bayswater, Queensway.

The white stucco terraces of Bayswater, with their houses, flats, small hotels and serviced apartments, stretch behind the Bayswater Road towards Paddington. The triangle of streets, squares, crescents and mews bounded by the Edgware Road and Sussex Gardens is sometimes referred to as **Tyburnia**, in reference to the ancient tributary of the Thames which flowed past here to Westminster and the notorious gallows which once stood on the site of Marble Arch (*see p. 322*). Edgware Road itself leads north from Marble Arch, following the ancient Roman Watling Street.

A Middle Eastern community has settled in Bayswater, with associated shops, restaurants and cafés, some with opportunities for sheesha-smoking in cordoned off sections of the pavement. Off Harrowby Street, a turning to the east off Edgware Road, an archway leads into the narrow **Cato Street**, famed as the meeting-place of the 'Cato Street Conspirators' (hanged at Newgate in 1820), whose object was the wholesale extermination of the Ministers of the Crown at a Cabinet dinner in Grosvenor Square.

Bayswater was developed as a comfortable middle-class housing estate, on land belonging to the Bishop of London, by S.P. Cockerell, beginning around 1805 and attracting artists and writers. In 1885 its nickname 'Asia Minor' was due to the number of colonial officers who settled here on their return from secondment in Asia. The small cluster of independent shops and businesses around Connaught Square (*map p. 634, C1*) is now known as 'Connaught Village'.

Lancaster Gate (*map p. 634, B1*), built in the mid-19th century, is the smartest part of Bayswater. The grand stucco terraces overlooking Hyde Park were designed with a wide boulevard between them (now a busy road) and the neo-Gothic Christ Church sited in a square. The church has now been converted into housing; the tower and spire remain. The church of **St James, Sussex Gardens** (*map p. 634, B1*) is a late work of G.E. Street (1881–2), building on an earlier, smaller church from the original 1840s' estate, which he realigned, placing the altar at the west end. It was designed to form part of a vista, with a triangular garden in front and Sussex Gardens beyond, splitting into separate crescents behind the church.

The Porchester Centre was originally a reading room and library as well as a baths complex. *The Reading Girl* statue, dating from the 1920s, is at the foot of the main stairs. Someone has given her a dab of lipstick.

PORCHESTER TERRACE AND QUEENSWAY

The Modernist 1950s' **Hallfield Estate** on Bishops Bridge Road (*map p. 634, A1*) was designed by the Tecton partnership and executed by Lindsay Drake and Denys Lasdun. The ten- and six-storey blocks, with landscaping in between, have chequered façades. At the western side is Lasdun's Hallfield School, also a landmark of its time.

In Leinster Gardens, nos 23 and 24 are sham fronts, built in the 1860s to hide the underground railway's steam condensers.

In **Porchester Terrace**, nos 3–5 are a pair of stucco houses designed as a 'double detached villa' by John Claudius Loudon, the gardening writer and architect. He built them for himself and his mother in 1823, a very early example of semi-detached housing (the glazed porch disguises the fact that the houses are a pair). In the **Porchester Centre** is an Art Deco leisure centre and spa, founded in 1923, with original features including a series of Turkish hot rooms. It is open to members and one can still have an authentic experience here. Ask at the reception desk if you can go upstairs to view the swimming pool from the gallery balcony.

Paddington Basin: view of the canal and the surrounding mixed-use developments.

Queensway and Westbourne Grove are at the heart of Bayswater, a lively multi-ethnic part of the city with numerous shops, bars and restaurants catering to a wide variety of tastes. In Queensway is **The Whiteley**, once London's premier department store, founded by William Whiteley in 1863 and expanding to 17 departments and 6,000 staff by 1900. The building is by Belcher and Joass (1908). The atrium and sweeping staircase are surviving original features. Today it is a mixed-use development with a hotel, retail units and residential flats.

Down Ilchester Gardens and St Petersburgh Place are three places of worship, all built in the 1870s but in different styles and for different faiths and denominations. On the corner of Moscow Road is the neo-Byzantine **Greek Orthodox Cathedral of St Sophia**, built for the Greek merchants of Bayswater by John Oldrid Scott (1877), son of Sir George Gilbert Scott. **St Matthew's** was built for the Church of England (J. Johnson, 1881) in Gothic Revival style. Diagonally opposite is the **New West End Synagogue** (George Audsley, 1877–9), in a 'Gothick' mix of styles.

PADDINGTON

Paddington Station (*map p. 634, B1*), the former terminus of the old Great Western Railway, opened in 1854. Its engineer was the great Isambard Kingdom Brunel. The first underground railway in the world, operated by the Metropolitan Railway Company, was opened in 1863 between Paddington and Farringdon. The popular series of children's books by Michael Bond, featuring a bear named Paddington, has led to endless souvenir spin-offs and there is a bronze statue of the bear on the station concourse itself.

The front of the station, formerly the Great Western Hotel by P.C. Hardwick (the son of Philip, who designed the Euston Arch; *see p. 386*), now forms the Hilton London Paddington Hotel. The area immediately surrounding the station is a mix of handsome stucco terraces bravely contending for a place beneath ever-higher, glassier and more beetling modern blocks. Much of the new development has taken place around **Paddington Basin**, where office, leisure and shopping complexes surround the L-shaped section of old canal, where houseboats are still moored alongside barge cafés and food trucks. This area, especially around the spacious Merchant Square, is a popular place for people to come and eat lunch, many of them staff from the nearby St Mary's Hospital. Here you will find Thomas Heatherwick's **Rolling Bridge** (2004), a hinged truss bridge which curls and uncurls to allow pedestrians to cross or boats to pass. Electric 'picnic boats' can be rented from here for a tour of the canals (*see goboat. co.uk*).

In Praed Street and South Wharf Road are the various buildings and departments of St Mary's Hospital. The great scientist Alexander Fleming discovered penicillin at St Mary's in 1928, when he noticed that a mould had grown on some of his bacterial culture dishes and that colonies of staphylococcus could not survive near it. The **Fleming Museum** (*visits by appointment; entrance on Norfolk Pl.*) includes a re-creation of Fleming's laboratory.

PADDINGTON GREEN

On the edge of Paddington Green, an expanse of garden north of the busy Westway (underpass from Paddington Station; *map p. 632, A4*), is **St Mary's church** (1791), the successor of the church in which Hogarth was secretly married in 1729 (*restricted opening hours; parishoflittlevenice.com*). The sculptors Thomas Banks (d. 1805) and Joseph Nollekens (d. 1823) and the painter Benjamin Robert Haydon (d. 1847), friend of Keats, have their tombs here. The actress Sarah Siddons is buried at the north end of the churchyard. In the adjoining recreation ground there is a statue of her (L.J. Chavalliaud, 1897), in a dramatic pose based on Reynolds' depiction of her as the Muse of Tragedy (a version of the portrait hangs in Dulwich Picture Gallery). She has cause to look tragic perhaps, turned as she is to face a ceaselessly roaring four-lane highway and a drab Premier Inn.

In 1829, the first London horse-drawn omnibus service began between Paddington Green and the Bank of England.

LITTLE VENICE

Little Venice (*map p. 628, C2*) is the name popularly given to the point where the Paddington arm of the Grand Union Canal meets the Regent's Canal. Do not expect the Rialto. The body of water here is scarcely bigger than a millpond, but brightly-painted narrowboats are moored here (some of them now functioning as cafés) and you can walk along the towpath to admire the picturesque villa architecture, or sit on a bench in the pleasant **Rembrandt Gardens**, on the waterfront below Warwick Avenue. The poet Robert Browning lived in Warwick Crescent in the 1860s, following his return from Italy after his wife Elizabeth Barrett Browning's death. His house overlooked the widest stretch of water, now known as **Browning's Pool**, and he is said to have rowed over to the small island (now likewise named after him) for poetry composition. It has also been suggested that Browning coined the name Little Venice: since he knew the *Serenissima* well, and in fact died there in 1889, in his son's home in Ca' Rezzonico on the Grand Canal, he would have been well aware of the inaccuracy of such a comparison and the attribution seems unlikely.

North of Little Venice is the residential district of **Maida Vale**. The name recalls the Battle of Máida of 1806, when the British expelled the French from Calabria, Italy. Opposite the Warwick Avenue Underground station is the **church of St Saviour**, with a fibreglass spire (Michael Biscoe, 1976). It replaces the Victorian church on this site which was deemed to large for its congregation. The section of Formosa Street between Warwick Avenue and Warrington Crescent is filled with shops and restaurants. At no. 2 Warrington Crescent is a blue plaque to Alan Turing, the computer scientist, who was born here in 1912. **Clifton Nurseries**, through a narrow corridor between two stuccoed mansions in Clifton Villas, opens out into a small and charming garden centre with plants, gifts and books and a café/restaurant. On the corner of Formosa St and Blomfield Rd is The Waterway, a popular canal-side pub with a large terrace overlooked by the tall spire of **St Mary Magdalene's church**, a fine example of Victorian ecclesiastical architecture by G.E. Street (1873).

Little Venice and Maida Vale merge to the northwest with Kilburn (*see p. 568*).

CANAL CRUISES AND EVENTS

At Blomfield Road, Jason's Trip offers rides in a 100-yr old canal boat to Camden Lock and back, passing through the Maida Hill Tunnel and Regent's Park (approx. 45mins; booking essential; jasons.co.uk). The London Waterbus Company also offers boat trips from Little Venice (londonwaterbus.com). The Puppet Theatre Barge puts on popular marionette shows; it is moored in Little Venice all year and tours the Thames during the summer (puppetbarge.com). For electric boats to rent for self-guided water tours, see goboat.co.uk. The annual Canalway Cavalcade, a festival when 100 narrowboats converge, takes place around the public holiday on 1st May.

NOTTING HILL

Map p. 628, B2–B3. Underground: Notting Hill Gate, Ladbroke Grove.

Notting Hill is a fashionable, mixed-residential area famous for its Saturday antiques market (Portobello Market) and the annual Notting Hill Carnival (*see below*), which takes place during the last weekend in August.

The church of St Saviour, Maida Vale (1976).

NOTTING HILL CARNIVAL

First held in 1965 as a simple Caribbean street parade with music, the Carnival is now Europe's biggest street party and indeed the biggest street festival in the world outside Rio. During the 1950s many West Indian immigrants came to settle in Notting Hill and their arrival was greeted with suspicion by an indigenous white working-class population: hostility exploded in August 1958 into some of the worst rioting seen in the UK. The Carnival started as a way to promote cultural unity in an area fraught with racial tensions. Today over a million visitors descend on Notting Hill during late August (the weekend known as the 'August Bank Holiday') to join in the festivities and to take part in the processions of floats, costume parades, dancers and soca, calypso and steel bands.

Notting Hill began life in the 1840s when the main landowners, the Ladbroke family, developed their estate with the intention of turning the area into a fashionable suburb. Streets and crescents of large, handsome, stuccoed terraced houses began to spring up, with private communal gardens; an aspect that appealed—and still does—to their wealthy, middle-class inhabitants. Artisans settled in streets of smaller, quainter cottages. By the end of World War Two, however, Notting Hill had become run-down. The big Victorian houses, now devoid of families and servants, were cheaply converted into multiple-occupancy tenements. Slum landlords, such as the infamous Peter Rackman, exploited tenants ruthlessly, moving entire West Indian immigrant families into substandard housing (stoking racial tensions) and coercing older tenants into giving up their properties by deliberately moving in noisy and intimidating neighbours.

In the late 1960s and '70s, Notting Hill began to attract an arty, bohemian community of writers, artists, journalists and actors. Musicians congregated around Ladbroke Grove (*map p. 628, B2*) and famous names who performed and recorded in the area include Van Morrison, Hawkwind, Nick Drake, Eric Clapton, The Clash and Bob Marley. Jimi Hendrix died at no. 22 Lansdowne Crescent in 1970. From the 1980s Notting Hill experienced a renaissance and in the 1990s it was made famous by the eponymous film starring Hugh Grant and Julia Roberts.

Today, Notting Hill is a sought-after area to live in. It is also an area full of contrasts: attractive, designer, multi-ethnic, edgy, scruffy, where rich coexists with poor—although the artists, writers and musicians are increasingly being supplanted by moneyed bankers, celebrities and politicians. The main streets are now tenanted by upmarket shops and restaurants, including the ubiquitous international chains. The area around Ladbroke Grove station tenaciously resists gentrification.

EXPLORING FROM NOTTING HILL GATE STATION

Holland Park Avenue (*map p. 628, B3*), which leads west towards Shepherds Bush, was developed in the 1860s. It is lined with large, Italianate detached villas by Francis Radford (*for the Campden Hill area, see p. 359*). Pembroke Road leads north to **Portobello**

Road (*map p. 628, B2*), which takes its name from the capture of Puerto Bello, in the Gulf of Mexico, by Admiral Vernon in 1739. On Saturdays this whole area plays host to the Portobello Market (*portobelloroad.co.uk*). Portobello Road, winding all the way to Ladbroke Grove, is crammed with stalls and with shoppers, who come to browse the antiques, jewellery, bric-à-brac, fruit, vegetables and fashion. There are plenty of interesting independent shops, cafés and pubs around here too, in particular along Westbourne Grove, Ledbury Road and Kensington Park Road. The **Electric Cinema** (*191 Portobello Rd, electriccinema.co.uk*) is one of the oldest cinemas in London and comprises an independent cinema, private-members' club and a popular bar/diner. In Lancaster Road (between Westbourne Park Road and Westway, *map p. 628, B2*) is the **Museum of Brands** (*museumofbrands.com*), crammed with consumerist ephemera from Victorian days to the present, presented through a 'Time Tunnel'.

THE LADBROKE GROVE ESTATE

The smart, good-looking streets and crescents fanning out from Ladbroke Grove (*map p. 628, B2*) form the Ladbroke Grove Estate, laid out in the 1840s (and as you will see, Notting Hill is indeed a hill). From the 1730s the land was owned by the Ladbroke family, one of whom, in 1873, opened a race course called the Hippodrome (commemorated by Hippodrome Place), erecting a circuit round the crest of the hill. It was not a success and closed in 1841. The subsequent housing development covered the hill with crescents in concentric circles, with St John's church slightly off-centre on the brow. The houses, by various developers, are large and impressive, some are attractively painted in pastel hues; they all have multi-million-pound price tags. There are private 'secret' gardens, for use by the residents, between the blocks. Before development the area was filled with piggeries and potteries: in Walmer Road is a surviving 19th-century conical kiln that once fired bricks and tiles from Notting Hill clay. Further north, tucked just below the Westway, is Bartle Road, which stands on the site of the former Rillington Place, made infamous by John Christie, who murdered several women there between 1943 and 1953.

AROUND LADBROKE GROVE STATION AND GOLBORNE ROAD

The area stretching north from Ladbroke Grove station, also known as North Kensington, mutely resists gentrification. Under the Westway, an ugly elevated motorway, is Portobello's fashion market. **Golborne Road** (*map p. 628, B2*), which forks right off the northern reaches of Portobello Road, is worth a look for its market, which has become an extension of the Portobello one. It also has small independent shops and cafés. Large Portuguese and Moroccan communities live around here.

At no. 5 Golborne Road, the forbidding **Trellick Tower** casts its shadow. This 31-storey concrete Brutalist skyscraper was designed by Ernő Goldfinger and completed in 1972. The lift and service shaft has walkways connecting it with the main block. The flats, designed as duplexes, each with its own balcony, were designed so that maximum light enters from both sides. Upon completion, the flats were given over to social housing and the Tower became a notorious hub for crime and anti-social behaviour in the 1980s. Today, the flats are mostly privately owned.

KENSINGTON, KNIGHTSBRIDGE & CHELSEA

The Royal Borough of Kensington and Chelsea, which includes Knightsbridge, is the smallest in London and arguably one of the most affluent. Home to film stars and international billionaires, this is the London of Harrods, Harvey Nichols and the expensive King's Road, as well as of the expansive Hyde Park and the voluminous collections of the South Kensington Museums. This is a place of contrasts, of discretion and exhibitionism. On a summer's

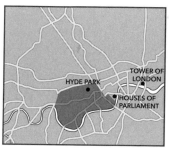

day in Hyde Park you will see Saudi women in all-concealing abayas manipulating pedalos on the Serpentine lake. In the depths of winter you will see Englishmen clad in skimpy Speedos disporting themselves in its glacial waters. London, in all its manifold madness and multifariousness, is distilled in this district.

Some highlights of the area

+ **Hyde Park** and **Kensington Gardens**, broad expanses of green with fine trees, flowerbeds and a boating lake;
+ **Harrods** and **Harvey Nichols**, two of the best-known high-end department stores in London;
+ The stunning collections of the **V&A**, **Natural History** and **Science museums**, institutions that all developed out of the Great Exhibition of 1851;
+ The exquisite **Chelsea Physic Garden**, whose café uses ingredients that are exclusively London-sourced.

PARK LANE & MARBLE ARCH

Park Lane (*map p. 635, D1–D2*), overlooking Hyde Park, was at its fashionable zenith in the 1820s and '30s, when private mansions lined the street. Today most of the great houses have gone, replaced by modern blocks. In 1963 Park Lane was widened, turning it into the relentless dual carriageway that it is now. There is nothing like thundering, deafening traffic to extinguish any lingering pretensions to aristocratic grandeur.

The Royal Albert Hall.

Set back from the road, at 47 Park Lane, the grey stone neo-Gothic building with elaborate tracery is **Stanhope House**, built by Romaine-Walker in 1901 for the soap magnate R.W. Hudson. At the time of writing it offered sanctuary to IBV Gold, international dealers in precious metals. In contrast is the smooth, white, relatively unadorned façade of the **Dorchester Hotel** (Owen Williams and William Curtis Green, 1931) on the site of Dorchester House, later Hertford House. The Dorchester is constructed from incredibly strong reinforced concrete, allowing for clean lines and spaciousness: when it opened it was considered dazzlingly modern. During the Blitz, it was one to the safest places to shelter and many of Mayfair's aristocratic residents took refuge at 'The Dorch'. In 1942 General Eisenhower moved in on a semi-permanent basis until the end of the War.

The huge **Grosvenor House**, between Mount Street and Upper Grosvenor Street, was conceived as serviced apartments and a hotel in four connected blocks (A.O. Edwards, 1929). It stands on the site of the London house of the Grosvenor family (later the Dukes of Westminster), the first of the grand houses to be demolished to make way for a hotel (the first to offer *en suite* bathrooms); Lutyens was consultant architect. The Great Room—London's biggest hotel banqueting venue—was used as a skating rink in 1929–34 and served as an American officers' mess in 1943.

Next door, across Upper Grosvenor Street, is 93 Park Lane, where Benjamin Disraeli lived from his marriage in 1839 until the death of his wife (to whom the house belonged) in 1872. The charming row of bow-fronted houses with 'Chinese' balconies (nos 93–99) survives from the 1820s. At no. 100 is **Dudley House**, a nine-bay, three-storey Neoclassical mansion with later cast-iron conservatory, built for the 1st Earl of Dudley in 1828 by William Atkinson. It is now owned by the Emir of Qatar (whose lavish renovations may have mollified the angry lady who reputedly haunts it).

On the green island between the two lanes of traffic (opposite an Aston Martin showroom) is the **Animals in War memorial** (David Backhouse, 2004). Dogs' homes and other charities leave wreaths here on Remembrance Day in November.

MARBLE ARCH

The name Marble Arch (*map p. 634, C1*) has come to denote the point where Oxford Street, Park Lane, Edgware Road and Bayswater Road converge. Here, at the centre of a busy traffic island, around which double-decker buses churn, stands the eponymous sugar-white **triumphal arch**, originally projected by the Regency architect John Nash as an entrance to Buckingham Palace. Modelled on the 4th-century Arch of Constantine in Rome, it was to have been a celebration of the victories of Wellington and Nelson, topped by a statue of George IV. Marble was brought from Seravezza near Carrara (a quarry favoured by Michelangelo) but the project was never completed. Sculpture and reliefs by Sir Richard Westmacott and others, which were not installed, now grace Buckingham Palace and the National Gallery and Chantrey's bronze equestrian statue of George IV stands on one of the plinths in Trafalgar Square. In 1850–1, when Buckingham Palace received a new east wing, the arch was brought here as a ceremonial entrance to Hyde Park. Road-widening in the 1960s cut it off completely.

Marble Arch stands close to the **site of Tyburn**, an early place of execution for the City of London and the county of Middlesex, to which the tumbrils of Newgate dragged many a victim, both innocent and guilty. The earliest execution here was of William FitzOsbert who was hanged here for sedition in 1196. The gallows known as the 'Tyburn Tree' was erected here in 1571 (a circular stone slab marks the spot). The first person to be hanged on it was Roman Catholic John Story, who was convicted of treason. He was one of many Catholics executed here between 1535 and 1681; their souls are still prayed for by the Tyburn Nuns, the 'Benedictine Adorers of the Sacred Heart of Jesus of Montmartre', in nearby **Tyburn Chapel** on the Bayswater Road (no. 19; *tyburnconvent.org.uk*). The body of one of these 'Tyburn Martyrs', John Southworth (executed 1654), may be seen in Westminster Cathedral. Among others who were dragged to this spot were Perkin Warbeck, pretender to Henry VII's throne, who claimed to be the younger of the two Princes in the Tower; Elizabeth Barton (the 'Holy Maid of Kent'), who warned Henry VIII that he would die within six months if he married Anne Boleyn; and Sir Thomas Culpeper, who unwisely became very close to Henry VIII's fifth wife, Catherine Howard, and was executed for adultery in 1541. Oliver Cromwell, John Bradshaw and Henry Ireton received 'posthumous' executions, when their bodies were exhumed from Westminster Abbey and brought to Tyburn to be beheaded for their part in the execution of Charles I. The last execution was that of the highwayman John Austin in 1783.

HYDE PARK & KENSINGTON GARDENS

Map p. 634, C2–A2. Underground: Hyde Park Corner, Knightsbridge, Marble Arch, Lancaster Gate. Park open daily 5am–midnight. For swimming and horse riding, see royalparks.org.uk. Deckchair hire from March–Oct. The park is amply supplied with cafés.

HISTORY OF HYDE PARK

Hyde Park stretches over 350 acres of land that once belonged to the monks of Westminster Abbey. After the Dissolution, Henry VIII appropriated it and turned it into a royal deer park. In the reign of Charles I, the carriage drive known as The Ring was built and in 1637 the park was opened to the public. Queen Caroline, wife of George II, created the lake known as the Serpentine by damming the Westbourne stream. From Decimus Burton George IV commissioned the monumental entrance gate from Hyde Park Corner, and at this time too the West Carriage Drive was driven across the water, formally dividing Hyde Park from Kensington Gardens.

In 1851, for the first Great International Exhibition, Joseph Paxton's Crystal Palace was built between Rotten Row and Knightsbridge (it was afterwards re-erected at Sydenham; *see p. 564*). The forged steel and bronze Queen Elizabeth Gate (also known as the Queen Mother Gates; by Giuseppe Lund with David Wynne) was opened in 1993. In 2005, near the Hyde Park Corner entrance, the 7th July Memorial was set up to the 52 victims of the London Bombings.

HYDE PARK LANDMARKS

At the northeast tip of the park is the famous **Speakers' Corner**, where stars of the soap box address the assembled multitude (on Sun). The right to speak here has existed since 1872 and anyone may say what they please provided that it is lawful and does not incite violence. Orators here have included Lenin, Orwell and Marx, and people still come here to try their rhetorical skills, offering a glimpse into a wide spectrum of world views, both radical and reactionary. However with the rise of social media, which offers a soapbox to all, the role of Speakers' Corner in providing a podium for the unrepresented has diminished significantly.

Rotten Row, a sand-track for horse riders, leads east–west across the southern part of the park. Its name is possibly a corruption of *Route du Roi*, 'King's Road', from its creation by William III, who travelled along it between his new palace at Kensington (*see below*) and the court at St James's. Because the park at night was infested with footpads, King William had 300 oil lamps installed along the length of Rotten Row, creating the first artificially illuminated street in England. East of The Dell, a green area watered by the now-underground Westbourne stream, is the **Holocaust Memorial** (1983). At Edinburgh Gate, outside the park on the other side of the road, is Jacob Epstein's sculptural group entitled ***Rush of Green*** (1959), showing a family and their dog sprinting towards the open space of the park, accompanied by Pan and his pipes. They might be fleeing in shock having just glimpsed the price tag for one of the apartments in One Hyde Park (Rogers Stirk Harbour + Partners), some of the most expensive on the planet. Sir Basil Spence's towering **Hyde Park Barracks** (1970) is a 33-storey concrete block which provides accommodation for the men and women of the Household Cavalry, who provide the Sovereign's Escort for Trooping the Colour and other state occasions.

The artificial lake known as the **Serpentine** (*boats and pedalos for hire Easter–Oct; royalparks.org.uk*) is home to a variety of water birds as well as to the **Lido**, set up in 1930 and still popular with swimmers (*open weekends in May, daily June–mid-Sept*). The Serpentine Swimming Club is the oldest swimming club in Britain: regulars come here for a dip at six o'clock in the morning, and every year on Christmas Day they hold a swimming race. The Lido Café Bar has tables on the water and is very pleasant in warm weather.

The **Diana, Princess of Wales Memorial Fountain** (Kathryn Gustafson, 2004) consists of an oval stream bed, measuring between 10ft to 20ft wide and following the gentle gradient of the ground on which it is built. Water brought up from underground flows around each side of the oval to a peaceful pool at the bottom. One side has a smooth finish, so that the water flows placidly and gently, while the other side has a series of steps, curves and contours which interrupt and break up the flow. The **bridge over the Serpentine** (1828) is the work of John Rennie the Younger and his brother George.

North of the Serpentine, just inside the railed-off bird sanctuary, is another work by Epstein: *Rima*, a relief carved as a memorial to the writer and ornithologist W.H. Hudson. When it was unveiled in 1925 it drew 'gasps of horror' from the assembled crowd and was swiftly dubbed the 'Hyde Park Atrocity'.

KENSINGTON GARDENS

Map p. 634, B2–A2. Underground: High Street Kensington, Lancaster Gate, Queensway.

Kensington Gardens, occupying an area of slightly under 300 acres, are separated from Hyde Park by the West Carriage Drive and by the portion of the Serpentine known as the Long Water. It was here, in 1816, that Harriet Westbrook, Shelley's first wife, drowned herself aged twenty-one.

KENSINGTON GARDENS LANDMARKS

The Serpentine Galleries (*map p. 634, B2; serpentinegalleries.org; free; restaurant*) are set in pleasurable open surroundings on either side of the water. The original **Serpentine Gallery** (to the south), founded in 1970, occupies a Neoclassical tea pavilion (J. Grey West, chief architect for His Majesty's Office of Works, 1934; renovated by John Miller + Partners, 1998). Just north of it stands the **Serpentine Sackler Gallery**, a brick-built, Doric-colonnaded ex-gunpowder store (1805) juxtaposed with a futuristic fly-away tensile structure (Zaha Hadid Architects, 2013) constructed of glass-fibre woven fabric, which seems to undulate in the wind ('a wedding marquee battling with a stiff breeze', as *The Guardian* put it). The former structure houses exhibition spaces; the latter the Magazine restaurant (named in honour of the old gunpowder store which yielded space to it). The Serpentine stages changing displays of modern and contemporary art, architecture, design and performance. The highlight is the annual Serpentine Summer

The tiny, clustering graves of the now-disused pet cemetery in Kensington Gardens.

Pavilion (June–Oct), which since 2000 has invited a different international architect or design team, who have never built in the UK previously, to create a temporary structure. The roll-call has included Zaha Hadid (2000), Daniel Libeskind (2001), Frank Gehry (2008), Ai Weiwei and Herzog & De Meuron (2012), Sumayya Vally (2021), Theaster Gates (2022) and Lina Ghotmeh (2023).

Henry Moore's travertine **Arch** (1979), looking like a great palaeontological pelvis, stands on the north bank of the Long Water. Through it is a splendid framed view of Kensington Palace (*see below*), of which this park was once the private grounds. The **Italian Gardens**, with their urns and fountains, were laid out for Prince Albert by Sir James Pennethorne. The **Pet Cemetery**, with its diminutive memorials, can be glimpsed near Victoria Gate (from the road side). It was opened in 1881 with the burial of a Maltese terrier named Cherry, but is now full and is closed to the public.

In the south part of the gardens is the **Albert Memorial** (*see p. 330*), behind which the charming Flower Walk leads west to the Broad Walk and Kensington Palace.

KENSINGTON PALACE

Map p. 643, A2. Admission charge. Café. Under restoration at the time of writing. hrp.org.uk.

The Jacobean mansion known as Kensington Palace was purchased by the Crown in 1689 and underwent a rapid architectural transformation under the supervision of Sir Christopher Wren, with Nicholas Hawksmoor as Clerk of the Works. As a new home for William III and Mary II, it was to be a winter retreat from the damp of Whitehall, a more suitable environment for the king, who suffered from asthma. It was always regarded as a private residence rather than a palace, though government business was conducted in the Council Chamber here in winter. The main **south front** of the palace was added by William III in 1695: a handsome design in red brick with four central Portland vases on the roofline carved by Caius Gabriel Cibber. Mary died at Kensington, of smallpox, in 1694, and it was to Kensington that William was carried following his fatal riding accident at Hampton Court.

His successor, Queen Anne, spent much time at Kensington, apparently hating the 'stinking and close' air around St James's. It was here that she nursed her husband, Prince George of Denmark, whose death in 1708 'flung her into an unspeakable grief'; and it was also here that Anne herself died in 1714. Following the accession of George I, an extensive new building programme saw the remodelling of the King's Apartments and their redecoration by William Kent. The apartments remain today as important early Hanoverian survivals. The **east façade**, part of George I's building campaign of 1718–21, is fronted by a seated marble statue of Queen Victoria, sculpted by her daughter Princess Louise (1893).

After the death of George II in 1760, Kensington ceased to be a seat of the reigning monarch. Family members continued to use it, however. The lower floors were remodelled for Edward, Duke of Kent, the fourth son of George III, and it was here that his daughter, the future Queen Victoria, was born. She received the news of her accession here in 1837. From 1981 until her death in 1997, the palace was the home of Diana, Princess of Wales. Today it is the offices and London home of the Prince and Princess of Wales, the Duke and Duchess of Gloucester, the Duke and Duchess of Kent and the Prince and Princess Michael of Kent.

The King's Apartments

The sequence of rooms that are open for public visits begins with the **King's Staircase**, with painted decoration carried out by William Kent in 1725–7 for George I. The figures crowding against the *trompe l'oeil* balustrade, as if welcoming the king as he mounts the stairs, represent figures from his court, including his Polish page, his two Turkish Grooms of the Chamber, Mustapha and Mehmet, and 'Peter the Wild Boy', found living in the woods near Hanover and brought to England as a curiosity to be tamed. Kent himself appears on the ceiling. The **Presence Chamber**, used for formal receptions, has Italian 'grotesque' decoration on the ceiling, with Apollo in his chariot in the centre. The carved Grinling Gibbons overmantel was moved from William III's King's Gallery; its cupids, one cheerful, the other mournful, are apparently reflective of the death of Mary II in 1694. The **Privy Chamber**, used for more intimate and select audiences, retains its Kent ceiling, which shows Mars and Minerva resting on clouds, with symbols of the Arts and Sciences. The 1623–4 Mortlake tapestries (*see p. 550*) were made for Charles I when Prince of Wales.

The **Cupola Room** was one of the most important of the new rooms for George I. Lavishly decorated, it was the principal state apartment and a showcase for Kent, whose work at Kensington began here. Ionic pilasters with gilded fluting alternate with marble niches containing gilded lead statues of Roman deities. The bas-relief above the fireplace, by Rysbrack, depicts a Roman marriage. The blue and gold feigned coffering on the ceiling, giving an illusion of height, with the Garter Star in the centre, in fact follows an earlier design by the great Baroque artist Sir James Thornhill. As the king's official history painter, Thornhill may have expected to be awarded the Kensington commission, but the promotion of the new Palladianism saw Kent triumph: although not a great artist, Kent was a gifted designer.

The **King's Drawing Room** was where the weekly court Drawing Rooms took place. Richly decorated with fine pictures from the Royal Collection hung against crimson damask, it has a fireplace and painted ceiling at its centre by Kent.

The **King's Gallery** retains its 1690s' carved cornice as well as the important wind-dial above the fireplace, made by Robert Morden in 1694. Points of the compass circle the map of the seas around Great Britain and a pointer, attached to the wind-vane on the roof, indicates the direction of the prevailing wind. The entire decorative scheme, of white and gold woodwork and crimson wall-hangings and curtains, is Kent's.

The Queen's Apartments

The apartments built for Queen Mary II in the early 1690s are the part of the palace which best retains its late 17th-century atmosphere. The **Queen's Staircase**, a plain and handsome space, was designed by Wren and retains some of its original sash windows. **Queen Mary's Gallery** was the richest and most grandly furnished of the Queen's rooms. Her taste for oriental porcelain was given free rein here. It was massed in symmetrical, towering displays on lacquer cabinets placed between the windows, as well as above the doors and chimneypieces. The latter displays were set against looking-glasses with elaborate carved surrounds, supplied by the royal cabinet maker Gerrit Jensen and by Grinling Gibbons. Displays of this nature were fashionable at the courts of Europe, and Mary was one of the chief promoters of the vogue in England. The richness of the room, with its expensive curtains (scarlet taffeta in winter; white flowered damask in summer), its porcelain and lacquerwork, would have been most apparent by candlelight.

The **Closet** contains portraits of Queen Anne in profile by Kneller, and George of Denmark by Michael Dahl (it was Anne's favourite image of her husband; she demanded to have it with her at St James's Palace after his death in 1708). It was in this room that Anne and her once-favourite, Sarah, Duchess of Marlborough, had their last, bitter quarrel in 1710. **Queen Mary's Drawing Room** (hung with pictures from the Royal Collection) and her intimate **Bedchamber** (with original elm floorboards) complete the suite of apartments.

The Orangery

The gardens at Kensington were once very elaborate but have long since disappeared. Queen Anne loved gardening and her most lasting achievement is the Orangery, designed by Hawksmoor (and altered by Sir John Vanbrugh), which housed plants in the winter and was used for entertainments in summer. It is now an elegant and airy restaurant with, at either end, two magnificent carved vases by Cibber and Edward Pierce, originally from the gardens at Hampton Court but now placed here, safe from further weathering.

KENSINGTON PALACE GARDENS

The street which bounds the west side of Kensington Gardens (*map p. 634, A2*) is famed for having the highest house prices in London; indeed, they are some of the highest in the world. Some of the buildings are used as embassies; others have become homes for the international super-rich. At no. 8 was the London Cage, an interrogation centre for German prisoners of war set up in 1940. Thackeray died in 1863, at no. 2 Palace Green, a house that he had partly designed himself, in a style that Queen Victoria had been persuaded would not damage the prospect from Kensington Palace.

ALBERTOPOLIS

The area of South Kensington around Exhibition Road (*map p. 634, B3*) is sometimes known as 'Albertopolis', after Albert, the Prince Consort, husband of Queen Victoria, who dreamed of bringing the Arts and Sciences together in a single, publicly-available cluster, an initiative inspired and in part financed by the Great Exhibition of 1851 (*see below*). His legacy includes the Royal Albert Hall, the V&A, the Natural History Museum, Science Museum and the Royal Colleges of Art and Music.

THE GREAT EXHIBITION

The Great Exhibition, planned by Albert, the Prince Consort, and Henry Cole (a man of pioneering spirit, who had worked on the introduction of postage stamps and is credited with inventing the Christmas card), took place in 1851 in Hyde Park. Its centrepiece was the Crystal Palace, a huge glass and iron building designed by Sir Joseph Paxton. Its aim was to showcase the products of human invention and ingenuity, in an age which was supremely confident of man's perfectibility and role in bettering society and the world, and in a country which believed unwaveringly in its own evangelising mission. 'Every conceivable invention' was on display at the Exhibition, as Queen Victoria noted proudly in her diary. A total of six million people from Britain and the world came to gape and marvel at natural and technical wonders of art and science. Many of the chief exhibits were subsequently purchased to go on display in the collections that would later grow into the three great museums that still draw great crowds on the edge of Hyde Park/Kensington Gardens today: the V&A, the Science Museum and the Natural History Museum. When the Exhibition closed, the Crystal Palace was moved to Sydenham (*p. 564*).

On Exhibition Road, which runs between the Natural History and Victoria & Albert museums, is the **Hyde Park Chapel** (1959–61), or Church of Jesus Christ of Latter-Day Saints (the Mormons), with a slim flèche covered in gold leaf. On either side of the road are buildings belonging to **Imperial College London** (The Imperial College of Science, Technology and Medicine), an independent university with a fine reputation. In Prince Consort Road is the **Royal College of Music**, occupying a building by Blomfield in 'French baronial' style (1884). The collection in their museum (*rcm.ac.uk*) includes musical instruments from 1500 to the present day: the 'clavicytherium' of c. 1480 is the oldest surviving stringed keyboard instrument in the world. Among the string collection are violins by Stradivari, the Amati Family and others. There are also portraits of former College pupils including Benjamin Britten, Imogen Holst, Ralph Vaughan Williams as well as many other musicians and composers. The manuscript collection includes the scores of works by Purcell, Mendelssohn and Liszt.

Opposite the Royal College of Music, the Queen Elizabeth II Diamond Jubilee Steps lead up past a bronze **statue of Prince Albert**, commemorating the Great Exhibition, curated by him '*in pulcherrimis illis hortis*'. Behind the statue stands the Royal Albert Hall.

ROYAL ALBERT HALL AND ALBERT MEMORIAL

A hybrid creation, part-Colosseum, part-Pantheon, the concert arena known as the **Royal Albert Hall** (*map p. 634, B2–B3; royalalberthall.com; Café Bar open to non-ticket holders; other restaurants are not*) was inspired by the architecture of ancient Rome. It was designed by two members of the Royal Engineers, Francis Fowke and Henry Scott, and opened in 1871 as the centrepiece of a cultural campus of the Arts and Sciences that had been planned by Prince Albert. Around the exterior drum of the shallow glass dome runs a continuous terracotta mosaic frieze depicting the continents of the Earth bringing forth the fruits of their labour, with an inscription proclaiming 'Glory be to God on high and on earth peace: this hall was erected for the advancement of the Arts and Sciences and works of Industry of all nations.' The interior auditorium has a capacity of over 5,000 and a Willis organ described by one of its hearers as possessing 'the voice of Jupiter'. The famous concert series known as the 'Proms' is held here annually from July–Sept. The name derives from the open-air 'promenade' concerts that took place in London's pleasure gardens.

Facing the Albert Hall is the **Albert Memorial** (*map p. 634, B3*), the national monument to Prince Albert of Saxe-Coburg Gotha, consort of Queen Victoria, who died in 1861 aged 42. The monument, unabashedly gaudy, was designed by Sir George Gilbert Scott in 1872 and unveiled by the Queen four years later. At the centre, beneath a canopy spire, is a seated statue of the prince (John Henry Foley, 1876), dazzlingly gilded and holding the catalogue of the Great Exhibition. The pedestal is decorated with a marble frieze of artists and scientists through the ages above which, at the four corners, are allegorical groups representing Agriculture, Engineering, Commerce and Manufacturing. The mosaics which decorate the canopy were designed by Clayton and Bell. Much of the decorative carving was carried out by William Brindley, who collaborated with George Gilbert Scott on St Pancras Station and whom the great architect described as 'the best carver I have met with and the one who best understands my views.' At the outer corners of the enclosure are further sculptural groups depicting the continents of Europe, Asia, Africa and America, each with a totem animal.

KENSINGTON GORE

Kensington Gore (*map p. 634, B2*) takes its name from Gore House, a property used as a restaurant by Alexis Soyer to feed visitors to the Great Exhibition. When the Exhibition closed, the building was pulled down to make way for the development of Albertopolis. Alexis Soyer took his culinary skills to the battlefields of the Crimea.

On the corner of Exhibition Road is the **Royal Geographical Society** (*rgs.org*), in a red-brick Queen Anne-style building by Norman Shaw (1874), built as a town residence for William Lowther, diplomat and member of parliament, and his wife Alice (their initials adorn a brick gable end, with a huge sunflower growing between them). The building was bought by the Society in 1912 and statues of Sir Ernest Shackleton and David Livingstone were added, on either side of the Exhibition Road corner. An old milestone is built into the wall at pavement level.

Across Exhibition Road, at no. 14 **Prince's Gate**, is a house once owned by John Pierpont Morgan, the New York banker and art collector. Many of the famous works acquired by him were once displayed here. Later, the young J.F. Kennedy lived here, while his father was ambassador to Britain (1937–40). The Iranian Embassy Siege of 1980 caused great damage to no. 16. At no. 20 is the **Polish Institute and Sikorski Museum**, with Polish art and archives (*pism.org.uk*).

On the west side of the Albert Hall is the Royal College of Art's **Darwin Building**, designed in the 1960s by a group of RCA members of staff, including Hugh Casson.

The Albert Memorial, with a detail of the sculpture group representing the continent of Africa.

The college has a prestigious history and numbers many famous alumni on its rolls. Queen Victoria's sculptor daughter Louise was one of them, when the college was known as the National Art Training School.

Further west is **Hyde Park Gate**, where at no. 18 Epstein had his studio (he died there in 1959). Sir Leslie Stephen, critic and scholar, lived at no. 22; his daughters Virginia Woolf and Vanessa Bell were born here. Winston Churchill died at no. 28 in 1965.

KENSINGTON & ITS MUSEUMS

Map p. 634, B2–B3. Underground: South Kensington, Gloucester Road, High Street Kensington, Knightsbridge.

Kensington is a largely residential area, leafy and well-mannered, containing some of the most desirable street addresses in London. It was made a royal borough after the death of Queen Victoria in 1901, in accordance with her express wish (she was born here), and in 1965 it was amalgamated with Chelsea. During the 19th century, artists and writers settled in Kensington, around Holland Park and further west, and many houses bear plaques commemorating famous literary residents: Macaulay, Browning, Thackeray, Henry James and Virginia Woolf were all either were born, died or resided here.

Brompton Road leads south through an area of stately squares and crescents (Alexander Place, Thurloe Square, Egerton Crescent) built in 1820–40. At Brompton Cross, where Brompton Road meets the Fulham Road, is the striking **Michelin House** (*map p. 602, C3*), previously headquarters for the Michelin Tyre Co., begun in 1909 and featuring colourful ceramic panels of racing cars and stained glass showing the 'Michelin Man' himself, Bibendum. It now houses a well-known restaurant and oyster bar.

Cromwell Road further north is named from a vanished house of Henry Cromwell, fourth son of the Protector. On the south side, opposite a flank of the V&A, stands the striking **Ismaili Centre** (Casson Conder Partnership, 1985), its teak and bevelled glass windows a nod to the *mashrabiyah* screen. It is a meeting point for Shia Ismaili Muslims (whose spiritual leader is His Highness the Aga Khan).

VICTORIA & ALBERT MUSEUM

Map p. 634, B3. Underground: South Kensington. Free except for special exhibitions. Café. vam.ac.uk.

The Victoria and Albert Museum (V&A) is one of the world's outstanding museums of applied arts. Its collection spans several centuries and encompasses sculpture, furniture, ceramics, glass, silver and metalwork, dress, textiles and jewellery. It is impossible to see even a tiny part of it on a single visit: but this is the joy of London's free museums. One can come again and again. The only scarce resource is time. The

V&A is a multi-site institution: the main collection is here and there is also Young V&A at Bethnal Green (*p. 114*) and V&A East, scheduled to open in Stratford (*see website for updates*).

HISTORY OF THE MUSEUM

The museum's origins lie in the School of Design, which opened in 1837 at Somerset House, established for the instruction of the application of art to industry. Works of ornamental art were collected by the school as teaching aids. In 1852 the school and its collection had come under the control of the Department of Science and Art, headed by the mighty figure of Henry Cole (1808–82) who, together with the Prince Consort, had masterminded the Great Exhibition of 1851, a phenomenally popular success: almost 100,000 visitors mobbed it on one of the days, flocking to view the raw and manufactured products of the nations of the world. With the Exhibition's profits, a plot of land was purchased in South Kensington and on the site of what is now the V&A, the South Kensington Museum was established. The School of Design and its collection moved here in 1857, partly accommodated in the Iron Building, nicknamed the 'Brompton Boilers'. Thus were displayed the V&A's first objects, a miscellaneous collection of sculpture, architecture, 'animal products' (fur, feathers, bristles, human hair etc.), 'patented inventions' and construction and building materials, jostling for space alongside items of ornamental art, all the finest examples of their kind, brought together to encourage excellence in British design. Internally there was gas illumination (this was the first museum in the world to be lit), which made evening opening possible—more convenient for working men and women. Attracting working people to visit was a cherished aim of Cole's, who saw museums as 'antidotes to brutality and vice'.

The building

Stretched over a twelve-acre site, the building itself is often said to be a work of art competing with the exhibits. The earliest permanent buildings are those that surround the central garden quadrangle. Built between 1857 and the early 1880s, they demonstrate what was to become known as the 'South Kensington style', their trademark being the use of ornamental terracotta. The museum's architect, Captain Fowke (architect of the Albert Hall), together with Godfrey Sykes (who was responsible for much of the early interior embellishment), were assisted by a band of pupils from the museum's Art Schools (now the Royal College of Art).

An arcaded corridor divided the **South Court** into two. On either side, below the roof, were balconies with large lunettes filled by frescoes by Leighton: *Industrial Arts as Applied to War* (1878–80; northeast) and *Industrial Arts as Applied to Peace* (1886; southeast). Today, the former magnificence of the South Court is hidden from view behind false walls but the Leighton frescoes, and the highly decorated soffits above them, can be viewed on the second floor.

The museum's ornamentation reached a peak of elaboration in Fowke's **Lecture Theatre Range** (north side of the central quadrangle), completed after Fowke's death in 1868. Internally and externally it is a showpiece of complex decoration. Its façade includes terracotta columns with figurative ornament, designed by Sykes and completed by his former pupils and successors. Filling the pediment is a mosaic representation of the Great Exhibition: different countries presenting exhibits to a central Queen Victoria. Inside, the **Ceramic Staircase** is an ornamental masterpiece, entirely encased in majolica and ceramic mosaic. Designed and modelled by Frank Moody, with students from the Art Schools, in Italian Renaissance style and executed by Minton in the new process of vitrified ceramic painting, its theme was the Arts, with stained-glass windows representing *Art* and *Science*. The mosaic portrait of Cole, in a majolica frame, marks his retirement from South Kensington in 1873. The **Silver Galleries**, a long vista flanked by majolica-clad columns with elaborate ceilings designed by Moody, were once equally lavish (now restored to their former magnificence as far as possible).

On the ground floor of the wing are the old **Refreshment Rooms** (the museum was the first to have such a facility). The Morris Room (originally the Green Dining Room) was entirely decorated by Morris, Marshall and Faulkner, the firm established by William Morris in 1861, with painted panels by Burne-Jones and stained glass designed by Burne-Jones and Philip Webb. The Gamble Room has ceramic tiles, mirrors and stained-glass windows designed by James Gamble (a pupil of Sykes). The upper ceramic frieze reads: 'There is nothing better for a man that he should eat and drink, and make his soul enjoy good in his labour' (*Ecclesiastes 2:24*). The chimneypiece, from Dorchester House, Park Lane, is by Alfred Stevens.

In 1890 Aston Webb won an architectural competition to bring sense and order to the museum complex. Regular, grand façades along Cromwell Road and Exhibition Road would be the new public face of the museum, with additional gallery space behind, joined to the existing buildings. On 17th May 1899, Queen Victoria laid the foundation stone, at the same time announcing that henceforth the museum would be known as the Victoria & Albert Museum. This was her last official public ceremony and the occasion was captured on a moving picture device, the Mutocscope (in the photography collection). By 1906 the works were largely complete. The **Cromwell Road central tower**, in the shape of an Imperial crown, is topped by a statue of *Fame*. Queen Victoria stands above the great arched entrance, flanked by *St George* and *St Michael*. Prince Albert stands directly above the doors, with representations of *Inspiration* and *Imagination* on either side. In a procession of niches along the façade, between the windows, are sculpture figures of great British artists. The new museum was officially opened by Edward VII in 1909.

The collections

The museum's vast holdings are displayed in two types of gallery: those that focus on a particular material or technique and those that examine a geographical region and/or historical period. Many techniques, such as sculpture, are exhibited in more than one gallery (*see V&A website for an interactive map*). The description below highlights some of the artefacts not to be missed.

The Gamble Room, the café in the V&A, with its stained-glass windows and ceramic tile decoration by James Gamble. It opened in 1868.

Galleries of materials and techniques

Sculpture

The **Cast Courts** were intended for the display of large-scale casts of the most famous examples of sculpture in the world (Michelangelo's *David* is a notable example). These vast spaces were—and still are—one of the museum's most extraordinary sites.

The post-Classical sculpture collection includes outstanding masterpieces, from highly important medieval ivory carvings to large-scale monuments. The Italian Renaissance collection is the best outside Italy (star exhibits are shown in the Medieval and Renaissance Galleries). Pre-eminent examples of British sculpture include works of the 18th and 19th centuries by Rysbrack, Roubiliac, Flaxman, Wilton and Banks. The **Gilbert Bayes Gallery**, an open corridor with magnificent vistas over both the Cast Courts, has smaller pieces, the displays emphasising materials and techniques and the process of sculpting in general.

Metalwork: iron, silver and gold

The museum's fine collection of silver and gold objects is spread throughout the museum, but also in the sumptuous **Silver Galleries**, one of the most lavish interiors of the 19th-century museum. Nineteenth-century interest concentrated on heavily decorated 15th–17th-century European pieces as well as on contemporary *tour-de-force* works. In the 20th century the museum started collecting English silver and its collection is now unrivalled. The displays include both ceremonial and domestic objects. Ceremonial salts are on show; a vast wine cistern by Thomas Jenkins (1677–8); elaborate candelabra; presentation cups and works by celebrated masters such as Paul de Lamerie, Charles Kandler and Matthew Boulton. The Ashburnham Centrepiece, or epergne, by Nicolas Sprimont (1747) is a major example of English Rococo silver. There is also an outstanding collection from southern Germany, one of the greatest centres of European silversmithing.

As well as silver, the museum has a large collection of cutlery, brass, pewter and ironwork. The **Metalwork Gallery** is famously described by H.G. Wells in his 1900 novel *Love and Mrs Lewisham*: 'The gallery is long and narrow…and set with iron gates, iron-bound chests, locks, bolts and bars, fantastic great keys, lamps and the like'. One of the major works is the 'Hereford Screen'. Designed by Sir George Gilbert Scott, it was hailed as 'the grandest, most triumphant achievement of modern architectural art' at the International Exhibition of 1862.

Ceramics and glass

The **Ceramics Galleries** make immediately apparent the astonishing range, depth and sheer magnitude of the collection: the history of pottery and porcelain manufacture can be studied here uninterrupted. The collection ranges from the Far East and Imperial China to the Ottoman Empire and Europe. Among the outstanding examples are nine pieces of Medici porcelain, the first European attempts at copying Chinese ware, which reached Europe in the 16th century. Made in the Grand Duke of Tuscany's workshops in Florence, only 60 of these rare and precious pieces are known.

Italian majolica, French Renaissance pieces and Limoges are also represented, and there are comprehensive collections of the works from the great English potteries: Lowestoft, Coalport, Wedgwood, Chelsea, Worcester and Bow. Twentieth-century pieces include British studio pottery, works by Bernard Leach and Lucie Rie, and European works such as Picasso's 1954 vase showing an artist at his easel.

The excellent **glass collection** ranges from ancient Egypt to the present, including commercial glass as well as works of art. On display are German goblets, Venetian and early English glass (including pieces by Jacopo Verzelini, who taught the art of glass-making in Elizabethan England), 18th-century drinking glasses, High Victorian pieces and modern items, including the rippling green stair and balcony balustrade by glass artist Danny Lane (1992). Of particular significance is the 'Luck of Edenhall', an exceptionally fine, pristinely preserved 14th-century Syrian beaker. In the main Rotunda Hall is Dale Chihuly's extraordinary lime green and turquoise Chandelier (2001; notoriously difficult to dust).

Jewellery

The Jewellery Gallery displays over 3,000 items tracing the history and development of Western jewellery from ancient times to the present day. It is one of the most comprehensive and important collections anywhere in the world. The wealth of antique jewels on display is particularly noteworthy. Before discoveries in the 19th century of seemingly inexhaustible supplies of precious metals, coloured gemstones and the

South African diamond mines, fine or high jewellery was a much rarer commodity. When fashions changed, jewellery was usually dismantled and remodelled rather than replaced by a new item; gold was melted down and the gems were re-set into the new design. The collection of Renaissance jewels is thus remarkable: enamelled gold pendants, which are really fanciful miniature sculptures decorated with gems and pearls, are cleverly displayed in Perspex cases so you may walk around them: the backs of the jewels are as important as the front. The art of goldsmithing was an important part of the Renaissance artist's training and there was a close relationship between sculptor and goldsmith. Note the **Heneage Jewel** (c. 1595), a gift from Elizabeth I to her loyal courtier Sir Thomas Heneage; it encloses a miniature of the Queen by Hilliard. Note also the jewels in frighteningly accurate Renaissance taste that are really the work of the 19th-century forger Reinhold Vasters. Since the discovery of vast numbers of design drawings, moulds, models and casts of Renaissance prototypes by known restorers and 'improvers' of antique jewellery, such as Vasters and Alfred André, jewels with previously uncontested Renaissance attributions in both private and museum collections have had to be re-examined—to the consternation and shuddering of jewellery historians worldwide. The **Canning Jewel** (a gem-set merman with a baroque pearl body) was one such casualty.

Also on show is a wide range of different types of jewel from the 19th century, including important Archaeological Revival pieces by Giuliano and Castellani, jewellers who worked from recently discovered Etruscan prototypes in order to rediscover the lost art of granulation. Here too are diamonds belonging to Catherine the Great and an emerald and diamond parure (1806 with 1820s' alterations) given by Napoleon to his adopted daughter. Also here are spectacular gem-set pieces from the greatest 20th-century jewellery houses and examples of work by 'artist' jewellers such as Lalique, whose innovative enamelling and use of non-precious materials defined Art Nouveau jewellery.

The V&A also invests in contemporary jewellery and there is a focus on works by living artists, including a pair of drop earrings, the Androecium Mobiles, designed and made by Sian Evans.

Fashion and textiles

The museum's collection of textiles (Spitalfields silks, Genoese velvets, upholstery fabrics etc.) was at first purely a learning resource. William Morris appears to have studied them, as elements of his designs are traceable to the specimens then exhibited. The serious collection of textiles began in the 1860s.

There are excellent examples of Indian and Persian carpets; an excellent lace collection (the largest in the world); and tapestries, including the **Devonshire Hunting Tapestries**, a group of four magnificent and enormous mid-15th-century Flemish pieces formerly in the collection of the Dukes of Devonshire.

Items from the Dress Collection are displayed throughout the period galleries, as well as in the **Fashion Gallery**. The European collection from Stuart times to the present day is particularly strong.

The museum's extensive **Theatre and Performance collections** were set to be redisplayed at the time of writing, with costumes, posters, props, designs and audio-visual recordings covering all areas of the performing arts.

Paintings, Prints and Drawings

Among the V&A's most celebrated possessions are the **Raphael Cartoons**, seven of the ten executed by Raphael in 1515–16 for tapestries depicting the Acts of the Apostles to decorate the Sistine Chapel (*see p. 550*). They are among the most important surviving examples of High Renaissance art. Distemper on paper, they were originally cut into strips to enable the weavers to use them as guides. Purchased by Charles I in 1623, they were put back together in 1699, restored and displayed at Hampton Court. Still in royal ownership, they have been on loan to the museum since 1865.

The V&A's **Paintings Collection** has at its core the Sheepshanks pictures, presented to the South Kensington Museum in 1857 and intended as the nucleus of a National Gallery of British Art. John Sheepshanks (1787–1863), a Leeds clothing manufacturer long settled in London, was acquainted with a wide circle of artists. His collection included fine works by Turner and Constable but his particular fondness was for early 19th-century genre pictures by Wilkie, Landseer and others, of which the collection has rich holdings. The V&A possesses a remarkable collection of oil sketches and works on paper by Constable, including a full-scale study for *The Haywain* (National Gallery).

The V&A houses the national collection of **portrait miniatures**. Among the many outstanding highlights by leading artists are Holbein's *Anne of Cleves*, with its carved ivory lid in the form of a rose; and pre-eminent works by Hilliard, including works with layered symbolism such as *Young Man Clasping a Hand from a Cloud*.

Changing displays are also shown from the **Prints, Drawings and Watercolours Collection**, an enormous and important resource. The principal collections are of Italian Old Master drawings; Dutch and Flemish works; and the national collection of British watercolours. The bulk of the latter collection is of 18th- and 19th-century works, the 'golden age' of British watercolour (Sandby, Cozens, Girtin, Cotman). The **Prints and Drawings Study Room** has the bulk of the collection and a fine collection of photographs by Julia Margaret Cameron.

Period Galleries

Medieval and Renaissance

Items from the collection, which spans the period c. 300–1600, are on display in various galleries. Pre-eminent objects include glassware, stained glass and a collection of highly important ivory carvings, including the '**Basilewsky Situla**', or Holy Water bucket (c. 980), probably presented to the Emperor Otto II on his visit to Milan in that year, an object of great rarity. The **Gloucester Candlestick** is an amazing survival of early 12th-century English medieval metalwork, a great masterpiece, with men and monkeys clambering through foliage, symbolic of the struggle between Good and Evil. Another major treasure is the **Becket Casket** (c. 1180), made to contain relics of St Thomas à Becket, the earliest, largest and best example in Limoges champlevé enamel showing Becket's martyrdom in shades of brilliant blue.

The silver-gilt **Burghley Nef** is a *tour de force* of Parisian goldsmiths' art of 1527. In the form of a ship, its body a nautilus shell balanced on the back of a mermaid, the tiny figures of Tristan and Isolde play chess at the foot of the main mast. Chief among the works of the Italian Renaissance are pieces by Donatello. His **Ascension with Christ Giving the Keys to St Peter**, from Palazzo Medici, Florence (c. 1428–30), is one of the finest surviving examples of *rilievo schiacciato* (very low relief carving).

British Galleries

The vast chronological scope of the British Galleries covers over 400 years of Britain's visual culture, bringing together the finest, most fashionable and most technically accomplished examples of sculpture, furniture, ceramics, silver, textiles and dress from the court of Henry VIII to the death of Queen Victoria. The incorporation of period interiors salvaged from important historic buildings lends the galleries particular authority and atmosphere.

One of the earliest objects on show is Pietro Torrigiano's famous painted terracotta **bust of Henry VII**, probably based on a death mask (*see p. 148*). Hilliard's famous **Young Man among Roses** is the quintessential image of the Elizabethan court, with its emphasis on complex emblems and symbolism. He is shown hand on heart, in devotion to the monarch, surrounded by eglantine roses (sweetbriar), the Queen's symbol.

The celebrated **Great Bed of Ware** (1590–1600), from an inn in Ware, Hertfordshire, mentioned in Shakespeare's *Twelfth Night*, is twice the size of any bed of the period known and was famous for the numbers it could hold. A rare duo is the Jacobean **portrait of Margaret Layton** (c. 1620) and, usually displayed alongside it, the very jacket she wears in the painting, with elaborate floral embroidery. Another outstanding item is the **bust of Thomas Baker** (c. 1638) by the great Baroque sculptor Bernini. Baker was commissioned to deliver to Bernini, in Rome, Van Dyck's portrait of Charles I in three positions, from which Bernini would sculpt a bust; while there, he took the opportunity to commission a bust of himself. A famous later sculpture is **Roubiliac's Handel** (1738), commissioned by Jonathan Tyers for his pleasure gardens at Vauxhall, with Handel in the guise of Orpheus, shown seated and plucking at his lyre. **Horace Walpole's limewood cravat** was carved by Grinling Gibbons c. 1690. Walpole famously once wore it when entertaining guests.

The 18th-century passion for Neoclassicism was stimulated by the young aristocrats, artists and connoisseurs who made Grand Tours and aesthetic pilgrimages to Italy to see Classical remains. There are many vases inspired by the antique, as well as candlestands and a mirror by **Robert Adam** adorned with Domus Aurea-inspired *grottesche*. Also by Adam is the plaster ceiling in delicate pastel shades from 5 Royal Terrace, part of the Adelphi development (*see p. 201*). When not in Edinburgh, Canova's magnificent **Three Graces** is on show, the famous marble sculpture commissioned by the Duke of Bedford for Woburn Abbey (it was purchased jointly with the National Museums and Galleries of Scotland after a national appeal in 1994). Examples of the Regency taste for rich luxuriance—and for Greek, rather than Roman, sources—include an 1806 bookcase from the Prince Regent's luxurious Carlton House. The plaster model for Nash's Marble Arch (c. 1826) is also here.

Important items by A.W.N. Pugin, the seminal figure in the history of the **Gothic Revival**, include a candelabrum made for the House of Lords.

Arts and Crafts objects include items by William Morris (wallpaper designs, furniture, tiles and textiles), a Charles Rennie Mackintosh high-backed armchair and wallpaper designs by Walter Crane.

Twentieth century

Twentieth-century art and design includes a chrome steel tubular lounger by Le Corbusier (1929), items from the Wiener Werkstätte, pieces of Art Deco household furniture and chairs by Charles and Ray Eames (in the Furniture Gallery).

Asia Galleries

A superb example of the art of Southeast Asia is the 14th–15th-century standing crowned Buddha, from the workshops of Ayutthaya, then the **Thai** capital. It was cast in bronze using the lost wax method and then gilded.

The **Indian Collection** has its origins in the Asiatic Society of Bengal (established 1784) and the museum of the East India Company, housed at the Company's headquarters in the City. One of the most famous works, 'Tippoo's Tiger' (c. 1790), is a wooden organ made for Tipu Sultan, ruler of Mysore, in the form of a tiger mauling a British officer (shrieking sounds emanate from it when played). An important example of Hindu sculpture is the sandstone *Bodhisattva Avalokitesvara*, called the 'Sanchi Torso' (c. 900), beautifully carved and exceptionally elegant, from the ruined temple of Sanchi in Madhya Pradesh. Sixteenth–18th-century Mughal art includes early Indian painting, gold ornamental jewellery and Mughal textile designs. Shah Jahan's exquisite white jade wine cup (1657), in the form of a ram's head flaring to a wide bowl, is perhaps the finest known example of Mughal hardstone carving. There is also an exquisite portrait of Shah Jahan, shown wearing a diaphanous skirt, by the Persian artist Muhammad Abed (c. 1632). The golden throne of Maharajah Ranjit Singh (shown with other Indian Empire treasures at the 1851 Great Exhibition) was part of the state property taken by the British in 1849 on the annexation of the Punjab.

The **Islamic Near East**, covering the art of Egypt, Turkey, Iran, Iraq and Syria, contains the famous Ardabil carpet (1539–40), one of the largest and most magnificent Persian carpets in the world, from the shrine of the same name in northwest Iran. Purchased in 1893, to William Morris it was 'of singular perfection'.

Highlights in the **China Gallery** include the 206 BC–AD 220 large head and partial torso of a horse, the largest animal carving in jade known. A bronze incense burner in the shape of an angry goose, its neck outstretched, dates from the Song or Yuan dynasty (1200–1300). The Ming-dynasty lacquer table (1425–36) is one of the only surviving pieces from the Imperial lacquer workshop set up to the northwest of Beijing's Forbidden City.

The **Korean Collection** includes beautiful examples of pale green celadon ware from the Koryo dynasty (935–1392) and fine examples of porcelain, furniture and decorative objects from the Choson dynasty (1392–1910), when Seoul became the capital. From **Japan** there is lacquerware, ceramics, ivory, textiles and netsuke.

NATURAL HISTORY MUSEUM

Map p. 634, B3. Underground: South Kensington. Free (except for some temporary exhibitions). Cafés. nhm.ac.uk. Often very crowded at weekends and during school holidays; at these times booking is recommended.

The Natural History Museum's collection was originally a department of the British Museum, where the myriad stuffed animals, fish, skeletons, botanical specimens, rocks and fossils were first displayed. Lack of space prompted the move to South Kensington, which took place in 1881, when Alfred Waterhouse's astonishing new building finally opened to the public. Since then the collection has grown immeasurably. Between them the five departments of Botany, Entomology, Mineralogy, Palaeontology and Zoology contain over 70 million natural history specimens and the museum is—as it has always been—one of the world's leading centres of taxonomic research. The museum gained independence from the British Museum in 1963. At the core of the collection is the hoard of natural history 'curiosities' of the eminent botanist and physician Sir Hans Sloane (including his magnificently carved pearly nautilus shell). These items were joined by the eye-opening specimens brought back from Captain Cook's great voyages of discovery to the South Pacific. Objects from Darwin's revolutionary voyage to the Galapagos Islands in HMS *Beagle* in 1831–6 also came to the museum as did, in 1856, the entire collection of the Zoological Society, soon followed by that of the East India Company.

The building

Waterhouse's magnificent building (1873–80), a great secular Romanesque cathedral clad in ornamental terracotta, incorporates in its design the ideas of Professor Richard Owen, a great comparative anatomist and palaeontologist and Superintendent of the Natural History Department from 1856. Owen was the prime agitator for a new museum and envisaged it as a great storehouse of divine creation. A broad flight of steps leads from the road up to the giant portal, centrally placed in the 680ft frontage, above which, surmounting the gable, Owen had placed a statue of Adam, man being creation's crowning glory (he fell off in the 1930s). Covering the façade and the interior is a veritable menagerie of birds and beasts cast in terracotta, symbolising the museum's function: designs of living animals to the west, where Zoology was displayed; extinct species to the east, where Geology and Palaeontology were housed. Extinct beasts line up on the entrance façade, monkeys scramble up arches in the entrance hall, fish swim in rippling water around columns where further up lizards lurk, and on the stairs animals and birds—including a beautiful pair of demoiselle cranes—peep from twining plants.

Waterhouse's dramatic entrance hall is conceived as a vast nave with a triforium above and, at the far end, the great staircase rising to the upper floors. Owen wished the Hall to be an 'Index' gallery, with displays of minerals, plants and invertebrates on one side and vertebrates on the other—a simple guide to the 'types' of the animal, plant and mineral kingdoms, carefully arranged according to the Linnaean system

The great neo-Romanesque portal of the Natural History Museum, by Alfred Waterhouse. It incorporates into its design the ideas of the comparative anatomist and palaeontologist Richard Owen, who had been a prime mover in the museum's foundation.

of classification. Owen's successor Sir William Flower introduced evolution to the display, a theory to which Owen had not wholly subscribed. In the centre were large mammals—whales, elephants and giraffes. Today the hall is dominated by the museum's most famous inhabitant, *Diplodocus carnegii*, 150 million years old and one of the largest land mammals which ever lived, cast from the original specimen at the Carnegie Museum, Pittsburgh and given to the museum in 1905. It is a fitting tribute to Owen, who coined the name 'dinosaur' in 1841.

Tour of the museum

The museum today offers a very different visitor experience from the museum which opened its doors in 1881. Instead of carefully arranged classified specimens in mahogany cases there are now interactive audio-visual Life- and Earth-Science displays on Ecology, Evolution and Man. This popular staging of science, which sometimes fits uneasily in a building designed for the scientific knowledge of a different era, was introduced to the museum in 1977 with the opening of the Human Biology display. It outraged scholars, who believed that the Victorian founding ideal, both to educate and to amuse, had been pushed too far in the latter direction. Who is to judge? Today the museum is extremely popular.

Life Galleries (Blue and Green Zones): The most famous display on the ground floor is the ever-popular Dinosaurs exhibit, including a vast animatronic *Tyrannosaurus rex*. The Mammal Hall is almost completely filled by the vast 91ft Blue Whale suspended from the ceiling, with the White Whale, Sperm Whale and dolphins alongside it. Of particular note in the Bird Gallery (first floor) are the two Mauritius dodos. On the second floor is a cross-section of a giant sequoia tree from the Sierra Nevada, California, 1,335 years old when felled in 1892.

Earth Galleries (Red Zone): The entrance to the Earth Galleries is from Exhibition Road. 'Earthquakes and Volcanoes' has an immensely popular earthquake simulator. 'From the Beginning' takes you from the Big Bang, the formation of Earth 4,560 million years ago, to the creation and sustaining of life. 'Earth's Treasury' has a display of minerals and gemstones. 'Lasting Impressions' explores the diversity of rocks and fossils, drawing on the museum's great mineralogy and palaeontology collections, which include 160,000 rocks and ocean bottom deposits, 3,000 meteorites and 30,000 ores, many collected on great expeditions such as Scott's second polar expedition (specimens brought back by the naturalist Edward Wilson proved that Antarctica had once been warm). 'Human Evolution' introduces us to our earliest ancestors, the first hominins from over seven million years ago, and explores human evolution. Here is the skeleton of Cheddar Man and a reconstruction of his face showing us what he would have looked like.

The Darwin Centre (Orange Zone): The Darwin Centre is the storehouse for the museum's zoological 'Spirit Collection': 22 million jarred specimens preserved in alcohol. Standing in the atrium you can look up seven storeys and see the extent of the storage. A small section on the ground floor is available for viewing, although you can take behind-the-scenes tours of other storerooms and the laboratories where over 100 scientists carry out taxonomic research.

The 'Cocoon' on the seventh floor (C.F. Møller Architects, 2009) features extraordinary wall displays of plants and insects, including exquisite butterflies.

SCIENCE MUSEUM

Map p. 634, B3. Underground: South Kensington. Often crowded at weekends and during school holidays. Free (except for some exhibitions and simulators). Cafés. sciencemuseum. org.uk.

Like the Victoria & Albert Museum, the origins of the Science Museum lie in the Great Exhibition of 1851. When it closed, the Museum of Manufactures was opened to maintain a permanent collection of selected Exhibition items, later transferred to the South Kensington Museum, the future V&A. In 1870, the Scientific and Educational Department of the South Kensington Museum merged with it and with the Patent

Office Museum collection, to form what became known as the 'Science Museum'. In 1924 the museum acquired the contents of James Watt's workshop (still on display) and four years later moved into its present site on Exhibition Road, where it has continued to grow, presenting the development of science, technology and medicine from the early 18th century to the present. The focus of acquisitions has been on artefacts that demonstrate developments in concepts and theory as well as practice, in the processes of discovery and invention, and in their relationship to economics and society. Artefacts associated with important historical events in science, individuals, groups of people and institutions have also found a home here. The exhibits cover an enormous range, from original items from the Great Exhibition to the latest in interactive technology; Charles Babbage and the earliest computers to the realms of 3D printing; Stephenson's *Rocket* to the Soyuz TMA descent module in which cosmonauts Tim Peake, Yuri Malenchenko and Tim Kopra were despatched to the International Space Station in 2015 and in which they returned in 2016. There is also the chance to try out the RAF Typhoon Jet simulator, as well as many other interactive activities.

On the fourth floor is a curiously fascinating series of tableaux and dioramas entitled 'Glimpses of Medical History', which show in great detail the development of medical practice from trepanning in Neolithic times to open heart surgery in our own day; amputations without anaesthetic in Nelson's time and early cataract operations. Curiosities in the museum's collection include Napoleon's silver-gilt toothbrush, Florence Nightingale's moccasins, Dr Livingstone's medicine chest and a microscope made for Lister.

KNIGHTSBRIDGE & BELGRAVIA

Map pp. 634, C2–635, D3. Underground: Knightsbridge, Hyde Park Corner.

Knightsbridge extends westwards from Sloane Street to Exhibition Road and from that axis stretches south approximately to Cadogan Square. Residentially speaking, it harbours some of the most exclusive streets in the world. It is also known as a luxury shopping district: these are the purlieux of Harrods and Harvey Nichols.

SLOANE STREET

Harvey Nichols (or Harvey Nics as it is sometimes affectionately known), on the corner of Knightsbridge and Sloane Street (*map p. 634, C2; harveynichols.com*), was founded on this site as a linen draper's by Benjamin Harvey in 1831. Today it is a luxury department store with branches around the world, including in Dubai, Riyadh and Kuwait. The present building dates from 1880. The Fifth Floor Foodmarket (with restaurant and café) is famous for its selection of national and international produce.

From here, Sloane Street extends south. Its upper part is lined with shops. At no. 55 is the **Danish Embassy**, designed by Arne Jacobsen (1978). The **Cadogan Hotel** at no. 75 (*cadogan.com*) was once the home of Lillie Langtry, mistress of Edward VII.

Colourful Doulton tiles of 1902 in the Harrods Food Hall, with a courtly fowler and a river teeming with fish.

After it became a hotel, it was patronised by Oscar Wilde, who was famously arrested here (from Room 118) for gross indecency in 1895. The hotel is owned by Charles, 8th Earl Cadogan, whose family own much of this part of London (his heir is styled Viscount Chelsea)—and have done since Elizabeth, daughter of Sir Hans Sloane (*see p. 375*), married the 2nd Baron Cadogan in 1717. The two families have lent their names to many of the streets in the area: Sloane Street, Cadogan Square, Hans Place. The building at no. 23 **Hans Place** stands on the site of the house where Jane Austen stayed with her brother Henry, while preparing *Emma* for publication. Hans Place today is entirely Victorian. It and the red-brick mansions of **Pont Street** (1870s) are built in a style for which Sir Osbert Lancaster coined the term 'Pont Street Dutch'. Strikingly positioned amid the gabled façades of Pont Street (corner of Lennox Gardens) is the Scottish church of **St Columba's** (*map p. 634, C3; stcolumbas.org.uk*), built by Sir Edward Maufe (1950–5) after the original church of 1884 was destroyed in the Blitz.

Beauchamp Place, leading into the Brompton Road, is lined with expensive boutiques. At no. 54 is the wonderful Map House, with an unrivalled collection of antiquarian maps, prints and globes (*themaphouse.com*). The business was founded in 1907 and once supplied maps of Antarctica to Shackleton.

HARRODS

This (*map p. 634, C3; harrods.com*) is the largest department store in London, a place where historically it was claimed that anything could be bought from a pin to an elephant. It was first established on this site in 1849 by Charles Henry Harrod, grocer.

Almost 200 miles from his country seat, Richard Grosvenor, Viscount Belgrave, pores over plans for the district of London which he was to develop in the 1820s: Belgravia.

Its present terracotta façade, strikingly picked out in lights at night, has become world-famous, as have the sage-green shopping bags with gold lettering. As Harrods developed into a department store, it began to aim at luxury: in 1898 the first 'moving staircase' in Britain was installed here and brandy and smelling salts were administered at the top to those for whom the automated journey had proved too gruelling. Harrods has remained at the top end of the market. The store is currently owned by the royal house of Qatar, who bought it from the Egyptian businessman Mohamed al-Fayed. The Egyptian Hall (with sculpted heads said to be modelled on the tycoon's own) was part of Al-Fayed's restoration and remodelling. The beautiful Food Hall remains famous, not only for what it sells but for the environment in which the goods are displayed. The hall is adorned with faïence tiles designed by W.J. Neatby and made by Doulton (1902), depicting birds and flowers, fish and game. There are golden flying ducks on the ceiling.

HOLY TRINITY AND THE BROMPTON ORATORY
The church of the **Holy Trinity** stands end-on at the top of an avenue of trees (*map p. 634, C3; htb.org.uk*). Built in 1827 (chancel added by Blomfield in 1879), it was once

the church of the rural parish of Brompton and is now known as the home of the evangelical Alpha course.

The imposing domed bulk of **Brompton Oratory** (*map p. 634, C3; bromptonoratory. com*), or the Church of the Immaculate Heart of Mary (1880–4, dome 1895–6), stands where Brompton Road meets Cromwell Road. Always known as the Brompton Oratory (though its correct name is the London Oratory), is one of the best-known Roman Catholic churches in the capital and the second largest in London. It is served by the Community of Fathers, secular priests of the Congregation of the Oratory, which was founded in Rome by St Philip Neri in 1575. Oratorians came to England under the auspices of Cardinal Newman in 1848 and the church here was founded by Father Wilfrid Faber, ancestor of Faber the publisher. The exterior of the dome, completed in 1896, is by George Sherrin, who worked as architect for the Metropolitan District Railway and designed Tube stations, among them parts of South Kensington. The church both inside and out is in opulent (if rather tenebrous) Roman Counter-Reformation style, to designs by Herbert Gribble. It is remarkable in its solemnity, with a nave wider than that of St Paul's. The painting over the altar in the Chapel of St Philip Neri (north side) is a copy of the original by Guido Reni at Chiesa Nuova, Rome, where St Philip Neri is buried. The original Oratory in Rome (next to Chiesa Nuova) gave its name to the musical genre known as oratorio. Entirely appropriately, the London Oratory is known for its music.

BELGRAVIA

Belgravia began to be developed in the 1820s by Richard, 2nd Marquess of Westminster, Viscount Belgrave and (from 1831), Earl Grosvenor. His surveyors were Thomas Cundy and his son, Thomas Cundy II, and his master builders were Thomas Cubitt, a former ship's carpenter who had already built speculative housing in other parts of London, and William Howard Seth-Smith. The district survives remarkably intact and gives a vivid impression of London town life at the period, with wide streets lined by patrician residences backed by narrow cobbled carriage mews and stables.

EXPLORING BELGRAVIA

Belgrave Crescent leads into the centrepiece of the district, **Belgrave Square**, formed of white stucco terraces of a chilly hauteur (designed by George Basevi) with detached mansions at the corners and a central garden planted with shrubs and statuary. Today it is the home of ambassadors and oligarchs. At the north end of the square is a statue of Grosvenor, shown consulting an architect's plan, his foot on a milestone showing the distance to Chester (his country seat) and on the plinth a quotation from Ruskin intimating immortality. Behind the statue, **Wilton Crescent** was laid out by Cundy, with a cobbled street of mews behind it, Wilton Row, where chauffeurs now nudge Bentleys into the old stables. The Grenadier pub here serves good bar snacks.

In Wilton Place stands one of the finest Victorian churches in London and one of two that bookend this district, dedicated to the two major apostles. This one is **St Paul's Knightsbridge** (*map p. 635, D2*), a High Anglican, Oxford Movement church by Thomas

Daniel Bell's ceramic-tile *Nativity* in the church of St Paul's Knightsbridge. The ox looks distinctly displeased by the usurper in its manger.

Cundy II, consecrated in 1843. Its interior is exceptionally rich. Around the walls are stories from scripture in ceramic tile, designed in the 1870s by Daniel Bell (brother of Alfred Bell, of the well-known Clayton and Bell stained-glass studio). A memorial commemorates members of the First Aid Nursing Yeomanry (FANY) who died during WWII while on secret intelligence work for the SOE. Among them are three holders of the George Cross, the highest award for gallantry that can be given to a civilian.

Leading off the further end of Wilton Crescent is pedestrianised **Motcomb Street**, a *bon-ton* parade of shops and restaurants. The Doric colonnaded Pantechnicon was built in 1830 by Seth-Smith as warehouses and wine vaults. Supposedly fireproof, it succumbed to a blaze in 1874 and had to be rebuilt

The **Carlton Tower Jumeirah Hotel** (1961, Michael Rosenauer), at no. 2 Cadogan Place, reopened in 2021 after a £100 million refurbishment. It incorporates copper panels by Elisabeth Frink, *Four Seasons*, on the south face. William Wilberforce, the campaigner against slavery, died at no. **44 Cadogan Place** in July 1833; the Slavery Abolition Act was passed in August of the same year.

Lowndes Street and then Chesham Place lead into **Lyall Street**, where Cubitt lived at no. 3 (*map p. 635, D3*) while building of this area was in progress. Lyall Street crosses Eaton Place (where the corner building at no. 99 has a plaque recording the first

London concert given by Chopin in 1848) and leads into **Eaton Square**. Named after the Grosvenors' country seat of Eaton Hall in Cheshire, it takes the form of a long stretch of gardens flanked by brick-and-stucco terraces and bisected by a busy road. Vivien Leigh and Laurence Olivier lived at no. 54 until their divorce in 1960. Leigh died here seven years later. At the north end, where Eaton Square becomes Upper Belgrave Street, is **St Peter's** (Henry Hakewill, 1827; enlarged by Blomfield, 1875; *map p. 635, D3*) with a tall and handsome Ionic portico. The church was gutted in an arson attack in 1987 and the interior (1990–1) is completely modern.

Eccleston Yards (named after another Grosvenor village in Cheshire), leading off Eccleston Place between Eccleston Place and Ebury Street, is a refurbished inner courtyard of low-rise brick buildings with cafés and shops.

CHELSEA

Map pp. 635, D3–634, B4. Underground: Sloane Square.

Chelsea is an extremely attractive residential suburb extending for about one and a half miles along the bank of the Thames. Once a small fishing village and—until the 19th-century transport and housing boom—covered in gardens and orchards of fruit trees, it was relatively isolated from the rest of London. It has been the home of many eminent people, especially artists, who came here for the good light and the riverscape. Today it is a very pleasant—but also a very expensive—place to live.

SLOANE SQUARE AND THE KING'S ROAD

Sloane Square (*map p. 635, D3*) was laid out in the 1770s by Francis Holland and named after the lord of the manor, Sir Hans Sloane, the physician whose collections formed the nucleus of the British Museum (*see p. 375*). Sloane bought the manor in 1712 from Sir Charles Cheyne, though he did not take up residence in Chelsea until about 1742. In the centre, beneath plane trees, the **Venus fountain** is by Gilbert Ledward (1953). An overhead pipe above the platform in **Sloane Square Tube station** carries the Westbourne stream, which runs from Hampstead through Hyde Park (where it was dammed to created the Serpentine) and joins the Thames near Chelsea Bridge. On the north side of the square, a short way up Sloane Street, is the important Arts and Crafts **church of the Holy Trinity** (John Dando Sedding, 1888–90), the widest in London. The architect, who died just a year after the church's completion and who is commemorated within, wished to fill the building with painting and sculpture of a 'frank and fearless naturalism', celebrating the beauty of God's creation. The huge east window, with its stained-glass panels of saints, is by Burne-Jones and William Morris.

On the west corner of the square stands the department store **Peter Jones**, part of the John Lewis Partnership (*see p. 299*). The Modernist curtain-walled building, one of the first in the UK (1936), is by William Crabtree, of Slater, Crabtree and Moberly.

THE KING'S ROAD

Chelsea was once a fashionable resort, much patronised by Charles II and his court. **King's Road**, Chelsea's main artery (*map p. 634, C4*), was built as a private royal way linking Hampton Court with St James's. Three hundred years later, in the 1960s, it was at the cutting edge of fashion, rivalling Carnaby Street and frequented by the 'Chelsea Set', who came for the boutiques, clubs and bars. It is still Chelsea's main shopping street and in the small side streets are many attractive cottages and villas.

Opening out on the left-hand side is **Duke of York Square**, a public space surrounded by shops and cafés. The Neoclassical porticoed building known as the Duke of York's Headquarters was built in 1801 by John Sanders, a pupil of Soane, and used for many purposes over the years including a school for soldiers' orphans and as the headquarters of the Territorial Army. The Ministry of Defence sold the building and its grounds to Cadogan Estates in 2000, and the **Saatchi Gallery** (*saatchigallery. com; free*) relocated here from County Hall in 2008. The gallery is a contemporary art space which exhibits pieces by emerging artists whose work is rarely seen in the UK.

On the other side of the road, in Blacklands Terrace, is the long-established **John Sandoe Books** (*johnsandoe.com*), a tiny warren crammed with tomes, often in piles on the floor (and yet the staff always know where everything is). It is all that an independent bookshop should be.

Set back from the King's Road at nos 152–154, behind an elaborate Georgian gateway with statues, is the former **Pheasantry**, so called because pheasants were once bred on the site for the royal household. The Russian ballet dancer Princess Seraphine Astafieva taught dance here from 1916; among her pupils were Alicia Markova and Dame Margot Fonteyn. Other famous residents have included Augustus John and Annigoni. A nightclub established in the basement was patronised by painters, writers and actors during the 1930s and '40s. The building is now a restaurant.

Chelsea Old Town Hall, in neo-Baroque style, is by J.M. Brydon (1885–7) with later work by Leonard Stokes (1904–8). Sydney Street, which links the King's Road to the Fulham Road, is home to **Chelsea Farmers' Market**—with not a tiller of the soil in sight: this is an enclave of restaurants, cafés and shops focusing mainly on fashion. **St Luke's Church** (J. Savage, 1820–4), in warm yellow stone, is an early example of the Gothic Revival. Charles Dickens married Catherine Hogarth here in 1836. Twenty-two years and ten children later, the couple were to separate, after Catherine accidentally intercepted a piece of jewellery intended by Dickens for another, much younger, woman.

CHELSEA EMBANKMENT, THE ROYAL HOSPITAL AND PHYSIC GARDEN

From Sloane Square, Lower Sloane Street leads to Chelsea Bridge Road, passing on the right Royal Hospital Road, with an entrance to the Royal Hospital Chelsea (*see below*) and then the green expanse of Ranelagh Gardens, part of the Hospital grounds.

Chelsea Embankment (*map pp. 634, C4–635, D4*), built in 1874 to a design by Bazalgette, extends from Chelsea Bridge to Battersea Bridge, a distance of over a mile. It is a picturesque reach of the river, unfortunately marred by incessant roaring traffic. Left of Chelsea Bridge, the Grosvenor Canal passes under the Embankment, near Bazalgette's attractive pumping station, with a tall chimney and a ship's keel roof. **Chelsea Bridge** itself was built in 1937, replacing an earlier structure which had become too narrow for the volume of traffic. It was the first self-anchored suspension bridge in Britain and was made using materials from around the British Empire.

Walk along the Embankment with the river on your left and the railings of Ranelagh Gardens on your right, until you come to an entrance to the Royal Hospital; here is a fine view of the beautiful brick buildings and gardens.

ROYAL HOSPITAL CHELSEA

The Hospital (*map p. 635, D4; guided tours of approx. 90mins can be booked Mon–Fri; admission charge; chelsea-pensioners.co.uk*) was conceived by Charles II, possibly in emulation of Louis XIV's Les Invalides in Paris, as a retirement home for soldiers 'broken by age or war'. Sir Christopher Wren was appointed architect and Sir Stephen Fox was charged with coming up with the necessary funds. The buildings were completed in 1692 and later added to by Robert Adam and Sir John Soane; they have been restored since bomb damage during both world wars. Among the first to be admitted were those injured at the Battle of Sedgemoor, 1685. The Hospital is home to around 400 pensioners, veterans of the British armed forces, who are boarded, lodged and nursed when ill, and who wear distinctive long scarlet coats. The first women were housed here in 2009. On Founder's Day, also known as Oak Apple Day, held around 29th May (as near to Charles II's birthday as possible), the Pensioners are reviewed by a member of the Royal Family. All participants wear sprigs of oak leaves in memory of Charles II, who hid in an oak tree after his escape from Parliamentarians at the Battle of Worcester in 1651; oak leaves are used to decorate Charles II's gilded statue (*see below*).

The central portion of the building, known as the **Figure Court**, dates from 1688. The Doric portico, flanked by a low colonnade with coupled columns, is surmounted by a small tower and cupola. The inscription along the colonnade commemorates the Hospital's foundation and establishment by Charles II and James II and its completion by William and Mary. In the projecting four-storey wings, known as **Long Wards**, are the pensioners' individual berths. The statue of Charles II as a Roman general is by Grinling Gibbons (1676); originally gilded, it was bronzed in the 18th century until re-gilding took place in 2002, in celebration of Queen Elizabeth II's Golden Jubilee.

The Figure Court leads to the **Chapel** (1681–7), with handsome oak carving by William Emmett, Grinling Gibbons's predecessor as royal carver. The organ case is by Renatus Harris. The painting of the *Resurrection* in the apse is by Sebastiano Ricci and his nephew Marco (1716, restored). The **Great Hall** is lined with portraits of monarchs and military heroes, including a huge equestrian portrait of Charles II, begun by Verrio and completed by Henry Cooke. The body of Wellington lay in state here in 1852. The Margaret Thatcher Infirmary (designed by Sir Quinlan Terry, opened 2009) is a care home for about 100 pensioners who can no longer live quite so independently within the hospital. The ashes of Margaret Thatcher and her husband Denis, who were great supporters of the hospital in the later years of their lives, were interred here.

Chelsea Embankment by night, viewed from across the Thames.

The grounds are beautifully maintained: to the south, overlooking the river, they were severely truncated by the construction of the Chelsea Embankment in 1874. Before this, they were one of the Hospital's proudest features, laid out in the 1690s by George London and Henry Wise, the royal gardeners, with canals and avenues providing glorious settings for Wren's gazebos and summer houses. The gardens to the east, **Ranelagh Gardens**, were formerly those of Ranelagh House (Lord Ranelagh was the first Hospital treasurer and built himself a house on the site). During the 18th century they were fashionable pleasure gardens; in the centre was a huge rotunda (1742), long since disappeared. The area hosts the annual Chelsea Flower Show during the third week of May.

In the Secretary's Office Block is the **Museum**, which has photographs, prints, uniforms, medals, pewter, arms, etc., and a portrait of the pensioner William Hiseland, who served 80 years in the army and died in 1732 at the age of 112.

The East Walk emerges in Royal Hospital Road beside the **graveyard** (closed in 1854), where Dr Charles Burney, Hospital organist, is buried (d. 1814).

NATIONAL ARMY MUSEUM AND TITE STREET

The **National Army Museum** (*map p. 634, C4 café; nam.ac.uk*) occupies a purpose-built building (1971) further west. Its collection illustrates, celebrates and records the history of the army from the 1640s to the present day, with over 2,500 objects arranged within airy permanent galleries arranged thematically (origins and organisation of the British army; a soldier's experience; the army's global role; conflict in Europe; and the army's home service.

Tite Street, whose enfilade of 19th-century mock-Queen Anne houses intersects Royal Hospital Road beyond the National Army Museum, was once home to a colony of writers and artists. It was the residence for 24 years of John Singer Sargent, who died at no. 31 in 1925. No. 34 was the home of Oscar Wilde from 1884–95. Opposite is the site of the White House, built for Whistler but occupied by him for a few months only in 1878–9; he lived also at no. 13 (in 1881–5) and at no. 46 (in 1888). Whistler is famous for his Thameside *Nocturnes*, painted in Chelsea in the 1870s (*for the famous libel case, see pp. 181–2*). A tablet at no. 23 Tedworth Square, to the north, marks the London residence of Mark Twain.

CHELSEA PHYSIC GARDEN

The entrance to this enchanting, secret garden is in Swan Walk (*map p. 634, C4; admission charge; café; chelseaphysicgarden.co.uk*). The Garden was founded in 1673 as the Apothecaries' Garden; the Society of Apothecaries used it to train apprentices in plant identification and it was sited near the river to create a microclimate favourable to the cultivation of non-native species from warmer climes. The apothecaries also used the river as a transport route, setting forth on their barge on 'herborising' expeditions. In 1685, John Evelyn noted the garden's heated greenhouse, probably the first in Europe. When the former apothecary student Sir Hans Sloane (a copy of whose 1733 statue by Rysbrack stands in the garden) purchased the Manor of Chelsea in 1714, he leased the four acres to the Society of Apothecaries for £5 a year in perpetuity, on condition that it was maintained as a physic garden forever. A deed of covenant of 1722 requested that 2,000 specimens of distinct plants grown in the garden should be sent to the Royal Society 'well dried and preserved', in annual instalments of 50—and the condition was amply fulfilled: by 1795 the Royal Society had received 3,700 specimens. Today the garden continues to publish an *Index Seminum* and exchanges seeds with several hundred botanic gardens around the world. Sloane appointed Philip Miller as Gardener (curator). Miller, whose *Gardener's Dictionary* became a seminal work, made the garden world famous and trained William Aiton, the first Gardener at Kew. In 1736 the Swedish botanist Linnaeus visited the garden to collect plants and specimens and Mrs Elizabeth Blackwell illustrated her *Curious Herbal* (1739) by drawing plants here.

Today, the garden is run as a charity and is open to the public. It follows a formal layout and the plants are grown according to their classification, with many rare specimens. Explore the rock garden, completed in 1733, and the herb garden and borders of perfumery plants. The Garden of World Medicine, in the northeast quadrant, includes 150 species from eight different cultures around the world. The glasshouses, which have been in constant use for a century, recently underwent a thorough restoration. The Physic Garden Café serves salads, steaks and fish, all London-sourced.

CHEYNE WALK TO CHELSEA WHARF

Meandering along Chelsea Embankment is historic **Cheyne Walk** (*map p. 634, C4*; pron. 'Chainy Walk'), with early 18th-century houses separated by narrow public gardens. No. 4 was occupied by George Eliot (d. 1880) during the last three weeks of her life. No. 16, the Queen's House, is erroneously connected with Catherine of Braganza, Charles II's consort, though it was not built until 1717, twelve years after her death. The fine railings are by Thomas Robinson. Dante Gabriel Rossetti lived at no. 16 in 1862–82, keeping his menagerie in the garden; later residents were Swinburne and George Meredith. Although known as Tudor House, it too was built in 1717 and later extended by Lutyens. A memorial fountain to Rossetti in the Embankment Gardens, with a medallion by Ford Madox Brown (1887), faces the house. At no. 18 was the celebrated 'Don Saltero's' coffee house, owned by a proprietor named Salter, who also exhibited a museum of curios here, some of them gifts from Sir Hans Sloane. On the site of nos 19–26 stood the manor house which Henry VIII gave to Catherine Parr, his sixth and final wife, as a wedding present (he acquired the Manor of Chelsea in 1536). Here Princess (afterwards Queen) Elizabeth seems to have spent the interval between the execution of her mother, Anne Boleyn, and the death of her father. Anne of Cleves, Henry's fourth wife, died here in 1557. A plaque records that the manor house was demolished in 1753, after the death of its last occupant, Sir Hans Sloane. The old manor house garden lies beyond the end wall of Cheyne Mews and is said to contain mulberry trees planted by Elizabeth I.

Cross over Oakley Street, with **Albert Bridge** (1873) on your left. The sculpture here, *Boy with a Dolphin*, is by David Wynne (1975), who studied Zoology before going on to become a self-taught sculptor, opening a studio in Campden Hill (*p. 359*). The model for the boy is Wynne's son, who tragically took his own life in 1999. Continuing west along Cheyne Walk, **nos 38 and 39** are by C.R. Ashbee, designer of many Chelsea homes (though few survive). In the gardens is a **statue of Thomas Carlyle** (Boehm, 1882), honouring the writer and historian known as the 'Sage of Chelsea'.

CARLYLE'S HOUSE

In Cheyne Row, a sedate Queen Anne terrace of 1708, is **Carlyle's House** (*map p. 634, C4; nationaltrust.org.uk*). The Scottish historian, essayist and philosopher Thomas Carlyle and his wife Jane, known for her beauty, intelligence and wit, moved here from Scotland in 1834 and remained until their deaths. The house is largely unchanged, with many of the original furnishings, and—though the couple's relationship was tempestuous—has an atmosphere of quiet simplicity. It was here that Carlyle wrote *The French Revolution* (1837) and *On Heroes, Hero Worship and the Heroic in History* (1841), in which he outlined his theories on the importance of powerful, conviction-led individuals.

The **Sitting Room/Parlour** is furnished much as it appears in Robert Tait's painting, *A Chelsea Interior* (c. 1857), which hangs here. Jane Carlyle was irritated that Tait had made her dog Nero look the size of a sheep (her death was caused by an attack of shock when Nero escaped from her carriage at Hyde Park Corner). Downstairs is the **Kitchen**, were Carlyle would smoke with Tennyson and where Jane Carlyle's domestic servant (she was a difficult woman to work for and got through several) slept. Upstairs is the **Library/Drawing Room**, where Carlyle wrote *The French Revolution*. The **Attic Study** was built for Carlyle by the firm of Cubitt in 1853 as a sound-proof retreat. Unfortunately it actually amplified noise from the Thames, but nevertheless Carlyle used it for twelve years, until his biography of Frederick the Great was complete. The **garden**, with its walnut and cherry trees and lilac bushes, is much as it would have been in Carlyle's day. Nero is buried about 5ft from the southeast corner.

Further north is **Glebe Place**. The house at no. 35 is by Philip Webb (1868). It was used as Uncle Monty's house in the 1987 film *Withnail and I*. No. 49 is by Charles Rennie Mackintosh (1920), his only London work.

CHELSEA OLD CHURCH

The red-brick Chelsea Old Church (*map p. 634, C4; entrance round the far corner in Old Church St; chelseaoldchurch.org.uk*) was probably founded in the 12th century. Along with its many fine funerary monuments, it was badly damaged by a parachute-bomb in the Second World War and has been largely rebuilt, its monuments painstakingly restored. Outside the church, in the gardens overlooking the river, is a seated **statue of Sir Thomas More** in black and gold (L. Cubitt Bevis, 1969). In the churchyard, in the corner plot behind railings, is the **tomb of Sir Hans Sloane** (*see pp. 349 and 375*).

Inside, by the first window on the right is a small **chained library** of books given to the church by Sir Hans Sloane, including two volumes of Foxe's *Book of Martyrs* (1684). Close by is a monument to Lord and Lady Dacre, with alabaster effigies (1595).

The South Chapel (or **More Chapel**) was almost undamaged by the bombing and dates from 1325; it was rebuilt by Sir Thomas More in 1528 for his private use. More settled in Chelsea around 1520; the site of his house, with extensive grounds stretching down to the river, is on Beaufort Street (*see below*). The archway between the chapel and the chancel is a reproduction of the 14th-century one but the capitals were carved in More's lifetime, c. 1528, and are similar to those on Pietro Torrigiano's tomb of Henry VII in Westminster Abbey. In the corner by the altar, on the right, is the tomb of Jane, Duchess of Northumberland (d. 1555), mother of Robert Dudley, Earl of Leicester (the favourite of Elizabeth I), mother-in-law of Lady Jane Grey, and grandmother of the poet Sir Philip Sidney. The tomb, which resembles Chaucer's in Westminster Abbey, has been much mutilated.

On the south side of the chancel is the **More Monument** (1532), designed by Sir Thomas More while still in royal favour, with a long inscription composed by him in memory of his first wife. It is almost certainly a cenotaph: More's head is in Canterbury and the whereabouts of his body are unknown. On the north side of the chancel is the tomb of Sir Edmund Bray (1539). Above it is the late 16th-century monument of Thomas Hungerford and his family. There is a wall-tablet to the novelist Henry James, who died in Chelsea 1916 and 'who renounced a cherished citizenship to give his allegiance to England in the first year of the Great War'.

The North Chapel (or Lawrence Chapel; 1325 but rebuilt) is entered by an archway of 1563; the arch is itself a monument to Richard Jervoise. The **monument to Charles Cheyne**, Viscount Newhaven and his wife Jane (1672), is by Paolo Bernini, son of the famous Gian Lorenzo, with an effigy by Bernini's great assistant Antonio Raggi. Henry VIII is said to have been secretly married here to Jane Seymour, some days before their public marriage.

CROSBY HALL

Past the junction with Danvers Street (*map p. 634, B4*) stands Crosby Hall, the surviving part of a medieval mansion brought from the City in 1910 and re-erected as far as possible with the careful retention of its original features. Its original site was on Bishopsgate (*map p. 639, E2*), where it was built in 1466–75 by Sir John Crosby, a rich textiles trader and freeman of the Grocers' Company. A later resident, in 1483, was Richard, Duke of Gloucester, soon to be Richard III. Around 1523 it was bought by Sir Thomas More—whose Chelsea garden coincidentally once included the plot on which the hall is sited today—and More's daughter and son-in-law Margaret and William Roper later occupied it. In the 16th century the mansion was considered sumptuous enough to be the abode of various ambassadors. It is the only example of a City merchant's residence in London.

Though the hall escaped the Great Fire, its fate was a chequered one until its purchase in 1908 by the University and City Association of London and its removal here by the architect Walter Godfrey, who added a 1920s' neo-Tudor block when it was used as the college hall of the British Federation of University Women. During the First World War it was a shelter for Belgian refugees. The interior (*no admission*) retains a fine oriel window and the original scissor ceiling covered in gold bosses, and contains a copy of Holbein's lost group of *Sir Thomas More's Family* (c. 1527). In 1989 it was bought by the millionaire Christopher Moran, who has recreated a Tudor palace around it. The name of the building is properly Crosby Moran Hall.

Over the junction with Old Church Street, in **Ropers Gardens** (named after Thomas More's son-in-law William Roper), is an unfinished bas-relief by Jacob Epstein, on the site of his studio (1909–14).

SIR THOMAS MORE

Thomas More was born into a prosperous family in the City of London in 1478. He studied first at Oxford before returning to London to study Law at Lincoln's Inn. As an adolescent he began to experience profound religious leanings—but More was ambitious as well as ascetic and in the end he married and took up a political career, becoming under-sheriff of London in 1510. Meanwhile he had met and befriended the Dutch Humanist Erasmus, and the two were to remain firm friends, collaborating on translations of works from Latin as well as producing original works of their own (More's *Utopia* and Erasmus' *In Praise of Folly*). More's abilities were greatly appreciated by Henry VIII, who noted his reputation for fairness and firmness. When Henry went to France to meet François I on the Field of the Cloth of Gold to discuss a lasting peace, he took More with him, and More helped Henry to compose his repudiation of Luther (for which Pope Leo X was to reward him with the title Defender of the Faith, a title still held by the British sovereign). More was knighted and numerous honours were heaped upon him. He was appointed Speaker of the House of Commons in 1523 and, after the downfall of Cardinal Wolsey in 1529, Lord Chancellor. But the same thorny thicket as had trapped Wolsey was to prove More's own undoing. More had not supported Henry's divorce proceedings; in 1533 he refused to attend the coronation of Anne Boleyn. In the spring of 1534, More refused to agree to the Act of Succession, which debarred Katherine of Aragon's daughter Mary from acceding to the throne; nor would he swear the Oath of Supremacy, recognising Henry as head of the Church of England. He was committed to the Tower, found guilty of treason, and beheaded the following year, alongside Bishop Fisher. In 1935 he was canonised by Pope Pius XI. He is the patron saint of lawyers.

WEST TO CHELSEA WHARF

Further west along the Embankment is **Beaufort Street** (*map p. 634, B4*), where Sir Thomas More's mansion once stood; fragments of his orchard wall border the gardens of the houses in Paulton's Square. **Battersea Bridge**, an iron structure of 1890, spans the river at the end of Beaufort Street; it replaced a picturesque old wooden bridge of 1771–2, which was a favourite subject with Whistler and other artists. The river, with many new blocks of flats opposite, here bends south, and has offered moorings for brightly-painted houseboats since the 1930s.

Beyond Beaufort Street is the western part of **Cheyne Walk**. Mrs Gaskell was born at no. 93 in 1810. Nos 95–100 make up Lindsey House (1674), the only surviving 17th-century mansion in Chelsea; it is now subdivided and largely invisible behind the high riverside fences. Whistler lived at no. 96 in 1866–78, and no. 98 was the home of the Brunels, father and son. The painter P. Wilson Steer died at no. 109 in 1942. At no. 119 J.M.W. Turner lived anonymously, in retirement, from 1846. He died here in 1851.

At the end of Cheyne Walk is **Lots Road** (at no. 114, the Lots Road Pub and Dining Room is good for a pit stop (*lotsroadchelsea.co.uk*); from here you can walk up to the King's Road). In the vicinity, the eight-acre site with its vast disused power station (1904; listed) has been redeveloped as **Chelsea Waterfront**, with over 700 new homes the first of its type in this area for over 100 years, designed by Sir Terry Farrell. **Chelsea Wharf** (*map p. 628, C3*) has been converted into workshops and design studios; the gates in the adjoining gardens are from Cremorne Gardens—a popular pleasure garden which closed in 1877. **Chelsea Harbour**, with the distinctive pagoda-like Belvedere Tower, was constructed on 20 acres of derelict land used as a coal depot. The development includes luxury flats, a marina, hotel, shops, restaurants and offices. Adjacent is a similar mixed-use modern development, Imperial Wharf (Imperial Wharf station operates train services across the river to Clapham Junction).

BROMPTON CEMETERY

Brompton Cemetery (*map p. 634, A4; Underground: West Brompton; royalparks.org.uk*), also known as the West London and Westminster Cemetery, opened in 1840 and is one of the Magnificent Seven of London's cemeteries, with some 205,000 graves. The memorials range from the simplest of headstones to glorious, elaborate mausolea. The central path, running from the Old Brompton Road entrance, is embraced by two asymmetrical colonnades and leads to the domed chapel. Beneath the colonnades are the catacombs, built to provide a cheaper alternative to burial than buying a plot; but the idea was never popular and only about 500 of the thousands of spaces were ever taken. The Royal Hospital Chelsea plot, where its residents are buried, is marked by an obelisk. Also buried here are Emmeline Pankhurst (d. 1928), her grave often decorated with purple, green and white flowers of the Suffragist movement; George Borrow (1881), author and traveller; Fanny Brawne (1865), Keats' muse, buried under her married name of Lindon; Henry Cole (1882), founder of the V&A; Samuel Cunard (1865), founder of the Cunard Line; the master mason Thomas Cundy (1895), who built so many of the streets and squares in this part of London; and John Snow (1858) who, as well as being an anaesthetist, made the connection between infected water with cholera. Among the most impressive memorials is the tomb of Frederick Richards Leyland, ship-owner and patron of the Pre-Raphaelites, whose burial place is marked by one of the finest Arts and Crafts funerary monuments in the country, designed by Edward Burne-Jones. The cemetery is also a haven for wildlife.

The southern end of the cemetery leads into Fulham Road, lined with shops and restaurants. Left (over a barely-noticeable bridge which takes you over Chelsea Creek) is Stamford Bridge, the grounds of **Chelsea Football Club**. On match days this whole area is choked with barely-moving traffic.

KENSINGTON HIGH STREET & HOLLAND PARK

Kensington High Street (*map p. 634, A2–A3; Underground: High Street Kensington*) is a busy and lively shopping street. Once home to three great department stores, Ponting's, Barker's and Derry and Tom's, it now offers nothing more adventurous than the usual selection of chain stores. But the bustling atmosphere can be invigorating, and it is much less crowded than Oxford Street.

In **Young Street** (*map p. 634, A2*) Thackeray lived at no. 16 from 1846–53 and wrote *Vanity Fair*. Young Street leads to **Kensington Square**, established in the late 17th century to be close to the court at Kensington Palace. Talleyrand lived here after his escape from Paris in 1792. The artist Burne-Jones lived at no. 41 for a short period. The sombre façade of the Maria Assumpta Chapel on the opposite side is pierced by an enormous rose window. J.S. Mill lived at no. 18.

The monumental Art Deco building that housed the **ex-Barker's department store** is now houses assorted shops. On the corner of the attractive Kensington Church Street stands **St Mary Abbots** (1869–81), a large church with a conspicuous spire, the tallest in London. It was built on the site of the much earlier parish church of the village of Kensington. When that became too small for the congregation, Archdeacon Sinclair called for something 'exceedingly magnifical' and enlisted George Gilbert Scott to provide. **Holland Street**, north of the church, is a charming street of early 18th-century houses built for the ladies-in-waiting at Kensington Palace.

CAMPDEN HILL

The area around **Campden Hill** (*map p. 628, B3–C3*) was a favourite residential area in the 17th century. A few of the fine houses in spacious grounds survive, though the gardens of many have been absorbed by Holland Park School. Swift, Gray and Queen Anne (as Princess) were among its famous inhabitants. The sculptor David Wynne had a studio in Campden Hill in the 1960s. **Aubrey Walk**, a colony of artists in Edwardian days, ends at the wooden gates of Aubrey House, built on the site of Kensington Wells, a spa established in the early 18th century and much esteemed for its curative waters. Aubrey Road leads downhill from here into **Campden Hill Square**, which slopes steeply away to the north. It was laid out in the 1820s by Joshua Hanson, who was a major developer of Regency Brighton. Here in the gardens, while staying at Hill Lodge (on the corner of Hillsleigh Road), Turner painted the sunset. Today, from some angles, you have a view of the infamous Trellick Tower (*p. 319*): thus two very different kinds of London housing contemplate each other.

The Windsor Castle pub at no. 114 Campden Hill Road dates from 1835 and has a pleasant beer garden. Close by, on the corner of Bedford Gardens, is a Bauhaus building that looks as if it has been transposed from Stuttgart or Rationalist Italy: an incongruity amid the Victoriana. It is '**The Mount**' (1962–4) by Douglas Stephen.

HOLLAND PARK

Holland Park (*map p. 628, B3*) is what remains of the grounds of a mansion built by John Thorpe in 1607 for Sir Walter Cope, Chancellor of the Exchequer under James I. The house passed by marriage to Henry Rich, created Earl of Holland (in Lincolnshire), who commissioned the surviving splendid **gateway** from Inigo Jones (executed by Nicholas Stone). Its piers of Portland stone are surmounted by worn griffins bearing the arms of Rich (the cross crosslets) and Cope (the rose). Lord Holland was executed by the Roundheads in 1649 and the house was occupied by the parliamentary general Fairfax, but was later restored to Holland's widow. Thereafter it was leased to a succession of tenants, among them William Penn and Joseph Addison. Eventually, the heir of the Rich family sold the house to Henry Fox (father of Charles James Fox), who was made Baron Holland in 1763. Under the 3rd Baron (and more particularly his imperious and strong-minded wife), the house became the centre of a Whiggish literary circle, the 'Holland House clique', to which Macaulay belonged. The house was badly damaged in World War Two and only the east wing remains.

The wooded park includes the former **gardens**. The Japanese Kyoto Garden was planted in 1991. The Orangery is used for exhibitions and other events and is popular for weddings. In the café are two sculptures of c. 1910: Eric Gill's *The Maid* and Epstein's *Sun God*. The area to the north is maintained as semi-natural woodland. The Open-Air Theatre stages opera performances and concerts in the summer. In 2013, cows were introduced into the park to graze down the woodland meadows.

THE DESIGN MUSEUM

Approached from Kensington High Street, at the south end of Holland Park, is the distinctive building of the former Commonwealth Institute. After a £17.5 million donation from Sir Terence Conran, the **Design Museum** (*map p. 628, B3; designmuseum. org*) opened here in 2016, bringing it within a short distance of Kensington's other museums. It is devoted to all elements of contemporary design. The collection includes a Mobil petrol pump dating from 1968, one of the earliest objects the museum acquired, and a pair of Nikecraft x Tom Sachs Mars Yards trainers. There are many temporary exhibitions and workshops.

LEIGHTON HOUSE

At no. 12 Holland Park Rd (south of Melbury Road, where Holman Hunt died in 1910, at no. 18) is Leighton House (*map p. 628, B3; joint ticket available with Sambourne House;*

rbkc.gov.uk), the home-cum-studio of the artist Frederic, Lord Leighton. High Victorian painter *par excellence*, and the first British artist to be given a peerage, Leighton created for himself an exotic 'Palace of Art', where he lived and worked for the last 30 years of his life. Construction was planned in collaboration with the architect George Aitchison, who designed the extraordinary **Arab Hall**, a room richly evocative of the artist's fascination with the Ottoman world. In the centre, above a fountain trickling into a pool cut from a single block of black marble, hangs an ornate copper chandelier. The dome was purchased in Damascus and decorated with a mosaic frieze designed by Walter Crane. Upstairs is the **Great Studio**, where Leighton produced most of his work. Several of his larger paintings hang on the north wall, notably his *Clytemnestra*. There is also *The Uninterpreted Dream* by Burne-Jones and a bronze bust of the artist by Sir Thomas Brock, who also sculpted Leighton's memorial in St Paul's Cathedral. In the apse of the west wall is a tall door through which large canvases could be lowered. Right of the archway at the east end is a door leading to a staircase to the servants' quarters, which was also used by the artist's models and (indicating their status in Leighton's eyes) by art dealers.

A ten-minute walk away, **Sambourne House** (*map p. 628, C3; admission by guided tour only; joint ticket available with Leighton House; rbkc.gov.uk*), at no. 18 Stafford Terrace, is the former home of the Punch cartoonist Edward Linley Sambourne and his wife, Marion Herapath. It is preserved in all its late Victorian detail, including William Morris and Japanese embossed wallpapers and a stunning stained-glass window of sunflowers which also incorporates, in its smaller panes, the Sambourne family emblem of a star and the Herapath lion. There is also a collection of Sambourne's drawings for *Punch* and the photographs which he consulted when creating his cartoons. The couple's daughter Maud, a talented artist in her own right, was the grandmother of Antony Armstrong Jones, the society photographer who would later marry Princess Margaret, sister of Elizabeth II. Their son is the furniture designer known as David Linley.

Centre Point, the Brutalist tower of 1966 that looms over the junction of Tottenham Court Road and Oxford Street.

FITZROVIA, BLOOMSBURY & THE BRITISH MUSEUM

Fitzrovia and Bloomsbury are both famed for their bohemian, artistic and literary associations. Fitzrovia was made famous by its avant-garde set (the artists Victor Pasmore and Augustus John and the poet Dylan Thomas), who lived here from the 1920s and frequented its bars, notably the Fitzroy Tavern on Charlotte Street. Bloomsbury is associated first and foremost with Virginia Woolf and her circle. It is also home to the famous British Museum and 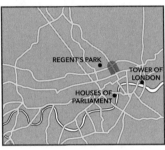 to UCL (University College London), making this a lively part of town with a large student population.

Some highlights of the area

✦ The **British Museum**, with its vast collections spanning the cultural history of the globe;

✦ The **Foundling Museum**, founded in the early 18th century, with its poignant displays on the care and education of destitute children;

✦ The **Charles Dickens Museum**, in a house once inhabited by the author whose vision of Victorian London has done so much to colour our own perceptions;

✦ Yet another museum, the **Petrie Museum of Egyptian and Sudanese Archaeology**, a cramped space overflowing with priceless treasures.

FITZROVIA

Fitzrovia, which takes its name from Fitzroy Square (*map p. 633, D4*), lies between Portland Place and Tottenham Court Road. The northern part was developed in the 18th century. A number of artists have chosen to live in Fitzrovia, among them the sculptor Nollekens (44 Mortimer St) and the painters Sir Edwin Landseer (33 Foley St) and Henry Fuseli (37 Foley St). Despite recent gentrification and increased rents, Fitzrovia manages to retain a diverse and scruffy charm. Several fashion wholesalers have their premises here, as do design studios and media companies.

FITZROY SQUARE

Fitzroy Square (*map p. 633, D4*) was built on land belonging to Charles Fitzroy, 1st Baron Southampton, who was a descendant of Henry Fitzroy, 1st Duke of Grafton, the illegitimate son of Charles II and his mistress Barbara Villiers. It was laid out speculatively in the 1790s; the elegant **east and south sides**, in Portland stone embellished with Venetian windows, medallions and anthemia, are by Robert Adam, continued after his death by his brothers James and William. The Adams never completed the square due to a property slump occasioned by the Napoleonic Wars. The stucco-fronted **north and west sides** were built in the 1820s–30s. Famous residents include Whistler (no. 8), the Bloomsbury Group artist Duncan Grant (no. 19), George Bernard Shaw and later Virginia Woolf (née Stephen; no. 29). Roger Fry established the Omega Workshops at no. 33 and Ford Madox Brown lived and entertained members of the Pre-Raphaelite Brotherhood at no. 37. On the corner of no. 40 is a statue of General Francisco de Miranda (1750–1816), Venezuelan soldier and campaigner for Spanish American independence, who lived for a time on Grafton Way. Miranda died in gaol near Cadiz and his body was buried in a mass grave. Opposite at no. 41, on the corner with Fitzroy Street, is the **YMCA Indian Student Hostel**, founded in 1920 to foster Anglo-Indian relations by accommodating Indian students in London as well as giving them a place to entertain their British classmates. The building, by Ralph Tubbs (1953), has an Indian canteen, open to all and popular at lunchtime (*indianymca.org*).

The **BT Tower**, south of Fitzroy Square, is surrounded by modern blocks. It is not open to the public; the best view of it is from Cleveland Mews. Commissioned by the General Post Office (GPO), it opened in 1964 as a telecommunications tower and at 627ft (including the aerial) was once the tallest building in London. Its narrow, cylindrical shape meant that it hardly moved in high winds and the tinted glass cladding prevented heat build-up. The revolving restaurant on the 34th floor closed after an IRA bomb attack in the 1970s. Plans to reopen it are perpetually put forward and then dropped.

ON AND AROUND CHARLOTTE STREET

Charlotte Street (*map p. 633, D4*), Fitzrovia's main thoroughfare, where Greeks and Italians settled after World War Two, is known for its mix of restaurants and pubs serving a wide variety of cuisine. At no. 16A is the famous **Fitzroy Tavern**, frequented by writers and artists from the 1920s until the 1940s such as Dylan Thomas, George Orwell and Augustus John. The range of restaurants continues round the corner in Goodge Street. Just before, the small pedestrianised Colville Street is filled with large tubs and planters of shrubs and flowers.

From Newman Street, the narrow Newman Passage leads to Rathbone Street. Here, the small pub on the corner, the **Newman Arms**, was frequented by George Orwell. Orwell, Thomas et al also drank in the Wheatsheaf pub in Rathbone Place.

BERNERS STREET AND MORTIMER STREET

Coleridge lived briefly at no. 71 Berners St (*map p. 633, D4*). At no. 50 is the **Sanderson Hotel**, with a Philippe Starck 'Cocteau-like dream-world' interior (white muslin curtains and red upholstered sofas designed to resemble pouting lips, etc.) and a Japanese-

Angels adoring the sign of the Cross. Byzantinesque mosaic in the Fitzrovia Chapel.

inspired courtyard garden by Philip Hicks. The 230ft frontage, in International Modernist style, was built as Sanderson House in 1958–60 by Slater, Moberly & Uren, a partnership also responsible for the Peter Jones and John Lewis department stores. It was originally the showrooms for Sanderson & Sons, manufacturers since 1860 of high-quality wallpaper, fabric and paint. The hotel is on the site of the house of a wealthy Mrs Tottenham, on whom a weird and unpleasant practical joke, the 'Berners Street Hoax', was allegedly played in or around 1810. Letters were sent out in her name to a wide variety of tradespeople and the ensuing traffic mayhem caused by horses and carts making endless attempts to deliver quantities of unwanted coal, fabric, pianofortes, jam tarts, meat, paintings, even a coffin, to her door, was widely reported in contemporary newspapers and alluded to in stage plays.

THE FITZROVIA CHAPEL

The **Fitzroy Place** development, offices and apartments bordered by Mortimer, Nassau, Riding House and Cleveland streets, occupies the site of the Middlesex Hospital, originally the Middlesex Infirmary, which first opened in the 1740s in buildings rented from a Mr Goodge, whose name is honoured by posterity in nearby Goodge Street. The hospital closed in 2005 and of its buildings little now remains except the old façade, 'The Middlesex Hospital Radium Wing', on Nassau Street, and its exceptionally fine chapel, now named the **Fitzrovia Chapel** (*map p. 633, D4; for opening times, see fitzroviachapel. org*), on Pearson Square, off Fitzroy Place. It was begun in 1891 by John Loughborough Pearson, an architect inspired by Gothic architecture (his other works in London include St Peter's church in Vauxhall and St Augustine's in Kilburn), and completed after his death in 1897 by his son Frank Pearson, whose enthusiasms were for the Early Christian and Byzantine. The interior is notable for the richness of its materials, including marble, alabaster and gold mosaic, assembled by Italian craftsmen. The beautiful ceiling was completed in 1939. As you enter the nave, the Baptistery Chapel is on your right and on the left is a chapel dedicated to the patron saints of doctors, with stained glass commemorating St Bartholomew, Sts Cosmas and Damian as well as the Knights Hospitallers and Good Samaritan. In the chancel, which has a beautiful Cosmatesque floor, Rudyard Kipling's body lay before being taken for burial to Westminster Abbey. He died at the Middlesex Hospital of a burst intestinal ulcer in 1936.

ALL SAINTS MARGARET STREET

At no. 63 Wells St you will find the **Cartoon Museum** (*map p. 633, D4; cartoonmuseum. org;*), with displays drawn from a collection of over 6,000 British cartoons, caricatures and comic strips, from their 18th-century origins to the present day. Great masters such as Gillray, Hogarth and Ronald Searle are represented. Around the corner on Margaret Street, the church of **All Saints** (William Butterfield, 1850–9; *allsaintsmargaretstreet.org. uk*) was built as a model church of the Oxford Movement, which sought within the Church of England a renewal of liturgical practice more in line with medieval traditions: in other words, less 'low church'. It is an important example of High Victorian Gothic Revival architecture and has hardly been altered since its consecration. The church, as well as a choir school and clergy house, is built on a confined site. The patterned red and black brick exterior with stone detailing and a slate roof, is dominated by a huge tower and spire, two feet taller than the western towers of Westminster Abbey; it can be seen from Primrose Hill. The interior is a riot of intense, brightly-coloured decoration: every available surface is adorned or revetted with stained glass, paintwork, tiling, inlaid hardstone and marble. The nave arches are of red Aberdeen granite. The multicoloured marble pulpit was installed in 1850 at huge expense, to accentuate the importance of preaching. The elaborate altarpiece (Ninian Comper, 1909) replaces the original by William Dyce, which had deteriorated; Comper also designed the Lady Chapel. The picture tiles running the length of the north wall were designed by Butterfield in 1873. The stained-glass west window was installed in 1877 under Butterfield's direction.

On Great Portland Street (*map p. 632, C4*), near the junction with Clipstone Street, is the **Central Synagogue**, founded in 1848. The building dates from 1958, replacing the former synagogue destroyed by the Luftwaffe (*entrance is normally from the back, on Hallam Street; visits by appointment; centralsynagogue.org.uk*).

There is a good view of the BT Tower up Clipstone Street. James Boswell lived nearby at no. 122 Great Portland St.

BLOOMSBURY: AROUND OLD ST GILES

Map p. 633, D4–E4. Underground: Tottenham Court Road, Goodge Street.

Bloomsbury, bounded by Tottenham Court Road, Euston Road, Grays Inn Road and High Holborn, is an attractive part of town, home to the British Museum as well as being the University of London's central precinct, with its colleges, subsidiary departments and divisions, as well as several medical and healthcare institutions. It is also an area associated with the arts, literature and publishing. It is inextricably linked with the names of Virginia and Leonard Woolf, Clive and Vanessa Bell, Lytton Strachey and others who, before the First World War, began here their unconventional association of intellectual and artistic interests later known as the Bloomsbury Group.

As was the case with so much of the West End, Bloomsbury was built up over fields and countryside by a succession of landlords; firstly by the Earl of Southampton in the 1660s and later by the Dukes of Bedford (the Russell family). The green squares date mainly from the 18th and early 19th centuries and handsome, well-proportioned terraced houses survive alongside newer buildings. Bloomsbury's architecture is grander than that of adjoining Fitzrovia, but in common with its neighbour, its charm lies in its lack of pretension, in its smattering of interesting independent shops (concentrated particularly in northeast Bloomsbury) and in its modest, convivial pubs and restaurants (although the ubiquitous coffee and sandwich chains have sneaked in). Many smaller hotels and student residences occupy houses here. 'A life of wealth does not appeal to me at all...All I want is a room in Bloomsbury,' sings Polly Browne in the 1954 musical *The Boyfriend*. Nevertheless, a top floor studio 'attic' today might have risen beyond Polly's price range.

OLD ST GILES

The area known as St Giles, now bisected by New Oxford Street (*map p. 635, F1*), was once a poverty-stricken and congested 'rookery' clustered around an old leper hospital that had been founded here in 1101 by Matilda, wife of Henry I. Disease long remained endemic in the area: one of the first cases of the Great Plague occurred among Flemish weavers in this parish in 1664. Just up **Denmark Street** (formerly London's answer to Tin-Pan Alley in New York and still with a string of shops selling electric guitars and other instruments) is the church of **St Giles-in-the-Fields**, built in 1730–4 by Henry Flitcroft. In the entrance vestibule is a carved oak relief of the *Resurrection* (1687) and opposite, halfway up the stairs, a memorial to Flaxman (carved by the sculptor), placed here in 1930. Inside the church, the late 17th-century organ and pulpit survive from the earlier church. Byron's daughter Allegra was baptised in the simple little font in 1818, as were Shelley's children William and Clara. Each of them died in Italy. Allegra, who was five when she died, lived longest. In the north aisle is a memorial to Andrew Marvell, extolling his political nous but never once mentioning his beautiful poetry. Next to it is the upper part of a pulpit used by John and Charles Wesley in 1743–91 (formerly in West Street Chapel; *see p. 282*) and beyond, a memorial to George Chapman (d. 1634), the translator of Homer who occasioned Keats' 'wild surmise'. Placed here by Inigo Jones, it is in the form of a Roman stele.

The **Central St Giles** development (St Giles High St and Dyott St) was Renzo Piano's first commission in the United Kingdom (2010). Its blocks are clad with tiles in primary-school shades of red, orange, yellow and green.

The plaza at the bottom of Tottenham Court Road, formerly St Giles Circus, is dominated by the Brutalist tower known as **Centre Point** (*map p. 635, F1*), the tallest

View from the Roof Terrace of the Post Building. The British Museum is prominent, with its Reading Room dome and glassed-over Great Court. In front of it is the eccentric spire of St George's and to the left the BT Tower, London's tallest building when it opened in 1964.

building in London's West End (R. Seifert and Partners, 1966), which is built over a former gallows. It stands at the junction of four key areas of the city: Soho (southwest); Covent Garden (southeast); Fitzrovia (northwest) and Bloomsbury (northeast). Now boasting newly refurbished residential apartments designed by Conran & Partners, it nevertheless remains a 34-floor concrete behemoth looming over the surrounding streets in a manner that never manages to be benevolent. Beyond it, under the cutaway corner chamfer of the golden cuboid **Now Building**, crowds gather to marvel at a vast screen showing visual effects. It seems a curiously controlled entertainment diet for a part of town that saw the spontaneous birth of punk rock.

TOTTENHAM COURT ROAD
Tottenham Court Road (*map p. 633, D4*) was once a byword for electronics and home furnishings. There are still some outlets left, though most have either gone online or moved to prefab warehouses further afield. At no. 46 (corner of Windmill St) is the Art Nouveau **Rising Sun pub**, by pub architects Treadwell and Martin (1896). On the other side of the road, Bayley Street leads to **Bedford Square** (*map p. 633, D4*), one of the first squares to be laid out on the Bedford Estate and built between 1775 and 1780 by Thomas Leverton and others. This is one of London's most complete 18th-century

squares: each side is designed as a terrace of brick houses with a 'palace front' at the centre; the central houses on the north and east sides are stuccoed and made prominent with a pediment and Ionic pilasters. Each house has a distinctive doorcase of Coade Stone (*see p. 466*) with regular vermiculated blocks and a bearded head at the keystone. Look closely and you will see variations in the fanlights and the ironwork balconies, and notice too that the windows have an irregular rhythm; this is because London terraces were rarely the work of just one architect and builder. These were private houses and were sold or rented by lawyers, doctors and architects; today they are mainly offices and the square is in demand as a period film set.

The bronze cat in Heal's department store.

Back on Tottenham Court Road, between Alfred Mews and Torrington Place, is **Heal's department store**, founded in 1810. The current building was designed by Smith and Brewer in 1917 and has a famous spiral staircase inside at the back, guarded by the shop's mascot, a bronze sculpture of a cat, which sits on a windowsill. Heal's original speciality was furniture, particularly bedding, and the building's exterior is adorned with motifs of crafts connected with interior design. The building was extended in 1938 by Sir Edward Maufe, whose wife, the designer Prudence Maufe, was a director of the store, and again in the 1960s, following the demolition of the Apollo Inn on the corner of Torrington Place.

Opposite, the **American International Church** (*amchurch.co.uk*) occupies the former Whitefield Memorial Chapel (E.C. Butler, 1956–8), which in turn was built on the site of a chapel erected for George Whitefield (1714–70), the cross-eyed evangelical preacher whose stentorian voice reportedly carried for miles and who preached many times in the American colonies and to American slaves.

BLOOMSBURY, RUSSELL & TAVISTOCK SQUARES

ST GEORGE'S AND BLOOMSBURY SQUARE

At 53 New Oxford Street (*map p. 635, F1*), at the junction of Bloomsbury Street and Shaftesbury Avenue, is **James Smith & Sons**, umbrella and walking stick merchants since 1830, still occupying their Victorian shop. Also on New Oxford Street, on the corner of Museum St, you will find the **Post Building**, a former sorting office-turned-office-space, which has a roof garden which can be visited (*look for the outside sign saying 'Public Roof Terrace'; go in and ask at the desk; ID needed*). The views from the top are excellent, taking in the eccentric spire of St George's Bloomsbury (*see below*), the British Museum roof and main façade, and clusters of towers in the City, the South Bank and around Elephant and Castle. When first opened, the idea had been to make this into a gin terrace overlooking Gin Lane. Today it is a quiet space articulated with concrete planters of flowers and grasses.

The church of **St George's Bloomsbury** in Bloomsbury Way (*map p. 633, E4; staffed by volunteers so visiting hours subject to change; stgeorgesbloomsbury.org.uk*) was built by Hawksmoor in 1716–31 as one of the new churches constructed after the 1711 New Churches Act (passed in reaction to the spread of Nonconformism). It is Hawksmoor's sixth and final London church. It has a grand Corinthian portico and its steeple, inspired by Pliny's description of the Mausoleum at Halicarnassus (modern Bodrum, Turkey), is constructed to resemble a stepped pyramid. Its base is borne by lions and unicorns and it is surmounted by a statue of George I. Its silhouette is clearly recognisable in Hogarth's famous satirical print *Gin Lane*.

Bloomsbury Square (*map p. 633, E4*) was developed in the 1660s for the 4th Earl of Southampton; it was one of the earliest squares in London to be laid out, though none of the original buildings remains. The terraces on the north side (Great Russell Street/ Bedford Place) date from c. 1800; at 3 Bloomsbury Place lived Sir Hans Sloane (*see p. 375*), physician and benefactor of the British Museum. In the garden, the bronze statue of Charles James Fox in Classical robes, holding a copy of the *Magna Carta*, is by Sir Richard Westmacott (1816).

RUSSELL SQUARE

Montague Place leads to Russell Square (*map p. 633, E4*), the largest of Bloomsbury's squares and one of the largest in London, laid out in 1800 by Humphry Repton. There are some original houses on the west side by James Burton, father of Decimus Burton, who was the contractor during this period for the Bedford family estates. The central gardens have been restored, based on Repton's original plan. A blue plaque at no. 24, in the northwest corner, commemorates T.S. Eliot, who worked here as poetry editor for Faber & Faber. Opposite, on the corner with the central gardens, the green hut is one of London's 13 remaining **cabmen's shelters**, which were built between 1875 and 1914 as places were taxi drivers could take a break and share a meal. On the east side, the French chateau-inspired **Hotel Russell**, festooned in terracotta, is by Charles Fitzroy Doll (c. 1900), whose design for the dining room on RMS *Titanic* is said to have been based on the hotel's opulent restaurant. Doll had been appointed Surveyor to the Bedford Estate in the 1880s; Burton's houses on the north and west sides, with their terracotta cladding of the 1890s, were presumably 'dolled up' under his direction. On the north side, the **Institute of Education**, with anodised aluminium panels, is by Denys Lasdun (1965–76).

GORDON SQUARE AND TAVISTOCK SQUARE

Gordon Square (*map p. 633, D4*) was developed by Thomas Cubitt from the 1820s as a pair with neighbouring Tavistock Square. At no, 46, the Bloomsbury Group was born: here the siblings Virginia, Vanessa, Adrian and Thoby Stephen held their Thursday evening salons, which were attended by Leonard Woolf, Lytton Strachey, Clive Bell, Duncan Grant and John Maynard Keynes, among others.

THE LONDON TOWNHOUSE

London is known for its terraces: street after street of contiguous houses stretching away to a distant vanishing point and thrusting myriad chimney pots into the sky. The continental European model, ubiquitous in cities like Vienna, of a single main entrance giving onto a wide communal courtyard from which stairways lead up floor by floor to individual apartments, is entirely unknown in London. Here (as was also the case in early New York) there are rows of individual houses, all seamlessly joined but each with its own separate entrance and hallway. The result is an arrangement of narrow abodes, standing side by side, sharing lateral walls, each accessed up a short flight of steps to an individual front door and with the interior rooms arranged steeply on multiple levels.

A row of terraced houses in London brick, each with its fanlit doorway, area steps behind black-painted railings, servants' rooms in the attics and banks of chimney pots.

The internal arrangement would have included a ground-floor hall (with steep stairs leading straight up from it) and dining room, a drawing room and parlour above, bedrooms above that, and servants' rooms in the attic. A bathroom often opened off one of the landings. The kitchens of the well-to-do houses were in the basement, accessed from within by the servants' stairs and from the street by the 'area', a narrow light-well beside and below the front-door steps, surrounded by railings and entered down a separate flight of stairs: housemaids in Edwardian novels are perpetually to be seen scrubbing the area steps with chillblained hands and buckets of carbolic soap.

Further out in the less affluent districts, the arrangements of terraces is similar, but the doorways are less magnificent. In the workers' and artisans' districts, the houses have no servants' attics and no areas: instead, the kitchen is typically a narrow galley at the back of the ground floor, with a tiny yard leading off it.

In the southwest corner of Gordon Square and Byng Place is the Catholic Apostolic Church known as the **Church of Christ the King**, a large Gothic Revival building in Bath stone and brick (Raphael Brandon, 1853). It was much admired by John Betjeman.

The church revived apostolic beliefs and appointed twelve leaders—or 'Apostles'—to guide its followers. The Book of Revelation was at the centre of its teaching and its core belief was that Christ's Second Coming was imminent; this church was built as a fitting place to receive Him. However, the belief in imminence meant that Apostles were not replaced when they died; after the last one passed away in 1901, the church gradually ceased to function. From 1963–92 it served as the base for the University of London's Anglican chaplaincy; today it is home to the Anglo-Catholic Forward in Faith movement and is only open at certain times. It has a highly polished encaustic-tile floor.

Opposite the church, in **Torrington Place**, is a neo-Gothic terracotta-clad terrace by Charles Fitzroy Doll (1907). It is interesting to compare it with his Russell Hotel (*see above*). The large branch of Waterstones here functions as the London University bookshop.

Tavistock Square (*map p. 633, D3–E3*) is largely surrounded now by functional mid-20th-century brick buildings. It boasts a bust of Virginia Woolf, whose house stood at no. 52, on part of the site now occupied by the Tavistock Hotel. Also in Tavistock Square is a statue of Mahatma Gandhi by Fredda Brilliant (1966); he stayed near here when in London studying law at UCL. A cherry tree commemorates the victims of Hiroshima and another monument honours the victims of a suicide bombing in 2005, as well as those who assisted them. The Tavistock Clinic, founded in 1920 by a psychiatrist who had treated WWI soldiers suffering from shell-shock and which came to prominence in the 2020s for its policy on gender reassignment therapy, used to have its headquarters in the square.

At 5–7 Tavistock Place (*map p. 633, E3*), **Mary Ward House** was built by Passmore Edwards in 1898 as a teaching and care centre for Mary Ward (better known as Mrs Humphry Ward), novelist, social reformer and aunt of Aldous Huxley.

LONDON UNIVERSITY

Map p. 633, D4. Underground: Goodge Street.

London was the last of the great European capitals to found a university. In 1836 a Royal Charter was granted constituting a University of London with the power of granting academic degrees, without religious tests, to students of University College (founded 1826), King's College, (founded 1829) and certain other affiliated institutions. In 1858 the examinations were thrown open to all male students without restriction; 20 years later the University of London became the first academic body in the United Kingdom to admit women as candidates for degrees on equal terms with men. Hitherto purely an examining body, it was reconstituted in 1898–1900 as a teaching university, instruction being given in existing colleges and schools. Today, the University of London is a federal body with 17 self-governing member institutions. Those in this part of town are Birkbeck (postgraduate research), SOAS (School of Oriental and African Studies),

UCL (University College London) and the London School of Hygiene and Tropical Medicine. In Malet Street looms **Senate House**, the administrative centre of London University, holding the University archive and extensive central library. It was London's first skyscraper, built in 1933–6 by Charles Holden (designer of many Underground stations). It inspired George Orwell's Ministry of Truth in *1984*.

SOAS
Opposite the main, sober brick SOAS (School of Oriental and African Studies) building on Thornhaugh Street is the **Brunei Gallery** (*map p. 633, E4*), a venue for exhibitions about Asia, Africa and the Middle East (*free; soas.ac.uk*). It has a Japanese roof garden.

UCL

Backing onto Gordon Street are the buildings of University College London, always known as UCL (*map p. 633, D4; main entrance round the corner in Gower St*). UCL was founded in 1826 with the title of University of London, with the object of affording 'at a moderate expense the means of education in literature, science and art' to students of any race, class or creed. King's College, on the Strand, was founded as an Anglican alternative to this 'Godless college on Gower Street'. Today UCL is proudly London's 'global' and 'multi-disciplinary' university, a centre of excellence with 25,000 students.

Through the lodge gates on Gower Street, at the back of the **main quad**, is the **central building**, with a Corinthian portico and dome, designed by William Wilkins in 1827–9; on all sides are extensions and additions. On your left (north) is the Slade School of Art (founded 1871), which produced Augustus and Gwen John, William Orpen, Stanley Spencer, David Bomberg and William Coldstream. Opposite the main college gates, is the red-brick neo-Gothic building known as the **Cruciform Building**, the former University College Hospital, founded in 1834. The building (Alfred and Paul Waterhouse, 1896–1906) was designed in an X-shape so as to provide maximum light and ventilation by separating the wards via long, hygienic corridors. Here Robert Liston, UCH's first Professor of Clinical Surgery, known for his speed and dexterity with a knife (crucial in an age before anaesthetic), performed the first operation in Europe under ether, in December 1846 (the first such operation in the world had taken place in Massachusetts three months earlier; to learn more about Liston, visit the Hunterian Museum in Lincoln's Inn Fields). UCH's huge new hospital, white with tinted green glass, ranges along Euston Road behind Euston Square Underground station.

The Pre-Raphaelite Brotherhood was founded at **no. 7 Gower Street**, in the home of John Everett Millais (corner of Gower Mews), in 1848. The Royal Academy of Dramatic Art (RADA) is also based here. Former residents of the street include Charles Darwin.

Exhibitions at UCL
UCL has several free exhibits that are open to the public during term time (*for access, see ucl.ac.uk/culture*). Under the Library dome is the **Octagon Gallery**, a space for changing exhibitions. On the level above is the **Flaxman Gallery**, with plaster casts by John Flaxman. The college holds an extensive collection of drawings and casts by the

Fragment of a relief of Princess Sitamun, from the mortuary temple of Amenhotep II, in the Petrie Museum of Egyptian and Sudanese Archaeology.

sculptor and more are on display in the **UCL Art Museum**, which houses a collection of 10,000 prints, drawings, sculptures and paintings from the 1490s to the present day. UCL also possesses the **preserved skeleton of Jeremy Bentham**, who sits fully clothed in a glass case. The philosopher and founder of Utilitarianism (d. 1830) asked that his body be dissected and preserved after his death; UCL has cared for it since 1850. The head is a wax version; the real one, deemed inappropriate for public display, is in safe storage. Part of the Geology Collection of rocks, minerals and fossils is in the **Rock Room** in the South Wing.

'The present has its most serious duty to history in saving the past for the benefit of the future.' So believed the great Egyptologist Sir Flinders Petrie—and he saved a very great deal, much of it charmingly displayed in the **Petrie Museum of Egyptian and Sudanese Archaeology**, located on the first floor of the DMS Watson Building in Malet Place. Here priceless pieces are crammed and crowded into old-fashioned display cabinets, some of them fitted with drawers which you can pull out to reveal yet more marvels. Here you will find jewellery, stelae, pottery, tools, ushabti figures, mummy portraits from the Fayyum, textiles and an intriguing bead and shell net dress in *eau-de-nil* green: this is a real trove. The portrait of Petrie is by Philip de Laszlo (1934).

The **Grant Museum of Zoology** (*21 University Street; opposite the main entrance*) holds 67,000 specimens, including the bones of a dodo.

THE BRITISH MUSEUM

Great Russell Street. Map p. 633, E4. Underground: Holborn, Tottenham Court Road, Russell Square. Free. Café. britishmuseum.org.

Founded in 1753, the British Museum is the oldest secular public museum in the world. Its vast collection spans over two million years of the world's cultural history and contains many objects of outstanding international importance. At the core of the collection are the curiosities of Sir Hans Sloane. Notions of contested heritage are playing a role today in determining the future for works of art not only here but in museums all over the world. In 2023 the director of the British Museum resigned after several artefacts, from uncatalogued holdings, were found to have been surfacing for sale on eBay.

SIR HANS SLOANE AND THE EARLY BRITISH MUSEUM

Sir Hans Sloane (1650–1753), botanist and scientist, was President of the Royal College of Physicians and of the Royal Society. His terracotta bust by Rysbrack (1736) is placed to the right of the British Museum's main entrance. In his will Sloane offered for sale to the Crown, for £20,000, his enormous and renowned collection of 'curiosities': botanical and natural history specimens, coins and medals, shells, paintings, books and manuscripts, the accumulations of a man of the scientific revolution intent on discovering and ordering the products of God's creation. A state lottery raised funds for its purchase together with the important manuscript collection of Robert Harley, Earl of Oxford (1661–1724). These collections, joined by the Cottonian manuscripts in 1700, were displayed not in a purpose-built museum but in Montagu House, a mansion of 1686. It was here that early visitors, including the young Mozart in 1765, who composed a motet, 'God is our refuge', dedicated to the museum, came to marvel. Cases of stuffed animals, fish, fossils and minerals, Classical antiquities and the museum's first Egyptian mummy were incongruously placed amid late 17th-century grandeur. Watercolours exist of the majestic grand staircase rising to meet three giant stuffed giraffes on the landing.

EXPANSION OF THE COLLECTION

A wave of major acquisitions in the late 18th and early 19th centuries necessitated the provision of suitable accommodation. In 1772 the great Greek vase collection of Sir William Hamilton (diplomat and archaeologist, and husband of Nelson's lover Emma) was acquired; in 1802 came the first significant haul of Egyptian antiquities, including the Rosetta Stone, followed in 1805 by the Townley Marbles. Too heavy for the delicate floors of Montagu House, they were placed in the adjoining Townley Gallery, purpose-built to accommodate them. Then, in

1816, came the purchase of the 'Elgin' Marbles, the most significant acquisition in the museum's history. A temporary structure of brick and wood was erected in the garden to house them, and it was here that the romantic Keats felt a 'dizzy pain' as he gazed upon 'these mighty things'.

The British Museum building

Between 1820 and 1823 Sir Robert Smirke produced plans for a vast new building. Greek Revivalist in style, austere and dignified, it reflected perceptions of the purity and rationalism of ancient Greece so admired by the English Neoclassicists. The building was conceived as a large quadrangle, with an imposing Ionic colonnaded entrance front and a massive portico. It was built wing by wing, parts of Montagu House coming down as the new edifice went up. Richard Westmacott's frieze of sculptures, *The Progress of Civilisation*, showing man's 'emergence from a rude state' to his embracement of the Arts and Sciences, shown gathered around the goddess Athena, was hoisted into place in the pediment above the entrance in 1851. But by then the original ideal of a 'universal' museum containing all branches of learning under one roof was understood to be a physical impossibility. The pictures, the nucleus of the National Gallery, had already been diverted to Trafalgar Square even before the first floor of the wing which was to have housed them was built. In the 1880s the natural history collections moved to South Kensington, where they became the Natural History Museum.

In 1998, with the removal of the British Library to St Pancras, the museum expanded into large areas previously occupied by books. Sydney Smirke's lofty **Reading Room** (1854–7), built in the centre of his brother Robert Smirke's quadrangle, is only 2ft smaller than the Pantheon in Rome. Many famous scholars have worked under its cream, blue and gold *papier mâché* dome. It retains its layout of reading desks and is now an exhibition space. The quadrangle itself, known as the **Great Court**, is covered by Norman Foster's vast glass roof.

The collections

It is not possible to view the museum's vast collections in a single visit, nor to give a comprehensive account of them. The holdings are displayed in a total of more than 60 galleries, arranged geographically or according to specific themes. Below is an outline of the museum's highlights.

The Age of Enlightenment

The restored **King's Library**, Smirke's magnificent Greek Revival space built to receive George III's library, donated to the museum by George IV in 1823, is the most imposing Neoclassical interior in London. It is 300ft long and decorated with an austere magnificence, with vast Corinthian columns of Aberdeen granite and a rich yet restrained plasterwork ceiling. Following the removal of the library to the British Library at St Pancras, the space has now been filled with a permanent exhibition looking at

The Arts and Sciences cluster around Athena in Westmacott's British Museum tympanum frieze of 1851.

the **Age of the Enlightenment**, the era of expanding knowledge, pioneering discovery and rational observation in which the museum was founded. The displays contain objects from all aspects of the museum's collections, making it an ideal introduction to the museum as a whole. The development of methods for ordering, classifying and understanding man's growing experience of the world is explored.

Ancient Egypt, Nubia, Sudan and Ethiopia

The museum's famous Egyptian collection covers the cultures of the Nile Valley from the Neolithic age (c. 10th century BC) to Coptic times (12th century AD). Although Sloane's foundation collection had included some Egyptian material, it was not until 1802 that major items, ceded to the British under the terms of the 1801 Treaty of Alexandria, began to arrive. First and foremost among these was the famous **Rosetta Stone**, an object of unparalleled importance in the history of Egyptology. Originally discovered by French scholars who accompanied Napoleon's expeditionary force to Egypt, the stone, bearing an inscription in three scripts—hieroglyphic, demotic Egyptian and Greek—held the key to the decipherment of hieroglyphs. The code was finally cracked by the French Egyptologist Jean-François Champollion in 1822, thereby enabling the translation of texts and inscriptions which opened the door to the hitherto mysterious 'lost' civilisation of ancient Egypt.

The first great piece of Egyptian sculpture to arrive was the **bust of Ramesses II**, 'the Younger Memnon', a colossal seven-ton sculpture (actually only the head) carved from a single block of granite, excavated from the king's vast mortuary temple, the Ramesseum, in Thebes. Presented to the museum in 1817 by Henry Salt, British Consul-General in Cairo, and Jean Louis Burckhardt, a Swiss explorer, it had been physically removed from its site by Giovanni Belzoni, a former strongman and hydraulic engineer, whose team had taken twelve days to haul it to the river's edge.

The upstairs galleries house the museum's renowned collection of papyri, mummies, tomb sculpture and funerary objects. The mummies and their elaborate cases, including the Roman-period **mummy case of Artemidorus** with its portrait of a young man from Hawara, are displayed alongside X-rays and CT scans, revealing amulets, scarabs and other sacred objects beneath the wrappings. Other grave goods such as jewellery, canopic jars and mummified animals are on show. There is a large collection of **Books of the Dead**, which offered spells to aid the dead in their passage through the underworld. The museum's most striking piece of tomb painting is the *Fowling in the Marshes*, a fragment from the tomb of Nebamun in Thebes (18th Dynasty, c. 1350 BC), showing Nebamun and his wife Hatshepsut in recreation in the afterlife.

Ancient Greece and Rome

The museum's collection of Greek and Roman antiquities is one of the finest in the world, ranging from the Bronze Age civilisations of the Cyclades and Minoan Crete to the late Roman Empire. The first major acquisition was the 1772 purchase of Sir William Hamilton's **Greek vase collection**, a large and valuable group mainly from southern Italy. In 1805 the Greek vases were joined by another major acquisition, the **Townley Marbles**, a group of mainly Roman sculptures which Charles Townley began collecting in 1768 when in Rome on the Grand Tour. Interest in Classical sculpture was then at its zenith, fuelled by dealers who excavated sites such as Hadrian's Villa at Tivoli and restorers who worked alongside them. During his lifetime Townley's collection was displayed in his cluttered house in Queen Anne's Gate, Westminster, where it became a celebrated attraction visited by scholars and connoisseurs. Among the highlights was the bust of 'Clytie', Townley's favourite sculpture, named after the nymph who was turned into a sunflower but which in fact perhaps represents Antonia, daughter of Mark Antony and Octavia.

The Townley collection had an immense impact on 18th-century British taste, but its reputation was eclipsed by the arrival in the 19th century of several examples of Greek sculpture which cemented in people's minds the primacy of ancient Greek art and civilisation over Roman. The arrival which caused the greatest stir was that of the **Parthenon Marbles**, acquired in 1816. Removed by Lord Elgin from the 5th-century BC Temple of Athena Parthenos on the Acropolis, Athens, these sculptures have long been admired as the greatest achievement of Greek art. In the 19th century they became the benchmark against which all art was measured. The marbles include sculptures from the east pediment, originally a rhythmic succession of figurative groups illustrating the birth of Athena; slabs from the sculpted frieze showing the Panathenaic procession held to celebrate the birthday of Athena, carved with amazing skill and finesse; and sculpted panels once placed above the colonnade showing with great vividness the fight between the Lapiths and the Centaurs. Also removed by Elgin was the **caryatid from the Erechtheion**'s south porch, also on the Acropolis. Although removed with the preservation of the marbles from the careless disregard of the Ottoman authorities in mind, even in the early 19th century Elgin was accused of robbery and plunder (by Byron). Visitors today will be well aware of the campaign for the marbles' repatriation. A specially designed museum in Athens has been awaiting their arrival for many years.

In 1845 slabs from the 4th-century BC **Mausoleum of Halicarnassus**, the tomb of Mausolus, King of Caria (modern Turkey), and one of the Seven Wonders of the ancient world, arrived at the museum. Another of the Seven Wonders, the **Temple of Artemis at Ephesus**, from where St Paul preached to the Ephesians, is represented by a vast sculpted column drum.

The well known **Portland Vase**, probably Roman (c. AD 5–25), was brought to England by Sir William Hamilton. It is a technical masterpiece of cobalt blue and white cameo glass decorated with a figurative frieze, famously copied by Josiah Wedgwood. In 1845 the vase was smashed into a hundred pieces by a drunken visitor, but successfully repaired.

The Middle East and Levant

The museum's material from the ancient civilisations of the Near East includes art and artefacts from ancient Mesopotamia, Iran (Persia), the Levant, Anatolia and Urartu (Armenia, east Turkey and Iran) and southern Arabia, spanning the Neolithic period to the arrival of Islam in the 7th century AD. It has at its heart one of the finest collections of Assyrian sculpture in the world.

It was the great excavator Sir Austen Henry Layard (1817–94) who opened the West's eyes to the truly magnificent civilisation of the Assyrians. The sculptures arriving in London from the 1840s from Nimrud and Nineveh caused a sensation. They included the **Black Obelisk of Shalmaneser III** (r. 858–824 BC) with its carved representation of Jehu paying tribute to the king, a tantalising reference to a biblical figure; from the Northwest Palace of Ashurnasirpal II (r. 883–859 BC), a colossal **human-headed winged lion** which guarded the entrance to the throne room; and carved slabs which lined the walls of the **Palace of Sennacherib** at Nineveh. Layard's local assistant, Hormuzd Rassam, continued to excavate on behalf of the museum, sending back astonishing discoveries from Ashurbanipal's North Palace at Nineveh, which he unearthed in 1852–4. From this richly-decorated palace came the famous Royal Lion Hunt slabs, in particular the **Dying Lion**, where the injured and bleeding animal is carved with incredible skill and observation. The discovery in 1872 that one of the cuneiform tablets (the **Flood Tablet**, 7th century BC) contained a Babylonian version of the biblical deluge riveted Victorian minds.

Africa

Exhibits include the 12th–14th-century bronze head of a Yoruba ruler, probably Oni, King of Ife on the River Niger; sophisticated **brass plaques from Benin**, produced for the Oba rulers in the 16th century; and a collection of goldwork collected in 1817 by Thomas Boldwich on a journey to the Asante kingdom (present-day Ghana). Asante's great wealth was based on its vast gold deposits: at Kumasi, Boldwich noted the sun glinting off the massy gold ornaments of the people.

The Americas

The museum still has the great ceremonial cloak of feathers and mother of pearl, which is probably the one presented to Cook in Tahiti in 1774. **Hoa Hakananai'a**, the museum's monumental Easter Island statue, was brought back by the crew of HMS *Topaze* from its surveying expedition of 1868. These great human figures known as *moai*, part of the island's statue cult, which flourished up until the 17th century, originally stood upright on platforms, surveying the remote island scenery from under their heavy brows.

From Mexico come the three pieces of **Mixtec-Aztec turquoise mosaic**, possibly part of the tribute given by Emperor Moctezuma II to the Spanish conquistador Hernán Cortés in 1519.

Asia

The large department covering the material remains of the Asian continent from Neolithic times to the present comprises the world's most comprehensive collection of sculpture from the Indian subcontinent; the best collection of Islamic pottery outside the Middle East; an outstanding collection of Chinese antiquities, including paintings, porcelain, lacquer and jade; the most important collection of Korean art in Europe; and, among the Japanese netsuke, samurai swords and ceramics (including tea ceremony ware), the finest collection of Japanese paintings and prints in the West. The gilt-bronze 9th-century Sri Lankan **Bodhisattva Tara** is one of the finest examples of Asian figural bronze-casting. The 133 1st–3rd-century delicately carved limestone **reliefs from the Great Stupa**, the Buddhist relic-house at Amaravati in Andhra Pradesh, southeast India, are one of the British Museum's greatest treasures.

The most important collection of Chinese artefacts was that of the Hungarian archaeologist and explorer of the Silk Route Sir Aurel Stein. Objects began to arrive from 1900, the most important of which was the group from the Tang period (AD 618–906): manuscripts, temple banners and paintings on silk and paper, including elaborate Paradise scenes, discovered in the **Valley of a Thousand Buddhas**, Dunhuang (Study Collection). Strategically placed on the Silk Route, the area had been an important centre for Buddhist pilgrims, who hollowed out over 1,000 cave shrines. In 1906, in Cave 17, closed since the early 12th century, Stein made his important discovery. In 1903 the museum purchased a major piece of Chinese art, the *Admonitions of the Instructress to the Court Ladies*, a painted scroll illustrating Zhang Hua's political parody attacking the excessive behaviour of the empress. The scroll is a valuable 6th–8th-century copy of the no-longer-extant original by the legendary artist Gu Kaizhi (AD 345–406), of whose work only a few not certainly attributed examples survive.

The excellent collection of **Japanese paintings and prints** includes fine pieces from the Kamakura period (1185–1333) and a great collection of Ukiyo-e (prints and paintings of the 'Floating World' school which flourished in the 17th–19th centuries), including the famous Mount Fuji woodblock print series by the leading artist of the late Edo period, Katsushika Hokusai (1760–1849).

Europe

The department spans a vast expanse of time, from the Palaeolithic and Neolithic eras, through the Bronze and Iron Ages and Celtic Europe, to Roman Britain and the Christian cultures of the Medieval, Renaissance and Modern ages. Archaeological discovery and the ancient law of Treasure Trove, refined by the Treasure Act (1996), have benefited the collection enormously. Buried 'treasure', defined as any object containing ten percent silver or gold, over 300 years old and placed in the ground with the intention of retrieval, is administered by the museum. Through this route came the 12th-century **Lewis Chessmen**, discovered in 1831 in a stone chamber under a sandbank on the Isle of Lewis, Outer Hebrides; the exceptional **Mildenhall Treasure**, a hoard of 34 pieces of superb Roman silver tableware of brilliant craftsmanship ploughed up in a field in Suffolk in the 1940s; and the great gold **Snettisham Torc**, a magnificent 1st-century BC example of early Iron Age British craftsmanship. Two magnificent works of Roman craftsmanship are the 1st-century silver **Warren Cup**, found near Jerusalem, depicting two male lovers observed by a young slave; and the 4th-century **Lycurgus Cup**, an intricate red and green glass drinking vessel of the type known as a cage cup.

The extraordinarily well preserved **Lindow Man** is a 1st-century AD man aged 25 who had been bludgeoned, garrotted and then had his throat cut, probably in a Druidic sacrifice.

One of the greatest archaeological excavations in Britain was the 7th-century Anglo-Saxon **ship burial at Sutton Hoo**, Suffolk, possibly the grave of Raedwald, King of East Anglia. Discovered in 1939 under windswept heathland, the astonishing rich treasure of silver and gold set with garnets, includes a perfectly preserved and intricate gold buckle and a finely-crafted helmet.

Prints and drawings

The national collection of Western prints and drawings is one of the top three collections of its type in the world. At its heart are the pieces collected by Sloane, including volumes of Dürer's watercolours and drawings which are among the museum's most important possessions. Among the other highlights are over 90 works by Michelangelo, including studies for great commissions such as the Sistine Chapel ceiling; 80 sheets of sketches and drawings by Rembrandt, as well as a collection of his etchings; a large body of excellent works by Rubens; and British watercolours, including works by John Sell Cotman. There are also works by Thomas Girtin, a young artist of great promise, recognised as a genius by Turner. He died before he was 30. The collection is made available through a programme of temporary exhibitions. The Print Room is open for research by appointment.

EAST BLOOMSBURY

The northeast side of Bloomsbury, away from the University and the British Museum and within easy walking distance of St Pancras and King's Cross, lies off the main tourist trail. It is a good place to wander as there are plenty of interesting independent shops, honest eateries and watering holes, especially around Marchmont Street and Lamb's Conduit Street.

In **Marchmont Street** (*map p. 633, E3–E4*), blue plaques dot the Georgian houses like patches on the face of a fashionable 18th-century beauty: no. 88 was the home of Kenneth Williams, star of the bawdy *Carry On* films; no. 47 was where one Mr Grey, manufacturer of artificial teeth, lived in 1817; at no. 43, Robert Dyas, ironmonger, first traded in the 1930s (shops bearing his name have swelled into a high-street chain).

Sir John Barbirolli (Giovanni Battista Barbirolli), conductor and cellist, lived on the site of the **Brunswick Centre**, between Marchmont and Hunter streets. A staggered-level complex by Patrick Hodgkinson, incorporating flats, shops and the Renoir Cinema, it was built in 1968–72 and serves as an example of what was in those days considered a model for new urban life. The flats, part private, part social housing, descend in two straight lines of terraces overlooking the shopping street; car parking is underneath. Never greatly popular with the public, it has nevertheless achieved listed status. The nihilistic Finnish rock band Lodger used it as inspiration for one of their songs: 'You came to the right place to lose your face: concrete, concrete, life is sweet. I wanna spend the rest of my days at the Brunswick Centre.'

ON AND AROUND BRUNSWICK SQUARE

Brunswick Square (*map p. 633, E3*), named after Caroline of Brunswick, consort of George IV, was laid out in 1800. The gardens in the centre are home to the second-oldest plane tree in London. In 1815, when Brunswick Square was still very new, Jane Austen received word that the Prince Regent would be pleased to accept the dedication of her next work. That novel, *Emma*, came out in December of the same year (the Prince Regent's copy is now in the library of Windsor Castle). In it, Brunswick Square receives fulsome mention from the mouth of Isabella Woodhouse, Emma's sister. Of the elegant buildings which once surrounded the square, not much survives.

In praise of Brunswick Square

'Our part of London is very superior to most others. You must not confound us with London in general, my dear sir. The neighbourhood of Brunswick Square is very different from all the rest. We are so very airy! I should be unwilling, I own, to live in any other part of the town; there is hardly any other that I could be satisfied to have my children in; but *we* are so remarkably airy!

Jane Austen, *Emma* (1815)

THE FOUNDLING MUSEUM

Next to the UCL School of Pharmacy, at no. 40 Brunswick Square, is the delightful Foundling Museum (*map p. 633, E3; foundlingmuseum.org.uk*), a remarkable institution which records the foundation, history and continuing work of the Foundling Hospital, a charitable home for illegitimate children established in 1739 by Captain Thomas Coram, whose statue stands outside. A humble Dorset man, Coram was a master mariner who had arrived back from the American colonies to be appalled by the plight of abandoned, orphaned and destitute children on the streets of London. In 1739, after 17 years of relentless campaigning, Coram persuaded George II to grant a Royal Charter to open 'A Hospital for the Maintenance and Education of Exposed and Deserted Young

Children'. An entirely secular organisation, the first of its kind, it was funded through private donations and subscription. Coram was supported by Hogarth, Handel and other well-known figures of the day.

All Foundling children were baptised on admission. The first child was named Thomas Coram and the first girl Eunice Coram, after Captain Coram's wife. In 1742 new buildings were begun. In 1749 Handel, who became a Hospital governor, conducted a concert to raise funds for the completion of the Hospital chapel, for which he composed the 'Foundling Hospital Anthem'. Fundraising concerts became a feature of the Hospital's calendar, with Handel conducting annual performances of the *Messiah*. A terracotta model by Roubiliac of his monument in Westminster Abbey is in the collection. The original building has been demolished but several of the finer rooms were carefully salvaged and re-erected within the new headquarters, completed in 1938.

The Hospital originally had official appointment days for receiving children, with desperate queues forming outside the gates with more children than could possibly be accommodated. A ballot method was introduced. On reception days mothers drew a ball from a bag, its colour deciding the fate of their child. Careful records were made of each child admitted, as well as of the identifying keepsakes which could be used to reclaim children. Several of these touching Foundling Tokens are now on show: metal tags with names, ribbons, buttons, a broken thimble and even a hazelnut shell. Also in the collection is Hogarth's great *March of the Guards to Finchley*, the scene set in Tottenham Court Road in the winter of 1745, where a band of guardsmen is moving off to Finchley before marching north against Bonnie Prince Charlie's rebels. The King's Head tavern has been commandeered by the notorious brothel-keeper Mother Douglas. Hogarth sold the picture by lottery: 167 of the unsold tickets were donated to the Hospital, which won the picture. By Hogarth also is the splendid **Captain Thomas Coram** (1740), a masterpiece of British art, which Hogarth presented to the Hospital. Coram is shown seated on a dais, with columns behind, holding the seal of the Hospital's Royal Charter: the composition is redolent of traditional Baroque pomp, and yet Coram appears wigless and ruddy-cheeked, a direct realism which gives the portrait its human appeal.

The **Handel Collection** on the top floor includes part of the fair copy of *Messiah* which Handel left to the Hospital. There are also acoustic armchairs, where you can sit and listen to selected works by the great composer.

The Hospital's old site, **Coram's Fields**, is now an enclosed seven-acre children's park where adults are not encouraged. A sign at the entrance on Guilford Street says adults may only enter if accompanied by a child under 16. Beside the gate is a niche flanked by columns and a mock architrave with triglyphs. This is where desperate mothers would once deposit their infants.

ST GEORGE'S GARDENS

In Heathcote Street (*map p. 633, E3*) is the entrance to St George's Gardens, which served as the burial grounds for St George the Martyr and St George's Bloomsbury from 1713. This atmospheric green space, with winding paths, mature plane trees and shrubs, is dotted with weathered monuments and tomb chests, one of which is to Anna Gibson (d. 1726), favourite daughter of Richard Cromwell and granddaughter of Oliver Cromwell. The terracotta figure of *Euterpe* (1898) is one of the nine Muses that once decorated the Apollo Inn, which stood on the corner of Tottenham Court Road and Torrington Place. Modern blocks now occupy that site.

SOUTH TO KINGSWAY FROM MECKLENBURGH SQUARE

Mecklenburgh Square (*map p. 633, E3*), with a private central garden, was named for Charlotte of Mecklenburg-Strelitz, wife of George III. It retains its elegant Georgian housing. Virginia Woolf lived on the site of no. 37 until her death by suicide in 1941.

THE CHARLES DICKENS MUSEUM

Doughty Street is a fine Georgian street leading to Gray's Inn; the writers Vera Brittain and Winifred Holtby lived at no. 52. At no. 48 is the Charles Dickens Museum (*map p. 633, F4; dickensmuseum.com*), in the house where Dickens lived for £80 a year between 1837 and 1839. It is his only surviving London residence, arranged now to paint an intimate picture of his domestic life, showing us the young husband and father as well as the writer and man of the theatre. Dickens lived here with his wife Catherine and their infant son Charles; the house also witnessed the birth of his daughters Mary and Kate as well as the completion of *The Pickwick Papers, Oliver Twist* and *Nicholas Nickleby*, the trio of publications which established his literary reputation.

The house holds a vast collection of Dickens memorabilia, including portraits, personal items, furniture and autograph letters and manuscripts. In the hallway a silhouette of Dickens, hand outstretched, welcomes the visitor. The basement contains a re-creation of the **Kitchen, Preparation Room and Wash House**, where one learns that the Victorians kept hedgehogs to control insects (the resident stuffed specimen is called Bill Spikes). The **Dining Room** plays host to a fictional dinner party: places are set for Thackeray, among others. Note the grandfather clock which belonged to Moses Pickwick, a coach proprietor of Bath, whose name Dickens took for his famous character. The **Morning Room** was principally used by Catherine Dickens, whose portrait, together with that of her husband, hangs over the fireplace; on display, too, is the couple's marriage licence (though the great idealiser of hearth and home was later to jilt Catherine for a woman 24 years her junior).

On the first floor is the spacious **Drawing Room**, used by Dickens to entertain his frequent visitors; here is the reading desk Dickens designed and took on tour with him around England and North America. On the second floor is the **Dickenses' Bedroom**, where Catherine Dickens gave birth to two daughters. The **Mary Hogarth Room** is the bedroom where Dickens' 'young, beautiful and good' sister-in-law, Mary Hogarth, died in 1837, aged just 17, an event which affected him profoundly and provided him with much material (for example, the death of Little Nell in *The Old Curiosity Shop*). The sketch of Dickens on his deathbed is by John Everett Millais.

In the third-floor **Nursery and Servant's Bedroom** the display enters the world of workhouses and prisons, illustrated by a grille from the debtors' prison at Marshalsea, where Dickens' father languished for three months (*see p. 456*). There are also earthenware jars from Warren's boot-blacking factory, where Dickens pasted on labels to earn his keep.

GREAT ORMOND STREET, RED LION SQUARE AND KINGSWAY

Lamb's Conduit Street (*map p. 633, E4*) is a pleasant, part-pedestrianised street where the Lamb, a Victorian pub at no. 94, is one of the many London hostelries where Dickens drank. Crossing Lamb's Conduit Street is **Great Ormond Street** and the well-known eponymous children's hospital, founded in 1852. J.M. Barrie donated the royalties of *Peter Pan* (1904) towards its funding. The hospital **Chapel of St Christopher** by E.M. Barry (1875), Italianate in inspiration, has stained glass by Clayton and Bell and a floor by the Venetian mosaicists Salviati. The building was moved wholesale to its present site in the 1980s, when the rest of the old hospital complex was demolished.

Queen Square was laid out in the early 18th century and named after Queen Anne. The church of St George the Martyr (1706) was part of the original plan; it survives today, though much altered in the 19th century. In the garden is a statue (c. 1775) of Queen Charlotte, previously thought to represent Queen Anne.

South of Theobalds Road, on the site now occupied by **Red Lion Square** (*map p. 633, E4*; formally laid out in 1684 by Nicholas Barbon), the bodies of Oliver Cromwell, Henry Ireton and John Bradshaw were displayed in 1661 after being disinterred from Westminster Abbey. Cromwell needs no introduction. Ireton was an uncompromising Parliamentarian army general. Bradshaw, a lawyer, led the trial of King Charles I that ended with his death sentence. The bodies

of the three men were taken the next day to Tyburn (*pp. 322–3*) where they were desecrated and the heads placed on poles at Westminster Hall. In the garden today is a bronze bust of Bertrand Russell by Marcelle Quinton (1980) and a bronze statue of the international peace campaigner Lord Brockway (1985). Several Pre-Raphaelite artists lived here: Rossetti at no. 17 in 1851, and Morris and Burne-Jones in 1856–9. In the northeast corner is Conway Hall (F. Herbert Mansard, 1929), the seat of the South Place Ethical Society, a pioneering institution of religious-humanist thought, founded in 1793.

Euterpe, Muse of lyric poetry and music. In her missing right hand she may once have held a flute. Terracotta statue in St George's Gardens.

A little to the west, at the junction of Southampton Row and Vernon Place, notice in the middle of the road the entrance to the **Kingsway Tram Tunnel** (now defunct) Behind the gates, you can still see the tram tracks on the slope leading into this part of secret, subterranean London. On Bloomsbury Way, notice **Sicilian Avenue**, a pedestrianised shopping street with buildings faced in terracotta (Robert Worley, 1910); the Ionic entrance screen gives it an exclusive, Italianate feel. **Kingsway** itself, which is the southern continuation of Southampton Row, opened in 1905 and was an impressive piece of Edwardian town planning: a wide boulevard with a tunnel for electric trams underneath it. Its breadth has now made it into a major traffic artery.

EUSTON ROAD, ST PANCRAS & KING'S CROSS

Map p. 633, D3–E3. Underground: Euston, Euston Square, King's Cross St Pancras.

Euston Road, the northern boundary of Bloomsbury, continues the line of Marylebone Road east to King's Cross. Forming part of the 'New Road' laid out in 1754–6 to connect Islington with Paddington, it now bears heavy traffic.

EUSTON STATION

Euston Station (*map p. 633, D3*) is the terminus of the London and Birmingham Railway, named after Euston Hall in Suffolk, the family seat of the Duke of Grafton. The railway engineer was Robert Stephenson, the station architect was Philip Hardwick and its builder Thomas Cubitt. Euston was one of the first—and perhaps the finest—of London's railway termini: at its entrance was Hardwick's colossal 70ft Doric propylaeum (1837; demolished), with lodges and bronze gates at either side, which became known as Euston Arch. It was so large that surviving drawings and photographs show the people and carriages at its base looking tiny and ant-like. It was designed to be both a physical and symbolic grand gateway from London to the Midlands—on arrival in Birmingham, passengers passed through a complementary Ionic arch, also designed by Hardwick (1838; it still stands). In the station proper, the Great Hall, by Hardwick's son, Philip Charles Hardwick (1849), had a sweeping double staircase and coffered ceiling. By the 20th century, however, due to increased numbers of passengers and the electrification of the railway, the old station was overstretched and outdated. In the 1960s, the Euston Arch and the Great Hall were demolished, against considerable opposition: John Betjeman, Nikolaus Pevsner, Sir Charles Wheeler (director of the RA), the Society for the Protection of Ancient Buildings, the Georgian Group and the London Society all stepped in to try to save it. Their attempts were fruitless and the buildings were pulled down to make way for what stands here now. Although considered an act of philistinism, the loss of this monument to Britain's railway age (branded the 'Euston Murder' by the *Architectural Review* in 1962) did open up a wider debate about how other historic buildings in the capital were being treated and did prevent others from being torn down in similarly brutal fashion. At the time of writing, Euston was once again being remodelled, to accommodate yet another controversial project, the HS2 high-speed railway link between London and Birmingham. A statue of Robert Stephenson by Marochetti (1871), which used to stand in the station forecourt, had at the time of writing been removed while construction work was in progress.

Meanwhile, the ghost of the Euston Arch refuses to rest. Much of its rubble was dumped in the Thames but some blocks of the hard Yorkshire stone have been retrieved.

THE WELLCOME COLLECTION AND ST PANCRAS PARISH CHURCH

At no. 183 Euston Road, diagonally opposite the railway station, is the **Wellcome Collection** (*map p. 633, D3*), part of the Wellcome Trust, a charitable foundation devoted to medicine and medical science, established by Sir Henry Wellcome (1853–1936). It has a library, café and free exhibition galleries (*wellcomecollection.org*). The Neoclassical building was built in 1932 to Wellcome's specifications. Beyond Gordon Street at no. 173 is the sober Neoclassical **Friends' House** (Hubert Lidbetter, 1926), the headquarters of the Society of Friends or Quakers.

Further east, on the corner of Upper Woburn Place and Euston Road, rises **St Pancras Parish Church**, sometimes referred to as St Pancras New Church (St Pancras Old Church is north of St Pancras station; *see p. 390*), a distinctive landmark built in neo-Greek style in 1819–22 by William and Henry Inward, father and son, who borrowed features from the Erechtheion in Athens. The church is defined by its twin caryatid porches, one at either side, each with four robust caryatids by J.C.F. Rossi. They are not stone but terracotta, built around cast-iron columns. Unfortunately they were too tall to fit and had to be shortened in the middle, hence their stocky appearance. The church steeple was inspired by the Tower of the Winds in the Athens agora. **Woburn Walk** and Duke Street are two charming surviving old London streets skirting the churchyard. The former street was built by Thomas Cubitt in 1822. It preserves quaint shopfronts, many of which are still in use by shops today. W.B. Yeats lived at no. 5 in 1895–1919.

In the **UNISON Centre** on the other side of the road (no. 130), on the ground floor of the former Hospital for Women founded by Elizabeth Garrett Anderson in 1872, is a small display on the life and work of the pioneering female doctor (*egaforwomen. org.uk*).

THE BRITISH LIBRARY

Formerly part of the British Museum, the British Library (*96 Euston Rd; map p. 633, E3; café and shop; bl.uk*) was housed until 1997 in the main Museum building, with magnificent purpose-built reading rooms. Having outgrown those premises, it moved here in 1998, to a building originally designed by Colin St John Wilson in 1977. The large **Piazza** in front the of the building has, crouching on one side, Eduardo Paolozzi's bronze, bespectacled *Newton* (1995), inspired by William Blake's image of the same. Surrounding the sunken 'amphitheatre' are the eight carved Swedish glacial boulders which make up Antony Gormley's *Planets*. The British Library is perhaps the sole surviving place where Britons still form an orderly queue. Before opening time, the line snakes in orderly single file around the Piazza.

The Victorian Gothic *palazzo* that is St Pancras Station (1868), with its grand carriage sweep in front and steepled clock tower.

The unprepossessing red-brick exterior makes the interior a complete surprise: a wonderful white, tall, airy space flooded with light, with broad steps leading up to the reading rooms. At the core of the Library's collections are the three foundation collections of the British Museum: those of Sir Hans Sloane (*see p. 375*); Sir Robert Cotton (d. 1631); and Robert Harley, 1st Earl of Oxford (d. 1724). Replica busts of Cotton and Sloane, as well as of the botanist Joseph Banks and the bibliophile Thomas Grenville, adorn the **Entrance Hall** (left wall). They have been provided with interpretative panels explaining each individual's role in the exploitation of people in other parts of the world. On the right-hand wall is a tapestry woven after R.B. Kitaj's *If not, not*. In the centre of the hall, encased in a six-storey tower block of bronze and glass and with their tooled leather and gold spines visible, are the 60,000 volumes of the **King's Library**, presented to the British Museum in 1823 by George IV.

The British Library has an exceptionally comprehensive collection and contains several treasures: two contemporary copies of *Magna Carta* (1215); the manuscript of the Anglo-Saxon epic *Beowulf*; the illuminated Northumbrian 'Lindisfarne Gospels' (c. 715–20); William Caxton's two editions of Chaucer's *Canterbury Tales* (1476 and 1483); the exceptional 'Sforza Hours' from Milan (c. 1490–1520); and the 'Codex Arundel' containing manuscript sheets of Leonardo da Vinci's mathematical notes and diagrams. The Codex was once owned by Thomas Howard, Earl of Arundel, who travelled to Italy with Inigo Jones, the architect who brought Classical notions of proportion and harmony to Britain. Jones was entranced by the ancient ruins he saw in Italy, as well as by the works of Palladio. Both men were repelled by the growing signs of the Baroque.

ST PANCRAS AND KING'S CROSS STATIONS

Next to the British Library towers a Victorian Gothic masterpiece, **St Pancras Station** (properly, St Pancras International; *map p. 633, E3*), from where Eurostar trains serve continental Europe. It opened in 1868 as the terminus connecting London with the Midlands and Yorkshire. The richly ornamented station front, with its clock tower facing Euston Road, is the former Midland Grand Hotel, by George Gilbert Scott, which opened in 1873 and was described as one of the most sumptuous hotels in the Empire. It lay neglected and empty for many years until in 2011 it finally reopened as the St Pancras Renaissance Hotel, restored to its former glory and now part of the Marriott's luxury collection. Inside is Gilbert Scott's grand staircase (guests only), which one may quickly peep at, and the Box Office 1869 bar-restaurant. Behind the hotel façade stretches the Victorian train shed by William Henry Barlow, and the new Eurostar terminal with further platforms serving UK destinations as well as shops, restaurants and Europe's longest champagne bar. Barlow's shed was one of the wonders of Victorian engineering, a 100ft-high glass and iron structure, 20ft above ground level and spanning 240ft, which at the time was the largest single-span roof in the world.

Next door, in contrast, **King's Cross Station**, built in the 1850s in yellow stock brick with large twin arches, appears deceptively diminutive. Appended to it is a modern concourse of 2012, topped with a hemidome. At the time of writing, a massive redevelopment project was underway in this area, once a deprived, run-down red light district, notorious for its high levels of homelessness, prostitution and drugs. The regeneration programme involves new houses, new streets and new public areas covering 67 acres of land, anciently a crossing on the river Fleet known as Battlebridge, north of (behind) the two stations. The *Guardian* and *Observer* newspapers now occupy multi-media suites and offices in King's Place, as do two of London's orchestras.

REGENT'S CANAL

North of St Pancras and King's Cross stations flows the Regent's Canal (*map p. 633, E2*), along which brightly-painted narrowboats, homes to their owners, are moored. The nine-mile canal, built in 1816–20, passes though Maida Vale, the Zoo at Regent's Park, Camden Town, Islington and Hackney to join the Thames at Limehouse. The **London Canal Museum** (*canalmuseum.org.uk*) in New Wharf Road is housed in the former house of Carlo Gatti, the Victorian entrepreneur who sold ice cream to the masses. It tells the story of London's waterways. There is good access for pedestrians and cyclists to the stretch of canal behind King's Cross, where a pleasant stroll can be taken along the towpath (there are cafés and restaurants too). Going east takes you towards Islington (although if going on foot, you have to leave the towpath when you reach the nearly 900m Islington Tunnel, and take the back streets). If you head northwest, you come to Camden, past the **Camley Street Natural Park**, an extraordinary 2-acre inner-city nature reserve where you might spot kingfishers and warblers. Boat trips can be taken on the canal (*see p. 578*), which is only four feet deep (non-swimmers need not fear).

ST PANCRAS OLD CHURCH

On Pancras Road, the continuation of Midland Road that runs between the British Library and St Pancras International, on a small grassy hillock—a site of great antiquity—stands the small, quaint St Pancras Old Church (*map p. 633, D2; stpancrasoldchurch.posp.co.uk*). Photographed from a certain angle, it looks like the country chapel it once was in the 17th century. In reality, it bravely stands its ground amidst new development, with high-speed Eurostar trains hurtling past its east end; despite this, it is a very tranquil, soothing spot. Of ancient origin, and nearly derelict by the 19th century, it was rebuilt in Victorian fashion. During rebuilding, workmen stumbled upon Elizabethan and Jacobean silver (booty stashed by Cromwell's troops during the Civil War) as well as the church's missing 6th-century altar stone.

In the churchyard is the **monument to Sir John Soane** (*see p. 221*), which takes the form of a central Grecian stele topped by a shallow convex roof (the inspiration for the red telephone box roof) and surmounted by a fircone. Also buried here (tall rectangular chest tomb) is Mary Wollstonecraft (d. 1792), author of *A Vindication of the Rights of Woman* and mother of Mary Shelley (author of *Frankenstein*). The twin slabs laid at a raked angle within railings are the graves of the Flaxman family. The famous '**Hardy Tree**' was an ancient ash that stood with a mass of headstones fanning around its base, seemingly growing amidst its roots. In actual fact, they were placed here during the 1860s, when the Midland Railway was being built over part of the churchyard. Tombs that were in the way were dismantled and their human remains exhumed under the direction of Arthur Blomfield. The tree, named after Thomas Hardy, who was Blomfield's assistant at the time (his first career, before he turned to literature, was as an architect) and who had a keen sense of the ghoulish, fell down in 2022.

LONDON CURIOSITIES

London is famous for its black taxicabs, its double-decker buses and for a handful of distinctive articles of street furniture: letter boxes, telephone kiosks (increasingly rare), boundary dragons, fire marks and commemorative plaques attached to housefronts.

As the use of postage stamps became widespread during the reign of Queen Victoria, people began to post their own letters in handily-positioned **letter boxes** erected for the purpose by the Royal Mail. The best known types, of which numerous examples survive, are the wall box and the pillar box. The latter is a free-standing cast-iron cylinder, painted bright red, typically with a crimped lid, and with the cypher of the reigning monarch embossed on the stem. 'VR' boxes are rare because of their age; 'EviiiR' examples even rarer because of the brevity of his reign.

The famous red **telephone boxes**, with their heavy and difficult-to-open doors, went through several design permutations since the first model in 1920. K2 was designed by Sir Giles Gilbert Scott in 1924. K6, designed in 1935, with a less articulated roof, became the most widespread. The roof was inspired by designs of Sir

Red telephone box, City of London boundary dragon, and fire mark denoting an insured property.

John Soane, who used the motif at Pitzhanger and for his own family tomb. Many old phone boxes have been purchased and preserved by private buyers.

The notion that passers-by will want to know who once resided in London's streets and squares is not a new one. The first **commemorative plaque** (to Sir Joshua Reynolds, in Leicester Square) went up in 1875. The most widespread type of plaque, of glazed clay coloured blue with a white border, belongs to the scheme administered by English Heritage. But plenty of other London councils operate their own schemes, with plaques variously coloured brown, red, green, blue and black. The City of London Corporation plaques are rectangular, composed of glazed tiles.

When people talk of the classic London **double-decker bus**, they are referring to the Routemaster, a model that first went into service in 1956. It was operated by a driver at the front, who had no contact with passengers, and a conductor in the bus itself, who went to and fro collecting fares. At the back was a hop-on, hop-off platform, making it easy to board or jump off wherever you chose (particularly welcome in frustratingly slow-moving traffic). Most of today's buses now stop only at designated bus stops and there are no conductors.

Early fire brigades in London were operated by insurance companies, who marked the properties covered by a policy by affixing their insignia to it. These embossed **fire insurance marks** can still be seen all over the city. Companies would only fight fires in properties which bore their mark.

All around the City of London, denoting its municipal border, **boundary markers** are placed. These take the form of cast-iron dragons rampant, painted silver and red, tongue extended and bearing the City shield. Look out for them, among other places, at Embankment, Temple Bar, Holborn, Broadgate, Aldgate and on London and Blackfriars bridges.

SMITHFIELD, CLERKENWELL & ISLINGTON

Islington, a district where North London can properly be said to begin, once lay on a drovers' road where cattle would come down from the countryside on their way to the great meat market at Smithfield. That market still operates, albeit on a reduced scale. Here too were the estates and priory of the Knights of the Order of St John, commemorated in the arterial St John Street. This is a part of the capital where the old City of London meets the earliest

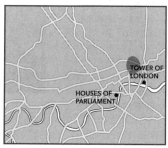

suburbs: lively areas with good places to eat give way to quieter residential streets and squares originally laid out for a newly prosperous 19th-century middle class, and threaded through with the patiently slow-flowing Regent's Canal.

Some highlights of the area

✦ The solemnly atmospheric **St Bartholomew the Great**, the most important Norman monument in London;

✦ Historic **Smithfield**, its market lively in the early morning, and some of its halls refitted to house the **Museum of London**.

ST BARTHOLOMEW'S & SMITHFIELD

Map p. 638, C2–B2. Underground: St Paul's, Barbican.

The street called **Little Britain** (*map p. 638, C2*) is where the poet John Milton lived in hiding after the Restoration in 1660. Off it is Bartholomew Close, where William Hogarth was born in 1697. At nos 87–88 is **Butchers' Hall** (1960), the livery hall of the Butchers' company. The block flanked by Little Britain and Giltspur Street is occupied by St Bartholomew's Hospital.

ST BART'S

St Bartholomew's Hospital (St Bart's; *map p. 638, C2*), a premier teaching and specialised treatment hospital, occupies the southeast side of Smithfield. It was founded, together with a priory for Augustinian canons, in 1123 by Rahere, a favourite courtier of Henry

The half-timbered St Bartholomew's gatehouse, leading through to West Smithfield.

I, in fulfilment of a vow made by him when on pilgrimage in Rome. Having fallen ill, Rahere had a vision of St Bartholomew and vowed to found a hospital for the poor on his return. It is the oldest charitable institution in London still extant on its original site. Dick Whittington, the famous mayor, bequeathed money for its repair in 1423. At the Dissolution, the priory was closed but the hospital was spared by Henry VIII, who granted it to the City and in 1547 endowed it with properties and income. Dr Roderigo Lopez became the hospital's first regular physician in 1567, later succeeded by Peter Turner (*see p. 86*). Lopez, a Portuguese Jew, was afterwards implicated in a plot against Elizabeth I and executed. It has been suggested that he was the inspiration for Shakespeare's Shylock. William Harvey, who discovered the circulation of the blood, was chief physician in 1609–43. In the 18th century a medical school was founded here and in 1877 a school of nursing. St Bart's was threatened with closure in the 1990s but was saved and now specialises in cancer and cardiac care.

The hospital buildings

The fine **Henry VIII Gateway**, where Giltspur Street meets West Smithfield, sports a statue of King Henry in a niche, standing in his characteristic swaggering pose, legs apart. It is the work of Edward Strong the Younger (1702) and is the oldest surviving part of the hospital. It was restored by Philip Hardwick in the 1830s. Just inside the gate (hard left) is the small octagonal church of **St Bartholomew the Less**, rebuilt (except for the striking 15th-century tower) in the 1790s by George Dance the Younger and restored in the 19th century by Thomas and Philip Hardwick. Inigo Jones was baptised here in 1573. Although the hospital itself escaped the Great Fire, the medieval buildings were demolished and the hospital rebuilt, in the name of medical modernity, as a quadrangle by James Gibbs, architect of St Martin-in-the-Fields, in 1730–69. Three out of Gibbs's four buildings survive. As you come through the gatehouse, straight ahead is his historic **North Wing** (1732). Pause in the archway and straight ahead again, the area with the fountain playing at the centre is what remains of the quadrangle; the two hospital wings left and right (east and west) were designed to house the hospital wards.

The museum and Hogarth paintings

The hospital has a small museum which is entered via the left-hand door under the North Wing archway (*open Tues–Fri 10–4, bartshealth.nhs.uk/bartsmuseum*). You can also view the grand staircase, hung with two vast paintings by William Hogarth, who was born nearby in Bartholomew Close and who donated them to the hospital. Both were painted in 1735–7. *The Pool of Bethesda* apparently features patients from the wards suffering from different sicknesses; the other painting depicts *The Good Samaritan*. (*Joining a guided tour gives you the chance to view the paintings in greater detail and to see more of this historic part of the hospital.*)

CLOTH FAIR

Cloth Fair, a tiny street skirting the north side of St Bartholomew's church, marks the site once occupied by the booths of drapers and clothiers at Bartholomew Fair. At nos 41 and 42, opposite the entrance to St Bartholomew's churchyard (*for the church, see below*), are fine examples of early 17th-century merchant's houses which have been well preserved and restored. The poet John Betjeman lived in Cloth Court (no. 43; blue plaque). At no. 1, just beyond St Bartholomew's churchyard, is **Founders' Hall**, belonging to the livery company of foundry workers. The company moved here in the 1980s from a site off Cannon Street. Their hall is decorated with cast-iron plaques.

At the far end of Cloth Fair, at no. 3 Cloth St, is the **livery hall of the Farmers and Fletchers** (Michael Twigg Brown, 1987).

ST BARTHOLOMEW THE GREAT

Map p. 638, C2. Free (donations welcome). Closed during services; greatstbarts.com.

The priory church of St Bartholomew the Great is the most important surviving 12th-century monument in London and is noted for its music. There are two approaches to it. From Cloth Fair, by the north side of the church, with its stone and flint chequerboard pattern and a statue of St Bartholomew with his flaying knife (the instrument of his martyrdom) above the door, is an entrance to the churchyard. From Little Britain, a small stone gateway with a half-timbered Tudor gatehouse above it—also adorned with a statue of St Bartholomew and his flaying knife—takes you down a passage to the main doorway beneath the church tower (with more flint and stone chequerboarding and yet another effigy of the saint and his knife).

On Good Friday, in accordance with a Victorian custom, 21 poor widows each received an old sixpence, which was laid on a flat tombstone in the churchyard here. The ceremony is now symbolic and the sixpences have been substituted by baskets of buttered hot cross buns, which are shared with the crowd who come to watch.

The brick entrance tower was built in 1628 to take the place of the tower over the crossing. The church has five pre-Reformation bells dating from 1510.

HISTORY OF ST BARTHOLOMEW'S
The church was part of a priory founded in 1123 by Rahere, a canon of St Paul's, and exists in fragment form. After the priory was dissolved in 1539, the Augustinian buildings and much of the church were pulled down or alienated, and of the original priory church only the choir, the crossing, one bay of the nave and the Lady Chapel remain. The stone gateway at the entrance to the churchyard was once the west door; another survival. The churchyard itself occupies the site of the nave (*see plan*). Restoration in the second half of the 19th century was mainly carried out by Sir Aston Webb, architect of the Victoria & Albert Museum.

Interior of St Bartholomew's
The shadowy, majestic choir of Rahere's priory church, with massive columns, piers and round arches, is in pure Norman style. The triforium is interrupted on the south side by **Prior Bolton's oriel window (a)**, added c. 1517 to communicate as a sort of

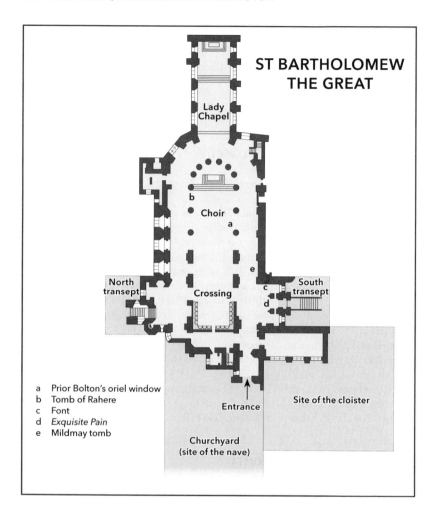

ST BARTHOLOMEW
THE GREAT

Lady
Chapel

b

Choir
a

e

North
transept · Crossing · c · South
transept
d

a Prior Bolton's oriel window
b Tomb of Rahere
c Font   Entrance   Site of the cloister
d *Exquisite Pain*
e Mildmay tomb

Churchyard
(site of the nave)

oratory with the prior's adjoining house. It bears Prior Bolton's rebus, a bolt and a tun (barrel). On the north side of the sanctuary is the early 15th-century **tomb of Rahere (b)** (d. 1143), founder of the church and hospital, with a coloured effigy beneath a rich canopy. Little is known of the facts of Rahere's life, though there are many legends about him and he appears as the king's jester in Rudyard Kipling's short story *The Tree of Justice*.

In the south transept stands the **font (c)** (c. 1405), one of only two pre-Reformation fonts in London, at which Hogarth (born nearby) was baptised in 1697. Next to it, on long loan to the church, is Damien Hirst's ***Exquisite Pain* (d)** (2006), a gilded statue of St Bartholomew, shown flayed and holding a scalpel. In the south aisle is the

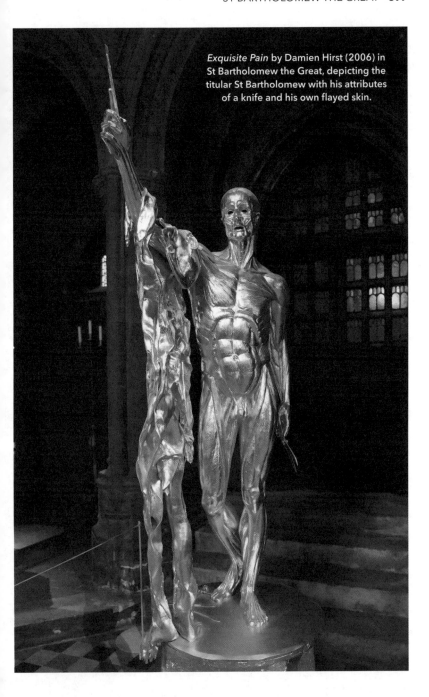

Exquisite Pain by Damien Hirst (2006) in St Bartholomew the Great, depicting the titular St Bartholomew with his attributes of a knife and his own flayed skin.

Prior Bolton's oriel window, in the church of St Bartholomew the Great, featuring the prelate's rebus, a play on his own name, consisting of a bolt shown piercing a tun (barrel).

alabaster **tomb of Sir Walter Mildmay** (d. 1589) **(e)**, founder of Emmanuel College, Cambridge, and his wife, Lady Mary Mildmay.

The **Lady Chapel**, the third on the site, was rebuilt in the 1890s. From 1539 it served variously as a private house, a printing press (where Benjamin Franklin worked in 1724) and as premises for lace and fringe makers until the property was bought back in 1885 and restored.

The **north transept** was a blacksmith's forge, where the clanging of hammer on anvil could be heard until 1884. Above the north transept screen is a 15th-century Florentine stucco *Virgin and Child*, probably from the workshop of Lorenzo Ghiberti.

What survives of the **cloister** (12th century, rebuilt c. 1405) was reconstructed in 1905–28. The arches in the wall mark the entrance to the former chapter house.

WEST SMITHFIELD

West Smithfield is an area that escaped both the Great Fire and the Blitz. Originally a spacious 'smoothfield' just outside the Roman city walls, it was used for events and tournaments. From 1133 until 1840 Smithfield was the scene of the annual Bartholomew Fair, horse and cloth fairs combined with several days of revelry, held around the feast of St Bartholomew (24th Aug), and until 1855 it was the chief live cattle market of London. It was also a place of execution. A memorial on the exterior wall of St Bartholomew's Hospital commemorates the Scottish patriot William Wallace, 'hanged, drawn and quartered' here in 1305. In 1381 the rebel Wat Tyler, leader of the Peasants' Revolt, was slain here by Sir William Walworth, the Mayor, in the presence of Richard II. Protestant martyrs were burnt at the stake here in the reign of Mary I.

Today the wide, circular space is surrounded by eateries and cafés. On the west side is the **Haberdashers' Hall** (2002) by the Hopkins partnership. In the centre are the Smithfield Rotunda Gardens, with a fountain and a figure of *Peace* by J.B. Philip (1873). The north side is filled with the elaborate building of the **old Central Meat Market** (Sir Horace Jones, 1867). A meat market has operated on this site for a thousand years and Smithfield is the only surviving wholesale meat market in Central London. It is also the largest in the country and one of the largest in Europe. Refrigerated lorries unload their carcases, which are then prepared by 'cutters' ready for selling from the very early morning. The market is open Mon–Fri and remains lively until midday, although most of the action is from 3am–9am. In Charterhouse Street, skirting the north side of the market, is the **Fox and Anchor** (*foxandanchor.com*), one of the many pubs with early opening hours. It has an Art Nouveau façade and serves a full breakfast from 7am. Many of the old warehouses that line the streets in this area have façades adorned with reliefs of livestock: bulls, sheep and cows. The market's future is uncertain, however, and calls for demolition, relocation and redevelopment continue to be made. At the time of writing, the Museum of London was preparing to move into the General Market Building.

THE MUSEUM OF LONDON
Closed at the time of writing while the site was being developed. museumoflondon.org.uk.
The Museum of London possesses over 1.1 million objects pertaining to the physical and social history of the city, from its origins in prehistory to the present day. At the time of writing the museum was in the process of moving to its new site in Smithfield. Selected highlights of the museum's holdings are given below.

Prehistory to the Middle Ages
Tools and ritual objects, some of them of exquisite craftsmanship, include flint hand axes and Mesolithic picks of a type known as the '**Thames pick**' from the sheer numbers of them dredged from London's river. **Roman Londinium** was at one time the largest city in Roman Britain. Artefacts include items of jewellery, sections of mosaic floor, three curses scratched on lead found in the drains of the Roman amphitheatre, and a famous pair of girl's leather underpants found at the bottom of an old well in Queen Street. Marble sculptures from the Temple of Mithras, discovered under Queen Victoria Street in 1954 (*see p. 44*), include a bust of Mithras dating to AD 180–220. Among the **Saxon artefacts** is a King Alfred the Great silver penny of c. 886. An 11th-century grave slab, beautifully carved with a lion and serpent in battle and with a Norse runic inscription, was possibly part of the tomb of an individual connected to the court of King Canute.

Items from **medieval London** demonstrate the cultural flowering of the capital and its extensive overseas mercantile links. There are a great many pilgrim badges, mementoes brought back from holy shrines, the most popular being that of St Thomas à Becket at Canterbury. A tangle of window leading from the vandalised stained glass of Merton Priory is a potent relic of the Reformation. The unquestionable highlight of the **Tudor collection** are the items from the astonishing **Cheapside Hoard**, over 230 pieces of jewellery recovered in 1912 from the site of Wakefield House, probably part of a goldsmith's trade stock.

From the Reformation to the modern metropolis
Artefacts from early Stuart and Reformation London include mortality bills from the time of the 1665 Great Plague. Oliver Cromwell's death mask is another highlight. As the city rose again from the ashes of the Great Fire, it became home to wealthy merchants and financiers, made rich through the great trading companies and the emerging financial market. The city developed into a centre for luxury trades, such as silk-weaving centred on Spitalfields. Alongside the wealth was great penury and hardship. The museum has a door from Newgate Prison, dating from c. 1780. Booth's poverty maps remind us that much of the East End was covered in slum tenements.

THE CHARTERHOUSE

The Charterhouse (*map p. 638, C1*), a charity and almshouse, occupies 16th–19th-century buildings behind a gatehouse off Charterhouse Square. A Carthusian priory was founded on the site in 1370 by Sir Walter de Manny, a distinguished soldier under Edward III. The monastery was brutally suppressed during the Dissolution and many monks were martyred at Tyburn (Marble Arch) before the priory surrendered. Sir Edward North, afterwards Lord North, to whom the property was granted in 1545, built a mansion on the site using material from the monastery buildings. It was sold to the Duke of Northumberland, who was executed in 1553 for his attempt to put Lady Jane Grey (his daughter-in-law) on the throne. Queen Elizabeth stayed here before her coronation in 1558. The property was considerably altered by a later owner, the 4th Duke of Norfolk, who was executed for complicity in a plot to put Mary, Queen of Scots on the throne. Elizabeth I paid further visits to the mansion (then known as Howard House). James I was entertained here by Thomas Howard, later Earl of Suffolk, to whom the property had passed in 1601. In 1611, the Charterhouse was bought for £13,000 by Thomas Sutton, a shrewd soldier, probably also a merchant-adventurer, who founded the 'Hospital of King James in Charterhouse'. This included a hospital for 80 poor brethren and a free school for 40 poor boys. The Charterhouse School rapidly developed into one of the best-known public schools in England and outgrew its premises. In 1872 it was transferred to Godalming in Surrey. Thackeray was a former, rather unhappy, pupil. From 1875 to 1933 the site of the school was occupied by the Merchant Taylors' School, founded in 1561 in Suffolk Lane, Upper Thames Street (this school is now at Moor Park, Hertfordshire).

One part of the Charterhouse is now let as private residences; the major part is used as a home for The Brothers, a community of single people over 60 from various professions in need of financial and social support. The Brothers (still known as such, though since 2018 there have been female members of the community) live privately but enjoy their meals together in the Great Hall—a little like the Carthusian brothers would have done when the house was first founded.

The Charterhouse may be visited on a private tour led by a qualified guide or by one of the Brothers. Tickets, which include visits to the chapel and small museum, must be pre-booked (*see thecharterhouse.org*).

CLERKENWELL

Map p. 638, B1. Underground: Farringdon.

Lively Clerkenwell, once a medieval monastic enclave, later a poor district on the edge of 'Little Italy' and close to Smithfield market, is now a fashionable and animated area, with designer offices and flats popularised and 'gentrified' by those in the arts and media and increasingly sought after by people with even bigger budgets. It has become

Mark Merer and Lucy Glendenning's cattle heads (1990s) on a building on Peter's Lane near Cowcross Street, a reference to the drovers and their herds who used to pass by here on their way to Smithfield Market.

a foodie destination too: delicious eating and fine-dining establishments abound. Former factories, warehouses and workshops have been converted into loft-style apartments, design studios, architects' practices, restaurants and bars. Many of these buildings have interesting façades.

Historically Clerkenwell is also associated with watch-making, jewellery and printing. From the 17th century several fine houses were built for merchants and the well-to-do. Among former residents were Izaak Walton (1650–61), Christopher Pinchbeck, inventor of the brass alloy that bears his name (1721), the Swedish theologian Emanuel Swedenborg and Oliver Cromwell.

Clerkenwell takes its name from the **Clerks' Well**, mentioned as early as 1174, around which the clerks of the parish used to perform miracle plays. The well survives and is housed inside Well Court (*14–16 Farringdon Lane*). It is visible through the plate glass but may be also be visited, free of charge, by appointment (*contact Islington Local History Centre, local.history@islington.gov.uk*).

THE FORMER HOSPITALLERS' PRIORY OF ST JOHN

On the south side of Clerkenwell Road is **St John's Gate** (*map p. 638, B1*), a castellated gatehouse spanning St John's Lane which once formed the main entrance to the Grand Priory of the Order of the Hospital of St John of Jerusalem (the Knights Hospitaller of the Crusades). Founded in the early 12th century, the Order was one of the last to be suppressed by Henry VIII (in 1540). The gatehouse was burnt down in Wat Tyler's Peasants' Revolt in the late 14th century and rebuilt in something resembling its present form by Prior Thomas Docwra in 1504. It was converted into the office of the Master of the Revels and later was variously the home of Hogarth; the offices of *The Gentleman's Magazine* (where Samuel Johnson worked); and the Old Jerusalem Tavern (where Dickens drank). In 1874 it was purchased by the British Order of St John (refounded as a Protestant Order in 1831) and now houses the **Museum of the Order of St John** (*museumstjohn.org.uk; free except tours*), exploring the history of the building, the Order of the Hospitallers in Jerusalem, Cyprus, Rhodes and Malta, and the work of St John's Ambulance. Among the exhibits is a 15th-century French limestone *St John the Baptist* and an 'Ashford litter' of 1910, an early form of hand-propelled ambulance, like an extended perambulator.

On the north side of Clerkenwell Road is another survival of the Hospitallers' tenure here, the **Priory Church of St John**, with an adjacent small garden, beautifully kept and planted with rosemary, acanthus and olives. The church served the Grand Priory (*see above*) since medieval times, though the building that stands today is an 18th-century reconstruction, incorporating the ancient choir walls. It has been restored since destruction in WWII. In the well-preserved 12th-century crypt is a fine 16th-century alabaster effigy of a knight of the Order, brought from Valladolid. **The Zetter** on St John's Square is a fine place for a cocktail (*thezetter.com*).

RADICAL CLERKENWELL AND CLERKENWELL GREEN

North of St John's church, Jerusalem Passage cuts through to St John's Square. The corner building at the top of the passage on the right stands on the site of the home of

Thomas Britton, the 'musical small-coal man', a charcoal vendor who fitted up his attic as a concert hall and held cramped but prestigious musical evenings every Thursday. It is rumoured that Handel was once among the company. Britton died in Clerkenwell in 1714, reputedly of fright after seeing a ventriloquist's act. His house is marked with a green plaque.

Historically, Clerkenwell has been associated with radicalism: during the 19th century Clerkenwell Green (*map p. 638, B1*), the old part of village Clerkenwell, became a political meeting place and the scene of Chartist marches. The house at no. 37A Clerkenwell Green (red door) was built in 1738 by James Steer as a Welsh charity school. The London Patriotic Society later based itself here until the Twentieth Century Press took up the lease for its Socialist printing works. William Morris and Eleanor Marx spoke here, and Lenin edited *Iskra* (1902–3). The **Marx Memorial Library** was established here in 1933 to commemorate the 50th anniversary of Marx's death and contains well over 100,000 books and manuscripts relating to Marxism, Socialism and the working class movement (*visitors are admitted as part of a tour; marx-memorial-library.org*).

Also on Clerkenwell Green, at no. 22, is the old **Middlesex Sessions Courthouse** (1779–82; red doors and railings), designed by Thomas Rogers with reliefs by Nollekens. It had a reputation for dispensing severe justice: in one year alone 200 people were convicted and transported to America and Australia. Nearby was a prison, the notorious House of Detention, constructed in the 17th century to relieve Newgate. Rebuilt in 1845, it became one of the busiest prisons in the capital.

In Clerkenwell Close is the parish church of **St James Clerkenwell**, with a steeple by James Carr (1788–91). It stands on the site of an early medieval nunnery. The church is open to visitors when the church office is open (*weekday office hours; ring doorbell for admittance*). The interior is very broad and fine, with an upper curved gallery. The monument to Thomas Crosse in the porch is by Roubiliac (1712).

To the left of the church, at **15 Clerkenwell Close**, is a striking block of flats composed of large squares outlined in raw quarried limestone and incorporating old columns and sections of mosaic (Amin Taha + Groupwork, 2017). Threatened with demolition shortly after it was built, it has since been reprieved.

Beyond Goswell Road, just north of Old Street, is the **deconsecrated church of St Luke** (*map p. 636, C1*) by John James, with an extraordinary fluted obelisk steeple by Hawksmoor (1727–33), a sort of proto-Shard. William Caslon (d. 1766), the typeface designer, is buried here, as is the architect George Dance the Elder (d. 1768). The church is now a music centre for the London Symphony Orchestra and is known as LSO St Luke's.

ON & AROUND HATTON GARDEN

Hatton Garden (*map p. 638, A1–A2*) is London's jewellery quarter. Diamond merchants, precious metal traders, jewellery wholesalers, retailers and dealers have clustered here since the 1870s. The street takes its name from the garden of a house made over to Sir

Christopher Hatton, Lord Chancellor under Queen Elizabeth I. His name lives on in the modern Sir Christopher Hatton pub at Waterhouse Square/Leather Lane.

At no. 5 Hatton Garden, a tablet between the first-floor windows, with a bas-relief portrait and a device of clasped hands, commemorates the residence of Giuseppe Mazzini, Italian patriot, who lived here in exile 1836 and re-founded his 'Young Italy' movement, aimed at securing national independence for his country. While in London, he befriended Thomas Carlyle (*see p. 355*).

ELY PLACE

Ely Place (1772; *map p. 638, B2*) occupies the site of the townhouse of the bishops of Ely. Queen Elizabeth I forced them to cede part of the property to Sir Christopher Hatton (at the yearly 'rent' of ten loads of hay, £10 and a single rose) but they regained it at the Restoration. The gardens were famous for their strawberries: in Shakespeare's *Richard III*, King Richard says to the Bishop of Ely, 'When I was last in Holborn, I saw good strawberries in your garden there. I do beseech you send for some of them (*Act III, Scene IV*). Part of Shakespeare's *Richard II* is also set here: John of Gaunt (who died here in 1399) makes his famous 'sceptred isle' speech from Ely Place. The street still officially belongs to the diocese of Ely in Cambridgeshire and it is not under the jurisdiction of the Metropolitan Police. It is closed at night and is guarded by its own uniformed watchmen, whose small lodge stands between the two sets of gates. Ye Olde Mitre Tavern in Ely Court was built in the 18th century on the site of a 16th-century inn. It is known for its good beer.

St Etheldreda's Church (*stetheldreda.com*), formerly the bishops' chapel, was founded here in 1290. The only surviving relic of the old bishops' house, it is the oldest Roman Catholic church in England (it returned to the Catholic rite in 1874) and has an atmosphere of serene and ancient sanctity, though much altered over the centuries, particularly following damage in the Blitz. The arcaded statue-niches in the walls and the tracery of the east and west windows are superb. The bright stained glass and statues of English martyrs are by Charles and May Blakeman (1952–64). The west window shows the five 'proto-martyrs' of English Catholicism, executed at Tyburn (*p. 323*) in 1535. Among their number is the prior of the nearby Charterhouse (*see p. 400*). The Blakemans also adorned the crypt with its fresco of the *Risen Christ*.

Ely Place leads into **Bleeding Heart Yard**, probably named from a tabernacle of the *Virgin of Sorrows* which once stood here but latterly the subject of an urban myth concerning a certain Lady Elizabeth Hatton, found murdered here with her heart torn out in the early 17th century.

ST PETER'S CHURCH

After 1863, when the Italian church of St Peter's (*italianchurch.org.uk; map p. 638, A1*) was built on Clerkenwell Road, the area came to be known as 'Little Italy'. Caruso performed here and Garibaldi was a visitor in 1864. The church, designed by the Irish architect Sir John Miller-Bryson, is modelled internally on the basilica of San Crisogono in Rome. It has the same system of a clerestory above the side aisles, supported by an Ionic colonnade. The Italian flavour of the district is now a thing of the past, though every year in mid-July a street procession in honour of Our Lady of Mount Carmel begins from St Peter's church. When it was first held in the 19th century, it was thought to be the first open-air Catholic celebration to take place in this country since the Reformation.

MOUNT PLEASANT AND EXMOUTH MARKET

Mount Pleasant (*map p. 638, A1*) is home to what was once the largest postal sorting office in the United Kingdom, built in 1900 on the site of the Coldbath House of Correction, a prison from 1794–1877. Partly still used as a post office and partly redeveloped for residential use, the site also includes a Postal Museum (*entrance on Phoenix Place; postalmuseum.org*), which features a ride on the so-called Mail Rail.

On the corner of Pine Street and Vineyard Walk, with one flank on Northampton Road (*map p. 633, F3*), is the Modernist **Finsbury Health Centre** (by Berthold Lubetkin/Tecton, 1935–8; their first public commission). **Exmouth Market**, a lively, semi-pedestrian street near the junction of Farringdon Road and Rosebery Avenue, is lined with bars and restaurants. Spa Fields, between Exmouth Market and Northampton Road, recalls the area's richness in water: Londoners would come for relaxation and treatments at Clerkenwell's many spas, which were built over natural mineral springs.

On the corner of Rosebery Avenue and Rosoman Street is the red-brick neo-Renaissance **Old Finsbury Town Hall** (1895).

ISLINGTON, BARNSBURY, CANONBURY & HIGHBURY

Map pp. 629 and 633. Underground: Angel, King's Cross St Pancras, Caledonian Road, Highbury & Islington. Overground: Caledonian Road & Barnsbury, Highbury & Islington, Canonbury.

'Up and down the City Road, in and out the Eagle, That's the way the money goes, Pop! goes the weasel.' The well-known verse of the old nursery rhyme is thought to refer to drinking at the Eagle tavern and then pawning ('popping') one's belongings. The wide **City Road** (*map p. 629, D2*) still runs past the Eagle tavern, immortalised in the song, though it is now dwarfed by the huge glass residential towers springing up around the Regent's Canal and its two basins, City Road Basin (1820; home of the Islington Boat Club) and Wenlock Basin. City Road ends at the Angel (a busy road junction named after another famous tavern, the long-demolished Angel coaching inn. This is where Islington begins.

Historically, Islington was a rural area where cattle were rested before being driven to market at Smithfield. In the 18th century it had become a pleasant countryside suburb near to Sadler's Wells spa and in the 19th it was developed with elegant terraces and squares and became a place where middle-class City workers lived, due to its proximity to the offices where they were employed. The area became overcrowded

View of the Regent's Canal from the bridge under Danbury Street, looking towards the entrance to the City Road Basin.

and less salubrious later in the 19th century, when the building of the railway at nearby King's Cross displaced large sections of a poor, working-class population, who overflowed into Islington. It was not until the 1960s, when an arty, predominantly left-wing intelligentsia began to rediscover Islington's attractions, that its houses began to be renovated. Today parts of the area are still poor, but on the whole it is a trendy, lively district with plenty of bars, restaurants and shops in its gentrified Georgian streets and squares.

ON AND AROUND THE ANGEL JUNCTION

On the Angel junction stands the late 19th-century former Angel Hotel, with a distinctive dome. South of the junction, on Rosebery Avenue, is **Sadler's Wells** (*sadlerswells.com*), a leading theatre for contemporary dance. The current purpose-built building opened in 1998 and incorporates an earlier 1930s' theatre. The first music hall, built in 1683 by Richard Sadler, was built around a medicinal well on this site. Opposite it, between Rosebery Avenue and St John Street, is the **Spa Green Estate** by Tecton, inventive multi-storey apartment blocks built over a former slum, designed before World War Two but not completed until 1950. The **Laboratory Building** at 177 Rosebery Avenue (1938), built for the Metropolitan Water Board, is now flats.

AROUND THE COURSE OF THE NEW RIVER

Running due north from Angel station is **Upper Street** (*map p. 629, D2*), lined with shops and restaurants, leading to Highbury and Holloway Road. Turn right off Upper Street down Duncan Street to reach **Duncan Terrace** and **Colebrooke Row**, attractive 18th-century streets which were developed to run either side of the **New River** (its course here indicated by the garden in front of Duncan Terrace; it was culverted in the 1890s). This man-made waterway, 10ft wide and 3ft deep, opened in 1613 to supply London with fresh drinking water from springs in Hertfordshire and Middlesex. It still supplies London with water, now treated before drinking, and flows from Hertford into reservoirs at Stoke Newington. Originally the New River terminated near the Sadler's Wells Theatre, where a play was staged in 1613 to mark its opening. It is still possible to walk along large sections of the New River, via the New River Path. At 64 Duncan Terrace lived the essayist Charles Lamb in 1823; his friend George Dyer, on leaving his house one day, fell into the New River and nearly drowned.

Where Duncan Street opens into Colebrooke Row, a ramp leads down to the **Regent's Canal Walk**. Here the canal enters the longest tunnel on its route, 960 yards, completed in 1818. There is no towpath and the towing horses were led along the stretch that is now Chapel Market while the bargees propelled their boats by 'legging': lying on their backs and pushing against the tunnel wall with their feet. A steam tug was introduced in 1826 and used until the 1930s. The canal emerges from the tunnel at Muriel Street near Caledonian Road (*map p. 633, F2*) and continues to Camden Town, Regent's Park and Paddington.

AROUND ISLINGTON GREEN

Camden Passage, a narrow pedestrian street running parallel with Upper Street on the right-hand side, has a mix of permanent shops and an antiques market with stalls on certain days. It leads into Essex Street, on the other side of which is the green triangle of **Islington Green**. In front of its narrow tip is a statue of Sir Hugh Myddleton (d. 1631), chief promoter of the New River. The statue is by John Thomas (1862). On Essex Road itself, on the corner of River Place (nos 161–169), is the Art Deco former **Carlton Cinema** (1930), now the Gracepoint church and meeting house. The building, by George Coles, is in the form of an Egyptian pylon temple, decorated with multi-coloured ceramic tiling.

Off Upper Street on the west, Berners Road leads to the **Business Design Centre**, an events venue partly housed in the former Royal Agricultural Hall. With its curved glass roof, it was built for cattle shows in 1861.

Further north on Upper Street, at no. 115 (left), is the **King's Head Pub and Theatre** (*kingsheadtheatrepub.co.uk*). Performances are held in a back room behind the bar, formerly a boxing ring. On the opposite side of the road, on the corner of Gaskin Street, is the red-brick Arts and Crafts former Islington Chapel (c. 1887). Next door is Islington's parish church of St Mary, with an 18th-century tower. The rest was rebuilt in the 1950s after serious war damage. At the rear are public gardens; in Dagmar Passage is the Little Angel Theatre, a puppet theatre for children.

The sphinxes of Richmond Avenue.

BARNSBURY, CANONBURY AND HIGHBURY

BARNSBURY

The residential area of attractive 19th-century streets between Upper Street and Caledonian Road is known as Barnsbury (*map p. 633, F1–F2*). Much rich architectural detail can be seen in Richmond Avenue, Thornhill Crescent, Thornhill Square and Barnsbury Square, all built in the 1820s–40s. **Richmond Avenue**, in particular, is noted for its houses adorned by pairs of guardian sphinxes, with stumpy obelisks behind them engraved 'Nile'. The reference is to Nelson's victory over the French at the Battle of the Nile in 1798. **Mountford Crescent**, looping out of Barnsbury Square (*map p. 633, F1*), has bow-fronted 1830s' stuccoed villas. **Barnsbury Wood** is an unexpected tiny plot of inner-city forest, a miniature nature reserve on the site of land once owned by the Thornhill family. The Kentish ragstone **church of St Andrew**, in Thornhill Square, was built in 1854 when the Thornhill family parcelled up their land, formerly occupied by dairy farms, for housing.

In the middle of Cloudesley Square (*map p. 633, F2*) stands an earlier church, the Gothic Revival **Holy Trinity** (1829) by Charles Barry, architect of the Houses of Parliament; it is based on King's College Chapel, Cambridge. **Lonsdale Square**, north of Cloudesley Square, was built collegiate-style in 1838–45 by R.C. Carpenter. To the west, **Gibson Square**, dating from the 1830s, has a long central garden, the housefronts at its corners articulated by giant orders of pilasters. In the garden is a ventilation shaft for the Victoria Line, disguised as a Neoclassical temple. Of **Milner Square** (Roumieu and Gough, 1838–44), the architecture historian John Summerson remarked, 'you still could not be absolutely certain that you have seen it anywhere but in an unhappy dream.' The design of long brick pilasters with squeezed-looking narrow windows between them is certainly original; proportionally a little strange. Beside no. 21, Almeida Passage leads to Almeida Street (*map p. 629, D2*); the **Almeida Theatre** was built by Roumieu and Gough as Milner Square's Literary and Scientific Institute.

ON AND AROUND CANONBURY SQUARE

Immediately north of the junction with Upper Street and Canonbury Lane (*map p. 629, D2*) is **Compton Terrace**, an attractive row of early 19th-century houses separated from Upper Street by their gardens. In the middle of the terrace, in Compton Avenue, is the dominatingly incongruous, red-brick neo-Gothic **Union Chapel** (James Cubitt, 1876–7); it is still a working church but also a music venue and a drop-in centre for the homeless (*unionchapel.org.uk*). To the east is **Canonbury Square**, with tall, very handsome townhouses built in 1805–30 around a central garden. Evelyn Waugh and George Orwell were former residents, in the 1920s and 1940s respectively, when the area was down-at-heel; it is far from that now. Along the north side, at no. 39A (Northampton Lodge), is the **Estorick Collection of Modern Italian Art** (*Underground: Highbury & Islington and 10mins walk; estorickcollection.com*), the finest assemblage of early 20th-century Italian art outside Italy. It was formed by the American-born sociologist, writer and art dealer Eric Estorick (d. 1993) and his wife Salome Dessau (d.1989), who began to collect Futurist works on their honeymoon in Switzerland and on their return to England via Milan. Futurism was launched in 1909 when the poet Filippo Tommaso Marinetti published his radical manifesto in *Le Figaro*. Turning its back on Italian heritage and tradition, the movement aimed to be the herald of a new century of technology, industry, energy, speed, action and dynamism. The Estorick has works by Umberto Boccioni, Carlo Carrà, Luigi Russolo, Giacomo Balla and Gino Severini. Chief among the paintings on display are Carrà's *Leaving the Theatre* (1910–11), Boccioni's *Modern Idol* (1911) and Balla's *The Hand of the Violinist* (1912). The collection also contains works by other well-known Italian modern artists, including De Chirico, Modigliani and Giorgio Morandi.

On the east side of the square rises **Canonbury Tower**, with attached buildings in swamp-green stucco. This red-brick 16th-century square tower, 66ft high, is the oldest building in the area, a relic from an ecclesiastical building built for Prior Bolton of St Bartholomew the Great in Smithfield (*p. 395*). After the Dissolution of the Monasteries, occupants of the manor house included Thomas Cromwell, Earl of Essex and John Dudley, Earl of Warwick. It was leased to Sir Francis Bacon in 1616–25 and Oliver Goldsmith lodged in rooms in the tower in the 1760s. The interior, with surviving period features, may be seen as part of a pre-booked guided tour (*islingtonguidedwalks.com*).

Beside the Tower, at the top of Alwyne Villas, is the attractive, late 18th-century Canonbury House and in **Canonbury Place**, a little cul-de-sac leading left, is a group of 1770s' villas in celadon green stucco (nos 1–5), built over the southern part of Prior Bolton's building. Weedon Grossmith, co-author of *Diary of a Nobody*, lived at no. 1.

Larger, Italianate villas on Alwyne Road overlook a stretch of the New River. From Canonbury Grove on the other side, you can join the **New River Walk** pathway, which passes alongside this original section of the channel; it is lush and green and overhung with trees.

HIGHBURY

Highbury (*map p. 629, D2*), once woodland belonging to the Knights Hospitallers, whose priory was a short way further south (*p. 402*), was developed from the 18th century as an entity distinct from both Islington and Canonbury; it has some very attractive streets.

Straight over Highbury Corner (the roundabout), leaving Highbury & Islington station and Holloway Road on your left, you come to **Highbury Fields**, an ancient open space saved from development in the 1880s by the Metropolitan Board of Works; it is surrounded by handsome late 18th-century terraces. Above the fields to the north is **Highbury Hill**, with an attractive little clock-tower at its centre, erected in 1897 to mark the Diamond Jubilee of Queen Victoria.

Highbury Square, near Arsenal Underground station, is the historic former home ground of Arsenal Football Club, one of the richest and most successful premier league clubs in the UK. After the club moved to their new stadium (the Emirates; *see below*), their original ground was turned into luxury flats incorporating the two listed Art Deco stands; the pitch has been landscaped into a garden.

The **Emirates Stadium**, with a capacity of 60,000, opened in Ashburton Grove in 2006, sponsored by Emirates Airlines. It is home to Arsenal Football Club, founded in 1886 by workers from the Royal Arsenal armaments factory in Woolwich (*see p. 573*) and known familiarly as the Gunners. When the team moved here, they asked the Royal Artillery Museum for two guns manufactured at the Royal Arsenal to stand guard outside the entrance. They are still there beside the roundabout.

REGENT'S PARK & CAMDEN

This area of north London, bisected by the Regent's Canal, includes green spaces that are reminders of its once-rural remoteness, to which their picturesque names (Primrose Hill, St John's Wood) still bear testimony. Here you will find London Zoo, the famous Lord's Cricket Ground, the equally famous zebra crossing which the Beatles famously trod, and the sprawling markets along Camden Lock.

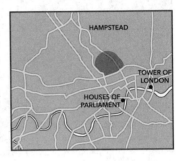

Some highlights of the area

+ **Regent's Park**, almost 500 acres of field and fountain, lawn and lake, incorporating **London Zoo**;
+ **Camden Market**, lively and crowded.

REGENT'S PARK & ITS NEIGHBOURHOOD

Map p. 632, B3. Underground: Regent's Park, Baker Street, Great Portland Street for the park itself; Camden Town for London Zoo. Park open daily 5am–dusk. Boats and pedalos can be hired April–Oct. Deckchairs for hire March–Oct. Numerous cafés. Performances in the Open-Air Theatre May–Sept. royalparks.org.uk.

Regent's Park, properly 'The Regent's Park', is a roughly square expanse of just under 500 acres, incorporating London Zoo. Originally known as Marylebone Park, it was appropriated by Henry VIII from the lands of Barking Abbey and turned into a royal hunting ground. It continued as such until Cromwell's day, when it was partially deforested. The Commonwealth government sold the timber to pay its debts from the Civil War. It was laid out in its present style as an aristocratic 'garden suburb' from 1812 by Nash, and it takes its name from the Prince Regent, son of George III, who contemplated building a country house here. Of Nash's projected 56 villas, only eight were ever built, and today only two remain standing: St John's Lodge and The Holme.

The park is encircled by a carriage road known as the Outer Circle, much of which is flanked by fine monumental Regency terraces in the classical style, mainly by Nash. In the southwest part of the park is the Boating Lake (with many water birds), while to the north runs the Regent's Canal, laid out by Nash in the 1820s. It links the London docks

Regent's Park in spring.

with the Grand Union Canal and was once a significant waterway, used for shipments of building materials and of imported goods from the docks. The well-kept greensward covering the greater part of Regent's Park is used as sports pitches. Also here is Regent's University, a postgraduate college. In mid-October the park hosts the Frieze Art Fair, a leading contemporary art show (*frieze.com*).

QUEEN MARY'S GARDENS
Queen Mary's Gardens, perfectly round and bounded by the carriage drive known as the Inner Circle, were occupied from 1840 to 1932 by the Royal Botanic Society. Their main entrance is through the grand Jubilee Gates on York Bridge. The gates were set up to commemorate the Silver Jubilee of George V in 1935 and the gardens are named after Queen Mary, his consort. They contain a famous rose garden (which includes the 'Royal Parks' variety), the Delphinium Border and Begonia Garden, in the centre of which is a statue of a boy with a frog by Sir William Reid Dick. The Open-Air Theatre is also here (*for programmes and tickets, see openairtheatre.com*).

West of the gardens, beyond the Inner Circle, is **The Holme**, one of the stately villas projected for the park by Nash. It was built by Nash's pupil Decimus Burton in 1818–19. When it was put on the market in 2023 (for £300m) it was described as London's most valuable house. **St John's Lodge** (1812), another Nash villa, is a private residence owned at the time of writing by a member of the Brunei royal family.

THE LONDON CENTRAL MOSQUE AND WINFIELD HOUSE

Hanover Gate (*map p. 632, A3*), which bears the name of the royal house to which the Prince Regent belonged, was once of the entrances to Regent's Park. Its gatehouse or lodge still stands. The Islamic Cultural Centre close by was opened by George VI in 1944. Adjoining it is the **London Central Mosque** (1978), its central prayer hall surmounted by a spectacular golden dome and lit by a monumental chandelier. Its architect was Frederick Gibberd, who is known for a number of other visually striking buildings, including Liverpool Metropolitan Cathedral ('Paddy's Wigwam').

H.G. Wells (1866–1946) lived and died at no. 13 Hanover Terrace, and Ralph Vaughan Williams lived at no. 11 from 1953–8.

Winfield House, on the Outer Circle (*map p. 632, A3*), stands on the site of Nash's Hertford Villa. In 1936 it was purchased by the American heiress Barbara Hutton, who pulled it down and commissioned Wimperis, Simpson and Guthrie (architects of Fortnum & Mason) to build this, which has the largest private garden in London after Buckingham Palace. It is now the residence of the US Ambassador.

View of the London Central Mosque from Hanover Gate. Its gilded dome surmounts a vast central prayer hall. The chandelier suspended from its ceiling is a prominent beacon, shining through the tall windows.

The Royal College of Physicians building by Denys Lasdun (1964).

EAST OF THE PARK

On the east side of the park, off the Outer Circle at the south end in St Andrew's Place, is the **Royal College of Physicians** (*map p. 632, C3*), occupying a striking, top-heavy modern building by Denys Lasdun (1964), architect of the National Theatre. It stands on the site of a Nash villa that was demolished following bomb damage in the Second World War. Demolition proceeded 'on the condition that the new building would harmonise with its surroundings'—and *voilà*! The flower beds outside it contain plants of the world associated with medicine. You can see something of the interior of the building when visiting the **College of Physicians' Museum** (*history.rcplondon.ac.uk*), which has a permanent collection of medical instruments, pharmacy jars, portraits (including one of William Harvey, best known for his description of the circulation of the blood). The museum also has six anatomical tables, similar to those kept at the Hunterian Museum (*see p. 221*), which were made in Padua (where Harvey qualified as Doctor of Medicine in 1602) in the 17th century, from bodies dissected at the anatomy theatre there, and show the intricate pathways of the human nervous and venous systems. The tables came to the College from the Earl of Winchilsea, an ancestor of whose had married Harvey's niece.

Also off the Outer Circle, further north, the neo-Gothic **St Katharine's church** (*map p. 632, C2*) has, since 1952, been the church of the Danish community in London (*danskekirke.org*). Before that it housed the St Katharine's Foundation, displaced from the East End (*see p. 123*).

LONDON ZOO

Map p. 632, B2. londonzoo.org.

London Zoo, one of the oldest zoos in the world, occupies the northern end of Regent's Park and is officially the Zoological Society of London (ZSL). It is a thriving concern and has adapted well to changing attitudes to keeping wild animals in captivity. ZSL is a respected international scientific and educational body: it has bred and released into the wild animals from 650 species, 112 of which are threatened. ZSL also works to preserve fragile habitats. Its sister zoo, Whipsnade in Bedfordshire (opened 1928), has wide open spaces for the larger animals.

HISTORY OF LONDON ZOO

The Zoological Society of London was founded by Sir Stamford Raffles and Sir Humphry Davy in 1826; when the Zoological Gardens opened in five acres of Regent's Park in 1828, it was only Fellows of the Zoological Society who were admitted. The general public was admitted in 1847 and the Zoo became a fashionable and very popular day out. London Zoo pioneered the exhibiting of exotic animals; it had the world's first reptile house, the first hippo seen in Europe, the first aquarium and the first insect house. It was also home to species which have since become extinct, including the quagga, a zebra sub-species native to South Africa that was ruthlessly hunted by white settlers. Several quaggas were sent to zoos but the creatures did not thrive and breeding programmes were unsuccessful: it was extinct in the wild by 1878 and extinct in captivity by 1883. London Zoo had three quaggas between 1831 and 1872. Five photographs, all taken at the Zoo, are believed to be of the second animal (her skin is now in the National Museums of Scotland and her skeleton at Yale). The skin of the Zoo's first quagga (d. 1834) is in the National History Museum in London. In 1931, the menagerie of animals kept in the Tower of London was presented to the Zoological Society and re-housed here. Today the Zoo does valuable conservation work, particularly with creatures threatened with extinction, and is continually updating its facilities to ensure the greatest possible comfort for its myriad inhabitants.

The Zoo has an interesting collection of animal buildings by leading architects, beginning with Decimus Burton, who laid out the original grounds. Surviving Burton buildings include the **Clock Tower** for the llama hut (1828, rebuilt; now a First Aid centre), the ravens' cage (1829; empty), the East Tunnel (1829–30; used as a bomb shelter during WWII). Burton's **Giraffe House** (1836–7), with 16ft doors and 21ft ceilings, is the only animal building serving its original purpose. The **Mappin Terraces** (1913–14), a mountainous landscape in reinforced concrete for bears, by Sir Peter Chalmers Mitchell and J.J. Joass, currently have emus and wallabies; underneath is the Aquarium (1923–4). The **Reptile House**, with carved snake detail, dates from 1926–7 (though the reptiles and amphibians were given new accommodation in 2024). The **Round House** (1932–3) is a Modernist gorilla house by Berthold Lubetkin's practice, Tecton; it now houses nocturnal creatures. Also by Tecton is the **Penguin Pool** (1934), the Zoo's most celebrated piece of architecture, currently unused because the penguins enjoy a bigger, deeper pool and beach elsewhere. The **aviaries**, by Lord Snowdon (1962–4), pioneered the use of aluminium and tension support and are well seen from Regent's Canal. Sir Hugh Casson designed the **Elephant and Rhino Pavilion** (1962–5), heavy and solid in textured concrete with green lanterns; these animals are now kept at Whipsnade.

The Zoo has had numerous celebrated residents. Guy the Gorilla, who arrived clutching a hot water bottle in 1947 and died in 1978, is commemorated by a sculpture. Winnie, an American black bear, lived at the Zoo from 1914. She came to the Zoo when her Canadian soldier owner went to fight in the trenches in France. She became the inspiration for A.A. Milne's stories of Winnie the Pooh and was visited here by the author with his son, Christopher Robin.

PRIMROSE HILL AND ST JOHN'S WOOD

Map p. 632, B2–A2. Underground: Camden Town, Chalk Farm, St John's Wood.

Primrose Hill was once as bucolic as its name suggests. William Blake writes of 'FIELDS from Islington to Marybone, to Primrose Hill and Saint John's Wood.' Today these areas are mainly covered by ROADS but Primrose Hill is still well-endowed with parkland and is lovely to visit: from the top of the hill (250ft) there is a fine view of London. Every September, white-robed druids congregate here to celebrate the autumn equinox (they celebrate the vernal equinox on Tower Hill and the summer solstice at Stonehenge). In the 1990s the 'Primrose Hill Set' was a group of locally-resident actors who collaborated on various projects. The area has many residents from the fields of literature and the media. Cecil Sharp House (2 *Regent's Park Rd*) is home to the English Folk Dance and Song Society (*efdss.org*) and the Vaughan Williams Memorial Library, the national collection of English folk music. A good place to eat is the popular and long-established Greek taverna Lemonia at 89 Regent's Park Rd (*www.lemonia.co.uk*).

ST JOHN'S WOOD

St John's Wood takes its name from the Knights of St John of Jerusalem, who owned the area when it was still thickly forested. Today it is residential, its streets lined with large and costly villas: the district's postcode (NW8) is one of the priciest in the city. St John's Wood is the home of the Marylebone Cricket Club (MCC), founded by Thomas Lord in 1787 (*see Dorset Square, p. 306*). **Lord's Cricket Ground** is here (*map p. 632, A3*) and has a museum with displays that all cricket fans will appreciate, such as gear worn by Donald Bradman. The famous Ashes Urn (the trophy that is battled over by England and Australia) is also housed here (*museum open on days when there is no match; lords.org*). Tours of the cricket ground can also be booked (*see website for details*).

On the Lord's Roundabout is the **church of St John** (Thomas Hardwick, 1814). It was here that a fanatic named Joanna Southcott, prophet and writer (1750–1814), was buried. In the last year of her life she declared herself pregnant with the new Messiah (Shiloh), for which she was ridiculed in the popular press, prompting Rowlandson's vulgar cartoon 'A Medical Inspection, or, Miracles Will Never Cease' showing her lifting her skirts to be examined by doctors.

The Beatles recorded their 1969 album *Abbey Road* (*map p. 628, C2*) at the eponymous studios; the pedestrian crossing on which the band were photographed for the album cover is a magnet for fans. Sir Paul McCartney still owns property in the area. Close by, at 108A Boundary Road, is the **Ben Uri Gallery** (*benuri.org.uk*), founded in Whitechapel in 1915 and home to a superb collection of art by European Jewish artists or artists of Jewish ancestry: Kitaj, Epstein, Chagall, Mark Gertler, Leon Bakst, Naum Gabo and many others. One of the founders of the gallery was the charismatic Mosheh Oved, owner of the extraordinary Cameo Corner, a shop on Bloomsbury's Museum Street, which sold all manner of antiques, curios, watches, *objets d'art*, Fabergé and jewellery. Oved typically appeared gowned in a velvet caftan with a huge cabochon amethyst pendant. In his shop's pre-World War Two heyday, its eclectic mix of customers included Nancy Cunard, Marghanita Laski, Jacob Epstein and Queen Mary (when her Daimler glided down the street, a moth-eaten red carpet would be rolled from the shop to the car door in homage).

CAMDEN

Map pp. 632, C2–633, D2. Underground: Camden Town, Mornington Crescent, Chalk Farm. Overground: Camden Road.

Camden Town, usually known simply as Camden, lies northeast of Regent's Park. It is a boisterous area, full of contradictions.

HISTORY OF CAMDEN

Camden takes its name from the landowner Charles Pratt, 1st Earl Camden (d. 1794) and was speculatively developed for housing from the late 18th century. By the 19th century its identity was shaped by industry: the Regent's Canal at its northern border opened in 1818–20 and in the 1830s the London and Birmingham Railway was built. Camden became 'the tradesman's entrance to the capital' and an important goods depot. Here working-class and immigrant communities settled, employed by the warehouses and factories lining the banks of the canal and spending their leisure time in the numerous music halls and pubs. Buildings which had initially been built for middle-class families became run-down, shabby and overcrowded. Camden was considered an underprivileged and unfashionable area at least until the mid-20th century.

Camden, on one hand, is venerated by counter-culture mavens for the live music that buzzes in the noisy bars, pubs and clubs; on the other, its sprawling network of markets along Camden Lock and Chalk Farm Road cater to something increasingly mainstream, providing a bucket-list destination for thousands of visitors who arrive each weekend in chaotic search for inspiration amongst the 'vintage' clothes, bric-à-brac, jewellery and junk, at the same time sampling what the food market has cooked up. Camden's grubby urban exterior may have smartened up in the past few years, and there may be more middle-class chain-shops in the High Street, but there is still a distinctly grungy throb at its heart. A step away from the melting pot of tourists, students, media-types and would-be Indie-kids, an altogether more dignified, bohemian feel is found in the side streets and at the peripheries. Here too, alongside belts of post-war social housing, are some very attractive streets and mews, home to respected figures in the arts.

ON AND AROUND CAMDEN HIGH STREET

Just south of Mornington Crescent Underground station (*map p. 633, D2*), on Hampstead Road, is the bright white neo-Egyptian **former Carreras 'Black Cat' Cigarette Factory** (Collins and Porri, c. 1926). The large black cats (restored) are in homage to the ancient Egyptian cult of cat-worship. The building is now Greater London House, offering 'warehouse-style' offices. Behind is **Mornington Crescent**, built in the 1820s; the artist Walter Sickert, founder of the Post-Impressionist Camden Town Group (*see below*), lived at no. 6.

THE CAMDEN TOWN GROUP

The Camden Town Group of Post-Impressionist artists staged three exhibitions between 1911 and 1913. Three of the painters most closely associated with the group are Spencer Gore, Harold Gilman and Walter Sickert. Their aim was to depict the real lives of the working class: Gilman's *Mrs Mounter at the Breakfast Table* (1917), showing a tight-faced elderly woman, wrapped in a shawl and with her hair bound in an orange headscarf, looking steadily out from behind a large brown teapot, is one such example. Another is *The Fried Fish Shop* (1907) by Stanislawa de Karlowska (not officially a Camden Town artist—women were barred from membership—but married to a member, Robert Bevan). Sickert's famous *Camden Town Murder* series, showing a naked woman stretched on a cheap bed with a fully-clothed man standing or sitting beside it, caused much comment and even led to rumours linking Sickert with the Jack the Ripper killings (though the artist never used the word 'murder' in his titles). Spencer Gore had a more vivid palette than some of the other artists, and many of his works were painted not in the studio but as *plein-air* studies, filled with warmth and sunlight. In 1913 the group joined forces with other artists, including a number of Vorticists, to challenge the precepts of the Royal Academy. Works by Camden Town Group artists can be seen at Tate Britain and in Fenton House (Hampstead).

Twin figures of Bastet, the ancient Egyptian cat-goddess, stand guard outside the former Carreras cigarette factory on Hampstead Road (c. 1926).

From the top of Hampstead Road, Camden High Street leads north to Camden Town. At the beginning of the street on the right is the **former Camden Palace** (1900), an old music hall with a green copper dome, now the live music venue KOKO. Here too is a statue of Richard Cobden, Liberal reformer and co-founder of the anti-Corn Law League. The statue was erected in the late 1860s, shortly after Cobden's death. Made of Sicilian marble, it is very badly worn, the face now little more than a ghoulish mask.

Three main roads leading north have their starting point at Camden Town Underground. Camden High Street (Chalk Farm Road) leads to Hampstead. Kentish Town Road (always choked with traffic) leads to the neighbouring suburbs of Kentish Town, Tufnell Park and Archway. Camden Road leads to Holloway and Holloway Road. The house at **39 Hilldrop Crescent**, west off the Camden Road (*just beyond map p. 633, D1*), is where the homeopath Dr Crippen is said to have disposed of the remains of his murdered wife.

ALBERT STREET AND OVAL ROAD

Parallel to Camden High Street is Albert Street (*map p. 632, C2*), with early Victorian terraced housing. Here at nos 129–31 is the **Jewish Museum** (*jewishmuseum.org. uk*), which traces the history of the Jewish community in Britain from 1066 (when William the Conqueror invited the Jews of Rouen to settle in London) and displays an outstanding collection of rare and beautiful Judaica.

Gloucester Crescent further north, with mid-19th-century Italianate villas, is one of Camden's most desirable addresses. At the top of it, at the junction with Oval Road, the distinctive circular building is Collard & Collard's **former piano factory**. Camden was once the centre of the now defunct British piano-making industry. In the early 20th century, several hundred companies associated with the trade were based here, making a range of instruments from mass-produced 'old Joannas' to concert pianofortes of superior quality. The nearby Regent's Canal provided supplies of timber for manufacture and a means of transport for the finished product. The British firm Challen supplied pianos to the BBC in the 1930s; when the Royal Festival Hall opened in 1951, its instruments were made by Danemann, a company based in nearby Islington.

Oval Road leads north to the canal, where you can join the towpath. Just before the bridge over the canal, low down on the right is (or was, at the time of writing) a blue and black stencilled piece of street art in the style of the celebrated Banksy.

CAMDEN LOCK AND CAMDEN MARKET

Camden Lock (*map p. 632, C2*) is a twin lock, constructed c. 1820. It is the only twin lock on the Regent's Canal. You can walk along the towpath here and the London Waterbus Company also offers cruises (*londonwaterbus.com*).

In converted former warehouses and buildings on the waterfront is **Camden Market** (*open daily from 10am; camdenmarket.com*), a combination of Camden Lock Market and Camden Stables Market, the latter in buildings which formerly housed the horses that towed the canal barges. There are masses of stalls, both indoor and out, extending all around and up Chalk Farm Road.

In Chalk Farm Road (near Chalk Farm Tube; *map p. 632, B1*) is the **Roundhouse**,

One of the main entrances to Camden Market.

built as a railway engine house and repair shed in the 1840s; it was also used as a bonded warehouse for storing gin. It is now a premier performance venue.

Other points of interest are **Rochester Square** and **Camden Square** (*map p. 633, D1*), dating from the 1840s. Flanking the latter are Camden Mews and Murray Mews, with architects' houses from the 1960s.

View south from Hampstead Heath to the towers of the City.

HIGHGATE & HAMPSTEAD

Highate and Hampstead, leafy and in parts delightfully bucolic, are the cream of the northern suburbs. Until the 19th century, they were very much separate from London. Today, largely due to their active conservation societies—who keep vigilant watch on new developments and on changes to the historic fabric—they still retain a distinct, villagey feel. These districts are lofty both literally and metaphorically: both are known for

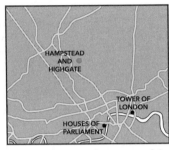

their free-thinking, intellectual residents, and both command outstanding views of the capital. Shops, pubs and restaurants abound and a day spent exploring the undulating, attractive streets is also excellent exercise. Both areas are spread along the edges of the almost-rural, 800-acre Hampstead Heath.

Some highlights of the area
✦ Atmospheric **Highgate Cemetery**, burial place of Karl Marx, among others;
✦ **Keats House** and the **Freud Museum**, with displays on the life and work of two very different residents of Hampstead;
✦ **Hampstead Heath**, for an exhilarating walk, with wide vistas towards the City of London and its towers and construction cranes;
✦ **Kenwood House**, containing paintings by Vermeer, Rembrandt, Van Dyck, Gainsborough and others; and **Fenton House**, with works by the Camden Town Group of artists.

HIGHGATE

Map p. 631. Underground: Archway, Highgate.

Leafy Highgate spreads across the hilltops north of Archway, with Hampstead Heath on its western side. The district takes its name from a 14th-century tollgate sited along the Old North Road, on land that adjoined the Bishop of London's hunting estate; the Gatehouse Inn, which has catered for travellers from the 1670s, commemorates this. Many famous people passed through the growing village along the road to the north, including, supposedly, Richard Whittington, four times Lord Mayor of London.

HIGHGATE HILL

Highgate Hill (*map p. 631, F2*) rises steeply from Archway, leading to Highgate High Street. Europe's first cable tramway was installed here in 1884, using the same technology that had been developed in San Francisco in the 1870s. Today, much of the traffic has been diverted along the Archway Road to the northeast, where the viaduct over the cutting (1897; the original was by Nash) affords terrific views.

Near Archway Underground station, at the bottom of Highgate Hill (corner of Magdala Ave.) is the diminutive **Whittington Stone** (middle of the pavement, outside the pub of the same name, behind railings), apparently marking the spot where Dick Whittington stopped and listened to the City's bells, 4½ miles away, summoning him back to London. The replica milestone dates from 1821; the cat was added in 1964. When Whittington died childless in 1423, he left money for a 'college' or almshouses (now relocated to Felbridge, Surrey) and the Whittington Charity also set up at his death still distributes money for the needy through the Mercers' Company.

St Joseph's Church, with its impressive green copper domes, lies just before the junction with Dartmouth Park Hill and Cromwell Avenue. Then, still on the left-hand side, you come to the start of the 29-acre **Waterlow Park**, 'the garden for the gardenless', bequeathed to London County Council in 1889 by Lord Mayor and philanthropic resident Sir Sydney Waterlow. The park stretches all the way down to Swain's Lane, where there is an exit opposite the main entrance to Highgate Cemetery (*see below*). In its grounds is the white stucco **Lauderdale House** (1582; much altered), where Nell Gwyn, Charles II's mistress, lived for a short time with her illegitimate son, the Duke of St Albans. John Wesley preached here in 1782. The house is now a community arts and education centre, with exhibition space and a café. Opposite its main entrance on Highgate Hill, note some handsome 18th-century houses (nos 106–110) and the 17th-century Cromwell House.

HIGHGATE HIGH STREET AND NORTH HILL

Highgate High Street (*map p. 631, E2*) is full of quaint shops and buildings—at least, it was until very recently; a few of the ubiquitous chain restaurants have now crept in. Highgate School, in North Road, was founded in the reign of Elizabeth I, in 1565. Sir John Betjeman was a pupil here. Opposite the school at no. 17, a Blue Plaque marks the house where poet A.E. Housman wrote 'A Shropshire Lad'. At the **Wrestler's Tavern** in North Road, dating from 1547, the tradition of the 'Swearing on the Horns' is kept alive in a biannual ceremony. The tradition, mainly enacted for the amusement of customers, was upheld in several of Highgate's pubs and inns from the 17th century. Visitors were granted the Freedom of Highgate after taking an oath of merriment and debauchery, which involved swearing by, kissing or saluting a set of animal horns held out to them by the landlord (*thewrestlershighgate.com*).

In North Hill is London's premier example of 1930s' Modernist housing: **Highpoint One and Two** (*map p. 631, E1*), built by Berthold Lubetkin for his design practice, Tecton. The apartment blocks were commissioned by Sigmund Gestetner, son of the Hungarian-born inventor of the cyclograph, a duplicating machine. Highpoint One, comprising 64 flats, was built in 1935, initially as working-class housing for Gestetner's employees, although they never moved in. The building was greatly admired by Le Corbusier, who visited it and was unequivocal in his praise; it expressed perfectly his vision of tower blocks in park settings. Highpoint Two was completed in 1938 and features caryatids. Both blocks pioneered the use of freely moulded, reinforced concrete, which the *Penguin Dictionary of Architecture* describes as 'prophetic of the 1950s'.

HIGHGATE VILLAGE CENTRE

The Grove and South Grove, with Highgate West Hill between them (*map p. 631, E2*), are at the centre of Highgate Village, preserving handsome 17th- and 18th-century houses. Coleridge lived at no. 3 **The Grove**. The poet had moved to Highgate, firstly to South Grove, in 1816, to live as a house patient with the family of his friend and physician, James Gillman, who helped him try to overcome his opium addiction. Here he continued to write and publish until his death in 1834. He was originally buried in the Old Graveyard, Highgate, but his remains, together with those of his wife and other members of his family, were buried in 1961 in the neo-Gothic **St Michael's Church**. Designed by Lewis Vulliamy (1832), it claims to be the highest standing church in London; as you enter it, you are at the same level as the cross on top of St Paul's Cathedral. The violinist Yehudi Menuhin also lived in The Grove (at no. 2). The art critic Roger Fry was born at no. 6.

The **Flask pub** (*77 Highgate West Hill*; not to be confused with the Flask in Hampstead) is one of the highway taverns at which travellers could purchase a refreshing flask of water filled from the area's mineral springs. The building dates from the 1720s and includes part of a 1660s' stable, with two horse boxes said to date to the 17th century. Dick Turpin, the highwayman, is said to have hidden in the cellar here. Byron, Shelley and Keats drank here when they visited Coleridge.

Pond Square, in the middle, is a pleasant bosky quadrangle; the ponds were filled in in the 19th century. Here, in 1626, Sir Francis Bacon is said to have conducted his famous experiment in refrigeration by stuffing a dead chicken with snow (the great empiricist consequently developed pneumonia and died a few days later). The vicinity is said to be haunted by the ghost of a squawking, half-plucked hen, which appears in extremely cold weather.

At no. 11 is the **Highgate Literary and Scientific Institution**, founded in 1839. Its archive of local history holds important documents and pictures from the 17th century to the present day; the library has collections relating to Coleridge and Betjeman.

Off Highgate West Hill is London's second-largest private residence (Buckingham Palace is the first): **Witanhurst**, overlooking Hampstead Heath. This 65-room super-mansion, set in eleven acres and now worth in the region of £300 million, was built in the early 20th century for Sir Arthur Crosfield, whose money came from soap and candles. It has been lavishly renovated by its secretive owner.

HIGHGATE CEMETERY

From South Grove, Swain's Lane descends very steeply (it is strongly recommended not to approach Highgate uphill from Swain's Lane) to Highgate Cemetery (*map p. 631, E2*), with the main entrances to both the east and west sections on opposite sides of the road.(*West Cemetery open for tours daily; at weekends you must book ahead, see highgatecemetery.org. On weekdays you are asked to turn up and join the next available tour. Tours last approx. 1hr. Tickets include entrance to the East Cemetery. For the East Cemetery alone, there is also an admission charge.*)

The **West Cemetery**, through the neo-Gothic gatehouse, is the secret, oldest section, no longer in use for burials. The rural hillside location, then part of the Forest of Middlesex, was a popular choice for the new cemetery in 1839, designed by the architect Stephen Geary. Initially it was the most expensive and exclusive in London. Here the fanciful high-Victorian funerary landscape is maintained in a romantic, overgrown state. Among the trees and bushes appear huge and ornate tombs and monuments; famous sights include the Egyptian Avenue, flanked by obelisks; the Colonnade; the Circle of Lebanon (around an ancient cedar tree); the Terrace Catacombs and the Mausoleum of Julian Beer, based on the Tomb of Mausolus at Halicarnassus.

The **East Cemetery** still functions as a working burial ground and you may wander here freely (though there is an admission charge; *see above*). It was opened in 1860. Here is the famous grave of Karl Marx (d. 1883)—a place of pilgrimage for visitors from all over the world. The inscription on the stone reads 'Workers of the World Unite' and the large bust, by Laurence Bradshaw, which dominates the cemetery, was added in 1956. Marx's wife Jenny, his domestic servant Helene Demuth, and the ashes of his daughter Eleanor, a Socialist activist who committed suicide in 1898, are also buried here. Buried nearby is George Eliot (as Mary Ann Cross; d. 1880). Many other literary figures have been laid to rest in this cemetery, including the author Beryl Bainbridge, the artist Lucian Freud, the novelist Radclyffe Hall, historian Lisa Jardine, murdered Russian dissident Alexander Litvinenko, singer-songwriter George Michael, the poet Christina Rossetti and her sister-in-law Elizabeth Siddal, wife and model of Dante Gabriel Rossetti and model for Millais' *Ophelia*.

HOLLY LODGE ESTATE

Continue descending Swain's Lane. The East Cemetery continues for some way on the left, where amongst the trees are row upon row of lichen-covered headstones interspersed with angels and crosses, overgrown with ivy. Soon on your right, a quiet, private estate composed of avenues of mock-Tudor mansion blocks or 'Tudor cliffs' (disconcerting, like a scene from a zombie film) comes into view. This is the **Holly Lodge Estate** (*map p. 631, E2*), which runs between Swain's Lane and Highgate West Hill. It was built in the grounds of an 18th-century villa, Holly Lodge, which was owned by the wealthy banking heiress and philanthropist Angela Burdett-Coutts. She gave more than £3 million to charitable causes and was known as the 'queen of the poor'. At her death in 1906, her body lay in state for two days and 30,000 people paid their respects. She is buried in Westminster Abbey. The estate was built in the 1920s as housing for female office workers; secretaries and clerks lived here in miserable-sounding bedsits that were considered very modern at the time. John Betjeman, who was brought up nearby, when the housing estate was still a garden, immortalised it in his poem 'NW5 & N6', writing of squirrels in the Burdett-Coutts estate and of bugging his nurse with questions about God. The copyright costs of reproducing a few lines from the poem in physical print make it impossible to do so here, but all five verses may be searched for and freely enjoyed online.

Further on is **Holly Village** (junction of Chester Road), a small, neo-Gothic group of houses, behind an elaborate gatehouse, built by Burdett-Coutts in the 1860s for senior workers on her estate.

HAMPSTEAD

Map p. 630. Underground: Hampstead. Overground: Gospel Oak, Hampstead Heath.

Scenic Hampstead, skirting the edges of Hampstead Heath, is one of the highest points in the capital. Its topography preserved it as a village until the arrival of the railway in the 1860s. From the 17th century, this countryside spot, with its clean, fresh air, medicinal spa waters and expansive heath, attracted convalescents and wealthy residents, especially in the summer months, and also inspired artists, musicians, writers and intellectuals of all kinds to settle here. They are nearly all remembered: Hampstead's buildings are simply pocked with blue plaques commemorating former illustrious inhabitants; a cartoon published by the local newspaper *Ham & High* in 1998 depicted a bemused tourist surveying a building plaque with the legend, 'The only house in Hampstead that nobody famous has lived in'.

Today, Hampstead is in effect a large, very wealthy suburban town. In the streets extending down towards the Finchley Road, bounded by Platts Lane, and in the area known as Belsize Park, there are substantial villas and mansions. Old Hampstead, or Hampstead proper, with its narrow, twisting, hilly lanes, still retains its village feel and is exceptionally pretty. Strong local interests have ensured that the many attractive houses and cottages have been preserved and that new development has been restricted. More of 21st-century Hampstead prospers along the High Street and down Rosslyn Hill towards Belsize Park, where independent businesses have been engulfed by up-market chains of coffee emporia, restaurants, cafés and boutiques that cater for a new strain of resident: bankers, business executives and wealthy expatriates. Property prices in Hampstead are now extremely high; there are said to be more millionaires per capita here than in the rest of London put together. The academic, artistic and literary community that built the area's reputation is being priced out of the market. In spite of this, old Hampstead may still be encountered if you explore the winding back streets, lanes and snickets; this is where you will be rewarded. There are many interesting things to see in Hampstead and a full day here is recommended.

ON AND AROUND HOLLY HILL

Hampstead Underground station opened in 1907; at 181ft, its lift-shaft is the deepest in London. From it, Heath Street leads south to **Church Row** (*map p. 630, B4*), a very handsome street of early 18th-century brick houses. Lord Alfred Douglas, Oscar Wilde's former lover, lived at no. 26. At the end is the parish church of **St John-at-Hampstead**, by John Sanderson, consecrated in 1747. The gates and railings are from Cannons, the Edgware stately home of the 'princely' Duke of Chandos (*see Cavendish Square, p. 301*). In the peaceful churchyard are buried many famous men and women, including John Constable (signposted) and the clockmaker John Harrison (*see p. 497*), in a tall chest tomb. The galleried church interior is overfull of austere grey-painted pews with tall bench ends surmounted by alternating devices of angled and segmental pediments.

In Holly Walk is the Catholic church of **St Mary** (1816; *map p. 630, B3*), its white façade and bell-cote squeezed into an ordinary terrace of houses; it was one of the first new Catholic churches to be built after the Reformation and was the centre of a community of *émigrés* who had fled the Terror of the French Revolution. Further on is the former **Hampstead Watch House**, where Hampstead's first police force was based in the 1830s.

At no. 7 **Mount Vernon** (Abernethy House, the corner of an elevated row of 1820s cottages), Robert Louis Stevenson stayed when he came to Hampstead to recuperate from illness in the 1870s. Mount Vernon Hospital opposite (now luxury flats) was built in the late 19th century to treat consumptives; its large scale, out of keeping with the rest of Hampstead's architecture, was largely deprecated.

No. 6 **Holly Hill**, a white weather-boarded house, formerly stables, now much altered, was owned and converted into a home and studio by painter George Romney in 1796; later the house became lecture rooms. Constable, Faraday and Elizabeth Fry all spoke here. In Holly Mount is the small and atmospheric **Holly Bush pub** (nooks, etched glass etc.; *hollybushhampstead.co.uk*), dating from the late 18th century and also converted from stables. Holly Bush Steps lead to Golden Yard and The Mount, a street of handsome 18th-century houses; Ford Madox Brown incorporated no. 6 into his painting *Work*, begun in 1852.

FENTON HOUSE

The handsome red-brick William-and-Mary-era Fenton House (*map p. 630, B3; admission charge; nationaltrust.org*) one of the best late 17th-century houses to survive in London, stands at the very top of Hampstead in one of the most attractive parts of the 'village'. From 1936 until her death in 1952, it was the home of Lady Binning, who bequeathed it to the National Trust along with her fine collection of porcelain. Also on display here is the important Benton Fletcher collection of early musical instruments. Music students often play them and it is a memorable experience to visit this airy house and beautiful garden, and to hear from a distant room the evocative sound of a harpsichord or spinet.

Little is known for certain about the early history of the house. It stands on manorial land which between 1682 and 1690 passed through the hands of four different lords, the last of them only six years of age. It was probably built by William Eades, the son of a master bricklayer, apparently without the help of an architect. In the early 18th century it was bought by Joshua Gee, a Quaker linen merchant who went into partnership with George Washington's father, importing pig-iron from Maryland. His initials and those of his wife, Anna Osgood, are worked into the handsome wrought-iron gates at the south entrance from Holly Hill. By 1786 the place was called Clock

House. Six years later it was bought by Philip Fenton, son of a coal merchant from Yorkshire, whose family owned it until 1834. During their time here, the Regency loggia between the wings on the east side, which now forms the main entrance, was added. Otherwise the house appears externally much as first built.

Apart from the porcelain and musical instruments, the house also contains paintings by the Camden Town Group of Post-Impressionists (*see p. 418*). The garden is extremely fine and there are 30 varieties of apple tree in the orchard.

ADMIRAL'S WALK TO THE HAMPSTEAD OBSERVATORY

Admiral's House in Admiral's Walk (1700; *map p. 630, B3*) was the home of Lieutenant Fountain North, who constructed the deck of a ship on the roof, from which he fired cannon in celebration of naval victories. Presumably Hampstead resident P.L. Travers was drawing on local knowledge when she created the character of Admiral Boon in *Mary Poppins* (scenes from the 1964 film were shot here). Sir George Gilbert Scott also lived here and next door, in Grove House, John Galsworthy completed the *Forsyte Saga*; he died here in 1933.

The views from **Judge's Walk** were painted by Constable, who lived for a time in Lower Terrace; Constable also painted Admiral's House in the 1820s. In Windmill Hill, the little 18th-century cottage called 'Capo di Monte' is where the actress Sarah Siddons stayed when she came to Hampstead for her health; in the 1940s it was the home of Sir Kenneth Clark and later of Marghanita Laski.

The **Hampstead Observatory** in Lower Terrace is open to the public on clear nights at certain times of year (*see hampsteadscience.ac.uk to check; visits are free*). It was opened by the Hampstead Scientific Society in 1910; the telescope dates from the 19th century.

EAST HAMPSTEAD AND THE WELLS

Flask Walk (*map p. 630, B3–C3*), a little pedestrianised street of shops near Hampstead Tube station, leads north from Hampstead High Street. Here is the popular Flask pub (the current building dates from the 19th century). In the original pub, the Lower Flask, Hampstead's spa water was bottled for sale. In **Well Walk**, further north, is the equally popular Wells Tavern (*thewellshampstead.co.uk*), on the site of a dance hall connected with the spa. The chalybeate spring, located on this street, is commemorated by a Victorian drinking fountain of 1882 (steps leading to Wells Passage); the spa's buildings were located opposite and also in Gainsborough Gardens, which has smart red-brick 1880s' houses. Notable residents of Well Walk included John Keats, John Masefield, J.B. Priestley, John Constable (Blue Plaque at no. 10), Margaret Llewelyn Davies (a campaigner who championed the right for women to divorce on the same terms as men) and Marie Stopes, pioneer of birth control.

Burgh House, in New End Square (*map p. 630, C3; burghhouse.org.uk*), built in 1703, was where the spa physician William Gibbons lived in the 1720s; the garden was designed by Gertrude Jekyll. It is now a community arts centre and holds the largest collection of works by Helen Allingham (1848–1926), illustrator and water-colourist.

HISTORY OF HAMPSTEAD SPA

From the 17th century, Hampstead was known for its iron-rich mineral springs, but it was not until the early 18th century that the waters were commercially exploited. In 1698 Susanna Noel, mother of the landowning Earl of Gainsborough (then an infant), bequeathed six acres of marshy land around Wells Walk on the understanding that it be used to benefit the poor of Hampstead; the Wells Trust (a charity that still exists today) was born. The charity leased the land, on which a chalybeate mineral spring was located, to a developer to build a health resort. The resulting spa town, called Hampstead Wells, had an assembly room for socialising and a pump room where the waters were imbibed; in Flask Walk the iron-rich water was bottled for sale in the City. The spa's success soon changed Hampstead from a quiet village into a small town: inns, lodging houses and shops were built to cater for the influx of revellers and invalids. Visitors to this first spa tended to be a rowdy, insalubrious lot, and were so unpopular with residents that in the 1720s the spa's lease was not extended. A second spa was run on much stricter lines, until its popularity finally flagged at end of the 18th century. Those who came to take the cure at this more genteel watering place included Alexander Pope, Dr Johnson and Fanny Burney (Hampstead features in Burney's novel *Evelina*, published in 1778). Today none of the spa buildings remain.

The area around **New End** was historically a working-class district. During Hampstead's periods of expansion—connected to the growth of the spa and the arrival of the railway—streets of mean, cramped houses were quickly erected to cope with the population surge; a cholera epidemic occurred in 1849. The buildings were then mostly swept away during a period of rebuilding and town planning the 1880s. The surviving old workhouse, Kendall's Hall, is today a luxury flat conversion.

In Well Road is a fantastical neo-Gothic mansion, '**The Logs**' (nos 17–20). Pevsner called it 'a formidable atrocity'.

WILLOW ROAD TO BELSIZE PARK

2 WILLOW ROAD

2 Willow Road (*map p. 630, C3; Underground: Hampstead and 10mins' walk; admission charge; visits must be pre-booked online; nationaltrust.org.uk*) is one of a terrace of three houses, important works by the Hungarian-born Marxist architect Ernő Goldfinger (1902–87), who was a leading exponent of the Modern movement in post-war Britain. Goldfinger designed the house in 1939 and lived here with his wife, the Crosse and Blackwell heiress Ursula Blackwell, their children and the nanny. It is said that the name of the titular villain in Ian Fleming's *Goldfinger* (1959) was a deliberate slight on the character and work of the architect for having demolished a row of cottages to make way for this Modernist ideal home. Controversial though Goldfinger's style was (and remains; Alexander Fleming House at Elephant and Castle, Trellick Tower in Ladbroke Grove and

Balfron Tower in Poplar have all been excoriated in their time), there is no better example than 2 Willow Road of the purity and sensitivity that Goldfinger could sometimes employ in his constructions. Far from being a piece of shocking Brutalism, the house shares many characteristics with the elegant Georgian antecedents of which Goldfinger was so enamoured: the brick-faced façade, the deftly-proportioned articulation of the exterior and the play of light inside. As Pevsner pointed out, the architecture is also complemented by a collection of modern art; there are works by contemporaries of Goldfinger such as Henry Moore, Max Ernst and Bridget Riley. The interior remains much as it was during Goldfinger's lifetime: the plywood chairs, wood-and-leather safari chairs and writing desk are all the work of this architect-cum-designer.

KEATS HOUSE

This house (*10 Keats Grove; map p. 630, C4; Underground: Hampstead, Belsize Park and 10mins' walk; for access, see cityoflondon.gov.uk*) is where John Keats, Romantic poet, the 'loveliest and the last' (Shelley, 'Adonaïs'), lived from Dec 1818 to Sept 1820. Brief though his residence was, it was here that he wrote some of his richest lyric poetry, including 'Ode to a Nightingale', 'Ode on a Grecian Urn' and 'Ode on Melancholy'. Here he fell in love with and became engaged to his 'Minx', Fanny Brawne, and here he became ill with the tuberculosis which would end his life the following year in Rome. He was not yet 26. Originally known as Wentworth Place, the building was constructed as two semi-detached houses in 1815. Keats lived in the smaller of the two, next door to his friend Charles Armitage Brown. Fanny, her siblings and disapproving mother subsequently moved in in Brown's place. The house was restored in 2009 and the garden now has three themed borders: 'Melancholy', 'Autumn' and 'Nightingale'. On display in the museum are Keats' death mask, the engagement ring he gave to Fanny, and letters between the young couple which reveal the poet's passion, insecurity and jealousy. The house also hosts poetry readings.

DOWNSHIRE HILL, ROSSLYN HILL AND BELSIZE PARK

On the corner of Keats Grove and Downshire Hill is the **church of St John** (*map p. 630, C3*), dating from the 1820s. **Downshire Hill** itself is lined with lovely 19th-century villas and gardens; at the end is the Freemason's Arms, which has a beer garden. Note no. 49A, by Michael Hopkins, an unobtrusive steel and glass box, partially sunken below the road; it won an RIBA award in the 1970s. Dante Gabriel Rossetti and Lizzie Siddal stayed in a house on the site of Hampstead Hill Mansions shortly after their marriage in 1860. Siddal had convalesced in Hampstead in the 1850s, after contracting pneumonia as a consequence of posing in a bath of freezing water for Millais's *Ophelia* (now at Tate Britain). A prominent aberration here is the towering 1970s' block in Pond Street, the **Royal Free** (an important teaching hospital, but nonetheless an architectural eyesore).

Rosslyn Hill (*map p. 630, C4*) descends to the area known as Belsize Park. It is along this street that 21st-century homogenisation has taken the strongest hold, in the form of coffee-shop, café, restaurant and boutique chains. The little takeaway crêpe stall outside the King William IV pub is now a Hampstead institution. In Belsize Park are several large 19th-century mansions, mostly converted into flats. In Lawn Road (*map p. 631, D4*) is the 1930s' white concrete apartment block known as the **Isokon Building**, which was built as communal living for professional workers. Agatha Christie and Walter Gropius were former residents.

FROGNAL TO THE FREUD MUSEUM

Frognal is a discreet residential enclave with some interesting architecture. In **Frognal Way** (*map p. 630, B3*) is a group of 1930s' houses. The most important architecturally is no. 9, Sun House, by Maxwell Fry (1935). Pevsner termed no. 4 'Hollywood Spanish-Colonial'; no. 5 was built by Sir George Gilbert Scott's grandson, Adrian Gilbert Scott, in 1930; no. 20, in Mediterranean style, was commissioned by the singer Gracie Fields in 1934. **No. 66 Frognal** (Connell, Ward & Lucas, 1937) caused a furore when built, its Modernist style offending Sir Reginald Blomfield, who had designed nos 49 and 51. Further down is the neo-Wren University College School (1905–7). Opposite, at no. 39, is the former home of the children's book illustrator Kate Greenaway (commemorated in the nearby Greenaway Gardens); it was built by Norman Shaw in 1884. Shaw's own house, which he designed for himself in 1874–6, is at no. 6 Ellerdale Rd.

In Arkwright Road is the **Camden Arts Centre** (*map p. 630, B4*), which runs education workshops and shows of contemporary art (*free; bookshop; camdenartscentre.org*). If you follow Arkwright Road in the other direction, you come to **Fitzjohn's Avenue** (*map p. 630, C4*), where a small plaque at the junction with Lyndhurst Road commemorates the Shepherd's Well, the purest natural water source in Hampstead. Further south, no. 3 Fitzjohn's Avenue (corner of Maresfield Gardens) was the home of another Hungarian-born Hampstead resident, the society portrait painter Philip de Laszlo.

THE FREUD MUSEUM

The Freud Museum (*20 Maresfield Gardens; map p. 630, C4; Underground: Finchley Road and 5mins' walk; admission charge; freud.org.uk*) occupies the house where Sigmund Freud lived for the final year of his life (1938–9), after fleeing Nazi oppression in his native Austria. His daughter Anna followed him into psychoanalytic practice, living and working here for 44 years, producing ground-breaking work in the field of child psychoanalysis and preserving her father's home as it had been left on his death.

The heart of the house is Freud's **Study and Library**. Here is the famous Biedermeier-style psychoanalytic couch, given to him by one of his Viennese patients in 1890. The rest of the room is decorated with rich warm rugs, over floor and tables, and with an array of antiquities, including a late 5th–early 4th-century BC Greek terracotta sphinx, a 1st or 2nd-century Roman bronze Venus and a Chinese Buddhist lion paperweight made of jade (Qing Dynasty, 18th–19th centuries). The study also contains the largest remaining part of Freud's personal library, which, along with his couch, was brought from Vienna. Goethe, Shakespeare and the novels of Balzac, Gogol and Anatole France were particular favourites.

On the first floor is the **Anna Freud Room**, with Anna's own analytic couch. On the **Landing** hang two portraits of Freud, one by fellow Austrian Ferdinand Schmutzer

(1926) and the other by Dalí, a death-foreshadowing image that he sketched on a visit to Freud in 1938, the meeting an historic one for both. Dalí had read *The Interpretation of Dreams* as a student in Madrid, and his art ever since had been driven by the Freudian concept of the unconscious. Freud, hitherto sceptical of being regarded as the father of Surrealism, recorded that 'The young Spaniard, with his candid, fanatical eyes and his undeniable technical mastery, has changed my estimate. It would indeed be interesting to investigate analytically how he came to create his paintings.'

HAMPSTEAD HEATH

Hampstead Heath (*map pp. 630–1*), rambling over 800 acres, commands superb views of London. It is beloved by Hampstead residents and Londoners alike and over the centuries its wild aspect has captured the imagination of numerous writers and artists. At one time, laundresses would spread their washing to dry on Hampstead Heath, making it look snow-capped from afar. Today it is a popular spot for walking, cycling, kite-flying, jogging, swimming and picnicking. From Parliament Hill, one of the highest points, one can spot numerous landmarks, including the Palace of Westminster and the dome of St Paul's Cathedral, as well as the dominating new skyscrapers in the City.

The land around Hampstead was anciently owned by the monks of Westminster, who had a farm here. In 1349, Abbott Simon de Barcheston inadvertently brought the Black Death to Hampstead, when he fled here to escape the epidemic in the City. The Heath is the source of three of London's 'lost' rivers: the Tyburn, the Westbourne and the Fleet (the latter still feeds its ponds), and its sand and clay composition also made it a rich source of mineral spring water. Improved transport links and the arrival of the railway in the 19th century led to Hampstead's popularity with day-trippers, who would come here to escape from London's heat, grime and squalor. During this period, Sir Thomas Maryon Wilson, lord of the manor, wished to turn Hampstead's popularity to his profit by building a network of villas across his land. The rural nature of the Heath would have been altered forever had his project not been vehemently opposed by the local population. Sir Thomas fought tooth and nail for his plans to be approved and the project was only finally given up on his death in 1869. His heir sold the land to the Metropolitan Board of Works, who vowed that it would 'forever keep the Heath open, unenclosed and unbuilt on…and at all times preserve, as far as may be, the natural aspect and state of the Heath, and to that end shall protect the turf, gorse, heather, timber and other trees, shrubs and brushwood thereon.' Today the precious Heath is protected and managed by the City of London Corporation. The Heath & Hampstead Society is also active in the area's preservation.

WHITESTONE POND AND THE VALE OF HEALTH
At the south edge of Hampstead Heath, the small **Whitestone Pond** (*map p. 630, B3*), screened from the road by a stand of reed, was named after a white milestone. At 440ft above sea level, this is the highest point in London (or so they say; but there are other points that claim this distinction, and it depends on how one defines 'London'). A flagpole marks the spot where the Armada Beacon was lit in 1588, one of several

torches that were illuminated on high points across the country, warning of the approach of Philip II's invading Spanish fleet.

The secluded hamlet known as the **Vale of Health** (*map p. 630, B3–C3*) was once swampy land known as Hatchett's Bottom. It was drained by 1801 and its new name, Vale of Health, may have been an attempt by its developers to obliterate its insalubrious reputation. In this enclave have lived many artists and writers including, briefly in 1915, D.H. Lawrence and his wife Frieda (1 Byron Villas). Stanley Spencer painted his *The Resurrection, Cookham* in the Vale in the 1920s (it is now in Tate Britain). At 3 Heath Villas lived the Bengali polymath and first non-European Nobel Prize-winner Rabindranath Tagore, in 1912.

Jack Straw's Castle (*map p. 630, B3*), clapboard-fronted and comedy-crenellated, was one of Hampstead's most famous pubs, where many artists drank (Dickens and Wilkie Collins are known to have visited). It was named after the rebel leader of the Peasants' Revolt in 1381, who is said to have taken refuge on the site until he was caught and executed. In 1673, the highwayman Francis Jackson was hanged near here and his remains were left to dangle for 18 years. Damaged in the Blitz, the current building dates from 1964. At the time of writing it housed offices of Group Nexus, 'delivering the future of parking'. Opposite, at the junction with Spaniards Road, is the 18th-century **Heath House**, once the home of the philanthropic merchant family of Hoare, who entertained William Wilberforce and Elizabeth Fry to dinner here.

NORTH END

Off North End Way is **Inverforth House** (formerly The Hill; *map p. 630, B2*) a huge, early 20th-century mansion built around a smaller property by the soap magnate Lord Leverhulme; it is now luxury apartments. Inverforth Close (left) leads to the Hill Garden and Pergola, also built by Leverhulme and now open to the public. This is one of Hampstead's secret gems; a raised terrace and colonnade, 15ft above the Heath, tumbling with fragrant climbing plants.

Towards the end of North End Way is the **Old Bull and Bush pub** (*thebullandbush. co.uk*), dating from the 17th century. A young William Hogarth is supposed to have helped plant the pub garden and Gainsborough, Reynolds and Garrick drank here. It gave its name to the music hall song 'Down at the Old Bull and Bush', made famous by Florrie Ford.

To the right off North End Road, on North End Avenue, is **Cedar Lodge**, home of the adventuress, philanthropist and benefactor of British aviation Lady Houston, whose fortune was estimated at £300 million in today's money. She lined the coffers of the British aviation team when they competed for the Schneider Trophy; this in turn stimulated the advancement of engine technology and the development of the Spitfire. Lady Houston died in 1936, just months after its maiden flight but it went to be used by the Allies during WWII (and was the backbone of the fighter command during the Battle of Britain). Also in North End Avenue, **Pitt House** stands on the site of the house where Prime Minister William Pitt, Earl of Chatham, lay ill for 18 months in 1766–7, refusing to see anyone, including King George III.

The great art historian and forensic cataloguer of England's architectural heritage, Sir

View of Hampstead Heath in winter, under a carpet of fresh snow.

Nikolaus Pevsner, lived at no. 2 **Wildwood Terrace** from 1936 until his death in 1983. In **Ivy House** (94–96 North End Rd) lived the prima ballerina Anna Pavlova; it is now the London Jewish Cultural Centre.

SPANIARDS ROAD

Spaniards Road (*map p. 630, B2–C2*) leads from Whitestone Pond all the way to Kenwood House and grounds; the road narrows at the summit of the hill, where an old tollgate still stands. Here is the quaint, oak-panelled **Spaniards Inn** (built 1585; *thespaniardshampstead.co.uk*), once the haunt of highwaymen. The Gordon Rioters stopped here on their way to burn Kenwood House in 1780 and were plied with drink by the landlord—a successful diversion. Others who have enjoyed drinking here include Keats, Shelley, Byron and—inevitably—Dickens.

KENWOOD HOUSE

Map p. 630, C2. Underground: Golders Green or Archway, then bus 210. Bus 210 also from Jack Straw's Castle, or 15mins brisk walk along the edge of the Heath. Free. Pleasant café, good light lunches. english-heritage.org.uk.

Kenwood, an elegant mansion set on a ridge of land with a magnificent prospect towards London, is one of the principal properties of English Heritage. The former house of c. 1700 was remodelled and redecorated in 1764–79 by the Adam brothers, Robert and James, for William Murray, 1st Earl of Mansfield and Lord Chief Justice, who lived here from 1754. The resulting elegant and imposing villa is a major piece of 18th-century Neoclassical architecture and interior decoration, which the Adam brothers regarded as one of their major commissions. The most magnificent of the ground-floor reception rooms created for Mansfield is the **Library**, regarded by many as Robert Adam's finest achievement. Shallow exedrae at both ends hold bookshelves. The painting at the centre of the pastel blue and pink stuccoed ceiling is by Antonio Zucchi. The wall at the far end has a mural of the *Aldobrandini Wedding* (1st-century BC original in the Vatican).

The 1st Earl began the landscaping of the park, which was continued by the 2nd Earl, aided by the great landscape gardener Humphry Repton, who was probably responsible for the ornamental flowerbeds of the west garden and the looped foliage passage near the front of the house. The grounds today are a beautiful combination of lawns, a lake, winding rhododendron walks among woodland (recorded here by 1806), an avenue of limes (a favourite resort of the poet Pope), the whole surrounded by Hampstead Heath.

In 1825 James Stanhope, a cousin of William Pitt, in constant pain from a wound sustained during the Peninsular War, hanged himself here in a fit of depression after the death of his wife (daughter of the 3rd Earl of Mansfield).

A sale of the house contents was held in 1922 and Kenwood today has none of its original furnishings, save for a few Adam pieces which have fortuitously returned. It is, however, home to the Iveagh Bequest, a major collection of paintings left to the nation in 1927, along with the house, by Edward Cecil Guinness, 1st Earl of Iveagh, who purchased Kenwood from the Mansfield family in 1925, together with 80 acres of grounds which were about to be sold as building plots. The house has been open to the public free of charge since 1928.

The paintings

Lord Iveagh, Chairman of Guinness Breweries—and on his death in 1927 reputedly the second richest man in the country—amassed an extraordinary collection of pictures between 1887 and 1891. The collection is particularly rich in 18th-century British portraiture and 17th-century Dutch and Flemish works. The conditions of his bequest have guaranteed that Kenwood will remain a free public art gallery. The 63 paintings are now displayed throughout Kenwood's historic interiors and include some world-famous masterpieces, such as Rembrandt's late *Self-Portrait* of c. 1663 and Vermeer's *Guitar Player*, probably a very late work and known to have been in the collection of his widow in 1676. Seventeenth-century works painted in Britain include De

Jongh's early topographical view of Old London Bridge (1630s), Van Dyck's *Henrietta of Lorraine* (1634), a noble full-length which belonged to Charles I, and works by Lely and Kneller. The succession of 18th-century British works, by Gainsborough, Reynolds, Romney, Hoppner, Angelica Kauffman, Lawrence, Raeburn and others, is extraordinary. Gainsborough's *Mary, Countess Howe* (c. 1763–4), one of Kenwood's treasures, dates from the artist's Bath period and is one of his loveliest portraits. The lyrical conversation piece *Going to Market* is a charming mid-period landscape. There are many portraits by Reynolds, including a self-portrait and *Kitty Fisher as Cleopatra*; Kitty Fisher was a notorious courtesan who died young, apparently of lead poisoning from cosmetics. There are two Romneys of Lady Hamilton, mistress of Nelson, and Romney's favourite muse. *Lady Hamilton at the Spinning Wheel* shows her demure, in the guise of a simple country girl. The celebrated actress Mrs Jordan (mistress of the future King William IV) appears as Viola in *Twelfth Night*, painted by Hoppner. Turner's *Iveagh Sea-Piece* (1802) is one of the earliest of his important marine paintings. There is also a delightful view of the bathing pond on Hampstead Heath by Constable (1821).

As well as the Iveagh Bequest, Kenwood has over 120 portrait miniatures and some superb examples of costume jewellery from the Georgian, Regency and Victorian periods. The collection dazzles with its use of semi-precious and replica stones and metal alloys and illustrates the incredible skill and craftsmanship of the designers and artisans. The pieces include brooches and pins, shoe buckles (donated by Lady Maufe, director of Heal's) and chatelaines—the chains from which the daily essentials of a lady's life depended: tiny scissors, a perfume bottle, a needle case.

GOLDERS GREEN
& HAMPSTEAD GARDEN SUBURB

Golders Green (*map p. 630, A1; Underground: Golders Green*) is a comfortable suburb developed in the 19th and 20th centuries, now home to a large Jewish community (some Orthodox), who settled here from the early 20th century onwards. It claims to offer some of the best kosher shopping in the whole of Europe. London's first crematorium was opened in Golders Green in 1902, in twelve acres of landscaped gardens. Sigmund Freud and Bram Stoker (who featured both Hampstead Heath and Jack Straw's Castle in his *Dracula*) were cremated here; here too repose the ashes of Ernő Goldfinger, Kingsley Amis, Enid Blyton, Anna Pavlova and Joe Orton.

Hampstead Garden Suburb (*map p. 628, C1; Underground: Golders Green, then bus H2 or 20mins' walk*) is a planned development, the brainchild of Dame Henrietta Barnett, a Whitechapel vicar's wife so horrified by housing conditions in the East End that she aimed to create a classless utopia. Building began in 1907, to designs by Raymond Unwin, who had laid out Letchworth Garden City in Hertfordshire. Around Central Square there are buildings by Lutyens, including the Free Church with its dome (interdenominational, in keeping with the founding spirit of the suburb) and the Anglican church of St Jude-on-the-Hill, with its conspicuous spire (1911).

Buildings lining the south bank of the Thames. The Oxo Tower, once a prominent landmark, is now dwarfed by The Mummy and the Southbank Tower.

THE SOUTH BANK, BANKSIDE, SOUTHWARK & BERMONDSEY

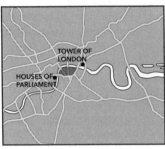

From Westminster Bridge to Tower Bridge, the south bank of the River Thames falls largely into the borough of Southwark, a historically prominent district with a fine and ancient cathedral. Southwark was also a place of bawdy entertainment outside the City limits. Theatres and bear-baiting arenas abounded from the Middle Ages and there were a great many breweries here too, with their corresponding taverns. The riverside is still a popular place of entertainment, with theatres and concert halls, waterfront pubs and cafés and the popular London Eye ferris wheel.

Some highlights of the area
+ **Tate Modern**, an exceptional collection of modern and contemporary art in a landmark building of industrial heritage;
+ **Shakespeare's Globe**, the reconstructed half-timbered playhouse where drama can still be enjoyed in the round;
+ **Southwark Cathedral**, an ancient place of Christian worship hard by the ever-popular and bustling **Borough Market**.

THE SOUTH BANK

Map p. 636, A3–B3. Underground: Waterloo; or Embankment and then walk across Hungerford footbridge.

The term 'South Bank' denotes the area running along the Thames opposite Victoria Embankment. A string of arts and performing arts venues covers the ground here from Westminster to Waterloo bridges and down towards the Oxo Tower.

Westminster Bridge (Thomas Page, 1854–62) is usually crowded, filled with souvenir vendors, buskers and tourists taking photographs. Extending along the river from the south end of Westminster Bridge to Jubilee Gardens is the grand, neo-Baroque **former County Hall building**, faced in Portland stone and with a 750ft concave river façade. Designed by Ralph Knott, it was begun in 1912, opened in 1922, but was not fully completed until the 1930s. Built to house the London County Council, later the Greater London Council, powerful—and now defunct—administrative bodies, the complex is now home to a hotel, flats and tourist attractions, including the Sea Life London Aquarium, the **London Dungeon** (a sort of glorified ghost train with an array of ghoulish shows; *thedungeons.com*) and the London Eye (*see below*). Eating and drinking establishments (mainly fast-food, with outdoor seating areas) line the heaving riverside terrace. Be prepared for long queues at all the attractions.

The **Sea Life London Aquarium**, occupying 170,000 square feet, is one of Europe's largest (*visitsealife.com*). A cascade of waters reveals the huge, crescent-shaped twin tanks devoted to the Atlantic and Pacific Oceans, supported by 40 additional exhibits on different regions of the world and different habitats—30,000 specimens in all representing over 350 species. Visitors descend a spiralling walkway through three levels to view the fish and marine life. A touch pool and beach pier allow visitors to handle some of the marine species. Experiences include sound effects, ocean-fresh aromas and a humid Rain Forest. The highlight of the visit is a face-to-face encounter with a shark.

THE LONDON EYE AND JUBILEE GARDENS
The **London Eye** (*map p. 636, A3; ticket office in County Hall; londoneye.com*) is a gigantic observation wheel overhanging the Thames, offering 30-min rides. The 443ft-high wheel, designed by the architects David Marks and Julia Barfield, opened in 2000 to celebrate the Millennium. The views of London and beyond, from the glass observation capsules, are outstanding, and on a clear day Windsor Castle can be seen (the Tower of London is more difficult to spot, even in optimum weather conditions, because of the encroaching skyscrapers). The Eye was assembled flat from parts made across Europe and delivered up the Thames by boat. The rim is connected by steel cables to the hub and spindle, which are held on A-frame legs buried deep under Jubilee Gardens. The last step was the attachment of the 32 capsules, which can hold up to 25 passengers, who step on and off during continuous rotation. The original plan was to dismantle it after five years, but it so captured the public's imagination that its tenure is now indefinite. The wheel is lit up at night, and on special occasions it is illuminated with colours and designs to reflect celebrations and anniversaries, for example in red, white and blue for the coronation of King Charles III. From the next-door pier, the 40-min London Eye River Cruises embark.

The open green space acting as a backdrop for the London Eye is **Jubilee Gardens**, first laid out in 1977 for Queen Elizabeth II's Silver Jubilee and now re-landscaped. The stone-clad, reinforced concrete Modernist blocks to the east, with grids of small windows (1953–63), make up the **Shell Centre**, one of the headquarters of the Anglo-Dutch oil and gas multinational. At the time of its completion it was the largest office space, by floor area, in Europe. Today, renamed Southbank Place, it has been redeveloped by the Canary Wharf Group and Qatari Diar with modernised offices, some still occupied by Shell, and the usual array of shops, restaurants and cafés, as well as a health club.

The London Eye in 2022, lit up in purple to celebrate the opening of the Elizabeth Line, the newest route on the London Underground transport network.

Hungerford Bridge (1864), on either side of which are the two Golden Jubilee footbridges, erected in 2002, carries trains from Charing Cross to Waterloo and the south. In one of the railway arches is the Archduke restaurant and wine bar, a pioneer of its kind when it opened at the end of the 1970s.

THE SOUTH BANK CENTRE, WATERLOO STATION & OXO TOWER

The Royal Festival Hall, Queen Elizabeth Hall, Purcell Room, Hayward Gallery and National Poetry Library collectively make up the body known as the South Bank Centre (*map p. 636, A3–B3*). The largest single-run arts body in the world, it attracts millions of visitors every year and has six resident orchestras, including the London Philharmonic. In addition to the main cultural programme, hundreds of free events are held in and around the venues each year. Along the pedestrian river terrace, known as Festival Riverside, there are bars, cafés and restaurants. Here too is Festival Pier, with riverboat services.

HISTORY AND DEVELOPMENT OF THE SOUTH BANK CENTRE

This once marshy area was drained in the 18th century and became variously a pleasure garden, the site for Lambeth Waterworks and then the Lion Brewery (*see South Bank Lion, p. 466*). After World War Two the land lay derelict and London County Council decided to develop it on a large scale. The South Bank Centre's history started in 1951 with the Festival of Britain, a scheme devised as a celebration and tonic for the nation, to cheer the country up after the deprivations and hardships of the War and its long aftermath of rationing and austerity. A large exhibition was laid out on the industrial wasteland between Westminster and Waterloo bridges, with the new Royal Festival Hall as its focus. Temporary buildings, where the Shell Centre (Southbank Place) now is, contained some remarkable structures including the Dome of Discovery and the 290ft high futuristic sculpture known as Skylon.

ROYAL FESTIVAL HALL

The **Royal Festival Hall** (*map p. 636, A3*) is a jolly structure in glass, stone and concrete, the sole surviving building from the Festival of Britain and the first new concert hall to be built in post-War Europe. It was designed in 1948–51 by the London County Council's chief architect Sir Robert Matthew, together with his deputy Sir Leslie Martin and a young team of designers; the riverside façade was altered by Sir Hugh Bennett in 1965 and in 2007 a multi-million pound refurbishment was completed. Its clever use of interior space, clad in wood, with large, multi-level foyers over which the main 'egg in a box' auditorium is suspended, was considered very innovative at the time. The main concert hall seats 2,500; Le Corbusier considered the design of the boxes, which look like pulled-out drawers, 'a very good joke'. The large foyer is used for exhibitions and there are several eating and drinking areas, with free lunch-time and evening entertainment. The Skylon cocktail bar and restaurant is on the first floor, with fine views of the river from the huge plate-glass windows.

The nearby concert and recital venues, **Queen Elizabeth Hall** (QEH) and the **Purcell Room**, and the **Hayward Gallery** modern art exhibition space, were added by architects of the Greater London Council in the late 1960s in a concrete Brutalist style. Once considered classic examples of the genre, the buildings have been generally disparaged over the years for their depressing greyness and for the incoherent—sometimes inaccessible—network of concrete staircases and walkways. In the undercroft of QEH is a skate-boarding area covered in graffiti art.

BFI Southbank, the British Film Institute (formerly known as the National Film Theatre), was established in 1933 and moved to its present site under Waterloo Bridge in 1958. It has an interesting programme of classic and contemporary film screenings from around the world (*see bfi.org.uk*) and also organises the annual London Film Festival. The BFI also has a restaurant and bar, as well as library facilities and the world's largest film archive. In front, on the riverside, is a second-hand market selling books, prints, postcards etc.

From **Waterloo Bridge** (Sir Giles Gilbert Scott, 1945) you can make out a remaining fragment of the Adams' Adelphi on the other side of the river (*see p. 201*). It forms an interesting contrast with Somerset House, built roughly at the same time.

THE NATIONAL THEATRE

East of Waterloo Bridge is The National Theatre (properly the Royal National Theatre; *map p. 636, B3; nationaltheatre.org.uk*), which opened in 1976. The building, an asymmetrical mix of concrete blocks, levels, terraces, struts, angles and flytowers, was designed by Sir Denys Lasdun. Many critics now consider it less Brutalist and more in the style of Le Corbusier; it is regarded by some as Lasdun's masterpiece. It was greatly admired by Sir John Betjeman, less so by Pevsner. King Charles, when Prince of Wales, called it 'a clever way of building a nuclear power station in the middle of London without anyone objecting'. The idea for a national theatre, with a challenging repertoire of contemporary and classic plays, was proposed as far back as 1848, a decade after the opening of the National Gallery, but its realisation was not to come until more than a century later. The National Theatre Company under Sir Laurence Olivier, its first artistic director, was set up in 1962 and took over the Old Vic as a temporary home. Building finally started on the current site in 1969. A statue of Olivier, portrayed as Hamlet (Angela Conner, 2007) stands at the corner of Theatre Square.

WATERLOO STATION

The Waterloo Bridge access road passes between BFI Southbank and the National Theatre and leads to a roundabout, where, in the middle, is the capital's first IMAX cinema (the **BFI IMAX**), the largest cinema screen in the UK (*map p. 636, B3*). Overlooking the roundabout is the neo-Greek **church of St John the Evangelist** (Francis Bedford, 1820s), a 'Waterloo' church (*see Glossary*), badly damaged in the Second World War and since restored.

    Waterloo Station (J.W. Jacomb-Hood, 1901–22) preserves a Victory Arch for the First World War, which is sadly hard to admire because of the teeming traffic on the roads surrounding the entrance and the ugly redundant office block which abuts it. Waterloo is one of London's busiest mainline terminals, serving the south coast as well as the commuter belt of Surrey and Hampshire. The station opened in 1848. In 1899 the direct Tube link with the City (to Bank Station) opened and still operates; it is popularly known as 'the Drain'. Nicholas Grimshaw designed the now defunct caterpillar-like, glass-roofed train shed which served the Eurostar services from 1993, before Eurostar moved to St Pancras.

THE OLD AND YOUNG VIC

On the corner of The Cut and Waterloo Road is the **Old Vic Theatre** (*map p. 636, B3; oldvictheatre.com*), opened in 1818 as the Royal Coburg. It was built in part from materials from the Savoy Palace on the Strand (*p. 203*), which had been demolished to make way for Waterloo Bridge. Rebuilt in 1833, it changed its name to the Royal Victoria, and then, rebuilt again, it re-opened in 1871 as the New Victoria, later becoming a temperance music hall for the working class. Lilian Baylis arrived in 1900 and took over the management in 1912, raising the standard of productions, particularly of Shakespeare, and making it one of London's leading theatres. It was damaged in 1941 but re-opened in 1950. In 1963 it became the temporary home of the National Theatre (*see above*). The first performance was *Hamlet*, directed by Sir Laurence Olivier with Peter O'Toole in the title role. After the National left for its new home on the South Bank, the Old Vic went through a difficult period until it was bought by Canadian entrepreneur Ed Mirvish, who returned the building to its Victorian splendour. It is now owned by the Old Vic Theatre Trust. During the Covid-19 pandemic, productions were live-streamed to replace lost box office revenue.

The **Young Vic**, its offshoot established by Frank Dunlop, occupies an octagonal building of 1970 further along The Cut. It aims to provide good theatre to young people at affordable prices. A plaque at the southeast corner commemorates the 54 people killed in 1941 while sheltering in the cellars of the building formerly on this site.

GABRIEL'S WHARF & OXO TOWER WHARF

The tiered building at **76 Upper Ground** (*map p. 636, B3*), formerly the headquarters of IBM, was designed by Denys Lasdun in 1985 to harmonise with his National Theatre next door. Next to it is an ex-studio complex formerly known as ITV Tower, after the independent terrestrial television company. The land around here lay derelict for many years after World War Two, until plans for offices were put forward in the 1970s. A planning battle took place between the local community and property developers, resulting in the property developers withdrawing their scheme. In 1984, a co-operative called the Coin Street Community Builders (CSCB) bought the 13-acre site with the aim of building affordable housing and workshops, opening up the river walkway and landscaping a riverside park. Some of that former atmosphere remains—the little half-timbered building opposite the Mulberry Bush pub, for example. But in the 21st century property developers have been more successful and the encroachment of their creations is loomingly obvious in the soaring glass panels of the Southbank Tower and 1 Blackfriars ('The Mummy'), which increasingly occupy the sky as one walks along.

Gabriel's Wharf and **Bernie Spain Gardens** (named after Bernadette Spain, a campaigning member of CSCB) took shape using open ground overlooking the Thames. Here are shops, cafés, restaurants, design studios and flats. Oxo Tower Wharf is another good mixed-use CSCB conversion. The wharf, built c. 1900, was acquired by Oxo, the meat extractors, as a cold store and processing plant. The **Oxo Tower** (A.W. Moore, 1928) was a successful attempt to defy the contemporary ban on outdoor advertising: letters spelling out the name of the famous stock cube were built into the ventilating louvres of the tower and were—and still are—lit up at night. Refurbished to a design by Lifschutz Davidson Sandilands, the building now has housing association flats on five upper floors and designer workshops and retail space on the ground, first and second floors. There is a restaurant on the top floor and a viewing platform which is free and open to the public. There was a time when looking out at London from an eighth floor gallery was quite unusual. Today it seems a little lowly. But the views are still good.

The South Bank Riverside Walk continues east to Blackfriars Bridge, past offices and the concrete-and-glass **Doggett's Coat and Badge pub**, named after the scarlet coat and silver badge awarded to the winner of the Doggett's Coat and Badge race; a five-mile rowing competition between newly-qualified Thames Watermen that takes place every July from London Bridge to Cadogan Pier, Chelsea. It commemorates Thomas Doggett, a comedian and manager of the Theatre Royal Drury Lane, who founded the competition in 1715. It is the world's oldest boat race.

Steps from here take you up onto Blackfriars Bridge, with a City of London boundary dragon in the centre of the roadway. Looking south you get a full-frontal view of the mixed-use skyscraper known as **The Mummy** (1 Blackfriars, Simpsonhaugh, 2018) and, a little to the right, the **Southbank Tower** (original building Richard Seifert, 1972; redeveloped and augmented in size by Kohn Pedersen Fox, 2015–17).

BANKSIDE

Map p. 636, C3. Underground: Southwark, Blackfriars, London Bridge.

During the 16th century, the area around Bankside was a place of ribald entertainment, with bear-baiting, cock-fighting and, after public plays were banned in the City, a clutch of theatres. The Rose was built in 1587, the Swan in 1595 and the Globe opened here in 1599. The area was also well known for its 'stews' (brothels) and all manner of illegal trading went on here, well away from the regulation of the City's livery companies. Perhaps unsurprisingly, the district also had many notorious prisons.

In 1550 it came under the jurisdiction of the City of London yet continued to enjoy its freedom from City restrictions, persisting in its wayward ways until the Puritans closed the theatres and cockpits down in 1642. Early 21st-century regeneration has lifted the area from its long post-War doldrums. Bankside is now a cultural 'destination', home of Tate Modern and the reconstructed Shakespeare's Globe Theatre.

HOPTON STREET

East of Blackfriars Bridge is the **Bankside Gallery** (*map p. 636, C3; 48 Hopton St; banksidegallery.com*), home of the Royal Watercolour Society and the Royal Society of Painter-Printmakers. As well as open exhibitions, it hosts selling exhibitions, mostly of contemporary watercolours and prints. On the riverbank behind the gallery, the **Founder's Arms** pub (*52 Hopton St*) is part of a modern office/housing development built on the site of a bell foundry where the bells of St Paul's were cast. From the terrace, bar and restaurant there are good views of St Paul's and other City landmarks.

Further down Hopton Street, overshadowed by the surrounding high-rises, are the **Hopton Street Almshouses** of 1752, founded by a fishmonger, Charles Hopton, and still home to some 20 pensioners in sheltered housing. There is a Committee Room used by all the residents for social gatherings and activities. The houses surround two garden squares with lawns and roses, creating a green haven in an otherwise somewhat bleak cityscape. There is a 100-year-old cattle trough on the pavement, where Hopton Street meets Southwark Street.

Diagonally across Southwark Street (left) are **Kirkaldy's Testing Works** (*99 Southwark St; for information on visiting, see testingworks.org.uk*), a building which houses the engineer David Kirkaldy's 350-ton materials testing machine, patented in 1863. The machine tests materials to determine their strength. Parts of bridges, aeroplanes and other civil engineering projects have been tested here. Kirkaldy's motto was 'Facts not opinions'.

THE MILLENNIUM BRIDGE

Designed by Foster & Partners with Arup & Partners and the sculptor Sir Anthony Caro, the bridge provides a pedestrian link between St Paul's Cathedral and Tate Modern. A flattened suspension bridge opened in 2000, it was the first Thames crossing to be constructed in over a century and is London's first pedestrian-only bridge. When first opened, it was found to have a tendency to wobble and after just one weekend had to be closed for adjustments. It is designed as a thin metal blade, high above the water, to give maximum views and thrills for those using it. It has a span of 320ft: the Thames is wider at this point than the Seine in Paris.

SHAKESPEARE'S GLOBE

In **Cardinal's Wharf** (*nos 49–52 Bankside*) are terraced houses dating from 1712, which have survived the surrounding redevelopment. No. 49 stands on the site of the Cardinal's Cap Inn, an Elizabethan tavern and brothel; an elaborate plaque falsely indicates that from here Wren watched the building of St Paul's.

Close by is the re-created **Shakespeare's Globe Theatre** (*map p. 636, C3; 21 New Globe Walk; guided tours approx. every 30mins, no need to book except for large groups; shakespearesglobe.com*). The original Globe stood in what is now Park Street, 200 yards away on the other side of Southwark Bridge. A small but lofty circular building, it was built by the Burbages and opened in 1599. Shakespeare was a shareholder and acted at the Globe for many years; several of his plays were produced there. In 1613 it burned down, when a spark caused its thatched roof to catch fire. It was immediately rebuilt, this second time with a tiled roof. The Puritans closed the theatre in 1642 and later demolished it. In 1970 the Shakespeare Globe Trust, headed by the American actor and film producer Sam Wanamaker (d. 1993), was set up to raise funds for the new Globe, which was completed in 1995. It is the first thatched building in central London since the Great Fire and traditional materials and building methods were used throughout—though always with modern safety precautions in mind. The reconstructed 20-sided polygonal building of oak and plaster is modelled closely on the original Globe and holds 1,500: 500 standing and the rest seated on wooden benches. The central part is open to the skies and performances take place through the summer months. The indoor theatre, the beautifully atmospheric, candlelit Sam Wanamaker Playhouse, operates year-round.

Bear Gardens, leading north from Park Street west of Southwark Bridge (*map p. 638, C4*) is the site of another early theatre, the Hope (1614), where Ben Jonson's *Bartholomew Fair* was first performed in October 1614. Bear-baiting began here before 1550 and continued in the theatre itself. Pepys was a visitor in 1666: 'After dinner, with my wife and Mercer to the bear-garden where...I saw some good sport of the bull's tossing of the dogs: one into the very boxes. But it is a rude and nasty pleasure.'

A plaque in **Rose Alley**, parallel with Bear Gardens to the east, recalls the Rose Theatre, put up by Philip Henslowe in 1587, the earliest theatre in the area and the first purpose-built playhouse to stage any of Shakespeare's plays, which were performed here along with those of Marlowe and Kyd. Edward Alleyn (*see p. 501*) was a leading actor. The theatre closed in 1606 and its remains were discovered in 1989 during archaeological excavations for a new office block. A performance and exhibition centre is planned.

TATE MODERN

Map p. 636, C3. Underground: Southwark, or Blackfriars or St Paul's and walk across the Millennium Bridge. For the Tate Boat, see p. 178. Free except for special exhibitions. Cafés, restaurant and shops. tate.org.uk.

Tate Modern is one of the most popular museums of modern art in the world. It opened in 2000 in the converted hulk of Sir Giles Gilbert Scott's Bankside Power Station, built after the Second World War to provide the City with electricity. An international architectural competition for the conversion of the site was won by the Swiss firm Herzog & de Meuron, who retained the stark industrial character of the building: a powerful horizontal mass of red brick, alleviated by immense vertical windows, is bisected by a tall central chimney. Externally it has been little altered. A two-storey light box, a gleaming white beam at night, has been added to the roofline, housing a restaurant with spectacular views over the river to the City and St Paul's Cathedral.

The entrance is either from the riverfront or through the great west entrance, down a vast concrete ramp straight into the **Turbine Hall**. Five hundred feet long and 150ft high, this is the heart of the building, the mighty nave of an industrial cathedral. Stripped of its turbine engines, the cavernous space is now a dramatic arena for the display of sculpture and installations of enormous scale, and pieces have been commissioned especially for it.

The **Natalie Bell Building**, the main boiler room of the old power station, is named after a local community leader and consists of three floors: one for temporary exhibitions and two others offering free displays from the Tate's collection.

The **Blavatnik Building**, named after the Blavatnik Family Foundation, which made one the largest donations ever received by the Tate, was opened in 2016 and provides more exhibition space and educational facilities. An oddly angled, slightly twisted building of brick openwork, this ten-storey extension to Tate Modern (also by Herzog & de Meuron) generated protests from residents of the neighbouring flats, who objected to the viewing gallery on the top storey from which visitors could look directly into their homes. The views beyond the flats are stunning.

The collection

Tate Modern is devoted to the Tate's collection of post-1900 international art and although Tate Britain is officially the home of British art, 20th-century British works are shown here too (*for the history of Tate as an institution, see p. 178*). There are many major works, spanning painting, drawing, sculpture, installation and conceptual art, as well as photography, film and video. The collection of Surrealist works is particularly strong, as is the modern and contemporary collection of British art—Henry Moore, Francis Bacon, David Hockney—which Tate represents comprehensively and in depth. The permanent collection displays are thematic rather than chronological. What follows is a selection of highlights.

The best-known artworks, from a variety of countries, include Henri Matisse's *The Snail* (1952–3), one of the gallery's major acquisitions, composed of vividly coloured rectangles of paper arranged roughly in the spiral of a snail shell. It is one of the artist's cut-outs, produced towards the end of his career when his hands were no longer steady enough for painting. Bridget Riley's *To a Summer's Day* (1980) is a series of coloured waves whose changes of colour and twisting pattern create an impression of rippling waves across the canvas. The iconic *IKB 79* by Yves Klein was described by the artist as 'a Blue in itself, disengaged from all functional justification', and he associated it with irrelevant standards beyond what can been seen or touched. *Standing Man* (1962, 1982) is a characteristic example of Michelangelo Pistoletto's mirror paintings. This back view of a life-size silk-screen image of a man in a dark suit is attached to a huge piece of highly polished steel, hung at or slightly above floor level to create illusionistic effects.

A number of the artworks belong within a social and political framework, some having been created as an immediate response to events and upheavals while others reflect on struggles of the past. Siah Armajani's *Room for Deportees* (2017) is a large-scale installation of a wooden sentry box guarding a barbed wire-topped chain-link fence separating two wooden chairs and a bench, the former occupants of which are suggested by the discarded hat and handbag.

Works such as Henri Matisse's *Studio Interior* (c. 1903–4) and Georges Braque's *Guitar and Jug* (1927) explore the relationship between the individual and the work of art. Another theme developed by the museum is the way in which artists use materials which were once considered unsuitable for art. In *Seamless* (1999), for example, Sarah Sze attaches everyday objects, plastic pots, pliers, office lamps and scrambled wires into a sweeping three-dimensional installation. Ana Lupaș's *Solemn Process* (1964–2008) preserves the large woven wreaths traditionally made for harvest festival celebrations in Transylvania. These were made from natural materials—hemp, straw, wood and clay—but as they and the tradition of making them declined, she sealed them in metal casings, preserving the traditional within the modern world.

The reaction of artists to the rise of mass media and new technologies is exemplified in a room with dimmed lighting, where Cildo Meireles' *Babel* (2001) is a striking circular tower created from old analogue radios, their station lights twinkling, tuned in to many different stations at a volume level at which they are just audible, thus creating an incomprehensible wall of low sound.

Tate Modern, occupying Sir Giles Gilbert Scott's former Bankside Power Station, with the extension known as the Blavatnik Building behind it. On the waterfront is the Founders' Arms pub, on the site of the foundry where the bells of St Paul's were cast.

A bridge across the Turbine Hall leads to the Blavatnik Building where, at the time of writing, 'How Art Became Active: 1960 to Now' offered a reflection of art over the last 50-plus years.

The Tanks in the foundations, which once held the oil which powered the generators, are now given over to live art, performance and cinema.

The Artist Rooms throughout the gallery are devoted to a nationwide touring collection of contemporary art by international artists, including Agnes Martin, Roy Lichtenstein and Ian Hamilton Finlay.

SOUTHWARK & BERMONDSEY

Map pp. 636–7. Underground: Southwark, London Bridge, Borough.

Southwark, on the south side of London Bridge, anciently in the county of Surrey, has as long a history as the City of London itself. The Roman London Bridge, built c. AD 43, connected what was then a series of marshy islands with Londinium on the other side of the river. Archaeological excavations have revealed that Southwark was a large Roman settlement, probably an extension of Londinium itself, where abattoirs, cemeteries and taverns were situated. Its name probably derives from 'Sudwerca', meaning a southern defensive fort in Old English. Southwark was the main entry point from the south and coaching inns and hostelries flourished in Borough, its commercial centre. Wharves and warehouses were built along the Thames and in the 18th and 19th centuries Southwark was an industrial centre with breweries and food factories. After serious damage in World War Two and with the decline in trade on the river, Southwark became very run-down until recent regeneration of the area.

SOUTHWARK BRIDGE, CLINK STREET AND ST MARY OVERIE DOCK

Southwark Bridge (*map pp. 639, D4*) was completed in 1921 (Sir Ernest George and Basil Mott), replacing a graceful cast-iron bridge by John Rennie, and is the least used by traffic of all the Thames bridges. East of it, in Park Street, a plaque marks the approximate **site of the original Globe Theatre** (*see p. 446*). At 34 Park St, overlooking the river, is the Anchor Inn, of 15th-century origin (the present building dates to the 18th century). Park Street was once the location for a number of breweries.

CLINK STREET

On the other side of the railway is Clink Street. Today it is a street of 19th-century former warehouses but once it was home to **Winchester Palace**, the town residence of the Bishops of Winchester from the 12th–17th centuries. Probably as grand as Lambeth Palace (*p. 463*), it was first built in 1144 by Bishop Henry de Blois, brother of King Stephen. In 1424 James I of Scotland and Joan Beaufort celebrated their wedding feast at the palace after their marriage in Southwark Cathedral; Henry VIII is said to have met his fifth wife, Catherine Howard, there. During the Civil War it was used as a Royalist gaol. The building burned down in 1814 but the remains of the Great Hall, including a beautiful 14th-century rose window (restored), survive near the Clink Prison Museum. The surrounding manor of 70 acres, attached to Winchester Palace, was known as the 'Liberty of the Clink' and a pleasure quarter sprang up outside the jurisdiction of the City. Here were the 'stews', largely inhabited by Dutch or Flemish prostitutes, and numerous bear gardens, used also for prize-fights, from which the Bishops of Winchester, as landlords, claimed rents (the prostitutes were known as 'Winchester Geese').

Here too was the **Clink Prison**, partly located below the palace. It was used by the bishops as a place of detention for heretics from the 16th century, and later for thieves and ruffians. The name Clink may have come from 'clinch' or 'clench', rivets hammered in a clinching iron, which held prisoners to the wall or floor. It has since become a term for prisons in general, hence the expression 'in the clink'. The prison was destroyed in the Gordon Riots of 1780 and never rebuilt. The Clink Prison Museum, in a former warehouse, tells the story of the old prison and the surrounding area (*admission charge; clink.co.uk*).

ST MARY OVERIE DOCK

St Mary Overie Dock (the name 'overie' means 'over the water') is said to date from the time of Winchester Palace. Today, lying rather incongruously between the modern buildings, you will find a full-scale reconstruction of Sir Francis Drake's ship the *Golden Hinde*, in which he circumnavigated the globe in 1577–80. This replica *Golden Hinde* was built in Appledore, Devon, using traditional skills and methods, and was launched in 1973. It had sailed more than 140,000 miles before berthing here in 1996. Actors in Tudor costume give guided tours (*goldenhinde.co.uk*).

SOUTHWARK CATHEDRAL

Map p. 639, D4. cathedral.southwark.anglican.org.

Southwark Cathedral is officially the Cathedral and Collegiate Church of St Saviour and St Mary Overie, Southwark. It has been the seat of a bishop since 1905, when the Diocese of Southwark was established, covering South London and East Surrey. Although much rebuilt and repaired, and seemingly rather hunkered down beside the temporal temptations of Borough Market, it is the oldest Gothic church in London. The first foundation here was a 7th-century nunnery, established, according to legend, by a ferryman's daughter. In 852–62 St Swithin, Bishop of Winchester, turned the convent into a house for Augustinian canons. In 1106 a priory was built, of which few traces survive.

Today the churchyard is usually full of people sitting and eating food purchased at Borough Market next door. An excavated area behind the Harvard Chapel, in the passage between the cathedral itself and the modern annexe, shows remains of a Roman road and parts of the Norman and medieval building fabric.

Interior of Southwark Cathedral

The grand and soaring nave was entirely rebuilt by Sir Arthur Blomfield in 1890–6. Its pews have been removed, replaced with modern, conference hall-style stacking chairs. The stained glass is mostly modern, replacing windows destroyed in 1941. Over the crossing rises a tall 15th-century tower and the transepts were also remodelled in the 15th century. The present choir and retro-choir were built by Peter des Roches, Bishop of Winchester, in 1207.

Nave: In the floor at the far west end is a large octagonal **plaque (A)** commemorating those who drowned in the *Marchioness* pleasure-boat disaster of 1989. To the left of it, beside the door to the tower, is a portion of **13th-century arcading (B)**. The splendid **carved wooden bosses** from the 15th-century roof, normally ranged along the wall

here, had been removed for restoration at the time of writing.

North side: In the north aisle is the much-restored **tomb of the poet John Gower** (1330–1408) **(C)**, a friend of Chaucer, with a recumbent effigy brightly painted with polychrome details. Gower was one of the earliest

Effigy of Lancelot Andrewes in Southwark Cathedral.

writers in English, a fact he alludes to in the Prologue of his *Confessio Amantis*:

And for that fewe men endite
In oure englissh, I thenke make
A bok for Engelondes sake,
The yer sextenthe of kyng Richard.
What schal befalle hierafterward
God wot...'

Behind the door into the vestry may be seen the jambs of a Norman door and an ancient **holy water stoup (D)**.

In the **north transept (E)** stands an oak dresser given to the church in 1588. The monuments here include one to John Lockyer (d. 1672), pill-maker, reclining wearily, with an amusing hyperbolical epitaph.

The **Harvard Chapel (F)** was restored and decorated in 1907 in memory of John Harvard, founder of Harvard University, Massachusetts, who was born in the parish and baptised in this church (1607). During the restoration a Norman column shaft (left of the altar) was discovered. The commemorative stained-glass window was presented in 1905. On the right, beside the entrance, a tablet commemorates the playwright and lyricist Oscar Hammerstein.

Choir and retro-choir: The fine **tombs** in the north choir are of **John Trehearne (G)** (d. 1618), gentleman-porter to James I; **Thomas Cure (H)** (d. 1588), his emaciated effigy a reminder that death must come to all; the wooden effigy of a **knight in chainmail (I)** (1280, restored) and the alderman **Richard Humble (J)** (d. 1616).

The vaulted **retro-choir (K)** has four chapels, dedicated to St Andrew, St Christopher, the Blessed Virgin, and SS

Elizabeth of Hungary and Francis of Assisi.

In the south choir aisle is the fine **tomb of Lancelot Andrewes (L)**, Bishop of Winchester (1555–1626), who oversaw part of the translation of the King James Bible, published in 1611. His *Nativity Sermon*, preached at Whitehall on Christmas Day 1622, in the presence of King James I, inspired one of T.S. Eliot's most famous poems.

The **altar-screen (M)**, erected by Bishop Fox in 1520, is a magnificent piece of work, though much damaged and restored. The statues in the niches date from 1905.

South transept and aisle: The **south transept (N)** was rebuilt in the 15th century by Cardinal Beaufort, whose niece, Joan Beaufort, was married to James I of Scotland in this church in 1424.

In the south aisle of the nave is Henry McCarthy's 1911 recumbent **alabaster figure of Shakespeare (O)**, usually holding a fresh rosemary 'quill'; Shakespeare's brother Edmond,

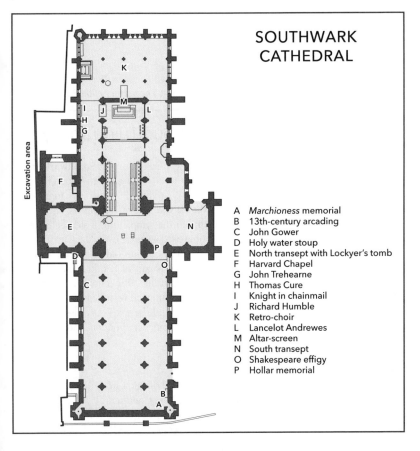

SOUTHWARK CATHEDRAL

A   *Marchioness* memorial
B   13th-century arcading
C   John Gower
D   Holy water stoup
E   North transept with Lockyer's tomb
F   Harvard Chapel
G   John Trehearne
H   Thomas Cure
I   Knight in chainmail
J   Richard Humble
K   Retro-choir
L   Lancelot Andrewes
M   Altar-screen
N   South transept
O   Shakespeare effigy
P   Hollar memorial

a 'player', was buried in the church in 1607. Above the monument is a memorial window to the playwright (C. Webb, 1954), On the pier diagonally opposite is a modern tribute to **Wenceslaus Hollar (P)**, the 17th-century engraver, one of whose famous views of London was taken from the top of Southwark Cathedral tower.

Lancelot Andrewes and T.S. Eliot

Last we consider the time of their coming, the season of the year. It was no summer progress. A cold coming they had of it at this time of the year, just the worst time of the year to take a journey, and specially a long journey. The ways deep, the weather sharp, the days short, the sun farthest off, in the very dead of winter.

Lancelot Andrewes *Nativity Sermon*, 1622

A cold coming we had of it,
Just the worst time of the year
For a journey, and such a long journey:
The ways deep and the weather sharp,
The very dead of winter.

T.S. Eliot *The Journey of the Magi*, 1927

BOROUGH MARKET AND BOROUGH HIGH STREET

Many breweries were based in Southwark from the 17th century. In **Southwark Street** (*map p. 638, C4*), developed by Bazalgette in the 1860s as a modern boulevard, part of the original **Hop Exchange** (R.H. Moore, 1866) survives. Its impressive long, white iron and stucco exterior stretches between the railway bridge and Stoney Street (*map p. 639, D4*). Note the sculpture of hop-picking in the tympanum. Inside is the large, naturally lit Exchange Hall. The building is now used as offices.

Borough Market (*map p. 639, D4*) is probably London's oldest market. A street market selling fruit and vegetables has existed in this part of London since the 13th century. The network of buildings mostly dates from the 19th century and today the specialist food stalls, cafés, restaurants and bars are thronged with tourists and foodies; delicious cooking smells permeate the whole area and the market is easily found by following your nose (*boroughmarket.org.uk; closed Mon*). The London Bridge attack of 2017 (*see p. 82*) spilled over into Borough Market.

BOROUGH HIGH STREET

To the south is Borough High Street (*map p. 637, D3*), which from Roman times was the great highway to the southeast of England and the Continent. It was the scene of countless processions and pageants in the Middle Ages and was trodden by the feet of many pilgrims on their way to the shrine of St Thomas à Becket in Canterbury. The

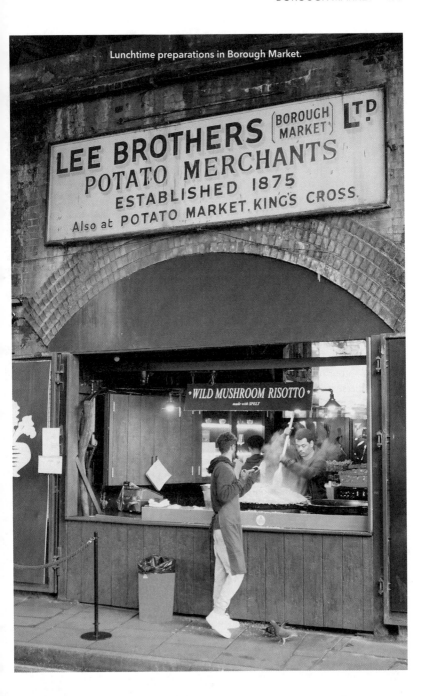

Lunchtime preparations in Borough Market.

street once abounded in hostelries and coaching inns, although few remain. Many were destroyed in the 'Little Fire of London' that laid waste the area in 1676 and the rest were made redundant after the coming of the railway in the 19th century. In a courtyard at no. 77 is the part-timbered **George Inn** (1676), the last galleried coaching inn left in London (still a pub but now owned by the National Trust; *nationaltrust.org. uk*). In **Talbot Yard** stood the most celebrated hostelry of all, the Tabard Inn, the 'Gentil hostelrye that highte the Tabard, faste by the Belle', the starting-point of Chaucer's Canterbury pilgrims. It survived (as the Talbot Inn) until 1876. The site is now marked with a plaque.

A short way further south, at **103 Borough High St**, was the Queen's Head Tavern (its memory preserved in the name of Queen's Head Yard), owned by the family of John Harvard (1607–38), who was born here and baptised in Southwark Cathedral (*see above*). The sale of this property before his emigration to America in 1637 augmented his fortune; at his death, he left money and books to a small Massachusetts college that would become Harvard University.

THE MARSHALSEA AREA

The area around **Newcomen Street** and **Mermaid Court** (*map p. 637, D3*) was the site of several prisons in the 18th and 19th centuries. It was here that debtors were held, as well as sailors accused of crimes at sea. Here was the Old Marshalsea prison, first mentioned in the 14th century and where Ben Jonson was imprisoned for sedition in 1597. Adjoining it to the south stood the Old King's Bench, the prison to which Judge Gascoigne is said to have committed Prince Henry (afterwards Henry V). Tobias Smollett, author of *Roderick Random*, was imprisoned here in 1739 for libel. In 1758 it was superseded by the New King's Bench, at the corner of Newington Causeway; John Wilkes was held there for libel in 1768–70. The prison was partially burned in the Gordon Riots (1780), fell into disuse in 1860 when imprisonment for debt was abolished, and was finally pulled down.

In **Union Street** to the west stood Horsemonger Lane Gaol, in which Leigh Hunt was confined for two years in 1813 for libelling the Prince Regent as a 'corpulent man of 50, a violator of his word, a libertine over head and ears in debt, a despiser of domestic ties, the companion of gamblers and demireps, a man who has just closed half a century without one single claim on the gratitude of his country' and where in 1849 Dickens witnessed the double hanging of a husband and wife, both convicted of murder. The jeers and hilarity of the crowd shocked him deeply.

In a public garden, before the church of St George the Martyr (*map p. 636, C3*), a small part of the walls survive of the **White Lion or Borough Gaol**, a 16th-century prison to which the New Marshalsea prison was transferred. Charles Dickens' father was imprisoned here in 1824 for failing to repay a baker £40 and 10 shillings. With the loss of family income, Dickens was forced to leave school at the age of twelve to work in a factory, an experience which influenced his writing and served as the inspiration for the prison scenes in many of his novels. While his father was incarcerated, the young Dickens lived in Lant Street. He later chose **St George the Martyr Church** (first mentioned in 1122, rebuilt in 1734–6 by John Price, and since restored; *stgeorge-*

themartyr.co.uk) as the scene of the christening and marriage of Little Dorrit (the street name Little Dorrit Court was chosen because of this). The church is based upon Wren's design for St James's Piccadilly.

Not far from here is the **London Fire Brigade Museum** (*94A Southwark Bridge Rd; closed for reorganisation at the time of writing; london-fire.gov.uk*), with a comprehensive collection of fire-fighting equipment and memorabilia.

THE LONDON BRIDGE QUARTER

The area between London Bridge and Tower Bridge is known as the London Bridge Quarter, with a section of riverside walk, refurbished warehouses and modern commercial developments. Close to its centre, towering over London, is Renzo Piano's **The Shard** (2013; *map p. 637, D3*). When it was built, this was the tallest skyscraper in Europe but it has since been eclipsed by a cluster of towers in Moscow and one in Warsaw. By the time this book goes to press, there will doubtless be others. The Shard is an immense glass icicle, conceived as a 'vertical city', and houses restaurants, bars, offices, a hotel, apartments and shops. Funded by Qatari money, it cost £1.2 billion to build and comprises 26 floors of office space, three floors of restaurants and bars. The 5-star Shangri-La Hotel occupies 18 floors and there are twelve floors of private apartments. A public viewing gallery ranges over floors 68–72. Teams of maintenance staff, in the form of abseilers, can often be seen dangling from its vertiginous exterior, cleaning the windows.

London Bridge Station (*map p. 637, D3*) is the terminus of one of the oldest railways in the world, opened in 1836 between Bermondsey (London Bridge) and Deptford. The station was completely rebuilt after extensive Second World War damage and again from 2013–18, in order to ease the passage of the 50 million people a year who use it.

OLD OPERATING THEATRE AND GUY'S HOSPITAL

St Thomas Street skirts London Bridge Station to the south. Before St Thomas's Hospital relocated from Southwark, its buildings and wards directly bordered the tower of **St Thomas's church** (1702–3), and an operating theatre and herbal pharmacy were created in the church's attic in 1821; female patients were operated upon here, without anaesthetic, in front of medical students. What is remarkable is that this space was forgotten about until 1956, when it was rediscovered and restored. Today, in the roof space of the church, up narrow, steep stairs, is the extraordinary **Old Operating Theatre Museum and Herb Garret** (*map p. 639, D4; admission charge; shop; oldoperatingtheatre. com*). It is the only known example of a Victorian operating theatre in existence; the operating table and spectators' benches are still *in situ*.

A little further down St Thomas Street stands **Guy's Hospital** (huge modern tower; *map p. 637, D3*), founded in 1726 by Thomas Guy (a City bookseller who made a fortune by his speculations in South Sea stock) to treat 'incurables' from nearby St Thomas's Hospital. John Keats studied here in 1815–16. In the courtyard, surrounded by original 18th-century buildings, is a brass statue of Thomas Guy, by Scheemakers (1733). Guy's Chapel, also 18th-century and recently restored, was designed by

Richard Jupp. It has a marble monument to Guy by John Bacon (1779), showing him attending a sick man on the ground while in the background a man is carried into the hospital on a stretcher. Eight mosaics dating from 1900 line the walls. They are in Arts and Crafts style and depict women in aspects of service. Brass plaques commemorate men and women associated with the hospital. The chapel was described by Pevsner as 'one of the noblest and most sensitive of its date in England.' It is the only 18th-century hospital chapel in England.

HAYS GALLERIA AND MORE LONDON

In Tooley Street, opposite London Bridge Station, is the entrance to **Hays Galleria** (*map p. 637, D3*), a conversion of shops, offices and restaurants, spanned by an iron and glass arched roof, leading out onto the riverside walk. These buildings were formally warehouses serving Hay's Wharf, built by William Cubitt in the 1850s. Tea clippers from India and China would enter an enclosed dock here to unload their cargoes. Inside, a kinetic bronze ship sculpture (1987) stands on the in-filled former dock, a reference to Hays Galleria's shipping past. The Horniman at Hays pub stands on the site of the tea warehouse of Frederick John Horniman (*see p. 505*). It contains friezes commemorating the life and travels of the great merchant and collector.

Continuing east towards Tower Bridge, the thriving 13 acres of modern glass offices, with a landscaped park and 'The Scoop' amphitheatre, is known as **More London**, a development conceived by Norman Foster in the late 1990s. The Kuwaiti property firm who originally developed the area bought the site in 2013 for an undisclosed sum (believed to be in the region of £1.6 billion). The armadillo-shaped structure irreverently dubbed 'the glass gonad' is **City Hall** (*map p. 637, E3*), the headquarters of the Mayor of London and the administrative body the GLA or Greater London Assembly. Designed by Foster + Partners, it opened in 2002; its unusual shape minimises the surface area exposed to sunlight and therefore the amount of energy it consumes. The Mayor of London should not be confused with the Lord Mayor of London, who is the head of the City of London Corporation (*see p. 19*). The Mayor of London holds responsibility for a much wider area, though within the City itself, the Lord Mayor takes precedence.

HMS *BELFAST*

HMS *Belfast* (*map p. 637, D3, iwm.org.uk*), the last surviving big gun World War Two armoured warship in Europe, is now part of the Imperial War Museum. An 'Edinburgh' class large light cruiser, she was designed during the mid-1930s in response to the threat posed by Japanese 'Mogami' class cruisers. Built by Harland and Wolff of Belfast, the vessel was launched on St Patrick's Day, 17th March, 1938. The ship itself and the displays inside her provide a compelling insight into the nature of war at sea.

On the outbreak of war in September 1939, HMS *Belfast* formed part of the maritime blockade of Germany, operating out of the Home Fleet's main base at Scapa Flow in the Orkney Islands. Badly damaged by a magnetic mine, she was completely refitted, eventually rejoining active service in 1943 on Arctic convoy duty. As the flagship of the Tenth Cruiser Squadron, she successfully provided close-range heavy cover for several convoys of the kind that supplied the Soviet Union with some four million tons

Shad Thames, with its former warehouses linked by overhead gantries.

of supplies during the course of the war, including 5,000 tanks and 7,000 aircraft. In the Battle of North Cape in December 1943, she engaged and contributed to the sinking of the German battle cruiser *Scharnhorst*. Only 36 men survived from that ship's complement of almost 2,000. On 6th June 1944, HMS *Belfast* was one of the first ships to open fire on German positions in Normandy in support of the D-Day landings. After 1945, she was occupied in peace-keeping duties in the Far East, helping to evacuate survivors of Japanese prisoner-of-war camps and Chinese civilian internment centres. A visit gives a vivid impression of life above and below deck in both war and peace.

BUTLER'S WHARF AND SHAD THAMES

The development of apartments and penthouses between Potter's Fields and Tower Bridge Road (*map p. 637, E3*) rejoices in the prestigious address 'One Tower Bridge'. On the east side of Tower Bridge is **Butler's Wharf**, a site of 1870s' warehouses and wharves which has been redeveloped into offices, restaurants, bars and loft-style apartments. The restaurants lining the river have outdoor terraces and good views of Tower Bridge, the City and Canary Wharf. Behind Butler's Wharf is **Shad Thames**. This atmospheric street lined with old warehouses connected by original iron gantries and overhead bridges now lends its name to the network of converted warehouses and docks in the vicinity. During the heyday of London's docks, the produce stored and traded here— tea, spices, coffee, dried fruits, etc.—was so plentiful and wide-ranging that the entire area was known as 'the larder of London'. The narrow canyon-like streets and inlets are interesting to explore, especially around St Saviour's Dock.

BERMONDSEY

Bermondsey was once the site of a great Benedictine Abbey dedicated to the Holy Saviour (hence the name St Saviour's Dock). On Bermondsey Wall East (*map p. 637, F3*) you will find **The Angel**, an inn originally built by the monks. Samuel Pepys was wont to pause here, on his journeys to and from Deptford to visit his friend John Evelyn (*see p. 483*). Here also are scant remains of a **manor house of Edward III**. It was near here that the engineer Bryan Donkin set up the first ever meat canning factory, on Southwark Park Road (*map p. 605, F4*) in 1813. The British Admiralty placed a large order. On Thurland Road is **St James's church** (*map p. 637, F4; godlovesbermondsey.co.uk*), with a fine bell-tower and a tall Ionic porch, built in 1829 following the petitions of a committee composed of a wool-stapler, two tanners and sundry others, formed with the aim of securing a new church for the district. This was one of seven 'Waterloo' churches in south London—and indeed its ten bells are cast from cannon abandoned by the French on the eponymous battlefield. The interior is serene and beautiful with fine pews.

ON AND AROUND BERMONDSEY SQUARE

Bermondsey Square (*map p. 637, D4–E4*) is the site of the once-great Cluniac **Abbey of Bermondsey**. Elizabeth, widow of Edward IV and the last Plantagenet queen, lived out her last days there. She had done her duty as a royal consort. Her two sons had vanished in the Tower of London (the 'Princes in the Tower') but her daughter had married Henry Tudor, the future King Henry VII. Bermondsey Square today is the scene of the **Bermondsey Square Antiques Market** (*Fridays from 6am; corner of Long Lane*). Until the laws of *marché ouvert* (which gave good title to purchasers of stolen goods) were abolished in the 1990s, Bermondsey Market had a reputation for skulduggery.

Bermondsey was also once a centre of the leather industry and many streets bear witness to this: Tanner Street, Morocco Street and Leathermarket Street (where the old **Leather Hide and Wool Exchange** building still stands; *map p. 637, D3–D4*). The old Leather Market is on Weston Street and there is an old tannery on Long Lane.

Between Morocco Street and Bermondsey Street is the Bermondsey branch of the **White Cube** (1970s and Casper Mueller Kneer, 2011; *map p. 637, D4; see p. 253*).

FASHION AND TEXTILE MUSEUM

The British designer Zandra Rhodes (b. 1940), who put the 'glamour into punk' in the 1970s with her jewelled safety pins and the artful rips in her jeans, established the museum in 2003 to showcase contemporary fashion, textiles and jewellery and to celebrate the work of textile designers, whom she regards as the 'Cinderellas of the business'. Exploding out against the tired greys of the surrounding building, the vividly-coloured museum (*83 Bermondsey St; map p. 637, D3; fashiontextilemuseum.org*) was converted from a 1950s' warehouse by the Mexican architect Ricardo Legorreta, his only commission in Europe. The UK's only museum of fashion and textile design, it has two permanent collections, the Fashion and Textile Museum Collection and the Zandra Rhodes Collection (*both may be viewed by appointment*). There is a continual run of temporary shows. Rhodes maintains a studio above the museum.

LAMBETH, VAUXHALL, BATTERSEA & BRIXTON

In centuries past, much of this area, south of the Thames, was a place of ecclesiastical power, with its archbishop's palace at Lambeth. Juxtaposed against this was Vauxhall, home of the famous Pleasure Gardens, one of the most popular places of public entertainment. Today the area around Battersea Power Station has been renewed. Further south stretch the mainly residential suburbs of Clapham, Brixton and Camberwell.

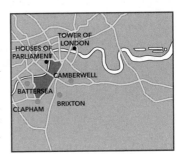

Some highlights of the area
✦ **The Imperial War Museum**, with material relating to Britain's experience of armed conflict;
✦ Two small, specialist museums, dedicated to the **Garden** and to **Florence Nightingale**;
✦ **Battersea Power Station**, an icon of early 20th century industrial power. Now a shopping mall (but its vast turbine hall is worth a look).

LAMBETH

Map p. 636, A4–B4. Underground: Waterloo, Lambeth North.

The name Lambeth is possibly derived from 'Lamb-hithe', meaning a place where lambs were docked, or from 'Loamhithe', a muddy harbour. Though badly bombed in WWII and today bisected by the railway lines that bring trains to and from the busy Waterloo Station, this is a historic area, home to the official residence of the Archbishop of Canterbury.

LAMBETH WALK
On the east side of the railway tracks is **Lambeth Walk** (*map p. 636, B4*), once a lively working-class street, made famous by the song in the 1937 musical *Me and My Girl* (its choreography inspired a strutting dance craze which reached America in 1938). Today the busy street market, with its costermongers, eel and pie shops and tripe dressers,

is long gone and the street is quietly occupied by modern social housing, though punctuated by relics from its past: a small parade of 1960s' shops; a tiny terrace of 19th-century cottages; small side streets with names such as Walnut Tree Walk (the ghost of a 17th-century country lane); and the elaborate, red-brick and stone-clad former Pelham Mission Hall (1910), now the Henry Moore Sculpture Studio. Above its door is an outdoor pulpit from where preachers once addressed shoppers and traders thronging the market below. The hot air that issues from it today is supplied by an extractor vent. Next door the yellow brick Chandler Hall has a plaque commemorating Charlie Chaplin, who was born and brought up in Kennington, which is in Lambeth borough. Part of his childhood was spent in the workhouse (*see p. 476*).

Lambeth Walk opens onto **Lambeth Road**, a busy thoroughfare running east–west. Beyond the junction with Kennington Road is the Imperial War Museum. At no. **100 Lambeth Rd**, part of a small Georgian terrace opposite the museum, lived Captain William Bligh, Commander of the *Bounty* (blue plaque); he is buried in the churchyard of St Mary-at-Lambeth (*see Garden Museum, below*).

THE IMPERIAL WAR MUSEUM

The Imperial War Museum (*map p. 636, B4; Underground: Lambeth North; café; iwm.org. uk.*) operates three sites in London: HMS *Belfast* (*see p. 458*), the Churchill War Rooms (*see p. 151*) and this, its main home. The displays illustrate and record the experience of armed conflict—with particular attention paid to the role played by Britain and the Commonwealth—since the start of the First World War in August 1914. The varied collections tell the story of military and civilian, Allied and enemy, tactical, strategic, social and political aspects of warfare by land, sea and air, employing an extraordinary array of memorabilia, fine art, film, sound archives, interactive displays and models. The vast atrium is given over to 'Witness to War' and displays objects like the Baghdad Car, the mangled remains of a vehicle destroyed in Mutanabbi Street book market in Baghdad and the four-storey high V2 rocket which would have terrorised the inhabitants of London and much of the southeast of England in 1944. The award-winning First World War galleries opened in 2014 to mark the centenary of the beginning of the 'Great War'; the reconstructed trenches give an idea of the conditions endured by soldiers on the various fronts. Other galleries cover the Second World War (the Holocaust Galleries tell the stories of some of the six million Jewish victims through jewellery, clothing, toys, letters and photographs) and the years 1945–2014, including the conflicts of Northern Ireland and the Falklands.

ST GEORGE'S CATHEDRAL AND HERCULES ROAD

On the corner of St George's Road and Lambeth Road, on the very spot where the 'No Popery' rioters (the Gordon Riots; *see Glossary*) assembled in 1780, stands **St George's Cathedral** of the Roman Catholic archdiocese of Southwark (*map p. 636, B4*), built by the Gothic Revival architect Augustus Pugin in 1840–8. Wrecked by bombs in 1941 it was freely rebuilt by Romilly Craze using the original design. A spacious edifice, brick outside and stone within, it mixes a profusion of Gothic styles. On St George's Road opposite the cathedral is a Georgian terrace, where at no. 131 lived the master builder

George Myers, who worked with Pugin on many of his projects, including Southwark Cathedral.

Christ Church, at the corner of Kennington Road and Westminster Bridge Road, has been rebuilt into an office block. At the junction of Westminster Bridge Road and Kennington Road, opposite Lambeth North Underground, stands the ragstone **Lincoln Tower**, designed by E.C. Robins, decorated with the Stars and Stripes emblem in red and white stone. It was erected by subscription from Americans as a memorial to President Lincoln, and opened in 1876.

In **Hercules Road**, a plaque on a modern red-brick block notes that William Blake lived on the site in 1793. Opposite it, alongside a charming fragment of Georgian terrace, in front of which stands a mature fir tree, Centaur Street leads through a clanging railway arch. Straight ahead, from Carlisle Lane off Royal Street, is an entrance to Archbishop's Park.

LAMBETH PALACE

Archbishop's Park (*map p. 636, A4*), opened to the public in 1901, was formerly part of the grounds of Lambeth Palace, the residence of the Archbishop of Canterbury, the Church of England's most senior prelate. The palace itself stands at the south end of its ancient grounds, close to the river and overlooking the Palace of Westminster: before the bridge crossings were built, the archbishops would travel to Westminster by ferry. Archbishop's Park affords a good view of the Bath stone residential wing of the Lambeth Palace, built by Edward Blore in the 1830s.

Lambeth Palace (*closed for refurbishment at the time of writing; archbishopofcanterbury. org*) has been the official London residence of the Archbishop of Canterbury for nearly 800 years. The building was begun by Archbishop Langton (1207–29). Altered many times by his successors, it suffered damage during the Civil War, when it was ransacked by Cromwell's men, and again in the Second World War. Thomas Cranmer wrote his *Book of Common Prayer* here (1549).

Interior of the palace

The early Tudor **gatehouse** (c. 1490), through which the palace is entered, resembles that of Hampton Court Palace, built in the same period. The **Great Hall**, rebuilt in medieval style by Archbishop Juxon in 1663, has a roof resembling that of Westminster Hall (it was described by Pepys in July 1665 as 'a new old-fashioned hall'). The **Library**, probably the oldest free public library in the country, contains some extraordinary treasures, including the 12th-century illuminated Lambeth Bible, Elizabeth I's prayer book, a copy of the Gutenberg Bible, a book of hours of Richard III and the letters that were on Archbishop Laud's desk at the time of his arrest. Laud (1573–1645) was the key advocate of Charles I's religious reforms. Arrested in 1640 by the Parliamentarians, he was executed in 1645 after being found guilty of treason. Also among the palace treasures is a fine series of portraits of archbishops by Holbein, Van Dyck, Hogarth, Reynolds, Romney, Lawrence and others. The small **Chapel** (c. 1230) preserves stalls and other fittings provided by Archbishop Laud (1634). The chapel was the scene of the second trial of Wycliffe in 1378 (the picturesque Lollards' Tower derives its name from the belief that the Lollards, Wycliffe's followers, were imprisoned in it). The beautiful **Crypt** is the oldest part of the building, perhaps as early as 1200.

LAMBETH BRIDGE AND THE GARDEN MUSEUM

Lambeth Bridge (Blomfield et al, 1932; *map p. 636, A4*) has red-painted arches and balustrades, supposedly to honour the red-upholstered benches in the House of Lords (Westminster Bridge, which is closer to the House of Commons, has a green colour scheme to match the Commons upholstery). On the south side of the bridge, in the deconsecrated church of St Mary-at-Lambeth, is the Garden Museum.

THE GARDEN MUSEUM

Founded in 1977 by the late John and Rosemary Nicholson, thus rescuing the church which houses it from demolition, this is the country's only museum dedicated to gardening and the history, art and design of gardens (*map p. 636, A4; admission charge; café; gardenmuseum.org.uk*). A refurbishment programme (Dow Jones Architects, 2017) provided more gallery space for displays of tools, photographs, paintings and gardening artefacts. At the core of the redevelopment is the Ark Gallery, a recreation of **Tradescant's Ark**, or cabinet of curiosities (*see box*). The museum also includes material on Joseph Banks (1743–1820), the first professional plant-hunter, who accompanied Captain Cook aboard HMS *Endeavour* and named Botany Bay. Artefacts (largely historical garden implements) include a collection of early garden gnomes, a canister of 'Slug Death' (an early pesticide), and two leather 'pony boots' worn by horses that pulled early lawn mowers, to stop their hooves from disfiguring the turf.

The glass and beaten copper **Garden Café**, whose floor is paved with old gravestones, overlooks a tranquil courtyard garden designed by Dan Pearson, inspired by the Tradescants' travels as plant collectors. In the garden you will find the elaborately carved **tomb chest of the Tradescant family**. The epitaph on the lid reads: 'A world of wonders in one closet shut, these famous Antiquarians that had been, both Gardiners to the Rose and Lily Queen, transplanted now themselves, sleep here.' The 'Rose and Lily Queen' is a reference to Henrietta Maria, consort of Charles I. As a princess of France she united, on her marriage, the *fleur-de-lys* and the rose of England. The elegant Coade Stone **tomb of Admiral William Bligh** (d. 1817), best known as the captain of the mutinous HMS *Bounty*, stands adjacent to that of the Tradescants. Bligh was engaged on a mission to transplant the first breadfruit trees to the West Indies from Tahiti, as an alternative food source for sugar plantation slaves, after American independence threatened the usual supplies. After the mutiny, he and his men were obliged to navigate 3,600 miles by sextant in an open boat for 41 days, living off raw fish, turtles and seabirds.

A viewing platform in the medieval **church tower**, the oldest part of the building, gives views across the Thames over to Westminster and beyond. During redevelopment, a vault containing 30 coffins was discovered, including those of five archbishops. Elias Ashmole and Elizabeth Boleyn (mother of Henry VIII's ill-fated wife Anne), were buried in the old churchyard.

THE TRADESCANTS AND THEIR 'ARK'

John Tradescant (c. 1580–1638) was gardener to Robert Cecil, the first Lord Salisbury, at Hatfield House, and later to Charles I and his consort Henrietta Maria. He was a keen collector of 'curiosities', unusual or unfamiliar objects—a feather, a shell, a religious object—anything which represented the art, nature and ways of life of other nations. He acquired some items on his travels around Europe and Russia, or they were given to him by ships' captains, botanists and friends, and obtained others from his son, John Tradescant the Younger. People were allowed to view his collection for sixpence. His Lambeth neighbour, the scholar and lawyer Elias Ashmole (1617–92), considered the Ark of huge significance and persuaded the Tradescant family to bequeath the collection to him. It became the basis of the Ashmolean Museum in Oxford and these objects have now returned to the Garden Museum on loan. John's son, John Tradescant the Younger (1608–62), was gardener to Charles II and became a freeman of the Worshipful Company of Gardeners in 1634. Three years later he made the first of three voyages to Virginia, bringing back the tulip tree, the Michaelmas daisy and the Virginia creeper, among other plants and shrubs.

THE RIVERSIDE WALK TO WESTMINSTER BRIDGE

On the west side of Lambeth Palace Road, the riverside walk leads north (right) to Westminster Bridge, affording excellent views of the Houses of Parliament on the opposite bank. In front of Lambeth Pier, from where boat services run up and down the Thames, is the **SOE Monument** (Karen Newman, 2009), commemorating all those who undertook perilous missions during World War Two. The SOE (Special Operations Executive, also known as Churchill's Secret Army) recruited male and female volunteers of all nationalities to conduct acts of sabotage in enemy-occupied countries. The bust is of British and French Resistance agent Violette Szabo, who was captured, tortured and then executed in Ravensbruck concentration camp in 1945. She was 23 years old. Szabo was posthumously decorated by both Britain and France.

The elaborate red-brick buildings behind the wall on the right are the surviving 19th-century ward pavilions of St Thomas's Hospital (*see below*). A plaque in the wall opposite Lambeth Palace commemorates Lt-Col John By, founder of Ottawa, who was born in Lambeth in 1779. Another plaque, just before Westminster Bridge, opposite 'Big Ben', commemorates the victims of CJD, the human form of 'Mad Cow Disease'.

Steps lead up to **Westminster Bridge** (Thomas Page, 1854–62), which replaces an 18th-century stone bridge. On its northern side it is guarded by the **South Bank Lion**, a large sculpture in Coade Stone (*see overleaf*). It was made in 1837 and formerly adorned the Lion Brewery (demolished in 1950 to make way for the Royal Festival Hall). It then stood outside Waterloo Station before being moved to its present site in 1966.

COADE STONE

This artificial, frost-resistant material was first manufactured by Mrs Eleanor Coade in 1769 in a factory on this site. Coade Stone was extolled in its day as the equal of marble for its sharpness of definition. The mixture, to which fine-ground quartz was added, was fired at very high temperatures so that it practically vitrified. In the 18th century its trade name was Lithodipyra, from the Greek meaning stone (*litho*) twice (*di*) fired (*pyra*). The stone, in fact, was semi-ceramic, the secret of its durability. The Coade family was originally from southwest England and it is surmised that they knew of and used china clay, which was—and still is—mined around St Austell in Cornwall. The success of Mrs Coade's enterprise came largely thanks to the enthusiasm for her product of influential architects and sculptors. Robert Adam, on his return from the

The Coade Stone South Bank Lion on Westminster Bridge.

Grand Tour, found it the ideal medium for producing the ornamental 'Grecian' urns which he made fashionable. Sir John Soane was another user. On the façade of his house in Lincoln's Inn Fields are two Coade Stone figures, and there are others at Pitzhanger Manor, his villa in Ealing. The sculptor John Flaxman also appreciated the material's qualities. His figures of *Tragedy* and *Comedy* on the Royal Opera House in Covent Garden are of Coade Stone.

Coade Stone ceased manufacture in 1840, but its presence still endures.

ST THOMAS'S HOSPITAL AND THE FLORENCE NIGHTINGALE MUSEUM

In Lambeth Palace Road, opposite the Houses of Parliament, is **St Thomas's Hospital** (*map p. 636, A4*). It is of ancient origin, possibly founded as early as 1106. It moved here from Southwark (where St Thomas Street still enshrines its memory; *map p. 637, D3*) and the foundation stone was laid by Queen Victoria in 1868. It was built on a 'pavilion' layout devised by Florence Nightingale: to aid ventilation and reduce the spread of disease, wards were organised in long blocks, linked by a corridor, with windows on both sides. Most of the pavilions were demolished when the hospital was rebuilt after the Second World War; the surviving chapel and three original pavilions have been restored.

In the hospital grounds is the **Florence Nightingale Museum** (*2 Lambeth Palace Rd; admission charge; florence-nightingale.co.uk*), exploring the achievements of the great nursing pioneer and health reformer both in this country and abroad. For her indefatigable campaigns to improve sanitation and hospital management, she became the first woman to receive the Order of Merit (in 1907). The exhibition space (stethoscope audio guides available) is arranged in three hospital 'pavilions', a system which she pioneered to improve ventilation and isolate patients with infectious diseases. The museum, whose exhibits include Nightingale's medicine chest, one of the famous lamps she used on her ward rounds and her pet owl Athena (which she rescued in Athens and carried in her pocket), documents her early life, her work in the Crimea and her legacy: 'Florence Nightingale—that Englishwoman whose name shall never die, but sound like music on the lips of British men until the hour of doom.' The tribute is from the pen of Mary Seacole, herself a Crimea veteran, whose work is also commemorated in the museum. There is also a register of nurses, listing the 229 women who served with Nightingale in Scutari (Üsküdar) and the Crimea. There is a **statue of Mary Seacole** (Martin Jennings, 2016) in the gardens between the Florence Nightingale Museum and the river.

VAUXHALL & BATTERSEA

Map p. 629, D3 and p. 635, F4. Underground: Vauxhall.

Opposite Vauxhall station is the busy traffic junction and bus shelter known as Vauxhall Cross. Straight ahead is **Vauxhall Bridge** (1906, Binnie and Fitzmaurice), replacing a 19th-century river crossing. It is decorated with allegorical bronze statues, twice life sized, representing *Pottery, Engineering, Architecture, Agriculture, Science*, the *Fine Arts* and the civic provisions of *Education* and *Local Government*. *Architecture*, which stands on the third iron pier on the up-stream side of the bridge as you travel from Vauxhall, holds a tiny but amazingly detailed model of St Paul's Cathedral in the palm of her hand (take care as you lean over the parapet!). On the right-hand side is Terry Farrell's Post-modern **SIS Building**, in cream stone and tinted green glass, opened in 1994. It is the home of Britain's intelligence service, SIS, generally known by its former title of MI6. The building's stepped geometric form supposedly echoes nearby Battersea Power Station, though it seems to owe more to ancient Babylon; the distinctive façade has featured in several James Bond films. Reflecting it, on the left-hand side of the bridge, is the **St George Wharf** housing development; seven acres of clear and tinted glass, with flock-of-seagulls rooftops. At its centre rises a tall cylindrical residential tower block. This part of South Lambeth, historically an industrial, working-class community, is today multi-ethnic and swiftly being gentrified: the former Elephant and Castle pub (left out of the station; note the sculptures of elephants with castles on their backs on the roofline) is currently a branch of Starbucks. The new riverside developments are popular with politicians because of their proximity to Westminster.

Industries that once flourished in Vauxhall were glass-making (commemorated by Glasshouse Walk, off Albert Embankment), porcelain (the Royal Doulton factory was also off the Embankment) and car manufacture. The Vauxhall Iron-works Co. (later Vauxhall Motors) built its first car in 1903; the factory was on Wandsworth Road, where the Sainsbury's supermarket now stands.

OLD VAUXHALL GARDENS

Behind Vauxhall Station, off Kennington Lane, is a modest green expanse (*map p. 629, D3*). This small rectangle of grassy hillocks with a tarmacked multi-use recreation ground, surrounded by housing estates and with the railway arches running along its western flank, is all that remains of Vauxhall Pleasure Gardens.

VAUXHALL PLEASURE GARDENS

'Vauxhall is the first pleasure in life!—I know nothing like it,' claims Mr Smith in Fanny Burney's *Evelina* (1778). Opened in 1661, the Pleasure Gardens' heyday was from 1729–67, when they were owned and run by the shrewd Bermondsey entrepreneur and arts patron Jonathan Tyers (a portrait of him and his family is held by the National Portrait Gallery), who turned them into a successful commercial enterprise. An entrance fee of one shilling (quite expensive for the times) was charged in the hope of discouraging prostitutes, pickpockets and other undesirables. The gardens featured the latest in Rococo design and decoration; visitors could stroll in landscaped grounds, dine in 'supper-boxes', dance, drink, listen to music, admire artworks, watch illuminations and firework displays and even go on balloon ascents. The Museum of London holds several original entrance tickets, from regular ivory passes to upmarket season tickets made of silver and decorated with Neoclassical scenes, the name of the guest engraved on the reverse. In 1738, Tyers commissioned Roubiliac to produce a life-size marble statue of Handel (now in the V&A) to greet guests in The Grove after they arrived by water. Handel's music was often performed here by the Gardens' resident orchestra; the dress rehearsal for Music for the Royal Fireworks took place at Vauxhall in 1749. Over the years, Vauxhall was visited by Pepys, Goldsmith, Boswell, Walpole, Fanny Burney, Frederick, Prince of Wales, Wordsworth and Charles Dickens. Dickens, in 1836, made the mistake of visiting the gardens by daylight, when all that had seemed so magical by night appeared tawdry and everyday: 'Our favourite views were mere patches of paint,' he wrote, in gloomy disillusion.

Along the eastern edge of the gardens, on Tyers Street, is the **Vauxhall City Farm** (*free, donations welcome; www.vauxhallcityfarm.org*). Following World War Two, the area was little more than a wasteland; this small farm was founded in 1976 as a place where members of the community could come and tend animals and grow their own

produce, a way of bringing nature to the inner city. Today the farm is home to horses, alpacas, pigs, goats, rabbits, ducks and geese, and offers therapeutic classes in riding and horticulture as well as educational and youth outreach programmes. A group of spinners spins wool from the sheep and alpacas, using vegetable dyes from plants grown on the farm.

Next door and behind the farm is the entrance to **St Peter's Church** (façade best seen from Kennington Lane; *stpetersvauxhall.org*). Its High Victorian, neo-Gothic design is by J.L. Pearson (1864) and it was built over the slum area that had developed from the former Vauxhall Pleasure Gardens; the altar is on the site of its Neptune Fountain. The restored, vaulted interior displays wall-paintings, mosaics by Salviati of Venice and carved stonework. The Vauxhall St Peter's Heritage Centre has exhibitions relating to the history of Vauxhall and Lambeth. The church is known for its music—an appropriate tradition, standing as it does on the site where Handel, Johann Christian Bach and Thomas Arne performed.

Detail of the ethylene tetrafluoroethylene panels that clad the US Embassy building on Nine Elms Lane.

NINE ELMS

Before becoming an industrial area based on the Nine Elms railway yard, Battersea served as a market garden for London; here were fields of watercress and lavender. The old yard is now home to the **new Covent Garden Market**. The famous produce and flower markets moved here on a wholesale basis from central London in 1974 (no retail traders). On Nine Elms Lane you will also find the **US Embassy**, which for security reasons took the decision to move here from Grosvenor Square in Mayfair. The building, by the US firm KieranTimberlake (2017), takes the form of a large cube with billowing lateral panels resembling mini spinnakers. They are made of ethylene tetrafluoroethylene, a kind of plastic designed to reduce solar gain. The grasses planted in the Embassy garden are intended to evoke the North American prairie.

BATTERSEA

Map p. 628, C3. Underground: Battersea Power Station.

Battersea, a former island in the Thames marshes, lying beside the river opposite Chelsea, is an ancient settlement, as indicated by the recovery in 1857 of the Iron Age Battersea Shield (now in the British Museum). Famous landmarks include Battersea Power Station and Battersea Park.

The first **Battersea Bridge** was built in the 18th century by Henry Holland; the present iron bridge was built by Bazalgette in the 1880s and replaced the wooden structure depicted in many paintings. Along the Thames here, many modern apartment complexes have been built.

In Old Battersea near the river, on the site of an Anglo Saxon church, stands **St Mary's Church** (Battersea Church Road), built by Joseph Dixon in 1775–6, in yellow brick with classical details. The east window has 17th-century heraldic glass and there are monuments from the earlier church. J.M.W. Turner was inspired to paint his Thames sunset by the view from the church window, and the poet William Blake married the daughter of a local market gardener here in 1792. The manor house which stood next to the church is now demolished. The Vicarage and Devonshire House are attractive 18th-century houses. In Vicarage Crescent is the 17th-century Old Battersea House. Battersea Square has upmarket shops and restaurants.

BATTERSEA PARK

Battersea Park (*open 8am–dusk; boats for hire in summer; fountain displays spring–autumn*) occupies the long riverside stretch between Albert Bridge and Chelsea Bridge. Before it was landscaped in the mid-19th century, it was notorious as Battersea Fields, according to one commentator 'a place that surpassed Sodom and Gomorrah in ungodliness and abomination', filled with illicit drinking dens frequented by such inveterate imbibers as Charles Dickens. Also here, in 1829, disagreement over the government's Catholic emancipation bill brought the Duke of Wellington (Prime Minister) and the Earl of Winchilsea (staunchly Protestant) to Battersea Fields to fight a duel (neither man was injured). The area became the centre for the new craze for bicycling in the 1890s and in 1951 was laid out as pleasure gardens for the Festival of Britain.

The 200-acre park today has attractive gardens, cafés and refreshment stands, a little zoo and a boating lake, a Herb Garden, Old English Garden and Winter Garden. Barbara Hepworth's *Single Form* (beside the lake) was made in commemoration of Dag Hammarskjöld, the UN Secretary General who was killed in an air crash in 1961. On the north side of the lake is Henry Moore's *Three Standing Figures*. The **Brown Dog** statue (Nicola Hicks, 1985), north of the English Garden, is a replacement for an earlier monument to a brown terrier who died in the vivisection laboratories of University College. The statue was destroyed after a 1907 riot by anti-vivisectionists.

The Victorian **Pump House** (1861) is now a contemporary art space. The **Peace Pagoda**, with wind-bells, overlooking the Thames and Chelsea, was erected by Japanese Buddhists in 1985.

The Death of Buddha, one of the gilded reliefs on the Battersea Peace Pagoda, brainchild of the Japanese monk Gyoro Nagase. It opened in 1985.

BATTERSEA POWER STATION

The four white, fluted, 335ft-high chimneys of **Battersea Power Station**, east of Chelsea Bridge, dominate the river skyline from many aspects. Although now the structure has achieved iconic status, it caused widespread public dismay when it opened in 1933, because of fears of pollution as well as its gigantic size. This 'Temple of Power' was designed by Sir Giles Gilbert Scott. Derelict for many years after it ceased to operate, it has now been developed, largely with Malaysian money, as a playground for shopping, eating and drinking, with a giant chess set on a patch of astroturf outside and a large range of shops within. Though the lofty old turbine hall is undeniably magnificent, the atmosphere provided by the background music and rows of branded-retail boutiques is very like that of a large international airport. You can also (for a fee) ride up one of the chimney in a lift made of glass, which pops out of the top and offers panoramic views to those not afflicted by claustrophobia or vertigo.

Around the power station there are tall residential and business blocks—and more storeys, containing flats and offices, have been added to the power station itself. There is a riverside walk linking the power station to Battersea Park and a plethora of places to eat and drink, including under the arches of the railway bridge. **Battersea Dogs' Home**, on Battersea Park Road, takes in over 20,000 stray dogs and cats a year and finds new homes for them.

CLAPHAM & BRIXTON

Map pp. 628, C3–629, D4. Underground: Clapham Common, Clapham South, Clapham North, Brixton.

There are many mainly residential districts south of the Thames, including Brixton and Clapham, grown up around former villages, estates and farms. Time was when it was a social embarrassment to live south of the river; today the areas are often prosperous and sought-after.

CLAPHAM
Over the course of this century Clapham, which sits astride the boroughs of Lambeth and Wandsworth along the line of a Roman military road, has become a desirable residential area. It has always had good links to the centre of the city: 'The man on the Clapham omnibus', a term first coined in a legal context in the late 19th century, is taken to stand for the average unexceptional, but reasonable and decent, human being. Today Clapham offers 'villagey' pockets of thriving independent bars, restaurants, shops and boutiques, most notably on Clapham High Street, Old Town and around the Common. Southeast of the Common, **Abbeville Road** has become a little enclave in its own right, filled with restaurants and referred to as 'Abbeville Village'. **Clapham Junction** is the busiest railway junction in the UK.

Clapham Common (*map p. 628–C4*) is recorded in the Domesday Book. It covers 220 acres and has never been cultivated. Once it was notorious as a cruising ground (in the 18th century the phrase 'been to Hadham and come home by Clapham' was slang for contracting gonorrhea). Today it is used for sports, fairs and circuses and general recreation. There is a bandstand in the centre. Around its perimeter are some attractive private houses dating back to the late 18th and early 19th centuries, when Clapham was 'a pretty suburb' (according to Thackeray). It still has a quasi-village appearance

Battersea Power Station, at dusk.

and an old horse trough sits at one edge of the Common. Samuel Pepys retired to Clapham and lived in a house in North Side, overlooking the Common, until his death in 1703; the mansion was demolished in 1754. On the site of no. 29, formerly 'The Elms', the architect Charles Barry lived, and died in 1860. At the northern tip of the common, surrounded by fine trees, stands the handsome church of the **Holy Trinity** (Kenton Couse, 1774; *holytrinityclapham.org*), built of milk-chocolate-coloured brick with a handsome clock-tower and a wide porch borne on Tuscan columns. Here the Clapham Sect, a group of evangelical Christians, met in the late 18th and early 19th centuries. Among their number were the vicar and curate of the church, John and Henry Venn, and, more famously, William Wilberforce. The sect, according to the commemorative plaque on the church exterior, 'rested not until the curse of slavery was swept away from all parts of the British dominions.'

BRIXTON

In origin, in common with other south London suburbs, Brixton (*map p. 629, D3–D4; Underground: Brixton*) was a fashionable residential area in the 18th and 19th centuries. Large villas along Brixton Hill and in Angell Town were built for City merchants and the arrival of the railway brought cheaper housing in densely-built terraces. Brixton at one time was known as the 'Oxford Street of the south', famed for its upmarket department

Windrush Square, Brixton, with the handsome main building of the Black Cultural Archives.

stores, Bon Marché and Quin & Axtens. Both are long gone and the life and culture of Brixton today is inextricably associated with immigrants from the West Indies. Many of the so-called 'Windrush Generation', British Commonwealth citizens who came to the UK between 1948 and 1971, settled here. The name comes from the *Empire Windrush*, a ship which docked in Tilbury, Essex in 1948, with 500 passengers aboard from Jamaica and other islands in the Caribbean. The visit of Nelson Mandela to Brixton in 1996 was a symbolic recognition of the district's role in the struggle for Black rights in Britain. Today around a quarter of Brixton's population is of African and Caribbean descent. The shops, street markets, pubs and restaurants all reflect this ethnic mix.

Brixton's most famous street is **Electric Avenue**, immortalised in a song of the early 1980s by Guyanese-born Eddie Grant. It took its name from the fact that it was one of the first London streets with electric lighting when it opened in 1888. Today its curving sweep is filled predominantly with small grocers and fishmongers selling okra, yams, aloe vera, plantains, tamarind and huge bags of rice in an array of grades and grain sizes. The roofline of **Brixton Market** on the corner of Electric Avenue and Electric Lane is adorned with large sculptures of foxes and cherries by Lucy Casson (2010).

Diagonally opposite Lambeth Town Hall, with its tall clock tower, is a survival of Brixton's stately past, the **Ritzy Cinema**, built in 1910. Next to it is the Tate Central Free Public Library, overlooking Brixton Oval and Windrush Square (with a somewhat neglected bust of the benefactor, Henry Tate, in front of it). Beyond, below a faded advertisement for Bovril, is a **memorial obelisk** to African and Caribbean members of the British Commonwealth forces in both world wars, and beyond that again, in a handsome Georgian building of 1824, are the **Black Cultural Archives** (*blackculturalarchives.org*), with an important collection documenting the history, culture and art of the African and Caribbean diaspora in Britain, particularly rich in oral histories. One of the collection founders was the Jamaica-born historian and educationist Len Garrison (1943–2003), who was determined to reveal the 'hidden history' of Black heritage in Britain. The Archives put on regular temporary exhibitions.

St Matthew's Church, with its massive Doric porch, is one of London's 'Waterloo' churches (*see Glossary*), consecrated in 1824. Former Prime Minister John Major was married here in 1970. Major's father, a vaudeville and music hall performer, had lived in Brixton at one time. The enormous Budd family mausoleum, facing the road intersection outside the churchyard, is indicative of the kind of consequence and fortune to which Brixton residents could aspire in the 19th century.

Brixton Windmill (*Blenheim Gardens, west off Brixton Hill*) was built as a flour mill in 1816 and was in use until 1934. Now restored to working order, it can be visited on open days (*see brixtonwindmill.org*).

Nearby **Brockwell Park and Hall** (20mins' walk; *map p. 629, D4*) provide a leafy retreat. Known for its swimming lido, the Park Estate is graced by a late Georgian mansion in a free Grecian style. It was built by D.R. Roper for John Blades, a glass manufacturer of Ludgate. The grounds are now a public park.

STOCKWELL AND KENNINGTON

Stockwell, north of Brixton (*map p. 629, D3; Underground: Stockwell*), has a sizeable Portuguese community. Famous residents included Van Gogh, who lived at 87 Hackford Rd in 1873 (he was 20). Here he fell in love with Eugenie Loyer, the daughter of his landlady, a love unrequited.

Near the Oval Underground station is **Kennington Park**, formerly an execution ground and also a popular public assembly point. The great radical preacher George Whitefield (*see p. 369*) addressed crowds numbering tens of thousands here in 1739. Chartists gathered here in 1848. Opposite rises **St Mark's church**, with its Doric portico and Ionic bell-tower. It is a 'Waterloo' church (*see Glossary*) built by D.R. Roper in 1824. Charlie Chaplin was born in Kennington in 1889, the son of an alcoholic music hall performer who died of dropsy aged 37. The last time his son saw him alive was in the Stag's Head on Kennington Road. The Surrey Cricket Club was established at the **Oval Cricket Ground** in 1845.

In Vassall Road, between Brixton Road and the Camberwell New Road, is the Anglo-Catholic church of **St John the Divine** (G.E. Street 1870–4; *sjdk.org*), admired by John Betjeman. The spire features gargoyles of prominent public figures, including the late Queen Elizabeth II (clutching a corgi) and King Charles, when he was Prince of Wales.

WALWORTH, PECKHAM & CAMBERWELL

Walworth, Peckham and Camberwell are suburbs with distinct characters. None of them is a destination in its own right, but all have features of interest.

ELEPHANT & CASTLE

Elephant and Castle (*map p. 636, C4; Underground: Elephant and Castle*) is a busy and somewhat chaotic area spreading around the large traffic roundabout of the same name. The skyline is punctuated by tall, glassy residential towers, including the semi-cylindrical **Strata**, whose angled tip features three large wind turbines. Lauded by some, dismissed as a gimmick by others, the building went up in 2010 and is not generally liked; in fact it was recently reported that the turbines, which were supposed to generate power for the block, are never switched on because they make the top-floor penthouse too noisy. **St Mary's Churchyard**, an area of green facing the busy road known as Newington Butts, was the site of a church demolished in the 1870s when the road was widened. The playwright Thomas Middleton (author of *Women Beware Women*) was buried here in 1627. A little further down Newington Butts, on Dugard Way off Renfrew Road (*just beyond map p. 636, C4*), is the **Cinema Museum** (*visits by guided tour; cinemamuseum.org.uk*). Housed in a handsome brick building of 1870, the former Lambeth Workhouse where Charlie Chaplin lived as a child, it is home to a rich collection of film, film-related equipment and memorabilia.

Near the Tube station on the east side of the roundabout is a Modernist block with blue balconies: Ernő Goldfinger's Alexander Fleming House, which was received with ecstasy in architectural circles in the 1960s, though loathed by those who had to inhabit it. It now goes by the name of **Metro Central Heights** and has been repurposed as a condominium, though alongside the tall slim towers that are going up around it, it looks small and shoddy and very much of its time.

The **Old Kent Road** (*map p. 637, D4*), formerly the Roman road to Dover, led from the Elephant and Castle to Canterbury. This was the route taken by Chaucer's pilgrims, who halted at 'St Thomas a Watering' (*site at 320 Old Kent Rd, corner of Albany Rd; map p. 629, D3*). An inn stood here for many years. At the time of writing the site was occupied by a Vietnamese restaurant. Ben Jonson once lived in lodgings on the Old Kent Road.

WALWORTH

The **Southwark Heritage Centre**, at 147 Walworth Rd (*beyond map p. 636, C4*), is home to the Southwark Archives, Art Collection and Cuming Collection. Between them Richard Cuming (d. 1870) and his son Henry (d. 1902) amassed an eclectic range of nearly 25,000 objects and curios encompassing natural history, ethnography, archaeology, decorative and popular art and British social history. Henry Cuming left the collection to the local borough, together with a sum of money for the employment of a curator, and the museum was opened in 1906 by Lord Rothschild. The 'Billy and Charleys' fakes are medieval pilgrim badges, small shrines and other oddments, forged by William Smith and Charles Eaton, two illiterate mudlarks from Shadwell, who duped the entire country in the 19th century. The museum continues to collect material relevant to the past and recent history of Southwark and its local communities.

Walworth is known for its **East Street Market** (*Tues–Sun*), along East Street which opens off the Walworth Road (*map p. 629, D3*). Officially the market has been running since 1880, though its origins are much older, from the days of the medieval drovers who would pasture their cattle on Walworth Common. The market sells mainly clothes and produce. Also opening off the Walworth Road is Liverpool Grove (*between East St and Albany Rd; map p. 629, D3*), which leads to **St Peter's church**, built by Sir John Soane in yellow stock brick with an Ionic screen porch (1825).

On Wells Way, which cuts through Burgess Park further south towards Camberwell, is the **former Public Baths and Library**, built of red brick with fine sculptural detail. It is one of the many public buildings endowed by John Passmore Edwards (1823–1911), a native Cornishman-turned-newspaper proprietor who became a passionate advocate for public education. He built 16 public libraries in London, many of them in the Camberwell area where he had been a resident. On the side wall is a ceramic tile depiction of a Camberwell Beauty butterfly (*see below*), dating from the 1920s. The butterfly had been adopted as the emblem of the Samuel Jones paper factory, founded in the early 19th century and known in particular for its gummed and adhesive products (they made the glue for the back of postage stamps). When the factory was demolished in the 1980s, the mosaic butterfly was saved and brought here. The former Waterloo church of St George just beyond has been converted to residential use.

CAMBERWELL

The inner city residential area of Camberwell (*map p. 629, D3; Overground: Denmark Hill*) was once empty and rural and appropriated as a hunting ground by King John. In the 18th century Camberwell was known for its market gardens. Terraced housing development began in the 1780s and in the 19th century the area became a fashionable, middle-class place to live. More recently it has been run-down and deprived, the place where Danny in the cult film *Withnail and I* invents a joint known as the Camberwell carrot. Today, however, Camberwell has experienced something of a resurgence and many of the Georgian and Victorian properties have been renovated. The area is enriched by the presence of Camberwell College of Arts and two important hospitals: the student buzz extends to a few lively bars and restaurants on Camberwell Church Street. Camberwell also gives its name to the Camberwell Beauty (*Nymphalis antiopa*), a butterfly that is a rare migrant to British shores and which received its English name when two specimens were seen here in 1748.

Camberwell Green, now a traffic island, was the site of fairs from 1279; they rivalled the popular events at Greenwich but were stopped in 1855. In **Denmark Hill** (south from Camberwell Green) are King's College Hospital (founded 1840) and the psychiatric Maudsley Hospital (founded 1923); in Champion Park is the William Booth Memorial Training College, designed by Sir Giles Gilbert Scott in 1932 with statues of the Salvation Army's founders, General and Mrs Booth, outside. John Ruskin lived at no. 28 Herne Hill, the continuation of Denmark Hill, and also at no. 163 Denmark Hill; both houses have gone but he is commemorated by **Ruskin Park**.

Some impressions of Camberwell's fashionable past may be glimpsed in **Camberwell Grove**, where the politician Joseph Chamberlain was born in 1836 (at no. 188). The Gothic Revival **parish church of St Giles** in Church Street was built in 1844 by Sir George Gilbert Scott on the site of an older church destroyed by fire. It has an exceptionally fine interior, tall and white, and the east window is filled with glass designed by John Ruskin and his friend Edmund Oldfield. Ruskin's inspiration, both for the subject matter and the rich colours of ruby red and violet, came from the great cathedrals of northern France. In the south transept are some fine old brasses, the earliest from the late 15th century, commemorating prosperous lords of the manor, many of whom received grants of land from Henry VIII following the dissolution of the monasteries.

On Peckham Road is the **South London Gallery**, known for its programme of contemporary and live art shows (*southlondongallery.org*). The building arose from the munificence of John Passmore Edwards (*see above*). Robert Browning was born in nearby Southampton Way in 1812.

PECKHAM AND NUNHEAD

Peckham (*map p. 629, E3; Overground: Peckham Rye or trains to Nunhead*) is named after the ancient River Peck. Along with Camberwell it was once a hunting ground of King John and later became an area of market gardens, where melons and figs were grown. Some fine houses were built here in the early 19th century. Thomas Tilling's first omnibus service ran from Peckham to the City in 1851, and in 1862 the railway arrived. **Peckham Rye Common**, where a young William Blake had a vision of angels, was saved from encroaching developments in 1868. The area has found its way into fiction with Muriel Spark's *The Ballad of Peckham Rye* (1960). By the late 20th century, Peckham had become a multi-ethnic neighbourhood, infamous for its complicated traffic system and large estates of council housing providing theatres for gang and gun crime. London press forecasts of gentrification, dubbed 'Peckhamania' in 2013, were perhaps over-enthusiastic, though a crop of bars, restaurants and shops sprang up around Bellenden Road, just behind Peckham Rye station, bordering East Dulwich. Frank's Café on **Rye Lane** opens during the summer months as a pop-up cocktail bar under a red tarpaulin on the 10th floor of a multi-storey carpark.

In **Meeting House Lane**, running north from Peckham High Street, stood the Meeting House used by the Quaker William Penn (founder of Pennsylvania) before his fiery tracts led to imprisonment in the Tower in 1668. Elizabeth Cadbury, Quaker and wife of the chocolate manufacturer, was also born in Peckham (in 1858).

Nunhead Cemetery (*map p. 629, E3*), between Linden Grove and Limesford Road, was founded in 1840 and is one of the largest of London's Victorian burial grounds. Part of the area is now a nature reserve, since over the years the tended lawns of the graveyard have turned to woodland and scrub; it has been described as the 'Highgate of the south'. The lodges and entrance gates (with cast-iron appliqué hour glasses and inverted torches, to symbolise the sands of time and life extinguished) are by James Bunning and the Kentish ragstone chapel is by Thomas Little. It is an evocative spot, popular with runners and dog-walkers. Among the lime trees is buried Thomas Tilling (d. 1893), who pioneered the horse-drawn bus. The Scottish Martyrs' Memorial, an obelisk erected in 1851, commemorates five political reformers (two of them Scots) who were transported to Australia for sedition in 1793.

The mock-Tudor Old Nun's Head pub on **Nunhead Green** (a good pit-stop if you need one; *theoldnunshead.co.uk*) stands on the site of a former convent.

GREENWICH & DULWICH

In the area immediately along the river, former naval dockyards and royal palaces survive to illustrate the ancient commercial and administrative prominence of this part of London. The foreports to Greenwich are Rotherhithe and Deptford, important areas of wharves and docks since early times. Greenwich fully merits a day trip and is rewarding at all seasons. Leafy Dulwich, where London begins to merge with Kent, is one of the suburbs of London that has best preserved its individual 'village' character.

Some highlights of the area

✦ The *Cutty Sark*, launched in 1869 and in her day the fastest of the tea clippers, now berthed on Greenwich harbourside;

✦ The **Old Royal Naval College**, an ensemble of buildings in historic Greenwich that is one of the finest expressions of the Baroque in England;

✦ The **National Maritime Museum** in Greenwich, home to a vast and varied collection on nautical history, with the exquisite **Queen's House**, a Baroque architectural gem displaying an important collection of paintings, and the **Royal Observatory**, site of the Prime Meridian, where you can stand with your feet in two hemispheres;

✦ **Dulwich Picture Gallery**, with some splendid masterpieces of European art in an architecturally important and influential building;

✦ The **Horniman Museum** in Forest Hill, founded by a prosperous tea merchant, with beautifully displayed collections of anthropology and natural history.

ROTHERHITHE & DEPTFORD

Rotherhithe: map p. 625, A2; Deptford: map p. 625, A3. Underground: Canada Water; Overground: Rotherhithe, Canada Water, Surrey Quays.

Neither Rotherhithe nor Deptford could claim to be tourist destinations in their own right but both serve as gateways to Greenwich and preserve interesting reminders of their historic past.

ROTHERHITHE

The Rotherhithe Peninsula juts into the Thames opposite Wapping, to which it is connected by a road tunnel (*see map p. 629, E3*). There are three old docks on the peninsula: Canada Water, Surrey Water and Greenland Dock. Russia Dock, where timber from Russia and Scandinavia was formerly unloaded, has now been filled in and is a woodland and nature park.

Rotherhithe Street skirts the peninsula close to the water. At its south end, **Surrey Docks Farm** (*map p. 625, A2*) is a working animal farm in the heart of London (*surreydocksfarm.co.uk*). Further on, the Doubletree Hilton London Hotel at Cuckold's Point (so named because King John is said to have donated the land to a local miller to compensate him for the seduction of his wife) occupies the old **Nelson Dock**, once a shipyard (it retains its dry dock and narrow draw dock). The Georgian Nelson House (1740s) in the hotel forecourt was probably once the home of a wealthy shipwright. On the peninsula tip are many restored riverside houses.

Lavender Pond Nature Reserve, just inland from the tip, contains a shallow pool once belonging to the old timber docks and used to prevent merchandise from drying out. It is now a wetland conservation area with walkways over the reed beds. The pond was formerly connected to the Thames by a channel, navigable by small boats and lighters. In 1928 the Port of London Authority built the Pump House to regulate water levels in the docks (previously subject to tidal fluctuations) and the channel was closed. The **Pump House** still stands (though the pump itself is now outside the Brunel Museum; *see below*) and until 2017 was a museum of Rotherhithe history including displays on Peek Frean biscuits (their factory was nearby). It is now a bilingual English and Mandarin nursery school.

ROTHERHITHE CENTRE

Historically, Rotherhithe was known as Redriff. Its centre, around the Overground station, is a tiny enclave of cobbled streets and converted mills and warehouses. In Tunnel Road, behind the station, is the **Brunel Museum** (*brunel-museum.org.uk; map p. 629, E3*). It occupies the former engine house (with slender tin smokestack) of Marc Brunel's Thames Tunnel (1825–43), the first underwater tunnel in the world, for the construction of which he invented the tunnelling shield. The museum offers a film and small exhibition on the construction of the tunnel, which almost cost Brunel's son Isambard his life when the Thames waters burst through the roof in 1828. The force of the water pushed him up the tunnel shaft and he had to be pulled to safety from a window. Brunel's Thames Tunnel was at first a foot tunnel and was later adapted for the railway. Today part of it can be seen at Wapping station and guided tours are sometimes organised (*see museum website for details*).

The 18th-century **Mayflower pub** (*mayflowerpub.co.uk*), which overlooks the river, was re-named to commemorate the famous ship which sailed from the Thames to Portsmouth and from there with the Pilgrim Fathers to America in 1620. The **Hope (Sufferance) Wharf** warehouse, in yellow stock brick, has been restored as flats. A sufferance wharf is one where dutiable goods may be unloaded to relieve congestion

Charity School pupil clutching her prayer book. Statue on the façade of the former Free School in Rotherhithe. Pairs of statues like this, with a girl on one side and a boy on the other, dressed in blue and white uniforms, adorn the exteriors of many former charity schools in London.

at licensed docks. The Anglo-Catholic **St Mary's Church** (*stmaryrotherhithe.org*) dates from 1715, though the tower and spire are later and all replace an earlier 12th-century structure. Prince Lee Boo, a native of the Pacific islands who died in Rotherhithe in 1784, is buried in the churchyard. The church interior is very fine, with a wooden-framed barrel roof held up by four massive pillars—tree trunks encased in a plaster shell and given gilded Ionic capitals. A clock ticks gently on the organ loft. The captain of the *Mayflower*, Christopher Jones, worshipped and was buried here (plaque at the end of the north aisle, beneath a fine sea captain's memorial).

Opposite the church is the **old Free School**, founded in 1613. The building is of the early 18th century and features statues of a girl and boy pupil in their uniforms at the first-floor level. The **Watchhouse Café** adjoins it, occupying the former house of the local parish Watch, whose job it was to keep an eye out for miscreants.

Rotherhithe has traditionally catered to the spiritual needs of Scandinavian seafarers. The Danish Seamans' Mission survives on Rope Street and on Albion Street are the Finnish Seamans' Mission and the Norwegian church of St Olav (by the entrance to the Rotherhithe Tunnel, a road tunnel built in 1904–8).

SURREY QUAYS

Between Rotherhithe and Deptford are the sprawling Surrey Quays (*map p. 629, E3*), a residential development and 'leisure park' on the site of once bustling docks: many are now filled in, though Canada Water, South Dock and Greenland Dock survive, with a marina and water sports centre. The first dock on the site was the Great Howland Dock, built in 1696. It was the largest commercial dock in the world when it was built, with berths for 120 ships. It became **Greenland Dock** in 1725, when the South Sea Company leased it for their whalers: the stench from the vats of boiling blubber being rendered down for soap drifted for miles. Today nothing more noxious wafts across the water than the smell of cooking oil from the Moby Dick pub. Later the docks complex was enlarged to receive timber from Canada, the Baltic and Scandinavia: Quebec Pond, Russia Dock and Norway Dock were added. The dockyard finally closed in 1970.

DEPTFORD

Deptford (*map p. 625, A4–A3*) takes its name from the 'deep ford' over the Ravensbourne, a tributary of the Thames. Its maritime past is commemorated by a large anchor planted in its High Street: Deptford's Royal Naval Docks were established by Henry VIII in 1513 and they have witnessed at least two scenes now immortalised by historians: the knighting of Sir Francis Drake by Queen Elizabeth I, and Sir Walter Raleigh's flinging his cloak across a puddle to prevent the muddying of the royal feet (though the latter stunt is also claimed by Greenwich). Deptford was the birthplace of the great shipwright Phineas Pett and his son Peter (*see Woolwich, p. 573*) and the docks were at the height of their prosperity in the 18th century, when the Victualling Yard was used for provisioning battleships during the Napoleonic Wars. In the 19th century the area fell into decline, as newer, larger ships needed docks of greater draught. The docks closed in 1869, the Victualling Yard in 1961. Deptford today has a rough reputation (a reputation sanctified by history: the playwright Christopher Marlowe was fatally stabbed here in 1593, possibly in a tavern brawl) but it is a lively district, proud of its High Street Market (produce, clothing, bric à brac). The High Street itself is a down-to-earth slice of old London: not a chain store in sight, and with an array of Vietnamese food shops.

WHAT TO SEE IN DEPTFORD

The Anglo-Catholic **St Paul's Church**, whose churchyard opens off Deptford High Street (*map p. 625, A4*), is a striking building by Thomas Archer (1730) with a tall spire and a semicircular porch of tall Tuscan columns. The interior (*open for services*) is very fine. In the churchyard is a plaque commemorating Mydiddee, a native of Tahiti who died in Deptford in 1793, having arrived here with Captain Bligh (of *Bounty* fame; *see p. 464*) aboard the *Providence*. There are also some characteristic tombs in the shape of sarcophagi with headstone and footstone, though many are now damaged. In the cobbled **Albury Street**, east off the High Street, is a row of 18th-century sea-captains' houses, the door hoods mounted on fine carved brackets.

St Nicholas's Church** on Deptford Green (*map p. 625, B3*) is the old parish church, dating from the late 17th century, with an earlier tower. Christopher Marlowe, after the fatal stabbing mentioned above, was buried here in an unmarked grave. Here too were buried George Shelvocke, father and son. The father, a captain in the Royal Navy and licensed privateer, published an account of a Pacific voyage on the *Speedwell* in 1719, during the course of which a sailor shot a 'disconsolate black Albitross', which seemed to jinx their weather. The incident was to inspire Coleridge's *Ancient Mariner*. The churchyard has more sarcophagus tombs.

From the top of Deptford Green, the **Thames Path** leads in two directions. To the right it passes the AHOY Centre on Borthwick Street, a charity offering ship-building apprenticeships and sailing courses to disadvantaged children. Beyond this is a wide foreshore of new housing, known in estate-agent speak as 'West Greenwich' (the domes of Greenwich and the masts of *Cutty Sark* are well seen from here). The promenade leads to a curious sculpture group of Peter the Great (Mikhail Shemyakin, 2001), at the corner where **Deptford Creek** enters the Thames. The first London railway, built between

Deptford and Bermondsey in 1836, had an extension to Greenwich added in 1838, across Deptford Creek on a drawbridge which took several men to operate.

In the other direction the Thames Path passes the site of the old docks and leads to **Sayes Court Park** (just off Evelyn Street; *map p. 625, A3*). It occupies the site of a house once owned by John Evelyn, where Pepys was entertained to dinner. Evelyn's daughter Elizabeth eloped with a young man from the dockyard, much to her father's chagrin. Grinling Gibbons also lived at Deptford, in a house rented from Evelyn. Marvelling at the wood carver's talent, Evelyn presented him to Sir Christopher Wren. Peter the Great stayed at Sayes Court in 1698 when he came to the Royal Dock incognito, to study the craft of shipbuilding. When he and his royal entourage left, it is reported that there was scarcely a window pane left intact, not a chair unsplintered nor a curtain unrent. The Thames Path leads towards Deptford Strand through the Pepys Estate, on the **site of the old Victualling Yard**, a housing development where the streets and tower blocks have been given nautical names such as 'Windlass Place' and 'Lanyard House'. It was acclaimed as 'an impeccable scheme' in 1967. A survival

Elaborate carved door-hood bracket in Deptford's Albury Street, where sea captains had their residences in the 18th century.

from more prosperous times is **The Colonnade**, leading off Grove Street (diagonally opposite Windlass Place; *map p. 625, A3*), a terrace of 18th-century houses for officers of the Victualling Yard.

GREENWICH

Greenwich was once a fishing village, lying along the line of the Roman Watling Street. Its pleasant location beside the Thames brought it to royal attention in the 15th century. Humphrey, Duke of Gloucester, son of Henry IV, built himself a mansion and enclosed the park as a hunting ground. It was from Greenwich that Willoughby and Chancellor set sail in search of the Northeast Passage in 1553; it was possibly here that Sir Walter Raleigh gallantly put down his cloak for Elizabeth I to walk over—and certainly here that he was arrested by James I on his return from Guyana, having failed to find the gold of El Dorado. George I landed here from Holland on his way to claim the crown of Great Britain and Ireland.

Today the magnificent buildings of the National Maritime Museum, the Old Royal Observatory, Queen's House and Old Royal Naval College have earned UNESCO World Heritage status under the soubriquet of 'Maritime Greenwich'. The views from either side of the river are exceptional: from the north bank at Island Gardens of the beautiful symmetry of Greenwich, or in the other direction, from Greenwich Hill, of the soaring geometry of Canary Wharf. Greenwich is a deservedly popular destination, often very full indeed on summer weekends. As well as the museums and historic buildings, there are some good pubs and restaurants, a market and of course the spacious park.

VISITING GREENWICH

Getting there: Map p. 625. DLR to Island Gardens (then through foot tunnel) or direct to Cutty Sark or Greenwich. Thames Clipper services to Greenwich Pier from Embankment, London Eye, Blackfriars, Bankside, London Bridge, Tower and Canary Wharf (journey time c. 40mins from Embankment).

Admission and Tickets: There are slightly different opening times and pricing policies for Cutty Sark, the National Maritime Museum, Queen's House, and Royal Observatory. For details, see visitgreenwich.org.uk, rmg.co.uk. For admission to the Naval College (Painted Hall, Nelson Room and Chapel), as well as for a timetable of services in the Chapel (usually Sundays at 11am) see ornc.org. Tickets from the Visitor Centre (see plan on p. 488). Guided tours can be booked.

CUTTY SARK AND THE THAMES WATERFRONT

The elegant masts and rigging of the **Cutty Sark** (*map p. 625, B3; rmg.co.uk/cutty-sark*) are a Greenwich landmark. *Cutty Sark* was the fastest of the great tea clippers, sleek ships which raced each other annually to bring back the lucrative new-season China tea crop from the Far East. She is now the only clipper to survive and is open to visitors. *Cutty Sark* was built by the firm Scott & Linton at their shipyard on the Clyde, and launched in 1869. Her name comes from the short shirt of Paisley linen worn by the witch Nannie in Robert Burns' poem 'Tam O'Shanter'. Nannie serves as the ship's figurehead, grasping the tail of Tam's grey mare in her hand. Elegant and sleek, with a great expanse of sail, *Cutty Sark* had a maximum crew of 28. At her fastest she covered 368 miles in a day. She worked in the China tea trade between 1870 and 1877, then carried coal from Shanghai to Sydney, wool between Melbourne and New York and, from 1885–95, wool between Australia and London. She has been in dry dock at Greenwich since 1954. Though damaged by fire in 2007, almost all her woodwork is still original. Her hull is now encased in the glass-walled lobby and shop, making her appear as if berthed on a crystal lilo.

Cutty Sark.

The glass-domed brick rotunda in front of *Cutty Sark* is the entrance to the **foot tunnel** under the Thames, completed in 1902 (there is a matching rotunda on the opposite bank). Access is via lift or stairs.

THE THAMES WATERFRONT

The **Thames Path** leads east past a couple of rib shacks and burger bars, passing an entrance to the Old Royal Naval College with a good view of the Queen's House. The walk continues all the way downstream to the Thames Barrier (*see p. 500*).

The **Trafalgar Tavern** (built 1837; *trafalgartavern.co.uk*), with iron balconies, overlooks the river. It became famous for its whitebait dinners, popular with ministers in Queen Victoria's reign. Other famous customers include Thackeray and the ubiquitous Dickens. The Thames Path leads behind it, past the cosy Yacht pub and a couple of rowing clubs, to emerge by the striking **Trinity Almshouses**, founded by Henry Howard, Earl of Northampton, in 1616. Behind it on Old Woolwich Road is **Greenwich Power Station** with its four tall chimneys, still in operation providing backup electricity for London Underground. The Cutty Sark pub is a few hundred yards further along (*signed*).

The **Greenwich Peninsula**, stretching north as the river bends around it, affords views of the O2 Arena concert venue. Close to it is **The Tide**, an elevated park and walkway raised on tall struts that look like giant cake stands. It boasts sculpture by Damien Hirst, who lived on the peninsula before it was redeveloped. The London Cable Car (officially the **IFS Cloud Cable Car**) runs from Greenwich Peninsula to the Royal Docks.

OLD ROYAL NAVAL COLLEGE

The main entrance to the Old Royal Naval College is via the west gates on King William Walk, which date from 1751 and were moved here in 1850. Their gigantic celestial and terrestrial stone spheres, 6ft in diameter, have their latitudinal and longitudinal lines marked in copper bands. Just inside on the left is the Visitor Centre and beyond it, just ahead, is the main complex of the old Greenwich Hospital, with a statue of George II by Rysbrack (1735) in the centre of the Grand Square (wrapped in polythene in winter). This is a good place to pause to get your bearings. There are four blocks or courts, each named after a monarch: Charles; Anne; William; Mary. The Painted Hall is in King William Court and the Chapel is opposite it. In King Charles Court is the Trinity Laban Conservatoire of Music and Dance (the pleasant tinkling of pianos can often be heard).

HISTORY OF GREENWICH

Greenwich has had royal associations since the 15th century, when Humphrey, Duke of Gloucester built the palace of Bellacourt. Here he came with his second wife Eleanor and enjoyed a life of ease and pleasure until Eleanor was arrested on charges of sorcery. Her alleged accomplice, the 'Witch of Eye', was burned at Smithfield and Eleanor dragged out the rest of her days a prisoner. Henry VII renamed the palace Placentia. It was the birthplace of Henry VIII and Elizabeth I, and a favourite location for jousting, tilting and hunting for Tudor and early Stuart monarchs. In 1614 James I presented Greenwich to his consort, Anne of Denmark, it is said in apology for having cursed her in public for accidentally shooting his favourite hound on a hunting jaunt. It was Anne who commissioned the Queen's House from Inigo Jones. The palace became the official reception point for important visitors, such as foreign ambassadors, who arrived downriver at Gravesend.

After the Restoration, Charles II demolished the Tudor buildings and began work on a vast new palace, designed by John Webb. Greenwich Park, which stretches up the hill beyond the Queen's House, was given axial tree-lined avenues, grass terraces, or Giant Steps (the remnants of which can be made out to the east of the Observatory), and an elaborate parterre with fountains designed by the French court garden designer André le Nôtre.

Greenwich is also the home of Greenwich Mean Time. The foundation of the Royal Observatory within the park in 1675, and the presence of the Navy on the palace site since 1694, placed Greenwich at the heart of astronomical discovery and maritime endeavour. The hospital was established by Queen Mary II in 1694 as the Royal Hospital for Seamen, a charitable institution for injured Royal Navy sailors, their widows and children. She gave over land at Greenwich for the purpose, John Webb's vast palace for Charles II having been abandoned in 1669 with the completion of only one block. Mary died in 1694 but her husband, William III, respected her wishes. Sir Christopher Wren was appointed Hospital Surveyor, with Nicholas Hawksmoor as Clerk of the Works. The Queen's House, however, remained in royal ownership and its vista to the river was to be preserved. Wren incorporated it in his plans as a distant visual centrepiece, with in front of it four symmetrical blocks, the two furthest from the river with matching domes and colonnades. Building was a piecemeal exercise which spanned 55 years and which witnessed successive surveyorships (Vanbrugh 1716, Colen Campbell 1726), but the resulting ensemble is one of the grandest Baroque sites in England. Greenwich Hospital's magnificence reflected the charitable munificence of the Crown and the importance of the Navy. The King Charles block, altered and enlarged, was the first to be completed; in 1705 the pensioners moved in.

In 1869 Greenwich Hospital closed and in 1873 the site became home to the Royal Naval College, which occupied the buildings until the mid-1990s. In 1997 the buildings were transferred to the Greenwich Foundation, established to administer the site and to oversee its conversion for the University of Greenwich (which now occupies the King William, Mary and Anne blocks) and Trinity Laban Music Conservatoire (King Charles block). Today the buildings of the Old Royal Naval College, together with the Queen's House, constitute a unique ensemble of works by leading architects: Inigo Jones, Wren, Hawksmoor. The magnificent river view of them inspired Canaletto (the view that he painted is in the Queen's House).

The Painted Hall

The Painted Hall occupies the length of one wing of King William Court. Painted by Sir James Thornhill in stages (for £3 per yard) between 1708 and 1726, it is one of the most magnificent and impressive Baroque painted interiors in the country, and Thornhill's masterpiece. Its hugely complicated iconography necessitated the publication of Thornhill's 'Explanation' of it in 1726/7.

The **entrance vestibule**, painted with cartouches inscribed with benefactors' names, with seated charity boys, was completed by 1726. It leads into the larger, **Lower Hall**, where the pensioners ate, and which was painted first, between 1708 and 1714. The

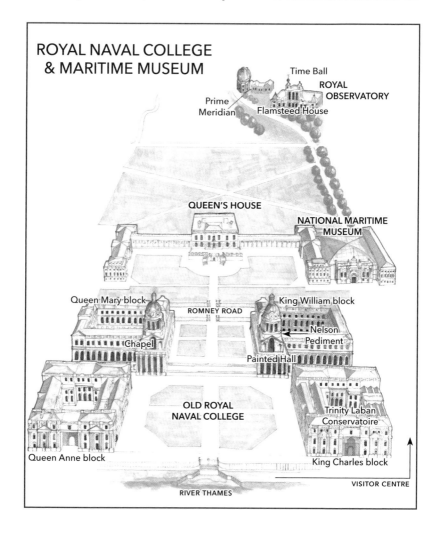

ROYAL NAVAL COLLEGE
& MARITIME MUSEUM

Time Ball

ROYAL OBSERVATORY

Prime Meridian

Flamsteed House

QUEEN'S HOUSE

NATIONAL MARITIME MUSEUM

Queen Mary block

ROMNEY ROAD

King William block

Nelson Pediment

Chapel

Painted Hall

OLD ROYAL NAVAL COLLEGE

Trinity Laban Conservatoire

Queen Anne block

King Charles block

VISITOR CENTRE

RIVER THAMES

The colonnaded King William block, part of the old Royal Naval College, a superb Baroque ensemble projected by Sir Christopher Wren.

ceiling is a glorification of the Protestant constitutional monarchy of William and Mary (*Peace and Liberty Triumph over Tyranny*), and the Naval and maritime foundation of Britain's power and mercantile prosperity. Large benches have been placed in the Hall, which visitors can lie back on to get a good view of the ceiling above. In the centre are the seated figures of the monarchs, with a cowering Louis XIV beneath them, clutching a broken sword, while symbols of the papacy and Catholicism tumble to perdition below. A figure representing Architecture points to a large elevation of the King William block. The appearance of Tycho Brahe, Copernicus and John Flamsteed on the ceiling (on the end nearest the entrance vestibule) alludes to the importance of astronomy to maritime navigation. Flamsteed holds a document inscribed 'Apr: 22 1715', the date of his predicted eclipse of the sun (which proved accurate).

The **Upper Hall**, where the officers ate, was completed in 1718–25. Queen Anne and her husband, Prince George of Denmark, Lord High Admiral, appear on the ceiling; the Prince of Orange, later William III, is welcomed by Britannia on the south wall (left), in grisaille, and on the north wall (right) George I lands at Greenwich. The great west wall, mainly the work of Thornhill's assistant Dietrich Ernst André, celebrates the Protestant Hanoverian succession, with George I and his family surrounded by Peace and Justice and other Virtues, with the great dome of St Paul's Cathedral, symbol of Anglicanism (and Thornhill's other great painting commission; *see p. 29*), rising in the background. Thornhill himself appears to the right of the steps.

Peace and Liberty (personified by William III and Mary II) triumph over Tyranny (Roman Catholicism, personfied by Louis XIV, who grasps a shattered sword while the papal tiara and apostolic Cross tumble out of the sky beneath him). Detail of James Thornhill's ceiling in the Painted Hall at Greenwich (1708-14).

THE BAROQUE IN ENGLAND

The art and architecture of the Baroque, with all its theatricality and direct appeal to the senses and emotions, took hold in Britain following the triumphant restoration to the throne of Charles II in 1660, when 'all arts seemed to return from their exile'. An international court language which bolstered the absolutist regimes of much of Europe, the Baroque flourished in Britain until the early 18th century. The period witnessed the architecture of Sir Christopher Wren, Nicholas Hawksmoor and Sir John Vanbrugh; the vast illusionistic mural paintings of Antonio Verrio, Louis Laguerre and Sir James Thornhill; and the virtuoso limewood carving of Grinling Gibbons. In 1660 Charles II and his courtiers set about equipping the Stuart monarchy with a magnificent setting suitable for the restored regime, inspired by the visual splendour witnessed at the courts of Europe. Baroque culture, with its emphasis on vastness of size, immense cost and grandeur, as well as the theatrical etiquette and ceremony which accompanied it, was used by the Stuart court to underline the power of the monarch and reinforce it in the minds of the people. Outside London, Verrio decorated the ceilings of the remodelled Windsor Castle with vast allegorical scenes celebrating the might of the Crown. In London, following the Great Fire of 1666, Sir Christopher Wren's new St Paul's Cathedral rose glorious from the ashes, a magnificent symbol of the Anglican nation, its great dome decorated by Thornhill. William and Mary created a splendid Baroque palace at Hampton Court, in conscious competition with Louis XIV's Versailles, with painted ceilings and sculpture symbolic of William as the Protestant victor of Europe. Greenwich Hospital, with Thornhill's supreme masterpiece, the Painted Hall, reflected the magnificence, munificence and charity of the Crown.

In an age which, following the 1688 Glorious Revolution, saw the curbing of the absolute authority of the Crown and the championing of civil liberty, Whig adherents increasingly viewed the reigns of the earlier Stuart monarchs as periods of aggressive Roman Catholicism, tyrannical government and extravagant ostentation. The Baroque fell from favour and in its stead came Palladianism, rooted in the ideals of ancient Rome and hailed as a purer and more restrained form of art. Symptomatic of this change was the renewed interest in the unsullied Classicism of the architecture of Inigo Jones, particularly championed by Lord Burlington and his circle, who saw in its 'still unravished' lines a style and culture which better reflected the decorum and gravitas of the new Augustan age.

From 4th–7th January 1806, Nelson's body lay in state in the **Nelson Room**, just off the Painted Hall, before being taken by funeral barge to St Paul's Cathedral. The room now houses a display on Nelson.

Outside in King William Court, above the colonnade (you have to be inside the courtyard to see it), is the **Nelson Pediment** (1810–12), designed and signed by

Benjamin West. Forty feet wide and ten feet high and stylistically heavily influenced by the Elgin Marbles, recently arrived in London, it shows Neptune delivering Nelson's mortal remains to Britannia. It is made of Coade Stone (*see p. 466*).

The Chapel

The Chapel is directly opposite the Painted Hall, in the Queen Mary block, the least magnificent of the four courts and externally a simpler (cheaper) version of the King William. Originally completed in 1750, the Chapel was gutted by fire in 1779 and remodelled by James 'Athenian' Stuart (author, with Nicholas Revett, of the influential *Antiquities of Athens*). The distinctive bracketed gallery repeats the earlier one, but the plasterwork ceiling is Stuart's design, its delicate neo-Grecian modelling in startling contrast to Thornhill's overwhelming Baroque. The 25ft altarpiece, *St Paul Shipwrecked at Malta*, was commissioned from Benjamin West in 1781, and the statues of *Faith, Hope, Charity* and *Humility* in the vestibule were also designed by him.

The Old Royal Naval College also preserves a charming **Skittle Alley**, built in 1864 to help pensioners in the hospital while away their time entertainingly and without resorting to drink. It is still in working order and can be visited (*ask at the Visitor Centre*).

THE NATIONAL MARITIME MUSEUM

The National Maritime Museum (*most direct entrance on Romney Road*), which opened in 1937, tells the story of the Royal Navy, of Britain as a seafaring power and of the history of maritime exploration, navigation, astronomy and the measurement of time. As well as the main museum, it includes the Royal Observatory and the historic Queen's House, where an important collection of art, much of it maritime, is displayed. The museum's 2.5 million objects include cartography, ship models and plans, an exceptional collection of scientific and navigational instruments, important collections relating to maritime heroes such as Nelson and Captain Cook (though recent interpretations view neither as unequivocally heroic), paintings and a valuable library housing books and manuscripts dating from the 15th century onwards.

THE MARITIME MUSEUM (MAIN BUILDING)

The main entrance takes you into The Square (Rick Mather, with the Building Design Partnership), a vast space spanned by a steel-framed glass roof where large-scale highlights from the collection are displayed, including a collection of figureheads and Prince Frederick's barge, a 'floating coach' designed by William Kent in 1732 with carved and gilded work by James Richards, the King's Master Carver. Used for state occasions on the Thames, it would have been accompanied by another barge with a 'set of Musick'.

Exhibition spaces and micro-galleries are arranged in and around The Square. One of them looks at the history of London as a trading capital tied to the Thames and contains an evocative painting of Deptford docks in 1794. In another, displayed on its own, is **Turner's** *The Battle of Trafalgar, 1805*, a magnificent work showing a clashing confusion of cloud and water and wooden hulks, with clots of desperate struggling men.

Opening off The Square is the Sammy Ofer wing, named after the Romanian-born Israeli businessman who donated many millions of pounds to the Maritime Museum and helped fund restoration of the *Cutty Sark* following fire damage in 2007. Money from the family foundation also secured two **paintings by Stubbs of a dingo and a kangaroo**, documenting discoveries by Captain Cook and representing the first depictions of the animals in Western art. Both works are now part of the 'Pacific Encounters' display on the first floor, along with a set of paintings by William Westall, artist on board the *Investigator*, which sailed to Australia in 1801–5. He was accused by later settlers of portraying the land as too hospitable. Also on the first floor is some fine **stained glass from the old Baltic Exchange building** in the City where the Gherkin now stands (*see p. 68*). Dating from 1922 and designed by John Dudley Forsyth, it features personifications of Virtues and a winged Victory.

The rise of the Navy and the status of the sailor is explored on the second floor, where rather frantic sound effects attempt to recreate the atmosphere of a warship in the thick of an engagement (many of the displays in the museum are particularly designed to appeal to school parties). A memorable exhibit is the deadly Spanish bar shot, which was fired at the *Victory* and arrived in spinning flight, slashing through rigging and killing eight men. Showcases include memorabilia connected to Britain's great naval commander, **Horatio Nelson**. The most compelling exhibits are the clothes he wore at the Battle of Trafalgar, the fatal musket ball hole visible just below the left epaulette of his coat. Touching personal items include a letter from his abandoned wife, Frances Nisbet, and Nelson's last letter to his daughter by Emma Hamilton, Horatia.

There are many treasures in the museum, among them the magnificent late 16th-century **Drake Jewel**, sun-shaped and decorated with rubies and opals, the reverse containing a miniature of Elizabeth I (it was presented to Sir Francis Drake by Elizabeth to mark his historic circumnavigation); and the **Drake Cup**, a coconut shell set elaborately in silver, the cover surmounted by an exquisite model of the *Golden Hind*. In some cases the artistry and craftsmanship struggle to stand out in displays which apologetically interpret Britain's maritime history as a tale of exploitation, greed and diplomatic ineptitude.

THE QUEEN'S HOUSE

The Queen's House, a perfectly proportioned architectural masterpiece, is usually taken as the first—and one of the finest—truly classical Renaissance buildings in England. Designed by the great architect Inigo Jones, who had returned from a trip to Italy in 1613 with influential ideas about Classical proportion, it symbolises the refined aesthetic of the early Stuart court. The Queen's House was in fact built in three main stages for successive queen consorts: Anne of Denmark, wife of James I; Henrietta Maria, wife of Charles I; and Catherine of Braganza, wife of Charles II. Anne of Denmark was granted Greenwich as her private residence in 1613 and commissioned the building in 1616. It stands almost exactly on the site of the gatehouse of the old Tudor palace, which marked the demarcation between the private palace gardens and

Greenwich Park, to which the queen desired easy access. The Queen's House is in fact two buildings, one on the palace side, the other on the park side, linked by first-floor bridges which span what was then a public highway. On Anne's death in 1619, only the bottom storeys of the two blocks were complete. In 1629 Greenwich was granted to Henrietta Maria, and work resumed. Between 1629 and 1638 the upper storeys were added, including the central bridge room and the elegant loggia overlooking the park, and a programme of elaborate interior decoration was undertaken.

The building

The double-height, single-cube galleried **Hall**, the centrepiece of the Queen's House, had its black and white marble floor laid in 1636–7, its pattern mirroring the white and gold compartmented ceiling above. The latter originally contained a cycle of nine canvases, *The Allegory of Peace and Arts under the English Crown*, by Orazio Gentileschi, a friend and follower of Caravaggio. Removed in 1708, when the Queen's House became the official residence of the Governor of Greenwich Hospital, they were re-installed at Marlborough House, where they still are today. Other important Gentileschis were commissioned for the house, including the large *Finding of Moses*, which was sold at the 1649 Commonwealth sale following Charles I's execution (it is now in the National Gallery). The Hall is an exceptionally pleasing space. Off the upper gallery are the principal rooms. The **Queen's Presence Chamber** has a coved ceiling painted with important Italianate grotesque work, possibly by John de Critz, Serjeant-painter to the King (the National Maritime Museum owns portraits by him of James I and Anne of Denmark). The most sumptuous room is the **King's Presence Chamber**. The beams of its compartmented ceiling bear festoons of fruit and flowers and the frieze and cornice cartouches have the monograms of Charles I and Henrietta Maria. At the time of writing the exit was via the so-called '**Tulip Stairs**' (though the motif in the fine wrought-iron balustrade is in fact probably intended as a *fleur-de-lys*, Henrietta Maria's family emblem).

The collection

The Queen's House displays many of the National Maritime Museum's excellent collection of paintings, including marine scenes, portraits of naval heroes and portraits and landscapes relevant to Greenwich's royal history. It is not possible to know which works will be on display at any given time (and some items from the collection are on show in the main Maritime Museum). Some highlights of the holdings include William Dobson's portrait of the elderly Inigo Jones (c. 1644); Lely's early portrait of Peter Pett, shipbuilder of Woolwich, with the *Sovereign of the Seas* in the background; a swaggering, almost comic, full-length of James II by Henri Gascars; and the exceptional '**Armada portrait**' of Elizabeth I. *The Somerset House Conference* (1604) shows delegates at the peace negotiations held between England and Spain after the death of Elizabeth I. Not to be missed is **Canaletto's view of Greenwich Hospital** (1750–2). Reynolds' portrait of Rear-Admiral the Hon. Augustus Keppel (1752–3) shows him full-length before a stormy sea and is said to be the picture which established Reynolds as a leading artist. Also among the portraits is Hudson's likeness of the unfortunate Admiral Byng, who failed to prevent the French capture of Minorca, was court-martialled and shot in 1757.

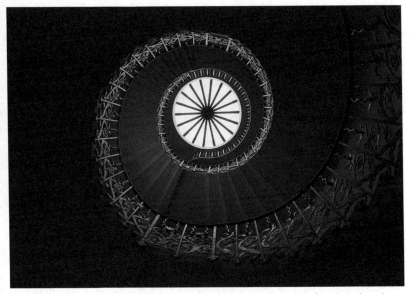

The 'Tulip Stairs' in the Queen's House. The wrought-iron 'tulips' are in fact thought to be lilies, emblems of Henrietta Maria, the 'Rose and Lily Queen', who united the French *fleur-de-lys* and the English rose on her marriage to Charles I.

A display is devoted to the **Elder and Younger Willem Van de Velde**, father and son, the first great marine artists to work in Britain. They settled in London in 1673/4 and were given a room on the lower floor by Charles II to use as a painting studio. There is also a seapiece by Dominic Serres, the only marine artist to be admitted as a founder member of the Royal Academy. Among the modern and contemporary works is Christy Symington's 2006 bust of the anti-slavery campaigner Olaudah Equiano.

THE ROYAL OBSERVATORY

Standing high on Observatory Hill, with a spectacular view over the Hospital, the Thames and London stretching into the distance, is Flamsteed House, the earliest building of the Greenwich complex, which comprises the Royal Observatory. Built in 1675–6 by Sir Christopher Wren, with the assistance of Robert Hooke, it was the first purpose-built scientific research facility in the country. The Observatory at Greenwich is no longer used to make positional observations (due to atmospheric pollution, the Royal Observatory began the move to Herstmonceaux, Sussex, in 1948), but its historic buildings remain a site of extraordinary significance for the history of astronomy, time-keeping and the calculation of longitude. At the International Meridian Conference in Washington in 1884, Greenwich was recognised as marking the Prime Meridian, Longitude 0°, and Greenwich Mean Time was internationally adopted. Today, at least in name, GMT has been largely supplanted by the international time standard known as UTC.

HISTORY OF THE OBSERVATORY

The Royal Observatory was the product of the 17th-century scientific revolution, a great era of investigation and discovery. One of the crucial problems demanding a solution was the calculation of longitude, vital for accurate navigation at sea which, for a maritime nation, was of obvious importance. The Royal Observatory was founded by Charles II, with John Flamsteed appointed the first 'Astronomical Observator' in 1675, with this specific task in mind. Flamsteed's aim was to facilitate the calculation of longitude through lunar observation, specifically the annual passage of the moon against the stars, by compiling accurate star catalogues and lunar tables. He moved into Flamsteed House, his official residence, in July 1676 and began his observations from the top floor observatory in September.

Outside the gates of the courtyard is the **Shepherd 24-hour clock**, erected in 1852, the year the Greenwich Time Service started sending signals. Greenwich is the official starting point of each new day. The large red Time Ball on the east turret of Flamsteed House is the world's first visual time signal. Since 1833 it has been hoisted half-way up the mast at 12.55, to the top at 12.58, and dropped at precisely 1pm.

On one side of the cobbled courtyard stands Flamsteed House and on the other the Meridian Building. A brass line in the ground marks the **Prime Meridian**. It runs straight through the Meridian Building, linking the North and South Poles and marking the division between the Eastern and Western Hemispheres. Visitors can thus stand astride the line, in two hemispheres at once (there are usually large numbers of people photographing each other doing so). The Meridian is seen most dramatically at dusk, when the green laser beam projected from the Observatory stretches into the evening sky, across Greenwich Hospital and the river towards the distant lights of the towers of Canary Wharf.

Flamsteed House

Upstairs is the spectacular **Octagon Room** (known by Flamsteed as his Octagonal Great or Star Room): Wren's fine, airy interior, with tall windows, was suitable for observing the heavens through long telescopes. The plasterwork ceiling has a frieze of roses, oak leaves and the royal arms, and there are full-length portraits of Charles II and James II after Lely (the latter a copy of 1984). The three clocks, with 13ft pendulums behind the walnut-grained wainscot, were used by Flamsteed for checking the regularity of the Earth's rotation. The original movements and dials were made by the great Thomas Tompion but in 1719, after Flamsteed's death, were sold by his widow (Flamsteed had paid for his own instruments). One was purchased by the British Museum in the 1920s and another was returned to the Observatory in 1994 and is displayed in a case with its movement and pendulum visible. Flamsteed's immense contribution to astronomical observation was published soon after his death (*Historia Coelestis Britannica*, 1725; *Atlas Coelestis*, 1729) and he is celebrated on the ceiling of Thornhill's Painted Hall (*see p. 489 above*).

Flamsteed House is also home to a display of historically important timepieces, particularly those which illustrate the **quest to calculate longitude**, given impetus after the drowning of Sir Cloudesley Shovell and his crew off the Scilly Isles in 1707. In separate cases are John Harrison's four ground-breaking marine chronometers (on loan from the Hydrographer of the Navy), which changed maritime navigation forever. Instead of using the moon as an astronomical clock, Harrison, a Yorkshire carpenter and self-taught clockmaker, worked towards the perfection of a clock that would keep accurate time while on a temperature-variable rolling ship at sea. His first prototype, H1 (1730–5), was based on his early wooden clocks but was fitted with a temperature compensation device. It was followed by H2 in 1737–40, and H3 between 1740 and 1759. The latter can be seen in the background of Harrison's portrait by Thomas King, as well as the precision pocket watch made for him, according to his specifications, by John Jefferys. H4 (1759) was Harrison's triumphal marine timekeeper. In the form of a compact watch, inspired by the Jefferys watch, it has pivot-holes of rubies and pallets of diamonds. It was H4 that was awarded the £20,000 prize for solving the Longitude problem, a prize which the Board of Longitude had been seeking to give away since 1714. Harrison is buried in Hampstead (*p. 428*).

The Meridian Building

Flamsteed had made further astronomical observations from the courtyard. Early views of the Observatory show his 60ft refracting telescope appearing above the courtyard wall. He also erected the northeast Summer House, his solar observatory; a Sextant House, for his seven-foot Equatorial Sextant; and a Quadrant House. The latter was added to by succeeding Astronomers Royal: Edmund Halley (d. 1742), of comet fame, and James Bradley. These buildings now make up the Meridian Building, where Bradley's Mural Quadrant and 12½-ft Zenith Sector Telescope (1727) can be seen; and successive Transit Instruments, culminating with Airy's Transit Circle. Observations made on the latter had the effect of moving the Greenwich Meridian 19ft east, the equivalent of .02 seconds, and its optical axis still defines the Greenwich Meridian. Inside the distinctive onion-shaped Dome of the Great Equatorial Building is Sir Howard Grubb's great 28-inch refracting telescope of 1893, which was used at Herstmonceaux until 1971 and then returned to Greenwich.

In 1894–9 two ornamental structures of red brick and terracotta were added to the complex: the Altazimuth Pavilion and the South Building. Between them is the **Planetarium** (*free admission*).

GREENWICH TOWN CENTRE

In the centre of Greenwich, **St Alfege**, in Church Street (*map p. 625, B4; st-alfege.org.uk*), marks the spot where Alphege, Archbishop of Canterbury, was murdered by invading Danish Vikings in 1012. Henry VIII was baptised in the medieval church; Thomas Tallis, the great composer of English sacred music, is buried in the vault and preserved at the west end is a keyboard that may have been played by him and by Princess

Elizabeth. The current church, designed by Hawksmoor and completed in 1714, was restored after heavy war damage. Also buried in the vault is James Wolfe, who lived in a house on Croom's Hill and who died claiming Quebec for the English. Just inside the entrance to the church is a plaque commemorating John Julius Angerstein, benefactor of the British Museum (*see p. 189*), another local resident, who was buried here in 1823.

Diagonally opposite the church, on Church Street, is an archway leading to **Greenwich Market**, in a covered Victorian market building. Once a produce market, its stalls now sell books, clothing, bric à brac and handicrafts, and more shops and food stalls line the periphery. An admonitory motto, 'A false balance is abomination to the Lord but a just weight is his delight' is inscribed over the exit to College Approach.

Croom's Hill has some attractive Georgian houses and, opposite the theatre, is the **Fan Museum**, dedicated to the history of fans and fan-making (*12 Croom's Hill; thefanmuseum.org.uk*). At the top of Croom's Hill is **Macartney House** (*map p. 625, C4*), where General Wolfe once lived. There are entrances along Croom's Hill to Greenwich Park.

GREENWICH PARK

Outside the Royal Observatory enclosure (*map p. 625, C4*) is a **statue of General Wolfe** by Tait McKenzie, presented by the Canadian nation in 1930 and unveiled—a nice touch—by the descendant of Montcalm, the commander of Quebec who met his death in the tussle with Wolfe. From here a broad, tree-lined avenue leads through Greenwich Park to Blackheath Gate. Greenwich is a royal park, first enclosed by Humphrey, Duke of Gloucester as a hunting ground in 1433. With its steep topography, it offers superb views of the Thames. It was laid out by Sir William Boreman to a plan by André le Nôtre, commissioned by Charles II in the 1660s. Signs indicate the park's salient features: the Flower Garden, Deer Enclosure, Roman remains (virtually nothing to see) and **Queen Elizabeth's Oak**, a tree under which Henry VIII is said to have danced with Anne Boleyn, and where Queen Elizabeth picnicked as a child. It collapsed in 1991 and now lies where it fell, enclosed by railings, a short walk southwest of Maze Hill Gate. Just outside Maze Hill Gate is **Vanbrugh Castle** (*map p. 625, C4–C3*), recognisable by its green turret, built in 1726 by Sir John Vanbrugh when he was Surveyor of the Royal Hospital.

On the west side of the park is a bronze sculpture by Henry Moore: *Large Standing Figure: Knife Edge* and a 6th–8th-century **Anglo-Saxon burial ground** and, south of it, the Ranger's House (*see below*). Close by are the remains of a **sunken bath house** built for Caroline of Brunswick, consort of George IV.

RANGER'S HOUSE

Standing on Chesterfield Walk, with fine views over Greenwich Park to the Royal Observatory, Ranger's House (*map p. 625, C4; english-heritage.org.uk*) is a handsome mansion built in 1723 for Captain, later Admiral, Francis Hosier. Due to its proximity to the royal palace, and later to the Naval College and surrounding shipyards, this was a spot favoured by courtiers and seafaring men. The core of the house is Hosier's, who made a fortune through the sale of ships' cargoes. The fine red-brick exterior has a Portland stone centrepiece, a modest Baroque flourish, with a carved mask of Neptune above the entrance door. In 1748 the house was owned by Philip, 4th Earl of Chesterfield, politician and wit and author of the celebrated letters to his son, who built the south wing of yellow brick. Chesterfield spent every summer here for the last 23 years of his life. The north wing was added in the 1780s. In 1807 the house was leased by Augusta, Dowager Countess of Brunswick, sister of George III, and in 1815 it became the official residence of the Ranger of Greenwich Park, by now purely an honorary office. The first Ranger to take up residence was Princess Sophia Matilda of Gloucester. Other occupants of the house include the young Prince Arthur of Connaught, Queen Victoria's third son, and Field Marshal Viscount Wolseley, who relieved General Gordon at Khartoum.

The Entrance Hall, with its chequered black-and-white stone floor, dates from Hosier's day. To the right of the Hall is Hosier's Crimson Camblet Parlour, used by Chesterfield for cards, which leads to the New Gallery, a spacious room with triple bow windows in the centre and at each end. Here Chesterfield displayed his Old Master paintings, with sculpture busts and porcelain in the niches. The 1710 Oak Staircase leads up to the Long Gallery or Passage, which retains its original early 18th-century panelling. Off it Hosier had a 'Cockloft', a gazebo from which he could train his telescope on ships on the Thames.

The Wernher Collection

The Wernher Collection of pictures, jewellery and *objets d'art* is on permanent loan here from the Wernher Foundation. Sir Julius Wernher (1850–1912) was a German diamond merchant who made his fortune (£11 million at his death) in South Africa in the 1870s when his operation merged with De Beers. He settled in England and in 1903 purchased the great Bedfordshire mansion Luton Hoo, which was redecorated in lavish style. Luton Hoo was sold in the 1990s and several of the most important items from the collection were auctioned. What remains is nonetheless impressive. There are pictures by Joos van Cleve, Hans Memling and Gabriel Metsu; English works by Reynolds, Romney and Hoppner; 18th-century French tapestries; Renaissance bronzes, ivories and enamels; and an important collection of enamelled and gem-studded Renaissance jewellery.

BLACKHEATH

Map p. 625, C4. Trains from London Bridge or Charing Cross to Blackheath in 15–20mins.

South of Shooter's Hill and Charlton Way is Blackheath, an attractive residential suburb. The heath on the edge of which it nestles is an almost treeless grassy plateau of some 280 acres. The Roman Watling Street crossed Blackheath and both Roman and Saxon remains have been found here. During the Peasants' Revolt in 1381, Wat Tyler assembled his supporters on the heath before advancing on London. It was the scene

The Thames Barrier.

of royal celebrations such as the welcome for Charles II in 1660. The heath also had a reputation for highway robberies. The Royal Blackheath Golf Club was the first in the country when it opened here in 1607 (it is now in Eltham). Blackheath Rugby Club prides itself on being the oldest in the world. Today the breezy heath is a favourite place for kite-flying. The start lines for the London Marathon are also ranged around Blackheath.

Around the east and south side of the heath are some handsome 17th- and early 18th-century villas. Morden College on St German's Place was built in 1695 by Wren with a colonnaded courtyard to house 'decayed Turkey Merchants who had fallen on hard times'. Sir John Morden, its benefactor, was himself a 'Turkey merchant'. It continues in the same spirit today, being a residential home for the elderly. The Princess of Wales pub on the south side of the heath (*1A Montpelier Row; princessofwalespub. co.uk*) is a good place to stop for a drink or a bite to eat.

THE THAMES BARRIER

Between Greenwich and Woolwich is the massive Thames Barrier (*map p. 629, F3*), which stretches across the river and is raised when necessary to protect London from surge tides. It is one of the largest moving flood barriers in the world, spanning 568 yards across the Thames, with ten massive steel gates. The Barrier came into operation in 1982, originally designed to be raised once every few years. The winter of 2014

broke all records for the number of consecutive occasions on which it was closed and there are fears that rising sea levels may mean that it will not be able to protect the capital for many more decades. The Thames Barrier Information Centre (*1 Unity Way; www.gov.uk/guidance/the-thames-barrier*) offers an audio-visual presentation and working models illustrating the history of the river and the threat of flooding.

DULWICH

Map p. 629, D4. Trains from Victoria to West Dulwich or from London Bridge to North Dulwich and 10mins' walk. Overground to Forest Hill and 20mins' walk through the park.

Dulwich is an attractive residential suburb, well kept with some handsome houses and an air of leafy prosperity. It is worth a visit for its tranquil atmosphere, superb art gallery and attractive park. In 967 King Edgar granted the manor of Dulwich to one of his followers; later it belonged to Bermondsey Abbey (*p. 460*) before the land was purchased by Edward Alleyn, the actor and theatre manager, in 1605. Alleyn founded Dulwich College, partly as a school for the poor and partly as almshouses. The College still survives. Dickens, who frequented the predecessor of the Victorian Crown and Greyhound pub, chooses Dulwich as the place of Samuel Pickwick's retirement, in 'one of the most pleasant spots

Sign giving toll charges on College Road, Dulwich—London's last surviving toll road.

near London'. The pub (73 *Dulwich Village; thecrownandgreyhound.co.uk*) makes a good place for lunch.

DULWICH VILLAGE

Dulwich still has the air of a village enclave. In the centre there are white-painted signposts whose arms are fashioned to look like pointing fingers. On College Road, with sedate houses set back behind picket or post-and-chain fences, is the **old toll-house** (corner of Grange Lane). A booth in the centre of the highway still collects tolls from cars: this is the last surviving toll-road in London. A noticeboard among the trees by the roadside notes that cars, motorcycles and carts pulled by horses or donkeys were all charged the same (sixpence). A little further up College Road on the opposite side is **Dulwich College**, designed by Charles Barry (son of the architect of the Houses of Parliament) in an ornate Italian style (1842 with extensions in 1870). The site includes the chapel in which Alleyn is buried. Famous former pupils include Raymond Chandler and P.G. Wodehouse. At no. 27 College Road is **Bell House**, with a handsome Georgian central section of five bays including a large Serlian window with octagonal glazing bars. Originally the country home of a prosperous paper and prayer-book merchant from London Bridge, it was due to open as a pottery at the time of writing. The eponymous bell was formerly used to alert the local fire brigade.

In the intersection of College and Gallery roads is **Edward Alleyn House**, with the original Dulwich College buildings. Alleyn's College of God's Gift was established as an educational and charitable foundation in 1619. Edward Alleyn (d. 1626) was an actor of renown and also wealth, manager of the Rose, Fortune and Hope playhouses (rivals to the Globe) and, alongside his father-in-law Philip Henslowe, joint master of the 'Royal Game of Bears, Bulls and Mastiff Dogs' (which incorporated lion-baiting). The old College complex has three wings surrounding an interior court with a WWI memorial cross and a bronze statue of Alleyn. The central wing contains the charming Christ's Chapel, which retains its pews. The wing on the left was formerly an almshouse and Dulwich College occupied the right-hand wing until it moved to its new premises.

DULWICH PICTURE GALLERY

According to the American architect Philip Johnson (1906–2005), 'the Dulwich Picture Gallery (*map p. 629, D4; admission charge; café; dulwichpicturegallery.org.uk*) set forever the way to show pictures'. Designed by Sir John Soane in 1811–13, this is the oldest public art gallery in the country. Purpose-built, it opened its doors to the public in 1817 (seven years before the National Gallery), and in June of that year its first annual dinner took place. Over 30 guests, including many Royal Academicians, feasted on turtle soup and venison. Today, Soane's great building sits in spacious grounds. The modern café wing (Rick Mather 2000) wraps itself round the east and north edges of the grounds, against the building of old Dulwich College.

HISTORY OF THE COLLECTION

Now an independent charitable trust, Dulwich was part of Alleyn's College of God's Gift (*see above*) until 1994. Alleyn bequeathed to his College his collection of pictures, which included a set of English monarchs. In 1686 the Alleyn pictures were joined by works from the collection of the actor William Cartwright, including a portrait of the actor Richard Burbage.

Sir Francis Bourgeois' bequest in 1811 of over 350 Old Master pictures transformed the collection. Bourgeois, an artist of moderate ability (several examples of his work are here), was the protégé of the ambitious art dealer Noel Desenfans, with whom he collaborated. Between 1790 and 1795 Desenfans was collecting on behalf of Stanislaw II Augustus, King of Poland, who wished to establish a National Gallery of Poland; but with the partition of that country and the King's forced abdication in 1795, Desenfans was left with the pictures. He passed them to Bourgeois, who in turn bequeathed them to Dulwich College to 'go down to Posterity for the benefit of the Public' (the educational impulse behind the gift remains present in the gallery's innovative educational programmes).

The building

Soane's task was to design a new gallery for the pictures which was also to incorporate a mausoleum for the tombs of Bourgeois and Desenfans and later Desenfans' wife (d.

1813), all of whom had been Soane's friends. This dual purpose, and the association between death and art, excited Soane, and Dulwich became his 'favourite subject'. Due to lack of funds, the actual building (which cost less than £10,000) is stark and austere, built of London stock brick with little embellishment. Though celebrated today, its appearance is not truly in accordance with Soane's wish. The mausoleum is centrally placed on the west side, originally flanked by almshouses (a key function of Alleyn's College), now converted to galleries. The contrast between the 'dull, religious light' of the mausoleum, filtered through Soane's signature amber glass, and the daylight clarity of the gallery, was deliberate and its eerie oddness is pure Soane. The main galleries, a succession of plain interlinked spaces, have top-lighting in the form of large lanterns, influential for later gallery design in Britain. Internally the gallery has been restored as far as possible to its original early 19th-century appearance, including the smoky dark red of some of the walls.

Collection highlights

The pictures at Dulwich include about 56 of those intended for Poland (others were sold at auction in 1802) and those Bourgeois continued to collect. Portraits of Bourgeois and Desenfans and his wife (the latter by Reynolds) are on display; the **mausoleum** faces you as you enter.

The collection has a particularly strong collection of **Dutch and Flemish pictures**: works by Cuyp, Ruisdael, Jan Steen, Gerrit Dou and Teniers the Younger. Aert de Gelder's *Jacob's Dream* is memorable, with its huge sky and angel appearing in a dazzling, bright light. By Rembrandt is the well-known *A Girl at a Window*, signed and dated 1645. There are several works by Rubens, including *Venus, Mars and Cupid*, and a memorable *Samson and Delilah* by Van Dyck.

Highlights of the **French works** include paintings by Claude; Charles Le Brun's *Massacre of the Innocents* and Poussin's *Nurture of Jupiter* and *Triumph of David*, showing David parading the head of Goliath through Jerusalem. **Italian pictures** include Guercino's *Christ and the Woman Taken in Adultery* (c. 1621), Sebastiano Ricci's *Resurrection* (an oil sketch for the painted apse in the chapel of the Royal Hospital, Chelsea), Veronese's *Saint Jerome and Girolamo Petrobelli* and a very striking portrait of a young man against a bright blue ground, attributed to Piero di Cosimo. There are two views of the Thames by Canaletto, one of London and the other of Westminster. Another popular work, and much copied, is Murillo's *Flower Girl*, possibly modelled by the artist's daughter Francisca, who later became a nun. Also by Murillo is *Three Boys*, showing a boy with a pitcher begging a second boy for a piece of pie while a third boy picks his pocket.

The **British pictures** include Van Dyck's extraordinary *Venetia Stanley, Lady Digby, on her Death-bed*, painted in 1633, two days after she died in her sleep, and William Dobson's portrait of the Royalist poet Richard Lovelace, hand on heart. *Mrs Siddons as the Tragic Muse* is a bitumen-browned replica of Reynolds's original now at the Huntington Art Gallery in California, which Desenfans ordered from the artist in 1789. Gainsborough's excellent full-length *The Linley Sisters*, portraits of the musical daughters of a friend of the artist, was bequeathed by William Linley in 1831. It is one of many portraits of members of this family.

Detail of Robert Anning Bell's mosaic on the main façade of the Horniman Museum: *Humanity in the House of Circumstance* (c. 1901).

Dulwich Park, with a lake and fine trees, is a pleasant place to stroll or have a picnic. You can walk across it to Forest Hill and the Horniman Museum in c. 20mins.

FOREST HILL

Map p. 629, E4. Overground: Forest Hill.

The suburb of Forest Hill, which became home to German merchants and artisans in the 19th century, is chiefly visited for the idiosyncratic Horniman Museum.

HORNIMAN MUSEUM AND GARDENS

As the plaque on the main façade indicates, the Horniman Museum and Gardens (*100 London Rd.; free except for aquarium; horniman.ac.uk*) were left to the people of London in 1901 'for ever as a museum for their recreation, instruction and enjoyment'. A museum of anthropology, natural history and musical instruments, it was established in 1888 by Frederick John Horniman (1835–1906), a Somerset-born Quaker tea merchant (his company was the largest in the world in its time), Liberal MP and avid collector. Horniman amassed around 30,000 objects in his lifetime, including birds and butterflies, musical instruments, glass and porcelain and Egyptian and Classical antiquities.

The building and gardens

The museum **building** (1901), a truly modern construction in its time, is an example of English free style architecture by Charles Harrison Townsend, who was dubbed one of 'the prophets of the new style' by the German architect Hermann Muthesius. The main feature of the façade is the large Byzantinesque mosaic by Robert Anning Bell, *Humanity in the House of Circumstance*, which symbolises the course of human life. 'Humanity' is flanked by the Gates of Life and Death and tended by figures personifying the Fine Arts, Poetry, Music, Endurance, Love, Hope, Charity, Wisdom, Meditation and Resignation.

Horniman opened the **gardens** to the public to mark the Diamond Jubilee of Queen Victoria in 1897. They spread over 16 acres and aim to recreate different habitats (e.g. meadows, grassland). There is also a Sunken Garden, a Medicinal Garden, a Dye Garden (with plants used to make colourings) and a Sound Garden, with large-scale musical instruments to play. Other features of note include the charming glass Conservatory (1894); the octagonal Bandstand (1912) designed by Charles Harrison Townsend; and the Dutch Barn (c. 1895), which Horniman transported back from Holland. The South Downs picnic area provides glorious views of Kent.

The collections

The **Natural History** gallery, on the ground and first floors, is wonderfully old-fashioned, suffused with a Victorian taxidermy aesthetic and is testimony to the vanguard work of the British naturalists of the 19th century. Its myriad glass cases filled with examples of the vertebrates and invertebrates that have inhabited and still inhabit the earth is usually surrounded by crowds of fascinated and delighted children. The ground-floor space is dominated by the overstuffed wrinkleless walrus from Hudson Bay, which has been on display since the museum's opening in 1901. Horniman's original collection boasts over 16,000 butterflies, beetles and insects, as well as rare birds in bell jars. The first-floor display has examples from the whole animal kingdom, classified according to the Linnaean system: protozoa to mammals by way of molluscs. Here too is the famed mid-19th-century German **Apostle Clock**, complete with mechanical figures of the Apostles which, apart from Judas, at 4pm each day, bow to the figure of Christ.

The basement **Aquarium** (*fee*) features seven aquatic habitats from around the world. Here are beautifully coloured poison-dart frogs from Central and South America, the grotesque giant frogfish, found in tropical coral reef areas such as the Red Sea, and the gorgeous moon jellyfish, an inhabitant of UK coastal waters.

The **World Gallery** presents a selection from the Horniman's anthropology and ethnography collections (there are an estimated 22,000 African and African-influenced objects alone) as a 'celebration of human creativity'. The museum possesses a number of fine brass artefacts from Benin (at the time of writing ownership had been officially transferred to Nigeria and discussion was in progress about their future long-term display).

The **Music Gallery**, arranged thematically, displays around 1,300 objects from the museum's collection of some 8,000 musical artefacts from all periods and cultures. It is the largest collection of its kind in the UK (audio tables are also available), a fascinating presentation of the ways in which mankind has acclaimed kings and praised divinity, celebrated rites of passage, entertained himself or generally filled the silence over many centuries and continents.

HAMMERSMITH, CHISWICK & EALING

Much of west London consists of suburbs—largely attractive and affluent ones. North of the river is hectic Hammersmith and west of it lies Chiswick, with its lovely vestiges. Further north is Ealing, once the heartland of the British film industry and home to an important architectural masterpiece.

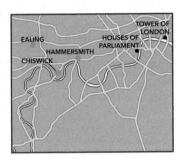

Some highlights of the area
+ **Chiswick House**, the country retreat of the 3rd Earl of Burlington, where he indulged his passion for Palladian architecture;
+ Another former country retreat, belonging to the architect Sir John Soane: **Pitzhanger Manor**, an expression of profound homage to Italy and ancient Rome.

HAMMERSMITH

Map p. 628, B3. Underground: Hammersmith.

Hammersmith is a busy commercial and residential West London suburb between the Thames and the A4, the Great West Road out of town. The concrete 1960s' Hammersmith Flyover, which dominates the centre, has caused optimists to liken Hammersmith to downtown Manhattan. Several international blue chip companies have their headquarters here and Hammersmith supports two Underground stations (Hammersmith & City and Circle lines, and the Piccadilly and District lines), a major bus terminus and a small shopping mall (Broadway Centre), two theatres (the Lyric and Riverside Studios), a music and comedy venue (the Eventim Apollo), several historic buildings and an attractive stretch of riverside townhouses, boating clubs and pubs. The influential **River Café** (*rivercafe.co.uk*), an Italian restaurant co-founded by Ruth Rogers (wife of the late architect Richard Rogers) and the late Rose Gray, is south of Hammersmith Broadway on Thames Wharf. More than one celebrity chef learned their craft in its kitchens. King Street, the main local shopping parade, leads west and eventually becomes the Chiswick High Road.

ST PAUL'S CHURCH

On one side of Hammersmith Flyover stands **The Ark** (*201 Talgarth Rd*), a striking office building in the shape of a plate-glass boat, designed by Ralph Erskine and built by Swedish developers Åke Larsson (1991).

In the other direction, in Queen Caroline Street, is **St Paul's Church** (*sph.org*). Dating to 1883, it has been heavily restored and a modern extension accommodates the needs of the swelling evangelical congregation. The church entrance is through the café and the combination of carpeted interior, electric musical instruments and amplifiers in front of the altar and walls lined with solemn Neoclassical monuments, is unexpected. On the north wall is a memorial to the civil engineer William Tierney Clark, who contributed much to Hammersmith's 19th-century infrastructure. He built the first Hammersmith Bridge (and also designed the famous Chain Bridge across the Danube in Budapest). The carved pulpit is from Wren's All Hallows, Thames Street. In the northwest corner, by glass doors leading to the porch, is a bust of Charles I, erected by the Royalist merchant trader Nicholas Crisp (d. 1666), who built the first chapel on the site. Upon his instructions, his embalmed heart was buried in the urn below the bust to be taken out each year and refreshed with wine (it has since been reunited with his remains elsewhere). The marble egg-cup font in the porch is from Crisp's chapel.

Bradmore House (facing St Paul's Church), now a work space and venue with an all-day café and bar, has a 17th-century façade which was restored in the 1990s. Original panelling from the house is held by the Museum of the Home in Shoreditch.

HAMMERSMITH BRIDGE AND THE RIVERSIDE WALK

Green-painted **Hammersmith Bridge**, London's first suspension bridge, was originally designed in 1824–7 by William Tierney Clark (*see above*). It soon became a popular vantage point from which to view the annual Oxford and Cambridge boat race. When it became too small for the volume of traffic, it was dismantled and the present structure, incorporating piers and abutments of Tierney Clark's bridge, was built by Sir Joseph Bazalgette in 1887.

Westwards from the bridge, the **Thames Path** forms a pleasant two-mile walk towards Chiswick. The **Blue Anchor pub** (*blueanchorlondon.com*) was founded in 1722 and was where Gustav Holst composed part of his *Hammersmith Suite*. Further on, **Furnival Gardens** provide breathing space between the river and the constant traffic of the Great West Road. Named after the social reformer and scholar Dr F.J. Furnivall (d. 1910), whose eponymous sculling club was based nearby, the gardens and small pier were built in 1951 to commemorate the Festival of Britain and to cover what was once 'Little Wapping', Hammersmith's old wharf. There was formerly a creek here, where Stamford Brook joined the Thames, allowing barges to sail as far as King Street at high tide.

Opposite, across the main road, stands the Art Deco **Hammersmith Town Hall** (E. Berry Webber, 1939). Note the double staircase flanked by sculptures of *Old Father Thames*. A pedestrian underpass allows closer access. The annexe, which backs onto King Street, was under redevelopment at the time of writing to create a 'civic campus' with a public square, a cinema and new housing.

The small paved alley with an entrance to the 18th-century **Dove Inn** (*dovehammersmith.co.uk*) is all that remains of old Hammersmith. The pub, once a coffee house, claims to be the smallest in London and is reputedly where Charles II had assignations with Nell Gwyn. It is also where James Thomson wrote the words to 'Rule, Britannia!'. He is buried in St Mary Magdalene church, Richmond. If you can get a place, the balcony offers a good aspect of the river. The other half of the building was where the Doves Press was located and a blue plaque commemorates this. Founded in 1900 by Thomas Cobden-Sanderson and Emery Walker (*see 7 Hammersmith Terrace below*), friends of William Morris, the Doves Press was renowned for its unique font, the Doves Type, which was used in its Arts and Crafts publications, including the Doves Bible. When the press closed in 1916, Cobden-Sanderson destroyed the type by throwing the blocks into the Thames from Hammersmith Bridge.

The alley leads into Upper Mall. William Morris lived at no. 26, **Kelmscott House**, from 1878–96 and died there; he named the house after his country home in Oxfordshire. The basement is home to the William Morris Society (*williammorrissociety. org*) and lectures and events take place here. Earlier it was home to Sir Francis Ronald, inventor of the telegraph (part of his original telegraph is in the Science Museum). Catherine of Braganza, wife of Charles II, lived in a house (now demolished) on Rivercourt Road after the death of her husband. Latymer Preparatory School (*36 Upper Mall*) stands on part of the site.

Some way further on, **Linden House** (c. 1730) is home to the London Corinthian Sailing Club and the Sons of the Thames Rowing Club. Continuing close to the Thames, you come to the **Old Ship Inn** (17th century and rebuilt 1850) and the **Black Lion pub** (c. 1793), standing on either side of what was the West Middlesex Waterworks (1906), also designed by Tierney Clark. Water was once pumped under the Thames from reservoirs across the river. Both pubs have outdoor seating overlooking the Thames and are popular all year round.

The path now doglegs into **Hammersmith Terrace**, a row of mid-18th-century townhouses. The English Arts and Crafts typographer and friend of William Morris, Emery Walker, lived at no. 7 and the interior has been preserved as it was in his lifetime (*for access and tours, see emerywalker.org.uk*). Another typographer lived at no. 3: Edward Johnston (1872–1944) who, in 1916, created the typeface still used (in a variant form) by London Underground.

CHISWICK

Map p. 628, A3–B3. Underground: Turnham Green then 20mins' walk; or Hammersmith and then along the Riverside Walk.

Old Chiswick, by the river, hemmed in by the busy A4, was once a rural community of fishermen, watermen and farmers (Chiswick means 'Cheese Farm' in Old English). Its setting made it popular from the 16th century as a country retreat for wealthy Londoners.

510 HAMMERSMITH, CHISWICK AND EALING

CHISWICK MALL

The riverside walk from Hammersmith continues into Chiswick Mall. Despite close proximity to the relentless main road, the setting is tranquil, with views of the wooded towpath on the opposite bank. Elegant 17th–19th-century villas line the cobbled street, many covered in climbing plants. Their lush private gardens are along the water's edge on the opposite side of the road (residents usually open their gardens to the public once a year in the spring). Parts of the Mall are unembanked and can flood during high tide (it is not uncommon to see swans swimming along it)—which is worth bearing in mind if driving or parking a car.

Walpole House, one of the finest villas on the Mall, was the home of Barbara Villiers, Duchess of Cleveland, Charles II's mistress, who died here in 1709, and is a fine example of the Restoration period. It was named after a later resident, the Hon. Thomas Walpole (d. 1803), nephew of Sir Robert Walpole, 1st Earl of Orford, the first Prime Minister of Great Britain. Walpole House later became a school and one of its pupils was the novelist William Makepeace Thackeray, who is said to have used it as the model for Miss Pinkerton's Seminary for Young Ladies in *Vanity Fair*.

On **Chiswick Eyot** (pronounced 'eight'), a small island in the Thames, osier willows were cultivated for basket-making until the 1930s.

Award-winning beer and real ale, such as Chiswick Bitter and London Pride, are brewed at **Fuller's Griffin Brewery** (Chiswick Lane; *for tours and tastings, see fullersbrewery.co.uk*). Beer has been brewed on this site for over 350 years, though Fuller's was bought in 2019 by the Japanese Asahi company. Tours start in the brewery's pub, the Mawson Arms, where Alexander Pope once stayed.

The famous Thornycroft boatyard was on Church Wharf (now 1980s' townhouses): the first torpedo gunboat with a water tube boiler (HMS *Speedy*) was built here in 1893 (she fell victim to a mine in the North Sea in 1914).

ST NICHOLAS'S CHURCH

At the end of the Mall stands the parish church of St Nicholas (*stnicholaschiswick.org*). It was rebuilt in the 1880s but the tower is from the 15th century. The churchyard contains **William Hogarth's tomb** (d. 1764; clearly visible on the left-hand side up the flight of steps), which is marked by a pedestal and urn with a palette and brushes on the side. The weathered epitaph, by Garrick, reads:

Farewell great Painter of Mankind
Who reach'd the noblest point of Art
Whose pictur'd Morals charm the Mind
And through the Eye correct the Heart.

Nearby is the bronze tomb chest of the artist Whistler (d. 1903). Two of Oliver Cromwell's daughters are buried here without monuments—as are, according to some, the headless remains of Oliver Cromwell himself (*for the fate of his head, see p. 142*). Also in the graveyard lies Henry Joy (d. 1893) the trumpeter who sounded the Charge of the Light Brigade.

CHURCH STREET AND THE HOGARTH ROUNDABOUT

The notorious 18th-century highwayman Dick Turpin is reputed to have frequented **The Old Burlington** on Church Street, an Elizabethan building, once the Burlington Arms tavern. Church Street leads to the congested **Hogarth Roundabout**. The construction of the Great Western Road (A4) was proposed in the 1930s but abandoned after strong local opposition. After the area sustained extensive bomb damage in World War Two, the planning finally went ahead in the 1950s, ripping through this part of historic Chiswick. Left off the roundabout is the tiny **Chiswick Square** (1680s), with Boston House (1740s) at its centre. A plaque on one wall states that 'into this garden Thackeray in "Vanity Fair" describes Becky Sharp as throwing the dictionary'. The claim to fame as the original Miss Pinkerton's Academy is disputed with Walpole House (*see above*).

Hogarth's House, on Hogarth Lane (*map p. 628, B3; hogarthshouse.org*), is a modest Queen Anne building, fragile and small amid the traffic. This is the 'little country box by the Thames' that the painter William Hogarth used as a summer retreat from 1749–64. A high wall surrounds the house and garden, where a mulberry tree from Hogarth's day survives. In 2020 the Mulberry Garden Project was completed, which involved re-landscaping and historic planting. The house contains Hogarth's palette, paintbox and punchbowl as well as prints and engravings. *The Man of Taste* mocks Lord Burlington and his favourite decorative painter, William Kent (who, through Burlington's promotion of him, won commissions from Hogarth's father-in-law, Sir James Thornhill). Burlington's support of Italianate art was a favourite subject of Hogarth's needling wit. His Palladian mansion (Chiswick House; *see below*) is in the park just to the southwest. To the north, at 3–7 Devonshire Rd, **La Trompette** offers fine French cuisine at less than West End prices (*latrompette.co.uk*).

CHISWICK HOUSE AND GARDENS

Map p 628, B3. Burlington Lane. Trains to Chiswick from Waterloo and Clapham Junction or 15mins' walk from Turnham Green, Chiswick Park or Gunnersbury Tube. The Duck Pond Market, held on the first Sun of the month in the forecourt, attracts small local businesses, artisans and a farmers' market. chiswick-houseandgardens.org.uk; duckpondmarket.com.

Chiswick House is the greatest architectural statement of Richard Boyle, 3rd Earl of Burlington (1694–1753), the early 18th-century 'Apollo of the Arts'. Heavily influenced by the architecture of ancient Rome and that of Palladio, which he had seen on his tours of Italy (returning from the second trip in 1719), as well as the architecture of the great Inigo Jones, Burlington conceived Chiswick as an embodiment of his architectural ideals. The villa, with ornate interiors and Jonesian ceilings painted by Burlington's protégé William Kent, was originally attached to the estate's Jacobean mansion (since demolished) and was used as a temple of the Arts, an intellectual retreat where Burlington displayed his fine pictures and sculptures and entertained friends, including the poet Alexander Pope. Kent also designed furniture especially for the villa to match its scale, the scallop-shell motifs being a signature for his work. Burlington's townhouse (now the Royal Academy; *p. 240*) was also decorated by Kent, in the same

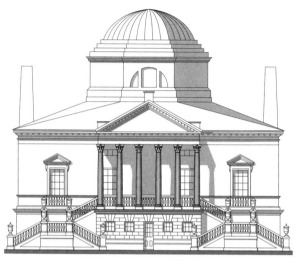

CHISWICK HOUSE: ENTRANCE FAÇADE

spirit. On Burlington's death the estate passed via his daughter to Lord Hartington, later 4th Duke of Devonshire. Throughout the 18th and 19th centuries the house was a centre of English social life. In 1809 Charles James Fox died here and Edward VII, as Prince of Wales, spent time here, as did the Tsars of Russia. The Chiswick estate remained with the Dukes of Devonshire until 1929. Burlington's pictures and much of the furniture designed for the house by Kent have either been dispersed or are in the Devonshire collection at Chatsworth. Several loans from the latter, however, and the odd chance purchase of important pieces original to the house, give a sense of the villa as it was in its 1730s' heyday.

Exterior of the villa

Palladio's Villa Rotonda outside Vicenza is usually cited as the main inspirational source, but in fact the villa is Burlington's own unique interpretation of several models. The central octagonal dome, lit by demi-lune 'thermal' windows inspired by those in the Baths of Diocletian in Rome, is flanked by four chimney stacks in the shape of obelisks, while an elaborate double staircase rises to the first-floor entrance, under a crisply carved Corinthian portico. At the foot of the staircase, to either side, are statues by J.M. Rysbrack (c. 1730) of Burlington's architectural heroes, Palladio and Inigo Jones.

Interior of the villa

A sequence of nine rooms of a studied, intellectual magnificence is arranged around the octagonal domed **Upper Tribune**, with light flooding in from its windows, its walls punctuated by four pedimented doorways, based on Jones designs. Classical busts sit on gilded brackets and above them hang large pictures from Burlington's collection. They include *Charles I and his Family*, after Van Dyck; *Liberality and Modesty*, after Veronese; *Louis XIII and Anne of Austria* by Poussin's master Ferdinand Elle; and Kneller's *The Moroccan Ambassador* (1684), an equestrian portrait of Mohammed Ohadu, famous for his displays of horsemanship in Hyde Park.

The **Gallery** runs the full length of the garden front and is one of the most important rooms in the house. A tripartite space with a rectangular, apsed centre, with flanking circular and octagonal cabinets, it is a rigorously controlled architectural enfilade. The actual dimensions are small but an effect of grandeur is achieved through the skilfully judged proportions and the richly carved and ornamented surfaces, decorated in white and gold. The ceiling painting, a copy of Veronese's *Defence of Smyrna*, is attributed to Sebastiano Ricci, who also decorated Burlington House (the Royal Academy). The surrounding ceiling panels, within compartments with ornamentation derived from Jones, are by Kent. The magnificent carved and gilded marble-topped tables, designed by Kent, were made for the house in 1730.

The **Green Velvet Room**, with marble chimneypieces based on Jones designs, contains eight charming paintings of the gardens commissioned by Burlington from Pieter Andreas Rysbrack, brother of the sculptor. The **Blue Velvet Room** has an elaborate ceiling design with console brackets with Kent's *Architecture* in the centre. The carved and gilded pedimented doorways are surmounted by portraits, held by putti, including Inigo Jones by William Dobson and Pope by Kent.

The gardens

The gardens at Chiswick mark a departure from the intricate, formal designs of the Baroque age in the direction of a more 'natural' landscape, with semi-contrived wildernesses, lakes and groves and expansive vistas, dotted with statuary. They have been hailed as the founders of the Landscape Movement, the inspiration for New York's Central Park and much besides. In the early 1730s, Kent was hired to complete for Burlington a suburban retreat. Many of the features can still be seen, including the broad **avenue lined with urns and sphinxes**, culminating in a semicircular **exedra**, originally of myrtle but now of yew, framing casts of Roman busts (originals inside the villa) of Caesar, Pompey and Cicero. The **bridge** over the canal was built by James Wyatt in 1774. At the canal's south end is the **Cascade**, two triple-arched storeys of rough masonry down which water flows. North of the house is the **Inigo Jones Gateway**, brought to Chiswick from Beaufort House, Chelsea, in 1736, a gift of Sir Hans Sloane and the subject of a verse by Pope. The **conservatory**, added in the early 18th century, is famous for its camellias.

STRAND-ON-THE-GREEN AND KEW BRIDGE

Strand-on-the-Green (*map p. 628, A3*), a dulcet stretch of fine riverside houses and a smattering of pubs, is best approached from Kew Bridge. Among its famous 18th-century residents was the artist John Zoffany, at no. 65 (1790–1810). **Kew Railway Bridge**, spanning the river, in green wrought-iron lattice, opened in 1869. On Kew Bridge Road, the tall chimney of the old Kew Pumping Station is prominent. The building now houses the **London Museum of Water and Steam** (*waterandsteam.*

org.uk), with restored beam engines of the Grand Junction Water Works, which began supplying water to west London in 1837. Here you will find the largest collection of stationary engines in the world, including Cornish pumping engines still in their original engine houses, and four rotative engines.

EALING

Map p. 628, A2–A3. Underground: Ealing Broadway.

Ealing is renowned as the 'Queen of the Suburbs', a reputation gained in the 19th century with the coming of the Great Western Railway (1838), turning what had been a sedate market-garden parish with Anglo Saxon origins into a bustling municipal borough—the first in the County of Middlesex—for the new Victorian middle classes.

EALING STUDIOS AND EALING GREEN

Ealing for many means the **Ealing Studios** on Ealing Green (*map p. 628, A3*). Film-making here dates back to the silent era and Ealing's is the oldest film studio in the world, though its golden age came in the late 1940s–mid-1950s with *Passport to Pimlico* (1949), *Kind Hearts and Coronets* (1949), *The Lavender Hill Mob* (1951) and *The Ladykillers* (1955). In the 1950s the BBC bought the studios and its film department was based here, with as many as 50 film crews producing dramas, comedy series and documentaries including *Dr Who*, *Cathy Come Home*, *Colditz* and *Monty Python*. The studios are now home to the Met Film School. There are five working studios, as well sound recording studios, used by artists such as Rihanna, Tinie Tempah and Sam Smith. North of the studios is **Pitzhanger Manor** (*see below*).

The continuation of Ealing Green to the south is St Mary's Road, where **St Mary's Church** (S.S. Teulon, 1866) is an extraordinary 'Byzantine shrine' on the site of a medieval church destroyed in the Civil War.

PITZHANGER MANOR

Map p. 628, A3. Underground: Ealing Broadway. Café. www.pitzhanger.org.uk

In 1800 Sir John Soane bought Pitzhanger Manor House. It was a homecoming for him, for, at the age of 15, he had been apprenticed to George Dance the Younger, who had built Pitzhanger's red-brick south wing extension. Soane later described Dance's interior as displaying a 'profusion of ornaments, exquisite in taste and admirable in execution'. He did little to alter it, and in fact used it as part of his house, demolishing the rest of the pre-1768 'incongruous mass of buildings' and over the next four years appending an Italianate villa to Dance's brick box, a villa which would advertise his fascination with ruins and the effects of space and light. For almost a decade Soane used it as a weekend family refuge, a house to entertain friends and a showcase for his

The Vestibule at Pitzhanger, with its roundel of Selene driving the chariot of the Moon into the sea, modelled on a relief on the Arch of Constantine in Rome.

ever-growing collection of art and antiquities. When it became clear that neither of his sons had the least interest in inheriting and continuing the project, Soane sold the house (in 1810) and its collection removed to Lincoln's Inn Fields (*see p. 221*).

Pitzhanger was purchased in 1843 by Spencer Horatio Walpole for his four unmarried sisters-in-law, all daughters of Spencer Perceval (*see below*). They lived at Pitzhanger on a peppercorn rent. During their tenure, Soane's courtyard, with its colonnade of mock-ancient columns, was demolished and replaced with a building which now houses the contemporary art gallery. Frederica, the youngest of the sisters, died in 1900.

The house

Soane's **façade** is still extant, of three bays in yellow London stock brick, across which stretches an Ionic screen: four columns with a massive, mannered entablature topped with sculptured figures of Coade Stone (*see p. 466*), modelled on the Erechtheion caryatids. The main doorway is flanked by Roman eagles, based on an ancient relief found near Trajan's Column in Rome.

The entrance **Vestibule** is surmounted by a central roof light, beautifully restored with yellow glass to confer a sherry-coloured sunlight effect at all seasons of the year. On the walls are huge roundels, copies of reliefs of *Selene* (the Moon) and *Sol* (the Sun) in their chariots, on the Arch of Constantine in Rome. The walls are painted dark green and yellow to resemble antique *verde antico* and *cipollino* marble. This marbling, as well as meticulously hand-painted Chinese wallpaper elsewhere in the house, faithfully reflect Soane's original design. Over-painting from the 1830s has been carefully stripped back in a return to Soane's colour schemes and some of Soane's structural elements have also been reinstated: a conservatory demolished in 1901 has been rebuilt, for instance. The **Breakfast Room** has a very shallow dome with Winged Victory figures in the corners and a central mock oculus, modelled on the Roman Pantheon, painted with a blue sky and scudding clouds. The **Dining Room** and **Drawing Room**, occupying the lower and upper levels of George Dance's wing, are handsome, well-proportioned rooms with plenty of natural light and preserving their original, pre-Soane graceful stuccoed ceilings. In the basement is the **Monk's Library**: as at Lincoln's Inn Fields, Soane liked to indulge in the fantasy of a resident hermit.

The **Gallery** is now a contemporary exhibition space.

Walpole Park

Walpole Park (*usually open 7.30–dusk*), named after Pitzhanger Manor's sometime owner, Spencer Horace Walpole, lies to the rear of the Manor and was once part of its grounds. In the mid-18th century it consisted of formal gardens, cedar trees and a rectangular kitchen garden (which can still be seen today). On his purchase of the manor house, Soane worked closely with the landscape architect John Haverfield and made notable changes, including a small serpentine lake (now a stream) with a rustic bridge arching over it, surfaced in flint, rubble and dressed stone to give an antique effect. His mock Roman ruins and fragments, which he left strewn around to give the impression that an ancient temple had been discovered in the grounds, are no longer extant and his planned melon grove did not materialise.

EALING COMMON AND GUNNERSBURY

The **church of All Saints** on Elm Grove Road on the south side of Ealing Common (*map p. 628, A3*), stands on the site of the home of Spencer Perceval, the only British Prime Minister to be assassinated, who lived there until his untimely end in 1812. The church was the bequest of his youngest daughter, Frederica, who lived at Pitzhanger. Among its possessions are Perceval's death mask and his official red leather attaché case.

MODERNIST TUBE STATIONS

Some of the finest examples of early 20th-century civic architecture in London can be seen in its Underground stations. Many of these were designed by Charles Holden (1875–1960), who was commissioned by the then-director of the Underground Electric Railways Company, Frank Pick. His work can be seen at Piccadilly Circus (the travertine-clad ticket hall), Chiswick Park, East Finchley and at  Arnos Grove and Southgate at the northern end of the Piccadilly Line, the latter two examples being inspired by Dutch and Scandinavian prototypes. Another architect to produce fine designs was Stanley Heaps (1880–1962), who designed the particularly successful Osterley and St John's Wood stations, and worked together with Holden on Ealing Common. The clutter of modern advertising panels, signage, automated turnstiles etc. does not always respect the streamlining of the designs but one can usually get a sense of how elegant—and modern—they once were, either in the outline of the main building itself, or with the addition of a tower, or in the graceful sweep of the platforms with their waiting rooms.

GUNNERSBURY

The Gunnersbury Park Museum (*map p. 628, A3; Underground: Gunnersbury Park; visitgunnersbury.org*) has a small local history collection housed in a 19th-century mansion, restored in 2018. Originally a Palladian villa stood here, built as a summer residence for Princess Amelia, daughter of George II. She made improvements to the grounds, originally laid out by William Kent: the Doric temple on the edge of the round pond is a survivor of her scheme. Her bath house, at a discreet distance from the main house, has also been restored. The villa was demolished in 1801 and the present Regency edifice (originally two separate houses) was built. In 1835 Nathan Meyer Rothschild bought the larger house and Sydney Smirke added the orangery. Later the Rothschilds also acquired the smaller mansion; they lived here until 1917. Today, there are displays on Ealing and Hounslow, from early history to the present. Ealing's association with cinema is covered and the original Victorian kitchens survive.

Wimbledon Windmill, the last surviving hollow-post flour mill in the United Kingdom.

KEW, ISLEWORTH, PUTNEY & WIMBLEDON

Riverside Kew is known first and foremost for its extensive and beautiful botanical gardens. On the opposite bank of the Thames are two fine houses with decoration by Robert Adam. Further east is riverside Putney, and Wimbledon with its famous tennis courts. The Heathrow flight path is very apparent in this part of London: jets fly low overhead in a continuous aerial stream, keeping pace with the flow of the Thames beneath.

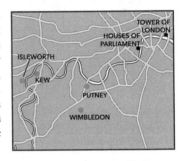

KEW

Map p. 628, A3. Underground: Kew Gardens. River boats from Westminster Pier in c. 90mins (no service in winter; for details, see thamesriverboats.co.uk).

It is to the existence of nearby Richmond Palace that Kew owes both its botanic garden and the attractive village setting at **Kew Green**. The handsome 18th-century houses surrounding a quintessentially English village green, where cricket is sometimes played, were built for members of the King's Court when the Hanoverian royal family made Kew their home.

The parish **church of St Anne's** was built in 1714 on a plot of land granted by Queen Anne. Buried here, along with many directors of Kew Gardens, are the painters Thomas Gainsborough (d. 1788) and John Zoffany (d. 1810), as well as Jeremiah Meyer, miniature painter to George III's consort Queen Charlotte, and Francis Bauer, his botanical artist. The stone mausoleum at the east end was the burial place of Prince Adolphus, Duke of Cambridge, son of King George and Queen Charlotte, who was buried here in 1850; his remains, and those of his wife, were removed in 1930 and buried in St George's Chapel, Windsor.

Across Kew Green at no. 22 a Blue Plaque marks where Impressionist artist Camille Pissarro stayed in 1892.

In Ruskin Avenue are the **National Archives** (formerly the Public Record Office), holding documents pertaining to a thousand years of British history, including the Domesday Book. The public may visit free of charge (*nationalarchives.gov.uk*) to consult original documents; only five percent of the records are online.

ROYAL BOTANIC GARDENS

There are entrances on three sides: the main Elizabeth Gate, on Kew Green; Victoria Gate on Kew Road (a short walk from the Tube station) and the Lion Gate south of it; and Brentford Gate on the Thames side, accessed from Ferry Lane. Cafés, restaurants. kew.org.

Kew's splendid 300-acre gardens, with glorious seasonal displays, both wild and exotic, occupy a bend in the Thames. They contain the largest and most diverse botanical collections in the world and grow over 30,000 species of plant and 9,000 species of tree; some of the rarest are under cover in the magnificent Victorian glasshouses. Kew is internationally recognised as a centre of botanical research and scientific excellence and is a world leader in plant conservation. Its 'unique cultural landscape', with several listed historic buildings, is a UNESCO World Heritage site.

HISTORY OF KEW GARDENS

The history of the gardens is really an amalgamation of several initiatives, but it is generally accepted that the foundations were laid in the 1750s when Augusta, Dowager Princess of Wales and mother of George III, developed a nine-acre garden around the White House, a Palladian villa by William Kent, that stood opposite what is now known as Kew Palace. Sir William Aiton was her head gardener and Sir William Chambers the architect. Over six years he built 25 ornamental buildings. Some of these mid-18th-century follies survive, including the Pagoda, the Orangery, the Ruined Arch, the Temple of Bellona and the Temple of Arethusa. The site was considerably enlarged by George III, who combined it with the Richmond Lodge estate and employed 'Capability' Brown to remodel the Old Deer Park. He and Queen Charlotte frequently stayed at Kew Palace (formerly the Dutch House). Sir Joseph Banks, who accompanied Captain Cook on his round-the-world voyage, was gardener from 1772–1819, when plants from South Africa, Australia and the Pacific were collected and cultivated. In 1841 the now extensive Kew Gardens were handed to the nation and expanded to 300 acres.

Among Kew's achievements were the introduction to the West Indies in 1791 of the bread fruit tree (the purpose of the *Bounty* voyage; fast-growing and nutritious, it was to provide food for plantation slaves), quinine to India in 1860 and rubber trees to Malaysia and Sri Lanka in the 1870s; in the late 19th century Kew played an important part in restoring the European wine-growing industry with imported American rootstock, after vines were destroyed by phylloxera.

KEW PALACE

The red-brick building (*closed in winter*) is a fine example of the 'artisan mannerist' style popular in the early 17th century. A royal residence from the early 18th century, it is all that remains of George II and George III's palace at Kew. It is the smallest of all the royal palaces. Formerly known as the Dutch House, it was built in 1631 for Samuel Fortrey, a

City of London merchant of Flemish descent. The date is carved in the brickwork above the door, as are Fortrey's initials, entwined with those of his wife in a lover's knot. By the mid-18th century this fine three-storey villa, with its ochre-washed Flemish-bond brickwork and Dutch gables, was being used as an annexe to the royal residence known as the White House or Kew House, built in the 1730s by Frederick, Prince of Wales. It was the childhood home of George III and later the nursery for his own children and his retreat during the onset of his nervous disorder, porphyria. Fanny Burney, Assistant Mistress of the Robes to King George's beloved wife, Queen Charlotte, wrote in 1786 that 'the Royal family are here always in so very retired a way, that they live as the simplest gentlefolks.' Queen Charlotte spent the last six months of her life here in 1818, a year in which the palace also saw the marriages of two of her sons, the middle-aged Duke of Clarence (the future King William IV) and the Duke of Kent. The latter parted unwillingly from his long-standing mistress in order to marry Princess Victoria of Saxe-Coburg. Their daughter, as Queen Victoria, opened the palace to the public in 1899.

Inside, the attractions include a waxwork of George III taken from Madame Tussaud's life cast; the shirt he wore during his illness; and a 1780s' dolls' house with tiny embroidered furnishings made by George III's daughters. The King and Queen were reluctant to let their daughters marry. Of the six of them, only one did, the eldest. Princess Sophia, the fifth daughter, in a letter to her brother the Prince of Wales, described herself and her sisters as 'wretches...old lumber to the country, like old clothes. I wonder you do not vote for putting us in a sack & drowning us in the Thames.' The wallpaper, carpets and curtains have been recreated from surviving fragments and contemporary descriptions, and the 18th-century brass door locks, engraved with the crest of Frederick, Prince of Wales, have been preserved. The suites of wood-panelled rooms on the second floor have good views of the Thames.

Behind the palace is the **Queen's Garden**, created in 17th-century style. Nearby are the recently restored **Royal Kitchens**, built in the 1730s to cater to Frederick, Prince of Wales and the royal family when they stayed here. The rusty hip bath in the silver scullery is alleged to have been used by George III. The **Orangery** (*now a restaurant*) was built by Chambers in 1761.

QUEEN CHARLOTTE'S COTTAGE AND THE PAGODA

Queen Charlotte's Cottage, on the other side of the gardens about a mile from Kew Palace, is an early example of a *cottage orné*, quaint and thatched. It was contrived and built by Queen Charlotte in 1771 as a rustic retreat. Here the royal family would come for breakfasts, to picnic and to take tea. In the upstairs Picnic Room the walls, ceiling and door frames are naïvely rendered as an arbour of nasturtiums and convolvulus. The artist is believed to have been Princess Elizabeth, a daughter of George III and Queen Charlotte, who painted similar decoration at Frogmore House, Windsor in 1805. The Cottage once overlooked a menagerie which in the 1790s had kangaroos; today the wooded grounds are a misty sea of flowering bluebells in May.

The ten-storey **Great Pagoda**, 164ft high, in the corner near the Lion Gate, was built by Sir William Chambers in 1761 as a surprise for Princess Augusta. It was built to one of the designs Chambers brought back to England after his journey to China. A major conservation project from 2015–18 aimed to restore as many of the original architectural and decorative features as possible. Eighty vividly coloured dragons once again adorn the roofs, created by using 3D technology. Eight on the lowest roof were hand-carved in cedarwood while those on the upper levels are made of a strong polyimide material, much lighter than wood, which would have been too heavy for the roofs. The building is once again painted in its original green and white, and the finials and terminal pole have been regilded.

THE GLASSHOUSES

Kew's collection of spectacular glasshouses is deservedly world-famous; between them they house four acres of the gardens and some of the rarest plants. Near the Pagoda, the enormous **Temperate House** was designed by Decimus Burton. Building started in 1860 but was not completed until 1898. After a five-year renovation programme it reopened in 2018 to house some 10,000 plants encompassing 1,500 different species, planted according to geographical zone. The temperature is kept at a steady 10°C. In the centre, the huge Chilean wine-palm (*Jubaea chilensis*) was raised from seed in 1846. *Encephalartos woodii*, a type of cycad extinct in the wild, is the rarest plant at Kew. The challenge is to get it to cone, because in the wild cycads bear male and female pollen on different plants and this plant is a lone male. The Toromiro, a small flowering tree from Easter Island, is also extinct in the wild. The **Evolution House** behind the Temperate House tells the story of plants from the first life forms 3.5 billion years ago.

In the centre of the gardens, is the **Treetop Walkway**, created by Marks Barfield Architects, the designers of the London Eye. It gives the opportunity to view the gardens from canopy level.

Near Victoria Gate, the **Palm House**, its distinctive curving roofs reflected in the nearby Palm House Pond, was completed in 1848 to a design by Decimus Burton and built by the engineer Richard Turner, who came up with the idea of wrought-iron ribs, as used in shipbuilding, to cover the maximum space without internal supports. Pevsner thought it was 'much bolder and hence aesthetically more satisfying than the Crystal Palace ever was.' It creates steamy, humid conditions similar to a tropical rainforest: tall palms reach up to the roof and underneath grow rubber trees, bananas, mangoes, jackfruits, breadfruits, durians and spices. Many of the plants grown here are threatened in the wild and some are extinct. Here too is an antique and massive pot plant, a South African cycad, brought to Kew in 1775. The Marine Display, in the basement, has seahorses and jellyfish as well as living algae, seaweed and coral. Outside the Palm House are the **Queen's Beasts**, replicas of statues created for the coronation of Queen Elizabeth II in 1953 and modelled on the King's Beasts at Hampton Court (*see p. 545*).

Next to the Palm House is the humid **Waterlily House**, designed and built in 1852, with ironwork by Richard Turner, to display the giant Amazonian waterlily (*Victoria amazonica*), quite a phenomenon of the day. The **Princess of Wales Conservatory** (1987) houses ten computer-controlled environments from desert heat to tropical rainforest under one glass roof. The cacti, succulents and lithops are one of the best collections of semi-arid plants in the world and there is an aquatic display of fish and

Gardeners at work in front of the Palm House at Kew Gardens, under a pewter sky. Some of the Queen's Beasts statues can be seen lining the path.

poison-dart frogs from South America. Nearby, on a tall plinth is *A Sower*, a bronze by Hamo Thornycroft. The model was a young Italian, Orazio Cervi, who posed for a number of artists, including Lord Leighton.

The **Davies Alpine House** (2006) won a RIBA award for its innovative design, which regulates the temperature to suit tender Alpine species. Also in this corner of the gardens, in an austere Neoclassical building, the **School of Horticulture**, originally the Museum of Economic Botany, founded in 1841 by the director of the Gardens Sir William Hooker. Hooker had a particular interest in the commercial usefulness of plants and the museum was the first of its kind in the world. The collections grew rapidly, with contributions encouraged from all corners of the Empire. Many items, such as an intricate Hindu temple carved out of vegetable ivory, were also received from the Great Exhibition of 1851 (*p. 329*). Changing selections from the collections are displayed in themed showcases.

ART GALLERIES AT KEW

When the **Shirley Sherwood Gallery** opened in 2008, it was the first gallery in the world dedicated exclusively to botanical art. Designed by Walters and Cohen, the blinds and glass automatically react to light in order to preserve the fragile paintings and drawings within. Here are exquisite works from Kew's premier—and hitherto little-known—collections of historic, scientifically accurate botanical illustrations; many have never been published. Francis Bauer (d. 1840), 'Botanick Painter to his Majesty' and tutor to Queen Charlotte and William Hooker, had such a precise eye that his drawing of a pollen grain was later proved by a scanning electron microscope to be entirely accurate. Works by Georg D. Ehret, Pierre-Joseph Redouté and Walter Hood Fitch are also shown and the Roxburgh drawings, presented to Kew by the East India Company in 1859, are sometimes on display. Fine contemporary botanical works from Dr Sherwood's extensive private collection are in the **Link Gallery**, which connects to the Marianne North Gallery next door.

The **Marianne North Gallery** is situated, at the artist's request, in a quiet corner away from the main gate. Red brick with a veranda, typical of European dwellings of that period in India, the building was expressly designed to display Marianne North's oil paintings, 832 studies of nature from life in countries all over the world, executed between 1871 and 1885. Many works were painted in circumstances of considerable discomfort and hardship, so North also wanted the gallery to remind visitors of the hospitality offered to the weary traveller in far-flung places. Neatly labelled and arranged geographically, her direct, colourful, uncomplicated oil paintings, none much larger than twelve inches by six, fill the walls completely above the dado, itself made of some 250 vertical strips of different types of timber.

ISLEWORTH, SYON PARK & OSTERLEY

Isleworth (*map p. 626, C3 and p. 628, A3*) became fashionable in the 18th century, when large residential properties were built along the river. Industry spread from Brentford (Pears Soap had a factory here until 1962) and council housing followed. There has been much redevelopment over the last half century, with riverside wharves restored as flats and new maisonettes now joining the estate tower blocks. The result is something of a jumble but Church Street is pretty, especially in sunny weather. It leads to a well-known pub, the **London Apprentice**, named after the apprentices who rowed up from the City on their day off. From the outside deck on the water there are views of Isleworth Ait, the islet in the middle of the river, of rowers out on the water, and the loading crane of an old dock. Inside there are a number of prints from original Hogarth drawings, including one subtitled 'The industrious 'prentice grown rich and Sheriff of London', showing him gourmandising at an official dinner while a black pageboy proffers a bumper of wine. Just beyond the pub is the modern **church of All Saints** (Michael Blee, 1969), incorporating the 15th-century tower of the previous church which was destroyed by fire in 1943, set by two schoolboys. There has been a church on the site since 695. Its prior at the time of the Reformation, John Haile, was executed at Tyburn in 1535 along with a monk from the nearby Syon Abbey. Both men are commemorated in the west window of St Etheldreda's church near Holborn (*see p. 404*).

On **Mill Plat** (a narrow snicket linking the river with Twickenham Road) you can see the former entrance to the old flour mill as well as a row of tiny almshouses founded by Sir Thomas Ingram in 1664.

SYON PARK AND HOUSE

Map p. 628, A3. Trains from Waterloo to Brentford or Syon Lane then 20mins' walk or bus 267 from Hammersmith to Brent Lea. Underground: Gunnersbury then bus 237 or 267. syonpark. co.uk. Café and restaurant in the adjoining Hillers Garden Centre.

The London seat of the Dukes of Northumberland, set in 200 acres of parkland, Syon is chiefly famous for its magnificent Adam interiors and furnishings, its collection of British historical portraits, and grounds laid out by Lancelot 'Capability' Brown. This is the only surviving ducal residence in Greater London. The somewhat gaunt exterior, comprising a castellated block with square corner turrets, dates from the mid-16th century and does nothing to prepare visitors for the splendours of Adam's state rooms. The Northumberland lion (made of lead) which tops the east front of the house is from Northumberland House on the Strand, the family's townhouse, demolished in 1874.

HISTORY OF SYON

The house occupies the site of a medieval abbey (named after Mount Zion in the Holy Land), founded by Henry V in 1415. After the Dissolution of the Monasteries the estate became Crown property, and it was at Syon that the unfortunate Catherine Howard, fifth wife of Henry VIII, was held between her trial and execution. Richard Reynolds, a monk at the abbey, is honoured as one of the five 'proto-martyrs', the first Catholics to be executed at Tyburn in 1535 (*p. 323*). In 1547 the estate was granted to Lord Protector Somerset (*see p. 206*), and after his execution in 1552 it was presented to John Dudley, Duke of Northumberland (no relation to the present family). His daughter-in-law, Lady Jane Grey, was offered the crown at Syon. The estate was acquired by the powerful Percys, Earls of Northumberland, in 1594. The 1st Duke of Northumberland commissioned Robert Adam to re-fashion the interiors in 1761.

The Adam rooms

Within the shell of the Jacobean house, Adam created a thoroughly Neoclassical interior. The **Great Hall**, in the form of a Roman basilica, is austerely decorated in tones of white and black, with Roman statuary and fine plasterwork. A striking contrast to this cool restraint is the lavish **Anteroom**. Twelve columns of *verde antico* marble (some ancient, dredged from the Tiber and brought to Syon in 1765), cleverly arranged to transform the rectangular space into a square, support jutting entablatures and heavily gilded free-standing classical figures. The richly coloured floor is a magnificent example of scagliola work. The **Dining Room**, Adam's first interior at Syon, is decorated in white and gold with copies of antique statues, ordered by Adam, in niches. The **Red Drawing Room**, next in the sequence, has a coved ceiling with intricately painted medallions by Cipriani, a fireplace with ormolu decoration by the silversmith and inventor Matthew Boulton, doorcases with large panels of ivory with applied gilded lead ornament, in Italian Renaissance style, and an exceptional Adam-designed carpet made by Thomas Moore of Moorfields, signed and dated 1769. This room also contains Sir Peter Lely's double portrait, *Charles I and James Duke of York*, painted probably in 1646 when the King was under house arrest at Hampton Court. Occasionally he was allowed to ride to Syon to see his children in the care of Algernon Percy, 10th Earl of Northumberland. The **Long Gallery**, with its intricate enrichment of almost every surface (in the words of Adam, decorated 'in a style to afford great variety and amusement'), is one of the highlights of the house. In the original Jacobean long gallery, Adam punctuated the wall with carefully-positioned doors and chimneypieces to detract from its vast length. Much of the furniture, as in the other rooms, was designed by Adam for this space.

ADAM STYLE

Fêted and derided in equal measure in the 18th century (he was even accused by one critic of 'debauching' buildings), Robert Adam (1728–92) was at his greatest as an interior designer. No other designer-architect of the period worked as closely as he did with artists and furnishers to achieve what has been called a 'unified style', a holistic approach which incorporated the architecture, interior design and furnishings of a building. Born in Kirkaldy, Fife, amidst the white heat of the Scottish Enlightenment, the second of four sons of the architect William Adam, his work was heavily influenced by the Grand Tours of 1755–7 and 1760–3, when, along with his brother James, he travelled to Italy and France, met important figures such as the artist-engraver Piranesi and Charles-Louis Clérisseau, under whose direction he published the lavish book *The Ruins of the Palace of the Emperor Diocletian at Spalatro* (1764). On his return to London, Adam's style developed from a Rococo classicism to something more akin to the Greek and Roman manner he had experienced abroad. A brief collaboration with the decorative colourist Giuseppe Manocchi and the subsequent publication (in 1768) of Sir William Hamilton's Greek vase collection (purchased by the British Museum in 1772), with their red- and black-figure decoration, inspired Adam's distinctive 'Etruscan manner'.

Many of Adam's architectural projects were undertaken in partnership with his brothers, James, John and William, while a group of specialist independent craftsmen was used to realise the meticulously-planned interiors. Every interior element was designed by the Adam office. Joseph Rose and his nephew, also Joseph Rose, provided plasterwork; Thomas Chippendale and other cabinet makers produced furniture; and the chief supplier of elaborate metal-cast ornament was Matthew Boulton. Patterned inlaid floors or carpets mirrored the design of the ceilings, richly painted in combinations of greens, blues, lilac and pink. Inset classical scenes were painted by Giovanni Battista Cipriani, Angelica Kauffman and Antonio Zucchi (who had travelled with Adam to Split—'Spalatro'). Kauffman, admired throughout Europe for her skill, worked with Zucchi on a number of Adam projects before their marriage and departure for Rome in 1781.

Other rooms and grounds

Non-Adam rooms include the **Print Room**, with Lely's portrait, as a child, of the great 17th-century heiress, Lady Elizabeth Percy, who was married three times between the ages of twelve and fifteen. Her second husband, Thomas Thynne of Longleat, was murdered in Pall Mall in 1681 by assassins hired by the Swedish Count Königsmark, a rival suitor (he is commemorated in Westminster Abbey; *no. 43 on plan on p. 137*).

In the grounds, which contain rare trees and plants, 'Capability' Brown swept away the formal walled gardens, establishing spacious lawns, vistas to distant trees and creating the ornamental lake. The **Great Conservatory** was built of gunmetal and Bath stone for the 3rd Duke in 1830 by Charles Fowler, designer of Covent Garden Market. Joseph Paxton is said to have studied it closely when designing the Crystal Palace.

THE GOLDEN MILE

North of Syon Lane station, on the Great West Road, is Gillette Corner (*map p. 628, A3*), the corner with Syon Lane, so named for the large Art Deco factory building, with its landmark central clock tower and ornate Victorian cast iron street lamps, that occupies the plot here. It was built in 1936–7 for the Gillette razor manufacturer. Heading eastwards from here towards Chiswick, you pass a stately enfilade of early 20th-century factory buildings of great architectural interest.

ART DECO LONDON

A number of striking buildings in London owe a debt to the principles of European Modernism. Many of them are to be found on the 'Golden Mile', the stretch of the Great West Road that runs from Syon Lane to Chiswick, through Brentford across the river Brent, which empties itself into the Thames. The Coty building at no. 941 is by Wallis, Gilbert and Partners (1932). At no. 981 is another fine building by the same architects (1929–30), built for the Pyrene fire extinguisher company.

The neo-Egyptian ex-Carlton Cinema in Islington.

Another Wallis, Gilbert and Partners building, Victoria Coach Station (1932), can be admired in central London, on Buckingham Palace Road. Close to it is a great towering pile adorned with sculpture by Gill and Epstein, rising above St James's Park Underground stations at 55 Broadway. This is in part the work of Charles Holden, an architect working in the Streamline Moderne style, who designed a number of Underground station. London University's Senate House is also by his hand (*see p. 373*)—though not in the streamline style, and less widely appreciated than his other work (Evelyn Waugh detested it).

Another architect, this time of Art Deco cinemas, was George Coles, a native Londoner, who designed the old Gaumont Cinema in Kilburn, the ex-Odeon in Woolwich, the neo-Egyptian ex-Carlton in Islington (1930; *pictured*) and cinemas in Southall (*p. 570*). The old Carreras tobacco factory, also in Islington and also neo-Egyptian, dates from a few years earlier (M.E. Collins et al, 1926–8).

The finest domestic building in the Art Deco style is Eltham Palace (*see p. 565*). On the Western Avenue (*map p. 628, A2*), which leads out of London towards Oxford, is the sleek, streamlined Hoover Building (Wallis, Gilbert and Partners, 1933; *Underground: Perivale*).

OSTERLEY

Designed by Charles Holden and Stanley Heaps, architects for the London Underground, **Osterley station** (*map p. 626, C3*) is one of number of Underground buildings erected in the 1920s and '30s according to a rational Modernist plan. Constructed of brick and concrete, it features a square-plan tower with an illuminated obelisk which at night transforms it into a sort of landlocked lighthouse. **Osterley Park and House** is a fine estate now in the keeping of the National Trust (*Jersey Road; Underground: Osterley and 15mins' walk; nationaltrust.org.uk; café*).

HISTORY OF OSTERLEY PARK

Set in 357 acres of parkland and formal gardens, Osterley owes its existence to the conspicuous consumption of three generations of a wealthy family, the Childs, as well as to the vision of the architect Robert Adam (*p. 526*) and the 18th-century fashion for collecting the Orient. Adam's manor house is a three-storey red-brick building, constructed around a raised courtyard, with a grand Ionic entrance portico. The first manor house on the site was built by Sir Thomas Gresham in 1562 (only the brickwork stables survive). Gresham (*p. 63*) used it both as a retreat from London and as a commercial enterprise: one of the earliest paper mills in England was established here. In 1713 the land and property passed into the hands of the goldsmith-banker Sir Francis Child, who had established Child's Bank on Fleet Street. His son Sir Robert, a director of the East India Company from 1719–20, was the first member of the family to live at Osterley but died unmarried in 1721. His younger brother Sir Francis, likewise a director of the East India Company, made substantial alterations to the estate. It is his nephews Samuel and Francis, the first of the Childs to have been brought up at Osterley, who are largely responsible for the architecture of the house today. In 1761 Sir Francis the Younger engaged Adam to remodel it. On his sudden death two years later, his 24-year-old brother Robert continued the work until 1772. The house and park were effectively transformed into what Horace Walpole called 'the palace of palaces…such expense! such taste! such profusion! and yet half an acre produces all the rents that furnish such magnificence. It is a jaghire got without a crime.'

In 1782 the only daughter of Robert Child eloped to Scotland with the Earl of Westmorland and was disinherited. Robert Child died—apparently from a broken heart—in the same year, leaving Osterley to his grandchild, Lady Sarah Sophia Fane, who married the 5th Earl of Jersey. In 1949 the 9th Earl of Jersey gave the property and some of its original contents to the National Trust.

Tour of the house

The house is approached through Adam's grand portico and across the screened courtyard into the severely formal **Hall**. Completed by Adam in 1767, rectangular with alcoves at either end intended to improve the original room's proportions, the design of the grey-and-white marble floor echoes the plasterwork ceiling. The elongated pilasters and shallow Greek-key frieze were inspired, like the ceiling of Adam's masterful Library at Kenwood (*p. 436*), by Diocletian's palace at Split. The niches in the apses display copies of Roman statues of Apollo, Minerva, Ceres and Hercules, and the Portland stone chimneypieces are surmounted by painted grisaille bas-reliefs by Giovanni Battista Cipriani depicting the *Triumph of Bacchus* and *Triumph of Ceres*. The austerity of the **Great Stair**, with its Corinthian and Ionic screens and wrought-iron balusters identical to those at Kenwood, is relieved by the ceiling, also designed by Adam for Rubens' *The Apotheosis of the Duke of Buckingham* (a copy replaces the original, which was removed in 1949 and later lost in a fire). Rubens' sketch for the painting can be seen in the National Gallery. Three lamps, probably made by Matthew Boulton to Adam's designs, hang between the Corinthian columns of the *piano nobile*.

The striking white-painted **Library**, monochromatic like the Hall at Syon (*see p. 524*), is more of a piece than many of the other rooms on this floor. The ceiling in very low relief is characteristic of Adam's middle years, with paintings by Antonio Zucchi set into the walls illustrating scenes from the lives of Classical writers. Above the door is *Britannia Encouraging and Rewarding the Arts and Sciences*. The marquetry furniture, inlaid with motifs emblematic of the liberal arts, is exceptionally fine.

The **Eating Room** was one of the first rooms designed by Adam for the house, in 1766, and is decorated up to the cornice in cheerful pinks and greens. As he later wrote of such rooms in his *Works in Architecture* (1772), 'Instead of being hung with damask, tapestry etc. they are always finished with stucco, and adorned with statues and paintings, that they may not retain the smell of the victuals.' The ceiling is decorated with appropriate Bacchic motifs. Above the remarkably large chimneypiece is Cipriani's *An Offering to Ceres*: women and children paying homage to the goddess of the harvest. Next door is the **Long Gallery**, running the full width of the garden front. It has been returned as far as possible to Adam's original pea-green colour scheme, with pier glasses for easier viewing of the paintings that hang here.

The **Drawing Room**, counterbalancing the Eating Room and designed around the same time, is much richer in concept, with a ceiling modelled on the Temple of the Sun at Palmyra. The carpet was designed by Adam in response to the ceiling and was manufactured by Thomas Moore of Moorfields. Horace Walpole considered the room 'worthy of Eve before the Fall'. The tall pier glasses are also by Adam, along with the inlaid, purely ornamental commodes. The grate in the chimneypiece, itself not entirely of a piece with the room, is made of paktong, an alloy of copper, zinc and nickel, the only one of such pieces by Adam to remain *in situ*. A number of Child family portraits are hung here, original to the house and on loan to Osterley from Lord Jersey. Among them is Allan Ramsay's *Francis Child III* (1758).

From here you enter the sumptuous **State Apartment**, already practically out of fashion when commissioned by Robert Child in 1772 but providing three superb examples of Robert Adam's style at its most confident and mature. The **Tapestry Room** has a delicate ceiling and the carpet was again designed by Adam to mirror it. On the walls are Gobelins tapestries designed by the painter François Boucher and representing the Four Elements in the shape of the loves of the gods: Venus and Vulcan

(Fire), Aurora and Cephalus (Air), and Vertumnus and Pomona (Earth). The mirror on the window wall stands in for Water. The eight armchairs are backed with oval frames holding Boucher's *Jeux d'Enfants*, designed for Madame de Pompadour in the early 1750s: the cartoons were not released for use by other clients until 1770.

The **State Bedchamber** is dominated by the domed State Bed of 1776, one of Adam's most ambitious pieces of furniture. The last room, the **Etruscan Dressing Room**, has striking wall decoration inspired by ancient Greek vases, Roman *grottesche* and the engravings of Piranesi. It is the only surviving example of this type of design by Adam.

PUTNEY

Map p. 628, B3. Underground: Putney Bridge (Fulham side of the river).

Putney is known for its heath (adjoining Wimbledon Common to the north) and for its bridge across the Thames. The original wooden bridge of 1729 was the first river crossing since London Bridge (though further out, at Kingston, there had been a bridge since the early Middle Ages). The current **Putney Bridge**, five spans in grey stone and Cornish granite, built by Bazalgette in 1882–6, links Putney with Fulham (*NB: Putney Bridge station is on the Fulham side of the river*). The **University Stone**, just upstream of Putney Bridge, marks the starting point of the Oxford and Cambridge boat race.

Putney was the birthplace of Thomas Cromwell in c. 1485; his early life here is reconstructed in Hilary Mantel's historical novel *Wolf Hall*. The church of **St Mary**, by the bridge, has a 15th-century tower; the rest was rebuilt in the 19th century and again after a fire in 1980. During the Civil War, Oliver Cromwell's New Model Army had their headquarters in Putney and the Putney Debates—a series of constitutional discussions—were held in the church in 1647. Edward Gibbon was born in Putney in 1737.

The **Embankment**, a picturesque spot on the water west of Putney Bridge, lined with small boathouses, a couple of pubs and gardens, overlooks the green expanse of Bishop's Park on the opposite bank (*p. 566*). At high tide the river often washes along here, in places ankle-deep. A path leads to Hammersmith Bridge (and a cut-off along the way, about a 30-min stroll, takes you to the London Wetland Centre; *see p. 563*).

All Saints' Church on Putney Common (south of Lower Richmond Road; consecrated in 1874) is richly decorated in the Victorian Arts and Crafts tradition. The architect was G.E. Street in collaboration with Edward Burne-Jones and William Morris; many of the stained-glass windows are by Morris & Co.

The poet Swinburne lived at 'The Pines' on Putney Hill from 1879 until his death in 1909, tended by his friend Theodore Watts-Dunton, whose aim was to save him from his alcoholism. In **Putney Vale Cemetery** (*map p. 628, B4; wandsworth.gov.uk*), the sculptor Joseph Epstein (d. 1959) is buried (Block AS, south of Alexander Way, southern boundary of the cemetery), as is Howard Carter (d. 1939), discoverer of the tomb of Tutankhamun (Block 12, south of Central Drive).

THE OXFORD AND CAMBRIDGE UNIVERSITY BOAT RACE

Each year in the raw weather of early spring, crowds throng the Tideway between Putney and Mortlake to see the Oxford and Cambridge eights battling with each other over the four-mile course. The race was first held in 1829 at Henley; today's course, from Putney to Mortlake, was established in 1845 (a victory for Cambridge). Since 1856 (also a victory for Cambridge) the Boat Race has been annual, interrupted only during the two World Wars and by the Covid-19 pandemic. It was cancelled in 2020 and in 2021 was relocated to the Great Ouse at Ely. Oxford wear dark blue shirts and Cambridge light blue, the same colour as their blades. The crew must be composed of members of the respective universities, graduate or undergraduate. The first woman took part in 1981, coxing Oxford to victory. The women's boat race, first run in 1927, was originally held separately from the men's but since 2015 both races have been held on the same day.

WIMBLEDON

Map p. 628, B4. Underground: Wimbledon, Southfields.

Wimbledon is one of the most attractive suburbs of London, part urban settlement, part country village, home of lawn tennis, site of the 'turfy plateau' of Wimbledon Common, and the inspiration for Elizabeth Beresford's burrow-dwelling, litter-picking Wombles, popularised in a succession of children's books and a TV series in the late 1960s and early '70s. The Common includes wooded areas, scrub and heathland, ponds, lawns and recreation facilities. The majority of the land is a conservation area due to its rich plant and animal life, including eight varieties of bat. In the past (due to its remoteness from London), Wimbledon Common was popular with duellists. The first recorded such contest was in 1652, when George Brydges, 6th Baron Chandos, killed Colonel Henry Compton over Mary Carey, Lady Leppington. In 1798, William Pitt the Younger fought the Whig MP George Tierney over his lack of patriotism, and in 1809 an argument over the deployment of British troops during the Napoleonic Wars led Lord Castlereagh (a crack shot) and George Canning (first time with a pistol) to exchange gunfire here. The latter was wounded in the thigh.

An unexcavated iron-age hill fort known as Caesar's Camp (no connection to the Romans) is situated on the Royal Wimbledon Golf Club (south part of the Common).

WIMBLEDON WINDMILL

Wimbledon Windmill, on the northeast edge of the Common, is the old village mill (*free; wimbledonwindmillmuseum.org.uk*), built in 1817 and the only hollow-post flour mill remaining in the country. It ceased working in 1864 when the 5th Earl Spencer wanted to enclose Wimbledon Common and build a manor house. Opposition to the plan rumbled on for six years, until the Wimbledon and Putney Commons Act of 1871 gave the land into the care of the local community. The windmill was converted into housing (for six families) until 1893, and was used as accommodation for the Common Rangers until 1975. Today it houses a museum of windmills, milling and local history (including displays of Girl Guide and Scouting memorabilia; Baden-Powell wrote part of *Scouting for Boys* here in 1908) and you can try your hand at milling flour with some grain, a saddle stone, a mortar and a hand quern.

SOUTHSIDE HOUSE

At the south edge of Wimbledon Common stands the two-storey Southside House (*3–4 Woodhayes Rd.; map p. 628, B4; virtual tours only; southsidehouse.com/gallery-tour*), faced in plum-coloured brick. The property is said to have been bought in 1665 by Robert Pennington, a Chancery official and loyal supporter of Charles II during his exile in Holland, who employed Dutch architects to create a William and Mary façade (the year 1687 is carved on one of the chimneypieces inside). The house has remained in the hands of the Pennington family ever since. In 1910 Hilda Pennington Mellor married the Swedish physician Dr Axel Munthe, author of the bestselling autobiography *The Story of San Michele* (1929). The house as it appears today owes most to the son of Hilda and Axel, the war hero Major Malcolm Munthe, who fought behind enemy lines in Sweden and Norway for the SOE and was awarded the Military Cross.

   The house boasts a fine small collection of British painting, including some elegant full-length portraits by Van Dyck and his studio and Burne-Jones's *St George and the Dragon* (1868). The house also contains a number of objects with colourful and elaborate provenances: Anne Boleyn's vanity case, which she had with her in the Tower before her execution; the pearl necklace which Marie-Antoinette wore at the guillotine and which was presented to John Pennington by Josephine Bonaparte; the emerald and gold ring of Alexander I, the last King of Serbia (assassinated in 1903), whose proposal of marriage Hilda Pennington Mellor declined; and a portrait and letter of Charles-Geneviève-Louis-Auguste-André-Timothée d'Éon de Beaumont, usually known as the Chevalier d'Éon (1728–1810), the French diplomat and spy who spent one half of his life dressed as a man and the other half attired as a woman. The sumptuous Prince of Wales Bedroom preserves the memory of the visits of Frederick, Prince of Wales, heir to George II. Lord Nelson, as well as Sir William Hamilton and his wife Emma, were guests at Southside when they were living at nearby Merton Place (demolished) in the years before Trafalgar. The platform upon which Lady Hamilton performed her classical 'attitudes' is in the Music Room, as is her portrait by Romney, for whom she sat over a hundred times.

WIMBLEDON VILLAGE

Some attractive old buildings survive in Wimbledon Village. On the High Street is the 17th-century **Rose and Crown pub**, where Swinburne was a regular before succumbing to alcoholic dysentery. On the same side of the High Street is the Dutch-gabled **Eagle House**, formerly the Rev. Thomas Lancaster's School for Young

Noblemen and Gentlemen, where the young Arthur Schopenhauer received a clumsy and inadequate education in 1803: no science of any kind was taught, canings were frequent, and the experience left him with a loathing of the Anglican Church. 'When English people display on the Continent their...stupid bigotry,' he later wrote, 'they should be treated with undisguised derision until they are shamed into common sense, for such things are a scandal to Europe.' North of the High Street, at 14 Calonne Rd, is the beautiful **Wat Buddhapadipa**, the first Buddhist temple to be built in the UK, by the Thai architect Praves Limparangsi (1979–82). It is open for visits daily (*buddhapadipatemple.org*).

Wimbledon's main fame, of course, comes from the annual championships at the **All England Lawn Tennis Club** on Church Road, held in June–July since 1877 (*Underground: Southfields and 15mins' walk; or Wimbledon and 20mins' walk; ticket-holders only during championships; admission charge; café; wimbledon.com*). The museum here explores the history and development of tennis from the gentlemanly pastime of 'real tennis' in 16th-century France to the multi-million dollar international business of today. There are autographed mementoes from Wimbledon champions such as Björn Borg and John McEnroe, once the *enfant terrible* of SW19. Of especial interest are the reconstructions of a wooden racquet-maker's workshop and a gentleman's changing room from c. 1900, and the costume gallery recording the changes to ladies' tennis dress over the past century and more. The museum can be seen as part of a tour which takes you to Court I, the Winter Gardens, the Press Interview Room and the International Box of the world-famous Centre Court.

RICHMOND & TWICKENHAM

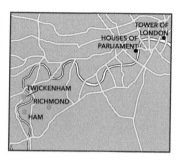

Richmond upon Thames is an attractive riverside suburb with a royal past that can still be traced. Its offering includes shops, plenty of pubs and restaurants, the Thames for riverside walks and boating, and Richmond Park for walking and cycling. Southwest of it lie two attractive riverside villages. Petersham (1 mile) and Ham (2 miles). On the other side of the river is Twickenham. These were favourite rural retreats in times past, for royalty and the well-to-do, and a number of mansions survive: Richmond Palace (in fragmentary form); Ham House and Orleans House, as well as the Palladian Marble Hill House and the neo-Gothic Strawberry Hill.

VISITING BY BOAT

Thames River Boats (wpsa.co.uk) operate services from Westminster Pier to Richmond, via Kew and continuing to Hampton Court (total journey time over 3hrs). Services are more regular between April and Oct; there are special sailings at other times of year. The family-run Hammerton's Ferry takes passengers between Ham and Twickenham for a very small fee (weekends only in winter; hammertonsferry.com).

RICHMOND UPON THAMES

Map p. 628, A4. Underground: Richmond

The area around **Richmond Green** is rich in history and architecture, making it an unspoilt and attractive green 'square'. There was jousting here in Tudor times, and two centuries later, cricket: as attested by the Cricketer's Inn. Shops fill the alleyways which lead through to George Street and the Quadrant. On the **Little Green** is the terracotta façade of Richmond Theatre, built by Frank Matcham, architect of the London Coliseum, in 1899.

On two sides of the Green and in adjoining alleyways are attractive 17th- and 18th-century houses, including Old Palace Terrace (1692), Old Palace Place (1700) and Old Friars (1687), on land which once belonged to the order of Friars Observant. The well-proportioned houses in Maids of Honour Row, fronting the Green, were built in 1724 for the ladies-in-waiting of Caroline of Ansbach, consort of the future George II.

RICHMOND PALACE

The remains of Richmond Palace are essentially rebuilt Tudor fragments, though the origins of a palace here go back further. Edward III built what was then known as Sheen (or Shene) Palace in the 14th century, but as early as 1125 Henry I had stayed in Richmond. After Sheen Palace was destroyed by fire in 1497, Henry VII had it rebuilt and renamed it Richmond Palace after his Yorkshire earldom. It became one of the favourite palaces of the Tudor monarchs. Elizabeth I kept a wardrobe of several thousand dresses here, and died here in 1603. After the execution of Charles I, the main buildings were demolished. The monarchy returned to Richmond in 1720 when George, Prince of Wales, the future George II, took over Richmond Lodge in the Old Deer Park. George III also used the lodge, but preferred Kew Palace.

Old Palace House and Palace Gatehouse were built into the surviving wall of Henry VII's palace. Next to them, turn left through a surviving arch of the Outer Gateway (above which is Henry VII's coat of arms) into Old Palace Yard. Here, the left-hand block is called The Wardrobe, renovated in the 1680s but retaining Tudor brickwork. At the bottom of the yard stands Trumpeter's House (1702–4), built on the former Middle Gate. Next door (right) is Trumpeter's Inn; it is in 18th-century style but was built in the 1950s. Past the bollards, Old Palace Lane, with attractive 19th-century cottages and the White Swan pub, leads left down to the Thames.

OTHER THINGS TO SEE IN RICHMOND

The attractive riverside is mainly a result of redevelopment in 1988 by Quinlan Terry and comprises some 20 buildings in different styles, pleasing in scale and arranged around four courtyards. It is popular and crowded in fine weather. **Asgill House** is built on the site of the water-gate of Richmond Palace. This fine mansion was designed by Sir Robert Taylor in 1757–8 for Sir Charles Asgill, Lord Mayor of London. Just before **Richmond Bridge**, a graceful curve with five arches (James Paine, 1777), are boathouses where one may hire rowing boats and bicycles.

In Paradise Road is **Hogarth House** (1748), home of Leonard and Virginia Woolf from 1915–24. It was here that they founded the Hogarth Press. In the Vineyard are three groups of pretty almshouses of various dates and in Ormond Road, just off Hill Rise, attractive 18th-century houses. The local parish church, **St Mary Magdalen**, on Church Walk in the centre of the town, dates from the early 13th century, with later restoration by Arthur Blomfield and G.F. Bodley. It has a 15th-century flint and stone tower. Among those buried here are the Shakespearean actor, Edmund Kean who died in 1883; James Thomson who wrote the lyrics of 'Rule, Britannia!' while at the Dove Inn, Hammersmith; and the actor and filmmaker Sir Richard Attenborough. The church of **St Matthias**, at the top of Richmond Hill, is by Sir George Gilbert Scott (1861–2). In the Old Town Hall on Whittaker Avenue is a **museum** where the local history of Ham, Petersham, Richmond and Kew is explored (*museumofrichmond.com*).

RICHMOND HILL

The view from Richmond Hill is famous: a fine prospect of the winding Thames with watermeadows, with Petersham Common and Ham on one side and Marble

Hill house and park on the other. At the top of Richmond Hill are two fine houses, both of the 1770s: The Wick, by Robert Mylne; and **Wick House**, built by William Chambers for Sir Joshua Reynolds. The huge neo-Renaissance **Star and Garter Home** (Sir Edwin Cooper, 1921–4), a dominant landmark from both the road and down on the riverbank, still houses invalid servicemen. Opposite is an attractive group of 18th-century terraces, now mostly hotels, and on the roundabout an elaborate **RSPCA fountain**, with gilded griffins (T.E. Collcutt, 1892), erected to quench the thirst of horses who had toiled up the hill.

RICHMOND PARK

Richmond Park comprises 2,500 acres of rolling natural parkland with historic trees. It was once a royal hunting ground, enclosed in 1637 by Charles I. Some oak trees are said to date back to the Middle Ages and several hundred red and fallow deer roam freely. There are also large flocks of screeching green parakeet; wilds birds not native to the UK but which now number several thousand in West London. In popular myth, they are said to be descendants of captive birds kept at Ealing or Isleworth studios, where *The African Queen* was filmed in 1951. In the centre of the park are the man-made Pen Ponds, where fishing is allowed by permit. The **Isabella Plantation** is impressive from March–May, when hundreds of azaleas and rhododendrons bloom.

Several buildings stand within the park, including the **White Lodge**, built in 1727–9 as a hunting lodge for George II, influenced by Chiswick House across the river. King Edward VIII was born at the house. It is now the Royal Ballet's Lower School.

Pembroke Lodge was the home of Lord John Russell and the childhood home of his grandson, the philosopher Bertrand Russell. It now houses a café and offers a splendid view over the Thames Valley; on a fine day one can make out Windsor Castle. Just north of it, a prehistoric barrow known as **King Henry's Mound** provides high ground from where it is said that Henry VIII watched the rocket announcing Anne Boleyn's execution. A telescope on the summit offers a protected view of St Paul's Cathedral, ten miles away in the City (really worth a look). The frame shows the famous cathedral standing alone, without the surrounding high-rises.

PETERSHAM & HAM

The neo-Gothic Petersham Hotel (1864) is by John James, an architect particularly associated with this part of London. **Petersham Nurseries** (*petershamnurseries.com*), reached by walking across the watermeadows, is a charming, rural-feeling garden centre, with a restaurant and café in its greenhouse (dishes are sprinkled with edible flowers).

HAM HOUSE

Ham House (*map p. 628, A4; bus 371 from Richmond to the Ham Street stop; admission charge; national-trust.org.uk*) is a remarkable 17th-century survival, having remained almost untouched since the 1670s. It preserves much of its original interior decoration and furniture (early inventories indicate how it was arranged) as well as its garden layout. The original 1610 Jacobean house, built by Sir Thomas Vavasour, Knight

Marshal to James I, was remodelled first by William Murray, 1st Earl of Dysart in 1637–9, and more substantially by Elizabeth, his daughter, and her second husband, John Maitland, Duke of Lauderdale, from 1672. Both periods of rebuilding and redecoration were according to the latest fashions, with no expense spared. The remarkable survivals from both these schemes make Ham a key house for the study and appreciation of grand 17th-century interior decoration. The Green Closet contains miniatures and cabinet pictures. There is also a reclining chair made for Catherine of Braganza.

TWICKENHAM

Map p. 628, A4 and p. 626, C3. Trains from Waterloo in c. 30mins to Twickenham or St Margaret's. Bus H37 from Richmond. You can also walk along the Thames Path from Richmond (about a 30-min stroll), or take the ferry from Ham (see p. 534).

Twickenham, the home of English rugby since 1909, is a prosperous riverside town. When Richmond and Hampton Court were royal palaces, courtiers came to live in Twickenham and some fine villas were built in the 17th–18th centuries. Famous past residents include Sir Francis Bacon and 'the three Yahoos of Twickenham' (so called by Lord Bolingbroke), John Gay, Jonathan Swift and Alexander Pope. Today, Twickenham has three fine houses to visit: Marble Hill House, Orleans House and Strawberry Hill House, and offers some pleasant riverside walking.

EXPLORING THE TOWN: WEST TO POPE'S GROTTO

On leaving Twickenham station, turn right, and about a 10-min walk along Whitton Road is **Twickenham Stadium**, known as 'Twickers', the headquarters of the Rugby Football Union. The World Rugby Museum (*admission charge, worldrugbymuseum.com*) has a collection of memorabilia and tours of the stadium are available.

Turning left out of Twickenham station, London Road leads to the river. In York Street, opposite the petrol station, is the entrance to **York House**, behind a wrought-iron gateway. It was built in the 17th century and owned by Lord Clarendon until 1689. Other residents include the sculptor Anne Damer (from 1817), the Comte de Paris (from 1864) and the Indian merchant Sir Ratan Tata, who designed the gardens (1906–13) in Italian style (*see below*). It is now council offices and has been much altered, with suburban red-brick extensions and white-painted shutters. Riverside leads east to Orleans House (*see below*).

In Church Street, surrounded by mature yew trees, is the church of **St Mary the Virgin**. The Kentish ragstone tower is medieval; the 18th-century red-brick Neoclassical main body, with pedimented projecting sides facing the village and river, was built by John James after the old church collapsed in 1713. Entry to the galleried interior, where Alexander Pope is buried, is limited (*stmarytwick.org.uk*). Also commemorated here are Mary Beach, Pope's nurse for 38 years, as well as the actress Kitty Clive and Thomas Twining of the tea family.

The Thames at Twickenham, 'where the eye is entertained by a thousand beauties' (Colen Campbell, Palladian architect, 1715). Eel Pie Island can just be glimpsed in the background. The red building to the left is Radnor House School, which stands on top of the famous grotto created by the poet Alexander Pope.

Church Street, with small shops and a couple of pubs, curves westwards, giving a sense of the old village. Continue down Church Lane to the river and at no. 25 The Embankment is the **Twickenham Museum** (*free; twickenham-museum.org.uk*), with local history archives. Across the water is **Eel Pie Island**, once only accessible by boat. From the 17th century it became a place of revelry and had its own public house. In the 19th century it catered for large boat parties who arrived by steamer to enjoy the famous eel pies; in the 1960s the Eel Pie Island Hotel attracted 'swinging' London, who came to party and to hear The Who and the Rolling Stones. Today the island is accessed by a footbridge and there is no pub or hotel, just boatyards, private residences and artists' studios.

Continue west and the **site of Alexander Pope's villa and grotto** is about 15–20mins' walk. Pope lived in Twickenham from 1719–44, leasing land beside the road now called Cross Deep. Here he built himself a Palladian villa (demolished 1808) and linked it with a riverside garden via a subterranean grotto. Much of the grotto still exists beneath buildings owned by Radnor House School but it may only be visited by special prior arrangement or during Twickenham's Festival Week in June each year (*requests for visits: popesgrotto.org.uk*).

YORK HOUSE GARDENS AND RIVERSIDE

Heading east, the Embankment leads past the Barmy Arms pub to the road called Riverside, from where there is access to the Italianate **gardens of York House**, laid out in 1910 by Sir Ratan Tata. Here, unexpectedly, is a fantastic statuary composition featuring enormous nude female nymphs clambering up a rockery-cum-cascade with scallop shells and leaping winged horses in white Carrara marble; mallard ducks float peacefully in the pool beneath all the fevered activity. A 'Chinese' stone bridge arches from the gardens across Riverside to York House itself.

Continue east along Riverside, under the bridge, and past attractive houses and villas. **Sion Row** is a pretty terrace dating from the 1720s; the White Swan pub (with riverside seating) also dates from the 18th century (NB: this area is prone to flooding at high tide). Soon you come to the pleasant woodland gardens of Orleans House.

ORLEANS HOUSE GALLERY

Map p. 628, A4. Trains to St Margaret's from Waterloo in c. 30mins and then 20mins' walk, or walk along the Thames Path from Richmond Bridge. Free. Café. orleanshousegallery.org.

Alas, the Octagon Room, designed by James Gibbs c. 1716–21, is all that remains of Orleans House, built by John James for James Johnston, Secretary of State for Scotland to King William III. The original two-storey red-brick house (demolished in 1926 by a firm of gravel merchants) was noted for its simplicity and for its Thames view. Gibbs's Baroque addition, the Octagon, owes much to his training under the Roman architect Carlo Fontana, a pupil of Bernini. Gibbs's task was to provide a fitting forum for a sumptuous dinner party for Caroline of Ansbach, consort of the future George II. The resultant domed room has an ornate plasterwork interior by the Swiss-born Giuseppe Artari and Giovanni Bagutti, whom Gibbs described as 'the best fret-workers that ever came to England'. Other notable features include portrait medallions of the future George II and his wife, probably by Rysbrack. A further portrait bust, above the east door, may represent Louis-Philippe, Duc d'Orléans, King of France from 1830–48, who lived here in 1800–14 and 1815–17 and after whom the house is now named.

On witnessing the demolition of Orleans House, the Hon. Mrs Nellie Ionides, a collector of Chinese porcelain who lived at Riverside House next door, came forward to save the Octagon Room, making regular use of it in the 1950s to host Edwardian-style dinner parties. She bequeathed it to the borough of Richmond on condition that it was used as a public art gallery. It now displays selections from its important collection of paintings, drawings and prints, mostly local topographical views including works by Leonard Knyff, Samuel Scott, Peter de Wint and Corot. Peter Tillemans' 18th-century *The Thames at Twickenham* is the earliest-known view of the area: it aims to capture what Colen Campbell, in his *Vitruvius Britannicus* (1715), called 'the most charming part of the Thames, where the eye is entertained by a thousand beauties'.

MARBLE HILL HOUSE

Map p. 628, A4. Trains to St Margaret's from Waterloo in c. 30mins and then 10mins' walk, or walk along the Thames Path from Richmond Bridge. Ferry from Ham. Free; café. Online tickets guarantee entry, otherwise entry subject to availability: english-heritage.org.uk.

Marble Hill (built 1724–9), set in 66 acres of public park is a fine example of an English Palladian villa, the fruit of the singular will of Henrietta Howard, Countess of Suffolk, mistress of George II. The design of the house has been attributed to both Henry Herbert, Earl of Pembroke, the 'architect earl', and the Palladian architect Colen Campbell (who remodelled Lord Burlington's town residence on Piccadilly, now the Royal Academy). The tripartite façade is divided both horizontally and vertically; it is faced with stucco and dressed in stone. The north front sports a giant Ionic order of four pilasters, complemented on the south front by a rusticated arched door. All sits compactly under a pyramidal roof. In 2015, a Heritage Lottery Fund grant enabled the conservation and revival of the house, reinstating its gracious Georgian colour schemes, and the restoration of its paintings and furnishing, as well as the development of sports facilities in the park.

The house and its mistress

Henrietta Howard (1688–1767), wife of Charles Howard, fifth son of the Earl of Suffolk, had become, at the accession of George I, a Woman of the Bedchamber to the Princess of Wales. From there she progressed to the bed of the Prince, the future George II, who by 1720 was said to be spending 'every evening of his life, three or four hours in Mrs Howard's lodging'. Doubtless Mrs Howard was seeking solace from her marriage to an uncongenial and spendthrift husband (she was once reduced to selling her own hair to keep creditors at bay). Her liaison with Prince George offered financial stability. The £11,500 worth of South Sea stock that he gave her was more than sufficient to purchase 25 acres next to the Thames to build her Palladian-style summer villa.

An early Hanoverian blue-stocking, Mrs Howard was said to keep a 'philosophical' expression and, in her own words, enforced 'every argument with that gesticulation of the hand for which I am so famous'. A patron and correspondent of men of letters, she gathered about her at Twickenham a circle of like-minded companions, including Alexander Pope, the Earl of Chesterfield, John Gay and Jonathan Swift. Pope's 'On a Certain Lady at Court' refers to Mrs Howard and his 'Bounce to Fop' is an epistle addressed to her lap-dog Fop from Pope's own Great Dane, Bounce. Her relationship with the king had ended in 1734, George reputedly bemoaning that she had become an 'old, dull, deaf, peevish beast' (she was 46). Her second marriage, to George Berkeley, was happy and she retired to Twickenham for the remainder of her life. Horace Walpole, her near neighbour at Strawberry Hill, was a regular visitor; between 1759 and 1766 he filled his notebooks with her conversation and anecdotes.

Tour of the house

The **Hall**, with its four columns, is decorated with marble profile reliefs of Jupiter, Juno, Ceres and Bacchus (French c. 1720), installed in the room in 1750–1. To the left is the **Breakfast Parlour**, symmetrically laid out and adorned with an acanthus-leaf frieze and decorated capitals on the columns. On the opposite side is the **Dining Parlour**, created for the Countess in 1750–1 by Matthew Brettingham.

The grand mahogany staircase leads to the first-floor **Great Room**, a perfect cube of 24ft with a coved ceiling, reputed to have been modelled on the double-cube room designed by Inigo Jones at Wilton House, Salisbury. The principal pictures here, including the *capriccio* views of Roman ruins by G.P. Panini (1738) set over the doors and chimneypiece, were returned to the house in stages, as they appeared on the art market. Copies after Van Dyck and Rubens, by Charles Jervas, were on display here in the Countess's day (the works after Van Dyck seen here now are not original to the house). The highlight of the room is the carved and gilded decoration by James Richards, Grinling Gibbons' successor as Master Carver to the Crown: friezes and panels of flowers and foliage above the pictures and pier glasses, eagles above the doors and antique masks in the cornice. Owls appear on the inside of the shutters and two large putti lean on the overmantel pediment. The marble-topped console table, with heavy Kentian gilded carving incorporating a peacock, the attribute of Juno, one of an original set of four, was returned to the house after its discovery in Australia.

Lady Suffolk's Bedchamber retains its screen of Ionic columns at the north end marking the bed space. There are two jib-doors, one of which leads to the service wing, the other to Miss Hotham's Bedchamber, where Henrietta's great-niece and companion once slept. From the mahogany staircase the Stone Staircase leads to the **Picture Gallery**, where visitors could originally view full-length portraits of George II, Queen Caroline and Henrietta herself—as well as enjoy a splendid panorama of the Thames and beyond, through the windows.

The gardens
In the gardens, laid out by Charles Bridgeman with the involvement of Alexander Pope, was a **grotto**, accidentally rediscovered in 1941 following the felling of a tree, and re-excavated in 1984. Now restored to an approximation of its original (c. 1739) appearance, it has walls lined with shells and a floor with circles of pebbles. The original cavern-mouth entrance was decorated with coral, flints and blue glass. Another garden feature, since disappeared, was the Priory of St Hubert, a 'gothic' barn dedicated to the patron saint of hunting, a sport which Henrietta is said to have pursued with a violent passion. Archaeologists found the remains of a bowling alley, at that time probably a game resembling *boules*, next to the house.

STRAWBERRY HILL HOUSE

Waldegrave Rd. Map p. 626, C3. Trains from Waterloo to Strawberry Hill in c. 30mins and then 10mins' walk (signposted). Tickets are timed-entry and self-guided; purchase from gift shop or online: strawberryhillhouse.org.uk.

In 1747 Horace Walpole, collector, antiquarian, man of letters, Whig politician (son of the Prime Minister Sir Robert Walpole) and coiner of the word 'serendipity', leased a modest house in Twickenham for use as his summer retreat. Twickenham, lying as it did between the royal palaces of Richmond and Hampton Court, was a fashionable resort during the 18th century and fine mansions and villas lined the banks of the Thames here; Walpole considered it an English Brenta (the canal that connects Venice with its hinterland and which is lined with Palladian summer villas). In contrast to the prevailing fashion for Palladianism, however, Walpole set about transforming his cottage, known locally as Chopp'd Straw Hall, into a diminutive Gothic castle. Over the next 40 years he clad and expanded the exterior with turrets, tracery and battlements and the interior was fancifully remodelled and Gothicised according to an amateur Committee of Style formed of himself, the architect John Chute, the illustrator Richard Bentley and Mr Robinson of the Board of Works, who took care of structural and building matters. Details from famous Gothic buildings including Old St Paul's, Canterbury Cathedral, Rouen Cathedral, York Minster and Westminster Abbey were copied and rendered in wood, *trompe l'oeil* and *papier-mâché*, but never so authentically as to be uncomfortable to live with. The prevailing themes were of mystery and surprise, light and shade, and of 'sharawaggi' or 'want of symmetry'; sheep and cows were grazed in the surrounding gardens and meadows to give a 'becoming' view.

At Strawberry Hill Walpole housed and exhibited his eclectic and vast collection of fine ceramics and porcelain, miniatures by Hilliard and Isaac and Peter Oliver, paintings by Reynolds, Lely, Poussin, Van Dyck, Hogarth and Gheeraerts. He also owned a number of curiosities such as the obsidian mirror of Dr Dee (*see p. 569*), now in the British Museum, the red hat of Cardinal Wolsey and the spurs that William III used on his horse Sorrel during the Battle of the Boyne. He entertained foreigners, royalty and members of the aristocracy and at one party greeted guests wearing leather gloves that had belonged to James I and a limewood cravat carved by Grinling Gibbons to resemble Venetian lace (now in the V&A). Walpole is documented as having been outbid at auction for Oliver Cromwell's nightcap. He wrote *The Castle of Otranto* while living here (1754–6) and printed it on his private printing press, the Strawberry Hill Press.

The house became famous in Walpole's own lifetime, not only as an avant-garde and influential work of Gothic Revivalism but also as a tourist attraction and folly. Visitors were shown around in groups of four by the housekeeper. Walpole catalogued the house and its contents and printed his *Description of the Villa* on his printing press. Today the *Description* provides a fascinating insight into Walpole's long-dispersed art collection and how it was displayed. It has been reprinted in its entirety and is available for purchase in the gift shop (an abridged version is part of the self-guided tour).

The house later passed to George, 7th Earl Waldegrave, who in 1842 sold off Walpole's collection in its entirety at a historic, 24-day auction. Today, the Strawberry Hill Trust has undertaken a restoration programme to return the house to its appearance of the 1790s. The garden is also being restored and has been replanted with an avenue of limes that existed in Walpole's day. Due to 20th-century development, however, there is no longer a river view. Nor are there cows.

Highlights of the interior

Past the Little Cloister, with the Abbot's Garden on your right, the visitor enters the 'gloomth' of the **Hall**, where the reproduction *trompe l'oeil* wall-paper is hand-painted with Gothic arches (during restoration some original fragments were uncovered). The windows on either side of the door were once fitted with 16th-century Flemish stained-glass saints; in the 1750s the shockwaves from a gunpowder explosion on Hounslow Heath (modern Heathrow Airport) were felt at Strawberry Hill and much of

Walpole's antique glass was blown out, including the saints, which Walpole described as having been 'martyred'. In the **Great Parlour**, leading off the Hall and used as the dining room, note the window-tracery design of the backs of the black chairs, which would have cast dramatic shadows on the walls by candlelight.

Back in the Hall, the elaborate **staircase**, with models of antelopes along the balustrade, was designed by Bentley and leads up to the splendid library with Gothic-arched fitted bookcases and a painted ceiling depicting Walpole's crusading ancestors. The **Holbein Chamber** was once hung with tracings of original drawings by Hans Holbein. Through a dusky corridor one arrives, in a burst of unexpected colour, into the **Gallery**, Walpole's state room, with its restored gilded fan-vaulted *papier-mâché* ceiling and crimson walls. The **Tribune Room** housed Walpole's treasured coins, medals, enamels and miniatures in a fine rosewood cabinet.

On the ground floor, the **Museum Room**, once the servants' hall, narrates the history of the house and its various owners via interactive displays. There is also access to Yale University's public database of Walpole's collections, which plans to list every artefact that was once at Strawberry Hill with its current location, if known.

HAMPTON COURT

Formerly the extravagant home of Cardinal Wolsey, Hampton Court was requisitioned by Henry VIII in 1528, following Wolsey's failure to obtain an annulment of Henry's marriage to Katherine of Aragon. It was here that Henry VIII was betrothed to his third wife, Jane Seymour and here, a year later, that Jane died giving birth to Edward VI. Shakespeare may have acted in his own *Measure for Measure* in the Great Hall. Hampton Court was a favoured royal residence of the later Tudors and early Stuarts, a pleasure palace with tennis courts, bowling alleys, a tiltyard and parks stocked with game. From 1645 Charles I was imprisoned here and, following his execution, it became Oliver Cromwell's country residence. From 1689 Hampton Court was transformed by Sir Christopher Wren into a modern Baroque palace for William III and Mary II, its size and splendour in conscious competition with Louis XIV's Versailles. Suites of King's and Queen's state apartments were created, outstanding ornamental gardens with topiary and fountains, and a maze which is still one of the palace's best-known features. The court last visited Hampton in 1737. The state apartments were opened to the public in the 19th century, shortly after the accession of Queen Victoria, while other parts of the palace were awarded as 'grace and favour' apartments to pensioners of the Crown and others.

GETTING THERE AND TICKETS

Map p. 626, C4. Trains from Waterloo to Hampton Court in c. 35mins. Underground: Richmond and then bus R68. Boats from Westminster Pier (thamesriverboats.co.uk). Admission charge. Cafés. hrp.org.uk.

HISTORY OF THE TUDOR PALACE

The first buildings at Hampton belonged to the Knights Hospitaller of St John of Jerusalem, who acquired the manor in 1236 and used it as a grange. By the 15th century the great barn had been replaced by residential buildings, used by the abbots as a rural retreat. In 1494 Sir Giles Daubenay, Henry VII's Lord Chancellor, purchased an 80-year lease on the property and transformed it into a major courtier house. It was in 1514–15 that Hampton Court's association with royalty and political life began, with the acquisition of a 90-year lease by Thomas Wolsey, Henry VIII's Lord Chancellor. Appointed Cardinal by Pope Leo X in 1515, Wolsey transformed Hampton Court into a place of international importance. As well as a private residence, he envisaged the palace as a show house for entertaining kings and prelates and for receiving foreign dignitaries.

Leading architects and master craftsmen gave Hampton Court innovative features and Renaissance embellishments not seen in England before. Its succession of courtyards and elaborate gateways provided accommodation for the court and lavish apartments for the king (which remained the apartments of the monarch until the reign of William and Mary). The long gallery, erected in 1515–16, was glazed on either side. Gardens were laid out and a moat and ponds constructed, the latter providing freshwater shrimps and carp. These major alterations were undertaken in two principal phases: in 1515–22, the last date being that of the visit to Hampton Court of the Holy Roman Emperor Charles V (nephew of Katherine of Aragon); and a second phase, until 1527, when Wolsey received the huge entourage of the French court. The palace was furnished with costly magnificence. Tapestries were purchased for staggering sums, while Wolsey's own apartments were hung with cloth of gold.

In September 1528 King Henry ordered Wolsey to vacate the palace for the duration of the visit of the papal delegation, who were in London to discuss the royal divorce. From that time on, Henry assumed ownership of Hampton Court. Alterations were made and practical improvements added, such as the construction of the Great House of Ease (communal lavatories).

Exterior of Hampton Court

The main entrance is through **Trophy Gate**, built for William III. At its far end is the **west front (1)** of the palace, built by Wolsey and completed and altered by Henry VIII. The central **Great Gatehouse**, of mellow brick with limestone dressings, was originally two storeys higher but nevertheless preserves an excellent sense of the imposing silhouette it would have presented to visitors. The fine moated bridge, built by Henry VIII, is guarded by the **King's Beasts**. On the turrets to either side are terracotta roundels by the Florentine sculptor Giovanni da Maiano, two of eight imported and set in place in 1521 (others appear in the succeeding courtyards). Henry VIII's arms were inserted in 1530. **Base Court (2)**, originally cobbled, remains much as Wolsey built it. Straight ahead is the **Anne Boleyn Gate (3)**, built by Wolsey but so called because the fan-vaulted ceiling was added after Anne became queen in 1533. It bears her badge of a falcon and the intertwined initials H and A. Its small 18th-century bell-tower contains an original bell of the Knights Hospitallers.

Though now much altered, **Clock Court (4)** was the principal court of Wolsey's palace. The west range has Wolsey's arms above the gate, supported by cherubs and surmounted by his cardinal's hat. Henry VIII's **Astronomical Clock**, made in 1540, its dial altered, shows the hour, month and day, the number of days passed since the beginning of the year, the houses of the Zodiac and the phases of the moon. The east side of the court, remodelled in Tudor style by William Kent in 1732, replaces the magnificent apartments constructed by Wolsey for Henry VIII, their former great feature being tall glazed windows which in their day would have amazed and

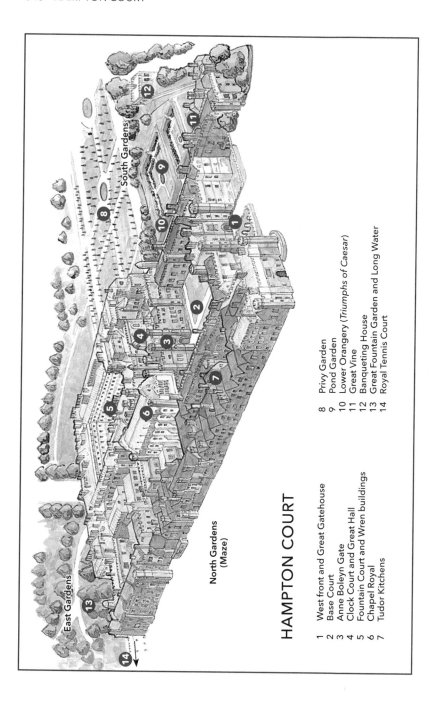

HAMPTON COURT

1 West front and Great Gatehouse
2 Base Court
3 Anne Boleyn Gate
4 Clock Court and Great Hall
5 Fountain Court and Wren buildings
6 Chapel Royal
7 Tudor Kitchens

8   Privy Garden
9   Pond Garden
10 Lower Orangery (*Triumphs of Caesar*)
11 Great Vine
12 Banqueting House
13 Great Fountain Garden and Long Water
14 Royal Tennis Court

North Gardens
(Maze)

South Gardens

East Gardens

astonished. On the north is the buttressed mass of Henry VIII's Great Hall (*see below*). The colonnaded south side was constructed by Wren for William III.

Eager to avoid the smog of London and the damp of Whitehall Palace (William III suffered from chronic asthma), William and Mary ordered Wren to 'beautify' Hampton Court in March 1689. Wren transformed it into a modern palace, architecturally influenced by Continental precedents. Continuing through to **Fountain Court (5)**, visitors find all trace of the Tudor palace supplanted by the arched cloisters and Baroque façades of Wren's new courtyard. The tall first-floor windows are those of the State Apartments. On the south side, carved wreaths surround twelve (much faded) *Labours of Hercules* by the French decorative artist Louis Laguerre, part of the heroic iconography glorifying William III that appears throughout the late Stuart palace. An exit on the east side leads to the gardens and Wren's imposing east and south fronts, among the most important examples of Baroque architecture in the country. The **east front** is architecturally the more elaborate, with a great central pediment filled with a sculptural relief, *Hercules Triumphing over Envy*, by Caius Gabriel Cibber, supported by giant Corinthian columns. The **south front**, which contains the King's Apartments, with views over the elaborate Privy Garden, has over the central window a carved trophy of arms with a Latin inscription, '*Gulielmus et Maria Rex et Regina Fecerunt*', glorifying William and Mary's building project.

The Tudor interiors

The surviving apartments of Henry VIII are approached via Clock Court, up the staircase in Anne Boleyn's Gate. They lead to the **Great Hall**, the largest room in the palace 106ft long, 40ft wide and more than 60ft high), begun in 1532. The remarkable hammerbeam roof, one of the finest in existence—but which serves no practical function—was designed by the King's Master Carpenter, James Nedeham, and is richly decorated with carved pendants, the royal arms and heraldic badges. The exceptional Flemish 'Story of Abraham' tapestries, woven in Brussels in the 1540s with silver and gold thread, were among the most expensive tapestries commissioned by Henry VIII. High in the roof are a series of carved and painted heads, the **Eavesdroppers**, who have kept watch over the hall over the centuries.

Beyond the Horn Room (where old Tudor antlers were stored at the time of William III) is the **Great Watching Chamber**, the only one of Henry VIII's state apartments to survive. It was a room at the heart of court life, where senior courtiers would have dined and where the Yeomen of the Guard were stationed, controlling access to the king in the Presence Chamber beyond. The decorated ceiling is original, as are the 16th-century tapestries, but the deep heraldic frieze has been whitewashed.

The **Pages' Chamber** was where courtiers waited before being presented to the king. The **Haunted Gallery** is named after the shrieking ghost of Catherine Howard said to inhabit it. Catherine, Henry VIII's fifth wife, was held at Hampton Court, in her lodgings, before her execution on charges of adultery (she was not yet twenty years old). Sixteenth-century Flemish tapestries, probably owned by Elizabeth I, show scenes from Virgil's *Aeneid*. Important Tudor pictures from the Royal Collection hang here, including (though the selection can change) the *Family of Henry VIII*, showing the King enthroned, flanked by Jane Seymour and his only son, the future Edward VI, with, to the sides, his daughters Mary and Elizabeth; and the famous *Field of the Cloth of Gold* and *The Embarkation of Henry VIII*, showing the English fleet preparing to leave for Calais.

The **Chapel Royal (6)** was built by Wolsey and is still in use (*chapelroyalhamptoncourt. org.uk*). Its most magnificent adornment is the astonishing fan-vaulted ceiling, carved and decorated with gilded pendants, installed by Henry VIII in 1535–6. The high altar, with its oak reredos by Grinling Gibbons and painted angels by Sir James Thornhill, was installed by Queen Anne, who also altered the upper Royal Pew, where the monarch would attend services. Its painted ceiling is also by Thornhill.

The Wolsey Rooms

The Wolsey Rooms occupy the site of Wolsey's private apartments, built in the 1520s. Refitted in the 18th and 19th centuries, they nevertheless retain some original Tudor features: linenfold panelling, plain early 16th-century fireplaces and a ribbed ceiling with early Renaissance decorative motifs. Important pictures (the display is liable to change) include Leonard Knyff's large bird's-eye panorama of Hampton Court, c. 1703.

The Tudor kitchens

The Tudor Kitchens **(7)** fed Henry VIII's court of 1,200 people, who dined in the Great Hall and the Great Watching Chamber. The **Boiling House** was the Tudor butchery, where great cauldrons of stock and stew were also prepared. **Fish Court** houses various kitchen departments, such as the Spicery, the Pastry House and the Fish Larder. The **Great Kitchens**, a vast, cavernous space with huge hearths and spits, is divided into three spaces, the third being the oldest, part of Wolsey's kitchens built c. 1514. Sometimes a fire is lit in the massive roasting fireplace and food is prepared over the flames, giving a vivid idea of the heat and the hard work. Dishes were elaborately dressed and garnished in the Dressers, then passed out to the Serving Place to be taken to diners via the North Cloister. The vaulted **Great Wine Cellar** contains great oak barrels hooped with willow.

Interiors of the late Stuart palace

The transformation of Hampton Court from an old-fashioned shrine to the Tudor monarchy into a great Baroque palace which challenged the supremacy of Louis XIV was undertaken for William and Mary from 1689 by a team of great architects and designers: Sir Christopher Wren, Nicholas Hawksmoor, the virtuoso carver Grinling Gibbons, William Talman and the leading Baroque decorative artist Antonio Verrio. Queen Mary had keenly overseen progress at the palace until her premature death, of smallpox, in 1694, when work virtually ceased until late 1697 when William, his European wars over, took a renewed, personal interest. In January 1698, after fire had virtually destroyed the chief royal residence, Whitehall Palace, Wren submitted an estimate for the completion of the interiors. Tapestries from the Royal Collection were used throughout the rooms, as well as pictures. The Master of the Great Wardrobe,

Ralph, Baron (later Earl, then 1st Duke of) Montagu, took charge of the furnishings. Former Ambassador in Paris, he promoted French Huguenot artists and craftsmen. Throughout the State Apartments is expensive carved giltwood furniture supplied by Jean Pelletier and exceptional mirrors by Gerrit Jensen. The court removed to Hampton for the first time in April 1700 and thereafter it was William's habit to spend spring and early summer and autumn here, until his death following a riding accident in the park in 1702.

The King and Queen had their own suites of rooms, reached by separate staircases. Access to the apartments was governed by strict court protocol. Most visitors could mount the Great Stairs and linger in the Guard Room, but further progression was governed by rank. The closer one got to the private apartments of the monarch, the more exclusive the room and the richer its furnishing and ornamentation. The King's Private Apartments, where only the most favoured were admitted, were the most lavish of all. All the state apartments at Hampton Court illustrate these conventions to rich and grand effect.

The King's Apartments

Meticulously restored after a fire in 1986, the rooms offer a sense of the exuberant and rich interiors of the time of William III. The spectacular **King's Staircase** was decorated by Verrio in 1700–2. An overwhelmingly Baroque space, designed to awe visitors, its walls and ceiling illustrate Alexander's triumph over the Caesars paralleled with William's over the Roman Catholic James II, celebrating the king as Protestant champion of Europe. *The Banquet of the Gods* is on the ceiling. The fine wrought-iron balustrade is by Jean Tijou. The **King's Guard Chamber** was where the Yeomen of the Guard were stationed, letting past into the state rooms only peers, officeholders, privy councillors or gentlemen of quality and fashion. The oak panelling is decorated with more than 3,000 pieces of arms, arranged in patterns by John Harris, Master Gunner of Windsor Castle.

The **King's Presence Chamber** was used for formal ceremonial occasions. Facing the entrance is the king's throne, made in 1700. Courtiers would bow three times in its direction, even when it was unoccupied. Opposite it is Sir Godfrey Kneller's enormous *William III on Horseback*, a prominent, heroic image of the monarch. The tapestries, the *Labours of Hercules* and *Triumph of Bacchus*, originally belonged to Henry VIII. The **King's Eating Room** was where the king dined in public, a ceremony not undertaken by William frequently. Above the chimneypiece is a portrait of Christian IV of Denmark, brother of James I's queen, Anne of Denmark, set within a majestic overmantel of carved limewood by Grinling Gibbons: brilliantly realised drops of leaves and flowers, with a cresting of arching wheat and palm fronds. The 'Acts of the Apostles' tapestries are of 17th-century Brussels manufacture (*see below*).

The **King's Privy Chamber** was the most important ceremonial room in the palace. It was here that the king received foreign ambassadors at their first, official, entrance and where other court functions, such as the performance of Birthday Odes, took place. The tapestries are part of Henry VIII's 'Story of Abraham' series intended for the Great Hall. The richly carved overmantel is by Gibbons.

THE 'ACTS OF THE APOSTLES' CARTOONS

Shortly after Giovanni de' Medici, son of Lorenzo the Magnificent, became Pope Leo X, he commissioned, in 1516, ten cartoons from Raphael, depicting the Acts of the Apostles, for tapestries for the Sistine Chapel. The tapestries were woven in Flanders in the workshops of Pieter van Aelst. Charles I purchased the cartoons in 1623, and had tapestries made up from them at Mortlake: lavish and costly items that made copious use of metallic thread. The Mortlake manufactory on the Thames (p. 569) had been set up by Royal Charter four years previously. It had 18 looms, an artist's studio, and employed over 50 Netherlandish weavers. Among them was Louis Dermoulen, who specialised in heads, and Pieter de Craigt, who specialised in flesh parts. Mortlake's golden era began in the 1620s, under the directorship of Francis Cleyn, who was chief designer there until his death in 1657. He was appointed on the strength of the new working cartoons which he produced from the Raphael series. Raphael's own cartoons were restored later in the century by order of William III and brought to Hampton Court. Monumental examples of High Renaissance art in England, they were held up as exemplars of artistic excellence. Sir James Thornhill studied them when working on the dome of St Paul's, and in 1729 he was granted a Royal Warrant to make copies. He hoped to make them more accessible to art students, and as such a focus for academic instruction. These great works of art—the gestures of the figures and their composition—made an impact on English art for generations.

Only court officeholders, privy councillors and Secretaries of State were admitted to the **King's Withdrawing Room**, where social gatherings would take place and cards would be played. This room signified the boundary between the King's public and private life. The tapestries are from the 'Acts of the Apostles' series. The carved overmantel is a masterpiece by Gibbons, with leaves and fruit hanging in dense ropes and crisply carved complex gatherings of fruit and flowers. The **King's Great Bedchamber** next door, one step further into the sanctum, admitted privileged courtiers only, by way of the King's Back Stairs. This magnificent space was a ceremonial room where the king was dressed in front of courtiers, who were kept at a distance behind a rail, and is fittingly one of the most sumptuous rooms in the palace. The gilded furniture and mirrors, by Gerrit Jensen, are the finest in the apartments, including one 13ft high, incorporating, in strips of blue glass, the king's monogram and crest. The great state bed, with plumed finials, soars towards the richly painted ceiling by Verrio, *Endymion in the arms of Morpheus*, Greek god of dreams and sleep. Below is a remarkable carved frieze by Gibbons, of scrolling acanthus, songbirds, blossoms, fruit and ears of wheat. The **King's Little Bedchamber**, where the monarch actually slept, is rather modest by comparison. Displayed on the chimneypiece are rare pieces of oriental porcelain from Mary II's collection. The Verrio ceiling, unusually well preserved, shows Mars and Venus, with cupids, billing doves and orange trees in the cove.

The **King's Closet** was his private study, where he would receive ministers and secretaries of state. The Back Stairs lead to the King's Private Apartments on the ground floor. Most of the paintings are from William's collection. The long and airy **Orangery** has a series of sculpture busts of philosophers by Hubert Le Sueur ('Praxiteles Le Sueur', as he liked to sign himself) and the original Privy Garden statuary (those in the garden now are copies). The **King's Private Dining Room**, where William entertained unofficially, is hung with Sir Godfrey Kneller's important *Hampton Court Beauties*, a series of full-length portraits of the principal court ladies, commissioned by Queen Mary.

The Queen's Apartments

Intended for Mary II, who died in 1694 before the completion of the palace, some of the Queen's Apartments, built on the site of Anne Boleyn's rooms, were used by William III but the rest remained empty. In 1715–18 they were set up for the use of the Prince and Princess of Wales, later George II and Queen Caroline, and on George II's accession to the throne they were redecorated and refurbished for Caroline. The **Queen's Staircase**, originally panelled and whitewashed, was painted by William Kent in 1734 to create a more lavish entrance. The vast allegorical oil painting, *Mercury Presenting the Liberal Arts to Apollo and Diana*, by Gerrit van Honthorst (1628), shows Charles I and Henrietta Maria as Jupiter and Juno with the Duke of Buckingham as Apollo. The **Queen's Guard Chamber** is where the Yeomen of the Guard were stationed to control access to the queen. They appear on the extraordinary chimneypiece, possibly made by Gibbons, the design sometimes attributed to Sir John Vanbrugh, who was also responsible for the room's architecture. The sober **Queen's Presence Chamber** was also designed by Vanbrugh, who was employed at the palace early in the reign of George I.

The **Public Dining Room** was used by George II and Queen Caroline when they dined in the presence of the court. The **Queen's Audience Chamber** was used for the reception of important visitors. It retains Queen Caroline's crimson throne canopy.

The **Queen's Drawing Room** is the central room on Wren's east façade. The view from the window shows the avenue of yews and other trees stretching into the distance. The queen's 'drawing rooms' took place here, where ladies of the court gossiped and played cards. The painted ceiling and walls, the latter in imitation of tapestries, were executed by Verrio and a team of assistants from 1703. Commissioned by Queen Anne, who succeeded William III, the theme is royal naval power. Anne's husband, Prince George of Denmark, features prominently as Lord High Admiral. Prince George was fond of Hampton Court and these apartments were set up for his use. This was Verrio's last commission—he was by this time an ageing man with poor eyesight—and the work has, with justification, been much criticised (although it is also much restored, George II having covered it up with wallpaper).

The **Queen's State Bedchamber** has its original bed, made in 1715, and a painted ceiling by Sir James Thornhill, *Leucothoë Restraining Apollo from entering his Chariot*, with oval portraits of members of the royal family in the cove. The **Queen's Gallery** was used by William III, who displayed here Mantegna's *Triumphs of Caesar* (see p. 553). The 18th-century Brussels tapestries, episodes from the story of Alexander the

Great, were hung here by George I. Here too are pieces of Queen Mary's Delftware which Queen Caroline also prized. The **Queen's Closet**, where private life took over from public duty, is hung with needlework panels made for Mary II, in the style of the French Huguenot Baroque designer Daniel Marot, who worked for Queen Mary when he was briefly in England.

The **Communication Gallery** was built for William III in the 1690s. It displays Sir Peter Lely's exceptional *Windsor Beauties*, a set of pictures of court ladies commissioned by Anne Hyde, first wife of James II, in the early 1660s. Notable figures such as Frances Stuart, Duchess of Richmond, and Charles II's mistress Barbara Villiers, are included. The **Cartoon Gallery**, built by Wren as William III's private picture gallery, was soon altered specifically to take Raphael's 'Acts of the Apostles' cartoons (*see p. 550*).

The Queen's Private Apartments were built by Wren for Mary II. They are presented today as occupied by Queen Caroline in the 1730s. The **Queen's Private Drawing Room** is hung with rare 18th-century crimson flock wallpaper and has a large 17th-century Isfahan carpet. Her **Private Bedchamber** is hung with Mortlake tapestries of c. 1685. Above the chimneypiece, set within a dense roundel of carved flowers by Gibbons, is a portrait of Queen Caroline by Joseph Highmore. The **Queen's Dressing Room and Bathroom** preserve a silver-gilt toilet service made c. 1695 by Daniel Garnier and engraved in 1740. The **Queen's Private Oratory**, with a lofty carved and moulded dome, is where Caroline would hear sermons and services from her chaplain.

The Cumberland Art Gallery

This changing display of paintings, mainly from the Royal Collection, is hung in rooms that were once the apartment of William Augustus, Duke of Cumberland, Queen Caroline's youngest and favourite son. They were designed and decorated by William Kent, who was greatly influenced by the latest Palladian style, while retaining elements of Tudor decoration. Displayed as near to their original arrangement as possible, the works have been chosen to reflect the royal tastes and lives of those who lived and died at Hampton Court and include Tudor and Renaissance portraits, Georgian landscapes and biblical and mythological allegories, heavy on implicit messages about royal power. Among the works are Van Dyck's *Portrait of Mary Stuart* (1637), showing the daughter of Charles I and mother of William III as a six-year-old girl. *A Flemish Fair* by Jan Brueghel the Elder (1600), shows a kermis or religious feast day, celebrated in a rustic street party. Caravaggio's *The Calling of Saints Peter and Andrew* (c. 1602–4) depicts the moment when the brothers are seized by Christ's words, 'Follow me and I will make you fishers of men', a moment which will change their lives forever. Christ is shown, unusually, clean shaven, his face and hands fully lit, while the brothers are in shadow, perhaps an indication of their uncertainty. A small, intimate room has 'postcard' views of Venice by Canaletto, bought by George III from Joseph Smith, English Consul at Venice and enthusiastic patron of the artist.

Incorporated within the Gallery is the **Wolsey Closet**, a much-restored fragment of Henry VIII's private chambers (the linenfold panelling was placed here when the room was opened to the public in 1889). The frieze, which was probably in another part of the Palace, bears Wolsey's motto, 'The Lord is my helper'.

The Palace Gardens

On a fine day it is tempting—and indeed possible—to spend as much time in the gardens as in the Palace itself. In Henry VIII's day there was a privy garden, a public garden, pleasure gardens and a tiltyard for jousting. Beyond lay parkland. The gardens today reflect their transformation under William and Mary, who laid out the great avenues of trees to the east as well as the elaborate parterre to the south and the Wilderness to the north. The formal gardens cover 60 acres and some 39 gardeners are employed here.

South Gardens

The **Privy Garden (8)**, magnificently symmetrical in design, was completed for William III in 1702. Recent restoration has re-established the great ornamental parterre, with its box and gravel arabesques, carefully placed clipped evergreens, its fountain basin at the centre, and elegant statuary. The great screens at the bottom of the garden, by the Thames, of wrought iron with elaborate gilded panels, are by Jean Tijou, originally made for the Fountain Garden. The **Pond Garden (9)** was where Henry VIII's freshwater fishponds were.

The **Lower Orangery (10)** houses Andrea Mantegna's magnificent *Triumphs of Caesar* (c. 1486–94), exceptional Italian Renaissance works made for the Gonzaga court at Mantua, purchased by Charles I in 1629. Their triumphal allegory reflected the king's military prowess. The **Great Vine (11)**, in its purpose-built glasshouse, is from a cutting of the Black Hamburg vine at Valentine's Park, Essex. Planted by 'Capability' Brown in 1768, it is the oldest vine in the world and is tended by a resident keeper. On the east-facing wall of the vine-keeper's house is the **Great Wisteria**, only a couple of decades younger.

The elegant **Banqueting House (12)**, a pleasure pavilion on the edge of the Thames, has three rooms richly decorated with Gibbons carving and Verrio decorative work.

East Gardens

Originally laid out for William III as an expansive semicircular parterre with twelve marble fountains, the **Great Fountain Garden (13)** was simplified by Queen Anne, who dug the encircling canal. The central **Long Water** was created for Charles II in the 1660s. The **Royal Tennis Court (14)**, built in the 1620s, is still in use today.

North Gardens

The northern gardens occupy the site of the **Wilderness** (in place by 1686 but to which William III made alterations, a plantation of hollies and bay trees with winding paths and openings in elaborate, symmetrical patterns, a great yew tree at its centre). It bursts into life in spring, with over one million flowering bulbs. The feature which remains today is the world-famous **Maze**, the oldest planted maze in the country (though renewed over the centuries). Originally of hornbeam, it was entirely replaced with yew in the 1960s. The **Royal Kitchen Garden** has rare and heirloom varieties of vegetables and fruit.

WINDSOR & ETON

Facing each other across the Thames are Windsor, with its famous royal castle, and Eton, with its equally famous boys' school. Windsor is easy to visit on a day trip. As well as Windsor Castle, rising majestically over the town, the attractions include shops, restaurants, hotels, a theatre, riverside walks and boat trips and a racecourse. Windsor is connected to Eton by footbridge.

GETTING TO WINDSOR

Map p. 626, A3. Trains from Waterloo to Windsor & Eton Riverside in c. 60mins. There are also trains from Paddington (often faster, though you have to change at Slough) to Windsor & Eton Central, very close to the castle. The Royal Windsor Information Centre (windsor.gov.uk/visitor-information) is in the Guildhall building on the High Street.

WINDSOR CASTLE

The castle is open to visitors all year, although is often wholly or partially closed. Always check before you visit: rct.uk/visit/windsor-castle. Tickets may be booked online. Changing of the Guard takes place on certain days only; check the website for schedules. The ceremony lasts approx. 45mins.

Anglo Saxon kings settled at Old Windsor, three miles from the current town, but after 1066, when the Norman conqueror William I built a fortress at New Windsor, the royal household moved here. The history of Windsor Castle spans a thousand years: it is the oldest and largest occupied castle in the world. Thirty-nine British monarchs have lived here; along with Buckingham Palace in London and Holyroodhouse in Edinburgh, it is one of the three royal residences. The monarch is in official residence at Windsor for the Garter Service (*see below*) in June. The King also uses the castle to entertain visiting heads of state and foreign dignitaries and members of the Royal Family host charitable receptions in the Royal Apartments, which are furnished with artworks from the Royal Collections. When the King is in residence, the royal standard flutters from the Round Tower.

Windsor Castle occupies a naturally defensive position, a chalk cliff rising 30m above the Thames. It was built by William I from 1070–86 to defend the western approach to London and formed part of a larger network of Norman fortifications. The original wooden fortress was built according to standard Norman motte-and-bailey design, although the keep that surmounts the artificial earth mound (motte) was unusually defended by two baileys (today the Upper and Lower Wards). Henry II rebuilt the castle in stone and in 1170 the wooden Norman keep was replaced with the Round Tower. Henry III improved and extended it (the D-shaped towers in the walls tend to be from Henry III's reign and the square towers from Henry II's) but preserved the original plan of two baileys and a motte hill. Under the 14th-century warrior king Edward III, William of Wykeham, Bishop of Winchester, transformed Windsor from a defensive fort into a Christian Gothic palace and built the royal apartments in the Upper Ward. During the Civil War, Windsor Castle was used as a Royalist prison; Charles I spent his last Christmas here as a prisoner (1648) before his execution the following January. After the Restoration in 1660, Charles II, influenced by what his cousin Louis XIV was doing at Versailles, turned the castle into a grand Baroque palace to glorify and accentuate the permanence of the restored monarchy. Gentleman-architect Hugh May oversaw the transformation. George IV created sumptuous royal apartments here and during his reign the exterior of the castle was re-Gothicised and towers and battlements were added to create a romantic castle ideal. The present aspect of the building dates from the extensive restorations undertaken by Jeffry Wyatt, who changed his name to Wyatville. During Queen Victoria's reign the castle fulfilled a twofold role of private royal retreat and magnificent palace for the ceremonial entertaining of visiting dignitaries. In the 1840s the state apartments were opened to the public.

THE ORDER OF THE GARTER

The Order of the Garter was founded by Edward III in 1348 and is the oldest and the highest British Order of Chivalry. Its motto is *Honi soit qui mal y pense* ('Shame on him who thinks ill of it'). The words were first spoken, according to the popular story, by Edward III when dancing with his daughter-in-law, whose garter slipped to the floor. Kind Edward picked it up and tied it around his own leg. Membership today consists of the Sovereign, the Prince of Wales and 24 'companions', either men or women, chosen by the Sovereign from among those who have held public office, who have contributed to national life or who have personally served the Sovereign. The patron saint of the Order is St George and its spiritual home is St George's Chapel, Windsor. In June, the Knights of the Garter gather at Windsor Castle, where new Knights take the oath and are invested with the insignia. A lunch is given in the Waterloo Chamber, after which the Knights process to a service in St George's Chapel, wearing their blue velvet robes (with the badge of the Order—St George's Cross within the Garter surrounded by radiating silver beams—on the left shoulder) and black velvet hats with white plumes.

In November 1992 a fire started in Queen Victoria's private chapel and spread to St George's Hall, the Grand Reception Room, the State Dining Room, the Crimson Drawing Room as well as rooms on neighbouring floors, causing millions of pounds' worth of damage. By fortunate coincidence, the rooms that were gutted and most badly damaged had been due for electrical rewiring so had been emptied of their contents, and thus many treasures survived. The castle has since been repaired and restored by teams of craftsmen, either in a neo-Gothic style using medieval building techniques, or as recreations of the way the rooms looked during the reign of George IV. Today the fabric of the castle is in better shape than it has been for two centuries. It was a favourite weekend retreat for her late Majesty Queen Elizabeth II.

Visiting the Castle

The Visitor Entrance is on Castle Hill, near St Alban's Street. The route circles the Middle Ward, where there is a good view of the Round Tower, built in 1170 by Henry II and extended upwards by George IV for pictorial effect. Today it houses the Royal Archives. The moat has always been dry and is planted as a lush ornamental garden with a small trickling waterfall on one side. In the Moat Room is a scale model of the castle as it would have appeared in 1377, the last year of Edward III's reign. Go through an archway in the curtain wall to enter the North Terrace, developed from the reign of Henry VIII, commanding splendid views towards Eton and beyond.

Queen Mary's Dolls' House

Queen Mary's Doll's House, never intended as a toy, was given to Queen Mary in 1924 and exhibited at the British Empire Exhibition the same year. It was designed by Sir Edwin Lutyens on a scale of 1:12 (it measures 8ft by 5ft) as an accurate replica of a contemporary aristocratic London house. It is fully plumbed with hot and cold running water, has electric lights, two lifts and is filled with miniature furnishings and objects made by leading artists, craftsmen and designers of the day. The wine in the cellar is genuine, the books in the walnut-panelled library were specially handwritten by prominent authors (including J.M. Barrie, Hilaire Belloc, Sir Arthur Conan Doyle and Rudyard Kipling), the tiny clocks are by Cartier, the silverware by Garrard and the provisions in the kitchen are all British brands in accurately reproduced packaging. In the maid's closet is the latest in cleaning devices: a working electric vacuum cleaner. The miniature garden was designed by Gertrude Jekyll and has birds nesting in the trees.

Drawings Gallery and China Museum

The **Drawings Gallery**, in a vaulted undercroft designed by James Wyatt for George III, holds temporary exhibitions of works from the Royal Collections. In the **China Museum** is the Rockingham Service, commissioned by William IV in 1830 from the Yorkshire pottery. This ambitious porcelain dinner service, decorated with symbols representative of Britain's far-reaching Empire, from Indian scenes to exotic fruits, sugar cane and pineapples, bankrupted the family who ran the pottery, but it was finally completed and delivered to Queen Victoria in 1837.

The Grand Staircase and Waterloo Chamber

Ascend the **Grand Staircase (1)**, with a huge statue of George IV (1832) by Chantrey

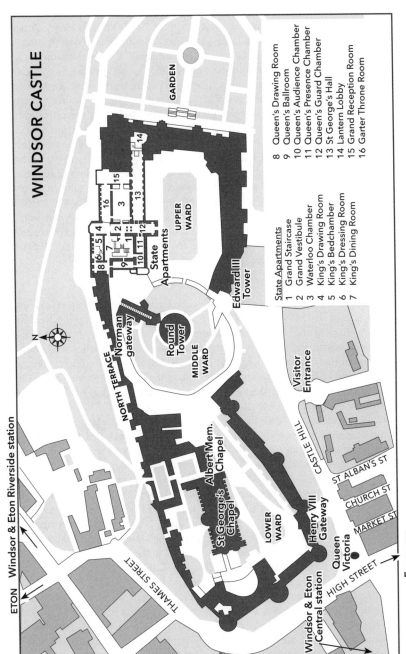

WINDSOR CASTLE

State Apartments

1 Grand Staircase
2 Grand Vestibule
3 Waterloo Chamber
4 King's Drawing Room
5 King's Bedchamber
6 King's Dressing Room
7 King's Dining Room
8 Queen's Drawing Room
9 Queen's Ballroom
10 Queen's Audience Chamber
11 Queen's Presence Chamber
12 Queen's Guard Chamber
13 St George's Hall
14 Lantern Lobby
15 Grand Reception Room
16 Garter Throne Room

on the half-landing, past suits of armour made for Henry VIII and Henry, Prince of Wales, to reach the **Grand Vestibule (2)**. Here, beneath James Wyatt's plaster fan-vaulted ceiling, a late work for George III, are displayed all manner of arms, armour and trophies, some intricately gem-set. In the showcase on your left is a relic from the magnificent palace of Tipu Sultan: a large gold tiger's head with rock crystal fangs which once adorned the great Tiger of Mysore's throne. In the showcase opposite is a mounted bullet: the very **musket ball that killed Lord Nelson**. It was extracted from Nelson's left shoulder on the deck of HMS *Victory* at his death in 1805; it is difficult to make out but it is said that a tiny fragment of Nelson's uniform is still attached to it.

The splendid **Waterloo Chamber (3)**, designed by Wyatville, displays superb portraits by Sir Thomas Lawrence of the monarchs, statesmen and commanders who contributed to the defeat of Napoleon Bonaparte. On the east wall is a portrait of the Duke of Wellington, leader of the allied forces at the Battle of Waterloo in 1815. The limewood carvings, by Grinling Gibbons and his assistants (1680s), are relics from the Royal Chapel demolished in the 1820s. The roof was designed and decorated by the firm of Crace, who worked for George IV at the Royal Pavilion, Brighton. This room was spared in the 1992 fire due to the thickness of its medieval walls.

The State Apartments

The State Apartments, now much altered, were built for Charles II and Catherine of Braganza between 1675 and 1678. They were richly decorated by the Neapolitan mural painter Antonio Verrio, with additional limewood carvings by Grinling Gibbons and his assistants and hung with sumptuous tapestries and textiles and recovered works of art that had once belonged to Charles I. Today the rooms display numerous masterpieces—paintings, furniture, objects—from the Royal Collections. In the **King's Drawing Room (4)**, where Charles II received important visitors, is Van Dyck's famous study for a bust of Charles I in three positions. The organ clock (c. 1740), with a rock crystal casket, plays ten tunes, five of which are arrangements by Handel. In the casket is the Bible used by General Gordon at Khartoum. The **King's Bedchamber (5)** was hung in crimson silk for George III; the bed was installed for a state visit by Emperor Napoleon III and Empress Eugénie; the green and mauve silk hangings are the colours of the Third Empire. The **King's Dressing Room (6)**, hung with Northern Renaissance paintings, including Brueghel's *Massacre of the Innocents* (1565–7), is probably where Charles II slept. In the **King's Closet**, Charles II's most private room, are fine Italian Renaissance paintings; Bronzino's *Portrait of a Lady in Green* (c. 1530) was originally in the collection of Charles I. In the wood-panelled **King's Dining Room (7)** is one of the three surviving ceilings by Antonio Verrio. Painted in the 1670s, it depicts a banquet of the gods. On the walls, the festoon carvings by Grinling Gibbons and his assistants incorporate life-like renderings of crustaceans and fish.

In the **Queen's Drawing Room (8)** are fine Tudor and Stuart royal portraits. The **Queen's Ballroom (9)** has a superb collection of portraits by Van Dyck, including *The Five Eldest Children of Charles I* (1637). Also worthy of mention is the solid silver furniture—tables and mirrors—the ultimate symbols of wealth and power and rare survivors from the late 17th century. The fashion for silver furniture was started by Louis

XIV at Versailles; many sets were subsequently melted down for currency. The **Queen's Audience Chamber (10)** and the **Queen's Presence Chamber (11)** both retain their painted ceilings by Verrio: Queen Catherine is depicted in glorified compositions at the centre of both. Both rooms also retain carving by Gibbons and his assistants; the tapestries are later acquisitions by George IV. The **Queen's Guard Chamber (12)**, which in the 17th century would have served as entrance to the queen's apartments, was altered to its current neo-Gothic appearance by Wyatville. Here is a large bust by Chantrey of Nelson (1835) and decorative wall displays of arms; the examples in the display cases came from George IV's collection at Carlton House. Above the busts of Wellington and Marlborough hang the annual rent banners for Stratfield Saye and Woodstock. The bust of Churchill is by Oscar Nemon (1953).

The 185ft **St George's Hall (13)**, created by Wyatville for George IV from two separate rooms, is used for state banquets, when it is filled by an enormous dining table that seats 160. The hall was gutted in the 1992 fire and has been restored; the neo-Gothic hammerbeam roof, by Giles Downes of the Sidell Gibson Partnership, was constructed in green oak using medieval techniques. It is decorated with hundreds of heraldic shields of Knights of the Garter since 1348; the plain white shields represent those of 'degraded' knights who have been struck from the Order over the centuries.

The **Lantern Lobby (14)**, formerly the Victoria Chapel, is where the 1992 fire started. Also by Downes, it is said to be inspired by the octagon in Ely Cathedral and the Abbey of Batalha in Portugal, and provides a processional route between the State and the Semi-State Apartments. It also functions as a treasury and displays fine examples of silver-gilt plate from the Royal Collections.

The Semi-State Apartments

The Semi-State Apartments, created by Wyatville as George IV's private rooms, are used by the monarch for entertaining and are not always open to the public. Though damaged by the 1992 fire, their contents—which had been moved out—survived and this was the chief impetus behind the decision to restore them to their late-Georgian gilded glory. What the visitor sees today is largely how the rooms would have appeared during the reign of George IV; some of the furnishings were originally at Carlton House.

The Rococo-revival **Grand Reception Room (15)** exemplifies George IV's own preferences for all things French, with 18th-century panelling imported from Paris. The parquet floor is original (singed blocks were turned over after the fire).

Finally, the **Garter Throne Room (16)** is where new Knights and Ladies of the Garter are invested. It was Queen Victoria's throne room, and it is here that she received visitors on the Indian ivory throne.

St George's Chapel

St George's Chapel, in the Lower Ward, is a superb Perpendicular building, begun in 1475 by Henry Janyns for Edward IV and continued in the early 16th century by William Vertue. It is one of the most perfect extant specimens of 15th–16th-century Gothic architecture in England. Eleven British monarchs are buried here. It was also here, in 2018, that Prince Harry, younger son of Charles III, married Meghan Markle.

The **west window** preserves pre-Reformation glass of 1503–9 depicting not only kings and their people, but also popes and saints. The nave has a fine ribbed vault with liernes and carved bosses bearing emblems of Henry VII. Between the nave and the north aisle is the **tomb of George V** (d. 1936) by Lutyens and Reid Dick, and of his consort Queen Mary (d. 1953), for whom the Dolls' House was made. In the **Urswick Chapel** (first north) is Matthew Wyatt's tomb of Princess Charlotte, George IV's only child, who died in childbirth in 1817, aged 21, occasioning a huge outpouring of public grief. She lies under an all-covering shroud from which only four fingers protrude, but also rises to heaven, accompanied by angels, one of whom carries the stillborn baby.

The quire is separated from the nave by a neo-Gothic screen (c. 1785–90). Off the north quire aisle is the **George VI Memorial Chapel**, where Queen Elizabeth II, her consort Prince Philip, as well her mother Queen Elizabeth, her father George VI and her sister Princess Margaret are interred. In the north quire aisle itself is the **Chantry Chapel of William, Lord Hastings**, with contemporary paintings of his execution in 1483. He was put to death by Richard III on charges of having conspired against the king's life. A superb pair of gates (1482) fronts the **tomb of Edward IV** (north of the high altar). Above the royal pew is a wooden oriel provided by Henry VIII for Katherine of Aragon to watch the Garter ceremonies.

In the centre of the floor of the **quire** is a vault containing the remains of Henry VIII and Jane Seymour (the wife who bore him a son) together with Charles I and a stillborn child of Queen Anne. In the Royal Vault are the remains of George III and Queen Charlotte, George IV and William IV. The three tiers of carved wooden stalls (1478–85 with 18th-century adjustments) are surmounted by the helmets, crests and banners of the Knights of the Garter, whose installations have taken place at Windsor since 1348. At a member's death their 'achievements' are removed but the brass stall plate, with the member's name, arms and date of installation, is retained as a memorial. The reverse stalls are those of the royal family, the sovereign's stall marked by the Royal Standard.

In the south quire aisle is the **Chantry of John Oxenbridge**, with paintings of 1522. It also contains the great sword of Edward III and a simple slab marking the **tomb of Henry VI**, founder of Eton College. On the south side of the high altar is the **tomb of Edward VII** and Queen Alexandra.

In the **ambulatory**, the east wall once formed the west front of Henry III's Chapel (1240–8) and retains its original doors.

Albert Memorial Chapel

South of the cloisters, the Albert Memorial Chapel was originally conceived by Henry VII as a burial place for Henry VI. It was later completed by Cardinal Wolsey but his tomb, which had never been used, was broken up during the Civil War (its black marble sarcophagus now forms part of Nelson's tomb in the crypt of St Paul's). Queen Victoria had the chapel converted into a memorial to her husband Prince Albert (d. 1861), who is buried at Frogmore (*see below*). The chapel also contains the tombs of Albert Victor, Duke of Clarence, eldest son of Edward VII, who died of influenza in 1892 aged 28 (tomb by Alfred Gilbert, sculptor of 'Eros' in Piccadilly); and of Leopold, Duke of Albany, Queen Victoria's haemophiliac son, who died in 1884 aged 30.

FROGMORE HOUSE

To the north and east of the Castle is the **Home Park**. In the south part is **Frogmore House** (*access along Windsor High St and then Park St; see rct.uk/visit/frogmore-house*), used as a retreat by Queen Charlotte, consort of George III, and her unmarried daughters. Queen Charlotte was a great botanist and created splendid gardens here. Queen Victoria loved Frogmore: the 'Indian Kiosk' in the garden is her addition. Also in the garden is the **Mausoleum**, a centrally-planned tomb chamber where the Prince Consort and Queen Victoria lie side by side in their sarcophagi. Also buried here are the Duke of Windsor (the former King Edward VIII; d. 1972) and his wife, the former Mrs Wallis Simpson (d. 1994).

The **Long Walk**, planted with elms by Charles II and replanted after 1945 with horse chestnut and plane trees, stretches for almost three miles, linking the Home Park to **Windsor Great Park**. At the end of the walk is a great statue of George III (known as 'The Copper Horse') by Westmacott. It shows the monarch in the Roman attitude of *acclamatio*, arm outstretched.

WINDSOR TOWN

Windsor Old Town consists of a network of cobbled streets and attractive and tightly-packed old houses. In Church Street, opposite Church Street Gardens (a small public square), is the **Old King's Head**, with a copy of Charles I's death warrant, signed by Oliver Cromwell, built into the wall. Next door is the red-brick Burford House (1640), where Nell Gwyn, mistress of Charles II, once lived.

At the junction of Castle Hill and the High Street, a **statue of Queen Victoria** by Sir Joseph Boehm (1887) stands on what was the centre of the medieval marketplace. The colonnaded **Guildhall**, on the High Street, opposite the Castle Hotel, was designed by Sir Thomas Fitch in 1686 and finished by Sir Christopher Wren in 1707. It is adorned with statues of Queen Anne and Prince George of Denmark, in niches at the short ends above the projecting portico, and has royal portraits and collections of Windsor's silver plate in its museum. The Information Office is also housed here.

The parish church of **St John the Baptist** in the High Street contains a *Last Supper* attributed to the painter and tapestry designer Francis Cleyn (*see p. 550*). The mosaics in the chancel and apse are by Antonio Salviati.

The **Household Cavalry Museum Archive** in Combermere Barracks, St Leonard's Road, can be visited by appointment (*householdcavalry.co.uk*).

North of Windsor Castle, **Windsor Town Bridge** (1824; *pedestrians and cycles only*) crosses the Thames to Eton. On the Windsor side of the river here is the terminal for river ferries to **Runnymede** (*map p. 626, A3*), where King John fixed his seal to *Magna Carta*, the great charter of English liberties, on 15th June 1215. The site is marked by a little columned rotunda.

SWAN UPPING

Swan Upping is the name given to the ceremony of the swan census which takes place every year on certain reaches of the Thames. It traces its origins back to the 12th century, when the sovereign claimed ownership of all Mute swans (*Cygnus olor*), a culinary delicacy. Swans are no longer eaten, but the census still takes place annually in the third week of July. Royal ownership of the swans is symbolically retained, and is held together with the Worshipful Companies of Vintners and Dyers, two of the City of London's ancient livery companies (*for more on these, see p. 19*). 'Swan Uppers' representing HM The King and the two livery companies, all clad in splendid scarlet uniforms, embark in six skiffs, propelled by oars, to find and mark all new cygnets on the Thames. When the skiffs row past Windsor Castle, the Swan Uppers utter the traditional salute: 'His Majesty The King, Seigneur of the Swans!' The ceremony takes five days. All cygnets are marked with a small nick in the beak, are examined for disease or injury (the King's Swan Warden is a qualified professor of ornithology), and are returned to the water.

The aura of bygone ritual, the prop-box costumes and the man-powered boats may make the ceremony appear little more than pantomime. But it fulfils an important function. Swans are not endangered but their habitats are threatened by increased river use by humans and their lives are put at risk by stray lengths of fishing line. The Swan Upping ceremony carefully and scientifically monitors how well they are faring and does much to ensure the survival of this wild species. Watching the ceremony, in any case, is a thrilling spectacle.

ETON

The pedestrian Windsor Town Bridge leads directly into Eton High Street, lined with shops and tearooms. Guided tours of Eton College can be booked (see etoncollege.com).

Eton College, probably the most famous school in England, was founded by Henry VI in 1440 to provide an education to poor scholars. It remains single-sex (boys only) and all its pupils are boarders. It is the best known of all the English public schools, famous for its uniform of morning coats and pinstripe trousers. The term 'public school' was originally used to indicate that entry was not subject to religious or professional restrictions. Today it means that a school is independent and fee-paying.

Over the centuries Eton has educated a great many statesmen, soldiers, poets, ne'er-do-wells and public servants. Famous old Etonians include the Duke of Wellington, Beau Brummell, George Gordon (instigator of the eponymous riots) and the poet Thomas Gray, who wrote his 'Ode on a Distant Prospect of Eton College' on seeing a group of schoolboys out on the playing field, laughing and shouting, full of the innocence and irresponsibility of youth. 'Alas, regardless of their doom, the little victims play!' he wrote, glumly: 'No sense have they of ills to come, nor care beyond today.'

APPENDIX

An alphabetical listing of districts of London, significant buildings, monuments and museums, mainly in outlying parts of the city not covered in the main chapters of the guide.

Alexandra Palace

Map p. 628, C1.

Familiarly known as 'Ally Pally', this entertainment venue set in an expansive park (*alexandrapalace.com*) is named after Alexandra, consort of Edward VII. It began life in 1873 as an exhibition centre inspired by the Crystal Palace (*see p. 329*) but burned down after only two weeks. Although it reopen ed two years later, it was never a commercial success. In 1936 it became the home of the BBC's TV service and the world's first high-definition television broadcast was made from here (the transmission antenna survives). Some of the original studios exist along with the producers' galleries and some of the Victorian stage machinery. The views of London from its elevated position are exceptionally good.

Barnet

Map p. 627, D1.

Barnet's location on the main road north from London stimulated local trade and many coaching inns sprang up here The Battle of Barnet, fought on Hadley Common in 1471, was a pivotal conflict of the Wars of the Roses. Warwick the Kingmaker was slain on the field and Edward IV's throne was secured. At 31 Wood St is the **Barnet Museum** (*free; barnetmuseum.co.uk*) with a display on the Battle of Barnet and curiosities including the glove of a Zeppelin pilot who crashed over Potters Bar during WWI. Barnet Fair (*first Mon in Sept*) is the descendant of the old

Horse Fair, from which the Cockney rhyming slang 'Barnet', meaning 'hair' is derived.

Barnes

Map p. 628, B3.

Until the opening of Hammersmith Bridge in 1827 and the coming of the railway in the mid-19th century, Barnes was an isolated rural area. It is still a tranquil riverside suburb, a picturesque, affluent 'village'. Its chief attraction is the **London Wetland Centre** (*wwt.org.uk*), a wildlife paradise in the midst of the capital, with terrific opportunities to spot interesting and sometimes rare wild birds. It is a first-class example of urban regeneration, successfully bringing the countryside to London—which is quite a feat, lying as it does beneath the Heathrow flight path. One of the Centre's rarer winter visitors—and the Holy Grail of birding—is the Great Bittern.

On the river near Hammersmith Bridge is the **Harrods Depository**, clad in distinctive orange terracotta tiles with twin cupolas and tinted blue windows. Built in 1894 to store large items of furniture for the eponymous department store in Knightsbridge, it was converted into luxury flats and penthouses in the 1990s as part of the Harrods Village estate.

Bedford Park

Map p. 628, B3.

North of South Parade and Flanders Road, Bedford Park is famed as being the first planned garden suburb in the world, with red-brick houses by a number of architects, including Norman Shaw. The green space across the road from Turnham Green station is the site of the Battle of Turnham Green, where a Parliamentarian army of some 24,000 soldiers fought the Royalist force of 13,000, winning a strategic though rather indecisive victory on 13th November 1642, during the English Civil War.

Canons Park
Map p. 626, C1.
Canons Park takes its name from the former home of James Brydges, 1st Duke of Chandos, patron of Handel (*see also pp. 301–2*). The mansion was destroyed in 1747 after the family fortune was lost in the South Sea Bubble. A short walk from Canons Park Tube station is the church of **St Lawrence, Whitchurch**, rebuilt for Chandos mainly by James Gibbs and containing Chandos's mausoleum. Work was completed in 1716 and it remains an important example of the Baroque in England. It is thought that Handel's psalm settings known as the *Chandos Anthems* were first performed here.

Charlton
Map p. 629, F3.
On Charlton Road is the Jacobean **Charlton House**, a fine mansion of brick with stone dressings, completed in 1612 for the tutor of Prince Henry, eldest son of James I. It is set in delightful grounds, which has a summer house attributed to Inigo Jones. The period interiors include fine plasterwork ceilings. Charlton is also known as the home of the Charlton Athletic football club.

Crystal Palace
Map p. 629, D4–E4.
The spacious park was designed by Sir Joseph Paxton in 1852 to complement the Crystal

Palace, the huge glass and iron building, also designed by Paxton, which had been the centrepiece of the Great Exhibition of 1851 (*p. 329*) and which was moved here in 1854. It perished in 1936 in a fire, which could be seen from as far away as Brighton. Only the grand approach stairways and parts of the parapets remain, the stone plinths mostly empty save for the statue of a turbanned man and the headless form of an elegantly-draped woman. Above these are two sphinxes. The **Crystal Palace TV transmitter** towers above one end of the terrace. John Logie Baird, the inventor of television, had studios here which were lost in the fire (the studios moved to Alexandra Palace; *see p. 563*). The **Crystal Palace Museum** on Anerley Hill is open at weekends (*crystalpalacemuseum.org. uk*). In the other direction (*signed*), is the **Dinosaur Park**, a pond with an island in its centre, inhabited by concrete models of huge prehistoric creatures designed by Benjamin Waterhouse Hawkins in 1854. They are quite an extraordinary sight. The **Crystal Palace Bowl** is a venue for concerts.

Dalston
Map p. 629, D2.
Dalston is known for its nightlife and for its 'clown service' on the first Sun in Feb, when jesters, fools and harlequins of all kinds congregate at Holy Trinity church on Beechwood Road for a service commemorating Joseph Grimaldi, the pantomime actor who developed the character of the modern clown. He died in Islington in 1837.

Eltham
Map p. 629, F4.
Ideally located on the way from London to the coast, Eltham was used by kings and their troops for 200 years, on their way to overseas battles. Well Hall Road leads north from

Eltham High Street for half a mile to **Well Hall Pleasaunce** (*wellhall.org.uk*), a small local park with a medieval moated garden, formerly the grounds of Well Hall mansion, the home of William Roper, who married Sir Thomas More's daughter Margaret in 1521. The 16th-century barn is now a restaurant and it preserves a small stained-glass window featuring Margaret Roper.

Court Yard, just off the High Street, leads to the remains of **Eltham Palace** (*english-heritage.org.uk*), once a royal manor and now one of London's finest Art Deco houses.

The manor of Eltham was one of the oldest estates belonging to the Crown and by the 14th century was one of the largest and most frequented of the English royal palaces. Originally a moated manor house, it was a favourite Christmas residence of English sovereigns from Henry III to Henry VIII. Chaucer was clerk of the works to Richard II here, and here Henry IV entertained the Byzantine emperor Manuel II Palaeologus. After Agincourt Henry V stayed at Eltham before his triumphal entry into London. The Great Hall, the most evident feature of the medieval palace which remains today, was constructed by Edward IV in 1475–80. Henry VIII was the last monarch to spend much time at Eltham, and after the Civil War both the palace and its grounds were given over to agricultural use. The Great Hall was used as a barn and romantic views of it as such were made by several artists, including Turner.

In 1933 the site was purchased by the wealthy Stephen Courtauld (brother of Samuel Courtauld, founder of the art institute) and his wife Virginia. They conceived a spectacular and luxurious house, designed by Seely & Paget. The aim was to construct a glamorous and modern home while retaining as much as possible of the medieval palace. The result is an extraordinarily eclectic mix. The interiors were created by a team of artistic advisers, personal friends of the Courtaulds, including Winifred Knights and her husband Thomas Monnington, the Swedish interior designer Rolf Engströmer (head of the Swedish company Jefta) and the Italian decorator Peter Malacrida. Malacrida, then working for the company White Allom, had been a neighbour of the Courtaulds in Grosvenor Square. The quality of the materials and craftsmanship was matched by the luxury of the innovative 1930s' technological features: an internal telephone system, concealed ceiling lights, underfloor heating, a centralised vacuum cleaner with sockets in each room and speakers which broadcast music throughout the ground floor. The house became the stage for extravagant weekend parties. The Courtaulds left Eltham in 1944.

The tour takes in the reception rooms, bedrooms, Virginia Courtauld's luxurious onyx bathroom, and Mah-Jongg's quarters, designed for the Courtaulds' pet ring-tailed lemur, bought at Harrods in 1923. 'Jongy' enjoyed central heating, a bamboo forest mural and a bamboo ladder leading down to the Flower Room. He accompanied his owners everywhere and had his own small deckchair for foreign cruises.

Finchley
Map p. 628, C1.
Finchley lies strung out along the Great North Road (also known as High Road). At no. 52 High Road is London's oldest working cinema, the **Phoenix**, in operation since 1910 (*phoenixcinema.co.uk*).

Forty Hall
Map p. 627, E1; fortyhallestate.co.uk.
The manor of **Forty Hall**, a red-brick mansion 'but a horse ride from the City' was built in 1629–32 for Sir Nicholas Rainton, Lord Mayor of London, President

of St Bartholomew's Hospital and a wealthy haberdasher (his name features on the plaque in the entrance to Haberdashers' Hall on West Smithfield). The exterior of Forty Hall is very handsome and the hipped roof is of particular interest, being advanced for its time and an important early example of the style. The interior has been much altered and restored, but some interesting features remain. The Entrance Hall has Rococo plasterwork of c. 1787, with medallions representing the Seasons. The fine carved panelling on the early 17th-century Hall Screen is an outstanding survival from the original house. Other rooms retain plaster ceilings with bold strapwork decoration.

In the grounds, scant remains have been found of Elsyng Palace, a Tudor royal manor and hunting lodge, where in 1547, in the presence of Princess Elizabeth, Edward VI received the news of the death of his father Henry VIII and of his consequent accession. Also on the estate is the Forty Hall Farm, with a variety of rare breed animals and an organic vineyard, the only commercial vineyard in London.

Rainton died at Forty Hall in 1646. In **St Andrew's church** in Enfield Town, set back from the market square, you can admire his fine family tomb, with stiffly reclining effigies.

At **Enfield Town railway station** you are treading on ground where Keats trod. The poet attended school in a building on this site from 1803–11. The headmaster's son, Charles Cowden Clarke, became Keats's great friend, to whom the poet acknowledged a debt of sincere gratitude: 'Ah! had I never seen or known your kindness, what might I have been?'

Fulham

Map p. 628, B3.
Fulham occupies a broad peninsula on the north bank of the Thames. Excavations near the river have revealed evidence of Neolithic and Roman settlements. White earthenware vases—Fulham Vases—were made by the Fulham Pottery (established 1672) on the New King's Road until the 1970s. In the 18th century, Fulham was a gentleman's retreat and several Georgian residences were built. From the late 19th century the area was built up with streets and terraces intended for the lower middle classes; by the mid-20th century Fulham was almost entirely a working-class community. Today, Fulham is ultra-respectable, especially popular with middle-class professionals. The small, former working-class terraces now command high prices and there are plenty of lively bars and restaurants.

On the north side of the curving grey **Putney Bridge**, opposite Putney's boat clubs, stretches Bishop's Park, home of Fulham Palace (*see below*). The parish church of **All Saints** (*allsaints-fulham.org.uk*) has a Kentish ragstone tower dating from the 1440s. The rest of the church was rebuilt in Gothic style in the 1840s and 1880s by Sir Arthur Blomfield. Inside there is a fine collection of monuments from the earlier church. Ten Bishops of London are buried here.

Fulham Palace, overlooking the Thames in **Bishop's Park**, was the official residence of the Bishop of London from 704 until 1973. The attractive red-brick Tudor quadrangle has Georgian additions and an adjoining Victorian chapel by William Butterfield, (1866–7). The buildings have been much restored and the early 19th-century wing, formerly the Bishop's dining room and library, houses the Museum of Fulham Palace (*fulhampalace.org*), which traces the history of the Bishops of London and Fulham Palace itself. The surrounding **botanical gardens** were made famous in the 17th century by Bishop Compton, who introduced many rare species, some never grown in Europe before.

Hackney

Map p. 629, E1–E2.

Hackney developed rapidly in the late 19th and early 20th centuries. After that it went into decline, becoming run-down and with a lingering atmosphere of threat. Furtive-looking men with pit bull terriers would stalk Victoria Park. Today **Victoria Park** is transformed and Hackney Marshes are proud to have the largest concentration of football pitches in Europe. South Hackney has become popular with young professionals and is well stocked with cafés and restaurants. It is also the site of one of London's burgeoning cluster of city farms, **Hackney City Farm** (*hackneycityfarm.co.uk*).

Sutton House survives largely intact from the early 16th century. The house (*2 & 4 Homerton High St; nationaltrust.org. uk*) was built in 1534–5 by Ralph Sadleir, a wealthy soldier and diplomat, secretary to Thomas Cromwell and later King Henry VIII's principal Secretary of State. It was first known as 'the bryk place', being one of the very few brick-built residences in the area (the ragstone tower of St Augustine's church nearby is the only other building to remain from the period). Constructed on the familiar Tudor 'H' plan, the building has been altered several times since—notably around 1620, in 1741–3 and in the early 19th century—but the original form remains remarkably intact. As such it represents an important London example of the development of the medieval hall house, with cross-wings and servants' quarters. The property later passed to Thomas Sutton, who according to John Aubrey was the type for Ben Jonson's *Volpone*. Of particular interest in the interior is the Linenfold Parlour, which is lined with very fine mid-16th-century carved oak panelling. Originally the wood was painted pale yellow with green in the folds, a colour scheme that can still be seen behind hinged panels in one wall. Quite possibly it was in this room that Sir Ralph Sadleir held negotiations during the Dissolution of the Monasteries, which carved up the wealth of the Church. Also on show are examples of artwork produced in the later 20th-century when the house was occupied by squatters. They named it the Blue House and it became a music venue for punk bands rejoicing in names like 'Sons of Bad Breath' and 'Flowers in the Dustbin'.

Holloway

Map p. 629, D1–D2.

The name Holloway may derive simply from 'hollow way', a road worn deep and tunnel-like by passing herds of cattle as they were driven south to Smithfield. Holloway was known for the women's prison in Parkhurst Road (top of Camden Road), originally built in 1852 as a house of correction for both sexes. Oscar Wilde was imprisoned here. It closed in 2016. In **Caledonian Road**, known locally as the Cally Road, is Pentonville Prison (just north of Wheelwright St; *map p. 633, E1–F1*), built in 1840. The district was developed and built up very quickly from the 19th century: Holloway is Mr Pooterland, where the fictional Victorian clerk lived and wrangled with uppity tradesmen and domestic servants (*Diary of a Nobody*, by George and Weedon Grossmith). Today it is multi-ethnic and densely populated.

Hoxton

Map p. 629, D2.

The district of Hoxton enjoyed a comet-like surge of glory for the twelve years that it was home to Jay Jopling's White Cube Gallery. It closed in 2012 and the White Cube now operates in St James's and Bermondsey in London, as well as in Hong Kong, Paris, New York and Palm Beach). On Pitfield Street is the 'Waterloo' church of **St John the Baptist** (1826), with a vast Edwardian ceiling painting of the *Apocalypse*. The architect was Francis Edwards, pupil of Sir John Soane. It is now home to an Evangelical congregation (*stjohnshoxton.org.uk*). **Hoxton Hall**, at 130 Hoxton St, is an old Victorian music hall still used for live performances (*hoxtonhall.co.uk*).

Kensal Green Cemetery
Map p. 628, B2.
One of London's oldest public burial places, opened in 1833. The design of the 72-acre grounds, with numerous listed monuments, is said to have been influenced by Père-Lachaise in Paris. Buried here are Marc Brunel (d. 1849), Isambard Kingdom Brunel (d. 1859), Thackeray (d. 1863), Trollope (d. 1882), Wilkie Collins (d. 1889) and the computer pioneer Charles Babbage (d. 1871).

Kilburn
Map p. 628, B2–C2.
Once a predominantly Irish area, now multi-ethnic. The Anglo-Catholic **St Augustine's church** in Kilburn Park Road (east off Kilburn High Road) is one of London's finest neo-Gothic Victorian churches (J.L. Pearson, 1898; *saugustinekilburn.org.uk*). It is referred to as the 'cathedral of North London' due to its large size and elaborate architecture: the soaring 254ft tower is an architectural triumph. In the High Road itself are a couple of good renovated Victorian pubs, the Black Lion and the North London Tavern. There are also few lingering working-men's pubs: a bit intimidating; the kind of places where everyone falls silent when a stranger enters.

Kingston upon Thames
Map p. 626, C4.
The Royal Borough of Kingston upon Thames is one of the oldest royal boroughs in London. The **Kingston Museum** on Wheatfield Road (*kingstonheritage.org.uk*) was opened in 1904 and houses three permanent

exhibitions. The **Eadweard Muybridge** exhibition celebrates one of Kingston's most famous past residents. Born Edward James Muggeridge in 1830, Muybridge moved to New York and later San Francisco to work in the book trade, becoming interested in landscape photography, from which profession he made his fortune. Challenged to establish whether a running horse ever has all four feet off the ground at any one time, Muybridge set up a camera shed at the stud farm of the tycoon and founder of Stanford University, Leland Stanford, and proved to the world that a horse can indeed fly. He later produced *Animal Locomotion* (1887), 751 plates of animal and human locomotion, based on studies carried out at the University of Pennsylvania. Muybridge bequeathed to the museum his lantern slides, his zoöpraxiscope (a device which could display photographic motion pictures) and a number of plates from *Animal Locomotion*.

Kingston's association with the pottery industry during the 13th and 14th centuries is illustrated in the collection of Surrey whiteware including jugs, dishes and plates used everyday by Londoners. The Marsh Collection has a collection of **Martinware and pottery by Bernard Leach**. The Martin Brothers, whose pottery was in Southall in the later 19th and early 20th century, produced highly distinctive studio pieces—the Wally Bird snuff jar is the star of the collection.

Mortlake
Map p. 628, A3–B3.
Turner painted two views of the Thames from Mortlake, a residential area bordering Barnes. They are now in the collections of the National Gallery of Washington and the Frick Collection, New York. The ancient manor of Mortlake, which included Putney and Wimbledon, was the property of the Archbishops of Canterbury until 1536,

when Cranmer transferred it to Henry VIII. The riverside location of the Stag/Budweiser brewery, with its distinctive chimney and redundant mid-Victorian buildings (off Mortlake High Street, near the roundabout and junction with Lower Richmond Road), is a site which would once have been the grounds of the Archbishops' residence. At the back of the brewery, down Ship Lane, is The Ship, a popular 18th-century riverside pub near the finishing line of the Oxford and Cambridge boat race (*see p. 531*).

Dr John Dee (d. 1608), scholar, mathematician and alchemist (the character of Prospero in Shakespeare's *Tempest* is said to have been based on him), was a local resident and is believed to be buried in the chancel of the **parish church of St Mary the Virgin**. His library was one of the finest in Europe and Elizabeth I came to Mortlake to consult him on matters of astrology. The obsidian mirror which Dee used for divination is in the British Museum. When at Cambridge, Dee devised 'miraculous' stage effects for a performance of a play by Aristophanes. People began whispering that he was a sorcerer, a reputation he never shook off. Aubrey describes him as 'tall and slender, a very handsome man,' with 'a long beard as white as milk'. A crystal which he used for cures, and which he claimed to have received from the Archangel Uriel, is held by the Science Museum.

In 1619, under James I, a **tapestry works** was established at Mortlake, staffed by Netherlandish weavers. The Prince of Wales, later Charles I, was a patron. The tapestry buildings stood along the river opposite the church: the lone survivor is no. 119. Despite the excellence of the tapestries produced, the works went into decline after the Civil War and by 1703, Queen Anne authorised their closure. Examples of Mortlake tapestry can be seen at Ham House, Kensington Palace and Hampton Court.

The extraordinary late 19th-century **mausoleum of Sir Richard Burton**, designed as an Arab tent, may be seen at the Catholic church of St Mary Magdalen, on North Worple Way. The butterscotch-coloured stone monument, with ruched exterior detail giving the impression of draped fabric, dominates the peaceful Victorian graveyard and is almost as high as the row of terraced cottages in the street behind. It is decorated with various Eastern and Christian motifs including a Star of Bethlehem, a Crucifix and gilded Muslim crescents. Inside are the coffins of Burton himself (1821–90), variously explorer, traveller and translator of *The Arabian Nights*, as well as of his wife Isabel. The various objects inside include an altar, Middle Eastern lamps, coloured glass vessels and camel bells, which were fixed to a battery in order that they would tinkle when the tomb door was opened. The interior may be viewed through a plate-glass window (originally stained glass) at the back, via a fixed iron step ladder. The tomb was erected by Lady Burton after her husband's death and she visited frequently, sometimes sitting inside amongst the tinkling bells. She was buried alongside him in 1896 (her coffin is the more ornate of the two).

Musical Museum

Map p. 628, A3; musicalmuseum.co.uk.
Specially designed museum and concert hall on Brentford High Street, which explains how music has been performed, recorded and reproduced. There is a collection of working instruments including Wurlitzers and pianolas, and a collection of 20,000 music rolls.

Neasden

Map p. 628, B2.
The 'Neasden Temple', officially the BAPS Shri Swaminarayan Mandir (*londonmandir. baps.org*), a vast Hindu temple in the northern

borough of Brent, was built using traditional materials and techniques (no steel is used). It opened in 1995 and is an artistic marvel, positively alive with figurative and non-figurative sculpture.

Pollock's Toy Museum

pollockstoymuseum.co.uk.
The collection takes its name from Benjamin Pollock (d. 1937), one of the last of the Victorian printers and publishers of toy theatres. The holdings include board games, mechanical toys, tin soldiers, marbles, wax dolls, puppets, toy theatres—and Eric, the museum's oldest teddy bear, dating from 1905. At the time of writing the museum was looking for new premises since the lease on their townhouse site in Fitzrovia expired.

Poplar

Map p. 625, B1.
An area of east London just north of the Isle of Dogs. Here, on the Brownfield Estate, on and near St Leonard's Road, are three Brutalist residential blocks by Ernő Goldfinger: **Balfron Tower** (1965), **Glenkerry House** (1977) and **Carradale House** (1970). Balfron Tower, an attempt to raise a Marxist Utopia from the streets of an East End slum, was in effect a dry-run for Trellick Tower (*p. 319*). All the towers share the architectural conceit of placing the lift and stairs in a separate shaft.

Ragged School Museum

In Copperfield Road, Stepney (*map p. 629, E2*) is the warehouse where Dr Barnardo opened his original 'Ragged School' in 1877, providing free education and meals for the poorest children in the area. It is now a museum (*raggedschoolmuseum.org.uk*), the main feature of which is the Victorian classroom, complete with serried ranks of desks, slate writing boards and dunce's hats.

Southall

Map p. 626, C3.
Southall, in the Borough of Ealing, is sometimes known as 'Little India' for the makeup of its population, many of whom have Punjabi roots (there is a large Sikh temple here). On the High Street is the **Southall Odeon**, an Art Deco cinema built by George Coles in 1936. An earlier cinema, on South Road, also by Coles, is the fanciful **ex-Himalaya Palace**, fashioned to resemble a Chinese temple. It opened in 1929.

Stamford Hill

Map p. 629, D1.
Stamford Hill, once just a sandy ford, was settled by wealthy merchants in the 18th and 19th centuries. Today, the most conspicuous aspect of the area is the number of ultra-orthodox Jews you will see going about their business: the square mile comes to bustling life on the Jewish Sabbath (Saturday). Ninety percent of the population here are Haredi Jews: this is the largest ultra-orthodox Jewish community outside Israel and Brooklyn. Behind the façades of the large Victorian and Edwardian houses are synagogues, single-sex schools, community centres and places of religious study, as well as homes. The Haredi live an insular, pious life; they were nearly wiped out during the Holocaust and thriving Eastern European communities were extinguished. The survivors settled in Israel, the USA and the UK, clinging to their centuries-old traditions and mistrustful of assimilation. Their primary language is Yiddish, religious study is pursued above all else and the trappings of modern secular life are eschewed. They set themselves apart most obviously by their dress. The men, with beards and long, curling side-locks, wear black frock coats and various forms of hat, which some of the married men exchange on Shabbat for the *shtreimel*: the large, circular,

real-fur hat that is worn come rain or shine on this holy day (during wet weather it is covered with a transparent plastic bonnet). The women dress modestly in long skirts, jackets, blouses and thick stockings and tend to marry young (at 18 or 20), after which they cover their hair with wigs. They bear an average of six children: fruitful family life is central to this closed community, which already numbers over 20,000 and is growing. The community has recently expanded out of Stamford Hill to Canvey Island at the mouth of the Thames.

Stoke Newington

Map p. 629, D1.

Once rural woodland, the village of Stoke Newington grew up around Stoke Newington Church Street. Edgar Allan Poe, who went to school here, described it as 'a dreamlike and spirit-soothing place', a place of 'deeply-shadowed avenues', where he would 'inhale the fragrance of its thousand shrubberies, and thrill anew with undefinable delight, at the deep hollow note of the church-bell, breaking, each hour.' Today, with its plethora of small independent shops, pubs, bars and restaurants, Stoke Newington's gentrified, villagey atmosphere is extremely well maintained. Stoke Newington High Street, part of the A10, is built over Ermine Street, the old Roman road to Lincoln and York.

For centuries Stoke Newington has been a place where outsiders and Nonconformists have settled. Its most famous Nonconformist resident was Daniel Defoe (a road and a pub are named after him), who wrote *Robinson Crusoe* while living in a house on the site of no. 95 **Stoke Newington Church Street**. At no. 184 (the local library) his tombstone from Bunhill Fields is preserved and on display. From the 18th century many wealthy Quakers lived in the area, including Anna Sewell, author of *Black Beauty*, who lived here

as a child. Jewish refugees arrived at the end of the 19th century, escaping the pogroms of Eastern Europe. The atmospheric **Abney Park**, to the east along Stoke Newington Church Street, was established around 1840 as a Nonconformist garden cemetery and arboretum; the wooded landscape had been laid out in the 18th century. John Loudon, gardener and writer (*see Porchester Terrace, p. 313*), very much admired it. It is now a public park and nature reserve. William Booth and his wife Catherine, founders of the Salvation Army, are buried here.

St Mary's Old Church in Stoke Newington Church Street dates from 1560. The 'new' church opposite was designed by Sir George Gilbert Scott in 1858. **Clissold Park**, to the west of the churches, formed the grounds of the local mansion, formerly Paradise House, built for the Quaker merchant and anti-slavery campaigner Jonathan Hoare, brother of Samuel Hoare, who lived at Heath House in Hampstead. Part of the New River, a man-made waterway opened in 1613 to supply London with fresh drinking water from springs in Middlesex and Hertfordshire, emerges in the park; further north, it feeds the east and west reservoirs. The **former Stoke Newington Pumping Station** in Green Lanes (skirting the west side of Clissold Park), a castle-like structure, is a valuable example of Victorian industrial architecture. Designed in 1854–6 by Chadwell Mylne, who took inspiration from Stirling Castle in Scotland, it once helped pump the waters of the New River.

Stratford

Map p. 629, E2.

The Olympic Park here was built for the 2012 Olympic Games. The swimming pool at the Aquatics Centre, designed by Zaha Hadid, is open to the public (*queenelizabetholympicpark. co.uk*). The Stratford Olympic Park is also the site of **V&A East**, an outpost of the Victoria & Albert Museum in South Kensington. At the time of writing, it was not yet open.

William Morris Gallery

Map p. 629, E1. wmgallery.org.uk.
The Water House at Lloyd Park in Walthamstow is a testament to the writer, social reformer, Socialist and designer William Morris (1832–96), famous for the phrase 'have nothing in your house that you do not know to be useful, or believe to be beautiful'. The designs of the objects of utility and beauty to which he refers, inspired by the forms of nature, traditional workmanship and the aesthetic of the medieval Gothic according to John Ruskin, and which his company Morris, Marshall, Faulkner and Co. produced from 1861 onwards, are applied to tiles, tableware, stained glass, furniture and wallpaper and are still produced to this day by Morris & Co.

Morris was born in Walthamstow, the son of a wealthy financier. He was a recalcitrant student at Marlborough College (Morris preferred to learn his own way, from the independent reading of antiquarian history books and the exploration of local prehistoric landscapes). When his father died in 1847, the family's straitened circumstances induced his mother to move with Morris and his eight siblings to the Water House, named after its ornamental moat in the grounds, where the Morris family would fish, boat and skate. Morris lived here from 1848–56 but today the open fields and countryside have been swallowed up by dense terraced housing, a process of suburban development which began in the 1870s with the extension of the railway. In Morris's words, Walthamstow became 'terribly cocknified and choked up by the jerry-builders'. The house was purchased by the publisher Edward Lloyd, the disseminator of sensationalist serials (known as 'penny dreadfuls') such as *Varney the Vampire or The Feast of Blood* (1845), the precursor to Bram Stoker's *Dracula* and reputedly one of the worst books written in a hundred years. After Lloyd's death the house and grounds passed into public hands.

Much of the contents of the museum comprise the collections of the artist Sir Frank Brangwyn (1867–1956), who was apprenticed to Morris, and A.H. Mackmurdo, an architect, designer and founder of the Century Guild, who had introduced Brangwyn to Morris (one of only five Fretwork chairs made by him is on display).

The nine galleries are thematically laid out, beginning with the early life and influences of William Morris, moving on to the establishment of his professional career as a designer, to later life as a poet, publisher and radical political activist, and concluding with his lasting legacy. Displays cover the Morris & Co. shop at 449 Oxford St and the famous Kelmscott Press, run from his house in Hammersmith (*see p. 509*), which published the *Works of Geoffrey Chaucer* (1896), with the typeface and page layout by Morris and illustrations by Burne-Jones. The story of the radicalisation of Morris in middle age is also told, showing how his work as a craftsman informed his political beliefs and covering his establishment of the Socialist League in 1884, as well as his arrest for disorderly conduct at a mass meeting of Socialists in 1885.

Wandsworth

Map p. 628, C4.
Wandsworth takes its name from the River Wandle, whose delta was first settled in the Bronze Age. The river was much exploited for industry: in the 18th century the arrival of Huguenot refugees led to a great growth in textile manufacture here; the Wandle came to support some 65 water mills between Wandsworth and Merton to the south.

Bleaching, dyeing and brewing were carried on here and there were also iron and copper foundries. The last brewery, Young & Co's Ram Brewery, closed in 2006, after 425 years. Today the riverside around **Wandsworth Bridge** (Thomas Peirson Frank, 1940) has been developed with modern apartment complexes and the riverside walk to Battersea has been opened up. The Ship Inn is an 18th-century pub with a river terrace. The Victorian streets behind Wandsworth Town station are attractive and gentrified and there are some good independent shops, bars and restaurants. The **Royal Victoria Patriotic Building**, a huge, mid-19th-century neo-Gothic former asylum by Rohde Hawkins, dominates the northern edge of Wandsworth Common; Rudolf Hess was interned here for a time during WWII.

Woolwich
Map p. 629, F3 and p. 627, F3.
Woolwich has a distinguished naval and military past and is also known for its football team, Arsenal (established by workers from the Royal Arsenal factory in 1886), which moved to north London in 1913. The **Woolwich Ferry** crosses the Thames here, a free service for vehicles and passengers operating every 5–10mins. A ferry crossing was first established here in the 14th century. You can also cross under the river via the Woolwich foot tunnel.

Henry VIII established a **dockyard** at Woolwich in 1512. The *Henri Grace à Dieu* or *Great Harry*, the fleet's flagship, was built here, as was the *Sovereign of the Seas*, designed in 1637 by Phineas Pett and his son Peter. The dockyard closed in 1869. Munitions manufacture began at Woolwich in 1696, at what became known as the **Woolwich Arsenal**, the Royal Ordnance Factory. In 1716 Vanbrugh was appointed to design new foundry buildings, after a severe explosion

at Moorfields (where guns were then made) made it imperative to transfer all works out of central London. During WWI some 80,000 workers were employed at the Arsenal; fear of air-raids during WWII caused manufacture to be spread more evenly throughout the country. The Arsenal closed in 1967. Until very recently Woolwich was known for its links with the Royal Regiment of Artillery or Royal Artillery, known colloquially as the 'Gunners', the artillery arm of the British Army with a distinguished history stretching back to the creation of two field companies in Woolwich in 1716. They occupied barracks at Woolwich until 2007. A museum in the regiment's honour was founded as a teaching collection here in 1776 by Lieutenant General Sir William Congreve. His son, Colonel Sir William Congreve, developer of the Congreve rockets used during the Napoleonic wars, succeeded his father as Superintendent of the Military Machines. The museum occupied the buildings of the Royal Arsenal but was closed in 2014 and is due to be reopened in a new site on Salisbury Plain. The Royal Arsenal complex has been turned into a mixed-use development with the usual complement of cafés, restaurants, events spaces and public sculpture.

The market at Woolwich received its first Royal Charter in 1618; today it thrives as **Beresford Square Market**, in the shadow of the old Arsenal gates (*daily except Sun*). It has stalls selling produce, flowers and general goods.

On Grand Depot Road, near the former Royal Artillery Barracks, are the ruins of the 19th-century **St George's Garrison Church** (*stgeorgeswoolwich.org*), which was damaged in WWII and not rebuilt. A canopy now protects the surviving (restored) mosaics. At the time of writing there was a project to create a garden here in honour of the Commonwealth and Gurkhas.

PRACTICAL INFORMATION

GETTING AROUND

TO AND FROM THE AIRPORTS

Heathrow

Heathrow Airport (*map p. 626, B3*) is well connected to central London. All its terminals are on the Piccadilly and Elizabeth lines of the Underground (the Elizabeth Line is much faster). A quicker (though more expensive and less frequent) way is to take the Heathrow Express train, non-stop between the airport and Paddington Station (*map p. 634, B1; journey time c. 15mins*). Tickets can be bought in the airport arrivals hall and on the Paddington station concourse; or online (*heathrowexpress.com*).

Gatwick

Gatwick Airport is 28miles south of London but with good connections. Frequent Gatwick Express trains (*gatwickexpress.com*) run from the airport to Victoria Station (*map p. 635, E3; journey time c. 30mins*). Tickets can be bought from the airport arrivals hall or from the Gatwick Express booths at Victoria railway station; or online. Slower but cheaper connecting coach services are operated by National Express, from Victoria Coach Station (*map p. 635, D3*). For these and other coach services, see the airport website (*gatwickairport.com*).

Luton

The airport is slightly over 30miles north of London. Trains link Luton Airport Parkway station with St Pancras International (*map p. 633, E3*) in c. 40mins (there are also trains to London Bridge and to Blackfriars, but they tend to be slower services). There is no exclusive Luton Airport train service: the route is served by national rail and this is a major commuter route to and from London—so if your journey from the airport is early in the morning or if you are travelling to the airport during the afternoon rush hour, you may find that the train is very crowded.

Luton Airport Parkway station is not the same as Luton Aiport, which is situated a mile or two further away. When buying tickets from London, make sure your final destination is Luton Airport. A shuttle service, the Luton Dart, makes the connection between the airport and the railway station. The fare is included in the rail ticket to Luton Airport. At Luton Airport itself, there are ticket machines in the terminal building. There are also coach services from Luton Airport to central London, operated to/from Victoria by easyBus (*journey time c. 70mins; easybus.com*) and National Express (*nationalexpress.com*). Both services serve other intermediate stops in central London.

Stansted

Stansted Express trains run frequently between London Liverpool Street (*map p. 637, D1*) and the airport (*journey time c. 50mins; stanstedexpress.com*), which is some 40miles north of London. Coaches operated by easyBus link the airport with London Victoria (*map p. 635, D3; journey time c. 1hr 45mins; easybus.com*) and other stops. There are also National Express coaches to/from the airport and Victoria, also with other stops in between (*nationalexpress.com*).

London City

Docklands Light Railway (DLR) trains link London City Airport (*map p. 629, F2*) with the centre of town.

USING PUBLIC TRANSPORT

All travel within London comes under a single umbrella, operated by Transport for London (*tfl.gov.uk*). A single type of ticket is valid on buses, the Underground, DLR, Elizabeth Line and National Rail services within London. Ticket machines are located in Underground stations; you cannot buy tickets directly from drivers. Buying tickets can be time-consuming and fiddly: there are often long queues at the machines. If you are going to be travelling quite a bit, or if you are in London for any length of time, it is a good idea to invest in a Travel Card or an Oyster Card, or use Contactless. Children aged eleven and under travel free with an accompanying adult.

Travel Cards

These are available for a single day, for 7 days, monthly or annually. Travel Cards are priced according to zone, and thus it is useful to work out which transport zones you will be visiting. London is divided into 9 zones, with Buckingham Palace and St Paul's Cathedral in Zone 1 (the most central) and Hampton Court in Zone 6, the outermost zone covered in this guide. Maps showing the zones are posted in all stations and at bus stops. Unless you are making multiple journeys a day, Oyster or Contactless will probably be a cheaper option.

Oyster Cards

These pay-as-you go cards can be purchased at Underground stations or online (*tfl. gov.uk*). You put a certain amount of money on the card when you buy it and top it up as needed, either at machines in the Underground stations or again online. They are convenient and time-saving, covering all zones and automatically calculating the cheapest fare. Place your Oyster Card on the sensor to open the turnstiles in the Underground, and touch it on the reader when you board buses. For rail journeys, you need to 'touch out' at the end of your journey (you will be charged the maximum fare if you forget to do this). On buses you do not need to touch out.

The **Visitor Oyster Card** also offers free travel on riverboats. For details, see the website (*tfl.gov.uk*).

Contactless

You can also pay directly with a contactless card or mobile phone, touching it against the reader. Cards not issued in the UK may be subject to extra charges, however. For details, see the website (*tfl.gov.uk*).

THE LONDON UNDERGROUND

The London 'Tube' is the oldest metropolitan underground system in the world. Its network of tunnels is vast, the number of passengers that it handles every day is vaster, and yet somehow it manages to operate (mostly efficiently) 365 days a year, despite a number of antiquated features, miles of tunnels to walk, long escalators, and frustrating numbers of stairs (frustrating if you are travelling with suitcases or pushchairs). Some stations have no escalators, only lifts (or stairs). It is also worth knowing that two of the lines (the Northern Line and the District Line) have split routes, and at times you need to change trains on the same line to get to the destination you want.

The Elizabeth Line, which opened in 2022, is a very vast driverless service running east–west. It also has split routes.

Maps of the Underground (based on a famous schematic design of 1931 by Harry Beck) are posted in all stations and there is also a London Tube Map app.

TRAVELLING ON OVERGROUND TRAINS

The '**London Overground**' is the name used to designate a network of suburban trains serving more outlying destinations. On Tube maps it is indicated by orange lines. Ordinary London Transport tickets are valid on these services. London Transport tickets may also be used on National Rail services within London but are not valid on the Heathrow Express, Stansted Express or Gatwick Express, or on National Rail airport services to Luton. The **Docklands Light Railway** (DLR, indicated by turquoise lines) serves destinations in east London including City Airport.

LONDON BUSES

The London double decker bus is famous and most visitors want to ride on one at least once. You board by the front door and swipe your travel pass at the machine. Tickets cannot be purchased on board.

TRAVELLING BY TAXI

London's **black cabs** are unique and famous. All the major railway stations have taxi ranks. Cruising cabs patrol the streets: look to see whether the orange light on the roof is illuminated. If it is, flag the cab down and the driver will stop where he (it is usually a he) conveniently may. It is customary to tell the driver where you want to go (speak to him through the front window) before you get in. In most cabs, there is a control panel which allows you to talk to the driver or seal yourself in hermetic silence. There is a meter, always placed so as to be readily visible from the back, which allows you to monitor the price of your journey. When you arrive at your destination, get out and pay the driver, again through the front window. It is customary (but not obligatory) to give a small tip. This need be no more than rounding up the fare to the nearest pound. If you have a large suitcase, the driver can stow it in the space beside him in the front. London taxis may also be booked in advance. For a list of numbers, visit the website: *www.tfl.gov.uk/modes/taxis-and-minicabs/book-a-taxi*.

Otherwise, you can hire an Uber or a Bolt.

DRIVING IN LONDON

Traffic often proceeds at a snail's pace through the capital's streets. Parking is difficult and most of the central areas of town are covered by the 'congestion charge', a fee levied on motor vehicles using central London roads on weekdays between 7am and 6pm and noon to 6pm at weekends. The Congestion Charge Zone is signed by a large white C inside a red circle. If you are going to be driving in London, you can pay the charge online. Other areas of the capital are designated 'low emission' or 'ultra low emission' zones (LEZ and ULEZ), indicated by green signs. For all details, see the website (*tfl. gov.uk*).

CYCLING AND WALKING IN LONDON

London is full of cyclists, and pedestrians and motorists alike should take care; they all too frequently take risks, cutting across traffic, weaving in and out of lanes and swerving onto pavements. The public cycle hire scheme (at the time of writing it was Santander Cycles) is efficient and docking stations are numerous (*see visitlondon.com/ traveller-information*).

London is a very walkable city. The Thames Path has been opened up along some stretches of the river and pavements everywhere are broad, giving the pedestrian ample space. A network of routes, chosen with the walker's enjoyment in mind (and also including a selection of nature trails), has been devised by Footways, with maps available either on paper or digitally. The latter option allows you to follow the routes on your mobile device, using the geolocator. For more information, see the website (*footways.london*).

GETTING AROUND BY WATER

Walking along the Thames in parts of the City of London or on the south side of the river, in Southwark, one gets a full appreciation of the tidal nature of the waterway. Wide expanses of the bank are exposed. In fine weather, the silty foreshore is colonised by sunbathers. Many boats ply the Thames, both pleasure craft and working commuter services.

Uber Boat (by Thames Clippers) runs commuter services between Putney and Barking, with many stops in between including the London Eye, Bankside (Tate Modern) and Greenwich. For details and timetables, see their website (*thamesclippers. com*) or consult the timetables at the river piers at any of the stops mentioned above, and also at Tower Pier, Millbank (Tate Britain), Embankment (Houses of Parliament), London Bridge, Canary Wharf and Chelsea Harbour. Thames Clippers also operate sightseeing cruises and the Tate Boat (*see p. 178*).

Thames River Boats operate services to Kew, Richmond and Hampton Court. Services run from Westminster Pier (*map p. 635, F2; wpsa.co.uk*).

There are a number of companies offering **Thames cruises**, including Thames River Sightseeing (*thamesriversightseeing.com*) and London Eye River Cruises (*londoneye.com*).

Waterbuses on the Regent's Canal, from Camden Lock (*map p. 632, C2*) or Little Venice (*map p. 628, C2*), all converted narrowboats, run approx. hourly April–Sept, less frequently in the colder months. They call at London Zoo (*for details, see londonwaterbus.com*). For details of the **Jason's Trip** canal tour, see p. 316. **Electric boats** for hire, for self-driven excursions from Paddington Basin or Canary Wharf, are offered by GoBoat (*goboat.co.uk*)

FOOD AND DRINK

Dining in London is extraordinarily good. The offering is plentiful and extremely varied, from the simplest street food to the most carefully crafted organoleptic extravaganza in one of the capital's 70-plus Michelin-starred restaurants. Surveys of the world's best places to dine regularly include a clutch of London establishments. At the time of writing there were five restaurants with three Michelin stars in London: Core by Clare Smith in Notting Hill; Hélène Darroze at the Connaught; Alain Ducasse at the Dorchester; Sketch in Mayfair and Restaurant Gordon Ramsay in Chelsea. However, this is only half the epicurean story because the gourmet on a budget may have an equally appetising time here: in London you can find any type of cuisine at any price level: French, Italian, Japanese, Moroccan, Lebanese, Chinese, Polish, Taiwanese, Vietnamese, Modern British, Pan European, North American, Spanish, Peruvian, Fusion, etc. The outward-looking nature of this famously 'insular' island race means that everything is given an airing, from eclectic and experimental to homely and unadorned—and all of it downright delicious. It is quite simply getting difficult to eat badly in London. The old joke about the reason for there being no English equivalent of 'Bon appétit' (because the British are realists) now wears a little thin. For inspiration, reviews and offers, see *squaremeal.co.uk* and *opentable.co.uk*.

As noted above, London eating can be frighteningly expensive; but it can also be astonishingly good value. Partly this depends on the area of town (Mayfair and Kensington are pricey; outlying districts much less so). But wherever you go, there are always plenty of simple cafés, sandwich bars, takeaway restaurants and street markets offering simple meals, as well as traditional pubs or high street chains (e.g. Côte) and eat-in fast food chains (Pizza Express, Zizzi, Franco Manca, Honest Burgers, Wagamama),

Bibendum, the 'Michelin Man', adorning the 1911 Michelin House between South Kensington and Chelsea (81 Fulham Rd). Appropriately enough, the building now houses a French restaurant.

where menus are comfortably affordable. In restaurants with more pretension, you can expect to pay around £70–100 a head for a two- or three-course dinner with wine. A number of places offer set menus, which tend to be good value. Note that in many establishments a service charge, typically of 12.5 percent, is automatically added to your bill. This will be indicated either on the menu or on the bill itself.

FIFTEEN PLACES TO EAT

Pubs and restaurants of interest are mentioned in each chapter and are listed in the Index (*under separate headings for Pubs and Restaurants*). In a city such as this, where the offering is so varied and so prone to change, no listing in a printed book can hope to cover all the possibilities or to remain reliably up-to-date. Below is a very short selection of places for a fine night out, chosen by the authors and editors of this guide, places where we have been well served and which we would happily visit again.

Price categories are as follows, intended only as an approximate guide:

£: *à la carte* main courses generally for under £20;
££: mains generally between £20 and £35;
£££: mains generally over £35.

£–££ **Moro**. Justly popular restaurant serving Iberian/Moorish cuisine, set up in 1997 by a husband-and-wife team who had taught themselves about the region's cuisine by visiting in their camper van. Opt either for tapas at the bar or a full meal in the restaurant. Highly recommended. *34–36 Exmouth Market, moro.co.uk. Map p. 633, F3.*

£–££ **Quality Chop House**. A traditional Victorian chop house, set up in 1869, still with some of its original fixtures and fittings and now serving the best of British fare—crab, turbot, and, of course, chops—with a dollop of Franco-Mediterranean influence to leaven the mix. Set weekday lunches. On the edge of lively Clerkenwell. *89–93 Farringdon Rd., thequalitychophouse.com. Map p. 633, F3.*

£–££ **St John**. Proper old-style English food. Eccles cake and Lancashire cheese for pud. Oysters or soused herring to start. Real nose-to-tail eating with interesting revivals of old recipes. At three locations, in Spitalfields (*94–96 Commercial St; map p. 639, F1*); Smithfield (*26 John St; map p. 638, B1*) and Marylebone (*98 Marylebone Lane; map p. 632, C4*). The Smithfield/John Street branch occupies a former bacon smokehouse. *stjohnrestaurant.com.*

££ **64 Goodge Street**. Good-looking restaurant in Bloomsbury offering broadly French-style cuisine. Everything is carefully prepared: menus are short. *64 Goodge St., 64goodgest.co.uk. Map p. 633, D4.*

££ **The Delaunay**. Large, popular place close to the Strand and Covent Garden.

The décor and menu aims to evoke the grand cafés of Central Europe. Good value *prix-fixe* pre- and post-theatre dinners. *55 Aldwych, the delaunay.com. Map p. 636, A2.*

££ **The London Shell Co**. A handsome narrowboat, the *Prince Regent*, offers set fish and seafood dinners on board as it plies its unhurried way along the Regent's Canal from Paddington Basin (*map p. 632, A4*). A fine way to spend an evening. *À la carte* menus on the static, non-cruising *Grand Duchess* are also on offer. They also have a fishmonger's on Swain's Lane in Hampstead (*map p. 631, E3*) which doubles as a seafood bar. *londonshellco.com.*

££ **Ognisko**. Central European, mainly Polish, cuisine, in a fine building that houses the Polish Hearth Club. Enjoy an ice-cold vodka at the bar before dinner in the restaurant with its lovely old-fashioned chairs. In summer, tables are laid in the charming garden. *55 Princes Gate, ognisko.com. Map p. 634, B2.*

££ **Toklas**. Unfussily furnished warehouse-style interior, pleasant terrace, deceptively simple broadly Italian-inspired menu. Between the Strand and the Thames. *1 Surrey St., toklaslondon.com. Map p. 636, A2.*

££ **The Wolseley**. Grand *belle-époque* style café-restaurant inspired by the continental Grand Café tradition. Good, affordable food and wine. Eggs Benedict and schnitzel are signature dishes. Usually humming. *160 Piccadilly (next to the Ritz), thewolseley.com. Map p. 635, E2.* They have a sister establishment in the City (*68 King William St., map p. 639, E3*).

££–£££ **Colbert**. Long-established, popular place to eat on Sloane Square. A French-style brasserie, convincingly pulled off. Good-value *prix-fixe* menus available. *50–52 Sloane Square, colbertchelsea.com. Map p. 635, D3.*

££–£££ **45 Jermyn Street**. Elegant contemporary décor and fine contemporary food, much of it modern takes on old classics. Good value pre-theatre dinners. *45 Jermyn St., 45jermynst.com. Map p. 635, E2.*

££–£££ **J. Sheekey**. Ever since the 1890s, when a Covent Garden stallholder named Joseph Sheekey obtained a licence from Lord Salisbury to serve fish and seafood in St Martin's Court (with an understanding that he also cater Lord Salisbury's post-theatre dinners), this restaurant and oyster bar has been serving fresh fish and *fruits de mer*. *28–32 St Martin's Court, j-sheekey. co.uk. Map p. 635, F1.*

£££ **Rules**. When Thomas Rule set up his restaurant in 1798, he may not have imagined that it would still be going over two centuries later, with a top-hatted doorman posted outside. London's oldest dining establishment, in the heart of Covent Garden, serves unabashedly English fare: oysters, puddings and pies, and plenty of game in season. Numerous luminaries have eaten here. It also features in several novels. *35 Maiden Lane, rules.co.uk. Map p. 635, F1.*

£££ **Scott's**. Smart seafood restaurant with a loyal following. Perch at the bar with oysters and champagne or book a table for fine *à la carte* dining. The best of Mayfair. *20 Mount St., scotts-mayfair. com. Map p. 635, D1.*

£££ **Wild Honey**. Broadly French-style fine dining (the restaurant has one Michelin star), where Gallic *savoir faire* is brought to bear on carefully sourced British produce. Very close to the theatres of Haymarket. The pre-theatre dinner menus are excellent value. *8 Pall Mall, wildhoneystjames.co.uk. Map p. 635, F2.*

STREET FOOD AND MARKETS

One does not have to eat expensively in London. Street food is extremely popular and there are stalls and sandwich bars all over the city catering to residents, office workers and visitors at lunchtime: Leather Lane in Holborn (*map p. 638, A2*), Strutton Ground in Westminster (*map p. 635, F3*) and Petticoat Lane in Spitalfields (*map p. 639, F2*) are three examples. One fine days, public gardens and green spaces everywhere are packed with people enjoying takeaway lunches. And most churches in the City have cafés or coffee bars attached where you can get a hot drink and a simple snack. London also plays host to a large number of local farmers' markets. Here you will find stalls selling fresh, seasonal produce to householders as well as freshly-prepared food for the casual and curious visitor to eat on the spot: pies, soups, scotch eggs, sandwiches, cakes and drinks. Farmers' markets are typically held from around 9am to 1 or 2pm. The calendar varies. For details and updates, locations and maps, and to find the market nearest to where you are, see *lfm.org.uk*.

Many of London's famous produce markets, notably Covent Garden but also Spitalfields and Greenwich, now host more crafts and gifts than fresh food but Borough Market on the south side of London Bridge still goes strong (*see p. 454*).

AFTERNOON TEA

This 'quintessential' English ritual came into being in the mid-19th century, as dinner times moved later and later into the evening and something was needed to fill the gap between luncheon and the evening meal, to avoid what the 7th Duchess of Bedford referred to as 'that sinking feeling'. Nearly every luxury or boutique hotel in town now offers their version of the congenial ceremony of the teapot and the plate of bread and butter—though most now mainly concentrate on the cakestand, laden with delicate fancies, and the pot of tea is supplemented with champagne or sparkling wine. One can while away a pleasurable afternoon in the consumption of finger sandwiches, scones with cream and jam, cakes and pastries and, of course, perfectly brewed loose-leaf tea. Top hotels in which to indulge in this ritual include The Savoy (*map p. 636, A2–A3; the savoylondon.com*); the Goring on Beeston Place (*map p. 635, E3*), which opened in 1910 and is still run by the Gorings; it is the last remaining family-operated hotel in London (*thegoring.com*); Durrant's on George Street (*map p. 632, B4*), elegantly discreet and privately owned (*durrantshotel.co.uk*); the Ritz (*map p. 635, E2; the ritzlondon.com*); Brown's in Albemarle Street, Mayfair, opened by an ex-valet to Lord Byron (*map p. 635, E1; brownshotel.com*); the Landmark Hotel on Marylebone Road, which offers tea in a grand palm court (*map p. 632, B4; landmarklondon.co.uk*) and Claridge's (*map p. 635, D1; claridges.co.uk*). The last, first opened by William Claridge in 1856, has been a favourite with crowned heads, deposed crowned heads, flappers and film stars ever since. Spencer Tracy famously said he would prefer to go to Claridge's than to heaven. Another place for tea *par excellence* is Fortnum and Mason (*map p. 635, E2; fortnumandmason.com*).

For more information, more venues (including themed afternoon teas) and tips on tea-related etiquette, there is a dedicated website (*afternoontea.co.uk*). Does it, however, answer the perennially tricky question of which should be spread on one's scone first, the jam or the cream? Opinions differ.

COCKTAILS

London may not be the city that invented the cocktail but it knows how to mix them and it enjoys drinking them. Order a gin and tonic and you will be offered a dizzying array of gins to choose from as well as different types of tonic. Blue Guides favour a London gin flavoured with juniper and nothing else, and a plain, classic, not-too-sweet tonic, served with lemon or lime and not too much ice.

Some of London's best dry Martinis (the vermouth makes brief contact with the glass, and is then discarded) can be had at Duke's Hotel in St James's Place (*map p. 635, E2; dukeshotel.com*). Another fine place is the Connaught, a famous luxury hotel in Mayfair, in business since 1815. General de Gaulle set up residence here in 1940 and it now has a restaurant with three Michelin stars (Hélène Darroze at the Connaught). For cocktails, the place to head for is its bar, which regularly features in lists of the world's best cocktail bars and which has a no-reservations policy (*map p. 635, D1; the-connaught.co.uk*). The Library Bar at the Lanesborough in Belgravia (*map p. 635, D2; oetkercollection.com*), a haven of Georgian settees, leather-bound books that no one has read and oil paintings of people that nobody knows, is another fine place for a drink (the Lanesborough has its own London gin). For something less *raffiné* (and less pricey), try the Alchemist, a small chain of cocktail bars offering innovative 'molecular mixology'. There are branches in Covent Garden (St Martin's Lane; *map p. 635, F1*), at Nine Elms on the South Bank (*map p. 628, C3*) and on Bevis Marks in the City (*map p. 639, F2; thealchemist.uk.com*). In Clerkenwell, the Zetter on St John's Square also has its *aficionados* (*map p. 638, B1; thezetter.com*).

FESTIVALS & EVENTS

There are events, festivals and pageants taking place in London all the time. Some of them are held annually, others occur on a pop-up basis. To find out what is going on, take a look at any one of the following websites: *timeout.com*, *visitlondon.com*, *londontown.com* or *allinlondon.co.uk*. For a list of public holidays, see p. 588. Below is a short list of some of the best, most famous and most traditional of the annual celebrations, events and fairs hosted by the city.

State Opening of Parliament: The State Opening of Parliament is a historic ceremonial pageant in which the three constituent parts of Parliament, the Sovereign, the House of Lords and House of Commons, meet to formally begin the parliamentary year. The ceremony occurs on the first day of a new parliamentary session or soon after a general election. The King, escorted by the Household Cavalry, processes from Buckingham Palace to the Houses of Parliament. He rides in Queen Victoria's Irish State Coach behind a coach transporting the royal regalia: the Imperial State Crown, the Cap of Maintenance and the Sword of State. The procession proceeds along the Mall, through Horse Guards Parade, along Whitehall and down Parliament Street and members of Britain's armed forces 'present arms' as he passes. When he enters the Palace of Westminster through the Sovereign's Entrance, a 41-gun artillery salute is fired in Hyde Park and at the Tower of London and the Royal Standard is raised to fly over Westminster for the duration of his visit. The King proceeds to the Robing Room where he assumes the Imperial State Crown and the Robe of State before leading the Royal Procession through the Royal Gallery to the chamber of the House of Lords. Black Rod, the King's parliamentary representative, then goes to summon MPs from the House of Commons. The doors to the Commons chamber are ritually slammed in his face to symbolise the Commons' right to exclude royal messengers; the last time the Sovereign entered the House of Commons was in 1642, when

Charles I attempted to arrest five MPs. After rapping three times, the doors are opened and Black Rod leads the members of the Commons to the Lords chamber, where both houses listen to the King's speech. The speech, which he delivers from the Throne, is in actual fact written by the government and sets out its proposed parliamentary agenda for the new parliamentary session. Afterwards, trumpeters sound the King's departure, the royal standard is replaced by the Union Jack and a new parliamentary session begins. Dates vary; *parliament.uk*.

University Boat Race: The popular annual rowing contest between Oxford and Cambridge University dates from 1829 and takes place at a weekend just before Easter. The four-mile course, following the bend in the Thames from Putney Bridge to Chiswick Bridge, is thronged with spectators and the riverside pubs overflow with revellers. The race is beamed live around the world by the BBC and large TV screens are erected in Bishop's Park (Fulham) and in Furnival Gardens (Hammersmith); a festival atmosphere reigns in both these open-air venues, with pop-up stalls selling refreshments. Both crews of eight are referred to as 'blues'; Oxford's colour is dark blue and Cambridge's is light blue. The coin toss before the race determines the side of the river on which the crews start. The Fulham/Chiswick side is known as Middlesex and the Putney/Barnes side is known as Surrey, and during the race each crew must stick to their side unless they obtain a 'clear water' lead, by which they may switch station. The race is timed to start on the incoming flood tide

and the crews compete for the fastest current in the middle of the river; if the boats become dangerously close and their blades look as though they might clash, the teams incur the wrath of the umpire, who warningly booms 'Oxford' or 'Cambridge' through the megaphone. The main race is preceded by the two competing reserve crews, Isis (Oxford) and Goldie (Cambridge). March or April; *theboatrace.org*.

Chelsea Flower Show: Britain's most prestigious annual flower show has been held in the grounds of the Royal Hospital, Chelsea since 1913. Organised by the Royal Horticultural Society, it is held over four or five days in May; members of the Royal Family attend the opening. British and international gardeners and horticulturalists compete for a range of prize medals. One of the most famous categories is the prize for the most original show garden. May; *rhs. org.uk*.

Trooping the Colour: This pageant is held every June on Horse Guards Parade as a public and official celebration of the King's birthday. The phrase 'trooping the colour' has its origins in ancient military tradition when the colours—flags—of regiments were used as rallying points on the battlefield. Thus it was vital for every soldier to recognise his colour, and to ensure he did so, ceremonies were held in which the colours of the regiment were processed—trooped— slowly down the ranks for all to see. Today's ceremony starts at approx. 11am, when the monarch and other members of the Royal Family process in carriages and on horseback from Buckingham Palace down Whitehall to Horse Guards Parade. The King is greeted by a royal salute, after which Foot Guards and the Household Cavalry perform a musical troop on the parade ground. The Sovereign rides or is driven in a carriage back to Buckingham Palace at the head of the Household Division and joins his family on the balcony of the palace to watch an RAF fly-past. June; *trooping-the-colour.co.uk*.

Wimbledon Lawn Tennis Championships: The prestigious international two-week tennis championships, held each summer, is the oldest tennis tournament in the world and the only remaining tennis championship to be held on grass. A quintessentially British affair, it has been held at the All England Club since 1877. Players abide by a strict all-white dress code—and if the King or the Prince of Wales is watching from the Royal Box, players are expected to bow or curtsey before play. Spectators gorge on strawberries and cream and nationalistically get behind the British underdog (Andy Murray won the men's singles title in 2013; the last British woman to win the singles title was Virginia Wade in 1977). Office workers find excuses to be off work in order to watch the BBC's live, back-to-back coverage. Play is often suspended due to the notoriously changeable British weather: Centre Court now has had a retractable roof which is closed when raining. June–July; *wimbledon.com*.

The Proms: The 'Promenade Concerts', always known as the Proms, are a festival of summer Classical music held at the Royal Albert Hall and in Hyde Park. They have been running since 1895, when they were founded by the impresario Robert Newman, who hired Henry Wood as conductor. Mid-July–mid-Sept; *bbc.co.uk/proms*.

Notting Hill Carnival: From small beginnings in 1965, this has risen to become Europe's biggest street party (*for details, see p. 318 and nhcarnival.org*). Aug.

Pearly Kings and Queens Harvest Festival: The London Pearly Kings and Queens Society Costermongers Harvest Festival Parade is the flagship event of London's Pearly royalty, usually held on the last Sunday in Sept. 'Pearlys' (*see p. 53*) from all London's boroughs dress up in their best mother-of-pearl finery and congregate in Guildhall Yard, where from 1pm traditional Cockney entertainment takes place. They then process, accompanied by marching bands, City dignitaries and donkeys and dogcarts laden with autumn produce, from the Guildhall to St Mary-le-Bow Church for a Harvest Festival service at 3pm. The event is free to the public but all donations go to charity. Sept; *pearlysociety.co.uk*.

London Open House: An annual event whereby members of the public may visit buildings, institutions and gardens that are otherwise closed. It is a fantastic way to get to see inside many of London's shuttered or secret architectural gems, free of charge. Buildings that have been opened in previous years include the Gherkin, the Foreign Office and 10 Downing Street, as well as many private houses. Usually held in Sept; *open-city.org.uk*.

Turner Prize: An exhibition of works by the four artists shortlisted for this prestigious contemporary art prize is hosted at Tate Britain, usually from Oct until shortly after the announcement of the winner in Dec. The prize was set up in 1984, to be awarded to any British artist under 50 whose output over the past year has been judged outstanding. The age restriction was lifted in 2017. The show always tries to raise eyebrows (its efforts to do so can sometimes seem predictable). Oct–early Jan.

The **Frieze London** contemporary art fair takes place in the first half of Oct in Regent's Park (*frieze.com*).

Bonfire Night: *'Remember, remember the fifth of November, Gunpowder, treason, and plot. I see no reason why gunpowder treason should ever be forgot.'* So runs the old rhyme. This annual event, held on 5th Nov, historically celebrates a failed attempt on the life of James I when a group of English Catholics planned to blow up the House of Lords during the State Opening of Parliament on 5th Nov 1605. After the so-called 'Gunpowder Plot' was discovered and foiled, Guy Fawkes, who was in charge of the explosives, and several of his co-conspirators, were hung, drawn and quartered. Thereafter, 5th Nov became a day of public commemoration and in communities across Britain schoolchildren would make an effigy of Fawkes, known as 'the Guy', to be ritually burned on a public bonfire. Today, very few bonfires are lit due to health and safety regulations but the event is marked by a series of impressive public firework displays held on the Sat nearest to Nov 5. The displays in Battersea Park are recommended. Nov.

Remembrance Sunday: Remembrance Sunday, the second Sunday in November, is when the nation remembers all those who have given their lives in defence of their country. A National Service of Remembrance is held at the Cenotaph in Whitehall, where a wreath is laid by The King. Members of the Cabinet, Opposition Party leaders, former Prime Ministers and certain other ministers and the Mayor of London are invited to attend, as are representatives of the Armed Forces, Merchant Navy, Air and Fishing Fleets, and members of faith communities. High Commissioners from Commonwealth countries also attend the ceremony and lay tributes. Sunday nearest to 11th Nov.

Lord Mayor's Show: Steeped in 800 years of history, this is one of London's premier pageants, usually held on a Saturday in early Nov. The newly elected Lord Mayor (*see p. 19*), accompanied by a procession over three miles long, processes from the City to Westminster where he or she swears allegiance to the Crown. The procession starts out at approximately 11am from Mansion House and makes its way, via St Paul's Cathedral, to the Royal Courts of Justice. It returns via the Embankment between 1–2.30pm. Afterwards fireworks are held on the river. Check website for details of the Lord Mayor's flotilla, an ancient part of the ceremony, which has recently been reintroduced. Nov; *lordmayorshow.org*.

New Year's Eve: Hordes of revellers line the banks of the Thames around Westminster, the South Bank and beyond, in anticipation of Britain's biggest and most spectacular fireworks display, which heralds the New Year after Big Ben tolls midnight. Afterwards the crowd comes together for a rendition of *Auld Lang Syne*. Space is very limited; it is recommended to plan well in advance and check for road, bridge, station, and Tube closures. The restaurants and bars along the South Bank usually have private viewing platforms and pedestrian access is restricted to diners; again, book well in advance. 31st Dec; *london.gov.uk*.

GENERAL INFORMATION

CHOOSING A SEASON

London is always crowded, particularly in the summer, when visitor numbers swell; and during school holidays and half terms, when long queues can form outside the more popular museums. The weather is famously changeable. Winter can be relentlessly raw and damp, summers disappointingly cool and wet. Crisp, sunny days in spring and autumn are the finest, when Constable-like formations of clouds scud across a bright blue sky and the green of the many parks and trees is truly glorious. Whatever the weather, though, there is never a shortage of things to keep the visitor to London entertained.

EMERGENCIES

For all emergencies, whether you require an ambulance, a fire engine or a police officer, T: 999: the switchboard will coordinate the help you need.

MUSEUMS AND GALLERIES

Many of London's finest and most famous museums can be visited free of charge: the British Museum, National Gallery, National Portrait Gallery, V&A, Natural History Museum and Science Museum are all examples. The same is true of most churches (though not all; the ticket prices for Westminster Abbey and St Paul's Cathedral are particularly hefty). Opening times for museums, galleries and other institutions all vary and are always subject to change; you should always check the website before you visit. This is particularly true of locations in high demand for official or corporate functions (the Royal Palaces are a good example). Tickets, if required, can almost always be purchased online.

OPENING HOURS

London is a city that seldom truly sleeps and most shops and restaurants are open all day, every day. For museums and other attractions, check the website before you visit. Parks are generally open from around 8am until dusk.

PUBLIC HOLIDAYS

England has relatively few public holidays and there is no National Day. Even on the days which are designated holidays, you will find that most shops, restaurants and major museums remain open. The curiously unhistoric-sounding tradition of the 'Bank Holiday', when banks were indeed closed, began in 1871. There are four of these, always occurring on a Monday so as to create a long weekend. Public holidays in England are as follows:

1st January	New Year's Day
Good Friday	(the Friday before Easter)
Easter Monday	Easter Bank Holiday
1st Monday in May	May Day Bank Holiday
Last Monday in May	Spring Bank Holiday
Last Monday in August	August Bank Holiday
25th December	Christmas Day
26th December	Boxing Day

SHOPPING

Napoleon might have sneered when he spoke of the British as a 'nation of shopkeepers', but London understands retail like nowhere else on the planet. The customer's convenience is paramount and endlessly attended to. Shops are open every day and sometimes well into the night; convenience stores abound; all manner of items are stocked under a single roof making one-stop shopping easy and normal; shop assistants leave you to browse on your own (but are available to help when required); no one minds if you leave without purchasing anything; and the quality of what is on offer is phenomenal: portable goods from every corner of the globe are available in this city. London is tirelessly and expertly commercial in its instincts.

The best-known **shopping districts** are St James's, with its traditional gentlemen's outfitters (*see p. 251*); Knightsbridge, which is home to Harrods, Harvey Nichols and Peter Jones (*see pp. 344–5 and 349*) and the King's Road. Regent Street and Bond Street are also filled with shops. Oxford Street, once home to a grand and glamorous enfilade of department stores, is still crowded and popular but it is tawdrier than it was and many of the shops are just branches of national or international chains, giving it something of the monotony of an ordinary provincial high street. The rise of online retail has made a big difference to footfall everywhere, but London is still a shopping city and every district has its shops, boutiques and malls. Quirky one-offs are still to be found, for example the splendid James Smith & Sons umbrella seller near the British Museum (*see p. 369*).

London is also home to a burgeoning number of **street markets**. The genuine bargains, cutting-edge fashions and plethora of individual traders have departed from Portobello Road, Carnaby Street and Covent Garden, whose names have become too famous now to sustain any kind of haphazard originality. However, there still are plenty of markets where it is fun to browse. These are mentioned in the text of this guide and for handy reference, are listed in the index.

THEATRES AND THEATRE TICKETS

The demand for tickets to West End shows is always high and competitive. One can buy direct from the theatre box office websites or via various general websites such as

Time Out (*timeout.com/london*), Lastminute (*lastminute.com/site/entertainment/theatre*), Ticket Master (*ticketmaster.co.uk*) or from the TKTS booth in Leicester Square (*map p. 603, F1*), which also offers tickets for selected shows at half-price or discounted rates (*see tkts.co.uk*). If you haven't booked anything in advance and feel like seeing a show, it is worth going along to see what is available. It is a good way to be spontaneous in a city where high demand makes spontaneity difficult.

To find out what's on, *Time Out* is probably the best source of listings information (*see website above*). Another good website, particularly for those less familiar with the city, is *visitlondon.com*.

TIPPING

Tipping is less bountiful in Britain than in North America. In restaurants the bill now increasingly includes service: always check whether this is the case before leaving a tip. If not, it is—or was—customary to leave the equivalent of ten percent of the total on the table to convey appreciation, although so many places now no longer accept cash that the practice of tipping in this way is atrophying. It is more usual to ask for the tip to be added to what you are paying by card. Taxi-drivers are very happy to be tipped but it is not automatically expected and it is fine just to round up the fare. In hotels, porters who show you to your room and help with your luggage will appreciate a small token of thanks.

VISITOR CARDS

The **London Pass**, a visitor card valid for 1, 2, 3 4, 5, 6, 7 or 10 days, allows free entrance to a number of top sights, including Westminster Abbey, Shakespeare's Globe, the Tower of London, London Zoo and Hampton Court. It is available either with or without a free travel pass on top. There are different prices for adults' and children's cards. Passes can also be bought online and shipped to you ahead of your trip. For details, see *londonpass.com*.

GLOSSARY OF TERMS

Annunciate, of the Virgin, shown receiving the news that she is to bear the Son of God

Anodised, treated with an electrolysing process to increase durability and resist corrosion

Anthemion (pl. anthemia), type of decoration originating in ancient Greece, resembling leaf or honeysuckle fronds fanning out from a central stem

Apulian, from Puglia, southern Italy

Architecture terrible, style recommended by the 18th-century French architect J.F. Blondel as suitable for prisons or houses of correction, for its dour and forbidding aspect

Architrave, the horizontal beam placed above supporting columns, the lowest part of an entablature (*qv*); the horizontal lintel above a door or window

Archivolt, moulded architrave carried round an arch

Art Deco Stylised, often geometric art and architecture of the 1920s and '30s

Art Moderne 'Machine Age' art, a 'poor man's Art Deco', stylised and geometric, of the late 1920s and '30s

Art Nouveau design style originating in the late 19th century, curving and feminine, asymmetrical, making use of floral motifs, leaves and vine tendrils

Arts and Crafts, design movement originating in the late 19th century emphasising handicrafts and artisanal workmanship, a reaction to the growth in mass production

Atlantes, sculpted figures of the god Atlas, used as supporting columns

Baldachin, canopy supported by columns or other uprights

Basilica, originally a Roman building used for public administration; in Christian architecture, an aisled church with a clerestory (*qv*) and apse

Bas-relief, sculpture in low relief

Bauhaus, design school founded by Walter Gropius which came to be associated with clear, clean, austere Rationalism

Boss, carved or otherwise decorated block at the join of two vault ribs

Caduceus, the staff of Hermes/Mercury, a winged rod with snakes twining around it

Canopic jar, ancient Egyptian urn used to preserve the entrails of the mummified deceased

Canted, inclined, oblique, slanted

Capital, the top or head of a column

Capitolium, in the Roman world, a temple dedicated to the 'Capitoline triad': Jupiter, Juno and Minerva

Capriccio, an artistic fantasy or caprice, typically a townscape incorporating buildings from different cities

Caryatid, supporting column in the form of a sculpted female figure

Cenotaph, literally 'empty tomb', a monument to someone whose body is lost or buried elsewhere

Champlevé, metalwork technique whereby elements of a design are scraped hollow, then filled with enamel before firing

Chancel, part of a church to the liturgical east of the crossing (*qv*), where the clergy officiate

Chiaroscuro, distribution of light and shade in a painting

Cloisonné, type of enamel decoration, where areas of colour are partitioned by narrow strips of metal

Clerestory, upper part of the nave wall of a church, above the side aisles, with windows

Coade Stone, artificial stone formerly manufactured at Lambeth (*see p. 466*)

Composite, order of architecture combining elements of the Corinthian and Ionic

Corinthian, ancient Greek and Roman order of architecture, a characteristic of which is the column capital decorated with sculpted acanthus leaves

Cosmati, Cosmatesque, decorative geometric inlay originating in 12th-century Rome, using pieces of stone and coloured glass to cover floors and other surfaces

Couchant, heraldic term to describe a beast as lying down

Cove, in a ceiling, concave ornamental moulding applied at the point where the ceiling and the wall meet

Crenellated, of a wall or parapet, indented with alternate crenels (the indented sections) and merlons (the sticking-up sections), so as to form a battlement

Crossing, the part of a church where the nave (central aisle) and transepts (side arms) meet

Curtain wall, a non-load-bearing wall, essentially an infill or screen between supporting piers or partitions

Decorated, late 13th–14th-century style of Gothic architecture characterised by rich, flowing tracery (*qv*)

De Stijl, the spare, geometric art and aesthetic of an avant-garde group of early 20th-century Dutch artists, among them Mondrian and Theo van Doesburg

Diaper, decorative style, particularly of brickwork, consisting in repeated geometric patterns of lozenges

Dissolution, in English history, this refers to the Dissolution of the Monasteries, the closure of religious houses orchestrated by Henry VIII between 1536 and 1541, after he had broken with the Church of Rome. Henry used the appropriated assets of the monasteries and convents to fund his military campaigns

Doric, ancient Greek order of architecture characterised by fluted columns with no base, and a plain capital

Entablature, the continuous horizontal element above the capital (consisting of architrave, frieze and cornice) of a Classical or Neoclassical building

Early English, Gothic architectural style of the 12th–13th centuries characterised by lancet (narrow, single-aperture, pointed) windows without tracery or plain Y-shaped tracery

Easter sepulchre, tomb recess in a church reserved for the ritual 'burial' of Christ in medieval Good Friday services

Evangelists, the writers of the gospels, Matthew, Mark, Luke and John, often represented in art by their symbols: a man's head, a lion, a bull and an eagle

Exedra, recessed area projecting from a room, a large alcove

Faïence, glazed decorative earthenware or terracotta, named after the town of Faenza, Italy, where it originated

Flemish bond, style of brickwork where the bricks in each row (course) are placed alternately long-short-long

Gordon Riots, several days of mayhem in 1780, when prominent buildings, including the Bank of England, were attacked, arson was rife and prisons were broken open. The uproar takes its name from Lord George Gordon, head of an association of Protestants who feared that new legislation aimed at emancipating Catholics would lead to the infiltration of Catholics into Establishment bodies where they could foment treason

Greek cross, cross with vertical and transverse arms of equal length

Grisaille, painting in tones of grey

Grotesque, grotesques (*grottesche*), painted or stucco decoration in the style of that discovered during the Renaissance in Nero's Golden House in Rome, then underground, hence the name, from 'grotto'. The delicate ornament usually includes patterns of flowers, sphinxes, birds, human figures etc, against a light ground

Guild church, a church that has no parish to care for but whose duties instead involve ministering to a non-resident congregation. A number of churches in the City of London are guild churches

Hammerbeam, type of roofing where the rafters are supported on short projecting struts

Hexastyle, having six columns

Inflected, of an arch, curving inwards before its point, a style much seen in Gothic and Moorish architecture

Ionic, an order of Classical architecture identified by its capitals decorated with volutes (scrolls)

Intarsia, inlay of wood, marble or metal

Krater, large ancient Greek vessel for mixing wine and water

Latin cross, cross where the vertical arm is longer than the transverse arm

Lierne, kind of ribbing in a vault producing an intense veined pattern, with ribs running out from each other

Listed, of a building, indicating that it has been placed on the roster of national monuments

Lost wax, method of metal casting whereby a mould is made around a wax model, which is then melted away so that molten metal can be poured in

Lunette, semicircular space in a vault or ceiling, often decorated with a painting or relief

Mascaron, decorative element in the form of a carved head or face

Mews, street of low-rise buildings behind larger townhouses, comprising former coach houses and stables

Misericord, decorated wooden block attached to the underside of the seat in a choir stall, against which choristers can lean for support during long periods of standing. From the Latin word for mercy

Norman, the name given to the Romanesque (*qv*) architecture of Normandy and Britain

Oculus, round window or other aperture

Ogee, of an arch, shaped in a double curve, concave above and convex below

Opus sectile, mosaic or paving of thin coloured marble slabs cut in geometric shapes

Oriel, a window projecting from an upper storey

Palladian, of architecture, pertaining to the ideas of Andrea Palladio (1508–80), whose airy, geometric, symmetrical forms sought to revive the architecture of ancient Rome

Pediment, gable above the portico of a classical building; also above a window, either triangular in form or curved (segmental)

Pendentive, concave spandrel (*qv*)beneath one of the four 'corners' of a dome

Perpendicular, 14th–15th-century style of Gothic architecture characterised by long horizontal and vertical elements dividing traceried panes

Pier, a square or compound pillar used as a support in architecture

Pilaster, shallow pier or rectangular column projecting only slightly from the wall

Pietre dure, hard or semi-precious stones, cut and inlaid to decorate cabinets, table-tops, etc.

Porphyry, an extremely hard, dark blue or purplish igneous rock

Putto (pl. putti), sculpted or painted figure, usually nude, of a baby boy

Quatrefoil, four-lobed

Quire, part of a cathedral reserved for the

singers, usually with stalls. Also written 'choir'

Quoins, from the French *coin* (corner), stones placed in courses at the outer corners of buildings

Ragstone, irregularly shaped blocks of hard grey limestone used as a facing

Rebus, a badge or device which indicates the surname of its user by means of a pun

Reredos, panel or screen behind an altar, which may stand alone or be part of a larger retable (*qv*)

Retable, screen behind an altar, often a frame or setting for the reredos

Rococo, frothy, highly ornamented design style of the 18th-century

Romanesque, architecture of the Western (not Byzantine) Empire of the 7th–12th centuries, preceding the Gothic. In England it is often known as Norman

Rood-screen, a screen below the Rood or Crucifix, dividing the nave from the chancel in a church

Royal peculiar, a place of worship under the jurisdiction of the sovereign instead of that of a bishop

Rustication, the grooves or channels cut at the joints between huge blocks of facing masonry (ashlar)

Scagliola, a material made from selenite, used to imitate marble or *pietre dure* (*qv*)

Sedilia, recessed bank of seats with stone canopies, for officiating clergy

Serlian window, tripartite window with a taller, arched central section flanked by two flat-topped apertures of lesser height

Sgraffito, decorative plasterwork whereby two-tone designs are etched onto a surface

Soffit, the underside of an arch

Spandrel, surface between two arches in an arcade or the triangular space on either side of an arch

Squint, angled aperture cut in the chancel wall to allow a sightline to the altar

Starling, bulwark around the piers of a bridge

Stoup, vessel for Holy Water, usually near the entrance of a church

Tessera (pl. tesserae), small cube of marble, glass, etc. used in mosaic work

Tondo (pl. tondi), a painting or sculpture in the form of a roundel

Tracery, system of carved and moulded ribs within a window aperture dividing it into patterned sections

Transenna, open grille or screen, usually of marble, in an early Christian church

Transept, the side arm of a church leading to right (liturgical south) or left (liturgical north) of the nave

Trefoil, decorated or moulded with three leaf or lobe shapes

Triforium, upper-level arcaded aisle, below the clerestory

Triton, a sea god

Trompe l'oeil, literally, a deception of the eye: illusionist decoration, painted architectural perspectives, etc.

Tuscan, plain order of architecture with an unfluted column rising from a base to an simple, unornamented capital

Tympanum, the area between the top of a doorway and the arch above it or the triangular space enclosed by the pediment

Ushabti, figurine from an ancient Egyptian tomb intended to perform manual tasks for the deceased in the afterlife

Verde antico, a green marble from Thessaly in Greece

Vermiculated, carved with a wormlike design

Vitrolite, opaque glass used as a structural component, typical of Art Deco

Volute, tightly curled spiral scroll

Waterloo church 'Waterloo' churches were part of a government moral improvements scheme inspired by the wave of national optimism that followed Wellington's victory over the French in 1815.

KINGS & QUEENS OF ENGLAND

HOUSE OF WESSEX

Edward the Confessor 1042–66
Harold II 1066 (killed in battle)

HOUSES OF NORMANDY–BLOIS

William I (the Conqueror) 1066–87
William II (Rufus) 1087–1100
Henry I (Beauclerk) 1100–35
Stephen 1135–54

HOUSE OF PLANTAGENET

Henry II 1154–89
Richard I (Coeur de Lion) 1189–99
John 1199–1216
Henry III 1216–72
Edward I 1272–1307
Edward II 1307–27
Edward III 1327–77
Richard II 1377–99 (deposed)
Henry IV 1399–1413
Henry V 1413–22
Henry VI 1422–61
Edward IV 1461–83
Edward V 1483 (?murdered)
Richard III 1483–5 (killed in battle)

HOUSE OF TUDOR

Henry VII 1485–1509
Henry VIII 1509–47
Edward VI 1547–53
Lady Jane Grey July 1553
(reigned 9 days, executed 1554)
Mary I 1553–8
Elizabeth I 1558–1603

HOUSE OF STUART

James I (James VI of Scotland) 1603–25
Charles I 1625–49 (beheaded)

INTERREGNUM: PROTECTORATE OF CROMWELL

HOUSE OF STUART (RESTORED)

Charles II 1660–85
James II 1685–9 (deposed)
William III and Mary II 1689–1702
and 1689–94
Anne 1702–14

HOUSE OF HANOVER

George I 1714–27
George II 1727–60
George III 1760–1820
George IV 1820–30 (Regent from 1811)
William IV 1830–7

HOUSE OF SAXE-COBURG GOTHA

Victoria 1837–1901
Edward VII 1901–10

HOUSE OF WINDSOR

George V 1910–36
Edward VIII 1936 (abdicated)
George VI 1936–52
Elizabeth II 1952–2022
Charles III 2022–

INDEX

Numbers in bold are major references. Numbers in italics refer to illustrations. Museums and galleries are listed under 'Museums', not by individual name.

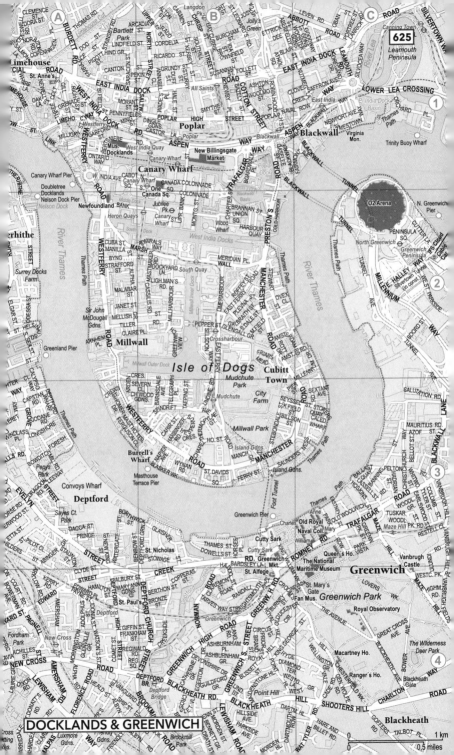

DOCKLANDS & GREENWICH

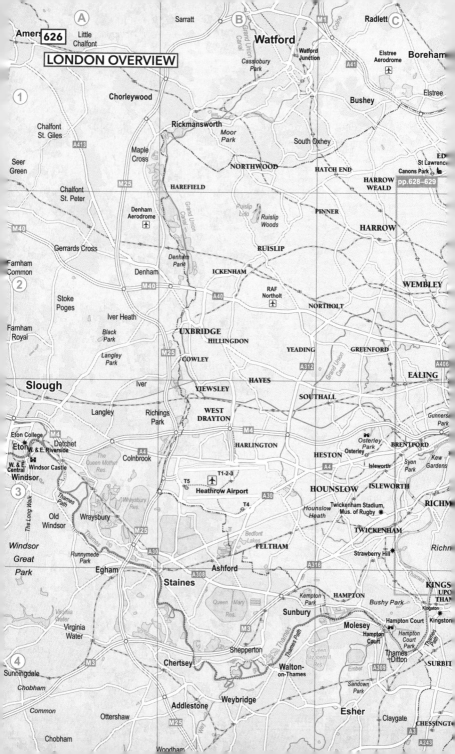

626

Amer. 626

A B C

Sarratt
Little Chalfont
Watford
Radlett
Boreham

Watford Junction
Elstree Aerodrome
Elstree

1

Chorleywood
Bushey

Rickmansworth
South Oxhey

Chalfont St. Giles
Moor Park

Seer Green

Maple Cross
NORTHWOOD
HATCH END
ED
St Lawrence
Canons Park
HARROW WEALD

pp.628–629

Chalfont St. Peter
HAREFIELD
RUISLIP
Lido
Ruislip Woods
PINNER

Denham Aerodrome
HARROW

Gerrards Cross
Denham Park
ICKENHAM

2

Farnham Common
RAF Northolt
WEMBLEY

Stoke Poges
Denham
NORTHOLT

Iver Heath
UXBRIDGE
HILLINGDON
YEADING
GREENFORD

Farnham Royal
Black Park
COWLEY
EALING

Langley Park

Slough
Iver
HAYES
SOUTHALL

VIEWSLEY

Langley
Richings Park
WEST DRAYTON

Eton College
W. & E. Riverside
Datchet
Colnbrook

Eton
W & E Central
Windsor Castle
The Queen Mother Res.
HARLINGTON
HESTON
Osterley Park
Osterley
BRENTFORD

Windsor
T5
T1-2-3
Heathrow Airport
Isleworth
Syon Park
Kew Gardens

3

Old Windsor
Wraysbury Res.
T4
HOUNSLOW
ISLEWORTH
RICH

Wraysbury
Hounslow Heath
Twickenham Stadium, Mus. of Rugby
RICHM

Thames Path
The Long Walk

Windsor Great Park
Runnymede Park
Egham
Ashford
FELTHAM
Bedfont Lakes
TWICKENHAM
Strawberry Hill

Virginia Water

Virginia Water
Staines
Queen Mary Res.
A316
KINGS UPO THAM

Sunbury
Kempton Park
HAMPTON
Bushy Park
Kingston

4

Sunningdale
Shepperton
Queen Elizabeth II Res.
Hampton Court
Molesey
Hampton Court
Hampton Court Park
Kingston

Chobham
Chertsey
Walton-on-Thames
Sandown Park
Ember
Thames Ditton
SURBI

Common
Addlestone
Weybridge
Esher
Claygate
CHESSINGT

Ottershaw

Chobham
Woodham

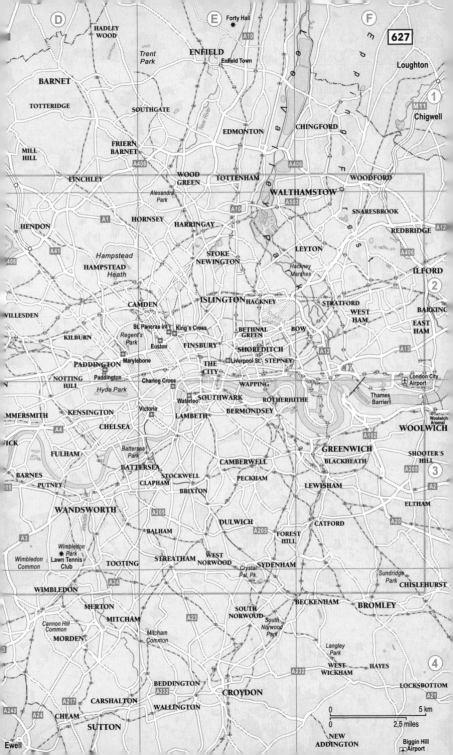

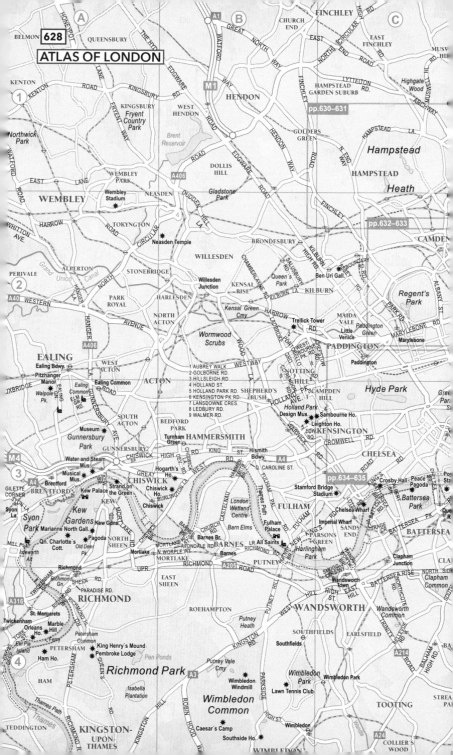

ATLAS OF LONDON

BELMON | QUEENSBURY | HONEYPOT LA. | THE HYDE | A1 | B | FINCHLEY | CHURCH END | EAST FINCHLEY | EAST FINCHLEY | MUSW HI | C

pp.630–631

pp.632–633

KENTON | KENTON ROAD | KINGSBURY ROAD | WEST HENDON | M1 | HENDON | NORTH CIRCULAR RD. | NORTH END RD. | ARCHWAY | Highgate Wood

Northwick Park | Fryent Country Park | Brent Reservoir | EDGWARE RD. | HENDON WAY | HAMPSTEAD GARDEN SUBURB | LYTTELTON RD. | N. END WAY | Hampstead

WATFORD RD. | EAST LANE | TRENT WAY | KINGSBURY | DOLLIS HILL | WEMBLEY PARK | A406 | GOLDERS GREEN | HAMPSTEAD LA. | Hampstead Heath

WEMBLEY | HARROW ROAD | TOKYNGTON | Wembley Stadium | NEASDEN | DUDDEN HILL LA. | Gladstone Park | HENDON WAY | FINCHLEY RD. | CAMDEN

WHITTON AVE. | PERIVALE | CIRCULAR RD. | ★ Neasden Temple | BRONDESBURY | KILBURN HIGH RD. | Regent's Park

A40 WESTERN | ALPERTON | STONEBRIDGE | WILLESDEN | Willesden Junction | KENSAL RISE | Queen's Park | SALUSBURY RD. | Ben Uri Gall. ★ | BOUNDARY RD. | MAIDA VALE | REGENT'S PARK RD. | ALBANY ST.

Grand Union Canal | HANGER LANE | NORTH CIRCULAR | PARK ROYAL | HARLESDEN | Kensal Green Cmy. | HARROW RD. | LADBROKE RD. | KILBURN LA. | KILBURN | Little Venice | Paddington Green | MARYLEBONE RD.

A406 | HANGER AVENUE | NORTH ACTON | Wormwood Scrubs | WOOD LANE | Trellick Tower ★ | MAIDA VALE | Marylebone | PADDINGTON | Paddington

EALING | Ealing Bdwy. | WEST ACTON | ACTON | WESTWAY | 1 AUBREY WALK | NOTTING HILL | Hyde Park | Gre Par

Pitzhanger Manor | Ealing Common | Ealing Common | 2 GOLBORNE RD. | 3 HILLSLEIGH RD. | 4 HOLLAND ST. | 5 HOLLAND PARK RD. | SHEPHERD'S BUSH | HOLLAND PK. AVE. | CAMPDEN HILL

Walpole Pk. ★ | GUNNERSBURY AVE. | SOUTH ACTON | BEDFORD PARK | 6 KENSINGTON PK RD. | 7 LANSDOWNE CRES. | 8 LEDBURY RD. | 9 WALMER RD. | Holland Park | Holland Park Design Mus. ★ Sambourne Ho. | Leighton Ho.

Museum ★ | Gunnersbury Park | GUNNERSBURY | CHISWICK | Turnham Green | HAMMERSMITH | KING ST. | H/smith Bdwy | WARWICK RD. | EDW. | KENSINGTON | CHELSEA | KING'S

M4 | Water and Steam Mus. | HIGH RD. | WEST | Hogarth's Ho. | FULHAM | Q. CAROLINE ST. | A4 | CROMWELL RD. | pp.634–635

GILETTE CORNER | A4 | Musical Mus. | GREAT | CHISWICK | Chiswick Ho. | BURLINGTON | London Wetland Centre | Stamford Bridge Stadium | Crosby Hall • Peace Pagoda | Po St

Brentford | Strand-on the Green | WEST | Chiswick | Thames Path | Barn Elms | Chelsea Wharf | Chelsea Wharf | Battersea Park | Que

Syon La. | BRENTFORD | Kew Palace ★ | KEW | Chiswick | CASTELNAU | Barnes Br. | Fulham Palace | Imperial Wharf | SANDS END | BATTERSEA

Syon Park | Marianne North Gall. ★ | Kew Gdns. ★ | Kew Gardens | NORTH SHEEN | CHURCH RD. | Barnes Br. | FULHAM RD. | KING'S RD. | Hurlingham Park | BATTERSEA PK. RD. | Clapham Junction

Qn. Charlotte's Cott. ★ | Pagoda ★ | Old Deer Pk | MORTLAKE | N. WORPLE WAY | Barnes | LR All Saints | PARSONS GREEN | BATTERSEA RISE | NORTH SIDE | CLA

MILL PLAT | Isleworth Ait | Richmond | Mortlake | RICHMOND ROAD | A205 | PUTNEY | Wandsworth Town | Clapham Common

Richmond Gn. | SHEEN | RD. | EAST SHEEN | UPR | RICHMOND | PUTNEY HILL | WANDSWORTH | Wandsworth Common

A316 | Twickenham | PARADISE RD. | RICHMOND | ROEHAMPTON | WEST HILL | HIGH ST. | TRINITY RD. | A214

St. Margarets | Orleans Ho. ★ | Marble Hill ★ | Petersham Common | King Henry's Mound | Putney Heath | SOUTHFIELDS | EARLSFIELD

YORK ★ | Eel Pie Island | ★ Fury | PETERSHAM | Pembroke Lodge ★ | Pen Ponds | KINGSTON RD. | Southfields | GARRATT LANE | BALHAM HIGH RD. | BA

Ham Ho. ★ | HAM | Richmond Park | Putney Vale Cmy. ★ | Wimbledon Park ★ | Wimbledon Park | A3 | Wimbledon Park | Lawn Tennis Club

Thames Path | Isabella Plantation | Wimbledon Common | Wimbledon | TOOTING | STREA A

KINGSTON-UPON-THAMES | Caesar's Camp ★ | Southside Ho. ★ | Wimbledon | A24 | COLLIER'S WOOD

TEDDINGTON | Thames | ROBIN HOOD LA. | KINGSTON HILL | HIGH ST. | WIMBLEDON

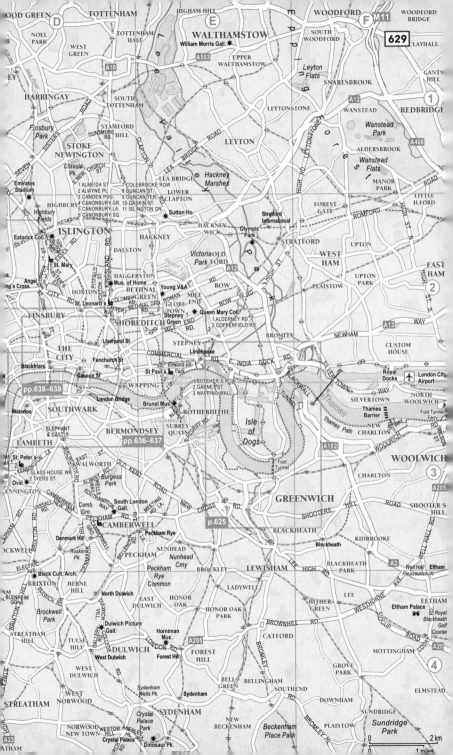

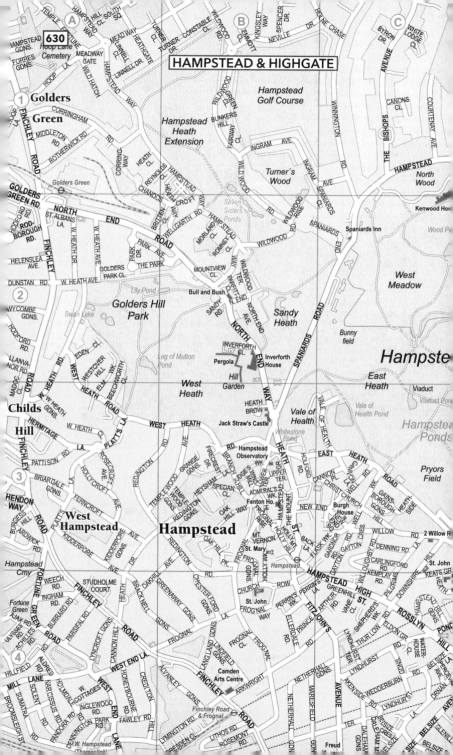

HAMPSTEAD & HIGHGATE

630

Grid references: A, B, C (columns) and 1, 2, 3, 4 (rows)

Golders Green (A1)

HAMPSTEAD GDNS. — TEMPLE FORTUNE HILL — HAMPSTEAD WAY — HOOP LANE Cemetery — MEADWAY GATE — MEADWAY — LINNELL DR. — LINNELL CL. — MELNMEL — HEATHGATE — WILDWOOD RD. — TURNER CL. — TURNER DR. — CONSTABLE WK. — WILDWOOD RD. — GREEN — MEMMOTT — KINGSLEY WAY — NEVILLE DR. — SPENCER DR. — BOURNE CHASE — BYRON DR. — WHITE LODGE CL.

Hampstead Golf Course

CANONS CL. — COURTENAY AVE. — THE BISHOPS AVE.

FORRES GDNS. — FINCHLEY ROAD — CORRINGHAM RD. — MIDDLETON RD. — ROTHERWICK RD. — CORRINGHAM RD. — WILD HATCH — HEATH CL. — REYNOLDS CL. — HAMPSTEAD WAY — HEATH CROFT — BRUTTEN — WELLGARTH RD. — HAMPSTEAD WAY — MORLAND CL. — ROMNEY RD. — FAIRWAY — BUNKERS HILL — INGRAM AVE. — WILDWOOD RD. — INGRAM AVE. — WINNINGTON RD. — SPANIARDS END

Hampstead Heath Extension

Turner's Wood

North Wood

Seven Sisters Ponds — WILDWOOD RISE — WILDWOOD RD. — SPANIARDS RD. — Spaniards Inn

Kenwood House — Wood Pk.

GOLDERS GREEN RD. — NORTH END — ROAD — ST. ALBANS LA. — W. HEATH DR. — W. HEATH AVE. — PARK DR. — PARK CL. — THE PARK — CHANDOS — HEATH CL. — MOUNTVIEW CL. — WILDWOOD TER. — PROFFIT — N. END — NORTH END AVE. — Bull and Bush — SANDY RD.

West Meadow

RODBOROUGH RD. — BO — HELENSLEA AVE. — DUNSTAN RD. — FINCHLEY ROAD — GOLDERS PARK CL. — Lily Pond

Golders Hill Park

Sandy Heath — Bunny field

Hampste...

WYCOMBE GDNS. — HODFORD RD. — LLANVANOR RD. — MADOC CL. — EDEN CL. — WESTOVER HILL — BEECHWORTH CL. — Swan Lake — Leg of Mutton Pond — INVERFORTH CL. — Pergola — Inverforth House — Hill Garden — NORTH END WAY

East Heath — Viaduct — Viaduct Pond

Childs Hill

HERMITAGE LA. — W. HEATH GDNS. — W. HEATH CL. — PLATT'S LA. — WEST HEATH ROAD — WEST HEATH AVE. — West Heath — HEATH BROW — Jack Straw's Castle — Vale of Health — Whitestone Pond — Vale of Health Pond

Hampstead Ponds

PATTISON RD. — BRIARDALE GDNS. — FINCHLEY ROAD — ROSECROFT AVE. — HOLLYCROFT AVE. — REDINGTON RD. — TEMPLEWOOD AVE. — TEMPLEWOOD GDNS. — GRANGE GDNS. — FIRECREST DR. — BRANCH HILL — JUDGE'S WK. — ADMIRAL'S WK. — UPPER TER. — HEATH — HOLFORD RD. — EAST HEATH ROAD — Pryors Field

HENDON WAY — BURGESS HILL — FERNCROFT AVE. — **West Hampstead** — REDINGTON RD. — HEYSHAM — SPEDAN CL. — OAK HILL WAY — Fenton Ho. — **Hampstead** — ST. MARY — MT. VERNON — HOLLY HILL — FROGNAL — HAMPSTEAD GR. — CANNON PL. — CANNON LA. — CHRISTCHURCH — NEW END — Burgh House — GAINSBOROUGH GDNS. — WILLOW RD. — 2 Willow Rd. — DENNING RD.

KIDDERPORE AVE. — KIDDERPORE GDNS. — FERNCROFT — FORTUNE GREEN ROAD — Hampstead Cmy. — OAK HILL PK. — St. Mary — CHURCH ROW — Hampstead — HAMPSTEAD HIGH ST. — PERRIN'S LA. — GREENHILL RD. — WILLOUGHBY RD. — CARLINGFORD RD. — KEMPLAY RD. — St. John — DOWNSHIRE HILL — ROSSLYN HILL — KEATS GR. — St. John

West Hampstead — WEECH RD. — INGHAM RD. — STUDHOLME COURT — BRACKNELL GDNS. — REDINGTON RD. — CHESTERFORD GDNS. — OAK HILL PK. — GREENAWAY GDNS. — FROGNAL — MT. VERNON — ST. MARY — HOLLY HILL — PERRIN'S LA. — PRINCE ARTHUR RD. — VANE CL. — SHEPHERD'S — LYNDHURST TER. — THURLOW RD. — ELDON GR. — WATERHOUSE — HAMPSTEAD HILL GDNS.

Fortune Green — AVAY RD. — ULYSSES RD. — ACHILLES RD. — FINCHLEY ROAD — BURRARD RD. — BURGESS HILL — ARDWICK RD. — CANNON HILL — LYNCROFT GDNS. — PARSIFAL RD. — FROGNAL GDNS. — FROGNAL LA. — FROGNAL — CHURCH ROW — PERRIN'S RD. — ELLERDALE RD. — PRINCE ARTHUR RD. — FITZJOHN'S AVENUE — LYNDHURST GDNS. — WEDDERBURN RD. — MARESFIELD GDNS. — LYNDHURST RD. — AKENSIDE RD. — BELSIZE

HILLFIELD — MILL LANE — SUMATRA RD. — SOLENT RD. — ALDRED RD. — NARCISSUS RD. — HOLMDALE RD. — WEST END LA. — INGLEWOOD RD. — DENNINGTON PARK RD. — FAWLEY RD. — HONEYBOURNE RD. — CREDITON HILL — LYMINGTON RD. — COMPAYNE GDNS. — FAIRHAZEL GDNS. — BRACKNELL GDNS. — ARKWRIGHT RD. — NUTLEY TER. — NETHERHALL GDNS. — NETHERHALL WAY — MARESFIELD GDNS. — AVENUE — DALEHAM GDNS. — BELSIZE CRES. — BELSIZE

PANDORA RD. — BROOMSLEIGH ST. — W. Hampstead (Thameslink) — LITHOS RD. — ROSEMONT — FINCHLEY ROAD — Camden Arts Centre — Finchley Road & Frognal — LYMINGTON RD. — CRESPIGNY RD. — LINDFIELD GDNS. — ARKWRIGHT RD. — Freud — BELSIZE

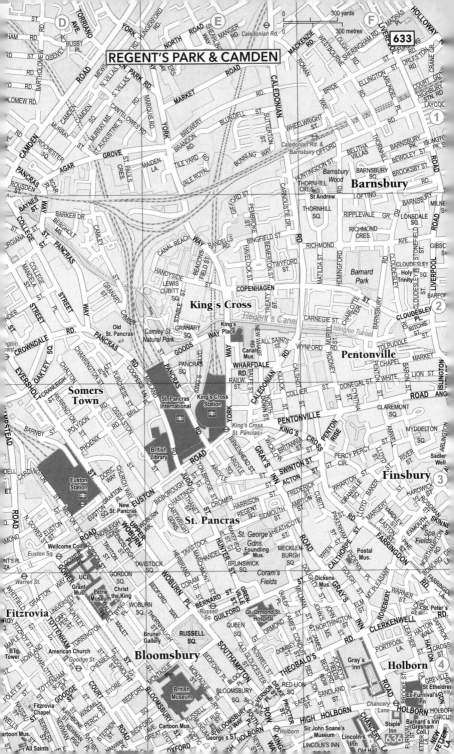

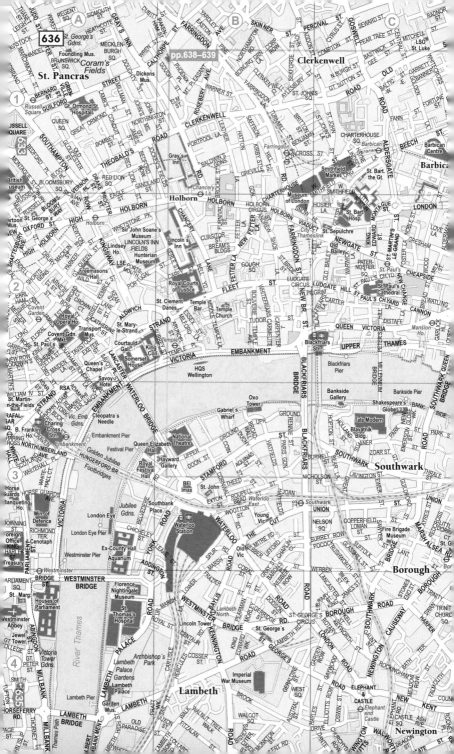

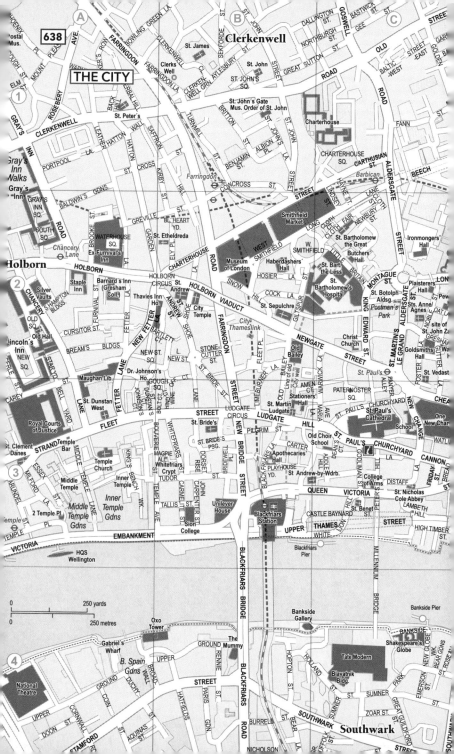

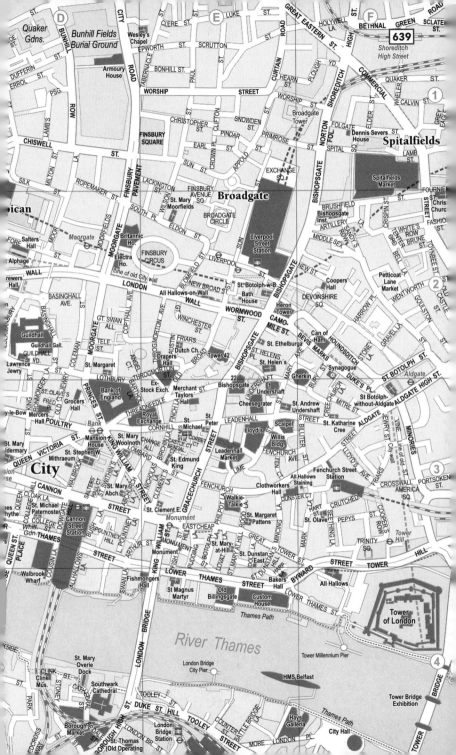